hugo

DUTCH
DICTIONARY

DUTCH-ENGLISH
ENGLISH-DUTCH

HUGO'S LANGUAGE BOOKS LTD

This impression 1991

©1969 Hugo's Language Books Ltd
ISBN 0 85285 079 4

Printed in Great Britain

hugo

WOORDENBOEK
ENGELS

NEDERLANDS-ENGELS
ENGELS-NEDERLANDS

VOORWOORD.

Hugo's Nederlands woordenboek is, zoals de ervaring zal leren, een zeer handig naslagwerkje in zakformaat. Het bevat in een klein bestek de dagelijks voorkomende woorden. Hugo's bekend systeem van nagebootste uitspraak is toegepast. Doordat de uitspraak op deze eenvoudige manier wordt weergegeven kan iedereen er zich onmiddelijk zonder de minste moeite van bedienen (zie blz. x). *Het is niet nodig zich eerst een ingewikkelde reeks van tekens eigen te maken.*

Woorden die tot dezelfde stam behoren en niet gegeven zijn in het Nederlands-Engels gedeelte kan men over het algemeen in het Engels-Nederlands gedeelte vinden. Deze methode is gevolgd om plaats te bieden aan een zo groot mogelijk aantal woorden.

iv

PREFACE.

Hugo's Dutch dictionary will be found to be a most serviceable pocket reference-book. It contains in a small space the words that are needed in everyday life. Hugo's well-known system of imitated pronunciation has been employed. This method of imparting the pronunciation is so simple that anyone can use it at once without the slightest trouble (see page xi). *There is no complicated key to be mastered.*

Words belonging to the same root not given in the Dutch-English Section will generally be found in the English-Dutch Section. This plan has been followed to provide space for the greatest possible number of words.

▼

VERGELIJKENDE TABELLEN

Maten. — **Gewichten.**

LENGTEMATEN

1 inch	1 fathom
(duim) = 0·025 m.	(vadem) = 1·828 m.
1 foot (voet) = 0·305 m.	1 furlong = 201·16 m.
1 yard = 0·914 m.	1 mile (mijl) = 1609·31 m.
1 knot (knoop) = 1852 m.	

VLAKTEMATEN

1 square inch = 6·45 cm²	1 square yard = 8361 cm²
1 square foot = 929 cm²	1 acre = 40·46 are

INHOUDSMATEN

1 pint (pint) = 0·568 liter
1 quart = 1·136 „
1 gallon = 4·546 „

GEWICHTEN (avoirdupois)

1 ounce (ons) = 28·35 gr.
1 pound (pond) = 453·59 gr.
1 stone = 6·35 kg.
1 hundredweight (centenaar) = 50·80 kg.
1 ton (ton) = 1016 kg.

(troy)

1 grain (grein) = 0·065 gr.
1 pennyweight = 1·555 gr.
1 ounce (ons) = 31·103 gr.
1 pound (pond) = 373·241 gr.

(vervolg op blz. viii)

COMPARATIVE TABLE

Measures.   **Weights.**

LINEAL MEASURE

1 millimeter = ·039 inch   1 centimeter = ·393 inch
1 decimeter = 3·93 inches
1 meter = 39·37 inches
1 kilometer (1000 meter) = 1093·63 yards

SQUARE MEASURE

1 vierkante meter = 1·196 sq. yards
1 are (100 vierkante meter) = 119·6 sq. yards
1 hectare (10,000 vierkante meter) = 2·471 acres

CUBIC MEASURE

Solids—1 kubieke meter = 1·308 cubic yards
Liquids—1 liter = 1·76 pint
1 hectoliter = 22·009 gallons

WEIGHTS
(avoirdupois)

1 ons (100 gram) = 3·527 ozs.
1 pond (500 gram) = 1·103 lbs.
1 kilogram (1000 gram) = 2·205 lbs.
1 ton (1000 kilogram) = 0·984 ton

(troy)

1 milligram = ·0154 grain
1 centigram = ·154 grain
1 gram = 15·43 grains

(continued on page ix)

(vervolg van blz. vi)

EQUIVALENTEN BIJ BENADERING

(De volgende tabel is zeer nuttig om een vlugge
berekening te maken)

1 inch	= ca. 0·025 m.
1 foot	= ca. 0·30 m.
1 yard	= ca. 0·91 m.
1 mile	= ca. 1600 m.
1 ounce	= ca. 28 gr.
1 pound	= ca. 454 gr.
1 pint	= een beetje meer dan ½ liter

THERMOMETER

32° Fahrenheit = 0° Celsius
212°   ,,   = 100°   ,,
9° Fahrenheit is gelijk aan 5° Celsius

Als men Celsius in Fahrenheit wil omrekenen,
vermenigvuldigt men met 9, deelt door 5 en voegt
er 32 bij.

———

(continued from page vii)

APPROXIMATE EQUIVALENTS
(For quick reckoning the following table will be found useful)

1 centimeter	=	about	two-fifths of an inch
1 meter	=	,,	39 inches
1 kilometer	=	,,	five-eighths of a mile
1 hectare	=	,,	two acres and a half
1 liter	=	,,	a pint and three quarters

THERMOMETER
0° Celsius = 32° Fahrenheit
100°   ,,   = 212°   ,,
5° Celsius are equivalent to 9° Fahrenheit

To convert Fahrenheit into Celsius subtract 32, multiply by 5, and divide by 9.

———

VERKLARING VAN DE NAGE-BOOTSTE UITSPRAAK

De nagebootste klanken spreke men uit alsof het Nederlandse klanken zijn, maar men schenke aandacht aan de volgende richtlijnen:

1. De **vetgedrukte** lettergreep heeft altijd de klemtoon.

2. De cursief-gedrukte *a* stelt een klank voor die ongeveer hetzelfde is als de a in vat, maar enigszins overhelt naar de u in dun.

3. **oa** wordt uitgesproken als **oa** in **loaten** in sommige Nederlandse dialecten (Brabants, Overijsels).

4. **e** op het einde van een lettergreep is stom zoals in **de**; **ee** wordt uitgesproken zoals ee in neem.

5. **eu** wordt uitgesproken zoals de **eu** van **freule** of zoals de **eu** van het Franse woord neuf.

6. **G** wordt uitgesproken zoals de g van garçon in het Frans of van gut in het Duits.

7. **èr** wordt uitgesproken zoals **èr** in **blèren**, maar men spreke de **r** nauwelijks uit.

8. In veel Engelse woorden is de klinker van een niet-beklemtoonde lettergreep nauwelijks hoorbaar en klinkt dan als de e in **winkel**, **koster**. Deze onbeklemtoonde klank wordt in de nagebootste uitspraak in veel gevallen met een komma (') aangeduid, b.v. **doctor** wordt **dok-t'r**.

9. Men onderscheidt in het Engels een stemloze en een stemhebbende **th**. In de nagebootste uitspraak is **th** de stemloze, **dh** de stemhebbende **th**. Voor de juiste uitspraak van deze klanken raadplege men een deskundige.

10. Dikwijls is de medeklinker in de nagebootste uitspraak verdubbeld b.v. **heroïne** wordt **her-ro-in**. Dit was noodzakelijk om duidelijk te maken dat de voorafgaande klinker kort is; men spreke echter deze verdubbelde medeklinker als één medeklinker uit.

EXPLANATION OF
THE IMITATED PRONUNCIATION

Read each syllable as if it were an English syllable, bearing in mind the following instructions:

a   (thick italic) indicates a sound similar to the English **a** in "**was.**"

EE indicates a sound similar to the French **u** in "**lune,**" or the German **ü** in "**grün.**" It is pronounced by uttering the English EE (as in "**seen**") with rounded lips.

HG (small capitals) must be pronounced gutturally like **ch** in the Scotch word "**loch.**"

er   to be pronounced as **er** in "**her.**"

ow to be pronounced as **ow** in "**now.**"

o   indicates the short **o** as in "**stock.**"

oh indicates the long **o** as in "**home.**"

r   (italic) must not be pronounced.

er   represents a sound like **e** in "**her,**" and u*r* like **u** in "**fur.**"

zh indicates the soft sound of **s** in "**measure.**"

ng must always be pronounced like **ng** in "**bring.**"

The stressed syllable is printed in **thick type.**

IMPORTANT.—The imitated pronunciation in the Dutch-English section, being for English-speaking people only, is framed in accordance with English "sound-spelling" principles. Users of this dictionary should beware of criticisms from foreigners who forget that this imitated pronunciation is not based upon their own phonetics.

Vice versa, the imitated pronunciation in the English-Dutch section is for Dutch-speaking people only.

AFKORTINGEN
IN DIT WOORDENBOEK.

Voor alle woorden die tot meer dan één rededeel, geslacht enz. behoren, worden de vereiste aanduidingen gegeven. B.v.: a. & adv., bijvoeglijk naamwoord en bijwoord; a. & p.p., bijvoeglijk naamwoord en verleden deelwoord; s.pl., zelfstandig naamwoord meervoud.

a.	(adjective) bijvoeglijk naamwoord	mil.	militaire term
		mus.	(musical) muziekterm
adv.	(adverb) bijwoord	n.	(neuter) onzijdig ("het"-woord)
art.	(article) lidwoord		
c.	(common gender) "de"-woord	naut.	(nautical) scheepsterm
conj.	(conjunction) voegwoord	p.p.	(past participle) verleden deelwoord
eccl.	(ecclesiastical) kerkelijke term	pl.	(plural) meervoud
fam.	(familiar) gemeenzaam	pop.	(popular) volks
		prep.	(preposition) voorzetsel
fig.	figuurlijk		
gram.	(grammar) spraakkunst	pron.	(pronoun) voornaamwoord
interj.	(interjection) tussenwerpsel	s.	(substantive) zelfstandig naamwoord
mech.	(mechanics) technische term	univ.	(university) universiteit
med.	(medical) geneeskundige term	v.	(verb) werkwoord
		vulg.	(vulgar) vulgair

N.B.—Een komma (,) scheidt in dit woordenboek twee of meer vertalingen van een woord als deze ongeveer dezelfde betekenis hebben. Een puntkomma (;) duidt aan dat er een andere betekenis volgt.

ABBREVIATIONS
USED IN THIS DICTIONARY

The appropriate indications are given against all words that may belong to more than one part of speech, gender, etc. Ex.: a. & adv., adjective & adverb; a. & p.p., adjective & past participle; s.pl., substantive plural.

a.	adjective	mus.	musical
adv.	adverb	n.	neuter
art.	article		("het-"word)
c.*	common gender	naut.	nautical
	("de"-word)	p.p.	past participle
conj.	conjunction	pl.	plural
eccl.	ecclesiastical	pop.	popular
fam.	familiar	prep.	preposition
fig.	figurative	pron.	pronoun
gram.	grammar	s.	substantive
interj.	interjection	univ.	university
mech.	mechanics	v.	verb
med.	medical	vulg.	vulgar
mil.	military		

* Comprises the nouns that were formerly masculine or feminine.

NOTE.—In this dictionary commas (,) separate two or more translations of a word where the meanings are similar. Semicolons (;) indicate different significations.

GEOGRAPHICAL NAMES
AARDRIJKSKUNDIGE NAMEN

Nagebootste uitspraak.	Imitated pronunciation.
Africa, **ef**-fri-ka	Afrika, **ah**-free-kah
America, e-**mer**-ri-ka	Amerika, ah-**may**-ree-kah
Asia, **ee**-sja	Azië, **ah**-zee-er
Australia, oas-**tree**-li-a	Australië, ow-**strah**-lee-er
Austria, **oas**-tri-a	Oostenrijk, oh-ster-reyk
Bavaria, be-**vee**-ri-a	Beieren, **bey**-er-rer
Belgium, **bel**-dzjum	België, **bel**-нGee-er
Bohemia, be-**hie**-mi-a	Bohemen, boh-**hay**-mer
Brazil, bre-**zil**	Brazilië, brah-**zee**-lee-er
Bulgaria, b**a**l-**Ger**-ri-a	Bulgarije,
	berl-**нGah**-rey-er
Canada, **ken**-ne-da	Canada, **kah**-nah-dah
China, **tsjai**-na	China, **shee**-nah
Denmark, **den**-maark	Denemarken,
	day-ner-mar-ker
Egypt, **ie**-dzjipt	Egypte, ay-**нGip**-ter
England, **ing**-Gl'nd	Engeland, **en**-нGer-lant
Europe, **joe**-rup	Europa, er-**roh**-pah
France, **fraans**	Frankrijk, **frank**-reyk
Germany, **dzjeur**-me-ni	Duitsland, **dowts**-lant
Great Britain,	Groot-Brittanië,
greet brit-t'n	**нGroht**-brit-**tah**-nee-er
Greece, **gries**	Griekenland,
	нGree-ker-lant
Holland, **hol**-l'nd	Holland, **hol**-lant
Hungary, **hang**-Ge-ri	Hongarije,
	hon-**нGah**-rey-er
India, **in**-di-a	India, **in**-di-ah
Indonesia; in-do-**nie**-si-a	Indonesië,
	in-do-**nay**-see-er
Ireland, **air**-l'nd	Ierland, **eer**-lant
Italy, **it**-te-li	Italië, ee-**tah**-lee-er
Japan, dzja-**pen**	Japan, yah-**pan**
Morocco, me-**rok**-ko	Marokko, mah-**rok**-koh
Netherlands,	Nederland, **nay**-der-rlant
nedh-'r-l'ndz	

New Zealand, njoe-**zie**-l'nd	**Nieuw-Zeeland,** nee-oo-**zay**-lant
Norway, noar-wee	**Noorwegen,** nohr-vay-HGer
Persia, peur-**sja**	**Perzië,** payr-**zee**-er
Poland, po-l'nd	**Polen,** poh-ler
Portugal, por-**tjoe**-Gel	**Portugal,** por-**TEE**-HGal
Prussia, pras-**sja**	**Pruisen,** prow-ser
Russia, ras-sja	**Rusland, rers**-lant
Scotland, skot-l'nd	**Schotland, sHGot**-lant
Spain, speen	**Spanje, span**-yer
Sweden, swie-d'n	**Zweden, zvay**-der
Switzerland, swit-z'r-l'nd	**Zwitserland,** zvit-serr-lant
Turkey, teur-ki	**Turkije,** teur-key-er
(The) United States, (dhe) joe-**nai**-tid steets	**(De) Verenigde Staten,** (der) verr-**ay**-niHG-der stah-ter
American, e-**mer**-ri-k'n	**Amerikaans, a.,** ah-may-ree-**kahns**
Australian, oas-**treel**-jun	**Australisch, a.,** ow-**strah**-lees
Belgian, bel-**dzjun**	**Belgisch, a.,** bel-HGees
British, brit-**tisj**	**Brits, a.,** brits
Canadian, ke-**nee**-djun	**Canadees, a.,** kah-nah-**days**
Danish, dee-nisj	**Deens, a.,** dayns
Dutch, datsj	**Nederlands, a.,** nay-derr-lants
English, ing-Glisj	**Engels, a.,** en-HGerls
French, frensj	**Frans, a.,** frans
German, dzjeur-m'n	**Duits, a.,** dowts
Irish, ai-risj	**Iers, a.,** eers
Italian, i-**tel**-jun	**Italiaans, a.,** ee-tah-lee-**ahns**
Norwegian, noar-**wie**-dzjun	**Noors, a,** nohrs
Portuguese, por-**tjoe**-Gies	**Portugees, a.,** por-tEE-HGays
Russian, ras-sjun	**Russisch, a.,** rers-sees
Scotch, skotsj	**Schots, a.,** sHGots
Spanish, spen-nisj	**Spaans, a.,** spahns

Swedish, **swie-disj**	Zweeds, a., zwayts
Swiss, swis	Zwitsers, a., **zwit-se**rrs
Antwerp, ent-weurp	Antwerpen,
	ant-vayr-per
Athens, edh-'ns	Athene, *a*-t*ay*-ner
Berlin, **beur**-lin	Berlijn, bayr-**leyn**
Bruges, broedzj	Brugge, brer-**HUG**er
Brussels, **bras**-sulz	Brussel, brers-serl
Cologne, ko-**loon**	Keulen, ker-ler
Flushing, **flas**-sjing	Vlissingen, **flis**-sing-er
Geneva, dzje-nie-va	Genève, jer-nay-ver
Genoa, dzjen-no-a	Genua, HGay-nee-ah
(The) Hague, (dhe) heeG	Den Haag, der hahHG
Liege, lie-eedzj	Luik, lowk
Lisbon, lis-b'n	Lissabon, lis-sah-bon
London, **lan**-d'n	Londen, **lon**-der
Moscow, mos-kau	Moskou, mos-kow
Naples, nee-p'ls	Napels, nah-perls
Nimeguen, **nim**-meeG-G'n	Nijmegen, ney-may-HGer
Paris, per-ris	Parijs, pah-reys
Venice, ven-nis	Venetië, ver-**nayt**-see-er
Vienna, vi-en-na	Wenen, vay-ner
Warsaw, **woar**-soa	Warschau, **war**-show
Alps, elps	Alpen, *al*-per
Atlantic Ocean,	Atlantische Oceaan,
et-len-tik o-sjun	*a*t-**lan**-tee-ser oh-say-ahn
Baltic Sea, **baol**-tik sie	Oostzee, **ohst**-zay
Black Sea, blek sie	Zwarte Zee,
	zvahr-ter zay
Danube, **den**-joeb	Donau, **doh**-now
(The) English Channel,	Het Kanaal,
(dhie) ing-Glisj **tsjen**-n'l	het kah-**nahl**
Mediterranean,	Middellandse Zee,
med-di-te-**reen**-jun	mid-der-**lant**-se zay
North Sea, north sie	Noordzee, **nohrt**-zay
Pacific Ocean,	Stille Zuidzee,
pes-**sif**-fik o-sjun	**stil**-ler **zowt**-zay
Pyrenees, pi-ri-**nies**	Pyreneeën,
	pee-rer-nay-er
Rhine, rain	Rijn, reyn
Scheldt, skelt	Schelde, **SHGel**-der
Thames, tems	Theems, tayms

xvi

DUTCH-ENGLISH DICTIONARY

aaien, ah-yer, v., to caress
aak, ahk, c., barge
aal, ahl, c., eel
aalbes, ahl-bess, c., currant
aalmoes, ahl-mooss, c., alms   [chaplain
aalmoezenier, ahl-moo-zer-neer, c., (mil.)
aambeien, ahm-bey-er, c. pl., piles, haemorr-
aan, ahn, prep., at, on, upon, in, to   [hoids
aanbeeld, ahn-baylt, n., anvil
aanbellen, ahn-bel-ler, v., to ring (the bell)
aanbevelen, ahn-ber-vay-ler, v., to recommend
aanbidden, ahn-bid-der, v., to adore, to worship
aanbieden, ahn-bee-der, v., to offer, to tender
aanbieding, ahn-bee-ding, c., offer, presentation
aanblik, ahn-blick, c., look, view, sight
aanbod, ahn-bot, n., offer   [strike (coal)
aanboren, ahn-boh-rer, v., to bore (a well); to
aanbouw, ahn-bow, c., building; cultivation
aanbranden, ahn-bran-der, v., to burn (in
   cooking)
aanbreken, ahn-bray-ker, v., to dawn; to come;
   to broach; to break into (one's savings)
aanbrengen, ahn-breng-er, v., to fix (up); to
aandacht, ahn-daHGt, c., attention   [denounce
aandachtig, ahn-daHG-terHG, a. & adv., attentive
aandeel, ahn-dayl, n., share; portion   [holder
aandeelhouder, ahn-dayl-how-der, c., share-
aandenken, ahn-den-ker, n., souvenir, keepsake
aandoen, ahn-doon, v., to put on (clothes); to
   cause
aandoening, ahn-doo-ning, c., malady; emotion
aandoenlijk, ahn-doon-luck, a. & adv., moving,
   pathetic   [tighten
aandraaien, ahn-drah-yer, v., to turn on; to
aandrang, ahn-drang, c., insistence; emphasis
aandringen, ahn-dring-er, v., to urge, to insist
aanduiden, ahn-dow-der, v., to indicate
aanduiding, ahn-dow-ding, c., indication
aaneen, ahn-ayn, adv., together, connected

aaneenbinden, ahn-ayn-bin-der, v., to bind together [fasten

aaneenhechten, ahn-ayn-hayHG-ter, v., to

aaneenschakelen, ahn-ayn-sHGah-ker-ler, v., to connect

aaneensluiten, ahn-ayn-slow-ter, v., to unite

aangaan, ahn-HGahn, v., to go on; to enter into; to concern

aangeboren, ahn-HGer-boh-rer, a., inborn, innate

aangedaan, ahn-HGer-dahn, a., affected, moved

aangelegenheid, ahn-HGer-lay-HGen-heyt, c., matter, affair

aangenaam, ahn-HGer-nahm, a. & adv., agreeable

aangespen, ahn-HGer-sper, v., to buckle on

aangeven, ahn-HGay-ver, v., to give; to hand; to reach; to mark; to notify; to declare

aangezien, ahn-HGer-zeen, conj., as, since

aangifte, ahn-HGif-ter, c., notification [adjoining

aangrenzend, ahn-HGren-zent, a., adjacent,

aangrijpen, ahn-HGrey-per, v., to seize; to assail

aanhalen, ahn-hah-ler, v., to fondle; to quote

aanhaling, ahn-hah-ling, c., quotation

aanhang, ahn-hang, c., supporters, followers

aanhanger, ahn-hang-er, c., follower, supporter

aanhangwagen, ahn-hang-vah-HGer, c., trailer

aanhankelijk, ahn-hahn-ker-luck, a., affectionate

aanhebben, ahn-heb-ber, v., to have on; to wear

aanhef, ahn-hef, c., start (of letter, speech)

aanhoren, ahn-ho-rer, v., to listen to

aanhouden, ahn-how-der, v., to hold; to detain

aanhoudend, ahn-how-dent, a., persistent

aanhouding, ahn-how-ding, c., detention;

aankijken, ahn-key-ker, v., to look at [seizure

aanklacht, ahn-klaHGt, c., accusation

aanklager, ahn-kla-HGer, c., accuser, plaintiff

aankleden, ahn-klay-der, v., to dress

aankloppen, ahn-klop-per, v., to knock (at door)

aanknopen, ahnk-noh-per, v., to enter into

aankomen, ahn-koh-mer, v., to arrive

aankomst, ahn-komst, c., arrival

aankondigen, ahn-kon-der-HGer, v., to announce

aankoop, ahn-kohp, c., purchase

aanleg, ahn-layHG, c., lay-out; gift, talent
aanleggen, ahn-layHG-er, v., to lay-out, to build
aanlegplaats, ahn-layHG-plahts, c., landing-stage
aanleiding, ahn-ley-ding, c., occasion; cause
aanlokkelijk, ahn-lock-ker-luck, a., alluring
aanlokken, ahn-lock-ker, v., to allure, to entice
aanmaken, ahn-mah-ker, v., to make; to light (a fire)
aanmanen, ahn-mah-ner, v., to exhort; to warn
aanmatigend, ahn-mah-ter-HGent, a., presumptuous
aanmelden, ahn-mel-der, v., to announce
aanmerkelijk, ahn-mayr-ker-luck, a. & adv.
aanmerking, ahn-mayr-king, c., remark [notable
aanmoedigen, ahn-moo-der-HGer, v., to encourage
aannemelijk, ahn-nay-mer-luck, a., acceptable
aannemen, ahn-nay-mer, v., to accept; to assume
aannemer, ahn-nay-mer, c., contractor
aanpakken, ahn-pak-ker, v., to seize; to tackle
aanpassen (zich), ahn-pas-ser (ziHG), v., to adapt (oneself)
aanplakbiljet, ahn-plak-bil-yet, n., poster
aanprijzen, ahn-prey-zer, v., to recommend
aanraden, ahn-rah-der, v., to advise
aanraking, ahn-rah-king, c., touch; contact
aanranden, ahn-ran-der, v., to assault, to assail
aanrijden, ahn-rey-der, v., to run into (with vehicle)
aanrijding, ahn-rey-ding, c., collision, smash
aanroepen, ahn-roo-per, v., to invoke (God); to hail (ship) [(subject)
aanroeren, ahn-roo-rer, v., to touch upon
aanschaffen, ahn-sHGaf-fer, v., to get, to procure
aanschijn, ahn-sHGeyn, n., appearance
aanschouwen, ahn-sHGow-er, v., to behold
aanslaan, ahn-slahn, v., to strike (note); to assess; to salute
aanslag, ahn-slaHG, c., touch (of pianist); attempt (to kill) [assessment
aanslagbiljet, ahn-slaHG-bil-yet, n., notice of
aansluiten, ahn-slow-ter, v., to connect, to join

aanspoelen, ahn-spoo-ler, v., to wash ashore
aansporen, ahn-spoh-rer, v., to incite, to urge
aanspraak, ahn-sprahk, c., claim, title
aansprakelijk, ahn-sprah-ker-luck, a., liable
aanspreken, ahn-spray-ker, v., to address; to accost
aanstaan, ahn-stahn, v., to please   [accost
aanstaande, ahn-stahn-der, a., next, coming.
    zijn, haar ——, zeyn, hahr ——, his, her
    fiancé(e)
aanstalten, ahn-stal-ter, c. pl., preparations
aansteken, ahn-stay-ker, v., to light; to infect
aansteker, ahn-stay-ker, c., lighter
aanstellen, ahn-stel-ler, v., to appoint; to pose
aanstellerig, ahn-stel-ler-rerHG, a., affected
aanstelling, ahn-stel-ling, c., appointment
aanstonds, ahn-stonts, adv., presently
aanstoot, ahn-stoht, c., offence   [stroke
aanstrepen, ahn-stray-per, v., to mark (with
aanstrijken, ahn-strey-ker, v., to strike (a match)
aansturen op, ahn-stEE-rer op, v., to make for;
    to aim at
aantal, ahn-tal, n., number   [(health)
aantasten, ahn-tas-ter, v., to attack; (to affect
aantekenboek, ahn-tay-ken-book, n., note-book
aantekenen, ahn-tay-ker-ner, v., to note; to
    register (letter)
aantonen, ahn-toh-ner, v., to show; to prove
aantreffen, ahn-tref-fer, v., to meet, to come
    across   [attractive
aantrekkelijk, ahn-treck-ker-luck, a. & adv.,
aantrekken, ahn-treck-ker, v., to attract; to
    tighten   [enter upon
aanvaarden, ahn-fahr-der, v. to accept; to
aanval, ahn-fahl, c., attack; fit
aanvallen, ahn-fal-ler, v., to attack; to assault
aanvang, ahn-fang, c., start, beginning
aanvangen, ahn-fang-er, v., to start, to commence
aanvankelijk, ahn-fan-ker-luck, a. & adv., at the
    outset
aanvaring, ahn-fah-ring, c., collision (of ships)
aanvoelen, ahn-foo-ler, v., to feel; to appreciate
aanvoer, ahn-foor, c., supply

aanvoerder, ahn-foor-der, c., commander
aanvraag, ahn-frahHG, c., demand, request
aanvragen, ahn-frah-HGer, v., to apply for
aanvullen, ahn-fEEL-ler, v., to fill up, to replenish
aanvuren, ahn-fEE-rer, v., to incite; to fire
aanwakkeren, ahn-vak-ker-rer, v., to stir
aanwenden, ahn-ven-der, v., to use, to employ
aanwennen (zich), ahn-ven-ner (ziHG), v., to fall into the habit of
aanwensel, ahn-ven-serl, n., habit; mannerism
aanwezig, ahn-vay-zerHG, a., present
aanwezigheid, ahn-vay-zerHG-heyt, c., presence
aanwijzen, ahn-vey-zer, v., to point out; to assign
aanzien, ahn-zeen, v., to look at; to consider. n., prestige, reputation [able
aanzienlijk, ahn-zeen-luck, a. & adv., consider-
aanzoek, ahn-zook, n., proposal; request
aap, ahp, c., monkey, ape
aar, ahr, c., ear (of corn)
aard, ahrt, c., nature, character; kind, sort
aardappel, ahrt-ap-perl, c., potato
aardbei, ahrt-bey, c., strawberry
aardbeving, ahrt-bay-ving, c., earthquake
aardbol, ahrt-bol, c., world, earth, globe
aarde, ahr-der, c., earth; soil, mould
aardewerk, ahr-der-vayrk, n., earthenware
aardig, ahr-derHG, a., nice, pleasant; witty
aardigheid, ahr-derHG-heyt, c., joke, fun
aardrijkskunde, ahr-dreyk-skEEn-der, c., geo-
aards, ahrts, a., earthly; worldly [graphy
aartsbisschop, ahrts-bis-sHGop, c., archbishop
aartsengel, ahrts-en-HGerl, c., archangel
aartsvader, ahrts-fah-der, c., patriarch
aarzelen, ahr-zer-ler, v., to hesitate
aas, ahss, n., bait. c., ace (in cards)
abonné, a-bon-neh, c., subscriber; season-ticket
abrikoos, ah-bree-kohss, c., apricot [holder
abt, apt, c., abbot
abuis, ah-bowss, n., mistake, error
accijns, ak-seynss, c., excise [(mus.) chord
accoord, ak-kohrt, n., agreement, settlement;
ach! aHG, interj., ah!, alas!

acht, *a*HGt, a., eight

acht, *a*HGt, c., attention. —— **slaan op,** —— slahn op, to pay attention to

achteloos, *a*HG-ter-lohss, a. & adv., careless

achten, *a*HG-ter, v., to respect; to consider

achter, *a*HG-ter, prep., behind, after [rear

achteraan, *a*HG-ter-ahn, adv., at the back, in the

achterbaks, *a*HG-ter-baks, a. & adv., underhand

achterblijven, *a*HG-ter-bley-ver, v., to stay behind

achterbuurt, *a*HG-ter-bEErt, c., slum

achterdocht, *a*HG-ter-doHGt, c., suspicion

achtereenvolgend, *a*HG-ter-ayn-fol-HGent, a., consecutive

achtergrond, *a*HG-ter-HGront, c., background

achterhalen, *a*HG-ter-hah-ler, v., to overtake

achterhouden, *a*HG-ter-how-der, v., to withhold

achterkant, *a*HG-ter-kant, c., back

achterlaten, *a*HG-ter-lah-ter, v., to leave behind

achterlicht, *a*HG-ter-liHGt, n., tail-light

achterlijk, *a*HG-ter-luck, a., backward (mentally)

achternaam, *a*HG-ter-nahm, c., surname

achterover, *a*HG-ter-oh-ver, adv., backward; on the back [to lean back

achteroverleunen, *a*HG-ter-oh-ver-ler-ner, v.,

achterpoot, *a*HG-ter-poht, c., hind leg

achterstallig, *a*HG-ter-stal-lerHG, a., overdue

achterstand, *a*HG-ter-stant, c., arrears

achtersteven, *a*HG-ter-stay-ver, c., stern

achteruit, *a*HG-ter-rowt, adv., backwards

achteruitgang, *a*HG-ter-rowt-HGanHG, c., decline

achtervoegsel, *a*HG-ter-fooHG-serl, n., suffix

achtervolgen, *a*HG-ter-fol-HGer, v., to persecute

achting, *a*HG-ting, c., regard, respect

achtste, *a*HGt-ster, a., eighth

achttien, *a*HGt-teen, a., eighteen

acte, *a*k-ter, c., document; deed; diploma

actueel, *a*k-tEE-ayl, a., topical

adder, *a*d-der, c., adder, viper

adel, ah-derl, c., nobility

adellijk, ah-derl-luck, a., noble

adem, ah-dem, c., breath

ademen, ah-der-mer, v., to breathe

ademloos, ah-dem-lohss, a., breathless
ader, ah-der, c., vein; artery
adres, ah-dress, n., address; petition
adresboek, ah-dress-book, n., directory
advies, at-veess, n., advice
advocaat, at-voh-kaht, c., barrister, counsel
af, af, adv., off, down; finished, done
afbeelding, af-bayl-ding, c., picture, portrait
afbetaling, af-ber-tah-ling, c., payment (by instalments)
afbeulen, af-ber-ler, v., to overwork (servants)
afblijven (van), af-bley-ver (fan), v., to leave alone
afbraak, af-brahk, c., demolition
afbranden, af-bran-der, v., to burn down; to burn off
afbreken, af-bray-ker, v., to demolish [burn off
afbrekend, af-bray-kent, a., destructive
afbrokkelen, af-brock-ker-ler, v., to crumble
afdalen, af-dah-ler, v., to descend
afdanken, af-dan-ker, v., to dismiss, to disband
afdeling, af-day-ling, c., section; branch
afdingen, af-ding-er, v., to bargain, to beat down
afdoen, af-doon, v., to finish, to settle
afdoende, af-doon-der, a., conclusive; effective
afdraaien, af-drah-yer, v., to turn off (tap)
afdragen, af-drah-HGer, v., to wear out (clothes)
afdrogen, af-dro-HGer, v., to dry; to wipe up
afdruipen, af-drow-per, v., to slink off
afdruk, af-drook, c., print
afdwalen, af-dvah-ler, v., to go astray; to depart
afdwaling, af-dvah-ling, c., digression [from
afdwingen, af-dvin-HGer, v., to extort; to command (respect)
afgelegen, af-HGer-lay-HGer, a., remote [(year)
afgelopen, af-HGer-loh-per, a., finished; past
afgemat; af-HGer-mat, a., worn out, exhausted
afgescheiden, af-HGer-sHGey-der, a., separate; (eccl.) dissenting
afgevaardigde, af-HGer-vahr-derHG-der, c.,
afgeven, af-HGay-ver, v., to deliver [deputy
afgezonderd, af-HGer-zon-dert, a. & adv., [secluded
afgifte, af-HGif-ter, c., delivery
afgodsbeeld, af-HGots-baylt, n., idol

afgrijselijk, af-HGrey-ser-luck, a., horrible

afgrond, af-HGront, c., precipice, abyss

afgunst, af-HGernst, c., envy

afgunstig, af-HGern-sterHG, a., envious, jealous

afhaken, af-hah-ker, v., to unhook; to uncouple

afhakken, af-hak-ker, v., to chop off, to lop off

afhalen, af-hah-ler, v., to call for; to meet

afhandelen, af-han-der-ler, v. to settle [(upon)

afhangen (van), af-hang-HGer (fan), v., to depend

afhankelijk, af-han-ker-luck, a., dependent

afkeer, af-kayr, c., aversion, dislike

afkerig, af-kay-rerHG, a., averse

afkeuren, af-ker-rer, v., to condemn, to reject

afkeuring, af-ker-ring, c., disapproval

afknappen, af-k'nap-per, v., to snap

afkoelen, af-koo-ler, v., to cool

afkomst, af-komst, c., origin, birth

afkondigen, af-kon-der-HGer, v., to proclaim

afkoopsom, af-kohp-som, c., ransom

afkorting, af-kor-ting, c., abbreviation

afladen, af-lah-der, v., to unload

afleggen, af-lay-HGer, v., to make (statement); to cover (distance); to pay (visit)

afleiden, af-ley-der, v., to divert; to distract

afleiding, af-ley-ding, c., derivation; amusement

afleren, af-lay-rer, v., to unlearn

afleveren, af-lay-ver-rer, v., to deliver

aflevering, af-lay-ver-ring, c., number, part (of afloop, af-lohp, c., end, result [publication)

aflossen, af-los-ser, v., to relieve; to pay off

afluisteren, af-low-ster-rer, v., to overhear [to kill

afmaken, af-mah-ker, v., to finish, to complete;

afmatten, af-mat-ter, v., to tire out

afmeting, af-may-ting, c., dimension

afnemen, af-nay-mer, v., to take away; to decrease

afpakken, af-pak-ker, v., to snatch away

afpersen, af-payr-ser, v., to extort

afraden, af-rah-der, v., to dissuade [to beat

aframmelen, af-ram-mer-ler, v., to rattle off;

afrastering, af-ras-ter-ring, c., fence

afrekenen, af-ray-ker-ner, v., to settle a bill

africhten, af-rerHG-ter, v., to train

afschaffen, af-SHGaf-fer, v., to abolish; to discard
afscheid, af-SHGeyt, n., departure, farewell
afscheiden, af-SHGey-der, v., to separate, to sever
afscheiding, af-SHGey-ding, c., partition
afschermen, af-SHGayr-mer, v., to screen
afscheuren, af-SHGer-rer, v., to tear off
afschrift, af-srift, n., copy [(loss)
afschrijven, af-srey-ver, v., to copy; to write off
afschrikken, af-srick-ker, v., to scare
afschudden, af-SHGerd-der, v., to shake off
afschuw, af-SHGEE, c., abhorrence, horror
afslaan, af-slahn, v., to knock off; to beat off; to refuse, to decline
afsluitboom, af-slowt-bohm, c., barrier
afsluiten, af-slow-ter, v., to lock; to close
afsnauwen, af-snow-er, v., to snarl at, to snap at
afspannen, af-span-ner, v., to unharness
afspiegeling, af-spee-HGer-ling, c., reflection
afspraak, af-sprahk, c., agreement; appointment
afspreken, af-spray-ker, v., to arrange, to agree
afspringen, af-spring-er, v., to jump down [upon
afstaan, af-stahn, v., to hand over; to cede
afstammeling, af-stam-mer-ling, c., descendant
afstamming, af-stam-ming, c., descent
afstand, af-stant, c., distance; cession; abdication
afstijgen, af-stey-HGer, v., to dismount
afstoffen, af-stof-fer, v., to dust
afstoten, af-stoh-ter, v., to push off; to repel
afstraling, af-strah-ling, c., radiation
afstuiten, af-stow-ter, v., to rebound
aftreden, af-tray-der, v., to resign, to retire
aftrek, af-treck, c., deduction; ready sale
aftrekken, af-treck-ker, v., to pull off; to deduct
aftreksel, af-treck-serl, n., infusion, extract
aftuigen, af-tow-HGer, v., to unharness
afvaardiging, af-fahr-der-HGing, c., deputation
afval, af-fal, c., waste, refuse, garbage
afvallige, af-fal-ler-HGer, c., renegade; deserter
afvaren, af-fah-rer, v., to sail away, to depart
afvloeien, af-floo-yer, v., to flow away
afvoeren, af-foor-er, v., to carry off (water)
afvragen(zich), af-frah-HGer(ziHG), v., to wonder

afwachten, *af-vaHG-ter*, v., to wait, to wait for
afwassen, *af-vas-ser*, v., to wash up
afwatering, *af-vah-ter-ring*, c., drainage, drain
afwenden, *af-ven-der*, v., to turn away; to avert
afweren, *af-vay-rer*, v., to parry, to ward off
afwerken, *af-vayr-ker*, v., to finish
afwerpen, *af-vayr-per*, v., to throw off; to cast off
afwezig, *af-vay-zerHG*, a., absent
afwijken, *af-vey-ker*, v., to deviate, to diverge
afwijzen, *af-vey-zer*, v., to refuse, to decline
afwikkelen, *af-vik-ker-ler*, v., to unwind; to settle
afwinden, *af-vin-der*, v., to wind off
afwisselen, *af-vis-ser-ler*, v., to alternate
afwisseling, *af-vis-ser-ling*, c., change
afzenden, *af-sen-der*, v., to send, to dispatch
afzetgebied, *af-zet-HGer-beet*, n., market
afzetten, *af-zet-ter*, v., to take off; to drop
(passenger); to amputate; to close (road); to
turn off (radio); to swindle
afzetter, *af-zet-ter*, c., swindler
afzichtelijk, *af-siHGt-ter-luck*, a., hideous
afzien (van), *af-seen (fan)*, v., to waive, to forgo,
to give up
afzonderen, *af-son-der-rer*, v., to separate, to
[isolate
agenda, *ah-HGen-dah*, c., agenda; diary
agentschap, *ah-HGent-sHGap*, c., agency
akelig, *ah-ker-lerHG*, a., lugubrious, wretched
akker, *ak-ker*, c., field
al, alle, *al*, *al-ler*, a., all, every
al, *al*, adv., already; yet; as early **as; as far back as.**
conj., although, even if
albast, *al-bast*, n., alabaster
aldaar, *al-dahr*, adv., there, at that place
aldus, *al-derss*, adv., thus, like this
[universal
algemeen, *al-HGer-mayn*, a. & adv., general,
alhier, *al-heer*, adv., here, at this place
alkoof, *al-kohf*, c., recess (in wall)
allebei, *al-ler-bey*, a., both
alledaags, *al-ler-dahHGs*, a., daily; commonplace
alleen, *al-layn*, a. & adv., alone, lonely; only
allegaartje, *al-ler-HGahrt-yer*, n., medley
allemaal, *al-ler-mahl*, a., all

allen, *al*-len, a., all of them, all   [of all
allereerst, *al*-ler-ayrst, a. & adv., very first; first
allerhoogst, *al*-ler-hohHGST, a., supreme
allerlei, *al*-ler-ley, c. & a., all kinds; of all kinds
alles, *al*-less, pron., everything, all
allesbehalve, *al*-less-ber-*hal*-ver, adv., anything
allicht, *al*-liHGt, adv., probably; obviously   [but
allooi, *al*-loh-e, n., alloy; kind; character
almachtig, *a*-*ma*HG-terHG, a., almighty
alomvattend, *a*-lom-*fat*-tent, a., all-embracing
als, *al*s, conj., as, like; when; if
alsof, *al*-sof, conj., as though, as if
althans, *al*-tans, conj., at any rate
altijd, *al*-teyt, **altoos,** *al*-tohss, adv., always, ever
alvorens, *al*-*voh*-renss, conj., before
alweer, *al*-vayr, adv., again, once more
alwetend, *al*-*vay*-tent, a., all-knowing
alzijdig, *al*-*zey*-derHG, a., universal, versatile
amandel, ah-*man*-derl, a., almond; tonsil
ambacht, *am*-baHGt, n., trade, craft   [nical school
ambachtsschool, *am*-baHGts-sHGohl, c., tech-
ambassade, am-bahs-sah-der, c., embassy
ambt, amt, n., office, post
ambtelijk, *am*-ter-luck, a. & adv., official
ambtenaar, *am*-ter-nahr, c., civil servant
ambtshalve, amts-*hal*-ver, adv., officially
ameublement, ah-mer-bler-ment, n., suite of
amicaal, a-mee-*kah*l, a., friendly   [furniture
amper, *am*-per, adv., scarcely, hardly
analphabeet, an-*al*-fah-bayt, c., illiterate
ananas, *a*-na-nas, c., pine-apple
ander, *an*-der, a., other, another
anderhalf, *an*-der-*half*, a., one and a half
anders (dan) *an*-ders (dan), a., other (than). adv.,
     otherwise. **iemand** ——, ee-*mant* ——,
     anybody else
andersom, *an*-der-som, adv., the other way about
anderzijds, *an*-der-zeyts, adv., on the other hand
andijvie, *an*-dey-vee, c., endive
angel, *ang*-erl, c., sting (of a bee); hook (for
angst, angst, c., fear, terror; agony   [fishing)
angstig, *ang*-sterHG, a., anxious, fearful

angstvallig, *angst-fal-ler*HG, a., scrupulous

angstzweet, *angst-svayt*, n., cold sweat

animo, *ah-nee-moh*, c., zest, heartiness, go

anjelier, *an-yer-leer*, c., pink, carnation

anker, *an-ker*, n., anchor

ansjovis, *an-shoh-viss*, c., anchovy

antenne, *an-teyn-ner*, c., aerial

antipathie, *an-tee-pah-tee*, c., dislike

antiquair, *an-tee-kveyr*, c., antiquarian; second-hand bookseller

antwoord, *ant-vohrt*, n., reply, answer

antwoorden, *ant-vohr-der*, v., to reply, to respond

apennootje, *ah-pen-noht-yer*, n., pea-nut

apotheek, *ah-poh-tayk*, c., chemist's; dispensary

appèl, *ah-payl* n., appeal; roll-call

appel, *ap-perl*, c., apple; pupil (of eye)

appelmoes, *ap-perl-mooss*, n., apple-sauce

appelwijn, *ap-perl-veyn*, c., cider

applaudisseren, *ap-plow-dis-say-rer*, v., to applaud, to clap

april, *a-pril*, c., April   [water-colour

aquarel, *ah-koo'ah-rel*, c., water-colour

arbeid, *ar-beyt*, c., work, labour

arbeiden, *ar-bey-der*, v., to work, to labour

arbeider, *ar-bey-der*, c., labourer, workman

arbeidsbeurs, *ar-beyts-berrs*, c., labour exchange

arbeidzaam, *ar-beyt-sahm*, a., industrious

archief, *ar-*HGeef, n., archives; filing cabinet

archipel, *ar-shee-pel*, c., archipelago   [records

archivaris, *ar-*HGee-vah-riss, c., keeper of

arend, *ah-rent*, c., eagle

argeloos, *ar-*HGer-lohss, a., innocent; unsuspecting

arglistig, *ar*HG-liss-ter*HG, a., cunning, crafty

argwaan, *ar*HG-vahn, c., suspicion, distrust

arm, *arm*, c., arm (limb); branch (of river, etc.); bracket (of lamp). a., poor

armband, *arm-bant*, c., bracelet

armelui, *ar-mer-low*, c. pl., poor lot, paupers

armenzorg, *ar-men-zor*HG, c., poor-relief

armleuning, *arm-ler-ning*, c., arm-rest

armoede, *ar-moo-der*, c., poverty   [shabby

armoedig, *ar-moo-der*HG, a. & adv., poor, needy;

armoedzaaier, ar-moo-tsah-yer, c., poor devil
armstoel, arm-stool, c., arm-chair, easy chair
armzalig, arm-zah-lerHG, a., pitiful
aroma, a-roh-mah, n., flavour
arreslede, ar-rer-slay-der, c., sleigh
arrest, ar-rest, n., custody; arrest; judgment
arrestant, ar-ress-tant, c., person in custody
arriveren, ar-ree-vay-rer, v., to arrive
arrogant, ar-roh-HGant, a., conceited; presumptuous   [trict
arrondissement, ar-ron-dis-ser-ment, n., dis-
artikel, ar-tee-kerl, n., commodity; clause
artisjok, ar-tee-shock, c., artichoke
arts, arts, c., general practitioner, physician
as, ass, c., axle, axis; shaft; spindle
as, ass, c., ash, ashes
asbak, as-bak, c., ash-pan; ash-tray
asbest, as-best, n., asbestos   [please
asjeblieft, a-sher-bleeft, interj., (pop.) if you
asperge, as-payr-zher, c., asparagus
asphalt, as-falt, n., bitumen, asphalt
aspirant, as-pee-rant, c., applicant   [goods)
assurantie, as-SEE-ran-see, c., insurance (life,
asyl, ah-zeel, n., asylum; shelter
atelier, a-terl-yeh, n., studio; workshop
athleet, at-layt, c., athlete
atoomenergie, ah-tohm-ay-nayr-zhee, c., atomic
attent, at-tent, a., attentive, considerate   [power
attest, at-test, n., testimonial
audiëntie, oh-dee-ent-see, c., audience
auditorium, oh-dee-toh-re-erm, n., auditory
augurk, ow-HGerrk, c., gherkin
augustus, ow-HGers-terss, c., August
aula, ow-lah, c., assembly hall
auspiciën, ows-pee-see-er, c. pl., auspices
auteur, oh-terr, c., author
auteursrecht, oh-terrs-rayHGt, n., copyright
auto, ow-toh, c., automobile, motor-car
autoband, ow-toh-bant, c., motor tyre
autobus, ow-toh-bers, c., motor-bus   [person
autodidact, ow-toh-dee-dakt, c., self-taught
automaat, ow-toh-maht, c., slot machine; robot

automobiel, ow-toh-moh-bíl, c., automobile
automobilist, ow-toh-moh-bee-list, c., motorist
autoped, ow-toh-pet, c., scooter
autoriteit, ow-toh-ree-teyt, c., authority
autoweg, ow-toh-vayHG, c., motor road
averechts, ah-ver-rayHGts, a. & adv., wrong,
averij, ah-ver-rey, c., damage; average [inverted
avond, ah-vont, c., evening; night. **'s avonds,**
    sah-vonts, in the evening, at night
avondblad, ah-vont-blat, n., evening paper
avondeten, ah-vont-ey-ter, n., supper [out
avondje, ah-vont-yer, n., evening party; night
avondmaal, ah-vont-mahl, n., evening-meal
avondrood, ah-vont-roht, n., red sunset [twilight
avondschemering, ah-vont-sHGay-mer-ring, c.,
avondtoilet, ah-vont-twa-let, n., evening-dress
avonturier, ah-von-tEER-reer, c., adventurer
avontuur, ah-von-tEER, n., adventure
avontuurlijk, ah-von-tEER-luck, a., adventurous
azen (op), ah-zen (op), v., to prey (upon), to feed
azijn, ah-zeyn, c., vinegar [(upon)
azuren, ah-zEE-rer, a., azure
azuur, ah-zEER, n., azure

ba! bah! ba, interj., bah!, pooh!
baai, bah'ee, c., bay; baize (material)
baaien, bah-yer, a., made of baize
baal, bahl, c., bale; sack, bag
baan, bahn, c., way, road, course, track, rink; orbit
baanbreker, bahn-bray-ker, c., pioneer
baantje, bahnt-yer, n., job; slide (on snow)
baanvak, bahn-fak, n., section (of railway)
baanwachter, bahn-vaHG-ter, c., signalman
baar, bahr, c., bar; stretcher; wave; ingot. a.,
baard, bahrt, c., beard [ready (money)
baardeloos, bahr-der-lohs, a., beardless
baars, bahrs, c., perch
baas, bahs, c., boss, master, governor
baat, baht, c., advantage; relief
baatzuchtig, baht-serHG-terHG, a., selfish
babbelaar, bab-ber-lahr, c., chatterbox, gossip
babbelen, bab-ber-ler, v., to babble, to chatter

babbelkous, bab-berl-kowss, c., chatterbox
babbelziek, bab-berl-zeek, a., talkative [gossip
bacil, ba-sil, c., bacillus [carrier
bacillendrager, ba-sil-lern-drah-HGer, c., germ-
bacteriën, bak-tay-ree-er, c. pl., bacteria
bad, bat, n., bath; bathe
baden, bah-der, v. to bath; to bathe
bader, bah-der, c., bather
badgoed, bat-HGoot, n., bathing-things
badkamer, bat-kah-mer, c., bath-room
badkuip, bat-kowp, c., bath-tub
badmantel, bat-man-terl, c., bath-robe [tume
badpak, bat-pak, n., bathing-suit, bathing-cos-
badplaats, bat-plahts, c., seaside resort; spa
bagage, ba-HGah-zher, c., luggage
bagagedepot, ba-HGah-zher-day-poh, n., cloak-
room
bagagedrager, ba-HGah-zher-drah-HGer, c.,
luggage-carrier [luggage-office
bagagekantoor, ba-HGah-zher-kan-tohr, n.,
bagagenet, ba-HGah-zher-net, n., luggage-rack
bagagereçu, ba-HGah-zher-rer-SEE, n., luggage-
ticket [gage-van (train)
bagagewagen, ba-HGah-zher-vah-HGer, c., lug-
bagatel, ba-HGah-tel, n., trifle
bagger, baHG-er, c., mud, mire, slush
baggeren, baHG-er-er, v., to dredge; to wade
(through mud)
baggerlaars, baHG-er-lahrss, c., wader (boot)
baggermolen, baHG-er-moh-ler, c., dredger
bajes, bah-yess, c., (pop.) quod, prison
bajonet, bah-yoh-net, c., bayonet
bak, bak, c., tank, trough, bucket; bin
bakbeest, bak-bayst, n., heavy, unwieldy object
bakboord, bak-bohrt, n., port (left side of ship)
baken, bah-ker, n., beacon
baker, bah-ker, c., dry-nurse [origin
bakermat, bah-ker-mat, c., cradle; place of
bakje, bak-yer, n., tray; cup (of coffee)
bakkebaard, bak-ker-bahrt, c., whiskers [tussle
bakkeleien, bak-ker-ley-er, v., (pop.) to romp, to
bakken, bak-ker, v., to bake; to fry

bakker, bak-ker, c., baker

bakkerij, bak-ker-rey, c., bakery, bakehouse

bakkes, bak-kess, n., (pop.) mug, face

bakpoeder, bak-poo-der, n., baking-powder

baksteen, bak-stayn, c., brick

bakvis, bak-fiss, c., (pop.) young girl, teenager

bal, bal, c., ball (in games). n., dancing party

balans, ba-lans, c., weighing scales; balance-

balcostuum, bal-kos-tEEm, n., ball-dress   [sheet

baldadig, bal-dah-derHG, a. & adv., wanton

baldakijn, bal-dah-keyn, n., c., canopy

balein, bah-leyn, c., n., whalebone

baliekluiver, bah-lee-klow-ver, c., loafer, idler

baljapon, bal-yah-pon, c., dance-frock

balk, balk, c., beam

balken, bal-ker, v., to bray

balkon, bal-kon, n., balcony; platform (tram)

ballade, bal-lah-der, c., ballad

ballast, bal-last, c., ballast; encumbrance

ballen, bal-ler, v., to clench (fist)

balling, bal-ling, c., exile-

ballingschap, bal-ling-sHGap, c., exile, banish-

ballon, bal-lon, c., balloon   [ment

balorig, ba-loh-rerHG, a., peevish

balsem, bal-sem, c., balm

balsemen, bal-ser-mer, v., to embalm

balspel, bal-spel, n., ball-game

balustrade, ba-lEE-strah-der, c., balustrade;

balzaal, bal-zahl, c., ball-room   [banisters

bamboe, bam-boo, n., c., bamboo

ban, ban, c., ban; excommunication

banaal, bah-nahl, a., trite, commonplace

banaan, bah-nahn, c., banana

band, bant, c., tie; tape; braid; hoop; tyre;
    binding; volume; bond

bandeloos, ban-der-lohs, a., riotous; licentious

bandiet, ban-deet, c., bandit, ruffian

banen, bah-ner, v., to clear; to pave (a way)

bang, bang, a. & adv., fearful, anxious, afraid of

bangerd, bang-ert, c., (pop.) funk

bangmakerij, bang-mah-ker-rey, c., intimidation

banier, bah-neer, c., banner, standard

bank, bank, c., bench, seat; pew (in church); bank (business)

bankbiljet, bank-bil-yet, n., banknote

banketbakker, ban-ket-bak-ker, c., confectioner

bankier, ban-keer, c., banker   [account

bankrekening, bank-ray-ker-ning, c., banking

bankroet, bank-root, a. & n., bankrupt

bankwerker, bank-vayr-ker, c., fitter (mechanic);

banneling, ban-ner-ling, c., exile   [turner

bar, bar, c., bar. adv., very

barak, bah-rak, c., hut; shed

barbaar, bar-bahr, c., barbarian

barbaars, bar-bahrss, a., barbarous

barbier, bar-beer, c., barber   [anxiety)

baren, bah-rer, v., to give birth to; to cause (stir,

baret, bah-ret, c., cap; beret

bargoens, bar-HGoenss, n., jargon, lingo

bark, bark, c., bark, barque

barmhartig, barm-har-terHG, a., charitable

barnsteen, barn-stayn, n., amber

barnstenen, barn-stay-ner, a., amber

barrevoets, bar-rer-foots, adv., barefooted

bars, barss, a. & adv., gruff, rough

barst, barst, c., burst, crack, flaw

barsten, bar-ster, v., to burst, to crack, to split

bas, bass, c., (mus.) bass

basalt, bah-zalt, n., basalt

bascule, bas-keel, c., weighing machine

baseren (op), bah-sey-rer (op), v., to base (upon)

bast, bast, c., bark (of tree); pod

bastaard, bas-tahrt, c., bastard; mongrel

bataljon, ba-ta-lyon, n., battalion

bate, bah-ter, c., benefit. **ten —— van,** ten

baten, bah-ter, v., to avail   [fan, in aid of

baviaan, ba-vee-ahn, c., baboon

bazaar, ba-zahr, c., bazaar, fancy fair; stores

bazelen, bah-zer-ler, v., to twaddle

bazig, bah-zerHG, a. & adv., masterful

bazuin, bah-zown, c., trombone; trumpet

beambte, ber-am-ter, c., officer, functionary

beamen, ber-ah-mer, v., to assent, to agree

beangst, ber-angst, a., alarmed, anxious

beangstigen, ber-*angs-terHGer*, v., to (cause) alarm   [to reply

beantwoorden, ber-*ant-vohr-der*, v., to answer,

bebloed, ber-*bloot*, a. & p.p., covered with blood

beboeten, ber-*boo-ter*, v., to fine

bebossen, ber-*bos-ser*, v., to plant with trees

bebouwen, ber-*bow-er*, v., to build on; to till

becijferen, ber-*sey-fer-rer*, v., to calculate   [(soil)

bed, *.bet*, n., bed

bedaard, ber-*dahrt*, a. & adv., composed, calm

bedacht (op), ber-*dacht* (op), a., mindful (of)

bedachtzaam, ber-*dacht-zahm*, a., thoughtful

bedanken, ber-*dan-ker*, v., to thank; to decline; to withdraw (membership)

bedaren, ber-*dah-rer*, v., to calm down, to abate

beddedeken, bed-der-*day-ker*, c., blanket

beddegoed, bed-der-*HGoot*, n., bed-clothes

beddelaken, bed-der-*lah-ker*, n., bed-sheet

bedding, bed-*ding*, c., bed (of river)

bedeesd, ber-*dayst*, a., timid, shy

bedekken, ber-*deck-ker*, v., to cover   [(threat)

bedekt, ber-*deckt*, a. & p.p., covered; veiled

bedelaar, bay-der-*lahr*, c., beggar

bedelbrief, bay-der-*breef*, c., begging-letter

bedelen, bay-der-*ler*, v., to beg   [(alms)

bedelen, ber-*day-ler*, v., to endow; to bestow

bedeling, ber-*day-ling*, c., distribution of alms

bedelven, ber-*del-ver*, v., to bury

bedenkelijk, ber-*den-ker-luck*, a., serious, grave

bedenken, ber-*den-ker*, v., to consider

bedenking, ber-*den-king*, c., objection; consid-

bederf, ber-*dayrf*, n., decay; corruption   [eration

bederfelijk, ber-*dayr-fer-luck*, a., perishable

bederven, ber-*dayr-ver*, v., to spoil; to corrupt

bedevaart, bay-der-*fahrt*, c., pilgrimage

bedevaartganger, bay-der-*fahrt-HGang-er*, c., pilgrim   [assistant

bediende, ber-*deen-der*, c., servant; clerk;

bedienen, ber-*dee-ner*, v., to serve; to handle

bediening, ber-*dee-ning*, c., service, attendance

beding, ber-*ding*, n., condition, stipulation

bedingen, ber-*ding-er*, v., to stipulate

bedlegerig, bet-lay-HGer-rerHG, a., bed-ridden

bedoelen, ber-doo-ler, v., to intend; to mean

bedoeling, ber-doo-ling, c., purpose; purport

bedompt, ber-domt, a., close, stuffy

bedorven, ber-dor-ver, a., spoiled (child); foul (air); tainted (food); depraved (morals)

bedotten, ber-dot-ter, v., to cheat

bedrag, ber-draHG, n., amount

bedragen, ber-drah-HGer, v., to amount to

bedreigen, ber-drey-HGer, v., to threaten

bedreiging, ber-drey-HGing, c., threat

bedremmeld, ber-drem-merlt, a. & adv., confused

bedreven, ber-dray-ver, a., skilful   [fused

bedrevenheid, ber-dray-ven-heyt, c., skill

bedriegen, ber-dree-HGer, v., to deceive

bedrieger, ber-dree-HGer, c., deceiver, fraud

bedriegerij, ber-dree-HGer-rey, c., deceit, deception

bedrieglijk, ber-dree-HGer-luck, a., fraudulent

bedrijf, ber-dreyf, n., business; industry; act (play)   [vehicle

bedrijfsauto, ber-dreyfs-ow-toh, c., commercial

bedrijfskapitaal, ber-dreyfs-ka-pee-tahl, n., working capital   [manager

bedrijfsleider, ber-dreyfs-ley-der, c., works

bedrijven, ber-drey-ver, v., to commit

bedrijvig, ber-drey-verHG, a., active

bedroefd, ber-drooft, a., sad, grieved

bedroefdheid, ber-drooft-heyt, c., sorrow, grief

bedroevend, ber-droo-vent, a., sad, deplorable

bedrog, ber-droHG, n., deceit, deception

bedrukt, ber-drerkt, a., (fig.) depressed

bedtijd, bet-teyt, c., bedtime

beducht, ber-derHGt, a., afraid   [clear

beduiden, ber-dow-der, v., to mean; to make

bedwang, ber-dvang, n., restraint, control

bedwelmd, ber-dvelmt, a., stupefied; intoxicated

bedwingen, ber-dving-er, v., to restrain

beëdigen, ber-ey-der-HGer, v., to swear in

beëindigen, ber-eyn-der-HGer, v., to finish

beek, bayk, c., brook

beeld, baylt, n., image, picture; statue

beeldhouwen, baylt-how-er, v., to sculpture

beeldhouwwerk, baylt-how-vayrk, n., sculpture

beeldroman, baylt-roh-man, c., strip cartoon

beeldschoon, baylt-sHGohn, a., lovely as a picture

beeldspraak, baylt-sprahk, c., metaphor

beeltenis, bayl-ter-niss, c., image, effigy

been, bayn, n., leg; bone

beenbreuk, bayn-brerk, c., fracture (leg or bone)

beenkappen, bayn-kap-per, c. pl., leggings

beer, bayr, c., bear; boar

beest, bayst, n., animal, beast; brute (person)

beestachtig, bays-taHG-terHG, a. & adv., beastly, brutish

beestenboel, bay-sten-bool, c., (fig.) piggery

beestenmarkt, bay-sten-markt, c., cattle-market

beet, bayt, c., bite; bit, morsel

beetje, bayt-yer, n., a little bit   [of

beetnemen, bayt-nay-mer, v., (pop.), to make fun

begaafd, ber-HGahft, a., gifted, talented

begaan, ber-HGahn, v., to commit (mistake, crime); to walk upon, to tread

begaanbaar, ber-HGahn-bahr, a., passable

begeerlijk, ber-HGayr-luck, a., desirable

begeerte, ber-HGayr-ter, c., desire; lust

begeleiden, ber-HGer-ley-der, v., to accompany

begeren, ber-HGay-rer, v., to desire, to covet

begeven (zich), ber-HGay-ver (ziHG), v., to go (to)

begieten, ber-HGee-ter, v., to water (plants)

begiftigen, ber-HGif-ter-HGer, v., to endow; to present

begin, ber-HGin, n., beginning, start   [present

beginletter, ber-HGin-let-ter, c., initial   [novice

beginneling, ber-HGin-ner-ling, c., beginner,

beginnen, ber-HGin-ner, v., to begin, to start

beginsel, ber-HGin-serl, n., principle   [pled

beginselloos, ber-HGin-serl-lohss, a., unprinci-

beginstadium, ber-HGin-stah-dee-erm, n., initial stage   [delusion

begoocheling, ber-HGoh-HGer-ling, c., spell,

begraafplaats, ber-HGrahf-plahts, c., cemetery

begrafenis, ber-HGrah-fer-niss, c., funeral

begraven, ber-HGrah-ver, v., to bury   [dered

begrensd, ber-HGrenst, a. & p.p., limited; bor-

begrijpelijk, ber-HGrey-per-luck, a., understand-
begrijpen, ber-HGrey-per, v., to understand [able
begrip, ber-HGrip, n., notion; comprehension
begroeid, ber-HGroo-it, a., overgrown
begroeten, ber-HGroo-ter, v., to greet, to welcome
begroeting, ber-HGroo-ting, c., greeting
begroting, ber-HGroh-ting, c., budget; estimate(s)
begunstigen, ber-HGun-ster-HGer, v., to favour
behaaglijk, ber-hahHG-luck, a., comfortable
behaagziek, ber-hahHG-seek, a., coquettish
behagen, ber-hah-HGer, v., to please. n., pleasure
behalen, ber-hah-ler, v., to obtain; to gain [from
behalve, ber-hal-ver, conj. & prep., except, apart
behandelen, ber-han-der-ler, v., to treat, to use;
    to deal with, to handle. (med.) to attend
behandeling, ber-han-der-ling, c., treatment;
    hearing (of lawsuit)
behang, ber-hang, n., wall-paper [festoon
behangen, ber-hang-er, v., to paper a room; to
behartigen, ber-har-ter-HGer, v., to look after
beheer, ber-hayr, n., management
beheerder, ber-hayr-der, c., manager; trustee
beheersen, ber-hayr-ser, v., to control (oneself);
    to rule, to sway; to master
behelpen(zich), ber-hel-per(zinHG), v., to make
behelzen, ber-hel-zer, v., to contain [shift
behendig, ber-hen-derHG, a. & adv., dexterous
behendigheid, ber-hen-derHG-heyt, c., dexterity
behept (met), ber-hept (met), a., afflicted (with)
beheren, ber-hay-rer, v., to conduct, to administer
behoeden, ber-hoo-der, v., to protect; to preserve
behoeder, ber-hoo-der, c., protector; preserver
behoedzaam, ber-hoot-sahm, a. & adv., prudent,
    wary [tion
behoedzaamheid, ber-hoot-sahm-heyt, c., cau-
behoefte, ber-hoof-ter, c., want, need. —— hebben aan, —— heb-ber ahn, to be in need of
behoeftig, ber-hoof-terHG, a., needy, destitute
behoeven, ber-hoo-ver, v., to want, to require
behoorlijk, ber-hohr-luck, a., proper, fitting
behoorlijkheid, ber-hohr-luck-heyt, c., propriety
behoren, ber-hoh-rer, v., to belong to

behoud, ber-howt, n., preservation; conservation

behouden, ber-how-der, v., to keep, to retain. a., safe (of arrival)

behoudens, ber-how dens, prep., except for

behuizing, ber-how-zing, c., housing; dwelling

behulp, ber-herlp, n., help, aid. met —— van, met —— fan, with the aid of

behulpzaam, ber-herlp-sahm, a., helpful

beiaard, bey-ahrt, c., carillon

beiaardier, bey-ahrt-deer, c., carillon player

beide, bey-der, a., both. geen van ——, HGayn fan ——, neither

beiderlei, bey-der-ley, a., of both sorts

beijveren(zich), ber-ey-ver-rer(ziHG), v., to do one's best [one's best

beitel, bey-terl, c., chisel

beitelen, bey-ter-ler, v., to chisel

beits, beyts, n., stain, wood-dye

beitsen, beyt-ser, v., to stain (wood)

bejaard, ber-yahrt, a., aged, elderly

bejammeren, ber-yam-mer-rer, v., to deplore

bejegenen, ber-yay-HGer-ner, v., to use; to treat

bejegening, ber-yay-HGer-ning, c., treatment

bek, beck, c., mouth, beak, bill, snout

bek-af, beck-αf, a., dog-tired

bekeerling, ber-kayr-ling, c., convert

bekend, ber-kent, a., known; wellknown. —— maken, —— mah-ker, to announce

bekende, ber-ken-der, c., acquaintance

bekendmaking, ber-kent-mah-king, c., announcement

bekennen, ber-ken-ner, v., to confess

bekentenis, ber-ken-ter-niss, c., confession

beker, bay-ker, c., cup, goblet

bekeren, ber-kay-rer, v., to convert

bekering, ber-kay-ring, c., conversion

bekeuren, ber-ker-rer, v., to summons

bekeuring, ber-ker-ring, c., summons

bekijken, ber-key-ker, v., to look at, to view

bekken, beck-ker, n., basin; bowl [cused

beklaagde, ber-klahHG-der, c., defendant; ac-

bekladden, ber-klahd-der, v., to bespatter; to slander

beklag, ber-klahHG, n., complaint [slander

beklagen, ber-klah-HGer, v., to pity; to lament

beklagenswaardig, ber-klah-HGens-**vahr**-derHG, a., pitiable

bekleeden, ber-klay-der, v., to cover, to drape; (fig.) to occupy a post

bekleeder, ber-klay-der, c., holder, occupant

bekleding, ber-klay-ding, c., covering, clothing

beklemtonen, ber-klem-toh-ner, v., to stress

beklimmen, ber-klim-mer, v., to climb, to ascend

beklinken, ber-klin-ker, v., to settle (a matter)

beknopt, berk-nopt, a., concise, brief

beknorren, berk-nor-rer, v., to chide, to scold

bekoelen, ber-koo-ler, v., to cool down

bekogelen, ber-koh-HGer-ler, v., to pelt (with eggs, etc.)

bekomen, ber-koh-mer, v., to receive; to recover

bekommerd, ber-kom-mert, a., concerned, anxious [to trouble

bekommeren(zich), ber-kom-mer-rer(ziHG), v.,

bekonkelen, ber-kon-ker-ler, v., to scheme

bekoorlijk, ber-kohr-luck, a. & adv., charming

bekoren, ber-koh-rer, v., to charm, to enchant

bekoring, ber-koh-ring, c., charm, fascination

bekorten, ber-kor-ter, v., to shorten; to abridge

bekostigen, ber-kos-ter-HGer, v., to bear the cost of

bekrachtigen, ber-kraHG-ter-HGer, v., to confirm

bekrompen, ber-krom-per, a., narrow-minded

bekronen, ber-kroh-ner, v., to crown; to award

bekroning, ber-kroh-ning, c., crowning; award

bekwaam, berk-vahm, a., capable; fit

bekwaamheid, berk-vahm-heyt, c., ability; skill

bel, bel, c., bell; bubble [lous

belachelijk, ber-la-HGer-luck, a. & adv., ridicu-

beladen, ber-lah-der, v., to load; to burden

belanden, ber-lan-der, v., to land; to arrive

belang, ber-lang, n., interest; importance

belangeloos, ber-lang-HGer-lohss, a. & adv., disinterested [party interested

belanghebbende, ber-lang-heb-ben-der, c.,

belangrijk, ber-lang-reyk, a., important

belangstellend, ber-lang-stel-lent, a., interested

belangstelling, ber-*l*ang-stel-ling, c., interest
belasten, ber-*l*ass-ter, v., to load; to tax; to charge
belasteren, ber-*l*ass-ter-rer, v., to speak evil of
belasting, ber-*l*ass-ting, c., taxation; load
belastingjaar, ber-*l*ass-ting-yahr, n., fiscal year
belastingplichtigen, ber-*l*ass-ting-pliHG-ter-
   HGer, c. pl., tax-payers
beledigen, ber-lay-der-HGer, v., to insult, to
   offend [insulting
beledigend, ber-lay-der-HGent, a., offensive,
belediging, ber-lay-der-HGing, c., insult, affront
beleefd, ber-layft, a. & adv., polite
beleefdheid, ber-layft-heyt, c., politeness
beleg, ber-layHG, n., siege
belegen, ber-lay-HGer, a., matured, seasoned
belegeren, ber-lay-HGer-rer, v., to besiege
beleggen, ber-layHG-HGer, v., to invest; to cover
belegging, ber-layHG-HGing, c., investment
beleid, ber-leyt, n., prudence; management;
   policy
belemmeren, ber-lem-mer-rer, v., to impede
belendend, ber-len-dent, a., adjacent
belet, ber-let, n., hindrance; (pop.) no entrance
beletsel, ber-let-serl, n., obstacle
beletten, ber-let-ter, v., to prevent
beleven, ber-lay-ver, v., to experience
belevenis, ber-lay-ver-niss, c., experience
belezen, ber-lay-zer, a., well-read [drel
belhamel, bel-hah-merl, c., (pop.) young scoun-
belichamen, ber-liHG-ah-mer, v., to embody
belichten, ber-liHG-ter, v., to throw light on
belichting, ber-liHG-ting, c., exposure (photos)
belijden, ber-ley-der, v., to avow; to profess
belijdenis, ber-ley-der-niss, c., confession; con-
   [firmation
bellen, bel-ler, v., to ring (bell)
beloeren, ber-loo-rer, v., to spy upon
belofte, ber-lof-ter, c., promise
belonen, ber-loh-ner, v., to reward
beloning, ber-loh-ning, c., reward
beloop, ber-lohp, n., course, way
belopen, ber-loh-per, v., to amount to
beloven, ber-loh-ver, v., to promise

belust, ber-lerst, a., eager   [possession of
bemachtigen, ber-maHG-ter-HGer, v., to take
bemannen, ber-man-ner, v., to man (ship, etc.)
bemanning, ber-man-ning; c., crew (of ship)
bemantelen, ber-man-ter-ler, v., (fig.) to veil
bemerken, ber-mayr-ker, v., to observe, to
bemesten, ber-mes-ter, v., to manure   [notice
bemiddelaar, ber-mid-der-lahr, c., mediator
bemiddeld, ber-mid-delt, a., well-to-do
bemiddeling, ber-mid-der-ling, c., mediation
bemind, ber-mint, a., beloved
beminnelijk, ber-min-ner-luck, a., lovable
beminnen, ber-min-ner, v., to love
bemodderd, ber-mod-dert, a., mud-stained
bemoedigend, ber-moo-der-HGent, a.; encour-
bemoeial, ber-moo-yal, c., busybody   [aging
bemoeien, ber-moo-yer, v., to interfere   [difficult
bemoeilijken, ber-moo'ee-luck-er, v., to make
bemoeiziek, ber-moo'ee-zeek, a., meddlesome
benadelen, ber-nah-day-ler, v., to harm
benaderen, ber-nah-der-rer, v., to approximate
benaming, ber-nah-ming, c., name, denomina-
benard, ber-nart, a., critical   [tion
benauwd, ber-nowt, a., stuffy; oppressed; fearful
benauwen, ber-now-er, v., to oppress
bende, ben-der, c., band, troop, gang
beneden, ber-nay-der, prep., below, beneath.
    adv., downstairs, down, below   [bottom
benedeneind, ber-nay-den-eynt, n., lower end,
benedenhuis, ber-nay-den-howss, n., ground
    floor   [(river)
benedenloop, ber-nay-den-lohp, c., lower course
benedenwaarts, ber-nay-den-vahrts, a. & adv.,
    downward(s)
benemen, ber-nay-mer, v., to take away
benepen, ber-nay-per, a., small-minded, timid
beneveld, ber-nay-verlt, a., (fig.) confused
benevens, ber-nay-venss, prep., in addition to
bengel, beng-erl, c., naughty boy
bengelen, beng-erl-er, v., to dangle, to swing
benieuwd, ber-nee'oot, a., curious. —— zijn,
    —— zeyn, v., to wonder

benig, bay-nerHG, a., bony
benijden, ber-ney-der, v., to envy
benodigd, ber-noh-derHGt, a., required
benodigdheden, ber-noh-derHGt-hey-der, c. pl.,
  requirements
benoemen, ber-noo-mer, v., to appoint
benul, ber-nerl, n., (pop.) notion
benutten, ber-nert-ter, v., to utilize
benzine, ben-zee-ner, c., petrol
benzinestation, ben-zee-ner-stah-see'on, n.,
  filling station   [(art, etc.)
beoefenaar, ber-oo-fer-nahr, c., practitioner
beoefening, ber-oo-fer-ning, c., study (science,
beogen, ber-oh-HGer, v., to aim at   [etc.)
beoordelaar, ber-ohr-day-lahr, c., critic, reviewer
beoordelen, ber-ohr-day-ler, v., to judge
beoorlogen, ber-ohr-loh-HGer, v., to wage war
bepaald, ber-pahlt, a., fixed; definite   [on
bepakking, ber-pak-king, c., (mil.) pack
bepalen, ber-pah-ler, v., to fix; to lay down; to
  determine; to confine
bepaling, ber-pah-ling, c., definition; clause; rule
beperken, ber-payr-ker, v., to limit
beperking, ber-payr-king, c., limitation
beperkt, ber-payrkt, a. & p.p., limited, confined
beplakken, ber-plak-ker, v., to paste (over)
beplanten, ber-plan-ter, v., to plant
bepleiten, ber-pley-ter, v., to plead
beploegen, ber-ploo-HGer, v., to plough
bepraten, ber-prah-ter, v., to talk about
beproefd, ber-prooft, a. & p.p., well-tried;
beproeven, ber-proo-ver, v., to try   [afflicted
beproeving, ber-proo-ving, c., trial; affliction
beraad, ber-raht, n., deliberation   [ate
beraadslagen, ber-raht-slah-HGer, v., to deliber-
beramen, ber-rah-mer, v., to devise, to plan
berechting, ber-rayHG-ting, c., trial (of criminal)
beredderen, ber-red-der-rer, v., to arrange
bereden, ber-ray-der, a., mounted (police)
beredeneren, ber-ray-der-nay-rer, v., to discuss
bereid, ber-reyt, a., ready; willing
bereiden, ber-rey-der, v., to prepare

bereidwillig, ber-*reyt*-vil-lerHG, a. & adv., ready

bereik, ber-*reyk*, n., reach; range [achieve

bereiken, ber-*rey*-ker, v., to reach; (fig.) to

bereisd, ber-*reyst*, a., widely-travelled

berekenbaar, ber-*ray*-ken-bahr, a., calculable

berekenen, ber-*ray*-ker-ner, v., to calculate; to charge

berekening, ber-*ray*-ker-ning, c., calculation

berg, bayrHG, c., mountain

bergachtig, bayrHG-*aHG*-terHG, a., mountainous

bergbeklimmer, bayrHG-ber-*klim*-mer, c., mountaineer

bergen, bayr-HGer, v., to store; to salve. **zich** ——, ziHG ——, to get out of the way

bergketen, bayrHG-*kay*-ter, c., mountain range

bergplaats, bayrHG-plahts, c., shed; depository

bergrug, bayrHG-rerHG, c., mountain ridge

bergspits, bayrHG-spits, c., mountain peak

bergtop, bayrHG-top, c., mountain top

bericht, ber-*riHGt*, n., report, message

berichten, ber-*riHG*-ter, v., to inform, to report

berichtgever, ber-*riHGt*-HGay-ver, c., reporter

berijdbaar, ber-*reyt*-bahr, c., passable

berijden, ber-*rey*-der, v., to ride (a horse)

berijder, ber-*rey*-der, c., rider, horseman

berispelijk, ber-*riss*-ter-luck, a., reprehensible

berispen, ber-*riss*-per, v., to rebuke

berisping, ber-*riss*-ping, c., rebuke, reprimand

berk, bayrk, c., birch (tree)

berm, bayrm, c., bank (road)

beroemd, ber-*roomt*, a., famous, illustrious

beroemdheid, ber-*roomt*-heyt, c., fame; celebrity

beroemen(zich), ber-*roo*-mer(ziHG), v., to boast of

beroep, ber-*roop*, n., calling, trade; appeal

beroepsofficier, ber-*roops*-of-fee-seer, c., regular officer [sional player

beroepsspeler, ber-*roops*-spay-ler, c., profes-

beroerd, ber-*roort*, a. & adv., wretched, bad

beroeren, ber-*roo*-rer, v., to disturb

beroering, ber-*roo*-ring, c., commotion

beroerte, ber-*roor*-ter, c., stroke, fit

berokkenen, ber-rock-ker-ner, v., to cause
berookt, ber-rohkt, a., smoke-stained
berouw, ber-row, n., repentance, remorse
berouwen, ber-row-er, v., to repent
berouwvol, ber-row-fol, a., repentant
beroven, ber-roh-ver, v., to rob, to deprive
beroving, ber-roh-ving, c., robbery
berucht, ber-rerHGt, a., notorious; disreputable
berusting, ber-rerss-ting, c., resignation
bes, bess, c., berry; currant
beschaafd, ber-sHGahft, a., civilized; cultured
beschaamd, ber-sHGahmt, a., ashamed; bashful
beschadigen, ber-sHGah-der-HGer, v., to damage
beschadiging, ber-sHGah-der-HGing, c., damage
beschamen, ber-sHGah-mer, v., to put to shame
beschamend, ber-sHGah-ment, a., humiliating
beschaven, ber-sHGah-ver, v., to civilize
beschaving, ber-sHGah-ving, c., civilization
bescheid, ber-sHGeyt, n., answer
bescheiden, ber-sHGey-der, n. pl., official papers. a., modest [esty
bescheidenheid, ber-sHGey-dern-heyt, c., mod-
beschermen, ber-sHGayr-mer, v., to protect
beschermer, ber-sHGayr-mer, c., protector; patron
beschermheilige, ber-sHGayrm-hey-ler-HGer, c., patron saint [patronage
bescherming, ber-sHGayr-ming, c., protection,
beschieten, ber-sHGee-ter, v., to fire upon
beschijnen, ber-sHGey-ner, v., to shine upon
beschikbaar, ber-sHGick-bahr, a., available
beschikken(over), ber-sHGick-ker(oh-ver), v.; to dispose (of)
beschikking, ber-sHGick-king, c., disposal; decree. **ter —— zijn,** tayr —— zeyn, to be available
beschimmeld, ber-sHGim-merlt, a., mouldy
beschimpen, ber-sHGim-per, v., to revile, to jeer
beschonken, ber-sHGon-ker, a., drunk
beschot, ber-sHGot, n., wainscoting; partition
beschouwen, ber-sHGOW-er, v., to look at
beschrijven, ber-srey-ver, v., to describe

beschrijving, ber-srey-ving, c., description
beschroomd, ber-srohmt, a. & adv., timid
beschuit, ber-sHGowt, c., rusk, biscuit
beschuldigde, ber-sHGerl-derHG-der, c., accused
beschuldigen, ber-sHGerl-der-HGer, v., to accuse
beschuldiging, ber-sHGerl-der-HGing, c., accusa-
beschutten, ber-sHGert-ter, v., to shelter [tion
beschutting, ber-sHGert-ting, c., shelter
besef, ber-sef, n., sense; realization
beseffen, ber-sef-fer, v., to realize
beslaan, ber-slahn, v., to shoe (horse); to occupy
beslag, ber-slaHG, n., horse-shoes; batter (dough);
seizure (of goods)
beslagen, ber-slah-HGer, a., shod; steamy; coated
beslissen, ber-slis-ser, v., to decide
beslissend, ber-slis-sent, a. & adv., decisive
beslissing, ber-slis-sing, c., decision
beslist, ber-slist, adv., absolutely; resolutely
beslommering, ber-slom-mer-ring, c., worry
besluipen, ber-slow-per, v., (fig.) to steal upon
besluit, ber-slowt, n., decision, resolve; decree
besluiteloos, ber-slow-ter-lohss, a., irresolute
besluiten, ber-slow-ter, v., to conclude; to decide
besmettelijk, ber-smet-ter-luck, a., contagious
besmetten, ber-smet-ter, v., to infect; to pollute
besmetting, ber-smet-ting, c., contamination
besmeuren, ber-smer-rer, v., to besmear
besparen, ber-spah-rer, v., to save
besparing, ber-spah-ring, c., saving
bespatten, ber-spɑt-ter, v., to splash
bespelen, ber-spay-ler, v., to play on
bespeuren, ber-sper-rer, v., to notice, to discover
bespieden, ber-spee-der, v., to spy upon
bespiegeling, ber-spee-HGer-ling, c., contempla-
tion [upon
bespionneren, ber-spee-on-ney-rer, v., to spy
bespoedigen, ber-spoo-der-HGer, v., to speed up
bespotten, ber-spot-ter, v., to ridicule
bespotting, ber-spot-ting, c., mockery, derision
bespreken, ber-spray-ker, v., to discuss; to book
(room, etc.)
besproeien, ber-sproo-yer, v., to water (plants)

bespuiten, ber-spow-ter, v., to squirt (water) upon

bessestruik, bes-ser-strowk, c., currant-bush

best, best, a., best, very good. adv., best, very well

bestaan, ber-stahn, v., to exist. —— uit, —— owt, to consist of. n., existence; subsistence

bestand, ber-stant, n., truce

bestanddeel, ber-stand-dayl, n., part; ingredient

besteden, ber-stay-der, v., to spend (money, time) [limit, scope

bestek, ber-steck, n., specification, estimate;

bestelbiljet, ber-stel-bil-yet, n., order form

bestelen, ber-stay-ler, v., to rob [office

bestelkantoor, ber-stel-kan-tohr, n., parcels

bestellen, ber-stel-ler, v., to order; to deliver

besteller, ber-stel-ler, c., postman; delivery man

bestelling, ber-stel-ling, c., delivery; order

bestelwagen, ber-stel-vah-HGer, c., delivery van

bestemmen, ber-stem-mer, v., to destine

bestemming, ber-stem-ming, c., destination

bestendig, ber-sten-derHG, a., constant; steady

bestijgen, ber-stey-HGer, v., to ascend; to mount

bestoken, ber-stoh-ker, v., to harass

bestormen, ber-stor-mer, v., to assault, to storm

bestorming, ber-stor-ming, c., assault; rush (on

bestralen, ber-strah-ler, v., to shine upon [bank)

bestraten, ber-strah-ter, v., to pave

bestrijden, ber-strey-der, v., to fight; to dispute

bestrooien, ber-stroh-yer, v., to sprinkle

besturen, ber-stEE-rer, v., to rule; to administer; to conduct; to drive; to steer; to fly

bestuur, ber-stEEr, n., government; administration; control; management

bestuurder, ber-stEEr-der, c., director; driver;

betaalbaar, ber-tahl-bahr, a., payable [pilot

betalen, ber-tah-ler, v., to pay

betaling, ber-tah-ling, c., payment

betamelijk, ber-tah-mer-luck, a., decent, seemly

betasten, ber-tas-ter, v., to handle, to feel

betekenen, ber-tay-ker-ner, v., to signify

betekenis, ber-tay-ker-niss, c., meaning; importance

beter, bay-ter, a. & adv., better, improved

beterschap, bay-ter-SHGap, c., change for the better   [strain

beteugelen, ber-ter-HGer-ler, v., to curb, to re-

beteuterd, ber-ter-tert, a. & adv., perplexed

betoger, ber-toh-HGer, c., demonstrator

betoging, ber-toh-HGing, c., demonstration

beton, ber-ton, n., concrete

betoog, ber-tohHG, n., argument   [charm

betoveren, ber-toh-ver-rer, v., to bewitch; to

betovering, ber-toh-ver-ring, c., spell, fascination

betrappen, ber-trap-per, v., (fig.) to catch, to detect

betreden, ber-tray-der, v., to enter (a room)

betreffen, ber-tref-fer, v., to concern, to affect

betreffende, ber-tref-fen-der, prep., concerning

betrekkelijk, ber-treck-ker-luck, a.&adv., relative

betrekken, ber-treck-ker, v., to move into; to involve

betrekking, ber-treck-king, c., relation; post

betreuren, ber-trer-rer, v., to regret; to mourn

betreurenswaardig, ber-trer-rerns-vahr-derHG, a., deplorable   [concerned

betrokken, ber-trock-ker, a. & p.p., overcast;

betrouwbaar, ber-trow-bahr, a., reliable

betuigen, ber-tow-HGer, v., to express (sympathy)

betweter, bet-vay-ter, c., pedant

betwijfelen, ber-tvey-fer-ler, v., to doubt

betwistbaar, ber-tvist-bahr, a., disputable

betwisten, ber-tviss-ter, v., to dispute

beu (van), ber (fan), a., sick (of)

beugel, ber-HGerl, c., strap, brace; clasp

beuk, berk, c., aisle (of church); beech (tree)

beuken, ber-ker, v., to beat, to pound

beul, berl, c., executioner. (fig.) brute

beunhaas, bern-hahss, c., dabbler

beurs, bers, c., purse; exchange; scholarship. a., oversoft (of apples)

beursvacantie, bers-fah-kan-see, c., bank holiday

beurt, bert, c., turn

beurtelings, ber-ter-lings, adv., in turn

beuzelaar, ber-zer-lahr, c., dawdler

beuzelachtig, ber-zer-laHG-terHG, a., trivial

bevaarbaar, ber-fahr-bahr, a., navigable
bevallen, ber-fal-ler, v., to please
bevallig, ber-fal-ler HG, a., graceful
bevalling, ber-fal-ling, c., confinement
bevaren, ber-fah-rer, v., to sail (seas)
bevattelijk, ber-fat-ter-luck, a., intelligent
bevatten, ber-fat-ter, v., to contain; to grasp
beveiligen, ber-fey-ler-HGer, v., to secure
beveiliging, ber-fey-ler-HGing, c., protection
bevel, ber-vel, n., order, command. **op —— van,
op —— fan**, by order of
bevelen, ber-vay-ler, v., to order, to command
bevelhebber, ber-vel-heb-ber, c., commander
bevelschrift, ber-vel-srift, n., warrant
beven, bay-ver, v., to tremble; to quiver (of voice)
bever, bay-ver, c., beaver   [confirm
bevestigen, ber-fess-ter-HGer, v., to fix; to
bevestigend, ber-fess-ter-HGent, a. & adv.,
affirmative   [(oneself)
bevinden (zich), ber-fin-der (ziHG), v., to find
bevinding, ber-fin-ding, c., experience
bevlekken, ber-fleck-ker, v., to stain; to defile
bevlieging, ber-flee-HGing, c., (pop.) caprice
bevochtigen, ber-foHG-ter-HGer, v., to moisten
bevoegd, ber-fooHGt, a., competent, qualified
bevolken, ber-fol-ker, v., to populate
bevolking, ber-fol-king, c., population
bevoordelen, ber-fohr-day-ler, v., to favour
bevooroordeeld, ber-fohr-ohr-daylt, a. & p.p.,
prejudiced
bevoorraden, ber-fohr-rah-der, v., to supply
bevoorrechten, ber-fohr-rayHG-ter, v., to favour
bevorderaar, ber-for-der-rahr, c., promoter
bevorderen, ber-for-der-rer, v., to further   to
promote
bevorderlijk, ber-for-der-luck, a., conducive
bevrachten, ber-fraHG-ter, v., to freight, to load
bevredigen, ber-fray-der-HGer, v., to satisfy
bevreemdend, ber-fraym-dent, a., surprising
bevreesd, ber-frayst, a., afraid, apprehensive
bevriend, ber-freent, a., friendly. **—— met,
—— met**, on friendly terms with

bevri-zen, ber-free-zer, v., to freeze
bevrijden, ber-frey-der, v., to liberate
bevrijding, ber-frey-ding, c., liberation [bitten
bevroren, ber-froh-rer, a. & p.p., frozen, frost-
bevuilen, ber-fow-ler, v., to soil; to defile
bewaarder, ber-vahr-der, c., keeper, caretaker
bewaarplaats, ber-vahr-plahts, c., storehouse
bewaarschool, ber-vahr-sHGohl, c., kindergarten
bewaken, ber-vah-ker, v., to guard, to watch over
bewaker, ber-vah-ker, c., keeper, guard
bewapenen, ber-vah-per-ner, v., to arm
bewapening, ber-vah-per-ning, c., armament
bewaren, ber-vah-rer, v., to keep; to maintain
bewaring, ber-vah-ring, c., preservation; custody
beweegbaar, ber-vayHG-bahr, a., movable
beweeglijk, ber-vayHG-luck, a., mobile; lively
beweegreden, ber-vayHG-ray-der, c., motive
bewegen, ber-vay-HGer, v., to move, to stir
beweging, ber-vay-HGing, c., motion; commotion
bewenen, ber-vay-ner, v., to weep over
beweren, ber-vay-rer, v., to allege, to assert
bewerken, ber-vayr-ker, v., to work, to fashion;
to till (ground); to adapt (play)
bewerkstelligen, ber-vayrk-stel-ler-HGer, v., to
bring about [shower praise
bewieroken, ber-vee-roh-ker, v., to incense; to
bewijs, ber-veyss, n., proof; certificate
bewijsstuk, ber-veys-sterk, n., title-deed
bewijzen, ber-vey-zer, v., to prove
bewind, ber-vint, n., rule, government
bewogen, ber-voh-HGer, a.& p.p., moved; affected
bewolkt, ber-volkt, a., clouded, overcast
bewonderen, ber-von-der-rer, v., to admire
bewondering, ber-von-der-ring, c., admiration
bewonen, ber-voh-ner, v., to inhabit, to live in
bewoner, ber-voh-ner, c., inhabitant, tenant
bewoordingen, ber-vohr-ding-er, c. pl., terms,
bewust, ber-verst, a., conscious [wording
bewusteloos, ber-vers-ter-lohss, a., unconscious
bewustzijn, ber-verst-zeyn, n., consciousness
bezadigd, ber-zah-derHGt, a., sedate
bezem, bay-zem, c., broom

bezemsteel, bay-zem-stayl, c., broomstick
bezeren, ber-zay-rer, v., to hurt, to injure
bezet, ber-zet, a., engaged, taken, occupied
bezeten, ber-zay-ter, a., possessed
bezetten, ber-zet-ter, v., to occupy; to fill (post)
bezetting, ber-zet-ting, c., occupation; cast (of
bezichtigen, ber-ziHG-ter-HGer, v., to view [play]
bezield, ber-zeelt, a., inspired, animated
bezieling, ber-zee-ling, c., inspiration, animation
bezien, ber-zeen, v., to view, to look at
bezienswaardig, ber-zeens-vahr-derHG, a., worth
bezig, bay-zerHG, a., busy; at work [seeing
bezigen, bay-zer-HGer, v., to use, to employ
bezingen, ber-zing-er, v., to sing (praises of)
bezinksel, ber-zink-serl, n., sediment; residue
bezinnen(zich), ber-zin-ner(ziHG), v., to reflect
bezit, ber-zit, n., possession, property
bezitten, ber-zit-ter, v., to possess, to own
bezitter, ber-zit-ter, c., owner, proprietor
bezoedelen, ber-zoo-der-ler, v., to soil, to defile
bezoek, ber-zook, n., visit, call
bezoeker, ber-zoo-ker, c., visitor, caller
bezoeking, ber-zoo-king, c., visitation; trial
bezorgd, ber-zorHGt, a., worried, anxious
bezorgdheid, ber-zorHGt-heyt, c., concern
bezorgen, ber-zor-HGer, v., to deliver; to procure
bezuinigen, ber-zow-ner-HGer, v., to economize
bezuiniging, ber-zow-ner-HGing, c., retrenchment
bezuren, ber-zEE-rer, v., (pop.) to pay dearly for
bezwaar, ber-zvahr, n., objection; drawback
bezwaarlijk, ber-zvahr-luck, a. & adv., difficult
bezweet, ber-zvayt, a., perspiring
bezweren, ber-zvay-rer, v., to swear; to exorcise
bezwijken, ber-zvey-ker, v., to succumb
bezwijming, ber-zvey-ming, c., faint, swoon
bibberen, bib-ber-rer, v., to shiver [brarian
bibliothecaris, bee-blee-oh-tay-kah-riss, c., li-
bibliotheek, bee-blee-oh-tayk, c., library
bidden, bid-der, v., to pray; to entreat
biecht, beeHGt, c., confession
biechtvader, beeHGt-fah-der, c., confessor
bieden, bee-der, v., to offer; to bid

biefstuk, beef-sterk, c., rumpsteak
bier, beer, n., beer
bierbrouwer, beer-brow-er, c., brewer
bies, beess, c., bulrush
biet, beet, c., beet
biezen, bee-zer, a., made of rushes
big, biHG, c., young pig
bij, bey, c., bee   [up to date
bij, bey, prep. & adv., by, with, near; advanced,
bijbel, bey-berl, c., bible
bijbetalen, bey-ber-tah-ler, v., to pay extra
bijblad, bey-blat, n., supplement (of newspaper)
bijblijven, bey-bley-ver, v., to keep pace
bijbrengen, bey-breng-er, v., to bring round
bijdehand, bey-der-hant, a., smart, bright
bijdoen, bey-doon, v., to add
bijdrage, bey-drah-HGer, c., contribution
bijeen, bey-ayn, adv., together   [together
bijeenbrengen, bey-ayn-breng-er, v., to bring
bijeendrijven, bey-ayn-drey-ver, v., to round up
bijeenkomst, bey-ayn-komst, c., meeting
bijeenroepen, bey-ayn-roo-per, v., to convene
bijenkorf, bey-en-korf, c., bee-hive
bijenwas, bey-en-vass, n., beeswax
bijenzwerm, bey-en-zvayrm, c., swarm of bees
bijgaand, bey-HGahnt, a., enclosed
bijgebouw, bey-HGer-bow, n., annex
bijgeloof, bey-HGer-lohf, n., superstition
bijgenaamd, bey-HGer-nahmt, a., surnamed
bijgevolg, bey-HGer-volHG, conj., therefore
bijhouden, bey-how-der, v., to keep, to keep up
bijkantoor, bey-kan-tohr, n., branch-office [again
bijkomen, bey-koh-mer, v., to come to oneself
bijkomstig, bey-kom-sterHG, a., unimportant
bijl, beyl, c., hatchet
bijleggen, bey-layHG-HGer, v., to settle (dispute)
bijna, bey-nah, adv., nearly. —— **geen,** ——
    HGayn, hardly any
bijnaam, bey-nahm, c., surname; nickname
bijslag, bey-slaHG, c., extra allowance
bijspringen, bey-spring-er, v., to help
bijstaan, bey-stahn, v., to help, to assist

bijstand, bey-stant, c., help, aid
bijt, beyt, c., gap in the ice
bijten, bey-ter, v., to bite
bijtend, bey-tent, a., caustic. (fig.) biting
bijtijds, bey-teyts, adv., in time
bijval, bey-fal, c., approval, applause
bijvalskreten, bey-fals-kray-ter, c. pl., cheers
bijvullen, bey-ferl-ler, v., to replenish
bijwerken, bey-vayr-ker, v., to touch up (pictures)
bijwonen, bey-voh-ner, v., to attend
bijzaak, bey-zahk, c., matter of minor importance
bijziend, bey-zeent, a., near-sighted
bijzijn, bey-zeyn, n., presence
bijzit, bey-zit, c., concubine
bijzonder, ber-zon-der, a. & adv., particular
bijzonderheid, ber-zon-der-heyt, c., detail
biljart, bil-yart, n., billiards; billiard-table
biljarten, bil-yar-ter, v., to play billiards
biljet, bil-yet, n., ticket
billijk, bil-luck, a., fair, just; moderate
binden, bin-der, v., to bind; to tie (up)
binnen, bin-ner, prep., within. adv., in, inside
binnenband, bin-ner-bant, c., inner tube
binnenbrengen, bin-ner-breng-er, v., to bring in
binnendringen, bin-ner-dring-er, v., to penetrate
binnengaan, bin-ner-нGahn, v., to enter
binnenhouden, bin-ner-how-der, v., to keep in-
binnenkant, bin-ner-kant, c., inside   [doors
binnenkomst, bin-ner-komst, c., entry, entrance
binnenkort, bin-ner-kort, adv., shortly
binnenland, bin-ner-lant, n., interior; home
binnenlands, bin-ner-lants, a., inland; home
  (affairs); home-made; internal
binnenlaten, bin-ner-lah-ter, v., to admit
binnenplaats, bin-ner-plahts, c., inner court
binnenroepen, bin-ner-roo-per, v., to call in
binnenshuis, bin-nerns-howss, adv., indoors
binnenste, bin-ner-ster, n., innermost
binnenstebuiten, bin-ner-ster-bow-ter, adv.,
  inside out   [inland waterways
binnenwateren, bin-ner-vah-ter-rer, n. pl.,
binnenzak, bin-ner-zak, c., inside pocket

binnenzee, bin-ner-zay, c., inland sea
binnenzijde, bin-ner-zey-der, c., inside
bioscoop, bee-os-kohp, c., cinema
bisdom, biss-dom, n., diocese
bisschop, bis-SHGOP, c., bishop
bisschopsstaf, bis-SHGOPs-staf, c., crosier
bits, bits, a. & adv., snappy, biting, tart
bitter, bit-ter, n., bitters. a., bitter; sore
bivak, bee-vak, n., bivouac
blaam, blahm, c., blame
blaar, blahr, c., blister
blaas, blahss, c., bladder
blaasbalg, blahss-balHG, c., bellows
blaasinstrument, blahss-ins-trEE-ment, n., wind-instrument
blad, blat, n., leaf, sheet; tray; newspaper
bladgoud, blat-HGowt, n., gold-leaf
bladzijde, blat-zey-der, c., page
blaffen, blaf-fer, v., to bark
blank, blank, a., white; fair; naked (sword)
blanke, blan-ker, c., white man (or woman)
blaten, blah-ter, v., to bleat
blauw, blow, a., blue. **een —— oog,** ayn ——
blazen, blah-zer, v., to blow [ohHG, a black eye
bleek, blayk, c., bleach-field. a., pale
bleken, blay-ker, v., to bleach, to whiten
bleu, bler, a., timid, shy
blij, bley, a., glad, pleased
blijdschap, bleyt-sHGap, c., joy, gladness
blijk, bleyk, n., token, proof, mark
blijkbaar, bleyk-bahr, a., apparent, evident
blijken, bley-ker, v., to be evident, to appear
blijspel, bley-spel, n., comedy
blijven, bley-ver, v., to remain, to stay
blijvend, bley-vent, a., lasting, permanent
blik, blik, c., look, glance. n., tin-plate; dustpan; tin (of food) [vegetables
blikgroenten, blik-HGroon-ter, c. pl., tinned
blikken, blik-ker, v., to look, to glance. a., made
bliksem, blik-sem, c., lightning [of tin
bliksemsnel, blik-sem-snel, a., quick as lightning
blikslager, blik-slah-HGer, c., tinsmith

blind, blint, n., shutter. a., blind
blinddoeken, blind-doo-ker, v., to blindfold
blinde, blin-der, c., blind person
blinken, blin-ker, v., to shine, to gleam
blocnote, bloc-noht, c., writing pad
bloed, bloot, n., blood
bloedarmoede, bloo-tar-moo-der, c., anæmia
bloedbad, blood-bat, n., massacre
bloeden, bloo-der, v., to bleed
bloedgeld, bloot-Hgelt, n., blood-money
bloedsomloop, bloot-som-lohp, c., blood circu-
bloedvat, bloot-fat, n., blood vessel   [lation
bloedverwant, bloot-fer-vant, c., (blood) re-
bloedzuiger, bloot-sow-Hger, c., leech   [lation
bloei, bloo-ee, c., bloom, flowering
bloeien, bloo-yer, v., to bloom. (fig.) to flourish
bloem, bloom, c., flower; flour
bloemblad, bloom-blat, n., petal
bloembol, bloom-bol, c., flower bulb
bloemist, bloo-mist, c., florist
bloemkool, bloom-kohl, c., cauliflower
bloemkweker, bloom-kveck-er, c., florist
bloemlezing, bloom-lay-zing, c., anthology
bloesemen, bloo-ser-mer, v., to bloom; to blossom
blok, block, n., block; log; chump
blokkade, blok-kah-der, c., blockade
blokken, blok-ker, v., to plod, to swot
blokkeren, blok-kay-rer, v., to blockade; to
blond, blont, a., blond, fair   [freeze (account)
blondine, blon-dee-ner, c., fair-haired lady
bloot, bloht, a., bare, naked
blootleggen, bloht-lay-Hger, v., (fig.) to expose
blootshoofds, bloht-hohfts, adv., bareheaded
blootstaan (aan), bloht-stahn(ahn), v., to be
exposed (to)   [expose (oneself)
blootstellen (zich), bloht-stel-ler (ziHG), v., to
blootsvoets, bloht-foots, adv., barefooted
blos, bloss, c., blush; flush; bloom
blozen, bloh-zer, v., to blush; to flush
bluffen, blerf-fer, v., to boast, to brag
blussen, blers-ser, v., to put out, to extinguish
bochel, bo-Hgerl, c., hump, hunchback

bocht, boHGt, c., bend, turn, curve. n., trash
bod, bott, n., offer, bid
bode, boh-der, c., messenger; beadle
bodem, boh-dem, c., bottom; territory
bodemloos, boh-dem-lohss, a., bottomless
boedel, boo-derl, c., estate; goods and chattels
boef, boof, c., knave, rogue
boeg, booHG, c., bow (of ship)
boei, boo'ee, c., shackle, fetter; handcuff; buoy
boeien, boo-yer, v., to shackle; to put in irons.
  (fig.) to grip, to enthral
boeiend, boo-yent, a., captivating
boek, book, n., book; quire (of paper)
boekbinder, book-bin-der, c., bookbinder
boekdeel, book-dayl, n., volume
boeken, boo-ker, v., to book; to register
boekenkast, boo-ken-kast, c., book-case   [seller
boekhandelaar, book-han-der-lahr, c., book-
boekhouden, book-how-der, n., book-keeping
boel, bool, c., lot, a great deal
boeman, boo-man, c., bogey-man
boemeltrein, boo-merl-treyn, c., slow train
boender, boon-der, c., scrubbing brush
boenen, boo-ner, v., to scrub; to polish
boenwas, boon-vass, n., beeswax
boer, boor, c., farmer, peasant
boerderij, boor-der-rey, c., farm
boerenkinkel, boo-ren-kin-kerl, c., rustic
boerenkool, boo-ren-kohl, c., kale
boerin, boo-rin, c., farmer's wife
boete, boo-ter, c., penitence; penalty, fine
boeteling, boo-ter-ling, c., penitent
boeten, boo-ter, v., to atone; to expiate
boetseren, boot-say-rer, v., to model
boetvaardig, boot-fahr-derHG, a., penitent
boezelaar, boo-zer-lahr, c., apron
boezem, boo-zem, c., bosom, breast; bay (sea)
bof, boff, c., stroke of luck; mumps
boffen, bof-fer, v., to be in luck
bok, bock, c., he-goat, buck; blunder. een ——
  schieten, ayn —— sHGee-ter, to make a
  blunder

bokkesprong, bock-ker-sprong, c., caper, capriole
bokkig, bock-kerHG, a., surly
bokking, bock-king, c., bloater
boksen, bock-ser, v., to box
bokspartij, bocks-par-tey, c., boxing match
bol, boll, c., ball, sphere, globe; bulb. a., convex,
    bulging; chubby (of cheeks)
bolhoed, boll-hoot, c., bowler hat
bolleboos, bol-ler-bohss, c., dab
bollenkweker, bol-lern-kveck-er, c., bulb-grower
bollenveld, bol-lern-felt, n., bulb-field
bolster, boll-ster, c., husk; bolster
bolwerk, boll-vayrk, n., rampart; (fig.) bulwark
bolwerken, boll-vayr-ker, v., (pop.) to manage
bom, bom, c., bomb   [bomb
bombarderen, bom-bar-day-rer, v., to shell, to
bomvrij, bom-frey, a., bomb-proof
bon, bon, c., ticket, voucher, coupon
bond, bont, c., union, league, alliance
bondgenoot, bont-HGer-noht, c., ally
bondig, bon-derHG, a. & adv., succinct, concise
bonenstaak, boh-nen-stahk, c., bean-stick
bonk, bonk, c., lump, chunk; bundle (of nerves)
bons, bonss, c., thump, thud; bump
bont, bont, n., fur. a., multi-coloured
bontjas, bont-yass, c., fur coat
bontwerker, bont-vayr-ker, c., furrier
bonzen, bon-zer, v., to throb; to batter; to bump
boodschap, boht-sHGap, c., message; errand
boog, bohHG, c., bow; arch; curve
booggewelf, bohHG-HGer-vaylf, n., arched vault
boom, bohm, c., tree; beam; punting pole; shaft
boomgaard, bohm-HGahrt, c., orchard
boomschors, bohm-sHGorss, c., bark (of tree)
boomstam, bohm-stam, c., trunk (of tree)
boomtak, bohm-tak, c., branch, bough (of tree)
boon, bohn, c., bean
boor, bohr, c., gimlet, drill
boord, bohrt, c., border, edge; bank (of river)
boordschutter, bohrt-sHGert-ter, c., air-gunner
boos, bohss, a., angry, cross
boosaardig, boh-zahr-derHG, a., malicious

boosdoener, bohz-doo-ner, c., malefactor
boot, boht, c., boat
bootsman, bohts-man, c., boatswain
bootwerker, boht-vayr-ker, c., docker
bord, bort, n., plate; blackboard
bordes, bor-dess, n., flight of steps (outside house)
borduren, bor-DEE-rer, v., to embroider
borduurwerk, bor-DEER-vayrk, n., embroidery
boren, boh-rer, v., to bore; to sink (a well)
borg, borHG, c., surety, guarantor; bail
borgstelling, borHG-stel-ling, c., security; bail
borrel, bor-rerl, c., small glass (of liquor)
borst, borst, c., breast, chest, bosom
borstbeeld, borst-baylt, n., bust; effigy (on coin)
borstel, bor-sterl, c., brush
borstelen, bor-ster-ler, v., to brush
borstplaat, borst-plaht, c., breast-plate
borstrok, borst-rock, c., undervest
borstwering, borst-vay-ring, c., parapet
bos, boss, n., wood, forest, c., bunch, bundle; tuft (hairs, etc.)
bosbouw, boss-bow, c., forestry
bosduif, boss-dowf, c., wood-pigeon
bosrijk, boss-reyk, a., wooded
bot, bot, n., bone. a., blunt (of knife); dull, stupid
boter, boh-ter, c., butter
boterbloem, boh-ter-bloom, c., buttercup
boterham, boh-ter-ram, c., slice of bread and butter
botervlootje, boh-ter-floht-yer, n., butter-dish
botje, bot-yer, n., small bone
botsing, bot-sing, c., collision; (fig.) clash
botvieren, bot-fee-rer, v., to give rein to
botweg, bot-vayHG, adv., bluntly, flatly
bougie, boo-zhee, c., sparking-plug
bout, bowt, c., bolt
bouw, bow, c., construction; building
bouwen, bow-er, v., to build; to construct
bouwkunde, bow-kern-der, c., architecture
bouwland, bow-lant, n., arable land
bouwterrein, bow-tayr-ren, c., building site
bouwvallig, bow-fal-lerHG, a., dilapidated

boven, boh-ver, prep., above, over, beyond. adv., upstairs; above; aloft

bovenaan, boh-ven-**ahn**, adv., at the top

bovendek, boh-ven-deck, n., upper deck [sides

bovendien, boh-ven-deen, adv., moreover, be-

bovenmenselijk, boh-ver-**men**-ser-luck, a. & adv., superhuman [adv., supernatural

bovennatuurlijk, boh-ven-nah-**teer**-luck, a. &

bovenop, boh-ven-op, adv., on top

bovenste, boh-ven-ster, a., uppermost, topmost

braadpan, braht-pan, c., frying pan

braadvet, braht-fet, n., dripping

braaf, brahf, a., good, honest. adv., well

braak, brahk, a., fallow

braakmiddel, brahk-mid-derl, n., emetic

braambes, brahm-bess, c., blackberry

brabbelen, brab-ber-ler, v., to jabber

braden, brah-der, v., to roast, to fry, to bake

brak, brak, a., brackish

braken, brah-ker, v., to vomit

brand, brant, c., fire

brandbaar, brant-bahr, a., inflammable

branden, bran-der, v., to burn, to be on fire

branding, bran-ding, c., breakers (on beach), surf

brandkast, brant-kast, c., safe [stigmatize

brandmerken, brant-mayr-ker, v., to brand; to

brandnetel, brant-nay-terl, c., stinging nettle

brandpunt, brant-pernt, n., focus

brandspiritus, brant-spee-ree-terss, c., methy-lated spirit [pile

brandstapel, brant-stah-perl, c., stake; funeral

brandstichter, brant-stiHG-ter, c., incendiary

brandstof, brant-stof, c., fuel

brandtrap, brant-trap, c., fire-escape

brandvrij, brant-frey, a., fire-proof

brandweer, brant-vayr, c., fire-brigade

brandweerman, brant-vayr-man, c., fireman

brandwond, brant-vont, c., burn; scald

brassen, bras-ser, v., to revel, to feast

breed, brayt, a., broad, wide

breedsprakig, brayt-**sprah**-kerHG, a., prolix

breedte, bray-ter, c., breadth, width; latitude

breedvoerig, brayt-foo-rerHG, a. & adv., ample
breekbaar, brayk-bahr, a., fragile
breekijzer, brayk-ey-zer, n., crowbar
breien, brey-er, v., to knit
brein, breyn, n., brain; intellect
breken, bray-ker, v., to break [to convey
brengen, breng-er, v., to bring; to take; to carry,
bretels, brer-telss, c. pl., braces
breuk, brerk, c., burst, crack; fracture; rupture
breukband, brerk-bant, c., truss
brevier, brer-veer, n., breviary
brief, breef, c., letter, epistle
briefkaart, breef-kahrt, c., postcard [spondence
briefwisseling, breef-vis-ser-ling, c., corre-
bries, breess, c., breeze
brievenbus, bree-ven-berss. c., letter-box, pillar-
brij, brey, c., porridge [box
brik, brick, c., brig; break (carriage); brick
bril, bril, c., pair of spectacles
brillenmontuur, bril-len-mon-tEEr, c., spec-
brilslang, bril-slang, c., cobra [tacle-frame
brits, brits, c., wooden couch
broche, brosh, c., brooch
broeden, broo-der, v., to brood
broeder, broo-der, c., brother; friar
broederschap, broo-der-sHGap, c., brotherhood
broeien, broo-yer, v., to sit brooding; to be sultry
broeierig, broo-yer-rerHG, a., sweltering [(of air)
broeikas, broo-ee-kass, c., hothouse
broek, brook, c., trousers. **korte** ——, kor-ter
—— , breeches, shorts
broekspijp, brooks-peyp, c., trouser-leg
broer, broor, c., brother
brok, brock, c. & n., piece, bit, morsel, lump
brokkelen, brock-ker-ler, v., to crumble
brombeer, brom-bayr, c., grumbler
bromfiets, brom-feets, c., autocycle
brommen, brom-mer, v., to grumble, to growl;
to hum, to buzz (of insects)
bromvlieg, brom-fleeHG, c., bluebottle
bron, bron, c., source, spring, well; (fig.) origin
brood, broht, n., bread; loaf

broodtrommel, broht-trom-merl, c., bread-tin
broodwinning, broht-vin-ning, c., livelihood
broos, brohss, a., brittle, frail
bros, bross, a., crisp, brittle
brouwen, brow-er, v., to brew; to plot
brouwer, brow-er, c., brewer
brouwsel, brow-serl, n., brew; concoction
brug, brerHG, c., bridge [bridge
bruggedek, brerHG-HGer-deck, n., roadway on
brugleuning, brerHG-ler-ning, c., parapet, railing
brugpijler, brerHG-pey-ler, c., pillar (of bridge)
bruid, browt, c., bride
bruidegom, brow-der-HGom, c., bridegroom
bruidsjapon, browts-yah-pon, c., wedding dress
bruidsmeisje, browts-mey-sher, n., bridesmaid
bruidsschat, browts-sHGat, c., dowry
bruikbaar, browk-bahr, a., useful, serviceable
bruikleen, browk-layn, n., free loan
bruiloft, brow-loft, c., wedding party
bruin, brown, a., brown [(of sea)
bruisen, brow-ser, v., to fizz (of drinks); to roar
brullen, brerl-ler, v., to roar
brutaal, brer-tahl, a., impertinent, impudent
brutaalweg, brEE-tahl-vayHG, adv., coolly
brutaliteit, brEE-tah-lee-teyt, c., impudence
bruto, brEE-toh, a., gross (of weight)
bruut, brEEt, c., brute
buffel, berf-ferl, c., buffalo
buffet, bEEf-fet, n., sideboard; buffet, bar
buffetjuffrouw, bEEf-fet-yerf-frow, c., barmaid
bui, bow, c., shower, squall (of weather); whim
  (of persons); fit (of laughter); temper
buidel, bow-derl, c., bag, pouch; purse
buideldier, bow-derl-deer, n., marsupial
buigbaar, bowHG-bahr, a., pliable, flexible
buigen, bow-HGer, v., to bend, to curve
buiging, bow-HGing, c., bow; curtsey
buiig, bow-erHG, a., gusty, showery
buik, bowk, c., belly, abdomen; stomach
buikpijn, bowk-peyn, c., stomach-ache
buikspreker, bowk-spray-ker, c., ventriloquist
buil, bowl, c., swelling; bump; bruise

buis, bowss, n., jacket. c., tube, pipe, conduit
buit, bowt, c., loot, spoils, booty
buitelen, bow-ter-ler, v., to tumble
buiten, bow-ter, n., country house. prep. & adv., outside, out of, beyond (reach); outdoors; without. van —— leren, fan —— lay-rer, to learn by heart
buitendeur, bow-ter-derr, c., street-door
buitengewoon, bow-ter-HGer-vohn, a. & adv., extraordinary
buitenkans, bow-ter-kans, c., stroke of good luck
buitenkant, bow-ter-kant, c., outside, exterior
buitenland, bow-ter-lant, n., foreign countries
buitenlands, bow-ter-lants, a., foreign
buitenlucht, bow-ter-lerHGt, c., open air
buitenplaats, bow-ter-plahts, c., country seat
buitenshuis, bow-tens-hows, adv., outdoors
buitensporig, bow-ter-spoh-rerHG, a., excessive
buitenstaander, bow-ter-stahn-der, c., outsider
buitenwijk, bow-ter-veyk, c., suburb
buitmaken, bowt-mah-ker, v., to seize, to capture
bukken, berk-ker, v., to bend; to stoop; to duck
buks, berkss, c., rifle
bulderen, berl-der-rer, v., to boom; to bluster; to bellow [to bellow
bulken, berl-ker, v., to bellow, to roar
bullebak, berl-ler-bak, c., bully, ogre
bult, berlt, c., hunch; hump; swelling
bundel, bern-derl, c., bundle; sheaf
burcht, berrHGt, c., citadel
bureau, bEE-roh, n., office; police station; writing [desk
burgemeester, berr-HGer-may-ster, c., burgo-master; mayor
burger, berr-HGer, c., citizen; civilian [class
burgerklasse, berr-HGer-klas-ser, c., middle-
burgerlijk, berr-HGer-luck, a., civil; civic
burgeroorlog, berr-HGer-ohr-loHG, c., civil war
burgerrecht, berr-HGer-rayHGt, n., citizenship
bus, berss, c., motor-bus; tin; box
buskruit, berss-krowt, n., gunpowder
buslichting, berss-liHG-ting, c., collection (postal)
buste, bEE-ster, c., bust
buur, bEEr, c., neighbour

buurt, bEErt, c., neighbourhood, vicinity
buurten, bEEr-ter, v., to visit neighbours

cacaopoeder, ka-kow-poo-yer, n., cocoa-powder
cactus, kak-terss, c., cactus
cadaver, kah-dah-ver, n., dead body, carrion
cadeau, kah-doh, n., present [keeper
caféhouder, ka-feh-how-der, c., coffee-house
cahier, kah-yey, n., exercise-book, copy-book
calqueerpapier, kal-kayr-pah-peer, n., tracing-paper
camoufleren, ka-moo-flay-rer, v., to camouflage
canapé, ka-na-pay, c., sofa, settee
candidaat, kan-dee-daht, c., candidate; applicant
cantine, kan-tee-ner, c., canteen
capaciteit, kah-pah-see-teyt, c., capacity; ability
capituleren, ka-pee-tEE-ley-rer, v., to surrender
capsule, kap-sEE-ler, c., capsule
carambole, ka-ram-bohl, c., cannon (at billiards)
caricatuurtekenaar, ka-ree-kah-tEEr-tay-ker-nahr, c., caricaturist
carrière, kar-ree-ay-rer, c., career
carrousel, kar-roo-sel, c., merry-go-round
cassa, kas-sah, c., cash; pay-desk; box-office
catalogus, ka-tah-loh-HGerss, c., catalogue
categorie, ka-tay-HGoh-ree, c., category
cavalerie, ka-vah-ler-ree, c., cavalry
cederhout, say-der-howt, n., cedar(-wood)
ceintuur, seyn-tEEr, c., belt, scarf
celibaat, say-lee-baht, n., celibacy
celibatair, say-lee-bah-tayr, c., celibate, bachelor
celstraf, sel-straf, c., solitary confinement; (mil.)
cementen, say-men-ter, a., cement [cells
censuur, sen-sEEr, c., censorship; censure
centrale, sen-trah-ler, c., power-station; (tele-phone) exchange. —— verwarming,
fer-var-ming, central heating
centrum, sen-trerm, n., centre
ceremoniemeester, say-rer-moh-nee-may-ster,
c., master of ceremonies [room
champignon, sham-pee-n'yon, c., edible mush-
chantage, shan-tah-zher, c., blackmail

chaos, HGah-oss, c., chaos, welter
chauffeur, shoh-ferr, c., chauffeur, driver
chef, shef, c., chief; principal; station-master
chequeboek, sheck-book, n., cheque-book
chic, sheek, a., smart, stylish
chirurg, shee-rerrHG, c., surgeon
christelijk, kriss-ter-luck, a. & adv., christian
cichorei, see-HGoh-ray, c., chicory
cijfer, sey-fer, n., figure; mark; cipher
cipier, see-peer, c., warder, jailer
circa, seer-kah, adv., about, approximately
circulaire, seer-KEE-layr, c., circular (letter)
circus, seer-kerss, n., circus, ring
cirkel, seer-kerl, c., circle
cirkelzaag, seer-kerl-zahHG, c., circular saw
citeren, see-tey-rer, v., to quote; to summon
citroensap, see-troon-sap, n., lemon-juice
civiel, see-veel, a., civil; reasonable (prices)
clandestien, klan-dess-teen, a. & adv., clandes-
classiek, klas-seek, a., classic(al)   [tine
coalitieregering, koh-ah-lee-tsee-rer-HGey-ring,
          c., coalition government
coiffeur, ko'ahf-ferr, c., hairdresser
cokes, kohks, c. pl., coke
colbertcostuum, kol-bayr-koss-tEEm, n., lounge-
collecte, kol-leck-ter, c., collection   [suit
collega, kol-lay-HGah, c., colleague
college, kol-lay-zher, n., college; lecture
colonne, koh-lon-ner, c., (mil.) column
combineren, kom-bee-nay-rer, v., to combine
comité, kom-ee-tay, n., committee, board
commandant, kom-man-dant, c., commander;
          (naut.) captain   [mand
commanderen, kom-man-day-rer, v., to com-
commentaar, kom-men-tahr, c., comment;
          commentary
commissaris, kom-mis-sah-riss, c., commission-
          er; chief constable   [mission
commissie, kom-mis-see, c., committee; com-
commode, kom-mohd, c., chest of drawers
compagnie, kom-pa-n'yee, c., (mil.) company
compagnon, kom-pa-n'yon, c., partner

compleet, kom-playt, a. & adv., complete
componist, kom-poh-nist, c., (mus.) composer
concentratiekamp, kon-sen-**trah**-see-kamp, n., concentration camp
concert, kon-sayrt, n., concert; concerto; recital
concierge, kon-see-ayr-zher, c., caretaker, door-keeper
concluderen, kon-klEE-day-rer, v., to conclude
concours, kon-koors, n., competition, match
concurrentie, kon-kEEr-ren-see, c., competition
conditie, kon-dee-see, c., condition; state
condoleren, kon-doh-lay-rer, v., to condole
conducteur, kon-derk-terr, c., guard; conductor
confectiepakje, kon-feck-see-pak-yer, n., ready-made suit
conferentie, kon-fer-ren-see, c., conference
congé, kon-zhey, n., dismissal
consequent, kon-ser-kvent, a. & adv., consistent
conserven, kon-sayr-ver, c. pl., preserves
consorten, kon-sor-ter, c. pl., confederates, associates [ascertain
constateren, kon-stah-tay-rer, v., to state; to
constructie, kon-strerk-see, c., construction
consulaat, kon-sEE-laht, n., consulate
consulent, kon-sEE-lent, c., adviser
consultatiebureau, kon-serl-tah-see-bEE-roh, n., health centre [ignition key
contactsleuteltje, kon-takt-sler-terlt-yer, n.,
contant, kon-tant, a., cash. —— e betaling, —— er ber-tah-ling, cash payment
contra-bas, kon-trah-bass, c., (mus.) double-bass
contributie, kon-tree-bEE-see, c., subscription
contrôle, kon-troh-ler, c., check, supervision
controleren, kon-troh-lay-rer, v., to check, to verify [versation lesson
conversatieles, kon-ver-zah-see-less, c., con-
copie, koh-pee, c., copy, duplicate [dress
costuum, koss-tEEm, n., costume; suit; fancy-
coulisse, koo-lees-ser, c., wing (theatre)
coupé, koo-pay, c., compartment (in train)
couplet, koo-plet, n., stanza [things]
couvert, koo-vayr, n., envelope; cover (dinner

crisis, kree-ziss, c., crisis, critical stage
critiek, kree-teek, c., criticism; review
cultureel, kerl-tEE-rayl, a., cultural
cultuur, kerl-tEER, c., culture; cultivation
curatele, kEE-rah-tay-ler, c., guardianship
cursief, kerr-seef, a. & adv., in italics   [i.um
cursus, kerr-serss, c., course (of study), curricu-
cycloon, see-klohn, c., cyclone
cylinder, see-lin-der, c., cylinder; top-hat
cynisch, see-neess, a. & adv., cynic, cynical

daad, daht, c., deed, act, action, feat
daags, dahHGs, a. & adv., daily, everyday
daar, dahr, conj., as, because. adv., there
daarbij, dahr-bey, adv., besides, moreover
daardoor, dahr-dohr, adv., through that   [hand
daarentegen, dah-ren-tay-HGer, adv., on the other
daargelaten, dahr-HGer-lah-ter, adv., leaving
daarheen, dahr-hayn, adv., there, thither   [aside
daarin, dah-rin, adv., in there
daarlangs, dahr-longss, adv., along there
daarmee, dahr-may, adv., with that
daarna, dahr-nah, adv., after that
daarnaar, dahr-nahr, adv., by that
daarom, dah-rom, adv., therefore
daaromheen, dah-rom-hayn, adv., around it
daaronder, dah-ron-der, adv., under it; among
daarop, dah-rop, adv., on that; thereupon   [them
daarover, dah-roh-ver, adv., over it; about that
daartegen, dahr-tay-HGer, adv., against that
daartoe, dahr-too, adv., for that
daartussen, dahr-ters-ser, adv., in between
daaruit, dahr-owt, adv., from that, thence
daarvan, dahr-fan, adv., of that, from that
daarvoor, dahr-fohr, adv., for that
daarvoor, dahr-fohr, adv., before that
dadel, dah-derl, c., date (fruit)
dadelijk, dah-der-luck, a. & adv., immediate
dader, dah-der, c., perpetrator, author
dag, daHG, c., day, day-time, daylight
dagblad, daHG-blat, n., daily newspaper
dagboek, daHG-book, n., diary

dagelijks, dah-HGer-lucks, a. & adv., daily

dagen, dah-HGer, v., to dawn; to summon

dageraad, dah-HGer-raht, c., dawn

daglicht, daHG-liHGt, n., daylight

dagloner, daHG-loh-ner, c., labourer

dagtaak, daHG-tahk, c., day's work   [to cite

dagvaarden, daHG-fahr-der, v., to summons,

dak, dak, n., roof

dakgoot, dak-HGoht, c., gutter

dakloos, dak-lohss, a., homeless

dakpan, dak-pan, c., tile

dakvenster, dak-fens-ter, n., garret-window

dal, dal, n., valley

dalen, dah-ler, v., to descend; to fall

daling, dah-ling, c., descent; drop, decline

dam, dam, c., dam, dike; barrage

damast, dah-mast, n., damask

dame, dah-mer, c., lady

dammen, dam-mer, v., to play draughts

damp, damp, c., vapour, fume

dampen, dam-per, v., to steam (of hot food)

dampkring, damp-kring, c., atmosphere

damspel, dam-sperl, n., draughts (game)

dan, dan, adv., then. conj., than

danig, dah-nerHG, a., very great. adv., greatly

dank, dank, c., thanks. geen ——! HGayn —— don't mention it!

dankbaar, dank-bahr, a., thankful

dankbaarheid, dank-bahr-heyt, c., gratitude

danken, dan-ker, v., to thank

dans, danss, c., dance

dansen, dan-ser, v., to dance

danspas, dans-pass, c., dancing-step

dapper, dap-per, a. & adv., brave, gallant

dapperheid, dap-per-heyt, c., bravery, valour

dar, dar, c., drone

darm, darm, c., intestine, gut

dartel, dar-terl, a., playful, frisky; skittish

das, dass, c., tie; scarf; badger

dasspeld, das-spelt, c., tie-pin

dat, dat, pron., that; which. conj., that

dateren, dah-tay-rer, v., to date

datum, dah-term, c., date
dauw, dow, c., dew
dauwdroppel, dow-drop-perl, c., dew-drop
daveren, dah-ver-rer, v., to boom, to resound; to shake
de, der, art., the
debat, der-bat, n., discussion, debate
debet, day-bet, n., debit
debiteur, day-bee-terr, c., debtor
december, day-sem-berr, c., December
declamator, day-klah-mah-tor, c., reciter
declameren, day-klah-may-rer, v., to recite
decor, day-kor, n., scenery (on stage)
decreet, der-krayt, n., decree
deeg, dayHG, n., dough
deel, dayl, n., part, portion; volume
deelgenoot, dayl-HGer-noht, c., sharer; partner
deelnemer, dayl-nay-mer, c., partner; competitor
deelneming, dayl-nay-ming, c., sympathy; participation
deels, dayls, adv., partly
deeltje, daylt-yer, n., particle
deemoed, day-moot, c., humility
deerlijk, dayr-luck, a. & adv., sad, pitiful
deernis, dayr-niss, c., pity
deerniswekkend, dayr-niss-veck-kent, a., pitiful
defileren, day-fee-lay-rer, v., to march past
deftig, def-terHG, a., dignified; fashionable
degelijk, dayr-luck, a. & adv., sound; thorough
degen, day-HGer, c., sword
degene, der-HGay-ner, pron., the person who
deinen, dey-ner, v., to heave
deining, dey-ning, c., swell; (fig.) commotion
dek, deck, n., cover, covering; deck (of ship)
deken, day-ker, c., dean; blanket
dekken, deck-ker, v., to cover; to lay (the table)
dekking, deck-king, c., cover; (fig.) cloak, screen
dekkleed, deck-klayt, n., cover
deksel, deck-serl, n., lid, cover
dekstoel, deck-stool, c., deck-chair
delen, day-ler, v., to divide; to share
delfstof, delf-stof, c., mineral
delict, der-lict, n., offence
delven, del-ver. v., to dig; to delve

demonteren, day-mon-tay-rer, v., to dismantle
dempen, dem-per, v., to deaden (sound); to fill
den, den, c., fir-tree   [(canal); to quell (revolt)
denkbaar, denk-bahr, a., conceivable
denkbeeld, denk-baylt, n., idea, notion
denkbeeldig, denk-bayl-derHG, a., imaginary
denken, den-ker, v., to think
denker, den-ker, c., thinker
dennenaald, den-ner-nahlt, c., fir-needle
dennenappel, den-ner-ap-perl, c., fir-cone
deponeren, day-poh-nay-rer, v., to put down; to deposit
deprimeren, day-pree-may-rer, v., to depress
derde, dayr-der, a., third
derderangs, dayr-der-rangs, a., third-rate
deren, day-rer, v., to harm, to hurt
dergelijk, dayr-HGer-luck, a., such
dertien, dayr-teen, a., thirteen
dertiende, dayr-teen-der, a., thirteenth
dertig, dayr-terHG, a., thirty
dertigste, dayr-terHG-ster, a., thirtieth
desem, day-sem, c., leaven
deserteur, day-zayr-terr, c., deserter
deskundig, dess-kern-derHG, a., expert
deskundige, dess-kern-der-HGer, c., expert
desnoods, dess-nohts, adv., if necessary
desondanks, dess-on-danks, adv., nevertheless
destijds, dess-teyts, adv., at that time
destilleerderij, dess-til-layr-der-rey, c., distillery
destilleren, dess-til-lay-rer, v., to distil
detail, day-ta-e, n., detail; retail trade
deugd, derHGt, c., virtue. **lieve** ——! lee-ver
  ——, good gracious!
deugdelijk, derHG-der-luck, a., sound
deugdzaam, derHGt-sahm, a., virtuous
deugniet, derHG-neet, c., good for nothing, rascal
deuk, derk, c., dent, dint
deukhoed, derk-hoot, c., trilby (hat)
deuntje, dernt-yer, n., tune, singsong, air
deur, derr, c., door
deurbel, derr-bel, c., door-bell
deurknop, derr-k'nop, c., door-handle, knob

deuropening, derr-oh-per-ning, c., doorway

deurwaarder, derr-vahr-der, c., usher

devies, der-veess, n., device, motto

deviezen, der-vee-zer, n. pl., foreign currency

deze, day-zer, pron., this, these

dezelfde, der-zelf-der, a., the same

diamant, dee-ah-mant, c. & n., diamond

diamantslijper, dee-ah-mant-sley-per, c., diamond-polisher

dicht, diHGt, a., closed (of door); dense (of fog)

dichtbij, diHGt-bey, adv., close by, near

dichtbinden, diHGt-bin-der, v., to tie up

dichtdoen, diHGt-doon, v., to shut, to close

dichtdraaien, diHGt-drah-yer, v., to turn off (tap)

dichten, diHG-ter, v., to write poetry

dichter, diHG-ter, c., poet   [poetical

dichterlijk, diHG-ter-luck, a. & adv., poetic,

dichtheid, diHGt-heyt, c., density

dichtknopen, diHGt-k'noh-per, v., to button up

dichtkunst, diHGt-kernst, c., art of poetry

dichtmaken, diHGt-mah-ker, v., to close   [down

dichtschroeven, diHGt-sroo-ver, v., to screw

dichtslaan, diHGt-slahn, v., to bang, to slam

die, dee, pron., that; those; which; who   [(door)

dieet, dee-eet, n., diet

dief, deef, c., thief

diefstal, deef-stal, c., theft, robbery, larceny

dienaar, dee-nahr, c., servant

diender, deen-der, c., (pop.) policeman

dienen, dee-ner, v., to serve (a master, etc.)

dienst, deenst, c., service. **tot uw ——! tot ƏƏ**

    ——, you are welcome!

dienstbode, deenst-boh-der, c., domestic servant

dienstig, deens-terHG, a., useful, serviceable

dienstknecht, deenst-k'nayHGt, c., man-servant

dienstmeid, deenst-meyt, c., maid-servant

dienstplicht, deenst-pliHGt, c., conscription

dienstregeling, deenst-ray-HGer-ling, c., time-table

dientengevolge, deen-ten-HGer-vol-HGer, adv.,

diep, deep, a., deep; profound   [hence

diepte, deep-ter, c., depth

diepzinnig, deep-seen-nerHG, a. & adv., profound
dier, deer, n., animal, beast
dierbaar, deer-bahr, a., dear, beloved
dierenopzetter, dee-rer-op-set-ter, c., taxider-
dierenriem, dee-rer-reem, c., zodiac   [mist
dierenrijk, dee-rer-reyk, n., animal kingdom
dierentemmer, dee-rer-tem-mer, c., tamer of
   animals
dierentuin, dee-rer-town, c., zoological garden
dierenvriend, dee-rer-freent, c., animal lover
dierkunde, deer-kern-der, c., zoology
dierlijk, deer-luck, a., animal; bestial
dievegge, dee-vayHG-er, c., female thief
dievenbende, dee-ver-ben-der, c., gang of thieves
dij, dey, c., thigh
dijbeen, dey-bayn, n., thigh-bone
dijk, deyk, c., dike, bank, dam
dik, dick, a., fat, stout, plump; thic:
dikte, dick-ter, c., thickness
dikwijls, dick-verls, adv., often
dilettant, dee-let-tant, c., amateur
dimmen, deem-mer, v., to dim (head-lights)
diner, dee-nay, n., dinner
dineren, dee-nay-rer, v., to dine
ding, ding, n., thing   [nahr, to compete for
dingen, ding-er, v., to bargain. —— naar, ——
dinsdag, dins-daHG, c., Tuesday
direct, dee-rect, adv., at once, directly
directeur, dee-rec-terr, c., manager; headmaster
dirigeerstok, dee-ree-HGayr-stock, c., (mus.)
   baton   [orchestra)
dirigent, dee-ree-HGent, c., conductor (of
disconto, diss-kon-toh, n., discount; bank rate
discreet, diss-krayt, a. & adv., modest; delicate
discretie, diss-kray-see, c., secrecy; discretion
discuteren, diss-KEE-tay-rer, v. to discuss, to
   argue
disponibel, diss-poh-nee-berl, a., available
dissel, dis-serl, c., pole, shaft
dissonant, dis-soh-nant, c., (mus.) discord
distel, diss-terl, c., thistle   [this
dit, dit, pron., this. —— alles, —— al-less, all

ditmaal, dit-mahl, adv., this time

diversen, dee-vayr-ser, c. pl., sundries

dobbelen, dob-ber-ler, v., to play dice; to gamble

dobbelsteen, dob-berl-stayn, c., die

dobber, dob-ber, c., float (of fishing line)

dobberen, dob-ber-rer, v., to float; to fluctuate

docent, doh-sent, c., teacher

doceren, doh-say-rer, v., to teach

doch, doHG, conj., but, however

dochter, doHG-ter, c., daughter

dode, doh-der, c., dead person

dodelijk, doh-der-luck, a. & adv., mortal, fatal

doden, doh-der, v., to kill

doedelzak, doo-derl-zak, c., bagpipe

doek, dook, c., cloth; shawl; sling. n., woven material; canvas; curtain (of theatre); screen (of cinema)

doel, dool, n., target; goal; (fig.) aim, purpose

doelbewust, dool-ber-verst, a., purposeful

doeleinde, dool-eyn-der, n., end, purpose

doelen (op), doo-ler (op), v., to aim at

doelloos, dool-lohss, a. & adv., aimless

doelmatig, dool-mah-terHG, a. & adv., appropriate; efficient

doelpunt, dool-pernt, n., goal (in game) [keeper

doelverdediger, dool-fer-day-der-HGer, c., goal-

doemen, doo-mer, v., to condemn; to doom

doen, doon, v., to do; to perform; to make

doende, doon-der, a., busy

doezelig, doo-zer-lerHG, a., hazy; drowsy

dof, dof, a., dull; dim

dok, dock, n., dock (for ships) [dock

dokken, dock-ker, v., to dock; to place into dry-

dokter, dock-ter, c., doctor, physician

dokwerker, dock-vayr-ker, c., docker, dock-labourer [fond of

dol, dol, a., mad; wild. — op, ——, op, very

dolblij, dol-bley, a., overjoyed

dolen, doh-ler, v., to roam, to wander

dolk, dolk, c., dagger, stiletto

dolleman, dol-ler-man, c., madman [stupid, dull

dom, dom, c., dome (of church); cathedral. a.,

domein, doh-meyn, n., domain; crown land
domheid, dom-heyt, c., stupidity
dominee, doh-me-nay, c., clergyman, parson
domkerk, dom-kayrk, c., cathedral
domkop, dom-kop, c., dunce, dullard
dommelen, dom-mer-ler, v., to doze, to drowse
dompelen, dom-per-ler, v., to plunge, to immerse
dompig, dom-perHG, a., close, stuffy
donder, don-der, c., thunder
donderbui, don-der-bow, c., thunder-storm
donderdag, don-der-daHG, c., Thursday
donderslag, don-der-slaHG, c., thunderclap
donker, don-ker, n., dark, darkness. a., dark,
dons, dons, n., down, fluff [sombre, obscure
donzig, don-zerHG, a., downy, fluffy
dood, doht, c., death. a., dead
doodarm, doht-arm, a., very poor [cool
doodbedaard, doht-ber-dahrt, a., very calm,
doodeenvoudig, doht-ayn-vow-derHG, a., very
doodgaan, doht-HGahn, v., to die [easy
doodgewoon, doht-HGer-vohn, a., quite common
doodgraver, doht-HGrah-ver, c., grave-digger
doodkist, doht-kist, c., coffin
doodmoe, doht-moo, a., tired to death
doodnuchter, doht-nerHG-ter, a., quite sober
doodsangst, dohts-angst, c., agony; mortal fear
doodsbericht, dohts-ber-riHGt, n., obituary notice
doodsklok, dohts-klock, c., death-bell, knell
doodskop, dohts-kop, c., skull
doodslag, doht-slaHG, c., manslaughter; homicide
doodsteek, doht-stayk, c., death-blow
doodsteken, doht-stay-ker, v., to stab to death
doodstil, doht-stil, a., dead silent
doodstraf, doht-straf, c., death penalty
doodsvijand, dohts-fey-ant, c., mortal enemy
doodvonnis, doht-fon-nerss, n., death-sentence
doodziek, doht-seek, a., mortally ill
doodzonde, doht-son-der, c., mortal sin
doof, dohf, a., deaf
doofheid, dohf-heyt, c., deafness
doofstom, dohf-stom, a., deaf and dumb
dooi, doh'ee, c., thaw

dooien, doh-yer, v., to thaw
dooier, doh-yer, c., yolk
doolhof, dohl-hof, c., labyrinth
doop, dohp, c., baptism, christening
doopnaam, dohp-nahm, c., Christian name
doopsgezinde, dohps-HGer-zin-der, c., baptist
doopvont, dohp-font, c., baptismal font
doopwater, dohp-vah-ter, n., baptismal water
door, dohr, prep. & adv., through, by, throughout.
—— en ——, —— en ——, thoroughly.
doorboren, dohr-boh-rer, v., to pierce; to stab
doorbraak, dohr-brahk, c., breach (in dike)
doorbreken, dohr-bray-ker, v., to break
doorbrengen, dohr-breng-er, v., to pass; to
spend (time)
doorbuigen, dohr-bow-HGer, v., to bend; to sag
doordacht, dohr-daHGt, a., well-considered
doordraven, dohr-drah-ver, v., (fig.) to rattle on
doordringen, dohr-dring-er, v., to penetrate
doordringen, dohr-dring-er, v., to pierce
doordringend, dohr-dring-ent, a., penetrating
doordrongen (van), dohr-drong-er (fan), a.,
impressed (with)
dooréén, doh-rayn, adv., mixed up, pell-mell
doorgaan, dohr-HGahn, v., to go on; to hold good
doorgaans, dohr-HGahns, adv., mostly; usually
doorgang, dohr-HGang, c., passage, thoroughfare
doorgeven, dohr-HGay-ver, v., to pass on (something)
doorgronden, dohr-HGron-der, v., to fathom
doorhalen, dohr-hah-ler, v., to cross out (words)
doorheen, dohr-hayn, adv., through
doorkneed, dohr-k'nayt, a., well read in
doorknippen, dohr-k'nip-per, v., to cut (through)
doorkomen, dohr-koh-mer, v., to get through
doorlaten, dohr-lah-ter, v., to let through
doorlezen, dohr-lay-zer, v., to read through
doorlopen, dohr-loh-per, v., to walk on; to pass
through
doorlopend, dohr-loh-pent, a., continuous
doorluchtig, dohr-lerHG-terHG, a., illustrious
doormaken, dohr-mah-ker, v., to experience

doormidden, dohr-**mid**-der, adv., in half
doorn, dohrn, c., thorn
doornat, dohr-**nat**, a., wet to the skin
doornhaag, dohrn-hahHG, c., thorn-hedge
doorpraten, dohr-**prah**-ter, v., to go on talking
doorreis, dohr-reyss, c., passage through
doorreizen, dohr-**rey**-zer, v., to travel through
doorschijnend, dohr-sHGey-nent, a., diaphanous
doorseinen, dohr-**sey**-ner, v., to transmit
doorsijpelen, dohr-**sey**-per-ler, v., to ooze through
doorslaand, dohr-slahnt, a., conclusive (proof)
doorslag, dohr-slaHG, c., carbon copy; strainer
doorsnuffelen, dohr-**snerf**-fer-ler, v., to rummage
doorstaan, dohr-stahn, v., to stand, to endure [in
doortastend, dohr-**ta**-stent, a. & adv., energetic
doortrapt, dohr-**trapt**, a., consummate (villain)
doortrokken, dohr-**trock**-ker, a., soaked, per-
doorvaart, dohr-fahrt, c., passage [meated
doorvoed, dohr-foot, a., well-fed
doorweekt, dohr-vaykt, a., soaked, sodden
doorweven, dohr-**vay**-ver, v., to interweave
doorworstelen, dohr-**vor**-ster-ler, v., to struggle
through (a book)
doorzenden, dohr-**zen**-der, v., to send on
doorzetten, dohr-**zet**-ter, v., to carry through
doorzicht, dohr-ziHGt, n., insight
doorzichtig, dohr-ziHG-terHG, a., transparent
doorzoeken, dohr-**zoo**-ker, v., to search, to
doos, dohss, c., box, case [rummage
dop, dop, c., shell, husk, pod; top, cover, cap
dopen, doh-per, v., to baptize; to dip, to sop
doperwt, dop-ayrvt, c., green pea
doppen, dop-per, v., to shell, to husk
dor, dor, a., barren, dry
dorp, dorp, n., village
dorpel, dor-perl, c., threshold
dorpeling, dor-per-ling, c., villager
dorps, dorpss, a., rustic [inn
dorpsherberg, dorps-hayr-bayrHG, c., country
dorpsmeisje, dorps-mey-sher, n., country girl
dorsen, dor-ser, v., to thresh
dorst, dorst, c., thirst

dorstig, dor-sterHG, a., thirsty
dosis, doh-zerss, c., dose, quantity
dot, dot, c., knot (of hair); tuft (of grass, etc.)
douane, doo-ah-ner, c., Customs, custom-house
douanerechten, doo-ah-ner-rayHG-ter, n. pl., [customs-duties
dove, doh-ver, c., deaf person
doven, doh-ver, v., to extinguish
dozijn, doh-zeyn, n., dozen
draad, draht, c., thread; wire; grain (of wood)
draadloos, draht-lohss, a., wireless
draagbaar, drahHG-bahr, c., stretcher
draagband, drahHG-bant, c., strap; sling
draaglijk, drahHG-er-luck, a., bearable, endurable
draagwijdte, drahHG-vey-ter, c., range (of guns, [etc.]
draai, drah-ee, c., turn, twist; winding [etc.]
draaibank, drah-ee-bank, c., lathe
draaibrug, drah-ee-brerHG, c., swing-bridge
draaideur, drah-ee-derr, c., revolving door
draaien, drah-yer, v., to turn; to spin; to twist
draaikolk, drah-ee-kolk, c., whirlpool
draaimolen, drah-ee-moh-ler, c., roundabout
draaiorgel, drah-ee-or-HGerl, n., barrel-organ
draak, drahk, c., dragon; sensational play
drab, drap, c., sediment; dregs, lees
dracht, drahGt, c., costume, dress
draf, draf, c., trot. op een ——, op ayn ——, at a [trot]
dragen, drah-HGer, v., to carry; to wear
drager, drah-HGer, c., carrier; porter
dralen, drah-ler, v., to linger; to hesitate
drang, drang, c., urgency, pressure
drank, drank, c., drink; liquor, spirits
drankje, drank-yer, n., medicine, potion
drankverbod, drank-fer-bot, n., prohibition
drassig, dras-serHG, a., marshy, swampy
draven, drah-ver, v., to trot
dreg, drayHG, c., drag
dreggen, drayHG-HGer, v., to dredge; to sweep
dreigement, drey-HGer-ment, n., threat, menace
dreigen, drey-HGer, v., to threaten
drek, dreck, c., dirt, muck
drempel, drem-perl, c., threshold [ing) person
drenkeling, dren-ker-ling, c., drowned (drown-

drenken, dren-ker, v., to drench; to water

drentelen, dren-ter-ler, v., to stroll; to loiter

dresseren, dres-say-rer, v., to train; to drill

dressoir, dres-so'ahr, c., dresser, sideboard

dreumes, drer-mess, c., mite, toddler

dreunen, drer-ner, v., to drone; to roar; to rumble

dribbelen, drib-ber-ler, v., to toddle; to trip

drie, dree, a., three

driedubbel, dree-derb-berl, a., treble, threefold

drieërlei, dree-er-ley, a., of three sorts

driehoek, dree-hook, c., triangle

driehoekig, dree-hoo-kerHG, a., triangular

driekleur, dree-klerr, c., tricolour   [Night

Driekoningen, dree-koh-ning-er, n., Twelfth

drieling, dree-ling, c., triplets

driemanschap, dree-man-sHGap, n., triumvirate

driest, dreest, a. & adv., audacious

drietand, dree-tant, c., trident

drievoet, dree-foot, c., tripod

driewieler, dree-vee-ler, c., tricycle

drift, drift, c., drift (of ship); anger, passion

driftig, drif-terHG, a. & adv., quick-tempered,

driftkop, drift-kop, c., hothead   [passionate

drijfkracht, dreyf-krahGt, c., motive power;.

   (fig.) driving force

drijfveer, dreyf-vayr, c., incentive, motive

drijfzand, dreyf-sant, n., quicksand

drijven, drey-ver, v., to float; to propel; to run

   (business); (fig.) to prompt

drijver, drey-ver, c., drover; beater (of game)

dril, drilboor, dril, dril-bohr, c., drill

drillen, dril-ler, v., to drill (soldiers)

dringen, dring-er, v., to push; to hustle

dringend, dring-ent, a. & adv., urgent

drinkbak, drink-bak, c., drinking-trough

drinkebroer, drink-er-broor, c., tippler

drinken, drink-er, v., to drink

drinkgelag, drink-HGer-laHG, n., drinking-bout

drinkwater, drink-vah-ter, n., drinking-water

droefgeestig, droof-HGay-sterHG, a., melancholy

droefheid, droof-heyt, c., sadness, sorrow

droesem, droo-sem, c., sediment, dregs, lees

droevig, droo-verHG, a., sad; mournful; pitiful

drogen, droh-HG**er**, v., to dry; to wipe

drogist, droh-HGïst, c., druggist

drogreden, droHG-ray-der, c., sophism

drom, drom, c., crowd, throng

dromen, droh-mer, v., to dream

dromer, droh-mer, c., dreamer, visionary

dromerig, droh-mer-rerHG, a. & adv., dreamy

drommel, drom-merl, c., deuce; devil. **arme ——!, ar-mer ——, poor devil!**

drommels! drom-merls, interj., the deuce!

dronk, dronk, c., draught, drink; toast

dronkaard, dronk-ahrt, c., drunkard

dronken, dron-ker, a., drunk; tipsy

droog, drohHG, a., dry; arid; parched

droogdok, drohHG**-dock**, n., dry-dock [reclaim

droogleggen, drohHG**-lay-**HG**er**, v., to drain; to

drooglijn, drohHG**-leyn**, c., clothes-line

droogrek, drohHG**-reck**, n., clothes-horse

droogte, drohHG**-ter**, c., drought

droom, drohm, c., dream

droombeeld, drohm-baylt, n., vision

drop, drop, c., drop; drip. n., liquorice

druif, drowf, c., grape

druilen, drow-ler, v., to mope; to pout

druilerig, drow-ler-rerHG, a., drizzling (weather)

druipen, drow-per, v., to drip; (pop.) to fail (in

druipnat, drowp-nat, a., dripping-wet [exam.]

druivennat, drow-vern-nat, n., grape-juice

druivenpers, drow-vern-payrss, c., wine-press

druk, drerk, a., busy, crowded, lively (of places); busy, bustling, noïsy (of persons); loud (of decoration)

druk, drerk, c., pressure; print; type; impression;

drukfout, drerk-fowt, c., misprint [edition

drukken, drerk-ker, v., to press; to print; (fig.) to weigh heavily upon

drukkend, drerk-kent, a., oppressive; sultry

drukker, drerk-ker, c., printer

drukkerij, drerk-ker-rey, c., printing-business

drukknop, drerk-k'nop, c., push-button

drukkunst, drerk-kernst, c., typography

drukpers, drerk-payrss, c., printing-press
drukproef, drerk-proof, c., proof
drukte, drerk-ter, c., stir, bustle; fuss
drukwerk, drerk-vayrk, n., printed matter
druppel, drerp-perl, c., drop (of water)
druppelen, drerp-per-ler, v., to drip
dubbel, derb-berl, a., double, twofold
dubbelganger, derb-berl-HGang-er, c., double
dubbelspoor, derb-berl-spohr, n., double track
dubbelzinnig, derb-berl-zin-nerHG, a. & adv.,
duchten, derHG-ter, v., to fear   [ambiguous
duchtig, derHG-terHG, a., fearful; strong
duf, derf, a., stuffy; musty
duidelijk, dow-der-luck, a. & adv., clear, obvious
duif, dowf, c., pigeon, dove
duik, dowk, c., dive
duikboot, dowk-boht, c., submarine
duikelen, dow-ker-ler, v., to tumble; to loop
duikeling, dow-ker-ling, c., somersault; tumble
duiken, dow-ker, v., to dive, to dip
duiker, dow-ker, c., diver
duikerklok, dow-ker-klock, c., diving-bell
duim, dowm, c., thumb
duin, down, n., dune
duister, dows-ter, a., dark, dim; mysterious
duisternis, dows-ter-niss, c., darkness, dark
duivel, dow-verl, c., devil, demon   [the deuce!
duivels, dow-verlss, a., devilish, diábolical. interj.,
duivelskunsten, dow-verls-kern-ster, c, pl., black
duivenhok, dow-ver-hock, n., dovecot   [magic
duiventil, dow-ver-til, c., dovecot, pigeon-house
duizelen, dow-zer-ler, v., to become dizzy
duizelig, dow-zer-lerHG, a., dizzy, giddy
duizeling, dow-zer-ling, c., fit of giddiness
duizend, dow-zent, a., a thousand
duizendpoot, dow-zent-poht, c., centipede
duizendste, dow-zent-ster, a., thousandth
duizendtal, dow-zent-tal, n., a thousand
dulden, derl-der, v., to tolerate; to endure
dun, dern, a., thin; scanty (hair); rare (air)
dunk, dernk, c., opinion
dunken, dern-ker, v., to think

duo, dEE-oh, c., pillion
duorijder, dEE-oh-rey-der, c., pillion-rider
duren, dEE-rer, v., to last
durf, derrf, c., daring, pluck
durfal, derrf-*al*, c., dare-devil
durven, derr-ver, v., to dare
dus, derss, adv., thus. conj., therefore
dusdanig, derss-dah-nerHG, a., such. adv., in such a way [ayn —— doon, to have a nap
dutje, dert-yer, c., nap, doze. een —— **doen**,
dutten, dert-ter, v., to doze, to snooze
duur, dEEr, c., duration. a., dear, expensive
duurzaam, dEEr-zahm, a. durable, hardwearing
duw, dEE, c., push
duwen, dEE-ver, v., to push, to thrust
dwaalbegrip, dvahl-ber-HGrip, n., fallacy
dwaalspoor, dvahl-spohr, n., wrong track
dwaas, dvahss, a., foolish, silly. c., fool
dwaasheid, dvahss-heyt, c., folly
dwalen, dvah-ler, v., to err; to wander
dwaling, dvah-ling, c., error
dwang, dvang, c., compulsion
dwangbevel, dvang-ber-vel, n., warrant, writ
dwarrelen, dvar-rer-ler, v., to whirl
dwars, dvarss, a., transverse; (fig.) wrong-headed
dwarsbalk, dvarss-*balk*, c., cross-beam
dwarsbomen, dvarss-boh-mer, v., to cross, to [thwart
dwarslat, dvarss-*lat*, c., cross-bar
dwarsweg, dvarss-vayHG, c., cross-road
dweepziek, dvayp-seek, a., fanatical; gushing
dweepzucht, dvayp-serHGt, c., fanaticism
dweil, dveyl, c., mop
dweilen, dvey-ler, v., to mop up, to swab
dwepen, dvay-per, v., to be fanatical
dweper, dvay-per, c., fanatic, zealot
dwerg, dvayrHG, c., dwarf
dwingeland, dving-er-*lant*, c., tyrant
dwingelandij, dving-er-lan-dey, c., tyranny
dwingen, dving-er, v., to force, to compel

eb, ep, c., ebb, ebb-tide. —— **en vloed**, —— **en floot**, ebb and flow

ebbenhout, eb-ben-howt, n., ebony

echt, ayнGт, c., marriage. a., real, genuine

echtbreekster, ayнGт-brayk-ster, c., adulteress

echtbreker, ayнGт-bray-ker, c., adulterer

echtelijk, ayнGт-ter-luck, a., conjugal; matrimonial

echter, ayнG-ter, adv., however, yet

echtgenoot, ayнGт-нGer-noht, c., husband

echtgenote, ayнGт-нGer-noh-ter, c., wife

echtpaar, ayнGт-pahr, n., married couple

echtscheiding, ayнGт-sнGey-ding, c., divorce

econoom, ay-koh-nohm, c., economist

edel, ay-derl, a., noble; precious (metals); vital
   (organs) [ous stone

edelgesteente, ay-derl-нGer-stayn-ter, n., preci-

edellieden, ay-derl-lee-der, c. pl., noblemen

edelman, ay-derl-man, c., nobleman

edelmoedig, ay-derl-moo-derнG, a., generous

eed, ayt, c., oath

eedaflegging, ayt-af-lенG-ing, c., taking an oath

eedafneming, ayt-af-nay-ming, c., swearing in

eedbreuk, ayt-brerk, c., perjury

eekhoorn, ayk-hoh-rern, c., squirrel

eeltig, ayl-terнG, a., callous, horny

eeltplek, aylt-playk, c., callosity

een, ayn, art., a. an. a, one

eend, aynt, c., duck; (fig.) goose

eendebout, ayn-der-bowt, c., leg or wing of duck

eendenvijver, ayn-der-fey-ver, c., duck-pond

eender, ayn-der, a., (pop.) equal, the same

eendracht, ayn-draнGт, c., concord, unity

eendrachtig, ayn-draнG-terнG, a., united

eenheid, ayn-heyt, c., unit; unity

eenhoorn, ayn-hoh-rern, c., unicorn

eenmaal, ayn-mahl, adv., once; one day

eenparig, ayn-pah-rerнG, a. & adv., unanimous

eens, ayns, adv., once; one day

eensgezind, ayns-нGer-zint, a. & adv., unanimous

eensklaps, ayns-klaps, adv., suddenly

eenstemmig, ayn-stem-merнG, a., (fig.) unanimous [unanimity

eenstemmigheid, ayn-stem-merнG-heyt, c.,

eentonig, ayn-toh-nerнG, a., monotonous

eenvoudig, ayn-vow-derHG, a. & adv., simple
eenvoudigheid, ayn-vow-derHG-heyt, c., simplicity
eenzaam, ayn-zahm, a., lonely, solitary
eenzaamheid, ayn-zahm-heyt, c., loneliness
eenzijdig, ayn-zey-derHG, a., one-sided
eer, ayr, c., honour; credit. adv. & conj., before
eerbaar, ayr-bahr, a., virtuous; honest
eerbewijs, ayr-ber-veyss, n., homage
eerbied, ayr-beet, c., respect
eerbiedig, ayr-bee-derHG, a., respectful
eerder, ayr-der, adv., before (in time); rather
eergevoel, ayr-HGer-fool, n., sense of honour
eergisteren, ayr-HGiss-ter-rer, adv., the day before yesterday
eerlijk, ayr-luck, a. & adv., honest, fair
eerlijkheid, ayr-luck-heyt, c., honesty
eerloos, ayr-lohss, a., infamous
eerroof, ayr-rohf, c., defamation
eerst, ayrst, a. & adv., first; early
eerstdaags, ayrst-dahHGs, adv., one of these days
eersteling, ayr-ster-ling, c., first-born
eerstvolgend, ayrst-fol-HGent, a., next, following
eertijds, ayr-teyts, adv., formerly
eervol, ayr-fol, a. & adv., honourable
eerzaam, ayr-zahm, a., honourable; modest
eerzucht, ayr-zerHGt, c., ambition
eerzuchtig, ayr-zerHG-terHG, a. & adv., ambitious
eetbaar, ayt-bahr, a., eatable
eetgerei, ayt-HGer-rey, n., dinner things
eetkamer, ayt-kah-mer, c., dining-room
eetlepel, ayt-lay-perl, c., table-spoon
eetlust, ayt-lerst, c., appetite
eetservies, ayt-sayr-veess, n., dinner-service
eetwaren, ayt-vah-rer, c. pl., victuals
eetzaal, ayt-sahl, c., dining-room
eeuw, ay'oo, c., century, age
eeuwfeest, ay'oo-fayst, n., centenary
eeuwig, ay'oo-verHG, a., eternal. adv., for ever
eeuwigheid, ay'oo-verHG-heyt, c., eternity
effecten, ef-feck-ter, n. pl., stocks, securities
effectenbeurs, ef-feck-ter-bers, c., stock exchange

effen, ef-fer, a., smooth; level; plain (of colour)
egel, ay-HGerl, c., hedgehog
ei, cy, n., egg
eiderdons, ey-der-donss, n., eider-down
eigen, ey-HGer, a., own; proper to
eigenaar, ey-HGer-nahr, c., owner   [peculiar
eigenaardig, ey-HGer-nahr-derHG, a. & adv.,
eigenares, ey-HGer-nah-ress, c., proprietress
eigenbelang, ey-HGer-ber-lang, n., self-interest
eigendom, ey-HGer-dom, n., property
eigendunk, ey-HGer-dernk, c., (self-) conceit
eigengebakken, ey-HGen-HGer-bak-ker, a., home-
    baked
eigengemaakt, ey-HGen-HGer-mahkt, a., home-
eigenlijk, ey-HGer-luck, a. & adv., proper [made
eigenmachtig, ey-HGer-maHG-terHG, a., high-
    handed
eigennaam, ey-HGen-nahm, c., proper name
eigenschap, ey-HGer-sHGap, c., quality; property
eigenwijs, ey-HGer-veyss, a., conceited
eigenzinnig, ey-HGer-zin-nerHG, a., self-willed
eigenzinnigheid, ey-HGer-zin-nerHG-heit, c.,
eik, eyk, c., oak   [wilfulness
cikel, eyk-erl, c., acorn
eiland, ey-lant, n., island
eilandbewoner, ey-lant-ber-voh-ner, c., islander
eind, eynt, n., end, close; extremity
einddoel, eynt-dool, n., ultimate object
eindelijk, eyn-der-luck, adv., at last; finally
eindeloos, eyn-der-lohss, a., endless
eindigen, eyn-der-HGer, v., to end, to conclude
eindje, eynt-yer, n., end; piece
eindresultaat, eynt-ray-zerl-taht, n., final result
eindstation, eynt-stah-see'on, n., terminus
eis, eyss, c., demand, claim; requirement
eisen, ey-ser, v., to demand, to claim
eiser, ey-ser, c., claimant; plaintiff
eiwit, ey-vit, n., white of an egg
ekster, eck-ster, c., magpie
eksteroog, eck-ster-ohHG, n., corn (on toe)
elders, el-derss, adv., elsewhere
elf, elf, a., eleven

elfde, elf-der, a., eleventh

elk, elk, a., every, each. c., everybody

elkaar, elkander, el-kahr, el-kan-der, pron., each other, one another

elleboog, el-ler-bohHG, c., elbow

ellende, el-len-der, c., misery, wretchedness

ellendeling, el-len-der-ling, c., wretch

ellendig, el-len-derHG, a. & adv., miserable, cizeboom, el-zer-bohm, c., alder-tree [wretched

email, ay-mah'ee, n., enamel

emailleren, ay-ma-yay-rer, v., to enamel

emmer, em-mer, c., pail, bucket

en, en, conj., and

eng, eng, a., narrow; tight; (pop.) creepy

engel, eng-erl, c., angel

engelachtig, eng-erl-aHG-terHG, a. & adv., angelic

engelenbak, eng-erl-er-bak, c., gallery (theatre)

engte, eng-ter, c., strait; narrow passage

enig, ay-nerHG, a., sole, single; unique

enigermate, ay-ner-HGer-mah-ter, adv., in some

enigst, ay-nerHGst, a., only, sole [measure

enigszins, ay-nerHG-sins, adv., somewhat

enkel, en-kerl, c., ankle. a., single. adv., merely

enorm, ay-norm, a., enormous, huge

enquête, an-kay-ter, c., inquiry

enten, en-ter, v., to graft

entree, an-tray, c., entrance, admission

entreebiljet, an-tray-bil-yet, c., admission ticket

entreeprijs, an-tray-preyss, c., entrance fee

entrepôt, an-trer-poh, c., bonded warehouse

epos, ay-poss, n., epic (poem)

equipage, ay-kee-pah-zher, c., crew (of ship)

er, ayr, adv., there

eraf, ayr-af, adv., off it, from it

erbarmelijk, ayr-bar-mer-luck, a., pitiful

erbarming, ayr-bar-ming, c., pity, compassion

ereburger, ay-rer-berr-HGer, c., freeman

eredienst, ay-rer-deenst, c., worship

eren, ay-rer, v., to honour, to revere

erewoord, ay-rer-vohrt, n., word of honour

erf, ayrf, n., farm-yard

erfdeel, ayrf-dayl, n., heritage

erfelijk, ayr-fer-luck, a., hereditary

erfenis, ayr-fer-niss, c., inheritance

erfgenaam, ayrf-HGer-nahm, c., heir

erfgename, ayrf-HGer-nah-mer, c., heiress

erflater, ayrf-lah-ter, c., testator

erfstuk, ayrf-sterk, n., heirloom

erfzonde, ayrf-son-der, c., original sin

erg, ayrHG, a., bad, evil. adv., badly

ergens, ayr-HGenss, adv., somewhere

ergeren, ayr-HGer-rer, v., to annoy   [annoying

ergerlijk, ayr-HGer-luck, a. & adv., offensive;

ergernis, ayr-HGer-niss, c., scandal; annoyance

erkennen, ayr-ken-ner, v., to admit; to recognize

erkenning, ayr-ken-ning, c., acknowledgment

erkentelijk, ayr-ken-ter-luck, a. & adv., grateful

ernst, ayrnst, c., earnestness; seriousness

ernstig, ayrn-sterHG, a. & adv., earnest; serious

erts, ayrts, n., ore   [experienced

ervaren, ayr-vah-rer, v., to experience. a.,

ervaring, ayr-vah-ring, c., experience

erven, ayr-ver, v., to inherit

erwt, ayrvt, c., pea

estafetteloop, ess-tah-fet-ter-lohp, c., relay race

etage, ay-tah-zher, c., floor, storey

etagewoning, ay-tah-zher-voh-ning, c., flat

etalage, ay-tah-lah-zher, c., show-window

etaleren, ay-tah-lay-rer, v., to display (goods)

eten, ay-ter, v., to eat; to dine. n., food; meal;

etiket, ay-tee-ket, n., label   [dinner

etmaal, et-mahl, n., period of 24 hours

etsen, et-ser, v., to etch

ettelijke, et-ter-luck-er, a., several, some

etter, et-ter, c., pus, matter

etterachtig, et-ter-*a*HG-terHG, a., purulent

etteren, et-ter-rer, v., to fester

euvel, er-verl, n., evil, fault

evangelie, ay-*v*an-HGay-lee, n., gospel

even, ay-ver, a., even, equal. adv., just, equally

evenaar, ay-ven-ahr, c., equator

evenals, ay-ven-*a*ls, conj., as well as, just like

evenaren, ay-ver-nah-rer, v., to equal

evenbeeld, ay-ver-baylt, n., picture, image

eveneens, ay-ven-aynss, adv., also, likewise
evenmin, ay-ver-min, adv., no more [portional
evenredig, ay-ver-ray-derHG, a. & adv., pro-
eventjes, ay-vert-yess, adv., only just
eventueel, ay-ven-tEE-ayl, a., contingent; possible
evenveel, ay-ver-fayl, a., as much, as many
evenwel, ay-ver-vel, adv., however, nevertheless
evenwicht, ay-ver-viHGt, n., balance [anced
evenwichtig, ay-ver-viHG-terHG, a., well-bal-
evenwijdig, ay-ver-vey-derHG, a., parallel
evenzeer, ay-ver-zayr, adv., as much
everzwijn, ay-ver-zveyn, n., wild boar
examen, eck-sah-mer, n., examination
exemplaar, eck-saym-plahr, n., specimen; copy
exerceren, eck-ser-say-rer, v., (mil.) to drill
exercitie, eck-ser-see-see, c., (mil.) drill
expediteur, ecks-pay-dee-terr, c., shipping-agent
expres, ecks-prayss, adv., on purpose
extase, ecks-tah-zer, c., ecstasy. in ——, in ——,
   enraptured
extrablad, ecks-trah-blat, n., special edition
ezel, ay-zerl, c., ass, donkey; easel
ezelachtig, ay-zerl-aHG-terHG, a., stupid [memory
ezelsbruggetje, ay-zerls-brerHG-ert-yer, c., aid to

faam, fahm, c., fame, reputation
fabel, fah-berl, c., fable; myth [fabulous
fabelachtig, fah-berl-aHG-terHG, a. & adv.,
fabricage, fah-bree-kah-zher, c., manufacture
fabriceren, fah-bree-say-rer, v., to manufacture
fabriek, fah-breek, c., factory, works, mill
fabrieksmerk, fah-breeks-mayrk, n., trade mark
fabrikaat, fah-bree-kaht, n., make
fabrikant, fah-bree-kant, c., manufacturer
factuur, fak-tEEr, c., invoice
facultatief, fah-kerl-tah-teef, a., optional
failliet, fa-yeet, n., bankruptcy. a., bankrupt
faillissement, fa-yee-ser-ment, n., bankruptcy
fakkel, fak-kerl, c., torch
falen, fah-ler, v., to fail
familienaam, fah-mee-lee-nahm, c., surname
familiestuk, fah-mee-lee-sterk, n., heirloom

fanfarekorps, fan-fah-rer-korps, n., brass band

fantaseren, fan-tah-zay-rer, v., to invent; to imagine things

fantasie, fan-tah-zee, c., phantasy, imagination

fat, fat, c., dandy, fop, swell

fatsoen, fat-soon, n., respectability

fatsoenlijk, fat-soon-luck, a. & adv., respectable

fatsoenshalve, fat-soons-hal-ver, adv., for decency's sake

fatterig, fat-ter-rerHG, a. & adv., foppish

fauteuil, foh-ter'ee, c., easy chair

fazant, fah-zant, c., pheasant

februari, fay-brEE-ah-ree, c., February

fee, fay, c., fairy

feeënrijk, fay-en-reyk, n., fairyland

feeks, fayks, c., vixen, shrew, virago

feest, fayst, n., feast, festivity

feestmaal, fayst-mahl, n., banquet

feestvieren, fayst-fee-rer, v., to feast

feilbaar, feyl-bahr, a., fallible

feilloos, feyl-lohss, a. & adv., faultless

feit, feyt, n., fact

feitelijk, fey-ter-luck, a., actual. adv., in fact

fel, fel, a. & adv., fierce; keen

felicitatie, fay-lee-see-tah-see, c., congratulation

feliciteren, fay-lee-see-tay-rer, v., to congratulate

ferm, fayrm, a., strong; stout; thorough

fielt, feelt, c., scoundrel, rogue

fier, feer, a. & adv., proud

fiets, feets, c., bicycle

fietsen, feet-ser, v., to cycle

fietser, feet-ser, c., cyclist

figuur, fee-HGEEr, c., figure

figuurlijk, fee-HGEEr-luck, a. & adv., figurative

figuurzaag, fee-HGEEr-zahHG, c., fret-saw

figuurzagen, fee-HGEEr-zah-HGer, v. to do fret-work. n., fret-work

fijn, feyn, a., fine, choice, lovely

fijngevoelig, feyn-HGer-voo-lerHG, a., delicate

fijnmaken, feyn-mah-ker, v., to pulverize, to crush

fijnmalen, feyn-mah-ler, v., to grind down

fijnproever, feyn-proo-ver, c., connoisseur

file, fee-ler, c., file, row, queue
filiaal, fee-lee-ahl, n., branch-office
filmjournaal, film-zhoor-nahl, n., news-reel
filmkeuring, film-ker-ring, c., film censorship
filmster, film-stayr, c., screen-star
financieel, fee-nan-see-ayl, a. & adv., financial
financiën, fee-nan-see-er, c. pl., finances
firma, feer-mah, c., firm, house
firmament, feer-mah-ment, n., firmament, sky
fiscus, fiss-kerss, c., treasury, exchequer
flacon, flah-kon, c., scent-bottle
fladderen, flad-der-rer, v., to flutter, to hover
flambouw, flam-bow, c., torch
flanel, flah-nel, n. & a., flannel
flanelletje, flah-nel-lert-yer, n., flannel vest or
flank, flank, c., flank, side   [shirt
flarden, flar-der, c. pl., tatters, rags
flater, flah-ter, c., blunder
flatgebouw, flat-HGer-bow, n., block of flats
flauw, flow, a., insipid; silly; faint
flauwte, flow-ter, c., swoon, faint
flegmatisch, flayHG-mah-teess, a. & adv., phleg-
flensje, flen-sher, n., thin pancake   [matic
fles, fless, c., bottle
flets, fletss, a., pale, faded, dim
flikflooien, flick-floh-yer, v., to coax, to cajole
flikkeren, flick-ker-rer, v., to flicker, to twinkle
flink, flink, a. & adv., goodly; sturdy; thorough
fluisteren, flows-ter-rer, v., to whisper
fluit, flowt, c., flute
fluiten, flow-ter, v., to whistle; to warble (of
fluweel, flEE-vayl, n., velvet   [birds)
foedraal, foo-drahl, n., case, cover
foei! foo'ee, interj., fie!
fokken, fock-ker, v., to breed, to rear (cattle)
folteren, fol-ter-rer, v., to put to the rack; to tor-
fonds, fonts, n., fund; club   [ture
fonkelen, fon-ker-ler, v., to sparkle
fontein, fon-teyn, c., fountain
fonteintje, fon-teynt-yer, n., (wash-)basin
fooi, foh'ee, c., tip, gratuity
foppen, fop-per, v., to fool, to cheat

forel, foh-rel, c., trout
formaat, for-maht, n., size
formaliteit, for-mah-lee-teyt, c., formality
formeel, for-mayl, a. & adv., formal; downright
formule, for-mEE-ler, c., formula   [tion)
formulier, for-mEE-leer, n., form (for informa-
fornuis, for-nowss, n., kitchener, kitchen-range
fors, forss, a. & adv., robust, vigorous, strong
fortuin, for-town, n., fortune
foto, foh-toh, c., photo
fout, fowt, c., mistake; fault
fraai, frah-ee, a., nice, pretty, handsome
fractie, frak-see, c., fraction; political group
framboos, fram-bohss, c., raspberry
franco, fran-koh, adv., post-free; carriage paid
franje, fran-yer, c., fringe, edging
frankeren, fran-kay-rer, v., to prepay; to stamp
fregat, frer-HGat, n., frigate   [(a letter)
fris, friss, a. & adv., fresh, refreshing; cool
frisheid, friss-heyt, c., freshness; coolness
fröbelschool, frer-berl-sHGohl, c., kindergarten
fronsen, fron-zer, v., to frown
fruithandelaar, frowt-han-der-lahr, c., fruiterer
fruitschaal, frowt-sHGahl, c., fruit-dish
fuif, fowf, c., (pop.) spree
fuiven, fow-ver, v., (pop.) to feast, to reve
functie, fernk-see, c., function
fundament, fern-dah-ment, n., foundation
funest, fEE-nest, a., disastrous
fut, fert, c., (pop.) spirit, pep
futloos, fert-lohss, a., (pop.) spiritless

gaaf, HGahf, a., sound, whole
gaan, HGahn, v., to go, to walk, to move
gaar, HGahr, a., done (meat)
gaarkeuken, HGahr-ker-ker, c., eating-house
gaarne, HGahr-ner, adv. willingly, gladly
gaas, HGahss, n., gauze; wire netting
gaatje, HGaht-yer, n., little hole
gadeslaan, HGah-der-slahn, v., to watch
gade, HGah-der, c., consort (husband and wife)
gaffel, HGahf-ferl, c., pitchfork

gal, HGal, c., gall, bile
galabal, HGah-lah-bal, n., state ball
galant, HGah-lant, a. & adv., gallant. c., fiancé
galanteriën, HGah-lan-ter-ree-en, c. pl., fancy-
galei, HGah-ley, c., galley   [goods
galerij, HGah-ler-rey, c., gallery
galg, HGalHG, c., gallows, gibbet
galm, HGalm, c., booming sound, reverberation
galmen, HGal-mer, v., to sound, to resound
galop, HGah-lop, c., gallop
galopperen, HGah-lop-pay-rer, v., to gallop
galsteen, HGal-stayn, c., gall-stone, bile-stone
gammel, HGam-merl, a., shaky, dilapidated
gang, HGanG, c., corridor; gait; course (meal)
gangbaar, HGang-bahr, a., current (money)
gangklok, HGang-klock, c., hall-clock
gangmaker, HGang-mah-ker, c., pace-maker
gans, HGanss, c., goose. a. & adv., whole, entire
ganzebout, HGan-zer-bowt, c., leg or wing of a
gapen, HGah-per, v., to yawn; to gape   [goose
gaping, HGah-ping, c., gap, hiatus
gappen, HGap-per, v., (pop.) to pinch, to pilfer
garage, HGah-rah-zher, c., garage
garantie, HGah-ran-see, c., guarantee, warrant
garderobe, HGar-der-rob-er, c., wardrobe;
garen, HGah-rer, n., thread   [cloakroom
garf, HGarf, c., sheaf
garnaal, HGar-nahl, c., shrimp   [jewels
garnituur, HGar-nee-tEer, n., trimming; set of
garnizoen, HGar-nee-zoon, n., garrison
gasaanval, HGass-ahn-val, c., gas-attack
gasbuis, HGass-bowss, c., gas-pipe
gasfabriek, HGass-fah-breek, c., gas-works
gasfornuis, HGass-for-nowss, c., gas-cooker
gaskraan, HGass-krahn, c., gas-tap   [pipes
gasleiding, HGass-ley-ding, c., gas-main; gas-
gasmasker, HGass-mass-ker, n., gas-mask
gasontploffing, HGass-ont-plof-fing, c., gas-
gast, HGast, c., guest; visitor   [explosion
gastheer, HGast-hayr, c., host
gasthuis, HGast-howss, n., hospital; hospice
gastmaal, HGast-mahl, n., feast, banquet

gastvrij, HGast-vrey, a. & adv., hospitable
gastvrijheid, HGast-vrey-heyt, c., hospitality
gat, HGat, n., hole, gap
gauw, HGow, a. & adv., quick
gauwdief, HGow-deef, c., thief, pickpocket
gave, HGah-ver, c., gift
gazel(le), HGah-zel(ler), c., gazelle
gazon, HGah-zon, n., lawn
geacht, HGer-aHGt, p.p. & a., esteemed, respected
geadresseerde, HGer-a-dres-sayr-der, c., ad-
   dressee; consignee   [affected
geaffecteerd, HGer-af-fec-tayrt, a. & adv.,
gearmd, HGer-armt, adv., arm in arm
gebaar, HGer-bahr, n., gesture, gesticulation
gebabbel, HGer-bab-berl, n., prattle, tittle-tattle
gebak, HGer-bak, n., pastry, cake(s)
gebakje, HGer-bak-yer, n., tart, fancy-cake
gebalk, HGer-balk, n., braying
gebazel, HGer-bah-zerl, n., silly prattle, twaddle
gebed, HGer-bet, n., prayer   [book
gebedenboek, HGer-bay-der-book, n., prayer-
gebeente, HGer-bayn-ter, n., bones   [tains
gebergte, HGer-bayrHG-ter, n., chain of moun-
gebeuren, HGer-ber-rer, v., to happen, to chance,
   to come about
gebeurtenis, HGer-berr-ter-niss, c., event
gebied, HGer-beet, n., territory, area, region
gebieden, HGer-bee-der, v., to command, to bid
gebit, HGer-bit, n., set of teeth
gebluf, HGer-blerf, n., boasting, bragging
geblaat, HGer-blaht, n., bleating
gebladerte, HGer-blah-der-ter, n., foliage
geblaf, HGer-blaf, n., barking
gebloemd, HGer-bloomt, p.p. & a., flowered
gebod, HGer-bot, n., command
geboorte, HGer-bohr-ter, c., birth   [rate
geboortecijfer, HGer-bohr-ter-sey-fer, n., birth-
geboortedag, HGer-bohr-ter-daHG, c., birthday
geboortejaar, HGer-bohr-ter-yahr, n., year of
geboren, HGer-boh-rer, p.p., born   [birth
gebouw, HGer-bow, n., building
gebraad, HGer-braht, n., roast meat

gebrek, HGer-breck, n., want, need; defect, fault.
bij —— aan . . ., bey —— ahn . . ., for want
of . . . [invalid

gebrekkig, HGer-breck-kerHG, a., defective;

gebroeders, HGer-broo-derss, c. pl., brothers

gebrom, HGer-brom, n., buzz, growl; grumbling

gebruik, HGer-browk, n., use; consumption;
custom [customary

gebruikelijk, HGer-brow-ker-luck, a., usual,

gebruiken, HGer-brow-ker, v., to use, to employ;
to take (food) [zing, c., directions for use

gebruiksaanwijzing, HGer-browks-ahn-vey-

gebruis, HGer-browss, n., effervescence; seething

gebrul, HGer-brerl, n., roaring, howling

gecompliceerd, HGer-kom-plee-sayrt, p.p. & a.,
complicated

gedaagde, HGer-dahHG-der, c., defendant

gedaante, HGer-dahn-ter, c., shape, form

gedachte, HGer-daHG-ter, c., thought, idea

gedachteloos, HGer-daHG-ter-lohss, a. & adv.,
thoughtless [of thought

gedachtengang, HGer-daHG-ter-HGang, c., trend

gedachtenis, HGer-daHG-ter-niss, c., memory;
souvenir

gedeelte, HGer-dayl-ter, n., part; instalment

gedeeltelijk, HGer-dayl-ter-luck, a. & adv.,
partial; partly

gedenkboek, HGer-denk-book, n., memorial book

gedenkdag, HGer-denk-daHG, c., anniversary

gedenken, HGer-den-ker, v., to remember, to
commemorate

gedenkteken, HGer-denk-tay-ker, n., memorial

gedenkwaardig, HGer-denk-vahr-derHG, a.,
[memorable

gedicht, HGer-diHGt, n., poem

gedienstig, HGer-deen-sterHG, a. & adv., obliging,
attentive

gedijen, HGer-dey-er, v., to thrive, to flourish

geding, HGer-ding, n., lawsuit, case

gedrag, HGer-draHG, n., conduct, behaviour

gedragen (zich), HGer-drah-HGer (ziHG), v., to
[behave

gedrang, HGer-drang, n., crowd; crush

gedrocht, HGer-droHGt, n., monster

gedrongen, HGer-drong-er, p.p. & a., compact

gedruis, HGer-drowss, n., noise, rush, roar

geducht, HGer-derHGt, a. & adv., formidable; tremendous

geduld, HGer-derlt, n., patience, forbearance

geduldig, HGer-derl-derHG, a. & adv., patient

gedurende, HGer-dEE-ren-der, prep., during

gedwee, HGer-dvay, a. & adv., submissive, meek

gedwongen, HGer-dvong-er, p.p. & a., enforced, constrained

geel, HGayl, a., yellow. n., yolk (of egg)

geen, HGayn, pron., no, not one

geenszins, HGayn-sinss, adv., not at all

geest, HGayst, c., spirit, mind; ghost

geestdrift, HGays-drift, c., enthusiasm

geestdriftig, HGays-drif-terHG, a. & adv., enthusiastic

geestelijk, HGays-ter-luck, a., spiritual; mental

geestelijke, HGays-ter-luck-er, c., clergyman

geestelijkheid, HGays-ter-luck-heyt, c., clergy

geestig, HGays-terHG, a. & adv., witty

geestkracht, HGayst-krαHGt, c., energy

geestvermogens, HGayst-fer-moh-HGenss, n. pl., mental faculties

geestverrukking, HGayst-fer-rerk-king, c., ecstasy

geeuw, HGay'oo, c., yawn [stasy

geeuwen, HGay'oo-er, v., to yawn

geflirt, HGer-flert, n., flirtation [ested; applicant

gegadigde, HGer-HGah-derHG-der, c., party inter-

gegevens, HGer-HGay-venss, n. pl., data

gegoed, HGer-HGoot, a., well-to-do

gegrond, HGer-HGront, p.p. & a., well-founded

gehaat, HGer-haht, p.p. & a., hated, detested

gehakt, HGer-hakt, n., minced meat

gehalte, HGer-hαl-ter, n., quality, standard

gehard, HGer-hαrt, p.p. & a., hardened; tempered

gehecht, HGer-hayHGt, p.p. & a., attached, devoted

geheel, HGer-hayl, a. & adv., entire, complete

geheelonthouder, HGer-hayl-ont-how-der, c., teetotaller

geheim, HGer-heym, n., secret. a., hidden

geheimschrift, HGer-heym-srift, n., cipher

geheimzinnig, HGer-heym-zin-nerHG, a., mysterious [tester

gehemelte, HGer-hay-merl-ter, n., palate; canopy;

gehoor, HGer-hohr, n., hearing; audience

gehoorzaam, HGer-hohr-zahm, a.&adv., obedient

gehoorzamen, HGer-hohr-zah-mer, v., to obey

gehucht, HGer-herHGt, n., hamlet

gehuil, HGer-howl, n., crying, howling

gehuwd, HGer-hEE'oot, p.p. & a., married

geïllustreerd, HGer-il-lers-trayrt, p.p. & a., illustrated

geit, HGeyt, c., goat, she-goat [illustrated

gejaagd, HGer-yahHGt, a. & adv., agitated

gejuich, HGer-yowHG, n., cheering, shouting

gek, HGeck, c., madman; fool. a. & adv., mad; queer

gekheid, HGeck-heyt, c., folly, foolery; joking

gekkenhuis, HGeck-ker-howss, n., madhouse

gekkenwerk, HGeck-ker-vayrk, n., madness, folly

geknoei, HGerk-noo-e, n., bungling; intriguing

gekreun, HGer-krern, n., groaning, moaning

gekscheren, HGayk-sHGay-rer, v., to joke

gekuch, HGer-kerHG, n., coughing

gekunsteld, HGer-kerns-terlt, a.,artificial, affected

gelaat, HGer-laht, n., countenance, face

gelaatskleur, HGer-lahts-kler, c., complexion

gelach, HGer-laHG, n., laughter [direct

gelasten, HGer-las-ter, v., to order, to charge, to

gelaten, HGer-lah-ter, a. & adv., resigned

geld, HGeylt, n., money

geldelijk, HGel-der-luck, a., monetary, financial

gelden, HGel-der, v., to cost; to be in force; to concern

geldgebrek, HGelt-HGer-breck, n., want of money

geldig, HGel-derHG, a., valid

geldigheid, HGel-derHG-heyt, c., validity

geldstuk, HGelt-sterk, n., coin

geldwolf, HGelt-volf, c., money-grubber

geldzaak, HGelt-sahk, c., money-affair

geleden, HGer-lay-der, adv., past

geleerd, HGer-layrt, p.p. & a., learned

geleerde, HGer-layr-der, c., learned man

gelegenheid, HGer-lay-HGer-heyt, c., opportunity

gelei, zher-ley, c., jelly; jam

geleide, HGer-ley-der, n., guidance; (mil.) escort
geleidelijk, HGer-ley-der-luck, a. & adv., gradual
geleiden, HGer-ley-der, v., to lead; (mil.) to escort
gelid, HGer-lit, n., joint (of body); (mil.) rank
geliefd, HGer-leeft, a., beloved, dear
geliefde, HGer-leev-der, c., sweetheart, lover
geliefkoosd, HGer-leef-kohst, a., favourite
gelieven, HGer-lee-ver, v., to please [conj., as, like
gelijk, HGer-leyk, n., right. a. & adv., identical
gelijken, HGer-leyk-er, v., to be like, to resemble
gelijkenis, HGer-leyk-er-niss, c., likeness; parable
gelijkgezind, HGer-leyk-HGer-zint, a., of one mind
gelijkmatig, HGer-leyk-mah-terHG, a. & adv.,
 equal, even
gelijknamig, HGer-leyk-**nah**-merHG, a., of the
 same name [genous
gelijksoortig, HGer-leyk-sohr-terHG, a., homo-
gelijkspelen, HGer-leyk-spay-ler, v., to draw (a
 game) [simultaneous
gelijktijdig, HGer-leyk-tey-derHG, a. & adv.,
gelijkvloers, HGer-leyk-floorss, a., on the same
 floor [same form
gelijkvormig, HGer-leyk-for-merHG, a., of the
gelijkwaardig, HGer-leyk-vahr-derHG, a.,equiva-
geloei, HGer-loo-e, n., lowing; roaring [lent
gelofte, HGer-lof-ter, c., vow, promise
geloof, HGer-lohf, n., faith, creed; credit [dentials
geloofsbrieven, HGer-lohfs-bree-ver, c. pl., cre-
geloofsleer, HGer-lohfs-layr, c., doctrine of faith
geloofwaardig, HGer-lohf-**vahr**-derHG, a., credible; reliable
geloven, HGer-loh-ver, v., to believe, to think
gelovige, HGer-loh-verHG-er, c., faithful, believer
gelui, HGer-low, n., ringing, tolling
geluid, HGer-lowt, n., sound, noise
geluidloos, HGer-lowt-lohss, a., soundless
geluidsfilm, HGer-lowts-film, c., sound film
geluk, HGer-lerk, n., happiness; blessing; luck
gelukken, HGer-lerk-ker, v., to succeed [lucky
gelukkig, HGer-lerk-kerHG, a. & adv., happy;
geluksvogel, HGer-lerks-foh-HGerl, c., lucky bird
gelukwens, HGer-lerk-venss, c., congratulation

gelukwensen, HGer-lerk-ven-ser, v., to congratulate   [bliss

gelukzaligheid, HGer-lerk-sah-lerHG-heyt, c.,

gelukzoeker, HGer-lerk-soo-ker, c., adventurer

gemaaktheid, HGer-mahkt-heyt, c., affectation

gemaal, HGer-mahl, n., grinding; pumping-engine

gemaal, HGer-mahl, c., husband, spouse

gemachtigde, HGer-maHG-terHG-der, c., proxy

gemak, HGer-mak, n., ease; comfort; facility

gemakkelijk, HGer-mak-ker-luck, a. & adv., easy; comfortable

gemaskerd, HGer-mas-kert, a., masked

gematigd, HGer-mah-terHGt, a., moderate

gember, HGem-ber, c., ginger

gemeen, HGer-mayn, a. & adv., common; vulgar; obscene   [course; connection

gemeenschap, HGer-mayn-sHGap, c., inter-

gemeenschappelijk, HGer-mayn-sHGap-per-luck, a., common, joint   [parish

gemeente, HGer-mayn-ter, c., municipality;

gemeentehuis, HGer-mayn-ter-howss, n., municipal house   [council

gemeenteraad, HGer-mayn-ter-raht, c., town

gemeenzaam, HGer-mayn-zahm, a., familiar

gemelijk, HGay-mer-luck, a., peevish, sullen

gemenebest, HGer-may-ner-best, n., common-

gemengd, HGer-mengt, p.p. & a., mixed   [wealth

gemeubiliseerd, HGer-mer-bee-lee-sayrt, p.p. & a., furnished

gemiddeld, HGer-mid-derlt, a. & adv., average

gemis, HGer-miss, n., want, lack

gemoed, HGer-moot, n., mind   [good-natured

gemoedelijk, HGer-moo-der-luck, a. & adv.,

gems, HGems, c., chamois

genaakbaar, HGer-nahk-bahr, a., accessible

genaamd, HGer-nahmt, p.p., named

genade, HGer-nah-der, c., grace, mercy

genadeslag, HGer-nah-der-slaHG, c., death-blow

genadig, HGer-nah-derHG, a. & adv., merciful

genaken, HGer-nah-ker, v., to approach, to draw near

gene, HGay-ner, pron., that, the former. **aan** — **zijde van,** ahn —— zey-der fan, beyond

geneesheer, HGer-nays-hayr, c., doctor

geneeskrachtig, HGer-nays-krahG-terHG, a., curative

geneeskunde, HGer-nays-kern-der, c., medical science

geneeslijk, HGer-nays-luck, a., curable [science

geneesmiddel, HGer-nays-mid-derl, n., remedy

genegen, HGer-nay-HGer, p.p. & a., inclined

genegenheid, HGer-nay-HGer-heyt, c., affection

generaal, HGay-ner-rahl, c., general

generen(zich), zher-nay-rer(ziHG), v., to feel embarrassed

genezen, HGer-nay-zer, v., to cure, to heal

genezing, HGer-nay-zing, c., cure, recovery

geniaal, HGay-nee-ahl, a. & adv., highly gifted

genie, zher-nee, n., genius. c., (mil.) engineering

geniepig, HGer-nee-perHG, a. & adv., sneaky

geniesoldaat, zher-nee-sol-daht, c., (mil.) engineer

genieten, HGer-nee-ter, v., to enjoy [gineer

genoeg, HGer-nooHG, a. & adv., sufficient

genoegdoening, HGer-nooHG-doo-ning, c., satisfaction

genoegen, HGer-noo-HGer, n., pleasure, delight

genoeglijk, HGer-nooHG-luck, a. & adv., pleasant

genootschap, HGer-noht-sHGap, n., society, association

genot, HGer-not, n., joy, delight; enjoyment

geoefend, HGer-oo-fent, p.p. & a., practised

geoorloofd, HGer-ohr-lohft, p.p. & a., lawful

gepaard, HGer-pahrt, adv., in pairs

gepast, HGer-past, a., becoming, fit, proper

gepeins, HGer-peyns, n., musing, pondering

gepensionneerde, HGer-pen-see-ohn-nayr-der, c., pensioner   [(fig.) salt, spiced

gepeperd, HGer-pay-pert, p.p. & a., peppered;

gepeupel, HGer-per-perl, n., mob, rabble

gepieker, HGer-pee-ker, n., brooding; puzzling

gepimpel, HGer-pim-perl, n., tippling

geplaag, HGer-plahHG, n., teasing, nagging [frame

geraamte, HGer-rahm-ter, n., skeleton; carcass;

geraas, HGer-rahss, n., noise, din

geraffineerd, HGer-raf-fee-nayrt, a., consummate
geraken, HGer-rah-ker, v., to get, to arrive
gerecht, HGer-rayHGt, n., court (justice); course (meals). a., just
gerechtelijk, HGer-rayHG-ter-luck, a. & adv., judicial; legal   [entitled
gerechtigd, HGer-rayHG-terHGt, a., authorized,
gerechtshof, HGer-rayHGts-hof, n., court (justice)
gereed, HGer-rayt, a., ready; finished, done
gereedmaken, HGer-rayt-mah-ker, v., to prepare
gereedschappen, HGer-rayt-sHGap-per, n. pl., tools
geregeld, HGer-ray-HGerlt, a. & adv., regular
gereserveerd, HGer-ray-zayr-vayrt, p.p. & a., reserved; reticent   [nient
geriefelijk, HGer-ree-fer-luck, a. & adv., conve-
gering, HGer-ring, a., small, scanty, slight
geringschatten, HGer-ring-sHGat-ter, v., to hold
gerinkel, HGer-rin-kerl, n., jingling   [cheap
geritsel, HGer-rit-serl, n., rustling
geroddel, HGer-rod-derl, n., talk, gossip
geroezemoes, HGer-roo-zer-mooss, n., buzz
gerommel, HGer-rom-merl, n., rumbling
geronnen, HGer-ron-ner, a., curdled; clotted
gerst, HGayrst, c., barley
gerucht, HGer-rerHGt, n., rumour; noise
geruim, HGer-rowm, a., considerable, ample
gerust, HGer-rerst, a. & adv., quiet, easy
gerustheid, HGer-rerst-heyt, c., peace of mind
geruststellen, HGer-rerst-stel-ler, v., to reassure
geschapen, HGer-sHGah-per, p.p. & a., created
gescheiden, HGer-sHGey-der, p.p. & a., separated; divorced
geschenk, HGer-sHGenk, n., present, gift   [occur
geschieden, HGer-sHGee-der, v., to happen, to
geschiedenis, HGer-sHGee-der-niss, c., history; story   [historian
geschiedschrijver, HGer-sHGeet-srey-ver, c.,
geschikt, HGer-sHGikt, a. & adv., fit, proper; able
geschiktheid, HGer-sHGikt-heyt, c., fitness; ability
geschil, HGer-sHGil, n., dispute   [skilled
geschoold, HGer-sHGohlt, p.p. & a., trained;

geschreeuw, HGer-sray'oo, n., cries, shrieks

geschrei, HGer-srey, n., weeping, crying

geschrift, HGer-srift, n., writing

geschut, HGer-sHGert, n., artillery, guns

gesel, HGay-serl, c., scourge; whip

geselen, HGay-ser-ler, v., to flog, to whip, to cane

gesis, HGer-siss, n., hissing

geslacht, HGer-slaHGt, n., generation; race; sex

geslachtelijk, HGer-slaHGt-ter-luck, a. & adv., sexual

geslachtsboom, HGer-slaHGts-bohm, c., pedigree

geslepen, HGer-slay-per, a. & adv., sharp; cunning

geslepenheid, HGer-slay-per-heyt, c., cunning

gesloten, HGer-sloh-ter, p.p. & a., closed, locked

gesmul, HGer-smerl, n., feasting

gesnork, HGer-snork, n., snoring

gesp, HGesp, c., clasp, buckle

gespierd, HGer-speert, a., muscular; (fig.) nervy

gespikkeld, HGer-spick-kerlt, p.p. & a., speckled

gesprek, HGer-spreck, n., conversation

gespuis, HGer-spowss, n., rabble, riff-raff

gestadig, HGer-stah-derHG, a. & adv., steady, continual

gestalte, HGer-stal-ter, c., figure, shape, build

gestamel, HGer-stah-merl, n., stammering [rock

gesteente, HGer-stayn-ter, n., (precious) stones)

gestel, HGer-stel, n., constitution

gesteldheid, HGer-stelt-heyt, c., state, condition

gesternte, HGer-stayrn-ter, n., constellation

gesticht, HGer-stiHGt, n., establishment. p.p. & a., founded [stumbling

gestommel, HGer-stom-merl, n., cluttering;

gestroomlijnd, HGer-strohm-leynt, p.p. & a., streamlined

gestreng, HGer-streng, see streng [stream-lined

gesuis, HGer-sowss, n., buzzing; soughing

gesukkel, HGer-serk-kerl, n., ailing; trudging

getaand, HGer-tahnt, a., tawny, tanned

getal, HGer-tal, n., number

getalm, HGer-talm, n., lingering, loitering

getier, HGer-teer, n., noise, clamour

getij, HGer-tey, n., tide

getik, HGer-tick, n., ticking; tapping

getiteld, HGer-tee-terlt, p.p. & a., titled; entitled

getjilp, HGer-tyeelp, n., chirping

getob, HGer-top, n., worry; drudgery

getroosten(zich), HGer-troh-ster(ziHG), v., to bear patiently

getrouw, HGer-trow, a., faithful, loyal

getuige, HGer-tow-HGer, c., witness; best man

getuigen, HGer-tow-HGer, v., to testify

getuigenis, HGer-tow-HGer-niss, n., evidence

getuigschrift, HGer-towHG-srift, n., certificate

geur, HGer, c., odour, smell, scent

geuren, HGer-er, v., to be fragrant

geurig, HGer-erHG, a., sweet-smelling, fragrant

gevaar, HGer-fahr, n., danger. op —— af van, op —— af fan, at the risk of

gevaarlijk, HGer-fahr-luck, a., dangerous, risky

geval, HGer-fal, n., case. in ieder ——, in ee-der ——, anyhow

gevangenbewaarder, HGer-fang-er-ber-vahr-der, c., warder

gevangene, HGer-fang-er-ner, c., prisoner

gevangenhouden, HGer-fang-er-how-der, v., to detain [prisonment

gevangenis, HGer-fang-er-niss, c., prison; im-

gevangenschap, HGer-fang-er-sHGap, c., captivity [imprison

gevangenzetten, HGer-fang-er-zet-ter, v., to

gevat, HGer-fat, a., quick-witted; clever

gevecht, HGer-fayHGt, n., fight, battle

gevechtsvliegtuig, HGer-fayHGts-fleeHG-towHG, n., fighter-plane

geveinsd, HGer-feynst, p.p. & a., feigned

geveinsdheid, HGer-feynst-heyt, c., hypocrisy

gevel, HGay-ferl, c., front

geven, HGay-fer, v., to give; to afford; to produce

gever, HGay-fer, c., giver, donor

gevest, HGer-fest, n., hilt

gevestigd, HGer-fess-terHGt, p.p. & a., established

gevit, HGer-fit, n., fault-finding [fixed

gevlei, HGer-fley, n., flattering, coaxing

gevloek, HGer-flook, n., swearing, cursing

gevoeglijk, HGer-fooHG-luck, adv., decently

gevoel, HGer-fool, n., feeling, touch; sentiment

gevoelen, HGer-foo-ler, n., feeling; opinion

gevoelig, HGer-foo-lerHG, a., sensitive, touchy

gevoelloos, HGer-fool-lohss, a., apathetic

gevogelte, HGer-foh-HGerl-ter, n., birds, fowls

gevolg, HGer-folHG, n., suite, train; result [clusion

gevolgtrekking, HGer-folHG-treck-king, c., con-

gevolmachtigde, HGer-fol-maHG-terHG-der, c., plenipotentiary; proxy

gevorderd, HGer-for-dert, p.p. & a., advanced

gewaagd, HGer-vahHGt, a., risky, hazardous

gewaand, HGer-vahnt, p.p. & a., supposed

gewaarwording, HGer-vahr-vor-ding, c., sensation, perception

gewapend, HGer-vah-pernt, p.p. & a., armed

gewas, HGer-vass, n., growth, harvest; plant

geweer, HGer-vayr, n., gun, rifle

gewei, HGer-vey, n., antlers, horns

geweifel, HGer-vey-ferl, n., hesitation

geweld, HGer-velt, n., violence; noise

gewelddaad, HGer-veld-daht, c., act of violence

geweldig, HGer-vel-derHG, a., violent; enormous

gewelf, HGer-velf, n., vault, arch, dome

gewennen, HGer-ven-ner, v., to accustom

gewenst, HGer-venst, p.p. & a., desired; desirable

gewerveld, HGer-vayr-verlt, a., vertebrate

gewest, HGer-vest, n., region, province

geweten, HGer-vay-ter, n., conscience [lous

gewetenloos, HGer-vay-ter-lohss, a., unscrupu-

gewetensbezwaar, HGer-vay-terns-ber-zvahr, n., conscientious objection

gewettigd, HGer-vet-terHGt, p.p. & a., justified

gewezen, HGer-vay-zer, a., former

gewicht, HGer-viHGt, n., weight, importance [tant

gewichtig, HGer-viHG-terHG, a., weighty, impor-

gewijd, HGer-veyt, p.p. & a., consecrated, sacred

gewild, HGer-vilt, a., in favour, popular

gewillig, HGer-vil-lerHG, a. & adv., willing

gewis, HGer-viss, a. & adv., certain, sure

gewoel, HGer-vool, n., bustle, stir; crowd

gewonde, HGer-von-der, c., wounded person

gewoon, HGer-vohn, a. & adv., usual, common, ordinary

gewoonlijk, HGer-vohn-luck, adv., as a rule

gewoonte, HGer-vohn-ter, c., custom, use; habit

gewoonweg, HGer-vohn-vayHG, adv., simply

gewricht, HGer-vriHGt, n., joint, articulation

gewrongen, HGer-vrong-er, p.p. & a., distorted

gezag, HGer-zaHG, n., authority, power, prestige

gezagvoerder, HGer-zaHG-foor-der, c., (naut.) master, captain [total

gezamenlijk, HGer-zah-mer-luck, a. & adv., joint;

gezang, HGer-zang, n., singing; song; hymn

gezant, HGer-zant, c., ambassador, envoy

gezantschap, HGer-zant-sHGap, n., embassy; legation

gezegde, HGer-zayHG-der, n., saying, phrase

gezel, HGer-zel, c., companion, fellow

gezellig, HGer-zel-lerHG, a. & adv., convivial; cosy

gezelschap, HGer-zel-sHGap, n., company, society

gezet, HGer-zet, p.p. & a., set, fixed; corpulent

gezicht, HGer-ziHGt, n., sight; face; looks

gezichtseinder, HGer-ziHGts-eyn-der, c., horizon

gezien, HGer-zeen, p.p. & prep., respected; in

gezin, HGer-zin, n., family, household [view of

gezind, HGer-zint, a., disposed, inclined [family

gezinshoofd, HGer-zins-hohft, n., head of the

gezinsleven, HGer-zins-lay-ver, n., family life

gezinstoeslag, HGer-zins-too-slaHG, c., family allowance [affected

gezocht, HGer-zoHGt, p.p. & a., in demand;

gezond, HGer-zont, a., healthy, wholesome

gezondheid, HGer-zont-heyt, c., health

gezondheidsdienst, HGer-zont-heyts-deenst, c., public health service

gezondheidstoestand, HGer-zont-heyts-too-stant, c., state of health

gezusters, HGer-zers-terss, c. pl., sisters

gezwel, HGer-zvel, n., swelling, tumour

gezwets, HGer-zvets, n., bragging

gezwollen, HGer-svol-ler, p.p. & a., swollen; bom-

gids, HGits, c., guide; guide-book [bastic

gier, HGeer, c., vulture; liquid manure

gierig, HGee-rerHG, a., avaricious, stingy

gierigaard, HGee-rer-HGahrt, c., miser [ness
gierigheid, HGee-rerHG-heyt, c., avarice, stingi-
gieten, HGee-ter, v., to pour; to cast; to found
gieter, HGee-ter, c., watering-can
gieterij, HGee-ter-rey, c., foundry
gietijzer, HGeet-ey-zer, n., cast iron
gif, gift, HGif, HGift, n., poison; venom
gift, HGift, c., gift, present, gratuity
giftgas, gifgas, HGift-HGass, HGif-HGass, n.,
giftig, HGif-terHG, a., poisonous [poison-gas
gij, HGey, pron., you
gijzelaar, HGey-zer-lahr, c., hostage
gil, HGil, c., yell, scream
gillen, HGil-ler, v., to yell, to shriek
ginds, HGints, a. & adv., yonder, over there
gips, HGips, n., plaster of Paris [dressing
gipsverband, HGips-fer-bant, n., plaster of Paris
gissen, HGis-ser, v., to guess, to surmise
gissing, HGis-sing, c., guess, conjecture
gist, HGist, c., yeast
gisten, HGiss-ter, v., to ferment
gisteren, HGiss-ter-er, adv., yesterday
gisterenavond, HGiss-ter-en-ah-vont, c., last
gitaar, HGee-tahr, c., guitar [night
gitzwart, HGit-svart, a., jet-black
glaasje, HGlah-sher, n., small glass
glad, HGlat, a. & adv., slippery; smooth; cunning
gladheid, HGlat-heyt, c., smoothness
gladmaken, HGlat-mah-ker, v., to smooth, to
glans, HGlanss, c., shine, gloss, glitter [polish
glansrijk, HGlanss-reyk, a. & adv., glorious,
glas, HGlas, n., glass; window-pane [brilliant
glasblazer, HGlas-blah-zer, c., glass-blower
glasblazerij, HGlas-blah-zer-rey, c., glass-works
glasscherf, HGlas-sHGayrf, c., piece of broken
glassnijder, HGlas-sney-der, c., glass-cutter [glass
glazen, HGlah-zer, a., glassy; glazed
glazenwasser, HGlah-zer-vas-ser, c., window-
gletscher, HGlet-sher, c., glacier [cleaner
gleuf, HGlerf, c., groove, slot, slit
glibberig, HGlib-ber-rerHG, a., slippery
glijbaan, HGley-bahn, c., slide (on play-ground)

glijden, HGley-der, v., to glide, to slide
glimlach, HGlim-laHG, c., smile
glimlachen, HGlim-laHG-er, v., to smile
glimmen, HGlim-mer, v., to shine, to gleam
glimworm, HGlim-vorm, c., glow-worm; firefly
glinsteren, HGlins-ter-rer, v., to glitter, to sparkle
globaal, HGloh-**bahl**, a. & adv., rough
gloed, HGloot, c., glow, blaze; (fig.) fervour
gloednieuw, HGloot-nee-oo, a., brand-new
gloeien, HGloo-yer, v., to glow
gloeilamp, HGloo'e-lamp, c., glow-lamp
glooiing, HGloh-ying, c., slope
glorie, HGloh-ree, c., glory, splendour
gluiperig, HGlow-per-rerHG, a. & adv., sneaky
gluren, HGlEE-rer, v., to peep, to peer; to leer
God, HGot, c., God
goddank! HGod-**dank**, interj., thank God!
goddelijk, HGod-der-luck, a. & adv., divine
goddeloos, HGod-der-lohss, a. & adv., godless
godenleer, HGoh-der-layr, c., mythology
godgeleerde, HGot-HGer-layr-der, c., theologian
godgeleerdheid, HGot-HGer-layrt-heyt, c., theology
godloochenaar, HGot-loh-HGer-nahr, c., atheist
godsdienst, HGots-deenst, c., religion
godsdienstig, HGots-deens-terHG, a. & adv., religious [c., divine service
godsdienstoefening, HGots-deenst-oo-fer-ning,
godslastering, HGots-las-ter-ring, c., blasphemy
godsvruchtig, HGots-frerHG-terHG, a. & adv., devout
goed, HGoot, n., goods; stuff; estate; property. a. & adv., good; correct; kind; well. —— **zo!** —— **zo**, well done! [natured
goedaardig, HGoo-**dahr**-derHG, a. & adv., good-
goeddunken, HGood-dern-ker, v., to think fit. n., approbation [ities
goederen, HGoo-der-rer, n. pl., goods, commod-
goederentrein, HGoo-der-rer-treyn, c., goods-train
goedertieren, HGoo-der-tee-rer, a., merciful
Goede Week, HGoo-der vayk, c., Holy Week
goedgeefs, HGoot-HGayfss, a., liberal

goedgelovig, HGoot-HGer-loh-verHG, a., credulous

goedhartig, HGoot-har-terHG, a. & adv., kind-hearted

goedheid, HGoot-heyt, c., goodness, kindness

goedig, HGoo-derHG, a. & adv., good-natured

goedkeuren, HGoot-ker-rer, v., to approve of

goedkeuring, HGoot-ker-ring, c., approval, assent

goedkoop, HGoot-kohp, a. & adv., cheap

goedpraten, HGoot-prah-ter, v., to gloss over

goedschiks, HGoot-sHGiks, adv., willingly

goedvinden, HGoot-fin-der, v., to think fit. n., [consent

gokken, HGock-ker, v., to gamble

gokker, HGock-ker, c., gambler

golf, HGolf, c., wave; bay, gulf. n., golf

golfbreker, HGolf-bray-ker, c., breakwater

golflengte, HGolf-leng-ter, c., wave-length

golvend, HGolf-fernt, a., waving, wavy, rolling

gondel, HGon-derl, c., gondola

gonzen, HGon-zer, v., to buzz, to drone

goochelaar, HGoh-HGer-lahr, c., juggler, conjurer

goochelen, HGoh-HGer-ler, v., to juggle, to conjure

gooien, HGoh-yer, v., to throw, to cast

goor, HGohr, a., dingy, nasty, sallow

goot, HGoht, c., gutter, drain

gordel, HGor-derl, c., girdle, belt; waist-band

gordijn, HGor-deyn, n., curtain; bed hangings

gorgelen, HGor-HGer-ler, v., to gargle

gort, HGort, c., groats, grits

goud, HGowt, n., gold

gouden, HGow-der, a., golden

goudkleurig, HGowt-kler-rerHG, a., gold-coloured

goudmijn, HGowt-meyn, c., gold-mine

goudsmid, HGowt-smit, c., goldsmith

goudvink, HGowt-fink, c., bull-finch

goudvis, HGowt-fiss, c., gold-fish

gouverneur, HGoo-ver-nerr, c., governor; tutor

graad, HGraht, c., degree; rank, grade

graaf, HGrahf, c., earl; count

graafschap, HGrahf-sHGap, n., county

graag, HGrahHG, a. & adv., eager; willingly

graan, HGrahn, n., corn, grain   [cereals

graangewassen, HGrahn-HGer-vas-ser, n. pl.,

graankorrel, HGrahn-kor-rerl, c., grain of corn

graat, HGraht, c., fish-bone

gracht, HGraHGt, c., canal; ditch

graf, HGraf, n., grave, sepulchre

grafkelder, HGraf-kel-der, c., family-vault

grafsteen, HGraf-stayn, c., gravestone

gramophoonplaat, HGra-moh-fohn-plaht, c., gramophone record

gramschap, HGram-sHGap, c., anger

granaat, HGrah-naht, c., (mil.) grenade; shell

granaatscherf, HGrah-naht-sHGayrf, c., splinter [of a shell

graniet, HGrah-neet, n., granite

grap, HGrap, c., joke; practical joke

grappenmaker, HGrap-pern-mah-ker, c., joker

grappig, HGrap-perHG, a. & adv., funny, comical

gras, HGrass, n., grass

grasperk, HGrass-payrk, n., lawn

gratie, HGrah-see, c., grace; pardon [elegant

gratieus, HGrah-see-erss, a. & adv., graceful,

gratis, HGrah-tiss, a. & adv., free of charge

grauw, HGrow, a., grey; (fig.) drab

graven, HGrah-ver, v., to dig; to sink (a well)

graveren, HGrah-vay-rer, v., to engrave

gravin, HGrah-vin, c., countess

gravure, HGrah-vEE-rer, c., engraving

grazen, HGrah-zer, v., to graze, to pasture

greep, HGrayp, c., grip; handful; handle

grendel, HGren-derl, c., bolt (door & rifle)

grendelen, HGren-der-ler, v., to bolt [wood

grenenhout, HGray-ner-howt, n., fir, deal, pine-

grens, HGrens, c., limit; bound; frontier

grensgebied, HGrens-HGer-beet, n., borderland

grensgeschil, HGrens-HGer-sHGil, n., frontier dispute [house

grenskantoor, HGrens-kan-tohr, n., custom-

grenspaal, HGrens-pahl, c., boundary-post

grenzenloos, HGren-zer-lohss, a., boundless

greppel, HGrep-perl, c., trench, drain

gretig, HGray-terHG, a. & adv., eager; greedy

grief, HGreef, c., grievance; offence

griep, HGreep, c., influenza

grieven, HGree-ver, v., to grieve; to hurt, to offend

griezelen, HGree-zer-ler, v., to shiver

griezelig, HGree-zer-lerHG, a., gruesome

griezelfilm, HGree-zerl-film, c., horror-film

griffeldoos, HGrif-ferl-dohss, c., pencil-case

grijns, HGreyns, c., grimace   [grin

grijnslachen, HGreyns-laHG-er, v., to sneer, to

grijpen, HGrey-per, v., to seize, to grasp, to grip

grijs, HGreyss, a., grey; grey-haired

grijsaard, HGrey-zahrt, c., grey-haired man

gril, HGril, c., caprice, freak

grillig, HGril-lerHG, a. & adv., capricious

grint, HGrint, n., gravel

groei, HGroo'e, c., growth

groeien, HGroo-yer, v., to grow

groen, HGroon, a., green

groente, HGroon-ter, c., vegetables

groenteboer, HGroon-ter-boor, c., greengrocer

groentesoep, HGroon-ter-soop, c., vegetable soup

groentetuin, HGroon-ter-town, c., kitchen-garden

groentewinkel, HGroon-ter-vin-kerl, c., green-   [grocer's

groep, HGroop, c., group, cluster, clump

groet, HGroot, c., greeting, salute

groeten, HGroo-ter, v., to salute, to greet

groeve, HGroo-ver, c., pit; quarry; furrow

grof, HGrof, a. & adv., coarse, rough

grond, HGront, c., ground, soil; land; bottom

grondbeginsel, HGront-ber-HGin-serl, n., basic   principle

gronden, HGron-der, v., to base, to found

grondgebied, HGront-HGer-beet, n., territory

grondig, HGron-derHG, a. & adv., thorough

grondslag, HGront-slaHG, c., foundation, basis

grondstof, HGront-stof, c., raw material

grondwet, HGront-vet, c., fundamental law

groot, HGroht, a., large; great; tall; vast. **in het**   ——, in het ——, on a large scale

grootbrengen, HGroht-breng-er, v., to bring up,   to rear   [trade

groothandel, HGroht-han-derl, c., wholesale

grootheid, HGroht-heyt, c., greatness; (fig.)   grandeur

groothertog, HGroht-hayr-toHG, c., grand duke

grootmoeder, HGroht-moo-der, c., grandmother
grootmoedig, HGroht-moo-derHG, a., magnanimous [parents
grootouders, HGroht-ow-derss, c. pl., grand-
grootspraak, HGroht-sprahk, c., boasting, brag-
grootte, HGroht-ter, c., size, extent [ging
grootvader, HGroht-fah-der, c., grandfather
gros, HGross, n., gross; mass
grossier, HGros-seer, c., wholesale dealer
grot, HGrot, c., grotto; cave [er part
grotendeels, HGroh-ten-dayls, adv., for the great-
gruis, HGrowss, n., grit; coal-dust
gruwel, HGree-verl, c., abomination, atrocity
gruwelijk, HGree-ver-luck, a. & adv., abominable
guirlande, HGeer-*lan*-der, c., garland, wreath
guit, HGowt, c., wag, little rogue
guitenstreek, HGow-ter-strayk, c., roguish trick
gul, HGerl, a. & adv., generous; frank
gulzig, HGerl-zerHG, a. & adv., greedy
gummi, HGerm-mee, n., india-rubber
gunnen, HGern-ner, v., to grant; not to grudge
gunst, HGernst, c., favour [favour
gunstbewijs, HGernst-ber-veyss, n., mark of
gunstig, HGern-sterHG, a. & adv., favourable
gutsen, HGert-ser, v., to gush; to stream
guur, HGEEr, a., bleak, inclement [school
gymnasium, HGim-*nah*-zee-erm, n., grammar-
gymnastiek, HGim-n*ass*-teek, c., gymnastics, drill
gymnastiekleeraar, HGim-n*ass*-teek-lay-rahr,
c., gymnastic instructor
gymnastiekzaal, HGim-n*ass*-teek-sahl, c., gymnasium, drill-hall

haag, hahHG, c., hedge, hedgerow
haai, hah'e, c., shark; (fig.) kite; hawk
haak, hahk, c., hook
haakpen, hahk-pen, c., crochet-needle
haakwerk, hahk-vayrk, c., crochet-work
haal, hahl, c., stroke (pen)
haam, hahm, c., collar (of horse)
haan, hahn, c., cock
haantje, hahnt-yer, n., young cock, cockerel

haar, hahr, n., hair. pron., their; (to) her; (to)
haarborstel, hahr-bor-sterl, c., hair-brush [them
haarbos, hahr-boss, c., tuft of hair
haard, hahrt, c., hearth, fireside; stove
haarfijn, hahr-feyn, a. & adv., minute; in detail
haarkam, hahr-kam, c., hair-comb
haarkloven, hahr-kloh-ver, v., to split hairs
haarkloverij, hahr-kloh-ver-rey, c., hair-splitting
haarlint, hahr-lint, n., hair-ribbon
haarspeld, hahr-spelt, c., hairpin
haarvlecht, hahr-flayHGt, c., plait; pigtail
haas, hahss, c., hare
haast, hahst, c., haste, hurry
haasten(zich), hahss-ter(ziHG), v., to hasten
haastig, hahss-terHG, a. & adv., hasty, in a hurry
haat, haht, c., hatred
haatdragend, haht-**drah**-HGent, a., resentful
hachée, ha-shey, c., hash, hashed meat
hachelijk, ha-HGer-luck., a., precarious, dangerous
hagedis, hah-HGer-diss, c., lizard
hagedoorn, hah-HGer-dohrn, c., hawthorn
hagel, hah-HGerl, c., hail; small shot
hagelbui, hah-HGerl-bow, c., hail-storm
hagelen, hah-HGer-ler, v., to hail
hagelwit, hah-HGerl-vit, a., (as) white as snow
hak, hak, c., heel; hoe; pickaxe
hakblok, hak-block, n., chopping-block
haken, hah-ker, v., to crochet; to hook, to hitch
hakenkruis, hah-ker-krowss, n., swastika
hakhout, hak-howt, n., coppice, copse
hakkelen, hak-ker-ler, v., to stammer, to stutter
hakken, hak-ker, v., to cut; to chop; to hash
hakmes, hak-mess, n., chopping-knife
hal, hal, c., hall; covered market   [pull
halen, hah-ler, v., to fetch, to go for; to draw, to
half, half, a. & adv., half, semi-
halfbloed, half-bloot, c., half-breed, half-caste
halfbroer, half-broor, c., half-brother
halfdonker, half-don-ker, n., semi-darkness
halfgaar, half-HGahr, a., half-done; (fig.) dotty
halfrond, half-rond, c., hemisphere
halfstok, half-stock, adv., at half-mast

halfwijs, **half-veyss**, a., half-witted
halm, halm, c., stalk; blade (of grass)
hals, halss, c., neck
halsband, halss-bant, c., (dog-)collar
halsdoek, halss-dook, c., scarf, neckerchief
halssnoer, hals-snoor, n., necklace
halsstarrig, hals-star-rerHG, a. & adv., headstrong
halster, hal-ster, c., halter
halte, hal-ter, c., stop, stopping-place
halvemaan, hal-ver-mahn, c., half-moon, cres-
halveren, hal-vay-rer, v., to halve   [cent
halverwege, hal-ver-vay-HGer, adv., half-way
ham, ham, c., ham
hamer, hah-mer, c., hammer, mallet
hamsteren, ham-ster-rer, v., to hoard (food)
hand, hant, c., hand
handappel, hant-ap-perl, c., eating apple
handboeien, hant-boo-yer, c. pl., handcuffs
handboek, hant-book, n., manual, handbook
handdoek, hand-dook, c., towel
handdruk, hand-drerk, c., handshake
handel, han-derl, c., trade; business
handelaar, han-der-lahr, c., merchant, dealer
handelbaar, han-derl-bahr, a., manageable
handelen, han-der-ler, v., to act; to deal
handeling, han-der-ling, c., act; action (play)
handelmaatschappij,   han-derl-maht-sHGap-
       pey, c., trading-company
handelsbetrekkingen,   han-derlss-ber-treck-
       king-er, c. pl., commercial relations   [paper
handelsblad, han-derlss-blat, n., commercial
handelsman, han-derlss-man, c., business man
handelsmerk, han-derlss-mayrk, n., trade mark
handelsvloot, han-derlss-floht, c., merchant fleet
handelwijze, han-derl-vey-zer, c., way of acting
handenarbeid, han-der-ar-beyt, c., manual
handgebaar, hant-HGer-bahr, n., gesture [labour
handgeld, hant-HGelt, n., earnest-money   [fight
handgemeen,hant-HGer-mayn, n., hand-to-hand
handgranaat, hant-HGrah-naht, c., hand-grenade
handhaven, hant-hah-ver, v., to maintain
handig, han-derHG, a. & adv., handy; clever

handkoffer, hant-kof-fer, c., hand-bag; suit-case
handlanger, hant-lang-er, c., accomplice
handleiding, hant-ley-ding, c., manual, guide
handpeer, hant-payr, c., eating pear
handschoen, hant-sHGoon, c., glove; gauntlet
handschrift, hant-srift, n., handwriting
handtasje, han-ta-sher, n., hand-bag, vanity-bag
handtekening, hant-tay-ker-ning, c., signature
handvat, hant-fat, n., handle
handvol, hant-fol, c., handful
handwerk, hant-vayrk, c., trade; needlework
handwerksman, hant-vayrks-man, c., artisan
handwijzer, hant-vey-zer, c., sign-post
handzaag, hant-sahHG, c., hand-saw
hanepoot, hah-ner-poht, c., scrawl
hangbrug, hang-brerHG, c., suspension-bridge
hangen, hang-er, v., to hang
hangkast, hang-kast, c., hanging wardrobe
hangklok, hang-klock, c., hanging clock
hanglamp, hang-lamp, c., hanging lamp
hangmat, hang-mat, c., hammock
hangslot, hang-slot, n., padlock
hansworst, hans-vorst, c., buffoon   [late
hanteren, han-tay-rer, v., to handle, to manipu-
hap, hap, c., bite, bit, morsel
haperen, hah-per-rer, v., to stammer; to stick
happen, hap-per, v., to snap, to bite
happig, hap-perHG, a., eager, keen
hard, hart, a. & adv., hard; harsh; loud
harden, har-der, v., to harden, to temper
hardgekookt, hart-HGer-kohkt, p.p. & a., hard-
boiled   [rude
hardhandig, hart-han-derHG, a. & adv., rough,
hardheid, hart-heyt, c., hardness; harshness
hardhorig, hart-hoh-rerHG, a., hard of hearing
hardlijvigheid, hart-ley-verHG-heyt, c., consti-
hardloper, hart-loh-per, c., runner   [pation
hardnekkig, hart-neck-kerHG, a. & adv., obstinate
hardop, hart-op, adv., aloud
hardrijderij, hart-rey-der-rey, c., skating-match
hardvochtig, hart-foHG-terHG, a. & adv., hard-
harig, hah-rerHG, a., hairy   [hearted

haring, hah-ring, c., herring
haringvisserij, hah-ring-vis-ser-**rey**, c., herring-
hark, hark, c., rake   [fishery
harken, har-ker, v., to rake
harlekijn, har-ler-keyn, c., harlequin, buffoon
harmonica, har-moh-nee-kah, c., accordion
harmoniëren, har-moh-nee-ey-rer, v., harmo-
harnas, har-nass, n., cuirass, armour   [nize
harp, harp, c., harp
harpoen, har-poon, c., harpoon
hars, harss, n., resin
hart, hart, n., heart; core
hartedief, har-ter-deef, c., darling, love
hartelijk, har-ter-luck, a. & adv., cordial
harteloos, har-ter-lohss, a. & adv., heartless
hartewens, har-ter-vens, c., heart's desire
hartkwaal, hart-kvahl, c., disease of the heart
hartroerend, hart-roo-rent, a. & adv., pathetic
hartstocht, harts-toHGt, c., passion
hartstochtelijk, harts-toHG-ter-luck, a. & adv.,
    passionate   [failure
hartverlamming, hart-fer-lam-ming, c., heart-
hartverscheurend, hart-fer-sHGer-rent, a., heart-
hartzeer, hart-sayr, n., grief   [rending
hatelijk, hah-ter-luck, a. & adv., spiteful, hateful
haten, hah-ter, v., hate
have, hah-ver, c., goods, stock
haveloos, hah-ver-lohss, a. & adv., ragged, shabby
haven, hah-ver, c., harbour; (fig.) haven
havenen, hah-ver-ner, v., to ill-treat, to batter
havengelden, hah-ven-HGel-der, n., pl., harbour-
havenhoofd, hah-ven-hohft, n., jetty, pier   [dues
havenloods, hah-ven-lohts, c., harbour-pilot
havenstad, hah-ven-stat, c., port town, port
havenstaking, hah-ven-stah-king, c., dock strike
haver, hah-ver, c., oats
havermout, hah-ver-mowt, n., oatmeal porridge
havik, hah-vick, c., hawk
hazardspel, hah-zahr-spel, n., game of chance
hazelaar, hah-zer-lahr, c., hazel-tree
hazelnoot, hah-zerl-noht, c., hazel-nut
hazenlip, hah-zer-lip, c., hare-lip

hazenwind, hah-zer-vïnt, c., greyhound
hazepeper, hah-zer-pay-per, c., jugged hare
hebben, heb-ber, v., to have
hebzucht, hep-serHGt, c., greed, cupidity
hebzuchtig, hep-serHG-terHG, a., greedy
hecht, hayHGt, a., solid, strong
hechten, hayHG-ter, v., to attach; to stitch up
hechtenis, hayHG-ter-niss, c., custody, detention
hechtpleister, hayHGt-pleys-ter, c., sticking-
heden, hay-der, adv., to-day [plaster
hedendaags, hay-der-dahHGs, a. & adv., present;
heel, hayl, a. & adv., whole, entire [nowadays
heelal, hay-lal, n., universe
heelhuids, hayl-howts, adv., unscathed
heen, hayn, adv., away. —— **en weer,** —— **en**
vayr, to and fro
heenreis, hayn-reyss, c., outward voyage
heer, hayr, c., gentleman; master
heerlijk, hayr-luck, a. & adv., lovely; delicious
heerlijkheid, hayr-luck-heyt, c., splendour, glory
heerschappij, hayr-sHGap-pey, c., mastery; rule
heersen, hayr-ser, v., to rule; to be prevalent
heerszucht, hayrs-zerHGt, c., lust of power
heerszuchtig, hayrs-zerHG-terHG, a., imperious
hees, hayss, a. & adv., hoarse
heester, hays-ter, c., shrub
heet, hayt, a. & adv., hot, torrid
heetbloedig, hayt-bloo-derHG, a., hot-blooded
heetgebakerd, hayt-HGer-bah-kert, a., quick-
heethoofd, hayt-hohft, c., hothead [tempered
hefboom, hef-bohm, c., lever
heffen, hef-fer, v., to raise; to levy (tax)
hefschroefvliegtuig, hef-sroo-fleeHG-towHG, c.,
heftig, hef-terHG, a. & adv., violent [helicopter
heftigheid, hef-terHG-heyt, c., violence
heg, hayHG, c., hedge
heide, hey-der, c., heath, moor; heather
heiden, hey-der, c., heathen, pagan
heil, heyl, n., welfare
Heiland, hey-lant, c., Saviour
heildronk, heyl-dronk, c., toast, health
heilig, hey-lerHG, a. & adv., holy

heiligdom, hey-lerHG-dom, n., sanctuary; relic
heilige, hey-ler-HGer, c., saint [a saint
heiligenbeeld, hey-ler-HGen-baylt, n., image of
heiligschennis, hey-lerHG-sHGen-niss, c., sacri-
heilloos, heyl-lohss, a., fatal, disastrous [lege
heilsleger, hoyls-lay-HGer, n., Salvation Army
heilstaat, heyl-staht, c., ideal state, Utopia
heilzaam, heyl-zahm, a. & adv., beneficial
heimelijk, hey-mer-luck, a. & adv., secret
heimwee, heym-vay, n., home-sickness
heining, hey-ning, c., fence, enclosure
hek, heck, n., fence, railing; gate
hekel, hay-kerl, c., dislike
hekeldicht, hay-kerl-diHGt, n., satire
hekelen, hay-ker-ler, v., to criticize
heks, hecks, c., witch; (fig.) vixen
hel, hel, c., hell. a., bright
helaas! hay-lahss, interj., alas!; unfortunately
held, held, c., hero
heldendaad, hel-der-daht, c., heroic deed
heldenmoed, hel-der-moot, c., heroism
helder, hel-der, a. & adv., clear, bright; clean
helderheid, hel-der-heyt, c., clearness; cleanness
helderziende, hel-der-zeen-der, c., clairvoyant
heldhaftig, helt-haf-terHG, a. & adv., heroic
heldin, hel-din, c., heroine
helemaal, hay-ler-mahl, adv., wholly, entirely
helen, hay-ler, v., to heal, to cure; to receive
heler, hay-ler, c., receiver [(stolen goods)
helft, helft, c., half
hellen, hel-ler, v., to incline, to slope, to slant
hellepijn, hel-ler-peyn, c., torments of hell
helling, hel-ling, c., slope; gradient
helm, helm, c., helmet; headpiece; caul
helpen, hel-per, v., to help; to avail; to attend to
helper, hel-per, c., assistant, helper, aid
hels, hels, a. & adv., hellish, infernal
hem, hem, pron., him
hemd, hemt, n., (under)shirt; chemise
hemdsmouw, hemts-mow, c., shirt-sleeve
hemel, hay-merl, c., heaven; sky, firmament
hemelhoog, hay-merl-bohHG, a. & adv., sky-high

hemellichaam, hay-merl-lee-HGahm, c., heavenly body
hemelrijk, hay-merl-reyk, n., kingdom of heaven
hemels, hay-merls, a. & adv., heavenly, celestial
hemelsblauw, hay-merls-blow, a., sky-blue, azure
Hemelvaartsdag, hay-merl-fahrts-daHG, c., [Ascension day
hen, hen, c., hen. pron., them
hengel, heng-erl, c., fishing-rod
hengelaar, heng-er-lahr, c., angler
hengelen, heng-er-ler, v., to angle. n., angling
hengsel, heng-serl, n., handle; hinge
hengst, hengst, c., stallion
hennep, hen-nerp, c., hemp
herademen, hayr-ah-der-mer, v., to breathe again
heraut, hay-rowt, c., herald
herberg, hayr-bayrHG, c., inn, public house
herbergen, hayr-bayr-HGer, v., to lodge
herbergier, hayr-bayr-HGeer, c., innkeeper, host
herbergzaam, hayr-bayrHG-sahm, a., hospitable
herboren, hayr-boh-rer, a., regenerate
herbouwen, hayr-bow-er, v., to rebuild
herdenken, hayr-den-ker, v., to commemorate
herdenking, hayr-den-king, c., commemoration
herder, hayr-der, c., shepherd, herdsman; pastor
herdershond, hayr-ders-hont, c., shepherd's dog
herdopen, hayr-doh-per, v., to rebaptize
herdruk, hayr-drerk, c., reprint, new edition
herenhuis, hay-rer-howss, n., gentleman's house
herexamen, hayr-ayk-sah-mer, n., re-examina- [tion
herfst, hayrfst, c., autumn
herfstweer, hayrfst-vayr, n., autumn weather
herhaaldelijk, hayr-hahl-der-luck, adv., repeat-
herhalen, hayr-hah-ler, v., to repeat [edly
herhaling, hayr-hah-ling, c., repetition
herinneren, hayr-een-ner-rer, v., to recall, to remind. **zich** ——, ziHG ——, to remember
herinnering, hayr-een-ner-ring, c., recollection; reminder; souvenir
herkauwen, hayr-kow-er, v., to ruminate
herkenbaar, hayr-ken-bahr, a., recognizable
herkennen, hayr-ken-ner, v., to recognize
herkiesbaar, hayr-kees-bahr, a., re-eligible

herkiezen, hayr-kee-zer, v., to re-elect
herkomst, hayr-komst, c., origin, descent
herkrijgen, hayr-krey-HGer, v., to get back
herleiden, hayr-ley-der, v., to reduce, to convert
hermelijnen, hayr-mer-ley-ner, a., ermine
hermetisch, hayr-may-teess, a. & adv., hermetic
hernemen, hayr-nay-mer, v., to take again; to resume [renovate
hernieuwen, hayr-nee-ver, v., to renew, to
hernieuwing, hayr-nee-ving, c., renewal
heroveren, hayr-oh-ver-rer, v., to recapture
herrie, hayr-ree, c., noise, uproar; row [fellow
herriemaker, hayr-ree-mah-ker, c., (pop.) noisy
herroepen, hayr-roo-per, v., to revoke, to recall; to repeal [to transform
herscheppen, hayr-sHGep-per, v., to re-create,
hersenen, hayr-ser-ner, c. pl., brain; brains
hersenpan, hayr-ser-pan, c., skull
hersens, hayr-senss, see hersenen [fancy
hersenschim, hayr-ser-sHGim, c., chimera, idle
hersenschimmig, hayr-ser-sHGim-merHG, a., chimerical [concussion of the brain
hersenschudding, hayr-sHGerd-ding, c.,
hersenvliesontsteking, hayr-ser-flees-ont-stay-king, c., meningitis
herstel, hayr-stel, n., reparation, recovery [able
herstelbaar, hayr-stel-bahr, a., curable, repair-
herstellen, hayr-stel-ler, v., to repair; to correct
herstellende, hayr-stel-len-der, c., convalescent
herstellingoord, hayr-stel-lings-ohrt, n., sana-torium
herstemming, hayr-stem-ming, c., second ballot
hert, hayrt, n., deer, stag
hertenkamp, hayr-ter-kamp, n., deer-park
hertog, hayr-toHG, c., duke
hertogdom, hayr-toHG-dom, n., duchy
hertrouwen, hayr-trow-er, v., to remarry
hervatten, hayr-fat-ter, v., to resume; to repeat
hervormd, hayr-formt, p.p. & a., reformed
hervorming, hayr-for-ming, c., reform; reforma-
herwaarts, hayr-vahrts, adv., this way [tion
herwinnen, hayr-vin-ner, v., to regain; to recover

herzien, hayr-zeen, v., to revise; to review

het, het, art. & pron., the; it; he, she

heten, hay-ter, v., to be called; to name; to order

hetgeen, het-HGayn, pron., that which; which

hetwelk, het-velk, pron., which

hetzelfde, het-selv-der, a., the same

hetzij . . . of, het-sey . . . of, conj., either . . . or; whether . . . or

heuglijk, herHG-luck, a., joyful; memorable

heup, herp, c., hip; haunch (of animal)

heus, herss, adv., truly, really

heuvel, her-verl, c., hill

heuvelachtig, her-verl-αHG-terHG, a., hilly

hevig, hay-verHG, a. & adv., vehement, violent

hevigheid, hay-verHG-heyt, c., vehemence, vio- [lence

hiel, heel, c., heel

hier, heer, adv., here. —— **en daar,** —— **en dahr,** here and there

hieraan, heer-ahn, adv., to this   [hereafter

hierachter, heer-αHG-ter, adv., behind (this);

hierbeneden, heer-ber-nay-der, adv., down here

hierbij, heer-bey, adv., enclosed, herewith

hierbinnen, heer-bin-ner, adv., within

hierboven, heer-boh-ver, adv., up here, above

hierbuiten, heer-bow-ter, adv., outside

hierdoor, heer-dohr, adv., through here

hierheen, heer-hayn, adv., here; this way

hierin, heer-in, adv., herein, in here

hierna, heer-nah, adv., hereafter

hiernaast, heer-nahst, adv., next door

hiernamaals, heer-nah-mahls, adv. & n., (the) hereafter

hierom, heer-om, adv., for this reason

hieromtrent, heer-om-trent, adv., about this

hieronder, heer-on-der, adv., below; at foot

hierop, heer-op, adv., upon this, hereupon

hierover, heer-oh-ver, adv., on this subject

hiertegen, heer-tay-HGer, adv., against this

hiertoe, heer-too, adv., for this purpose

hiertussen, heer-ters-ser, adv., between these

hieruit, heer-owt, adv., hence

hiervan, heer-fαn, adv., of this, about this

hiervoor, heer-fohr, adv., for this; before this

hij, hey, pron., he

hijgen, hey-HGer, v., to pant, to gasp (for breath)

hijsen, hey-ser, v., to hoist, to pull up

hik, hick, c., hiccough

hikken, hick-ker, v., to hiccough

hinde, hin-der, c., hind, doe

hinder, hin-der, c., hindrance, obstacle

hinderen, hin-der-rer, v., to hinder; to trouble

hinderlaag, hin-der-lahHG, c., ambush [venient

hinderlijk, hin-der-luck, a., annoying, incon-

hindernis, hin-der-niss, c., hindrance, obstacle

hinken, hin-ker, v., to limp, to hobble

hinniken, hin-ner-ker, v., to neigh

historicus, hiss-toh-ree-kerss, c., historian

historisch, hiss-toh-reess, a., historic(al)

hit, hit, c., pony, nag, cob

hitte, hit-ter, c., heat

hittegolf, hit-ter-HGolf, c., heat-wave

hobbelen, hob-ber-ler, v., to rock, to toss, to jolt

hobbelig, hob-ber-lerHG, a., rugged, bumpy

hobbelpaard, hob-berl-pahrt, n., rocking-horse

hobo, hoh-boh, c., oboe

hoe, hoo, adv., how

hoed, hoot, c., hat; bonnet

hoedanigheid, hoo-dah-nerHG-heyt, c., quality

hoede, hoo-der, c., guard; protection

hoededoos, hoo-der-dohss, c., hat-box

hoeden, hoo-der, v., to tend, to guard, to look after

hoedenborstel, hoo-der-bors-terl, c., hat-brush

hoedenmaakster, hoo-der-mahk-ster, c., milliner

hoedenwinkel, hoo-der-vin-kerl, c., hat-shop

hoedje, hoot-yer, n., little hat

hoef, hoof, c., hoof

hoefijzer, hoof-ey-zer, n., horseshoe

hoefsmid, hoof-smit, c., shoeing-smith

hoek, hook, c., angle, corner; hook

hoekig, hoo-kerHG, a., angular

hoekje, hook-yer, n., corner

hoekkast, hook-kast, c., corner cupboard

hoeksteen, hook-stayn, c., corner-stone

hoektand, hook-tant, c., canine tooth

hoen, hoon, c., hen, fowl

hoenderhok, hoon-der-hock, n., poultry-house

hoenderpark, hoon-der-park, n., poultry-farm

hoentje, hoont-yer, n., chicken

hoep(el), hoop(-erl), c., hoop

hoepelen, hoo-per-ler, v., to play with a hoop

hoepelrok, hoo-perl-rock, c., hoop-petticoat, [crinoline

hoest, hoost, c., cough

hoestbui, hoost-bow, c., fit of coughing

hoesten, hoo-ster, v., to cough

hoeve, hoo-fer, c., farm

hoeveel, hoo-fayl, pron., how much, how many

hoeveelheid, hoo-fayl-heyt, c., quantity

hoewel, hoo-vel, conj., although

hoezee! hoo-zay, interj., hurrah!

hoezeer, hoo-zayr, conj. how(ever) much

hof, hof, c., garden. n., court

hofbeambte, hof-ber-am-ter, c., court-official

hofdame, hof-dah-mer, c., lady in waiting

hoffelijk, hof-fer-luck, a. & adv., courteous

hoffelijkheid, hof-fer-luck-heyt, c., courtesy

hofhouding, hof-how-ding, c., royal household,

hofmeester, hof-mays-ter, c., steward [court

hofnar, hof-nar, c., court-jester

hofstede, hof-stay-der, c., homestead, farmstead

hogepriester, hoh-HGer-prees-ter, c., high-priest

Hogerhuis, hoh-HGer-howss, n., Upper House

hogerop, hoh-HGer-rop, adv., higher (up)

hogeschool, hoh-HGer-sHGohl, c., university

hok, hock, n., kennel, pen, sty, cage, shed

hol, hol, n., cave; hole, den. a., hollow, empty

holderdebolder, hol-der-der-bol-der, adv., head over heels

hollen, hol-ler, v., to run, to scamper

holte, hol-ter, c., hollow, cavity

hommel, hom-merl, c., drone; bumble bee

homp, homp, c., lump, chunk

hompelen, hom-per-ler, v., to hobble, to limp

hond, hont, c., dog, hound [home

hondenasyl, hon-der-ah-zeel, n., (lost) dogs'

hondenhok, hon-der-hock, n., kennel

hondenleven, hon-der-lay-ver, n., dog's life

hondenwacht, hon-der-*va*HGt, c., (naut.) mid-
watch   [weather
hondenweer, hon-der-vayr, n., (pop.) beastly
honderd, hon-dert, a., a (one) hundred
honderdduizend, hon-dert-dow-zent, a., a (one)
hundred thousand   [years old
honderdjarig, hon-dert-yah-rerHG, a., a hundred
honderdste, hon-dert-ster, a., hundredth
honderdtal, hon-dert-*tal*, n., a (one) hundred
honderdvoudig, hon-dert-fow-derHG, a., a
hundredfold
honds, honts, a. & adv., doggish; brutal
hondsbeet, honts-bayt, c., dog-bite
hondsdagen, honts-dah-HGer, c.pl., dog-days
hondsdolheid, honts-dol-heyt, c., rabies
hondsheid, honts-heyt, c., brutality
honen, hoh-ner, v., to jeer at; to insult
honend, hoh-nent, a., scornful, derisive
honger, hong-er, c., hunger. —— **hebben,** ——
heb-ber, to be hungry   [starvation
hongerdood, hong-er-doht, c., death from
hongerig, hong-er-rerHG, a., hungry
hongerkuur, hong-er-*k*EEr, c., hunger cure
hongerlijder, hong-er-ley-der, c., starveling
hongerloon, hong-er-lohn, n., starvation wages
hongersnood, hong-ers-noht, c., famine
hongerstaking, hong-er-stah-king, c., hunger
honing, hoh-ning, c., honey   [strike
honingbij, hoh-ning-bey, c., honey-bee
honingraat, hoh-ning-raht, c., honeycomb
honingzoet, hoh-ning-zoot, a., honey-sweet
honorarium, hoh-noh-rah-ree-erm, n., fee
hoofd, hohft, n., head; chief; heading
hoofdambtenaar, hohft-*am*-ter-nahr, c., high
official   [article
hoofdartikel, hohft-*ar*-tee-kerl, n., leading
hoofdbestuur, hohft-ber-stEEr, n., managing
committee   [objection
hoofdbezwaar, hohft-berz-vahr, n., main
hoofdbrekend, hohft-bray-kernt, a., puzzling
hoofdbureau, hohft-bEE-roh, n., head-office;
police-office

hoofdconducteur, hohft-kon-derk-terr, c., guard (in train)

hoofddader, hohft-dah-der, c., chief culprit

hoofddeksel, hohft-deck-serl, n., head-dress

hoofddoek, hohft-dook, c., kerchief, turban

hoofddoel, hohft-dool, n., main object

hoofdeinde, hohft-eyn-der, n., head (of bed)

hoofdgebouw, hohft-HGer-bow, c., main building

hoofdgebrek, hohft-HGer-breck, n., principal fault

hoofdhaar, hohft-hahr, n., hair (of the head)

hoofdingang, hohft-in-HGang, c., main entrance

hoofdkaas, hohft-kahss, c., (pork) brawn

hoofdkantoor, hohft-kan-tohr, n., head-office

hoofdknik, hohft-k'nick, c., nod (of the head)

hoofdkussen, hohft-kers-ser, n., pillow [quarters

hoofdkwartier, hohft-k'var-teer, n., (mil.) head-

hoofdletter, hohft-let-ter, c., capital letter

hoofdlijn, hohft-leyn, c., main line

hoofdman, hohft-man, c., chief, leader

hoofdonderwijzer, hohft-on-der-vey-zer, c., headmaster

hoofdpijn, hohft-peyn, c., headache [town

hoofdplaats, hohft-plahtss, c., capital; principal

hoofdprijs, hohft-preyss, c., first prize [editor

hoofdredacteur, hohft-ray-dak-terr, c., chief

hoofdschotel, hohft-sHGoh-terl, c., principal dish

hoofdstad, hohft-stat, c., capital; chief town

hoofdstraat, hohft-straht, c., main street

hoofdtoon, hohft-tohn, c., (mus.) key-note

hoofdweg, hohft-vayHG, c., main road

hoofdzaak, hohft-sahk, c., main point (thing)

hoofdzakelijk, hohft-sah-ker-luck, adv., mainly,

hoofs, hohfss, adv., courtly [chiefly

hoog, hohHG, a. & adv., high, lofty; tall

hoogachten, hohHG-aHG-ter, v., to esteem

hoogachting, hohHG-aHG-ting, c., esteem, respect

hoogdravend, hohHG-drah-vernt, a. & adv., (fig.) bombastic [mountains

hooggebergte, hohHG-HGer-bayrHG-ter, n., high

hooghartig, hohHG-har-terHG, a., proud, haughty

hoogheid, hohHG-heyt, c., height. Zijne Hoog-

heid, zey-ner ——, His Highness

hooghouden, hohHG-how-der, v., to maintain
hoogleraar, hohHG-lay-rahr, c., professor
hoogmoed, hohHG-moot, c., haughtiness
hoogmoedig, hohHG-moo-derHG, a., haughty
hoogoven, hohHG-oh-ver, c., blast-furnace
hoogschatten, hohHG-sHGat-ter, v., to esteem
highly [respect
hoogschatting, hohHG-sHGat-ting, c., esteem,
hoogspanning, hohHG-span-ning, c., high tension
hoogst, hohHGst., a. & adv., highest; top
hoogstaand, hohHG-stahnt, a., eminent, distinguished [at best
hoogstens, hohHG-stenss, adv., at (the) most,
hoogstwaarschijnlijk, hohHGst-vahr-sHGeyn-
luck, adv., most probably
hoogte, hohHG-ter, c., height; elevation [point
hoogtepunt, hohHG-ter-pernt, n., culminating-
hoogtezon, hohHG-ter-zon, c., artificial sunlight
hoogverraad, hohHG-ferr-raht, n., high treason
hoogvlakte, hohHG-flak-ter, c., plateau
hoogwaardig, hohHG-vahr-derHG, a., venerable
hoogwater, hohHG-vah-ter, n., high tide
hooi, hoh'ee, n., hay
hooiberg, hoh'ee-bayrHG, c., haystack
hooien, hoh'yer, v., to make hay
hooikoorts, hoh'ee-kohrts, c., hayfever
hooiopper, hoh'ee-op-per, c., haycock
hooischuur, hoh'ee-sHGEér, c., haybarn
hooizolder, hoh'ee-zol-der, c., hayloft
hoon, hohn, c., scorn, scoffing, taunt
hoongelach, hohn-HGer-laHG, n., scornful laugh-
hoop, hohp, c., hope; heap; lot; crowd [ter
hoopvol, hohp-fol, a., a hopeful
hoorbaar, hohr-bahr, a., audible
hoorn, hoh-rern, c., horn; (mil.) bugle
hoorspel, hohr-spel, n., radio play
hoos, hohss, c., water-spout
hop, hop, c., hop. interj., gee-up!
hopeloos, hoh-per-lohss, a. & adv., hopeless,
hopen, hoh-per, v., to hope [desperate
hopman, hop-man, c., scout-master
horde, hor-der, c., horde, troop; hurdle

horen, hoh-rer, v., to hear; to learn   [zontal
horizontaal, hoh-ree-zon-**tahl,** a. & adv., hori-
horloge, hor-**loh**-zher, n., watch   [chain
horlogeketting, hor-loh-zher-ket-ting, c., watch-
horlogemaker, hor-loh-zher-mah-ker, c., watch-
hortend, hor-**ternt,** a., jerky   [maker
horzel, hor-zerl, c., horse-fly
hospita, hoss-pee-tah, c., landlady
hospitaal, hoss-pee-**tahl,** n., hospital
hostie, hoss-tee, c., (eccles.) host
hotelhouder, hoh-tel-how-der, c., hotel-keeper
houdbaar, howt-**bahr,** a., tenable, maintainable
houden, how-der, v., to hold; to keep; to contain;
    to observe. —— **van,** —— fan, to be fond of
houder, how-der, c., holder, bearer
houding, how-ding, c., carriage, bearing, attitude
hout, howt, n., wood; timber
houtduif, howt-dowf, c., wood-pigeon
houten, how-ter, a., wooden
houthakker, howt-hak-ker, c., wood-cutter
houthandel, howt-han-derl, c., timber-trade
houthandelaar, howt-han-der-lahr, c., timber-
    merchant
houtmijt, howt-meyt, c., wood-stack; pile
houtskool, howts-kohl, c., charcoal
houtsnijder, howts-ney-der, c., wood-carver
houtvester, howt-fess-ter, c., forester
houtzagerij, howt-sah-HGer-rey, c., saw-mill
houvast, how-**vast,** n., handhold, grip; hold,
houw, how, c., cut, gash, slash   [support
houweel, how-vayl, n., pickaxe
houwen, how-er, v., to hew; to cut
hovaardig, hoh-vahr-derHG, a. & adv., proud
hoveling, hoh-ver-ling, c., courtier
huichelaar, how-HGer-lahr, c., hypocrite
huichelachtig, how-HGer-laHG-terHG, a. & adv.,
    hypocritical
huichelarij, how-HGer-lah-rey, c., hypocrisy
huichelen, how-HGer-ler, v., to simulate, to sham
huicheltaal, how-HGerl-tahl, c., hypocritical
huid, howt, c., skin, hide, pelt   [language
huidig, how-derHG, a., of the present day

huidje, howt-yer, n., skin, film
huidkleur, howt-klerr, c., colour, complexion
huidziekte, howt-seek-ter, c., skin-disease
huifkar, howf-kar, c., hooded cart
huilbui, howl-bow, c., crying-fit
huilebalk, how-ler-balk, c., whiner; weeper
huis, howss, n., house, home. van —— tot ——,
  fan —— tot ——, from house to house
huisarts, howss-arts, c., family doctor
huisbaas, howss-bahss, c., landlord
huisbel, howss-bel, c., street-door bell   [taker
huisbewaarder, howss-ber-vahr-der, c., care-
huisbezoek, howss-ber-zook, n., house-to-house
  call
huisdeur, howss-derr, c., street-door, house-door
huisdier, howss-deer, n., domestic animal
huisdokter, howss-dock-ter, c., family doctor
huiseigenaar, howss-ey-HGer-nahr, c., landlord
huiselijk, how-ser-luck, a., domestic; homelike
huisgenoot, howss-HGer-noht, c., inmate
huisgezin, howss-HGer-zin, n., household
huishoudelijk, howss-how-der-luck, a., domestic; thrifty   [housekeeping
huishouden, howss-how-der, n., household;
huishoudgeld, howss-howt-HGelt, n., house-
  keeping money
huishoudster, howss-howt-ster, c., housekeeper
huishuur, howss-hEEr, c., house-rent
huisje, how-sher, n., small house; shell (of snail)
huisjesslak, how-shers-slak, c., snail
huiskamer, howss-kah-mer, c., sitting-room,
  living-room   [family
huismoeder, howss-moo-der, c., mother of the
huismus, howss-merss, c., sparrow; (fig.) home-
  bird   [the house
huisnummer, howss-nerm-mer, n., number of
huisonderwijs, howss-on-der-veyss, n., private
huisraad, howss-raht, n., furniture   [tuition
huissleutel, hows-sler-terl, c., house-key
huisvesten, howss-fess-ter, v., to house; to take in
huisvesting, howss-fess-ting, c., lodging, housing
huisvriend, howss-freent, c., family friend

huisvrouw, howss-frow, c., housewife
huiswaarts, howss-vahrts, adv., homeward
huiswerk, howss-vayrk, n., home-work
huiveren, how-ver-rer, v., to shiver, to shudder
huiverig, how-ver-rerHG, a., chilly
huivering, how-ver-ring, c., shiver, shudder
hulde, herl-der, c., homage   [believe in
huldigen, herl-derHGer, v., to pay homage to; to
hullen, herl-ler, v., to wrap (up), to envelop
hulp, herlp, c., help, assistance; relief
hulpbehoevend, herlp-ber-hoo-vent, a., invalid;
hulpbron, herlp-bron, c., resource   [needy
hulpeloos, herl-per-lohss, a. & adv., helpless
hulpgeroep, herlp-HGer-roop, n., cry for help
hulpkantoor, herlp-kan-tohr, n., sub-office
hulpmiddel, herlp-mid-derl, n., expedient
hulpmotor, herlp-moh-tor, c., assisted cycle
hulptroepen, herlp-troo-per, c. pl., auxiliary
      troops   [helpful
hulpvaardig, herlp-fahr-derHG, a., ready to help,
hulpverlening, herlp-fer-lay-ning, c., assistance
huls, herlss, c., pod, husk; straw case
hulst, herlst, c., holly
humeur, hEE-merr, n., temper, mood, humour
humeurig, hEE-mer-rerHG, a., moody, sulky
humor, hEE-mor, c., humour   [humorous
humoristisch, hEE-moh-riss-teess, a. & adv.,
hun, hern, pron., their; them   [crave (for)
hunkeren (naar), hern-ker-rer (nahr), v., to
hunnerzijds, hern-ner-zeyts, adv., on their part
huppelen, herp-per-ler, v., to hop, to frisk
huren, hEE-rer, v., to hire, to rent; to engage
hurken, herr-ker, v., to squat
hut, hert, c., cottage, hut, hovel; (naut.) cabin
hutkoffer, hert-kof-fer, c., cabin-trunk
hutspot, herts-pot, c., hotchpotch
huur, hEEr, c., rent, hire; wages; lease
huurder, hEEr-der, c., hirer; tenant, lessee
huurhuis, hEEr-howss, n., hired (rented) house
huurkoetsier, hEEr-koot-seer, c., cabman
huurkoop, hEEr-kohp, c., hire-purchase
huurtijd, hEEr-teyd, c., term of lease

huwbaar, HEE-bahr, a., marriageable
huwelijk, HEE-ver-luck, n., marriage, wedding
huwelijksfeest, HEE-ver-lucks-fayst, n., wedding-party
huwelijksreis, HEE-ver-lucks-reyss, c., honey-moon (trip)
huwen, HEE-ver, v., to marry   [moon (trip)
huzaar, HEE-zahr, c., hussar
hygiëne, hee-HGee-ey-ner, c., hygiene, hygienics
hygiënisch, hee-HGee-ey-neess, a. & adv.,
hymne, him-ner, c., hymn   [hygienic
hypnotiseren, hip-noh-tee-zay-rer, v., to hyp-notize
hypnotiseur, hip-noh-tee-zerr, c., hypnotist
hypotheek, hee-poh-tayk, c., mortgage
hysterisch, hiss-tay-reess, a. & adv., hysterical

ideaal, ee-day-ahl, n., ideal. a., ideal
idee, ee-day, n., idea, notion   [identity card
identiteitskaart, ee-den-tee-teyts-kahrt, c.,
idioot, ee-dee-oht, c., idiot. a. & adv., idiotic
ieder, ee-der, a., every, each
iedereen, ee-der-rayn, pron., everybody
iemand, ee-mant, pron., somebody, anybody
iep, eep, c., elm-tree
iets, eets, pron., something, anything. adv., a little
ijdel, ey-derl, a. & adv., vain; idle
ijdelheid, ey-derl-heyt, c., vanity; futility
ijlen, ey-ler, v., to hasten; to be delirious
ijlings, ey-lings, adv., hastily
ijs, eyss, n., ice; ice-cream
ijsbeer, eyss-bayr, c., white (polar) bear
ijsbreker, eyss-bray-ker, c., ice-breaker
ijscoman, eyss-koh-man, c., ice-cream vendor
ijselijk, ey-ser-luck, a. & adv., horrible, dreadful
ijskoud, eyss-kowt, a., icy-cold
ijsschol, eys-sHGol, c., ice-floe, flake of ice
ijver, ey-fer, c., diligence, ardour
ijverig, ey-fer-rerHG, a. & adv., diligent, zealous
ijverzucht, ey-fer-zerHGt, c., jealousy
ijzel, ey-zerl, c., glazed frost
ijzer, ey-zer, n., iron; blade (of skate)
ijzererts, ey-zer-ayrts, n., iron ore

ijzergieterij, ey-zer-HGee-ter-**rey,** c., ironfoundry
ijzingwekkend, ey-zing-**veck**-kent, a., gruesome,
ik, ick, pron., I   [ghastly
illusie, eel-**LEE**-zee, c., illusion
illustratie, eel-lee-HGrah-**see,** c., illustration
imker, im-ker, c., bee-keeper
immigratie, im-mee-HGrah-**see,** c., immigration
immoreel, im-moh-**rayl,** a. & adv., immoral
impasse, im-**pas**-ser, c., deadlock
importeren, im-por-**tay**-rer, v., to import
in, in, prep., in, into, within; at; on
inachtneming, in-**a**HGt-nay-ming, c., observance
inademen, in-ah-der-mer, v., to breathe, to inhale
inbeelden(zich), in-**bayl**-der(ziHG), v., to imagine
inbeelding, in-**bayl**-ding, c., imagination
inbeslagneming, in-ber-slaHG-nay-ming, c.,
inblazer, in-**blah**-zer, c., prompter   [seizure
inboedel, in-**boo**-derl, c., furniture, household
    effects
inboezemen, in-**boo**-zer-mer, v., to inspire
inboorling, in-**bohr**-ling, c., native
inborst, in-**blah**-zer, c., character, nature
inbraak, in-**brahk,** c., burglary
inbreken, in-**bray**-ker, v., to commit burglary
inbreker, in-**bray**-ker, c., burglar
inbreuk, in-**brerk,** c., infringement, violation
incluis, in-**klowss,** a., included
inclusief, in-klee-**zeef,** a. & adv., inclusive
inconsequent, in-kon-ser-**kvent,** a. & adv.,
    inconsistent
indachtig, in-**da**HG-terHG, a., mindful of
indelen, in-**day**-ler, v., to divide; to classify
inderdaad, in-der-**daht,** adv., indeed, really
inderhaast, in-der-**hahst,** adv., hurriedly
indien, in-**deen,** conj., if   [ward
indienen, in-**dee**-ner, v., to bring in, to put for-
individu, in-dee-vee-**dEE,** n., individual
indompelen, in-**dom**-per-ler, v., to plunge in
indringen, in-**dring**-er, v., to enter by force
indringer, in-**dring**-er, c., intruder, interloper
indringerig, in-**dring**-er-rerHG, a. & adv., intru-
indruk, in-**drerk,** c., impression   [sive

indrukwekkend, in-drerk-veck-kent, a., impress-
industrie, in-ders-tree, c., industry   [ive
indutten, in-dert-ter, v., to doze off   [gether
ineendraaien, in-ayn-drah-yer, v., to twist to-
ineenfrommelen, in-ayn-from-mer-ler, v., to
     crumple up
ineenkrimpen, in-ayn-krim-per, v., to shrink
ineenstorten, in-ayn-stor-ter, v., to collapse
inenten, in-en-ter, v., to vaccinate
infanterie, in-fan-ter-ree, c., infantry
infectieziekte, in-feck-see-zeek-ter, c., infectious
inflatie, in-flah-see, c., inflation   [disease
influisteren, in-flows-ter-rer, v., to whisper, to
     prompt   [inquiry
informatie, in-for-mah-see, c., information;
informeren, in-for-may-rer, v., to inquire
ingaan, in-HGahn, v., to enter; to become
ingang, in-HGang, c., entrance, way in [effective
ingebeeld, in-HGer-baylt, a., imaginary pre-
     sumptuous
ingeboren, in-HGer-boh-rer, a., innate, inborn
ingemaakt, in-HGer-mahkt, a, & p.p., preserved,
ingenieur, in-zhay-nee-err, c., engineer [pickled
ingenomen (met), in-HGer-noh-mer (met), a.,
     pleased (with)   [uous; inten-
ingespannen, in-HGer-span-ner, a. & adv., stren-
ingetogen, in-HGer-toh-HGer, a. & adv., modest,
ingeval, in-HGer-val, conj., in case   [quiet
ingevallen, in-HGer-val-ler, a., hollow, sunken
ingeven, in-HGay-ver, v., to administer; to suggest
ingewanden, in-HGer-van-der, n. pl., bowels
ingewijd, in-HGer-veyt, a., initiated
ingewikkeld, in-HGer-vick-kelt, a., intricate
ingieten, in-HGee-ter, v., to pour in   [fere
ingrijpen, in-HGrey-per, v., to intervene; to inter-
ingrijpend, in-HGrey-pent, a., radical, drastic
inhalen, in-hah-ler, v., to fetch in, to gather in; to
inhalig, in-hah-lerHG, a., grasping, greedy [inhale
inham, in-ham, c., creek, bay, inlet
inhameren, in-hah-mer-rer, v., to hammer in
inhechtenisneming, in-hayHG-ter-niss-nay-
     ming, c., arrest

inheems, in-**haymss**, a., native; home-bred

inhoud, in-**howt**, c., contents; purport

inhouden, in-**how**-der, v., to contain; to restrain

inhuldiging, in-**herl**-der-HGing, c., installation

initiatief, ee-nee-see-ah-teef, n., initiative

inkeer, in-kayr, c., repentance

inkepen, in-kay-per, v., to indent; to nick

inkijken, in-key-ker, v., to look in; to glance over

inkomen, in-koh-mer, v., to come in. n., income

inkomstenbelasting, in-kom-ster-ber-las-ting, c., income tax

inkoopsprijs, in-kohps-preyss, c., cost price

inkorten, in-kor-ter, v., to shorten

inkrimping, in-krim-ping, c., shrinking; dwind-inkt, inkt, c., ink [ling

inktvis, inkt-fiss, c., cuttle-fish

inkwartieren, in-kvar-tee-rer, v., to billet

inlander, in-lan-der, c., native

inlands, in-lants, a., indigenous; home (-grown,

inlassen, in-las-ser, v., to insert [-made)

inlaten, in-lah-ter, v., to let in. zich — met, ziHG — met, to have dealings with

inleggen, in-lay-HGer, v., to put in; to deposit

inleiding, in-ley-ding, c., introduction; preamble

inleveren, in-lay-ver-rer, v., to give in; to deliver

inlichting, in-liHG-ting, c., information [up

inlijven, in-ley-ver, v., to incorporate

inmaakfles, in-mahk-fless, c., preserving-bottle

inmenging, in-meng-ing, c., meddling, interference

inmiddels, in-mid-deriss, adv., in the meantime

innemen, in-nay-mer, v., to take in; to occupy

innemend, in-nay-ment, a., pleasing, attractive

inneming, in-nay-ming, c., taking [cheque)

innen, in-ner, v., to collect (debts); to cash (a

innerlijk, in-ner-luck, a., inward, inner

innig, in-nerHG, a. & adv., hearty, tender

inoogsten, in-ohHG-ster, v., to gather in, to reap

inpakken, in-pak-ker, v., to pack (up); to wrap up

inpikken, in-pik-ker, v., (pop.) to pinch; to pick up

inprenten, in-pren-ter, v., to inculcate, to impress

inrichten, in-riHG-ter, v., to fit up; to arrange

inrichting, in-riHG-ting, c., arrangement; structure; furnishing; establishment

inrijden, in-rey-der, v., to run in (a car); to break in (a horse)

inroepen, in-roo-per, v., to call in, to invoke

inruilen, in-row-ler, v., to barter, to exchange

inrukken, in-rerk-ker, v., to march into; to turn in

inschakelen, in-sHGah-ker-ler, v., to switch on

inschenken, in-sHGen-ker, v., to pour out

inschepen, in-sHGay-per, v., to ship, to embark

inschikkelijk, in-sHGik-ker-luck, a., obliging

inschrijven, in-srey-ver, v., to book, to enter; to inscribe [powder

insectenpoeder, in-seck-ter-poo-der, n., insect-

insigne, in-see-n'yer, n., badge

inslaan, in-slahn, v., to drive in (nail); to dash in

inslapen, in-slah-per, v., to fall asleep [to stock

inslikken, in-slick-ker, v., to swallow

insluimeren, in-slow-mer-rer, v., to doze off

insluiten, in-slow-ter, v., to enclose; to lock in

insmeren, in-smay-rer, v., to oil, to smear

insnijden, in-sney-der, v., to cut in(to)

insnuiven, in-snow-ver, v., to inhale

inspannen, in-span-ner, v., to exert, to strain.
zich ——, ziHG ——, to do one's utmost

inspanning, in-span-ning, c., effort; strain

inspecteur, in-speck-terr, c., inspector, super-

inspuiting, in-spow-ting, c., injection [intendent

instaan (voor), in-stahn (fohr), v., to answer (for), to vouch (for)

instandhouding, in-stant-how-ding, c., upkeep

instantie, in-stan-see, c., instance; authority

instappen, in-stap-per, v., to get in

instelling, in-stel-ling, c., establishment: [men:

instemming, in-stem-ming, c., approval, agree-

instinctmatig, in-stinkt-mah-terHG, a. & adv., [instinctive

instorten, in-stor-ter, v., to collapse

instorting, in-stor-ting, c., collapse; down-fall

nstuderen, in-stEE-day-rer v., to practise, to rehearse

intact, in-takt, a., unimpaired, intact [trary

integendeel, in-tay-HGen-dayl, adv., on the con-

intekenen, in-tay-ker-ner, v., to subscribe
interessant, in-ter-rers-sant, a. & adv., interesting
interesseren, in-ter-rers-say-rer, v., to interest.
  zich —— voor, ziHG —— vohr, to be interested in
internaat, in-tayr-naht, n., boarding-school
interneringskamp, in-ter-nay-rings-kamp, n., internment camp
intiem, in-teem, a. & adv., intimate; inner
intomen, in-toh-mer, v., to curb; to restrain
intrede, in-tray-der, c., entrance, entry; coming
intreeprijs, in-tray-preyss, c., admission-fee
intrekken, in-treck-ker, v., to draw in; to move in
intrige, in-tree-HGer, c., intrigue, scheming
introduceren, in-troh-dΕ-say-rer, v., to introduce
intussen, in-ters-ser, adv., in the meantime [duce
inval, in-fal, c., invasion; idea, thought
invalide, in-vah-lee-der, c., invalid [enter
invallen, in-fal-ler, v., to drop in; to set in, to
inventaris, in-ven-tah-rerss, c., inventory; stock-
invloed, in-floot, c., influence [in-trade
invoegen, in-foo-HGer, v., to put in, to insert
invoer, in-foor, c., import, importation
invoeren, in-foo-rer, v., to import; to introduce
invoerrechten, in-foor-rayHG-ter, n. pl., import duties
invreten, in-fray-ter, v., to corrode [release
invrijheidstelling, in-frey-heyt-stel-ling, c.,
invullen, in-ferl-ler, v., to fill in; to fill up
inwendig, in-ven-derHG, a. & adv., inner, inward
inwerken (op), in-vayr-ker (op), v., to act (upon); to affect
inwerking, in-vayr-king, c., influence, action
inwijden, in-vey-der, v., to inaugurate; to initiate
inwikkelen, in-vick-ker-ler, v., to wrap up, to cover up [grant
inwilligen, in-vil-ler-HGer, v., to comply with, to
inwisselen, in-vis-ser-ler, v., to change (bank-notes)
inwoner, in-voh-ner, c., inhabitant, resident;
inwrijven, in-vrey-ver, v., to rub in [inmate
inzage, in-zah-HGer, c., examination, inspection

inzakken, in-zak-ker, v., to sink down, to cave in
inzamelen, in-zah-mer-ler, v., to collect, to
        gather (in)   [bless
inzegenen, in-zay-HGer-ner, v., to consecrate, to
inzender, in-zen-der, c., correspondent, contri-
inzepen, in-zay-per, v., to soap, to lather   [butor
inzetten, in-zet-ter, v., to put in, to set in
inzicht, in-ziHGt, n., insight; opinion, view
inzien, in-zeen, v., to see, to realize; to glance over
inzinking, in-zin-king, c., relapse, decline, sinking
inzuigen, in-zow-HGer, v., to suck in (up)
inzwelgen, in-zvel-HGer, v., to swallow (up)
ironisch, ee-roh-neess, a. & adv., ironical
irreëel eer-ray-ayl, a., unreal [pl., irrigation works
irrigatiewerken, eer-ree-HGah-see-vayr-ker n.
irriteren, eer-ree-tay-rer, v., to irritate
ivoor, ee-vohr, n., ivory
ivoren, ee-voh-rer, a., ivory
ivoorsnijder, ee-vohr-sney-der, c. ivory-cutter

ja, yah, adv., yes; indeed
jaar, yahr, n., year
jaarbeurs, yahr-berrss, c., industries fair
jaarboek, yahr-book, n., year-book
jaargang, yahr-HGang, c., volume; file; vintage
jaargetij(de) yahr-HGer-tey-(der), n., season
jaarlijks, yahr-lucks, a. & adv., yearly
jaartelling, yahr- tel-ling, c., era
jaarverslag, yahr-fer-slaHG, n., annual report
jaarwedde, yahr-ved-der, c., annual salary [suit
jacht, yaHGt, n., yacht, c., hunt(ing), chase; pur-
jachtgeweer, yaHGt-HGer-vayr, n., sporting-gun
jachthond, yaHGt-hont, c., hound, sporting-dog
jachtopziener, yaHGt-op-see-ner, c., gamekeeper
jachtvliegtuig, yaHGt-fleeHG-towHG, n., fighter
        (plane)
jacquet, zhah-ket, n., morning-coat   [drive
jagen, yah-HGer, v., to hunt, to shoot; to race; to
jager, yah-HGer, c., hunter, sportsman; rifleman
jakhals, yak-hals, c., jackal
jakkes! yak-kess, interj., bah!
jaloers, yah-loorss, a. & adv., envious, jealous

jaloersheid, yah-loorss-heyt, c., envy, jealousy
jaloezie, zhah-loo-zee, c., jealousy; Venetian blind
jammer, yam-mer, c., misery, distress. hoe —— !
  hoo ——, what a pity!
jammeren, yam-mer-rer, v., to lament, to wail
jammerlijk, yam-mer-luck, a. & adv., wretched
janboel, yan-bool, c., (pop.) mess, muddle
janken, yan-ker, v., to whine, to yelp
januari, yah-nee-ah-ree, c., January
japon, yah-pon, c., gown, dress, frock
jarenlang, yah-rer-lang, a. & adv., of years; for
jarig, yah-rerHG, a., a year old   [years together
jarretelle, zhar-rer-tel, c., (stocking-) suspender
jas, yass, c., coat, jacket
jawel, yah-vel, adv., yes; indeed
jawoord, yah-vohrt, n., consent, yes
je, yer, pron., you; your
jegens, yay-HGenss, prep., towards, to; with
jekker, yeck-ker, c., jacket; pilot-coat
jenever, yer-nay-ver, c., gin, Hollands
jeneverstokerij, yer-nay-ver-stoh-ker-rey, c.,
jeugd, yerHGt, c., youth   [gin-distillery
jeugdherberg, yerHGt-hayr-bayrHG, c., youth-
jeugdig, yerHG-derHG a. & adv., youthful   [hostel
jeugdvereniging, yerHGt-fer-ay-ner-HGing, c.,
  youth-association
jeuk, yerk, c., itching   [to scratch oneself
jeuken, yer-ker v., to itch. zich —— ziHG ——,
jichtaanval, yiHGt-ahn-val, c., attack of gout
jichtlijder, yiHGt-ley-der, c., sufferer from gout
jij, yey, pron., you
jochie, yoHG-ee n., boy, kid laddie
Jodenbuurt, yoh-der-beert, c., Jewish quarter
Jodenkerk, yoh-der-kayrk, c., synagogue
jodium, yoh-dee-erm n., iodine
jokken, yok-ker, v., to fib, to tell stories
jolig, yoh-lerHG a., jolly, merry
jolijt yoh-leyt, c., joy, fun, merry-making
jong, yong, c., young one; cub. a. young
jongeling, yong-er-ling, c., youth, young man
jongelui, yong-er-low, c. pl., young people, young
jongen, yong-er, c. boy lad   [men

jongensachtig, yong-ens-*a*HG-terHG, a. & adv., boyish

jongensschool, yong-ens-sHGohl, c., boys' school

jonger, yong-er, a., younger, junior

jongetje, yong-ert-yer, n., little boy

jonggezel, yong-HGer-zel, c., single man

jongst, yongst, a., youngest, latest

Jood, yoht, c., Jew, Hebrew

Joods, yohts, a., Jewish; Judaic

jou, yow, pron., you

jouw, yow, pron., your

joviaal, zhoh-vee-ahl, a. & adv., jovial, genial, [sporting

jubelen, yEE-ber-ler, v., to jubilate, to exult

juffrouw, yerf-frow, c., lady; madam; miss; Mrs.

juichen, yow-HGer, v., to shout; to cheer

juist, yowst, a. & adv., right, exact; just

juk, yerk, n., yoke, cross-beam

juli, yEE-lee, c., July

jullie, yerl-lee, pron., you, you people

juni, yEE-nee, c., June

jurist, yEE-rist, c., jurist, lawyer

jurk, yerrk, c., dress, frock, gown

jurylid, zhEE-ree-lit, n., member of the jury

jus, zhEE, c., gravy

juslepel, zhEE-lay-perl, c., gravy-spoon [police

justitie, yerss-tee-see, c., judicature; the law; the

juweel, yEE-vayl, n., jewel, gem; (fig.) treasure

juwelierswinkel, yEE-ver-leers-vin-kerl, c., jeweller's shop

kaai, kah-ee, c., wharf, quay; embankment

kaaiman, kah-ee-m*a*n, c., alligator

kaak, kahk, c., jaw(-bone); cheek; gill (of fish)

kaakslag, kahk-sl*a*HG, c., slap in the face

kaal, kahl, a., bald; bare; callow; threadbare

kaalhoofdig, kahl-hohv-derHG, a., baldheaded

kaalkop, kahl-kop, c., baldhead

kaap, kahp, c., cape, promontory, headland

kaars, kahrss, c., candle; taper

kaarslicht, kahrss-liHGt, n., candlelight

kaarsvet, kahrss-fet, n., candle-grease, tallow

kaart, kahrt, c., card; map; chart; ticket

kaartje, kahrt-yer, n., card; ticket
kaartlegster, kahrt-leHG-ster, c., fortune-teller
kaartspel, kahrt-spel, n., game of cards
kaas, kahss, c., cheese
kaasboer, kahss-boor, c., cheese-maker
kaasmarkt, kahss-markt, c., cheese-market
kaatsen, kaht-ser, v., to play at ball
kabaal, kah-bahl, n., hubbub, hullabaloo, noise
kabbelen, kab-ber-ler, v., to babble, to ripple
kabel, kah-berl, c., cable; (naut.) hawser
kabelballon, hah-berl-bal-lon, c., captive balloon
kabeljauw, kah-berl-yow, c., cod(-fish)
kabelspoorweg, kah-berl-spohr-veHG, c., cable-railway
kabinet, ka-be-net, n., cabinet; lavatory
kabouter, ka-bow-ter, c., goblin, elf, gnome, imp
kachel, kaHG-erl, c., stove; (electric) heater
kader, kah-der, n., (mil.) cadre; (fig.) framework
kadetje, kah-det-yer, n., French roll
kadettenschool, kah-det-ter-sHGohl, c., cadet-school [school]
kaf, kaf, n., chaff
Kaffer, kaf-fer, c., Kaffir; (fig.) boor
kaft, kaft, c., (paper) cover, wrapper
kaftpapier, kaft-pah-peer n., wrapping-paper, brown paper [ster ——, saloon]
kajuit, kah-yowt, c., cabin. eerste ——, ayr-
kakelen, kah-ker-ler, v., to cackle; (fig.) to chatter
kakkerlak, kah-ker-lak, c., black-beetle, cock-roach [roach]
kalender, kah-len-der, c., calendar
kalf, kalf, n., calf; (fig.) booby, ninny
kalfsgehakt, kalfs-HGer-hakt, n., minced veal
kalfskop, kalfs-kop, c., calf's head; (fig.) block-head [head]
kalfsleer, kalfs-layr, n., calf-leather
kalfsvlees, kalfs-flayss, n., veal
kalk, kalk, c., lime; mortar
kalkgroef, kalk-HGroof, c., limestone quarry
kalkoen, kal-koon, c., turkey
kalkoven, kalk-oh-ver, c., limekiln
kalm, kalm, a. & adv., calm, quiet, cool
kalmeren, kal-may-rer, v., to calm, to appease
kalmpjes, kalmp-yess, adv., quietly. —— aan!, ——ahn, steady! easy!

kalmte, **kalm**-ter, c., calm(ness), composure
kam, kam, c., comb; crest; ridge
kameel, kah-**mayl**, c., camel
kameleon, kah-may-lay-**on**, c., chameleon
kamer, kah-mer, c., room, chamber
kameraad, kah-mer-**raht**, c., comrade, companion, mate   [maid
kamermeisje, kah-mer-mey-sher, n., chamber-
kamerplant, kah-mer-pl*a*nt, c., indoor plant
kamfer, kam-fer, c., camphor
kamgaren, kam-HGah-rer, n. & a., worsted
kamillethee, kah-mil-ler-tay, c., camomile-tea
kammen, kam-mer, v., to comb. zich ——,
—— , to comb one's hair   ziHG
kamp, kamp, n., (mil.) camp. c., fight
kampeerterrein, kam-payr-tayr-reyn, n., camp-
ing-ground
kampen, kam-per, v., to fight, to struggle
kamperen, kam-pay-rer, v., to camp out
kamperfoelie, kam-per-foo-lee, c., honeysuckle
kampioen, kam-pee-**oon**, c., champion; (fig.)
advocate   [pionship
kampioenschap, kam-pee-oon-sHG*a*p, n., cham-
kampvuur, kamp-fEEr, n., camp-fire
kan, kan, c., jug, jar, can, mug
kanaal, kah-**nahl**, n., canal; channel
kanarie, kah-nah-ree, c., canary
kandelaar, k*a*n-der-lahr, c., candlestick
kandijsuiker, kan-dey-sow-ker, c., sugar-candy
kaneel, kah-nayl, c., cinnamon
kangoeroe, kan-HGoo-roo, c., kangaroo
kanjer, k*a*n-yer, c., whopper, spanker, bouncer
kanker, k*a*n-ker, c., cancer; canker
kankeraar, k*a*n-ker-rahr, c., (pop.) grumbler
kano, kah-noh, c., canoe
kanon, kah-non, n., gun, cannon
kans, kanss, c., chance, opportunity
kanselier, k*a*n-ser-leer, c., chancellor
kant, k*a*nt, c., lace; side, border; margin
kantelen, k*a*n-ter-ler, v., to tilt; to turn over
kantoor, kan-tohr, n., office   [office-clerk
kantoorbediende, k*a*n-tohr-ber-deen-der, c.,

kantoorbehoeften, kan-tohr-ber-hoof-ter, c. pl.,
stationery [c., stationer's
kantoorboekhandel, kan-tohr-book-han-derl,
kantoorkruk, kan-tohr-krerk, c., office-stool
kap, kap, c., cap; hood; cowl; top; roof
kapel, kah-pel, c., chapel; (mus.) band
kapelaan, ka-per-lahn, c., chaplain, curate
kapelmeester, ka-pel-mays-ter, c., (mus.) bandmaster [pinch
kapen, kah-per, v., (naut.) to capture; (pop.) to
kapitaal, kah-pee-tahl, n., capital (money). a.,
substantial [c., investment
kapitaalbelegging, kah-pee-tahl-ber-leHG-ing,
kapitein, kah-pee-teyn, c., captain; skipper
kaplaars, kap-lahrss, c., top boot
kapmes, kap-mess, n., chopper, chopping-knife
kapot, kah-pot, a., broken; in holes; broken-
kappen, kap-per, v., to fell, tc chop [hearted
kapper, kap-per, c., hairdresser; feller, chopper
kapperswinkel, kap-perss-vin-kerl, c., hair-
kapseizen, kap-sey-zer, v., to capsize [dresser's
kapsel, kap-serl, n., hair-dress, head-dress
kapstok, kap-stock, c., hat-stand, coat-stand
kar, kar, c., cart
karaf, kah-raf, c., decanter; water-bottle
karakter, kah-rak-ter, n., nature, character
karakterloos, kah-rak-ter-lohss, a. & adv., un-
principled [strength of character
karaktervastheid, kah-rak-ter-vast-heyt, c.,
karavaan, kah-rah-vahn, c., caravan
karbonade, kar-boh-nah-der, c., cutlet, chop
karbouw, kar-bow, c., buffalo
kardinaal, kar-dee-nahl, c., cardinal. a., cardinal
karig, kah-rerHG, a. & adv., scanty, meagre, frugal
karmozijn, kar-moh-zeyn, n., crimson
karnemelk, kar-ner-melk, c., buttermilk
karpet, kar-pet, c., carpet
karretje, kar-rert-yer, n., small cart
karton, kar-ton, n., cardboard; pasteboard
kartonnen, kar-ton-ner, a., cardboard; paste-
karwei, kar-vey, c., job, piece of work [board
kas, kass, c., hothouse; cash; pay-desk; fund

kasboek, kass-book, n., cash-book   [grapes
kasdruiven, kass-drow-ver, c. pl., hothouse
kasgeld, kass-HGelt, n., cash in hand, till-money
kassier, kas-seer, c., cashier; banker
kast, kast, c., cupboard; wardrobe; cabinet; chest
kastanje, kass-ta-n'yer, c., chestnut. **wilde** ——
     vil-der ——, horse-chestnut
kastanjebruin, kass-ta-n'yer-brown, a., auburn,
kasteel, kass-tayl, n., castle   [bay, chestnut
kastelein, kah-ster-leyn, c., innkeeper, publican
kastijden, kass-tey-der, v., to chastise
kat, kat, c., cat, tabby-cat
kater, kah-ter, c., tom, tom-cat
kathedraal, kah-tay-drahl, c., cathedral
Katholiek, kah-toh-leek, a. & c., Roman Catholic
katoen, kah-toon, n., cotton   [mill
katoenfabriek, kah-toon-fah-breek, c., cotton-
katoentje, kah-toont-yer, n., print dress
katrol, kah-trol, c., pulley
kattekwaad, kat-ter-k'vaht, n., mischief
katterig, kat-ter-rerHG, a., chippy
kattig, kat-terHG, a., cattish
kauw, kow, c., jackdaw   [munch
kauwen, kow-er, v., to chew, to masticate, to
kauwgom, kow-HGom, c., chewing gum
kaviaar, kah-vee-ahr, c., caviar, caviare
kazemat, kah-zer-mat, c., casemate
kazerne, kah-zayr-ner, c., barracks
keel, kayl, c., throat, gullet
keelpijn, kayl-peyn, c., pain in the throat
keer, kayr, c., turn, change; time. **twee** ——, tvay
keerkring, kayr-kring, c., tropic   [——, twice
keerpunt, kayr-pernt, n., turning-point, crisis
keerzijde, kayr-zey-der, c., reverse; (fig.) dark
keet, kayt, c., shed, shanty; salt-works   [side
keffen, kef-fer, v., to yelp, to yap; (fig.) to squabble
kegel, kay-HGerl, c., cone; skittle, ninepin; icicle
kei, key, c., boulder; paving-stone; (fig.) dab
keizer, key-zer, c., emperor; pass-key, master-key
keizerlijk, key-zer-luck, a. & adv., imperial
keizerrijk, key-zer-reyk, n., empire
kelder, kel-der, c., cellar

kelderverdieping, kel-der-fer-dee-ping, c., basement [ment

kelk, kelk, c., cup, chalice

kellner, kell-ner, c., waiter; (naut.) steward

kemphaan, kemp-hahn, c., fighting-cock

kenbaar, ken-bahr, a., recognizable

kenmerk, ken-mayrk, n., characteristic

kenmerken, ken-mayr-ker, v., to characterize

kennelijk, ken-ner-luck, a. & adv., obvious,
apparent [with

kennen, ken-ner, v., to know, to be acquainted

kenner (van), ken-ner (fan), c., connoisseur (of)

kennis, ken-niss, c., knowledge; acquaintance

kennisgeving, ken-niss-HGay-ving, c., announcement [ment

kenteken, ken-tay-ker, n., badge, token

keren, kay-rer, v., to turn; to stop; to sweep

kerk, kayrk, c., church; chapel [register

kerkboek, kayrk-book, n., prayer-book; church

kerkdienst, kayrk-deenst, c., divine service

kerker, kayr-ker, c., jail; dungeon

kerkhof, kayrk-hof, n., churchyard, cemetery

kerkklok, kayrk-klock, c., church-bell; church-
clock

kerktoren, kayrk-toh-rer, c., church-steeple

kermen, kayr-mer, v., to groan, to moan, to whine

kermis, kayr-miss, c., fun fair

kern, kayrn, c., kernel, stone; nucleus

kernachtig, kayrn-αHG-terHG, a. & adv., terse

kernspreuk, kayrn-sprerk, c., aphorism

kerrie, kayr-ree, c., curry

kers, kayrss, c., cherry; cress

kerseboom, kayr-ser-bohm, c., cherry-tree

Kerstavond, kayrst-ah-vont, c., Christmas Eve;
Christmas Evening

Kerstboom, kayrst-bohm, c., Christmas-tree

Kerstdag, kayrst-dαHG, c., Christmas Day.
tweede ——, tvay-der ——, Boxing-day

Kerstfeest, kayrst-fayst, n., Christmas (feast)

Kerstgeschenk, kayrst-HGer-sHGenk, n., Christ-
mas-present

Kerstmis, kayrst-miss, c., Christmas

Kerstvacantie, kayrst-fah-kαn-see, c., Christ-
mas-holidays

kersvers, kayrss-fayrs, a., quite new

ketel, kay-terl, c., kettle, copper; (mech.) boiler

keten, kay-ter, c., chain; (fig.) bond, fetter

ketteren, ket-ter-rer, v., to rage, to swear, to

ketting, ket-ting, c., chain; warp   [storm

keu, ker, c., billiard-cue

keuken, ker-ker, c., kitchen; cooking   [range

keukenfornuis, ker-ker-for-nowss, n., kitchen-

keukengerei, ker-ker-HGer-rey, n., kitchen-uten-

keukenmeid, ker-ker-meyt, c., cook   [sils

keur, kerr, c., selection, choice, pick

keuren, ker-rer, v., to examine; to taste; to inspect

keurig, ker-rerHG, a. & adv., exquisite, choice

keuring, ker-ring, c., examination, inspection

keurtroepen, kerr-troo-per, c. pl., picked troops

keus, kerss, c., choice, selection

keuterboer, ker-ter-boor, c., small farmer

keuvelen, ker-ver-ler, v., to chat; to prattle

kever, kay-ver, c., beetle

kibbelen, kib-ber-ler, v., to squabble

kieken, kee-ker, n., chicken. v., to take a snapshot

kiel, keel, c., blouse; (naut.) keel

kiem, keem, c., germ; (fig.) seed, bud

kier, keer, c., narrow opening, chink. **op een** ——,
    op ayn ——, ajar   [considerate

kies, keess, c., (back) tooth. a. & adv., delicate,

kieskeurig, kees-ker-rerHG, a., dainty, particular,

kiespijn, keess-peyn, c., toothache   [nice

kiesrecht, keess-reHGt, n., franchise, suffrage

kietelen, kee-ter-ler, v., to tickle

kiezel, kee-zerl, n., gravel, shingle

kiezer, kee-zer, c., voter, elector

kijken, key-ker, v., to look, to peep

kijker, key-ker, c., spectator; opera-glass

kijkgat, keyk-HGat, n., loop-hole, spy-hole

kijven, key-ver, v., to quarrel, to wrangle

kikker, kikvors, kick-ker, **kick**-fors, c., frog

kil, kill, c., channel. a., chilly

kim, kim, c., horizon

kin, kin, c., chin

kind, kint, n., child, baby, infant   [childish

kinderachtig, kin-der-aHG-terHG, a. & adv.,

kindergek, kin-der-HGek, c., lover of children
kinderjaren, kin-der-yah-rer, n. pl., infancy
kinderliefde, kin-der-leef-der, c., love of children
kinderlijk, kin-der-luck, a., childlike
kinderloos, kin-der-lohss, a., childless
kindermeid, kin-der-meyt, c., nursemaid
kinderwagen, kin-der-vah-HGer, c., pram
kindje, kind-yer, n., baby, little child
kinds, kints, a., doting
kindsheid, kints-heyt, c., childhood, infancy; [dotage
kinkel, kin-kerl, c., boor, lout
kiosk, kee-osk, c., kiosk; band-stand
kip, kip, c., chicken, hen, fowl
kippenhok, kip-per-hock, n., poultry-house
kippensoep, kip-per-soop, c., chicken-broth
kippenvel, kip-per-fel, n., hen-skin; (fig.) goose-[flesh
kist, kist, c., chest, box; coffin
kittelen, kit-ter-ler, v., to tickle
kittelorig, kit-ter-loh-rerHG, a., touchy
klaar, klahr, a. & adv., ready; finished; evident
klaarblijkelijk, klahr-bley-ker-luck, a. & adv.,
    obvious
klaarmaken, klahr-mah-ker, v., to prepare
klacht, klæHGt, c., complaint; accusation
klad, klat, c., stain, blot. n., rough copy
kladschrift, klat-srift, n., rough-copy book
klagen, klah-HGer, v., to complain; to lament
klam, klam, a., damp, moist
klandizie, klan-dee-zee, c., clientele, customers
klank, klank, c., sound, ring
klant, klant, c., customer, client
klap, klap, c., slap, smack, blow
klaploper, klap-loh-per, c., parasite, sponger
klappen, klap-per, v., to smack, to clap; to tell
    tales   [tattler] rattle; index; register
klapper, klap-per, c., coconut; squib, cracker;
klapperen, klap-per-rer, v., to rattle, to chatter,
klaproos, klap-rohss, c., corn-poppy   [to flap
klapstoel, klap-stool, c., folding chair
klarinet, klah-ree-net, c., clari(o)net
klasgenoot, klass-HGer-noht, c., class-mate
klasse, klas-ser, c., class; form; class-room

klassiek, klas-seek, a. & adv., classic, classical
klateren, klah-ter-rer, v., to splash; to rattle
klauteren, klow-ter-rer, v., to climb
klauw, klow, c., claw; talon
klaver, klah-ver, c., clover, shamrock, trefoil
klavier, klah-veer, n., keyboard; piano; (fig.) paw
kleden, klay-der, v., to dress, to clothe
klederdracht, klay-der-draHGt, c., dress, costume
kleed, klayt, n., garment; carpet; table-cover
kleedje, klayt-yer, n., rug; table-centre; frock
kleerborstel, klayr-bor-sterl, c., clothes-brush
kleerhanger, klayr-hang-er, c., coat-hanger
kleerkast, klayr-kast, c., wardrobe; clothes-press
kleermaker, klayr-mah-ker, c., tailor
klei, kley, c., clay
klein, kleyn, a., little; short; undersized. **in het
——,** in het ——, in a small way
kleindochter, kleyn-doHG-ter, c., grand-daughter
kleineren, kley-nay-rer, v., to belittle   [minded
kleingeestig, kleyn-HGay-sterHG, a., narrow-
kleingeld, kleyn-HGelt, n., small change
kleinhandelaar, kleyn-han-der-lahr, c., retailer
kleinigheid, kley-nerHG-heyt, c., trifle
kleinkind, kleyn-kint, n., grandchild
kleinood, kley-noht, n., trinket, jewel
kleintje, kleynt-yer, n., baby   [pain; touchy
kleinzerig, kleyn-zay-rerHG, a., frightened of
kleinzielig, kleyn-zee-lerHG, a., petty-minded
kleinzoon, kleyn-zohn, c., grandson
klem, klem,'c., emphasis; catch, trap [pinch; to jam
klemmen, klem-mer, v., to clench; to tighten; to
klemtoon, klem-tohn, c., emphasis, accent
klep, klep, c., valve; flap; peak (of a cap)
klepel, klay-perl, c., clapper, tongue (of bell)
kleppen, klep-per, v., to clap; to toll
klerk, klayrk, c., clerk
kletsen, klet-ser, v., to splash; to talk nonsense
kletser, kletskous, klet-ser, kletss-kowss, c.,
    chatterbox
kletsnat, kletss-nat, a., soaking wet   [clatter
kletteren, klet-ter-rer, v., to clang, to clash; to
kleur, klerr, c., colour; complexion; suit (at cards)

kleuren, kler-rer, v., to colour; to blush, to flush
kleurenblind, kler-rer-blint, a., colour-blind
kleurkrijt, klerr-kreyt, n., coloured chalk
kleurling, klerr-ling, c., coloured person
kleurloos, klerr-lohss, a., colourless; (fig.) drab
kleuter, kler-ter, c., toddler, kid(dy)
kleuterschool, kler-ter-sHGohl, c., infant school
kleven, klay-ver, v., to cleave, to cling, to stick
kleverig, klay-ver-rerHG, a., sticky, viscous,
klier, kleer, c., gland; (fig.) a pig   [gummy
klikken, klick-ker, v., to tell tales, to sneak
klikspaan, klick-spahn, c., telltale
klimaat, klee-maht, n., climate
klimmen, klim-mer, v., to climb, to mount
klimop, klim-op, n., ivy
klingelen, kling-er-ler, v., to tinkle
klink, klink, c., latch (of a door)
klinken, klin-ker, v., to sound; to clink glasses
klinkend, klin-kernt, a., sounding
klinker, klin-ker, c., vowel; brick
klip, klip, c., crag, rock
klipgeit, klip-HGeyt, c., chamois
klodder, klod-der, c., clot
kloek, klook, c., mother hen. a. & adv., brave, bold
klok, klock, c., bell; clock; bell-jar. interj., cluck!
klokhen, klock-hen, c., mother hen, clucking hen
klokkengieter, klock-ker-HGee-ter, c., bell-
founder   [bells]
klokkenspel, klock-ker-spel, n., chimes, peal (of
klokketoren, klock-ker-toh-rer, c., bell-tower
klomp, klomp, c., clog; lump; nugget (of gold)
klontje, klont-yer, n., lump (sugar); clod (earth)
klonter, klon-ter, c., clot (blood); lump (in
porridge)
kloof, klohf, c., cleft, rift; chap (on the skin)
klooster, klohss-ter, n., cloister; monastery;
convent
kloosterzuster, klohss-ter-zerss-ter, c., nun
kloppartij, klop-par-tey, c., scuffle, scrap
kloppen, klop-per, v., to knock; to tap; to beat.
—— **met,** —— met, to agree with
klopping, klop-ping, c., beating, throbbing

klos, kloss, c., bobbin, reel, spool

kloven, kloh-ver, v., to split, to chop

klucht, klerHGt, c., farce

kluchtig, klerHG-terHG, a. & adv., farcical

kluif, klowf, c., knuckle of pork; bone (to pick)

kluis, klowss, c., strong-room, safe-deposit; cell

kluitje, klowt-yer, n., lump, clod

kluiven, klow-ver, v., to gnaw, to nibble

kluizenaar, klow-zer-nahr, c., hermit

klungelen, klerng-er-ler, v., to bungle; to tinker

knaagdier, k'nahHG-deer, n., rodent

knaap, k'nahp, c., lad, youth, youngster

knabbelen, k'nab-ber-ler, v., to nibble, to gnaw

knagen, k'nah-HGer, v., to gnaw [to peck

knakken, k'nak-ker, v., to crack; to snap; to in-

knakworst, k'nak-vorst, c., small sausage [jure

knal, k'nal, c., explosion, bang

knallen, k'nal-ler, v., to crack, to bang

knap, k'nap, a. & adv., handsome; clever, smart

knapheid, k'nap-heyt, c., good looks; skill

knarsen, k'nar-ser, v., to creak, to grate; to grind

knarsetanden, k'nar-ser-tan-der, v., to gnash

knecht, k'neHGt, c., man-servant [one's teeth

kneden, k'nay-der, v., to knead; (fig.) to fashion

kneep, k'nayp, c., pinch; dodge [to oppress

knellen, k'nel-ler, v., to pinch, to squeeze; (fig.)

knetteren, k'net-ter-rer, v., to crackle, to sputter

kneuzen, k'ner-zer, v., to bruise

knevel, k'nay-verl, c., moustache; whiskers

knevelarij, k'nay-ver-lah-rey, c., extortion

knevelen, k'nay-ver-ler, v., to gag; to pinion; to

knie, k'nee, c., knee [extort

knielen, k'nee-ler, v., to kneel

kniesoor, k'nees-ohr, c., mope

kniezen, k'nee-zer, v., to mope, to fret; to sulk

knijpen, k'ney-per, v., to pinch, to nip; (fig.) to

knijptang, k'neyp-tang, c., pincers [squeeze

knik, k'nick, c., nod; crack

knikkebollen, k'nick-ker-bol-ler, v., to doze

knikken, k'nick-ker, v., to nod

knikker, k'nick-ker, c., marble

knikkeren, k'nick-ker-rer, v., to play at marbles

knip, k'nip, c., catch; snap; cut, clip; fillip

knipogen, k'nip-oh-HGer, v., to wink [punch

knippen, k'nip-per, v., to cut; to trim; to clip; to

knobbel, k'nob-berl, c., knob; bump; knot

knoei, k'noo-ee, c., mess, muddle

knoeien, k'noo-yer, v., to make a mess; to bungle

knoeier, k'noo-yer, c., bungler, muddler, dabbler

knoest, k'noost, c., knot, gnarl

knoflook, k'nof-lohk, n., garlic

knokkel, k'nock-kerl, c., knuckle

knol, k'nol, c., tuber; turnip; jade (horse)

knoop, k'nohp, c., button; stud; knot

knoopsgat, k'nohps-HGat, n., button-hole

knop, k'nop, c., knob; handle; peg; pommel; button; bud

knopen, k'noh-per, v., to tie, to knot, to button

knorren, k'nor-rer, v., to grunt, to growl

knorrig, k'nor-rerHG, a., peevish, growling, grum-knots, k'nots, c., cudgel, club, bludgeon [bling

knuffelen, k'nerf-fer-ler, v., to cuddle, to hug

knul, k'nerl, c., (pop.) booby, lout, fellow

knuppel, k'nerp-perl, c., cudgel, club; (fig.) lout

knus, k'nerss, a. & adv., snug

knutselen, k'nert-ser-ler, v., to potter

koddig, kod-derHG, a. & adv., droll, comical

koe, koo, c., cow

koek, kook, c., gingerbread; cake [pastry-cook

koekbakker, kook-bak-ker, c., confectioner

koekepan, koo-ker-pan, c., frying-pan

koekje, kook-yer, n., small cake; (sweet) biscuit

koekoek, koo-kook, c., cuckoo; skylight

koel, kool, a. & adv., cool; (fig.) cool, cold

koelbloedig, kool-bloo-derHG, a. & adv., cold-koelen, koo-ler, v., to cool (down) [blooded

koelkast, kool-kast, c., refrigerator

koelte, kool-ter, c., coolness

koen, koon, a. & adv., daring; hardy

koepel, koo-perl, c., dome; summer-house

koerier, koo-reer, c., courier [course

koers, koorss, c., direction; rate, price; (fig.)

koestal, koo-stal, c., cow-shed [tain; to nurse

koesteren, kooss-ter-rer, v., to cherish; to enter-

koeterwaals, koo-ter-vahlss, n., gibberish

koets, kootss, c., coach, carriage

koetsier, koot-seer, c., driver, coachman, cabman

koevoet, koo-foot, c., crowbar [case

koffer, kof-fer, c., trunk; box; (hand-)bag, (suit-)

koffie, kof-fee, c., coffee; lunch [to lunch

koffiedrinken, kof-fee-drin-ker, v., to take coffee;

koffiekamer, kof-fee-kah-mer, c., refreshment-

koffiekan, kof-fee-kan, c., coffee-pot [room

kogel, koh-HGerl, c., bullet (of a rifle)

kogelvrij, koh-HGerl-frey, a., bullet-proof

kok, kock, c., cook. eerste ——, ayr-ster ——

koken, koh-ker, v., to cook; to boil [chef

koker, koh-ker, c., boiler, cooker; sheath, case,

kokosnoot, koh-koss-noht, c., coconut [socket

kolen, koh-ler, c. pl., coal(s) [merchant

kolenhandelaar, koh-ler-han-der-lahr, c., coal-

kolenkit, koh-ler-kit, c., coal-scuttle

kolenmijn, koh-ler-meyn, c., coal-mine, coal-pit

kolf, kolf, c., butt-end (of a rifle); bat; club

kolom, koh-lom, c., column

kolonel, koh-loh-nel, c., colonel

kolonie, koh-loh-nee, c., colony, settlement

kom, kom, c., basin, bowl

komedie, koh-may-dee, c., comedy, play; theatre

komen, koh-mer, v., to come. laten ——, lah-

ter ——, to send for

komiek, koh-meek, c., (low) comedian. a. & adv.,

comical, funny

komkommer, kom-kom-mer, c., cucumber

kommerlijk, kom-mer-luck, a., needy, indigent,

pitiful [ful

kommervol, kom-mer-fol, a., wretched, distress-

kommetje, kom-mert-yer, n., small cup, bowl

kommies, kom-meess, c., custom-house officer

kompas, kom-pass, n., compass

komplot, kom-plot, n., conspiracy, plot

komplotteren, kom-plot-tay-rer, v., to plot, to

conspire [op —— zeyn, to be coming

komst, komst, c., arrival, coming. op —— zijn,

konijn, koh-neyn, n., rabbit, bunny

konijnevel, koh-ney-ner-fel, n., rabbit-skin; cony

koning, koh-ning, c., king
koningin, koh-ning-in, c., queen
koningsgezind, kog-nings-HGer-zint, a., royalist
koninklijk, koh-nink-luck, a. & adv., royal, regal
koninkrijk, koh-nink-reyk, n., kingdom [ing
konkelarij, kon-ker-lah-rey, c., plotting, schem-
konkelen, kon-ker-ler, v., to plot, to scheme
konvooi, kon-voh-ee, n., convoy
kooi, koh-ee, c., berth, bunk; cage; fold
kookboek, kohk-book, n., cookery book
kookkunst, kohk-kernst, c., art of cooking
kookpunt, kohk-pernt, n., boiling-point
kool, kohl, c., cabbage; coal; charcoal
koolraap, kohl-rahp, c., swede
koolteer, kohl-tayr, c., coal-tar [sale
koop, kohp, c., purchase. te ——, ter ——, for
koopje, kohp-yer, n., bargain
koopman, kohp-man, c., dealer, merchant
koopprijs, kohp-preyss, c., purchase-price
koopvaardij, kohp-fahr-dey, c., merchant service
koopvaardijvloot, kohp-fahr-dey-floht, c., mercantile marine
koopwaar, kohp-vahr, c., merchandise
koor, kohr, n., choir; chorus; chancel
koord, kohrt, n., string, cord, rope
koorddanser, kohrt-dan-ser, c., rope-dancer
koordirigent, kohr-dee-ree-HGent, c., choir-
koorts, kohrts, c., fever [master
koortsachtig, kohrts-aHG-terHG, a. & adv., fever-
  ish; (fig.) hectic
koortsigheid, kohrt-serHG-heyt, c., feverishness
koorzanger, kohr-zang-er, c., chorister
kop, kop, c., head; headline; cup; litre
kopen, koh-per, v., to buy
koper, koh-per, c., buyer. n., copper; brass
koperdraad, koh-per-draht, n., brass-wire
kopererts, koh-per-ayrts, n., copper-ore
kopijrecht, koh-pey-reHGt, n., copyright
kopje, kop-yer, n., cup; head
koplamp, kop-lamp, c., head-light
koppel, kop-perl, c., leash; belt. n., couple; brace
koppelen, kop-per-ler, v., to couple; to join

koppeling, kop-per-ling, c., coupling; clutch
koppig, kop-perHG, a. & adv., obstinate; heady
koppigheid, kop-perHG-heyt, c., obstinacy
koptelefoon, kop-tay-ler-fohn, c., earphone
koraalvisser, koh-rahl-fis-ser, c., coral-diver
kordaat, kor-daht, a. & adv., bold, plucky
koren, koh-rer, n., corn, grain
korenaar, koh-rern-ahr, c., ear of corn
korenbloem, koh-rer-bloom, c., cornflower
korenschoof, koh-rer-sHGohf, c., sheaf of corn
korenschuur, koh-rer-sHGEEr, c., granary
korf, korf, c., basket, hamper; hive
korfbal, korf-bal, n., basket-ball
kornet, kor-net, c., cornet
kornuit, kor-nowt, c., comrade, companion
korporaal, kor-poh-rahl, c., corporal
korrel, kor-rerl, c., grain; pellet (of shot)
korrelig, kor-rer-lerHG, a., granular
korreltje, kor-rerlt-yer, n., grain, granule
korset, kor-set, n., corset
korst, korst, c., crust; rind; scab (on wound)
korstachtig, korst-aHG-terHG, a., crusty
kort, kort, a. & adv., short
kortademig, kort-ah-der-merHG, a., asthmatic
kortaf, kort-af, a. & adv., abrupt
korten, kor-ter, v., to shorten; to crop; to deduct
kortheid, kort-heyt, c., shortness, briefness
korting, kor-ting, c., deduction; rebate, discount
kortom, kor-tom, adv., in short
kortsluiting, kort-slow-ting, c., short-circuit
kortstondig, kort-ston-derHG, a., of short dura-
kortweg, kort-veHG, adv., in short, shortly [tion
kortwieken, kort-vee-ker, v., to clip the wings of
kortzichtig, kort-siHG-terHG, a., short-sighted
korzelig, kor-zer-lerHG, a. & adv., crabbed, crusty
kost, kost, c., food, fare, board; living, livelihood
kostbaar, kost-bahr, a., expensive; valuable
kostbaarheden, kost-bahr-hay-der, c. pl., valu-
kostbaas, kost-bahss, c., landlord [ables
kostelijk, koss-ter-luck, a. & adv., exquisite
kosteloos, koss-ter-lohss, a. & adv., free, gratis
kosten, koss-ter, v., to cost. c. pl., expense(s)

koster, koss-ter, c., sacristan, verger, **sexton**
kostganger, kost-gang-er, c., boarder
kostgeld, kost-HGelt, n., board
kosthuis, kost-howss, n., boarding-**house**
kostprijs, kost-preyss, c., cost-price
kostschool, kost-sHGohl, c., boarding-school
kostwinner, kost-vin-ner, c., wage-earner
kostwinning, kost-vin-ning, c., livelihood
kot, kot, n., cot; pen; sty; kennel; (pop.) quod
koud, kowt, a. & adv., cold; frigid
koudbloedig, kowt-bloo-derHG, a., cold-blooded
koude, kow-der, c., cold. **een —— vatten,** ayn
—— fat-ter, to catch a cold
kous, kowss, c., stocking
kouseband, kow-ser-bant, c., garter
kousje, kow-sher, n., wick; (incandescent) mantle
kouten, kow-ter, v., to talk, to chat [chilly]
kouwelijk, kow-er-luck, a., sensitive to cold,
kozijn, koh-zeyn, n., window-frame
kraag, krahHG, c., collar; tippet
kraai, krah-ee, c., crow
kraaien, krah-yer, v., to crow
kraakstem, krahk-stem, c., grating voice
kraal, krahl, c., bead
kraam, krahm, c., booth, stand, stall
kraambed, krahm-bet, n., childbed
kraaminrichting, krahm-in-riHG-ting, c., ma-
ternity home
kraan, krahn, c., derrick; cock, tap; (pop.) dab
kraanvogel, krahn-foh-HGerl, c., crane (bird)
krab, krap, c., crab; scratch
krabbelen, krab-ber-ler, v., to scratch; to scribble
krabben, krab-ber, v., to scratch; to scrape
kracht, kraHGt, c., strength, vigour, power
krachtdadig, kraHGt-dah-derHG, a. & adv.,
strong, energetic [invalid]
krachteloos, kraHG-ter-lohss, a., powerless;
krachtens, kraHG-terns, prep., in virtue of
krachtig, kraHG-terHG, a. & adv., strong, energetic
krachtsinspanning, kraHGts-in-span-ning, c.,
effort [station]
krachtstation, kraHG-stah-see'on, n., power-

krachtverspilling, krаHGt-fer-spil-ling, c., waste of energy

krakelen, krah-kay-ler, v., to quarrel

krakeling, krah-ker-ling, c., cracknel

kraken, krah-ker, v., to crack; to creak; to crunch

kralensnoer, krah-ler-snoor, n., bead necklace

kramp, krаmp, c., cramp; spasm

krampachtig, kram-pаHG-terHG, a. & adv., spasmodic

kranig, krah-nerHG, a. & adv., brave, bold

krankzinnig, krаnk-sin-nerHG, a., insane, crazy

krankzinnige, krаnk-sin-ner-HGer, c., lunatic

krankzinnigengesticht, krаnk-sin-ner-HGern-HGer-stiHGt, n., lunatic asylum

krans, krаns, c., garland, wreath

krant, krаnt, c., (news)paper

krantenhanger, krаn-ter-hang-er, c., newspaper-rack

krantenjongen, krаn-ter-yong-er, c., newsboy

krantenpapier, krаn-ter-pah-peer, n., newsprint

krantenverkoper, krаn-ter-fer-koh-per, c., newsvendor

krap, krаp, a. & adv., narrow, tight

kras, krаss, c., scratch. a. & adv., strong; drastic

krassen, krаs-ser, v., to scratch; to grate; to croak

krater, krah-ter, c., crater [screech, to

kreeft, krayft, c., lobster; crayfish

kreet, krayt, c., shriek, scream

kregelig, kray-HGer-lerHG, a. & adv., peevish

krekel, kray-kerl, c., cricket

kreng, kreng, n., carrion; (fig.) blighter

krenken, kren-ker, v., to offend; to injure

krenkend, kren-kernt, a. & adv., injurious, insulting

krent, krеnt, c., (dried) currant

krentenbroodje, kren-ter-broht-yer, n., currant-bun

krenterig, kren-ter-rerHG, a. & adv., stingy

kreuk, krerk, c., crease, wrinkle

kreukelen, krer-ker-ler, v., to crease, to wrinkle

kreunen, krer-ner, v., to groan, to moan

kreupel, krer-perl, a., lame

kreupelhout, krer-perl-howt, n., thicket, underwood

kribbe, krib-ber, c., manger; cot; jetty

kribbig, krib-berHG, a. & adv., peevish; fretful

kriebelen, kree-ber-ler, v., to tickle; to itch

kriebelig, kree-ber-lerHG, a., ticklish; itching

kriek, kreek, c., black cherry

krielhaantje, kreel-hahnt-yer, n., bantam cock

krijgen, krey-HGer, v., to get; to receive; to catch

krijgsdienst, kreyHGs-deenst, c., military service

krijgsgevangene, kreyHGs-HGer-fang-er-ner, c., prisoner of war   [sHGap, c., captivity

krijgsgevangenschap, kreyHGs-HGer-fang-er-

krijgshaftig, kreyHGs-haf-terHG, a., martial

krijgslist, kreyHGs-list, c., stratagem

krijgsmacht, kreyHGs-maHGt, c., military forces

krijgsman, kreyHGs-man, c., warrior

krijgstucht, kreyHGs-terHGt, c., military discipline

krijsen, krey-ser, v., to shriek, to scream   [line

krijt, kreyt, n., chalk; crayon

krimpen, krim-per, v., to shrink; to shiver

kring, kring, c., circle, ring; district   [cycle

kringloop, kring-lohp, c., circular course; (fig.)

krioelen, kree-oo-ler, v., to swarm; to teem. —— **van,** —— fan, to bristle with

kristal, kriss-tal, n., crystal

kristallen, kriss-tal-ler, a., crystalline

kritiek, kree-teek, c., criticism. a., critical

kroeg, krooHG, c., public house

kroes, kroos, c., mug; cup; crucible. a., frizzled

krokodil, kroh-koh-dil, c., crocodile

krom, krom, a., crooked, bent; curved

krommen, krom-mer, v., to curve, to bow

kromming, krom-ming, c., bend, curve, winding

kronen, kroh-ner, v., to crown

kroniek, kroh-neek, c., chronicle

kroning, kroh-ning, c., coronation, crowning

kroningsplechtigheid, kroh-nings-pleHG-terHG-heyt, c., coronation-ceremony

kronkel, kron-kerl, c., twist, coil

kronkelen, kron-ker-ler, v., to wind, to twist

kronkelig, kron-ker-lerHG, a., winding, meandering

kroon, krohn, c., crown; top; chandelier   [ing

kroonjuwelen, krohn-yee-vay-ler, n. pl., crown-jewels

kroonprins, krohn-prinss, c., prince royal

kroost, krohst, n., issue, offspring

kroot, kroht, c., beetroot

krop, krop, c., crop, gizzard; head (of cabbage)

kropgezwel, krop-HGer**-zvel,** n., goitre
kropsla, krop-slah**,** c., cabbage-lettuce
krot, krot, n., hovel; den; kennel
krotwoning, krot-voh-ning, c., slum dwelling
kruid, krowt, n., herb; medicinal herb
kruiden, krow-der, v., to season, to spice
kruidenier, krow-der-neer, c., grocer
kruidenierswaren, krow-der-neers-vah-rer, c.
  pl. groceries   [grocer's
kruidenierswinkel, krow-der-neers-vin-kerl, c.,
kruidnagel, krowt-nah-HGerl**,** c., clove
kruien, krow-er, v., to push a wheelbarrow; to
kruier, krow-er, c., porter   [drift (ice)
kruik, krowk, c., pitcher, jar. **warme ——, vahr-**
  mer **——,** hot-water bottle
kruimel, krow-merl, c., crumb
kruimelen, krow-mer-ler, v., to crumble
kruin, krown, c., crown, top
kruipen, krow-per, v., to creep
kruis, krowss, n., cross; (fig.) trial, affliction
kruisbeeld, krowss-baylt, n., crucifix
kruisbes, krowss-bess, c., gooseberry
kruisen, krow-ser, v., to cross (arms; animals;
kruiser, krow-ser, c., cruiser   [plants]
kruisigen, krow-ser-HGer**,** v., to crucify
kruisiging, krow-ser-HGing**,** c., crucifixion
kruising, krow-sing, c., cross-breeding; crossing
  (of roads)   [ing
kruispunt, krowss-pernt, n., intersection; cross-
kruisverhoor, krowss-fer-hohr, n., cross-
  examination   [the Cross
kruisweg, krowss-veHG**,** c., cross-road; Way of
kruiswoordraadsel, krowss-vohrt-raht-serl, n.,
  cross-word puzzle
kruit, krowt, n., (gun)powder
kruiwagen, krow-vah-HGer**,** c., wheelbarrow;
  (fig.) influence   [stool
kruk, krerk, c., handle (of door); crutch; perch;
krul, krerl, c., curl; shaving; scroll
krulhaar, krerl-hahr, n., curly hair
krullen, krerl-ler, v., to curl, to frizz
krultang, krerl-tang, c., curling-irons

kublek, KEE-**beek,** a., cubic. n., cube

kuchen, ker-HGer, v., to cough

kudde, kerd-der, c., herd, flock

kuieren, kow-er-rer, v., to stroll, to saunter

kuif, kowf, c., tuft, crest; forelock

kuiken, kow-ker, n., chicken; (fig.) simpleton, dolt

kuil, kowl, c., pit, hole; (naut.) waist

kuiltje, kowlt-yer, n., hole; dimple

kuip, kowp, c., tub, barrel, vat

kuiperij, kow-per-rey, c., coopery; (fig.) intrigue

kuis, kowss, a. & adv., chaste, pure

kuisheid, kowss-heyt, c., chastity, purity

kuit, kowt, c., calf (of the leg); spawn, roe

kundig, kern-derHG, a., clever, able, capable

kunnen, kern-ner, v., to be able to

kunst, kernst, c., art; trick, knack, feat

kunstbeen, kernst-bayn, n., artificial leg

kunstenaar, kernss-ter-nahr, c., artist

kunstenmaker, kernss-ter-mah-ker, c., acrobat

kunstgebit, kernst-HGer-bit, n., denture

kunstgeschiedenis, kernst-HGer-sHGee-der-niss, c., history of art

kunstgevoel, kernst-HGer-fool, n., artistic feeling

kunstgreep, kernst-HGrayp, c., trick, knack

kunsthandel, kernst-han-derl, c., picture-shop

kunstig, kernss-terHG, a. & adv., ingenious, clever

kunstje, kernsst-yer, n., trick, dodge

kunstleer, kernst-layr, n., imitation leather

kunstlicht, kernst-liHGt, n., artificial light [ficial

kunstmatig, kernst-**mah**-terHG, a. & adv., arti-

kunstnijverheid, kernst-ney-ver-heyt, c., arts and crafts

kunstrijder, kernst-rey-der, c., circus-rider

kunstschilder, kernst-sHGil-der, c., painter, artist [feat

kunststuk, kernst-sterk, n., masterpiece; (clever)

kunstverzameling, kernst-fer-zah-mer-ling, c., art-collection

kunstwerk, kernst-vayrk, n., work of art

kunstzijde, kernst-sey-der, c., artificial silk, **rayon**

kurk, kerrk, c., cork

kurkdroog, kerrk-drohHG, a., bone-dry

kurketrekker, kerr-ker-treck-ker, c., corkscrew
kus, kerss, c., kiss
kussen, kers-ser, v., to kiss. n., cushion; pillow
kussensloop, kers-ser-slohp, c., pillow-case
kust, kerst, c., shore, coast
kustwacht, kerst-*va*Hgt, c., coast-guard (service)
kuur, kEEr, c., whim, caprice; cure
kwaad, kvaht, n., evil, wrong; harm. a., bad, evil;
    angry; malignant   [malignant
kwaadaardig, kvah-dahr-derHG, a., malicious;
kwaadheid, kvaht-heyt, c., anger
kwaadspreken, kvaht-spray-ker, v., to talk
    scandal. —— **van**, —— fan, to slander
kwaadspreker, kvaht-spray-ker, c., slanderer
kwaadsprekerij, kvaht-spray-ker-rey, c., back-
kwaal, kvahl, c., disease, complaint   [biting, slander
kwadraat, kvah-draht, n., square. a., square
kwajongen, kvah-yong-er, c., naughty boy, urchin
kwajongensstreek, kvah-yong-erns-strayk, c.,
    practical joke
kwaken, kvah-ker, v., croak; quack
kwakkel, kv*a*k-kerl, c., quail   [(down)
kwakken, kv*a*k-ker, v., to dash, to dump, to flop
kwakzalver, kv*a*k-s*a*l-ver, c., quack; (fig.) char-
kwal, kv*a*l, c., jelly-fish   [latan
kwalijk, kvah-luck, adv., amiss; scarcely
kwaliteit, kvah-lee-teyt, c., quality, character;
kwantiteit, kv*a*n-tee-teyt, c., quantity   [grade
kwart, kv*a*rt, n., fourth part; (mus.) crotchet
kwartaal, kv*a*r-tahl, n., quarter of a year
kwartier, kv*a*r-teer, n., quarter (hour, etc.)
kwast, kv*a*st, c., brush; tassel; lemon-squash
kweekschool, kvayk-sHGohl, c., training college
kwekeling, kvay-ker-ling, c., pupil; pupil-teacher
kweken, kvay-ker, v., to cultivate; (fig.) to foster
kwellen, kvel-ler, v., to torment, to vex, to annoy
kwelling, kvel-ling, c., vexation, torment
kwestie, kvess-tee, c., question, matter; quarrel
kwetsbaar, kvetss-bahr, a., vulnerable
kwetsen, kvet-ser, v., to injure, to hurt, to wound
kwetsuur, kvet-sEEr, c., injury, wound
kwetteren, kvet-ter-rer, v., te twitter, to chirp

kwezel, kvay-zerl, c., bigot, pietist
kwezelachtig, kvay-zer-laHG-terHG, a., bigoted
kwiek, kveek, a., (pop.) spry, bright, nimble
kwijlen, kvey-ler, v., to drivel, to slaver
kwijnen, kvey-ner, v., to languish, to pine (away); to wither [forgive
kwijtschelden, kveyt-sHGel-der, v., to remit, to
kwik, kvick, n., quicksilver, mercury
kwikstaart, kvick-stahrt, c., wagtail
kwinkslag, kvink-slaHG, c., witticism, joke
kwispelstaarten, kviss-perl-stahr-ter, v., to wag the tail
kwistig, kviss-terHG, a. & adv., lavish, liberal
kwistigheid, kviss-terHG-heyt, c., lavishness, liberality
kwitantie, kvee-tan-see, c., receipt [liberality

laag, lahHG, c., layer, bed; coat (of paint). a., low; (fig.) base, mean, vile
laaghartig, lahHG-har-terHG, a. & adv., vile, base
laagheid, lahHG-heyt, c., baseness, meanness
laagvlakte, lahHG-flak-ter, c., low-lying plain
laagwater, lahHG-vah-ter, n., low tide
laakbaar, lahk-bahr, a., blamable
laan, lahn, c., avenue; alley
laars, lahrss, c., boot
laat, lahrt, a. & adv., late. **hoe —— is het?,** hoo —— iss het, what's the time? [day
laatst, lahtst, a.; last; latest. adv., lately, the other
laatstgenoemd, lahtst-HGer-noomt, a., latter
lach, laHG, c., laughter
lachbui, laHG-bow, c., fit of laughter
lachen, la-HGer, v., to laugh
laconiek, lah-koh-neek, a. & adv., laconic
ladder, lad-der, c., ladder
laden, lah-der, v., to load
lading, lah-ding, c., load; cargo
laf, laf, a., insipid; cowardly
lafaard, laf-ahrt, c., coward, poltroon
lafheid, laf-heyt, c., cowardice; insipidity
lager, lah-HGer, a., lower, inferior
Lagerhuis, lah-HGer-howss, n., House of Com-
lak, lak, n., sealing-wax; seal; lacquer [mons

laken, lah-ker, v., to blame, to find fault with. n., sheet; cloth

lakken, lak-ker, v., to lacquer, to varnish; to seal [(a letter)

laks, lakss, a., slack, indolent

lakschoenen, lakss-HGoo-ner, c.pl., patent leather [shoes

laksheid, lakss-heyt, c., laxity, slackness

lam, lam, n., lamb. a., paralysed; awkward

lambrizering, lam-bree-zay-ring, c., wainscot

lamheid, lam-heyt, c., paralysis, palsy

lamlendig, lam-len-derHG, a. & adv., miserable

lamp, lamp, c., lamp; bulb; valve (wireless)

lampekap, lam-per-kap, c., lamp-shade

lampetkom, lam-pet-kom, c., wash-hand basin

lampion, lam-pee-on, c., Chinese lantern

lamsbout, lamss-bowt, c., leg of lamb

lanceren, lan-say-rer, v., to launch; to start

land, lant, n., land; field; country; estate

landbezitter, lant-ber-zit-ter, c., landowner

landbouw, lant-bow, c., agriculture

landbouwer, lant-bow-er, c., farmer

landbouwschool, lant-bow-sHGohl, c., agri-cultural college

landelijk, lan-der-luck, a., rural; national

landen, lan-der, v., to land, to disembark

landerijen, lan-der-rey-er, c.pl., landed property

landgenoot, lant-HGer-noht, c., compatriot

landgoed, lant-HGoot, n., country-seat, estate

landhuis, lant-howss, n., country-house

landing, lan-ding, c., landing; disembarkation

landkaart, lant-kahrt, c., map

landloper, lant-loh-per, c., vagabond, tramp

landmacht, lant-maHGt, c., land-forces

landmijn, lant-meyn, c., land-mine

landschap, lant-sHGap, n., landscape

landstaal, lantss-tahl, c., mother tongue

landstreek, lant-strayk, c., district, region

landsverdediging, lantss-fer-day-der-HGing, c., national defence

landverhuizer, lant-fer-how-zer, c., emigrant

landverraad, lant-fer-raht, n., high-treason

landweg, lant-veHG, c., country-road

lang, lang, a., long, tall, high. adv., long

langdradig, lang-drah-derHG, a., tedious, long-winded [tracted

langdurig, lang-dEE-rerHG, a., prolonged, pro-

langs, langss, prep., along; by; past

langslaper, lang-slah-per, c., late riser

languit, lang-owt, adv., at full length

langwerpig, lang-vayr-perHG, a., oblong

langzaam, lang-zahm, a. & adv., slow, lingering

langzamerhand, lang-zah-mer-hant, adv., little by little

lankmoedig, lank-moo-derHG, a., patient, long-suffering [suffering

lans, lanss, c., lance

lantaarn, lan-tah-rern, c., lantern; lamp

lantaarnpaal, lan-tah-rern-pahl, c., lamp-post

lanterfanten, lan-ter-fan-ter, v., to loiter, to idle

lanterfanter, lan-ter-fan-ter, c., loiterer, idler, loafer [slice (of meat); slap

lap, lap, c., piece (of cloth); rag; patch; remnant;

lapwerk, lap-vayrk, n., patchwork

larie, lah-ree, c., (pop.) humbug, nonsense

lassen, las-ser, v., to weld, to join

last, last, c., load, burden; trouble; command

lastdier, lass-deer, n., beast of burden

laster, lass-ter, c., slander, calumny

lasteraar, lass-ter-rahr, c., slanderer

lasteren, lass-ter-rer, v., to slander, to calumniate; to blaspheme [blasphemous

lasterlijk, lass-ter-luck, a. & adv., slanderous,

lasterpraatjes, lass-ter-praht-yerss, n. pl., slanderous talk [date

lastgeving, last-HGay-ving, c., instruction, man-

lastig, lass-terHG, a., difficult; inconvenient

lastpost, last-post, c., nuisance; bore

lat, lat, c., lath; slat (of a Venetian blind)

laten, lah-ter, v., to let, to permit. —— **vallen**, —— fal-ler, to drop

later, lah-ter, a., later. adv., later, afterwards

latwerk, lat-vayrk, n., lath-work; trellis

laurier, low-reer, c., laurel, bay

lauw, low, a., tepid; (fig.) half-hearted

laven, lah-ver, v., to refresh

lavendel, lah-ven-derl, c., lavender

laving, lah-ving, c., refreshment
lawaai, lah-vah-ee, n., tumult, uproar, noise
lawaaischopper, lah-vah-ee-sHGop-per, c., noisy
lawine, lah-vee-ner, c., avalanche   [fellow
lectuur, lec-tEER, c., reading-matter; reading
ledematen, lay-der-mah-ter, n. pl., limbs
lederwaren, lay-der-vah-rer, c. pl., leather goods
ledigen, lay-der-HGer, v., to empty
ledigheid, lay-derHG-heyt, c., emptiness; idleness
ledikant, lay-dee-kant, n., bedstead
leed, layt, n., sorrow; harm; injury
leedwezen, layt-vay-zer, n., regret
leeftijd, layf-teyd, c., age; lifetime
leefwijze, layf-vey-zer, c., manner (way) of living
leeg, layHG, a., empty; vacant; idle [drain (a glass)
leegdrinken, layHG-drin-ker, v., to empty, to
leeghoofd, layHG-hohft, c., empty-headed person
leeglopen, layHG-loh-per, v., to idle; to empty
leegloper, layHG-loh-per, c., loafer; idler
leegpompen, layHG-pom-per, v., to pump dry
leegstaan, layHG-stahn, v., to be empty
leegte, layHG-ter, c., emptiness, void, blank
leek, layk, c., layman
leem, laym, n., loam, clay
leenbank, layn-bank, c., loan-office
leep, layp, a. & adv., cunning, sly, shrewd
leer, layr, n., leather. c., doctrine, theory
leerboek, layr-book, n., text-book, manual
leergierig, layr-HGee-rerHG, a., studious
leerjongen, layr-yong-er, c., apprentice
leerkracht, layr-krant, c., teacher, master
leerling, layr-ling, c., pupil, disciple; apprentice
leerlooier, layr-loh-yer, c., tanner
leerplicht, layr-pliHGt, c., compulsory education
leerzaam, layr-zahm, a., instructive; studious
leesbaar, layss-bahr, a., legible; readable
leesbibliotheek, layss-bee-blee-oh-tayk, c., lend-
    ing-library
leesboek, layss-book, n., reading-book
leest, layst, c., last, boot-tree; figure, waist
leeszaal, lays-sahl, c., reading-room
leeuw, lay-oo, c., lion

leeuwendeel, lay-ver-dayl, n., lion's share
leeuwenmoed, lay-ver-moot, c., courage of a lion
leeuwerik, lay-ver-rerk, c., (sky)lark
lef, lef, n., pluck, nerve; swagger, swank
legaat, ler-HGaht, n., legacy. c., legate
legende, ler-HGen-der, c., legend, myth
leger, lay-HGer, n., army; bed; lair. —— **des heils**, —— dess heylss, Salvation Army
legerafdeling, lay-HGer-af-day-ling, c., (mil.) unit   [bulletin
legerbericht, lay-HGer-ber-riHGt, n., army-
legeren, lay-HGer-rer, v., to alloy; (mil.) to en-
leggen, leHG-er, v., to lay; to place   [camp
legioen, lay-HGee-oon, c., legion
lei, ley, c., slate
leiden, ley-der, v., to lead; to conduct; to direct
leider, ley-der, c., leader; manager; guide
leiding, ley-ding, c., leadership; conduit-pipe
leidraad, ley-draht, c., guide-book
leidsel, leyd-serl, n., rein
lek, leck, n., leak, leakage. a., leaky
lekken, leck-ker, v., to leak
lekker, leck-ker, a. & adv., nice, delicious, sweet
lekkerbek, leck-ker-beck, c., gourmet   [tasty
lekkernij, leck-ker-ney, c., delicacy, titbit
lekkers, leck-kerss, n., sweets, sweetmeats
lelie, lay-lee, c., lily
lelieblank, lay-lee-blank, a., lily-white
lelijk, lay-luck, a. & adv., ugly; plain; nasty
lelijkheid, lay-luck-heyt, c., ugliness
lende, len-der, c., loin
lenen (aan), lay-ner (ahn), v., to lend (to). —— **van**, —— fan, to borrow from
lener, lay-ner, c., lender; borrower
lengte, leng-ter, c., length; height; size
lenig, lay-nerHG, a., supple, lithe, limber
lenigen, lay-ner-HGer, v., to alleviate
lening, lay-ning, c., loan
lente, len-ter, c., spring
lentetijd, len-ter-teyt, c., spring-time
lepel, lay-perl, c., spoon; ladle
leperd, lay-pert, c., shrewd fellow

leraar, lay-rahr, c., master, teacher

leren, lay-rer, v., to teach; to learn

les, less, c., lesson

lesrooster, less-roh-ster, c., time-table

lessen, les-ser, v., to quench (one's thirst)

lessenaar, les-ser-nahr, c., desk; writing-desk

letsel, let-serl, n., harm, injury; damage

letter, let-ter, c., letter, character

lettergreep, let-ter-нgrayp, c., syllable

letterkunde, let-ter-kern-der, c., literature [man

letterkundige, let-ter-kern-der-нger, c., literary

letterlijk, let-ter-luck, a. & adv., literal

leugen, ler-нger, c., lie, falsehood

leugenaar, ler-нger-nahr, c., liar

leugentje, ler-нgent-yer, n., fib

leuk, lerk, a. & adv., jolly, funny, droll

leunen, ler-ner, v., to lean [a chair)

leuning, ler-ning, c., rail; banisters; back, arm (of

leuningstoel, ler-ning-stool, c., arm-chair

leus, lerss, c., watch-word, device, slogan

leuteren, ler-ter-rer, v., to dawdle; to twaddle

leven, lay-ver, v., to live. n., life; noise, tumult

levend, lay-vent, a., living, alive

levendig, lay-ven-derнg, a. & adv., lively, brisk

levenloos, lay-ven-lohss, a., inanimate [keen

levenmaker, lay-ven-mah-ker, c., noisy fellow

levensbehoeften, lay-vens-ber-hoof-ter, c. pl., necessaries of life [tion of life

levensbehoud, lay-vens-ber-howt, n., preserva-

levensbeschrijving, lay-vens-ber-srey-ving, c., biography [life

levensgevaar, lay-vens-нger-vahr, n., danger of

levensgroot, lay-vens-нgroht, a., life-size(d)

levenslang, lay-vens-lang, a., (imprisonment) for life [life

levensloop, lay-vens-lohp, c., career, course of

levenslustig, lay-vens-lerss-terнg, a., full of life

levensmiddelen, lay-vens-mid-der-ler, n. pl., provisions [livelihood

levensonderhoud, lay-vens-on-der-howt, n.,

levensopvatting, lay-vens-op-fat-ting, c., conception of life

levensstandaard, lay-vens-stan-dahrt, c., standard of living [life-assurance

levensverzekering, lay-vens-fer-zay-ker-ring, c.,

levenswijze, lay-vens-vey-zer, c., way of living

lever, lay-ver, c., liver

leverancier, lay-ver-ran-seer, c., supplier

leveren, lay-ver-rer, v., to supply; to deliver

levering, lay-ver-ring, c., supply; delivery

levertraan, lay-ver-trahn, c., cod-liver oil

leverworst, lay-ver-vorst, c., liver sausage

lezen, lay-zer, v., to read; to gather, to glean

lezer, lay-zer, c., reader; gleaner, gatherer

lezing, lay-zing, c., reading; lecture; version

liberaal, lee-ber-rahl, c., liberal. a., liberal

lichaam, liHG-ahm, n., body; frame [body

lichaamsdeel, liHG-ahms-dayl, n., part of the

lichamelijk, liHG-ah-mer-luck, a. & adv., bodily

licht, liHGt, n., light. a. & adv., light; slight; mild

lichtboei, liHGt-boo-ee, c., light-buoy

lichtbundel, liHGt-bern-derl, c., beam of light

lichtelijk, liHGt-ter-luck, adv., slightly

lichten, liHG-ter, v., to lift; to dawn; to give light

lichtgelovig, liHGt-HGer-loh-verHG, a. & adv., credulous

lichtgeraakt, liHGt-HGer-rahkt, a., touchy

lichting, liHG-ting, c., (mil.) draft; collection (letters)

lichtkogel, liHGt-koh-HGerl, c., fire-ball

lichtvaardig, liHGt-fahr-derHG, a. & adv., rash

lichtzinnig, liHGt-sin-nerHG, a. & adv., frivolous

lichtzinnigheid, liHGt-sin-nerHG-heyt, c., frivol-

lid, lit, n., limb; joint; phalanx; member [ity

lidmaatschap, lit-maht-sHGap, n., membership

lied, leet, n., song; hymn

lieden, lee-der, c. pl., people, men

liederlijk, lee-der-luck, a. & adv., dissolute

liedje, leed-yer, n., song, tune

lief, leef, a. & adv., dear; amiable; sweet; nice

liefdadig, leef-dah-derHG, a. & adv., charitable

liefde, leef-der, c., love; charity

liefdeblijk, leef-der-bleyk, n., token of love

liefdedienst, leef-der-deenst, c., act of charity

liefdeloos, leef-der-lohss, a., uncharitable
liefdevol, leef-der-fol, a., loving
liefelijk, leef-er-luck, a. & adv., lovely
liefhebben, leef-heb-ber, v., to love
liefhebber, leef-heb-ber, c., lover, amateur
liefhebberij, leef-heb-ber-rey, c., hobby
liefje, leef-yer, n., darling, sweetheart
liefkozen, leef-koh-zer, v., to fondle, to caress
liefkozing, leef-koh-zing, c., caress, endearment
liefkrijgen, leef-krey-HGer, v., to grow fond of
liefst, leefst, a., dearest. adv., rather
lieftallig, leef-tal-lerHG, a. & adv., lovable, sweet
liegen, lee-HGer, v., to tell lies
lier, leer, c., lyre; (naut.) winch
lieveling, lee-ver-ling, c., darling, dear, love
liever, lee-ver, a., dearer. adv., rather, sooner.
** ---- niet!,** ---- neet, I'd rather not!
lift, lift, c., lift, elevator
liften, lif-ter, v., to hitch-hike
liggen, liHG-er, v., to lie; to be situated
ligging, liHG-ing, c., position, situation
ligstoel, liHG-stool, c., long chair
lijden, ley-der, v., to suffer, to bear
lijder, ley-der, c., sufferer, patient
lijdzaamheid, leyt-sahm-heyt, c., patience
lijf, leyf, n., body; bodice
lijfrente, leyf-ren-ter, c., (life-)annuity
lijfwacht, leyf-vɑHGt, c., body-guard
lijk, leyk, n., corpse
lijkdienst, leyk-deenst, c., funeral service
lijken, ley-ker, v., to seem, to appear; to look like
lijkrede, leyk-ray-der, c., funeral oration
lijkschouwer, leyk-sHGow-er, c., coroner
lijkverbranding, leyk-fer-brɑn-ding, c., crema-
lijkwagen, leyk-vah-HGer, c., hearse [tion
lijm, leym, c., glue; bird-lime
lijmen, ley-mer, v., to glue; to talk over
lijmerig, ley-mer-rerHG, a., sticky; (fig.) drawling
lijn, leyn, c., line; string, cord, rope
lijnolie, leyn-oh-lee, c., linseed oil
lijnrecht, leyn-reHGt, a. & adv., straight
lijntrekken, leyn-treck-ker, v., (pop.) to go slow

lijst, leyst, c., list; frame; edge, border
lijster, leyss-ter, c., thrush
lijvig, ley-verHG, a., corpulent; bulky; fat
likeur, lee-kerr, c., liqueur
likken, lik-ker, v., to lick
linde, lin-der, c., lime(-tree)
liniaal, lee-nee-ahl, c., ruler
linkerbeen, lin-ker-bayn, n., left leg
linkerhand, lin-ker-hant, c., left hand
links, linkss, a., left; left-handed; (fig.) clumsy.
naar ——, nahr ——, to the left
linksaf, links-af, adv., to the left   [linen
linnen, linnengoed, lin-ner, lin-ner-HGoot, n.,
linnenkast, lin-ner-kast, c., linen-cupboard
lint, lintje, lint, lint-yer, n., ribbon
lintworm, lint-vorm, c., tapeworm
linze, lin-zer, c., lentil
lip, lip, c., lip
lippenstift, lip-per-stift, c., lipstick
liquideren, lee-kvee-day-rer, v., to wind up, to
lis, liss, c., iris, flag   [liquidate
lispelen, liss-per-ler, v., to lisp
list, list, c., ruse, trick; cunning, slyness
listig, liss-terHG, a. & adv., sly, crafty, cunning
lits-jumeaux, lee-zHEE-moh, n. pl., twin beds
litteken, lit-tay-ker, n., scar
loeien, loo-yer, v., to low; to moo; to bellow; to
loens, loonss, a., squinting, squint-eyed   [roar
loeren, loo-rer, v., to peer, to leer, to spy
lof, lof, c., praise, eulogy. n., benediction
loffelijk, lof-fer-luck, a. & adv., laudable
log, loHG, a. & adv., unwieldy, heavy, lumbering
loge, lozh-er, c., (freemasons') lodge; box (in a
logé, loh-zhay, c., guest, visitor   [theatre)
logeerkamer, loh-zhayr-kah-mer, c., guest-room
logenstraffen, loh-HGen-straf-fer, v., to give the
lie to   [up
logeren, loh-zhay-rer, v., to stay; to put (a person)
logies, loh-zheess, n., accommodation, lodging
logisch, loh-HGeess, a. & adv., logical
lok, lok, lock, c., lock, curl
lokaal, loh-kahl, n., room, hall; locality

lokaas, lock-ahss, n., bait, decoy

loket, loh-ket, n., booking-office, box-office

lokken, lock-ker, v., to entice, to decoy, to lure

lol, lol, c., fun, lark

lollig, lol-lerHG, a. & adv., jolly, funny

lommerd, lom-mert, c., pawnbroker's shop

lomp, lomp, c., rag, tatter. a. & adv., rude; clumsy

lomperd, lom-pert, c., lout, boor, churl

lonen, loh-ner, v., to reward, to pay

long, long, c., lung

longontsteking, long-ont-stay-king, c., pneu- [monia

lonken, lon-ker, v., to glance, to ogle, to leer

lont, lont, c., match, fuse

loochenen, loh-HGer-ner, v., to deny

lood, lohd, n., lead; plumb-line

loodgieter, loht-HGee-ter, c., plumber

loods, lohtss, c., (naut.) pilot; shed; hangar

loodzwaar, loht-zvahr, a., leaden, heavy as lead

loof, lohf, n., foliage

loom, lohm, a., slow, slack; close; oppressive

loomheid, lohm-heyt, c., slackness, lassitude

loon, lohn, n., pay, wages; reward [increase

loonsverhoging, lohnss-fer-hoh-HGing, c., wage-

loontrekker, lohn-treck-ker, c., wage-earner

loop, lohp, c., walk, gait; course; run. op de —— zijn, op der —— zeyn, to be on the run

loopbaan, lohp-bahn, c., career

loopgraaf, lohp-HGrahf, c., (mil.) trench

loopjongen, lohp-yong-er, c., errand-boy

loopplank, lohp-plank, c., gangway

loos, lohss, a., dummy, false; sly, cunning, crafty

lopen, loh-per, v., to walk; to run; to go

lopend, loh-pent, a., running; current

loper, loh-per, c., runner; messenger; carpet; [pass-key

lor, lor, c., rag; (fig.) trash

lorgnet, lor-n'yet, n., eye-glasses

los, loss, a. & adv., loose, undone; (fig.) loose

losbandig, loss-ban-derHG, a., dissolute, loose

losbarsten, loss-bar-ster, v., to break out

losbarsting, loss-bar-sting, c., outbreak, burst

losbol, loss-bol, c., rake, libertine

losbreken, loss-bray-ker, v., to break loose

losdraaien, loss-drah-yer, v., to unscrew
losgespen, loss-HGess-per, v., to unbuckle
loshangen, loss-hang-er, v., to hang loose
losknopen, loss-k'noh-per, v., to untie; to unbutton
loslaten, loss-lah-ter, v., to release, to let go
loslippig, loss-lip-perHG, a. & adv., flippant
losmaken, loss-mah-ker, v., to loosen, to untie
losprijs, loss-preyss, c., ransom
lossen, loss-ser, v., to unload; to fire; to discharge
lostrekken, loss-treck-ker, v., to pull loose
lot, lot, n., lottery-ticket; fate, destiny
loten, loh-ter, v., to draw lots
loterij, loh-ter-rey, c., lottery, draw, raffle
lotgenoot, lot-HGer-noht, c., fellow-sufferer
lotgevallen, lot-HGer-fal-ler, n. pl., adventures
loting, loh-ting, c., drawing of lots; draw
loupe, loop, c., magnifying-glass
louter, low-ter, a., mere, pure, sheer
loven, loh-ver, v., to praise, to extol, to glorify
lucht, lerHGt, c., air; sky; scent, smell
luchtaanval, lerHGt-ahn-fal, c., air-raid
luchtafweer, lerHGt-af-vayr, c., air defence
luchtalarm, lerHGt-ah-larm, n., air-raid warning
luchtbescherming, lerHGt-ber-sHGayr-ming, c.,
Civil Defence
luchten, lerHG-ter, v., to air; (fig.) to vent
luchtgesteldheid, lerHGt-HGer-stelt-heyt, c., atmosphere; climate
luchthaven, lerHGt-hah-ver, c., air-port
luchtig, lerHG-terHG, a. & adv., airy; light
luchtkasteel, lerHGt-kass-tayl, c., castle in the air
luchtledig, lerHGt-lay-derHG, a., void of air
luchtlijn, lerHGt-leyn, c., air-line
luchtmacht, lerHGt-maHGt, c., air force
luchtpost, lerHGt-posst, c., air mail
luchtreiziger, lerHGt-rey-zer-HGer, c., air-trav- [eller
luchtvaart, lerHGt-fahrt, c., aviation [tion
luchtverversing, lerHGt-fer-fayr-sing, c., ventila-
lucifer, lEE-see-fayr, c., (safety) match [match-box
lucifersdoosje, lEE-see-fayrss-doh-sher, n.,
lui, low, c. pl., people. a. & adv., lazy, idle

luiaard, low-ahrt, c., sluggard; sloth
luid, lowt, a. & adv., loud
luiden, low-der, v., to ring, to peal; **to sound**
luidkeels, lowt-kaylss, adv., aloud
luidruchtig, lowt-rerHG-terHG, a. & adv., noisy
luidspreker, lowt-spray-ker, c., loud-speaker
luier, low-er, c., (baby's) napkin
luieren, low-ay-rer, v., to be idle, to loaf
luiheid, low-heyt, c., laziness, idleness
luik, lowk, n., trap-door; shutter; (naut.) hatch
luim, lowm, c., mood, humour; caprice; freak
luimig, low-merHG, a. & adv., humorous; capri-
luis, lowss, c., louse [cious
luister, lowss-ter, c., lustre, pomp, splendour
luisteren, lowss-ter-rer, v., to listen (in); to obey
luisterrijk, lowss-ter-reyk, a. & adv., brilliant
luistervink, lowss-ter-fink, c., eavesdropper
luitenant, low-ter-nant, c., lieutenant
lukraak, lerk-rahk, adv., at random
lummel, lerm-merl, c., lout, booby
lus, lerss, c., loop; noose; tag; strap
lust, lerst, c., delight; desire; appetite; lust
lusteloos, lerss-ter-lohss, a. & adv., listless
lusten, lerss-ter, v., to like, to fancy
lustig, lerss-terHG, a. & adv., cheerful, merry
luwen, lEE-ver, v., to abate, to fall, to die down
luxe, lEEk-ser, c., luxury
lyriek, lee-reek, c., lyrics, lyric poetry

maag, mahHG, c., stomach
maagd, mahHGt, c., virgin, maid(en) [enly
maagdelijk, mahHG-der-luck, a., virginal, maid-
maagpijn, mahHG-peyn, c., stomach-ache
maaien, mah-yer, v., to mow; to cut; to reap
maal, mahl, n., meal, repast. c., time
maalstroom, mahl-strohm, c., whirlpool, **eddy**
maaltijd, mahl-teyt, c., meal, repast
maan, mahn, c., moon
maand, mahnt, c., month
maandag, mahn-daHG, c., Monday
maandblad, mahnt-blat, n., monthly (magazine)
maandelijks, mahn-der-luckss, a. & adv., monthly

maansverduistering, mahns-fer-dows-ter-ring, c., eclipse of the moon

maar, mahr, conj. & but. adv., but, merely

maarschalk, mahr-SHGalk, c., marshal

maart, mahrt, c., March

maas, mahss, c., stitch; mesh (net)

maat, maht, c., measure; size; mate, partner

maatregel, maht-ray-Herl, c., measure, decree

maatschappelijk, maht-SHGap-per-luck, a. & adv., social [pany

maatschappij, maht-SHGap-pey, c., society; com-

maatstaf, maht-staf, c., standard, gauge

machinaal, mah-shee-**nahl,** a. & adv., mechanical

machine, mah-shee-ner, c., engine, machine

machinegeweer, mah-shee-ner-HGer-vayr, n., machine-gun [(naut.) engineer

machinist, mah-shee-**nist,** c., engine-driver;

macht, maHGt, c., power; authority [less

machteloos, maHG-ter-lohss, a., powerless, help-

machthebber, maHGt-heb-ber, c., ruler, man in power [(food)

machtig, maHG-terHG, a. & adv., powerful; rich

machtigen, maHG-ter-HGer, v., to authorize

made, mah-der, c., grub, maggot

madeliefje, mah-der-leef-yer, n., daisy [house

magazijn, mah-HGah-zeyn, n., warehouse, store-

mager, mah-HGer, a., thin, lean; (fig.) poor

magneet, maHG-nayt, c., magnet; magneto

mahoniehout, mah-hoh-nee-howt, n., mahogany

maïs, ma-iss, c., maize, Indian corn

majesteit, mah-yess-teyt, c., majesty

majestueus, mah-yess-tEE-erss, a. & adv., majestic

majoor, mah-yohr, c., (mil.) major

mak, mak, a., tame, gentle, tractable

makelaar, mah-ker-lahr, c., broker

maken, mah-ker, v., to make; to do; to mend. **het maakt niets, het mahkt neets,** it does not matter

maker, mah-ker, c., maker, author

makker, mak-ker, c., comrade, companion

makreel, mah-krayl, c., mackerel

mal, mal, a. & adv., foolish, mad; silly

malen, mah-ler, v., to grind, to mill
mallemolen, mal-ler-moh-ler, c., merry-go-
mals, mals, a., tender; mellow, soft [round
man, man, c., man; husband
manchet, man-shet, c., cuff; wristband
mand, mant, c., basket, hamper [attorney
mandaat, man-daht, n., mandate; power of
mandarijntje, man-dah-reynt-yer, n., tangerine
manege, mah-nay-zher, c., riding-school [ment
manen, mah-ner, c. pl., mane. v., to press for pay-
maneschijn, mah-ner-sHGeyn, c., moonlight
mangel, mang-erl, c., mangle [brave
manhaftig, man-haf-terHG, a. & adv., manly
maniak, mah-nee-ak, c., maniac; faddist
manie, mah-nee, c., mania, rage, fad
manier, mah-neer, c., manner, way, fashion
mank, mank, a., crippled
mankeren, man-kay-rer, v., to fail; to be absent
manmoedig, man-moo-derHG, a. & adv., manly
mannelijk, man-ner-luck, a., male; manly
mannentaal, man-ner-tahl, c., manly language
mannetje, man-nert-yer, n., little man; male (of
animals)
manslag, man-slaHG, c., homicide; manslaughter
mantel, man-terl, c., lady's coat; mantle, cloak
mantelpak, man-terl-pak, n., coat and skirt
manufacturen, mah-nEE-fak-tEE-rer, c. pl.,
draper's goods [drapery shop
manufactuurzaak, mah-nEE-fak-tEEr-zahk, c.,
map, map, c., stationery-case, portfolio
marcheren, mar-shay-rer, v., to march
marechaussée, ma-rer-shohs-say, c., constabu-
mare(n)tak, mah-rer-tak, c., mistletoe [lary
marine, mah-ree-ner, c., navy
marinier, mah-ree-neer, c., marine
markies, mar-keess, c., marquess; awning
markt, markt, c., market; market-place
marktplein, markt-pleyn, n., market-square
marmer, mar-mer, n., marble
marmeren, mar-mer-rer, a., marble. v., to
marble; to grain [quarry
marmergroeve, mar-mer-HGroo-ver, c., marble-

marmot, m*a*r-mot, c., marmot; guinea-pig
mars, m*a*rs, c., (mil.) march; (pedlar's) pack
marsepein, m*a*r-ser-peyn, n., marzipan
marskramer, m*a*rss-krah-mer, c., pedlar,
martelaar, m*a*r-ter-lahr, c., martyr [hawker
martelen, m*a*r-ter-ler, v., to torture
marteling, m*a*r-ter-ling, c., torture
marter, m*a*r-ter, c., marten
masker, m*a*ss-ker, n., mask; (fig.) disguise
massa, m*a*s-sah, c., mass, crowd
masseren, m*a*s-say-rer, v., to massage; to knead
massief, m*a*s-seef, a., massive, solid
mast, mast, c., mast; (climbing-)pole [ing
mastklimmen, m*a*st-klim-mer, n., pole-climb-
mat, mat, c., (door-)mat. a., tired, weary; dead,
dull [immense
mateloos, mah-ter-lohss, a. & adv., boundless,
materiaal, mah-tay-ree-ahl, n., material(s)
materieel, mah-tay-ree-el, a. & adv., material.
n., material(s) [sober
matig, mah-ter*HG*, a. & adv., moderate, frugal,
matigen, mah-ter-*HG*er, v., to moderate, to
mitigate [temperance
matigheid, mah-ter*HG*-heyt, c., moderation,
matras, mah-trass, c., mattress
matroos, mah-trohss, c., sailor [sailor suit
matrozenpak(je), mah-troh-zer-pak(-yer), n.,
mattenklopper, m*a*t-ter-klop-per, c., carpet-
beater [c., speed limit
maximumsnelheid, m*a*k-see-merm-snel-heyt,
mazelen, mah-zer-ler, c. pl., measles
me, mer, pron., me, to me [(clock, etc.)
mechaniek, may-kah-neek, n., mechanism; works
medaille, mer-d*a*l-yer, c., medal [locket
medaillon, mer-d*a*l-yon, c., medallion; inset;
me(d)e, may, adv., also, too, likewise, as well
me(d)ebrengen, may-breng-er, v., to bring
(along); to entail [municative
mededeelzaam, may-der-dayl-zahm, a., com-
mededelen, may-der-day-ler, v., to communicate
mededeling, may-der-day-ling, c., communication

mededinger, may-der-ding-er, c., rival, com- [petitor
me(d)edoen, may-doon, v., to join in
me(d)egaan, may-HGahn, v., to accompany
me(d)egeven, may-HGay-vay, v., to send along with; to yield
medegevoel, may-der-HGer-vool, n., sympathy
me(d)ehelpen, may-hel-per, v., to assist
medelijden, may-der-ley-der, n., pity, com-passion. —— **hebben met,** —— **heb-ber met,** to sympathize with
medemens, may-der-menss, c., fellow-man
me(d)enemen, may-nay-mer, v., to take along with [complice
medeplichtige, may-der-pliHG-ter-HGer, c., ac-
me(d)eslepen, may-slay-per, v., to drag along
medespeler, may-der-spay-ler, c., fellow-player
medestudent, may-der-stEE-dent, c., fellow-student
medewerker, may-der-vayr-ker, c., co-operator
medeweten, may-der-vay-ter, n., knowledge
medicijn, may-dee-seyn, c., medicine [student
medicus, may-dee-kerss, c., doctor; medical
medisch, may-deess, a. & adv., medical
mediteren, may-dee-tay-rer, v., to meditate
medogenloos, may-doh-HGen-lohss, a., pitiless
meegaand, may-HGahnt, a., pliable, yielding
meel, mayl, n., meal, flour
meelfabriek, mayl-fah-breek, c., flour-mill
meer, mayr, n., lake. a., more
meerder, mayr-der, a., greater, more
meerderheid, mayr-der-heyt, c., majority
meerderjarig, mayr-der-yah-rerHG, a., of age
meermalen, mayr-mah-ler, adv., frequently
mees, mayss, c., tit
meesmuilen, mayss-mow-ler, v., to smirk, to
meest, mayst, a., most. adv., mostly [simper
meestal, mayss-tal, adv., mostly; usually
meester, may-ster, c., master
meesterknecht, may-ster-k'neHGt, c., foreman
meesterstuk, may-ster-sterk, n., masterpiece
meetkunde, mayt-kern-der, c., geometry
meeuw, may-oo, c., (sea-)gull

meevallen, may-fal-ler, v., to exceed expectations
meevaller, may-fal-ler, c., windfall
mei, mey, c., May
meid, meyt, c., (maid-)servant; girl
meidoorn, mey-doh-rern, c., hawthorn
meikever, mey-kay-ver, c., cockchafer, may-bug
meineed, mey-nayt, c., perjury
meisje, mey-sher, n., girl; fiancée; servant
melaatse, mer-laht-ser, c., leper
melaatsheid, mer-lahts-heyt, c., leprosy
melden, mel-der, v., to mention, to report
melig, may-lerHG, a., mealy, floury; woolly
melk, melk, c., milk
melkboer, melk-boor, c., milkman; dairy-farmer
melken, melk-er, v., to milk
melkinrichting, melk-in-riHG-ting, c., dairy
melkkan, melk-kan, c., milk-jug
melkmeid, melk-meyt, c., milkmaid, dairymaid
melkpoeder, melk-poo-der, n., milk-powder
melksalon, melk-sah-lon, n., creamery
melkweg, melk-veHG, c., Milky Way
melodie, may-loh-dee, c., melody, tune, air
meloen, mer-loon, c., melon
men, men, pron., people, one, we, you, they
menen, may-ner, v., to mean; to suppose
mengelmoes, meng-erl-moos, n., medley, jumble
mengen, meng-er, v., to mix, to mingle, to blend
mengsel, meng-serl, n., mixture, blend
menie, may-nee, c., red lead
menig, may-nerHG, a., many, several   [often
menigmaal, may-nerHG-mahl, adv., many a time,
menigte, may-nerHG-ter, c., crowd, multitude
menigvuldig, may-nerHG-ferl-derHG, a. & adv.,
     manifold
mening, may-ning, c., opinion, view, idea
meningsverschil, may-ningss-fer-sHGil,   n.
     difference of opinion
mens, menss, c., man; woman. **de mensen,** der
     men-ser, people, mankind
menselijk, men-ser-luck, a., human   [cannibal
menseneter, men-sen-ay-ter, c., man-eater,
mensenhater, men-sen-hah-ter, c., misanthrope

mensenschuw men-sen-SHGEE, a., shy
mensheid, menss-heyt, c., mankind [anthropy
menslievendheid, menss-lee-vent-heyt, c., phil-
menu, mer-NEE, n., menu, bill of fare
mep, mep, c., (pop.) slap, smack, blow
merel, may-rerl, c., blackbird
merendeels, may-rer-daylss, adv., mostly
merg, mayrHG, n., marrow; pith
mergelgroeve, mayr-HGerl-HGroo-ver, c., marl- [pit
merk, mayrk, n., mark; brand, sort, quality
merkbaar, mayrk-bahr, a. & adv., perceptible
merken, mayr-ker, v., to mark; to notice
merkteken, mayrk-tay-ker, n., token, mark, sign
merkwaardig, mayrk-vahr-derHG, a. & adv.,
merrie, mayr-ree, c. mare [remarkable
mes, mess, n., knife [knife
mesje, mess-sher, n., blade (safety-razor); small
messteek, mess-stayk, c., knife-thrust, knife-stab
mest, mest, c., dung, manure, fertilizer [(animals)
mesten, mess-ter, v., to manure; to fatten
mesthoop, mest-hohp, c., manure-heap
met, met, prep., with, by, in
metaal, may-tahl, n., metal [foundry
metaalgieterij, may-tahl-HGee-ter-rey, c.,
meteen, met-ayn, adv., at the same time: pre-
    sently. **tot ——! tot ——,** so long!
meten, may-ter, v., to measure; to gauge
meter, may-ter, c., godmother; metre; measurer
metgezel, met-HGer-zel, c., mate, companion
metselaar, met-ser-lahr, c., bricklayer
metselen, met-ser-ler, v., to lay bricks; to build
metterdaad, met-ter-daht, adv., indeed, in fact
metworst, met-vorst, c., German sausage
meubel, mer-berl, n., piece of furniture [maker
meubelmaker, mer-berl-mah-ker, c., furniture-
meubileren, mer-bee-lay-rer, v., to furnish, to fit
mevrouw, mer-frow, c., lady; madam; Mrs. [up
miauwen, mee-ow-er, v., to mew, to miaul
middag, mid-daHG, c., midday, noon; afternoon
middagdutje, mid-daHG-dert-yer, n., after-
    dinner nap [dinner
middageten, mid-daHG-ay-ter, n., midday-meal,

middel, mid-derl, n., means; remedy; waist

middelbaar, mid-derl-bahr, a., middle; secondary (school) [ages

middeleeuwen, mid-derl-ay-ver, c. pl., middle

middeleeuws, mid-derl-ay-ooss, a., medieval

middelmatig, mid-derl-**mah**-terHG, a. & adv., mediocre

middelpunt, mid-derl-pernt, n., centre

middelste, mid-derl-ster, a., middle

midden, mid-der, n., middle, centre

middenstand, mid-der-stant, c., middle classes

middernacht, mid-der-naHGt, c., midnight

mier, meer, c., ant

mij, mey, pron., me, to me

mijden, mey-der, v., to avoid, to shun

mijmeren, mey-mer-rer, v., to muse; to brood

mijlpaal, meyl-pahl, c., mile-stone; (fig.) landmark

mijn, meyn, pron., my. c., mine [mark

mijnbouw, meyn-bow, c., mining

mijnenlegger, mey-ner-leHG-ér, c., mine-layer

mijnenveger, mey-ner-fay-HGer, c., mine-sweeper

mijnheer, mer-nayr, c., gentleman; sir; Mr.

mijnramp, meyn-ramp, c., mining-disaster

mijnwerker, meyn-vayr-ker, c., miner

mijt, meyt, c., mite (insect); stack, pile

mijter, mey-ter, c., mitre

mikken, mick-ker, v., to aim, to take aim

mikpunt, mick-pernt, n., aim; (fig.) butt, target

mild, milt, a. & adv., generous, liberal; genial

milddadigheid, mil-dah-derHG-heyt, c., generosity

milieu, meel-yer, n., surroundings [osity

militair, mee-lee-tayr, a., military. c., soldier

millioen, meel-yoon, n., a million

milt, milt, c., milt, spleen

mimiek, mee-meek, c., mimic art

min, min, c., (wet-)nurse. a., mean, low. adv., less

minachten, min-aHG-ter, v., to disdain

minachting, min-aHG-ting, c., contempt, disdain

minder, min-der, a. & adv., fewer; inferior

minderheid, min-der-heyt, c., minority

minderjarig, min-der-yah-rerHG, a., under age

minderwaardig, min-der-vahr-derHG, a., inferior

minister, mee-niss-ter, c., minister, secretary (of State). —— **-president,** —— **-pray-zee-dent,** prime minister

ministerie, mee-niss-tay-ree, n., ministry, department

minnaar, min-nahr, c., lover [partment

minnetjes, min-ner-tyess, adv., poorly

minst, minst, a. & adv., fewest, least; smallest

minstens, mins-tens, adv., at (the) least

minuut, mee-nEEt, c., minute

minzaam, min-zahm, a. & adv., affable, suave

mis, mis, c., Mass. adv., wrong

misboek, miss-book, n., missal

misbruik, miss-browk, n., abuse

misbruiken, miss-browk-er, v., to misuse

misdaad, miss-daht, c., crime, offence

misdadig, miss-dah-derHG, a., criminal, guilty

misdadiger, miss-dah-der-HGer, c., criminal

misdoen, miss-doon, v., to offend, to do wrong

misdrijf, miss-dreyf, n., offence, misdemeanour

misgunnen, miss-HGern-ner, v., to (be)grudge

mishandelen, miss-han-der-ler, v., to ill-treat

miskennen, miss-ken-ner, v., to undervalue

miskraam, miss-krahm, c., miscarriage, abortion

misleiden, miss-ley-der, v., to mislead, to deceive

misleider, miss-ley-der, c., impostor, deceiver

mislukkeling, miss-lerk-ker-ling, c., failure

mislukken, miss-lerk-ker, v., to fail, to miscarry

mislukking, miss-lerk-king, c., failure

mismaakt, miss-mahkt, a., deformed

misnoegd, miss-nooHGt, a. & adv., displeased

misoogst, miss-ohHGst, c., bad harvest

misplaatst, miss-plahtst, a., misplaced, mistaken

mispunt, miss-pernt, n., (pop.) good-for-nothing fellow [tion

misrekening, miss-ray-ker-ning, c., miscalculation

misschien, mis-SHgeen, adv., perhaps

misselijk, mis-ser-luck, a. & adv., sick; (fig.) sickening

missen, mis-ser, v., to miss; to lack; to do without

missie, mis-see, c., mission [out

misslag, mis-sl*a*HG, c., miss; (fig.) fault

misstaan, mis-stahn, v., to be unbecoming

misstap, mis-st*a*p, c., false step; lapse, slip

mist, mist, c., fog; mist

mistig, miss-terHG, a., foggy; misty

mistroostig, miss-trohs-terHG, a., dejected

misverstand, miss-fer-st*a*nt, n., misunder-
standing

misvormen, miss-for-mer, v., to disfigure

mitrailleur, mee-tr*a*-yerr, c., machine gun

mits, mits, conj., provided that   [tion

mobilisatie, moh-bee-lee-zah-see, c., mobiliza-

modder, mod-der, c., mud, mire, sludge

modderig, mod-der-rerHG, a., muddy; miry

modderpoel, mod-der-pool, c., slough, quagmire

mode, moh-der, c., fashion   [article] novelty

modeartikel, moh-der-*a*r-tee-kerl, n., fancy-

modegek, moh-der-HGeck, c., dandy, fop

model, moh-del, n., model, pattern

moderniseren, moh-dayr-nee-zay-rer, v., to
modernize   [milliner's

modezaak, moh-der-zahk, c., fashion-house;

modiste, moh-diss-ter, c., milliner, dress-maker

moe, moo, a. & adv., tired, weary

moed, moot, c., courage, spirit   [dent

moedeloos, moo-der-lohss, a., dejected, despon-

moeder, moo-der, c., mother; matron; dam

moederlijk, moo-der-luck, a. & adv., motherly

moederschap, moo-der-sHG*a*p, n., motherhood

moedertaal, moo-der-tahl, c., mother tongue

moedervlek, moo-der-flayk, c., birth-mark

moedig, moo-derHG, a. & adv., courageous, brave

moedwillig, moot-vil-lerHG, a. & adv., wanton

moeheid, moo-heyt, c., fatigue, weariness

moeilijk, moo'ee-luck, a. & adv., difficult, hard

moeilijkheid, moo'ee-luck-heyt, c., difficulty

moeite, moo'ee-ter, c., difficulty; trouble

moer, moor, c., dam (of animals); dregs

moeras, moo-r*a*ss, n., marsh, swamp

moerassig, moo-r*a*ss-serHG, a., marshy, boggy

moerbei, moor-bey, c., mulberry

moes, mooss, n., mash; stewed fruit or vegetables

moesje, moo-sher, n., mummy; beauty-spot (on the face); spot (on materials)

moestuin, mooss-town, c., kitchen-garden

moeten, moo-ter, v., to have to

mof, mof, c., muff; (mech.) sleeve, socket

mogelijk, moh-HGer-luck, a. & adv., possible. **zo spoedig ——,** zoh spoo-derHG ——, as soon as possible

mogelijkheid, moh-HGer-luck-heyt, c., possibility

mogen, moh-HGer, v., to be permitted

mogendheid, moh-HGent-heyt, c., power (nation)

mokken, mock-ker, v., to sulk, to pout

mol, mol, c., mole; (mus.) flat

molen, moh-ler, c., mill

molenaar, moh-ler-nahr, c., miller

molensteen, moh-ler-stayn, c., millstone

mollig, mol-lerHG, a., plump, chubby; soft

molmachtig, molm-aHG-terHG, a., worm-eaten

molshoop, molss-hohp, c., mole-hill

momenteel, moh-men-tayl, adv., at the moment

mompelen, mom-per-ler, v., to mutter

mond, mont, c., mouth

mondeling, mon-der-ling, a. & adv., oral, verbal

mondig, mon-derHG, a., of age

monding, mon-ding, c., mouth (of a river)

mondstuk, mont-sterk, n., mouthpiece

mondvoorraad, mont-fohr-raht, c., provisions

monnik, mon-nerk, c., monk, friar

monster, mons-ter, n., monster; pattern

monsteren, mons-ter-rer, v., to muster

montagewoning, mon-tak-zher-voh-ning, c., prefabricated house

monter, mon-ter, a. & adv., lively, cheerful

monteren, mon-tay-rer, v., to erect; to assemble (car, etc.); to stage (a play)

monteur, mon-terr, c., mechanic; fitter

montuur, mon-tEEr, c., frame; setting (of a jewel)

mooi, moh'ee, a. & adv., handsome, pretty

mooiprater, moh'ee-prah-ter, c., flatterer

moord, mohrt, c., murder [assault

moordaanslag, mohrt-ahn-slaHG, c., murderous

moorddadig, mohrd-dah-derHG, a., murderous

moordenaar, mohr-der-nahr, c., murderer

moot, moht, c., slice (meat, etc.); fillet (fish)

mop, mop, c., joke; biscuit; blot (of ink); pug-dog

moppentapper, mop-per-t*a*p-per, c., regular joker

mopperaar, mop-per-rahr, c., grumbler, grouser

mopperen, mop-per-rer, v., to grumble, to grouse

moreel, moh-rayl, a. & adv., moral. n., (mil.) morale

morgen, mor-HGer, c., morning. adv., to-morrow

morgenblad, mor-HGen-bl*a*t, n., morning paper

morgenrood, mor-HGen-roht, n., red of dawn

mormel, mor-merl, n., monster, freak

morren, mor-rer, v., to grumble, to murmur

morsdood, mors-doht, a., stone-dead, stark-dead

morsen, mor-ser, v., to make a mess

morsig, mor-serHG, a., dirty, grimy, grubby

mortier, mor-teer, n., (mil.) mortar

mos, moss, n., moss

mosachtig, moss-*a*HG-terHG, a., mossy

moskee, moss-kay, c., mosque

mossel, mos-serl, c., mussel

mosterd, moss-tert, c., mustard

mot, mot, c., moth

motgaatje, mot-HGaht-yer, n., moth-hole

motie, moh-see, c., motion; vote

motief, moh-teef, n., motive

motor, moh-tor, c., motor; engine

motorboot, moh-tor-boht, c., motor-boat

motorfiets, moh-tor-feets, c., motor-cycle

motorpech, moh-tor-peHG, c., engine trouble

motorrijder, moh-tor-rey-der, c., motor-cyclist

motregen, mot-ray-HGer, c., drizzle

mottig, mot-terHG, a., moth-eaten

mousseline, moos-ser-leen-er, n., muslin

mout, mowt, n., malt

mouw, mow, c., sleeve

mozaïek, moh-zah-eek, n., mosaic (work)

muf, muffig, merf, merf-ferHG, a., musty, stuffy

mug, merHG, c., midge; gnat

muggenzifter, merHG-er-zif-ter, c., hair-splitter

muil, mowl, c., mouth; slipper

muildier, mowl-deer, n., mule
muilpeer, mowl-payr, c., (pop.) slap, box on the [ear
muis, mowss, c., mouse
muisstil, mows-stil, a., as still as a mouse
muiten, mow-ter, v., to rebel
muiterij, mow-ter-rey, c., rebellion
muizenval, mow-zer-fal, c., mousetrap
mul, merl, a., loose. c., mould (earth)
munitie, mEE-**nee-**see, c., ammunition
munt, mernt, c., coin; coinage; mint
murmelen, merr-mer-ler, v., to murmur; to
    purl; to babble
murw, merrv, a., tender, soft
mus, merss, c., sparrow
musicus, mEE-zee-kerss, c., musician
muskaatnoot, merss-kaht-noht, c., nutmeg
muskaatwijn, merss-kaht-veyn, c., muscatel
muskiet, merss-keet, c., mosquito
muts, mertss, c., bonnet; cap
muur, mEEr, c., wall
muziek, mEE-zeek, c., music
muziekgezelschap, mEE-zeek-HGer-zel-sHGap,
    n., musical society
muziekleraar, mEE-zeek-lay-rahr, c., music- [master
muzikaal, mEE-zee-kahl, a., musical
muzikant, mEE-zee-kant, c., musician
mysterieus, mees-tay-ree-erss, a., mysterious
mystiek, mis-teek, a. & adv., mystic. c., mysticism

na, nah, prep.; after. adv., near. —— **elkaar,** ——
    el-kahr, one after the other
naad, naht, c., seam; suture (of a wound)
naaf, nahf, c., nave
naaidoos, nah'ee-dohss, c., sewing-box
naaien, nah-yer, v., to sew, to do needlework
naaigaren, nah'ee-HGah-rer, n., sewing-thread
naaimachine, nah'ee-mah-shee-ner, c., sewing-
    machine
naaister, nah'ee-ster, c., needlewoman
naakt, nahkt, a., naked, bare, nude
naald, nahlt, c., needle
naam, nahm, c., name, reputation

naambord, nahm-bort, n., name-plate
naamdag, nahm-d*a*HG, c., saint's day, name-day
naamgenoot, nahm-HG*a*y-noht, c., namesake
naamkaartje, nahm-kahrt-yer, n., (visiting-) card
naamloos, nahm-lohss, a., nameless, anonymous
naamplaatje, nahm-plaht-yer, n., door-plate
naäpen, nah-ah-per, v., to imitate
naäperij, nah-ah-per-rey, c., aping, imitation
naar, nahr, a. & adv., unpleasant; horrible, nasty
naar, nahr, prep., to, for, at; according to; after
naarmate, nahr-mah-ter, prep., according as, as
naarstig, nahr-sterHG, a. & adv., industrious, diligent [beside
naast, nahst, a., nearest, next. prep., next (to),
naastbestaanden, nahst-ber-stahn-der, c. pl., next of kin
naaste, nahss-ter, c., neighbour, fellow-man
nabij, nah-bey, adv., close by, close to, near
nabijgelegen, nah-bey-HGer-lay-HGer, a., neighbouring
nabijheid, nah-bey-heyt, c., neighbourhood
nabootsen, nah-boht-ser, v., to imitate
naburig, nah-bEE-rerHG, a., near by, neighbouring
nacht, n*a*HGt, c., night. in de ——, in der ——, at night
nachtegaal, n*a*HG-ter-HGahl, c., nightingale
nachtelijk, n*a*HG-ter-luck, a., nocturnal
nachtmerrie, n*a*HGt-mayr-ree, c., nightmare
nachtvlinder, n*a*HGt-flin-der, c., night-moth
nadat, nah-d*a*t, conj., after
nadeel, nah-dayl, n., disadvantage, drawback; harm, hurt
nadelig, nah-day-lerHG, a., injurious, detrimental
nadenken (over), nah-den-ker (oh-ver), v., to think (about) [pensive
nadenkend, nah-den-kent, a. & adv., thoughtful,
nader, nah-der, a., nearer; further. adv., nearer
naderen, nah-der-rer, v., to approach, to draw
naderhand, nah-der-h*a*nt, adv., afterwards [near
nadering, nah-der-ring, c., approach
nadoen, nah-doon, v., to imitate

nadruk, nah-drerk, c., emphasis, stress; reprint.

—— **verboden,** —— fer-boh-der, copyright,
all rights reserved [emphatic

nadrukkelijk, nah-drerk-ker-luck, a. & adv.,

nagaan, nah-HGahn, v., to follow; to trace

nagedachtenis, nah-HGer-daHG-ter-niss, c.,

nagel, nah-HGerl, c., nail [memory

nagelborstel, nah-HGerl-bors-terl, c., nail-brush

nagellak, nah-HGerl-lak, n., nail varnish [feit

nagemaakt, nah-HGer-mahkt, p.p. & a., counter-

nagenoeg, nah-HGer-nooHG, adv., almost, all but

nagerecht, nah-HGer-reHGt, n., dessert

nageslacht, nah-HGer-slaHGt, n., posterity, issue

nagluren, nah-HGlEE-rer, v., to peep (peer) after

naïef, nah-eef, a. & adv., naïve, ingenuous

naijver, nah-ey-ver, c., emulation; envy

naijverig, nah-ey-ver-rerHG, a., emulous; envious

najaar, nah-yahr, n., autumn

najagen, nah-yah-HGer, v., to chase, to pursue

najouwen, nah-yow-er, v., to hoot after

nakijken, nah-key-ker, v., to look after; to look
over (lessons); to revise (proofs); to correct
(exercises); to overhaul (cars, etc.)

nakomeling, nah-koh-mer-ling, c., descendant

nakomen, nah-koh-mer, v., to follow; to fulfil

nalaten, nah-lah-ter, v., to leave (behind); to
omit; to fail; to leave off; to neglect (one's
duties) [inheritance

nalatenschap, nah-lah-ten-sHGap, c., estate;

nalatig, nah-lah-terHG, a., negligent, careless

naleven, nah-lay-ver, v., to live up to; to observe

nalopen, nah-loh-per, v., to follow, to run after

namaak, nah-mahk, c., imitation, counterfeit

namaken, nah-mah-ker, v., to imitate, to counterfeit

namelijk, nah-mer-luck, adv., namely, viz.

namens, nah-mens, adv., in the name of

namiddag, nah-mid-daHG, c., afternoon

naoorlogs, nah-ohr-loHGss, a., post-war

napraten, nah-prah-ter, v., to repeat the words of

nar, nar, c., fool, jester

narcis, nar-siss, c., daffodil, narcissus

narcose, nar-koh-zer, c., narcosis [reckon up

narekenen, nah-ray-ker-ner, v., to verify; to

narennen, nah-ren-ner, v., to run after

narigheid, nah-rerHG-heyt, c., misery [(at)

naroepen, nah-roo-per, v., to call after; to hoot

naschrift, nah-srift, n., postscript [plagiarize

naschrijven, nah-srey-ver, v., to copy, to

naslagwerk, nah-slaHG-vayrk, n., book of refer-

nasleep, nah-slayp, c., aftermath [ence

nasmaak, nah-smahk, c., after-taste [to search

nasnuffelen, nah-snerf-fer-ler, v., to rummage;

naspel, nah-spel, n., afterpiece; (fig.) sequel

naspeuren, nah-sper-rer, v., to trace, to investi-

gate [tracing

nasporing, nah-spoh-ring, c., investigation,

nastaren, nah-stah-rer, v., to stare after, to eye

nastreven, nah-stray-ver, v., to pursue, to strive

nat, nat, a., wet; damp; moist [after

natie, nah-see, c., nation

naturaliseren, nah-tEE-rah-lee-zay-rer, v., to

naturalize

natuur, nah-tEEr, c., nature; disposition; scenery

natuurgetrouw, nah-tEEr-HGer-trow, a., true to

nature

natuurkunde, nah-tEEr-kern-der, c., physics

natuurkundige, nah-tEEr-kern-der-HGer, c.,

physicist [course

natuurlijk, nah-tEEr-luck, a., natural. adv., of

natuurvorser, nah-tEEr-for-ser, c., naturalist

nauw, now, n., straits. a. & adv., narrow; tight;

(fig.) close

nauwelijks, now-er-lucks, adv., scarcely

nauwgezet, now-HGer-zet, a. & adv., conscienti-

ous; punctual [exact

nauwkeurig, now-ker-rerHG, a. & adv., accurate,

navolgen, nah-fol-HGer, v., to follow, to imitate

navorsen, nah-for-ser, v., to investigate

navraag, nah-frahHG, c., inquiry; demand

nazeggen, nah-zeHG-er, v., to repeat

nazien, nah-zeen, v., see nakijken

nécessaire, ney-sess-sayr, c., dressing-case

neder, neer, nay-der, nayr, adv., down

ne(d)erbuigen, nayr-bow-HG**er,** v., to bend down
ne(d)erdalen, nayr-dah-ler, v., to come down
nederig, nay-der-rerHG**,** a. & adv., humble, modest
ne(d)erknielen, nayr-k'nee-ler, v., to kneel down
nederlaag, nay-der-lahHG**,** c., defeat; overthrow
ne(d)erlaten, nayr-lah-ter, v., to lower; to drop
ne(d)erwerpen, nayr-vayr-per, v., to throw down
ne(d)erzetten, nayr-zet-ter, v., to put down
nederzetting, nay-der-zet-ting, c., settlement
neef, nayf, c., nephew; cousin
neen, nayn, adv., no. —— **maar!** —— **mahr,**
well I never!

neergooien, nayr-HG**oh-yer,** v., to throw down
neerhurken, nayr-herr-ker, v., to squat down
neerleggen, nayr-leHG**-er,** v., to lay down; to
neerliggen, nayr-liHG**-er,** v., to lie down [resign
neerschieten, nayr-sHG**ee-ter,** v., to shoot down
neerslaan, nayr-slahn, v., to strike down
neerslachtig, nayr-sl*a***HG-ter**HG**,** a., down-hearted
neerslag, nayr-sl*a***HG,** c., precipitation [crash
neerstorten, nayr-stor-ter, v., to fall down; to
neervellen, nayr-fel-ler, v., to strike down; to fell
negatief, nay-HG**ah-teef,** n., negative. a. & adv.,
negen, nay-HG**er,** a., nine [negative
negende, nay-HG**en-der,** a., ninth
negentien, nay-HG**en-teen,** a., nineteen
negentiende, nay-HG**en-teen-der,** a., nineteenth
negentig, nay-HG**en-ter**HG**,** a., ninety
neger, nay-HG**er,** c., negro
negeren, nay-HG**er-rer,** v., to bully
negeren, ner-HG**ay-rer,** v., to ignore
négligé, ney-glee-zhey, n., morning dress
neigen, ney-HG**en,** v., to bend, to bow, to incline
neiging, ney-HG**ing,** c., inclination, tendency
nek, neck, c., nape of the neck
nemen, nay-mer, v., to take, to accept; (mil.) to
nerf, nayrf, c., nerve; rib; vein [capture
nergens, nayr-HG**ens,** adv., nowhere
nerveus, nayr-verss, a. & adv., nervous, nervy
nest, nest, n., nest; litter
nestelen, ness-ter-ler, v., to nest
net, net, n., net; string bag; network, system

net, net, n., fair copy. a. & adv., tidy, clean; neat, smart; decent

neteldoek, nay-terl-dook, n., muslin

netelig, nay-ter-lerHG, a., thorny, ticklish

netheid, net-heyt, c., neatness; cleanness

netjes, net-yess, adv., neatly; properly; nicely

netschrift, net-srift, n., fair copy

netto, net-toh, adv., net (weight, proceeds, cash)

neuriën, ner-ree-er, v., to hum

neus, nerss, c., nose; toe-cap; nozzle

neusbloeding, nerss-bloo-ding, c., bleeding from [the nose

neusgat, nerss-HGɑt, n., nostril

neushoorn, nerss-hoh-rern, c., rhinoceros

neusklank, nerss-klank, c., nasal sound

neutraal, ner-trahl, a., neutral; secular (school)

nevel, nay-verl, c., haze, mist, fog [foggy

nevelachtig, nay-verl-ɑHG-terHG, a., hazy, misty,

nevengeschikt, nay-ver-HGer-sHGikt, a., co-ordinate [ordinate

nicht, niHGt, c., niece; cousin

nIemand, nee-mant, pron., nobody, no one, none

niemendal, nee-men-dɑl, adv., nothing at all

nier, neer, c., kidney

nierziekte, neer-zeek-ter, c., renal disease

niet, neet, adv., not. n., nothing, nought. **om ——,** om ——, gratis

nietig, nee-terHG, a., null and void; paltry

nietigheid, nee-terHG-heyt, c., insignificance; [nullity

niets, neets, pron., nothing

nietswaardig, neets-vahr-derHG, a., worthless

nietszeggend, neets-zeHG-ent, a., meaningless

niettegenstaande, neet-tay-HGen-stahn-der, prep., notwithstanding. conj., (al)though

niettemin, neet-ter-min, adv., nevertheless

nieuw, nee'oo, a., new; fresh; recent; modern

nieuweling, nee-ver-ling, c., new-comer

nieuwerwets, nee-ver-vets, a., new-fashioned

nieuwigheid, nee-verHG-heyt, c., novelty

nieuwjaar, nee'oo-yahr, n., New Year

nieuws, nee'ooss, n., news, tidings; novelty

nieuwsbericht, nee'ooss-ber-riHGt, n., news report [curious

nieuwsgierig, nee'ooss-HGee-rerHG, a. & adv.,

nieuwtje, nee′oot-yer, n., piece of news; novelty
niezen, nee-zer, v., to sneeze
nijd, neyt, c., envy
nijdig, ney-derHG, a. & adv., angry, cross
nijdigheid, ney-derHG-heyt, c., anger
nijging, ney-HGing, c., bow, curtsy
nijlpaard, neyl-pahrt, n., hippopotamus
nijpen, ney-per, v., to pinch, to nip
nijpend, ney-pent, a., nipping; biting; acute
nijptang, neyp-tang, c., pincers
nijverheid, ney-ver-heyt, c., industry
niks, nicks, pron., (pop.) nothing
nimf, nimf, c., nymph
nimmer, nim-mer, adv., never
nis, niss, c., niche; alcove; recess (in a wall)
niveau, nee-voh, n., level
nobel, noh-berl, a. & adv., noble (-minded)
noch . . . noch, noHG, conj., neither . . . nor
nochtans, noHG-tanss, conj., nevertheless
nodeloos, noh-der-lohss, a. & adv., needless
nodig, noh-derHG, a. & adv., necessary, needful.
—— **hebben,** —— **heb-ber,** to be in need of
noemen, noo-mer, v., to name, to call; to mention
nog, noHG, adv., yet, still; further, besides
nogal, noHG-al, adv., rather, fairly
nogmaals, noHG-mahls, adv., once more
nok, nock, c., ridge (of a roof)
non, non, c., nun
nonchalant, non-shah-lant, a. & adv., careless
nonnenklooster, non-nen-klohss-ter, n., nunnery
nood, noht, c., necessity, need, want
noodbrug, noht-brerHG, c., temporary bridge
noodhulp, noht-herlp, c., temporary help
noodkreet, noht-krayt, c., cry of distress
noodlanding, noht-lan-ding, c., forced landing
noodlijdend, noht-ley-dent, a., necessitous
noodlot, noht-lot, n., destiny
noodlottig, noht-lot-terHG, a. & adv., fatal
noodmaatregel, noht-maht-ray-HGerl, c., emergency measure
noodrantsoen, noht-rant-soon, n., (mil.) iron
noodrem, noht-rem, c., safety-brake   [ration

noodsein, noht-seyn, n., distress-signal, SOS
noodtoestand, noht-too-stant, c., state of emergency   [exit
nooduitgang, noht-owt-HGang, c., emergency
noodverband, noht-fer-bant, n., first dressing
noodweer, noht-vayr, n., heavy weather
noodwoning, noht-voh-ning, c., emergency dwel-
noodzaak, noht-sahk, c., necessity   [ling
noodzakelijk, noht-sah-ker-luck, a. & adv.,
          necessary
noodzaken, noht-sah-ker, v., to compel
nooit, noh-it, adv., never
noordelijk, nohr-der-luck, a., northern
noorden, nohr-der, n., north
noorderling, nohr-der-ling, c., northerner
noordoostelijk, nohr-oh-ster-luck, a., north-
noordpool, nohrt-pohl, c., north pole   [easterly
noordpoolreiziger, nohrt-pohl-rey-zer-HGer, c.,
          arctic explorer
noordster, nohrt-stayr, c., polar star   [westerly
noordwestelijk, nohrt-vess-ter-luck, a., north-
noot, noht, c., note; (mus.) note; nut, walnut
nootmuskaat, noht-merss-kaht, c., nutmeg
nopen, noh-per, v., to induce
norm, norm, c., standard, rule
nors, norss, a. & adv., surly, grumpy
nota, noh-tah, c., account, bill
notabelen, noh-tah-berl-er, c. pl., notabilities
notaris, noh-tah-riss, c., notary (public)
noteboom, noh-ter-bohm, c., walnut-tree
notedop, noh-ter-dop, c., nutshell
notenkraker, noh-ter-krah-ker, c., nut-crackers
notie, noh-see, c., notion
notitie, noh-tee-see, c., note; notice
november, noh-vem-berr, c., November
nou, nu, now, NEE, adv., now. **nu en dan, NEE en**
          dan, now and then
nuchter, nerHG-ter, a., sober
nuchterheid, nerHG-ter-heyt, c., soberness
nuffig, nerf-ferHG, a., prudish, prim
nuk, nerk, c., freak, whim
nukkig, nerk-kerHG, a., freakish, whimsical

nul, nerl, c., nought, zero   [gram]; size
nummer, nerm-mer, n., number; item (of pro-
nummerplaat, nerm-mer-plaht, c., number-
    plate
nummerschijf, nerm-mer-sHGeyf, c., dial (of
nurks, nerrkss, a., peevish, gruff   [telephone]
nut, nert, n., use, benefit, utility
nutteloos, nert-ter-lohss, a. & adv., useless
nuttig, nert-terHG, a. & adv., useful   [(a meal)
nuttigen, nert-terHG-er, v., to take, to partake of
nuttiging, nert-terHG-ing, c., consumption;
    Communion

oase, oh-ah-zer, c., oasis
obligatie, oh-blee-HGah-see, c., debenture, bond
och!, oHG, interj., oh! ah!
ochtend, oHG-tent, c., morning
ochtendblad, oHG-tent-blat, n., morning paper
october, ock-toh-ber, c., October
octrooi, ock-troh'ee, n., patent; charter
oefenen, oo-fer-ner, v., to practise, to train
oefening, oo-fer-ning, c., practice; prayer-meeting
oefenwedstrijd, oo-fen-vet-streyt, c., practice
oerwoud, oor-vowt, n., virgin forest   [match
oester, ooss-ter, c., oyster
oesterkwekerij, ooss-ter-kvay-ker-rey, c., oyster-
oever, oo-ver, c., shore; bank   [farm
of, of, conj., or; if, whether. of . . . of, either . . .
    or; whether . . . or
offer, of-fer, n., offering, sacrifice; victim
offeren, of-fer-rer, v., to sacrifice, to offer up
officieel, of-fee-see-el, a. & adv., official
officier, of-fee-seer, c., officer
officieus, of-fee-see-erss, a. & adv., semi-official
ofschoon, of-sHGohn, conj., (al)though
ogenblik, oh-HGer-blick, n., moment, instant
ogenblikkelijk, oh-HGer-blick-ker-luck, a. &
oksel, ock-serl, c., armpit   [adv., immediate
olie, oh-lee, c., oil
olienootje, oh-lee-noht-yer, n., pea-nut
olieverf, oh-lee-fayrf, c., oil-paint
olifant, oh-lee-fant, c., elephant

olijfboom, oh-**leyf**-bohm, c., olive-tree
olijfolie, oh-**leyf**-oh-lee, c., olive-oil
olijk, oh-**luck**, a. & adv., sly, roguish
olmboom, **olm**-bohm, c., elm
om, om, prep., round, about; at; for; in order to
oma, oh-**mah**, c., grandmother, granny
omarmen, om-**ar**-mer, v., to embrace
omblazen, om-**blah**-zer, v., to blow down
ombrengen, om-**breng**-er, v., to kill
ombuigen, om-**bow**-HGer, v., to bend
omdat, om-**dat**, conj., because, as, since
omdraaien, om-**drah**-yer, v., to turn round; to twist
omgaan, om-**HGahn**, v., to go about; to pass; to take place. —— **met**, — met, to associate with; to handle
omgang, om-**HGang**, c., social intercourse; cession
omgangstaal, om-**HGangs**-tahl, c., colloquial language
omgekeerd, om-**HGer**-kayrt, a., turned upside down; reversed
omgeving, om-**HGay**-ving, c., surroundings
omgooien, om-**HGoh**-yer, v., to upset; to throw on
omhaal, om-**hahl**, c., fuss, ceremony
omhakken, om-**hak**-ker, v., to cut down
omheen, om-**hayn**, adv., round about
omheining, om-**hey**-ning, c., enclosure, fence
omhelzen, om-**hel**-zer, v., to embrace
omhoog, om-**hohHG**, adv., aloft; up(wards)
omhooggooien, om-**hohHG**-HGoh-yer, v., to throw up
omhoogheffen, om-**hohHG**-hef-fer, v., to raise
omhoogtrekken, om-**hohHG**-treck-ker, v., to pull up
omhulsel, om-**herl**-serl, n., wrapper, cover
omkantelen, om-**kan**-ter-ler, v., to topple over
omkeer, om-**kayr**, c., change; revolution; turn
omkeren, om-**kay**-rer, v., to turn (up, over, upside down) round
omkijken, om-**key**-ker, v., to look back, to look
omkleden (**zich**), om-**klay**-der (ziHG), v., to change (one's clothes)
omkomen, om-**koh**-mer, v., to perish; to finish
omkopen, om-**koh**-per, v., to bribe, to corrupt

omkoperij, om-koh-per-rey, c., bribery, corruption [below

omlaag, om-lahHG, adv., below, down, down

omliggend, om-liHG-ent, a., neighbouring

omlijsting, om-leys-ting, c., frame; framing

omloop, om-lohp, c., circulation; revolution (of the earth)

ommezijde, om-mer-zey-der, c., back. zie ——, zee ——, please turn over

omploegen, om-ploo-HGer, v., to plough

ompraten, om-prah-ter, v., to talk over

omringen, om-ring-er, v., to surround, to enclose

omroep, om-roop, c., broadcast(ing) [crier

omroeper, om-roo-per, c., announcer; (town)

omroepstation, om-roop-stah-see'on, c., broadcasting station

omroeren, om-roo-rer, v., to stir (tea, etc.)

omruilen, om-row-ler, v., to exchange [over

omschakelen, om-sHGah-ker-ler, v., to change

omschoppen, om-sHGop-per, v., to kick down

omschrijving, om-srey-ving, c., definition

omsingelen, om-sing-er-ler, v., to encircle

omslaan, om-slahn, v., to knock down; to turn over; to turn up

omslachtig, om-slaHG-terHG, a., long-winded

omslag, om-slaHG, c., cuff; turn-up; wrapper

omslagdoek, om-slaHG-dook, c., shawl, wrap

omsmijten, om-smey-ter, v., to knock down

omspitten, om-spit-ter, v., to dig (up)

omstander, om-stan-der, c., bystander [in detail

omstandig, om-stan-derHG, a., detailed. adv.,

omstandigheid, om-stan-derHG-heyt, c., circumstance [over

omstreeks, om-straykss, adv., about [cumstance

omstrengelen, om-streng-er-ler, v., to enlace, to entwine [neighbourhood

omtrek, om-treck, c., outline; circumference;

omtrent, om-trent, prep., about, concerning

omvallen, om-fal-ler, v., to fall over; to (be) upset

omvang, om-fang, c., circumference; extent

omvangrijk, om-fang-reyk, a., extensive, bulky

omvatten, om-fat-ter, v., to enclose; to comprise

omver, om-fayr, adv., down, over

omverduwen, om-fayr-dee-ver, v., to push over

omverwerpen, om-fayr-vayr-per, v., to upset; to overthrow

omvormen, om-for-mer, v., to remodel, to [transform

omwassen, om-vas-ser, v., to wash up

omweg, om-vehg, c., roundabout way, circuit

omwenden, om-ven-der, v., to turn

omwenteling, om-ven-ter-ling, c., revolution, rotation, turn [write; to dig up

omwerken, om-vayr-ker, v., to remodel; to re-

omwikkelen, om-vick-ker-ler, v., to wrap up

omwisselen, om-vis-ser-ler, v., to change, to exchange

omzagen, om-zah-HGer, v., to saw down

omzet, om-zet, c., turnover; sale [over tax

omzetbelasting, om-zet-ber-last-ing, c., turn-

omzichtig, om-ziHG-terHG, a. & adv., cautious

omzien, om-zeen, v., to look back [border

omzomen, om-zoh-mer, v., to hem; (fig.) to

onaangemeld, on-ahn-HGer-melt, a., unan-nounced [disagreeable

onaangenaam, on-ahn-HGer-nahm, a. & adv.,

onaannemelijk, on-ahn-nay-mer-luck, a., un-acceptable [adv., unattractive

onaantrekkelijk, on-ahn-treck-ker-luck, a. &

onaanzienlijk, on-ahn-zeen-luck, a., inconsider-able

onaardig, on-ahr-derHG, a. & adv., unpleasant

onachtzaam, on-aHGt-sahm, a. & adv., inatten-tive [continuous

onafgebroken, on-af-HGer-broh-ker, a. & adv.,

onafhankelijk, on-af-han-ker-luck, a. & adv., independent [independence

onafhankelijkheid, on-af-han-ker-luck-heyt, c.,

onafscheidelijk, on-af-sHGey-der-luck, a. & adv., inseparable [unselfish

onbaatzuchtig, on-baht-serHG-terHG, a. & adv.,

onbarmhartig, on-barm-har-terHG, a. & adv., merciless

onbeantwoord, on-ber-ant-vohrt, a., unanswered

onbebouwd, on-ber-bowt, a., waste (ground)

onbedorven, on-ber-dor-ver, a., unspoiled; sound

onbedreven, on-ber-**dray**-ver, a., inexperienced

onbeduidend, on-ber-**dow**-dent, a., insignificant

onbedwingbaar, on-ber-**dving**-bahr, a., indomitable [passable

onbegaanbaar, on-ber-**HGaahn**-bahr, a., im-

onbegrensd, on-ber-**HGrenst**, a., unlimited

onbegrijpelijk, on-ber-**HGrey**-per-luck, a., incomprehensible

onbehaaglijk, on-ber-**hahHG**-luck, a., unpleasant

onbeheerd, on-ber-**hayrt**, a., ownerless; vacant

onbeholpen, on-ber-**hol**-per, a. & adv., clumsy

onbehoorlijk, on-ber-**hohr**-luck, a. & adv., unbecoming

onbekend, on-ber-**kent**, a., unknown [from care

onbekommerd, on-ber-**kom**-mert, a. & adv., free

onbekwaam, on-ber-**k'vahm**, a., incapable

onbelangrijk, on-ber-**lang**-reyk, a., unimportant

onbeleefd, on-ber-**layft**, a. & adv., impolite

onbelemmerd, on-ber-**lem**-mert, a., unhindered

onbemerkt, on-ber-**mayrkt**, a. & adv., unnoticed

onbemiddeld, on-ber-**mid**-delt, a., without means

onbemind, on-ber-**mint**, a., unloved

onbenullig, on-ber-**nerl**-lerHG, a., inane

onbepaald, on-ber-**pahlt**, a., indefinite, uncertain

onbeperkt, on-ber-**payrkt**, a. & adv., unrestrained

onberaden, on-ber-**rah**-der, a. & adv., inconsiderate

onbereikbaar, on-ber-**reyk**-bahr, a., unreachable

onberekenbaar, on-ber-**ray**-ken-bahr, a., incalculable [blameless

onberispelijk, on-ber-**riss**-per-luck, a. & adv.,

onbeschaafd, on-ber-**sHGahft**, a., ill-bred; uncivilized [pudent

onbeschaamd, on-ber-**sHGahmt**, a. & adv., im-

onbeschaamdheid, on-ber-**sHGahmt**-heyt, c., impudence [damaged

onbeschadigd, on-ber-**sHGah**-derHGt, a., un-

onbescheiden, on-ber-**sHGey**-der, a. & adv., immodest, indiscreet

onbeschoft, on-ber-**sHGoft**, a. & adv., impertinent

onbeschrijfelijk, on-ber-**srey**-fer-luck, a., indescribable

onbeschroomd, on-ber-srohmt, a. & adv., fear-
onbeslist, on-ber-slist, a., undecided [less
onbesuisd, on-ber-sowst, a. & adv., rash, reckless
onbetaalbaar, on-ber-tahl-bahr, a., unpayable
onbetamelijk, on-ber-tah-mer-luck, a. & adv.,
unbecoming
onbetrouwbaar, on-ber-trow-bahr, a., unreliable
onbevaarbaar, on-ber-fahr-bahr, a., innavigable
onbevangen, on-ber-fang-er, a., unconcerned
onbevlekt, on-ber-fleckt, a., unstained; immaculate [patent
onbevoegd, on-ber-fooHGt, a. & adv., incom-
onbevooroordeeld, on-ber-fohr-**ohr**-daylt, a.,
unprejudiced
onbevredigd, on-ber-fray-derHGt, a., unsatisfied
onbevreesd, on-ber-frayst, a. & adv., fearless
onbewaakt, on-ber-vahkt, a., unguarded
onbeweeglijk, on-ber-vayHG-luck, a. & adv.,
motionless
onbewimpeld, on-ber-vim-perlt, a. & adv., frank
onbewogen, on-ber-voh-HGer, a., untouched
onbewolkt, on-ber-volkt, a., cloudless [unmoved
onbewoonbaar, on-ber-**vohn**-bahr, a., uninhabitable
onbewoond, on-ber-vohnt, a., uninhabited
onbezet, on-ber-zet, a., unoccupied; vacant (post)
onbezonnen, on-ber-zon-ner, a. & adv., rash
onbezorgd, on-ber-zorHGt, a. & adv., free from
onbillijk, on-**bil**-luck, a. & adv., unjust [care
onblusbaar, on-blerss-bahr, a., inextinguishable
onbrandbaar, on-**brant**-bahr, a., incombustible
onbreekbaar, on-brayk-bahr, a., unbreakable
onbruik, on-browk, n., disuse
onbruikbaar, on-**browk**-bahr, a., useless
onbuigzaam, on-bowHG-sahm, a., inflexible
ondank, on-d**a**nk, c., ingratitude
ondankbaar, on-d**a**nk-bahr, a. & adv., ungrateful
ondanks, on-d**a**nks, prep., in spite of
ondeelbaar, on-dayl-bahr, a., indivisible
ondenkbaar, on-**denk**-bahr, a., unthinkable
onder, on-der, prep., under; during; among, adv.,
below. —— **ons**, —— ons, between ourselves

onderaan, on-der-ahn, prep., at the foot of

onderaards, on-der-ahrtss, a., subterranean

onderafdeling, on-der-*af*-day-ling, c., sub-division [adv., subconscious

onderbewustzijn, on-der-ber-verst-seyn, a. &

onderbreken, on-der-bray-ker, v., to interrupt

onderbrengen, on-der-breng-er, v., to shelter

onderbroek, on-der-brook, c., pants; drawers

onderdaan, on-der-dahn, c., subject

onderdak, on-der-dak, n., shelter, home

onderdanig, on-der-dah-nerHG, a. & adv., sub-missive [unit

onderdeel, on-der-dayl, n., lower part; (army)

onderdompelen, on-der-dom-per-ler, v., to immerse [to suppress; to stifle

onderdrukken, on-der-drerk-ker, v., to oppress;

onderduiken, on-der-dow-ker, v., to dive; to hide oneself [sun) to perish

ondergaan, on-der-HGahn, v., to sink; to set (of

ondergaan, on-der-HGahn, v., to undergo

ondergang, on-der-HGang, c., setting (of sun); ruin [dinate

ondergeschikt, on-der-HGer-sHGikt, a., subor-

ondergetekende, on-der-HGer-tay-ken-der, c., undersigned

ondergoed, on-der-HGoot, n., underwear

ondergronds, on-der-HGronts, a., underground.
—— **e spoorweg**, —— **-er** spohr-veHG, c., underground railway [negotiate

onderhandelen, on-der-han-der-ler, v., to

onderhevig (aan), on-der-hay-verHG (ahn), a., subject (to) [versation

onderhoud, on-der-howt, n., maintenance; con-

onderhoudend, on-der-how-dent, a., amusing

onderin, on-der-in, adv. & prep., at the bottom (of)

onderkant, on-der-kant, c., bottom

onderkomen, on-der-koh-mer, n., shelter

onderlijf, on-der-leyf, n., abdomen, belly

onderlijfje, on-der-leyf-yer, n., under-bodice

onderling, on-der-ling, a. & adv., mutual

onderlip, on-der-lip, c., lower lip

onderlopen, on-der-loh-per, v., to get flooded

ondermijnen, on-der-**mey**-ner, v., to undermine, to sap   [undertake

ondernemen, on-der-**nay**-mer, v., to attempt, to

ondernemend, on-der-**nay**-ment, a., enterprising

ondernemer, on-der-**nay**-mer, c., undertaker; owner   [missioned officer

onderofficier, on-der-of-fee-**seer**, c., non-com-

onderpand, on-der-**pant**, n., pledge, guarantee

onderricht, on-der-**riHGt**, n., instruction, tuition

onderrok, on-der-**rock**, c., underskirt; petticoat

onderschatten, on-der-**sHGat**-ter, v., to underrate

onderscheid, on-der-**sHGeyt**, n., difference

onderscheiden, on-der-**sHGey**-der, v., to distinguish   [tion; award

onderscheiding, on-der-**sHGey**-ding, c., distinc-

onderscheppen, on-der-**sHGep**-per, v., to intercept

onderschrift, on-der-**srift**, n., subscription

onderste, on-der-**ster**, a., lowest, undermost

ondersteboven, on-der-ster-boh-ver, adv., upside down

onderstel, on-der-**stel**, n., under-carriage

onderstelling, on-der-**stel**-ling, c., supposition

ondersteunen, on-der-**ster**-ner, v., to support

ondersteuning, on-der-**ster**-ning, c., support

onderstrepen, on-der-**stray**-per, v., to underline

ondertekenen, on-der-**tay**-ker-ner, v., to sign

ondertekening, on-der-**tay**-ker-ning, c., signature

ondertrouw, on-der-**trow**, c., notice of (intended) marriage

ondertussen, on-der-**ters**-ser, adv., meanwhile

onderverdeling, on-der-**fer**-day-ling, c., subdivision

ondervinden, on-der-**fin**-der, v., to experience

ondervinding, on-der-**fin**-ding, c., experience

ondervoeding, on-der-**foo**-ding, c., malnutrition

ondervoorzitter, on-der-**fohr**-zit-ter, c., deputychairman   [rogate

ondervragen, on-der-**frah**-HGer, v., to inter-

onderweg, on-der-**veHG**, adv., on the way

onderwereld, on-der-**vay**-rerlt, c., underworld

onderwerp, on-der-**vayrp**, n., subject, topic

onderwerpen, on-der-**vayr**-per, v., to subject

onderwijs, on-der-**veyss**, n., instruction; education [teach

onderwijzen, on-der-**vey**-zer, v., to instruct, to

onderwijzer, on-der-**vey**-zer, c., teacher, master

onderzeeër, on-der-**zay**-er, c., submarine

onderzoek, on-der-**zook**, n., inquiry, investigation

onderzoeken, on-der-**zoo**-ker, v., to inquire, to examine

ondeugd, on-derHGt, c., vice; mischief

ondeugend, on-der-HGent, a. & adv., naughty

ondiep, on-deep, a., shallow

ondier, on-deer, n., monster, brute

ondoenlijk, on-**doon**-luck, a., unfeasible

ondoordacht, on-dohr-daHGt, a., thoughtless

ondoordringbaar, on-dohr-**dring**-bahr, a., impenetrable [inscrutable

ondoorgrondelijk, on-dohr-HGron-der-luck, a.,

ondraaglijk, on-drah-HGer-luck, a. & adv., unbearable

ondrinkbaar, on-**drink**-bahr, a., undrinkable

ondubbelzinnig, on-derb-berl-**zin**-nerHG, a. & adv., unequivocal [distinct

onduidelijk, on-**dow**-der-luck, a. & adv., inonecht, on-eHGt, a., not genuine; false

oneer, on-ayr, c., dishonour, disgrace

oneerbiedig, on-ayr-**bee**-derHG, a. & adv., disrespectful

oneerlijk, on-ayr-luck, a. & adv., unfair

oneffen, on-**ef**-fer, a., uneven, rough, rugged

oneindig, on-**eyn**-derHG, a. & adv., endless

onenigheid, on-ay-nerHG-heyt, c., discord

onervaren, on-ayr-**vah**-rer, a., inexperienced

oneven, on-**ay**-ver, a., odd (number)

onevenwichtig, on-ay-ven-**viHG**-terHG, a., unbalanced [indecent

onfatsoenlijk, on-**fat**-soon-luck, a. & adv.,

onfeilbaar, on-**feyl**-bahr, a. & adv., infallible

onfortuinlijk, on-for-**town**-luck, a., unlucky

ongaarne, on-**HGahr**-ner, adv., reluctant

ongastvrij, on-**HGast**-frey, a., inhospitable

ongeacht, on-**HGer**-aHGt, prep., irrespective of

ongebaand, on-HGer-**bahnt,** a., unbeaten (road), untrodden   [(fig.) licentious

ongebonden, on-HGer-**bon-der,** a., unbound;

ongebruikt, on-HGer-**browkt,** a., unused, idle

ongedeerd, on-HGer-**dayrt,** a., uninjured

ongedierte, on-HGer-**deer-ter,** n., vermin

ongeduldig, on-HGer-**derl-derHG,** a. & adv., impatient   [strained

ongedwongen, on-HGer-**dvon-HGer,** a., unre-

ongeëvenaard, on-HGer-**ay-ver-nahrt,** a., unequalled   [prepaid

ongefrankeerd, on-HGer-**fran-kayrt,** a., not

ongegrond, on-HGer-**HGront,** a., unfounded

ongehinderd, on-HGer-**hin-dert,** a., unhindered

ongehoord, on-HGer-**hohrt,** a., unheard of

ongehoorzaam, on-HGer-**hohr-zahm,** a. & adv., disobedient   [c., disobedience

ongehoorzaamheid, on-HGer-**hohr-zahm-heyt,**

ongehuwd, on-HGer-**hEEt,** a., unmarried

ongekleed, on-HGer-**klayt,** a., undressed   [artless

ongekunsteld, on-HGer-**kern-stelt,** a. & adv.,

ongeldig, on-HGel-**derHG,** a., invalid; void

ongelegen, on-HGer-**lay-HGer,** a. & adv., inconvenient

ongelijk, on-HGer-**leyk,** a., unequal, different.
          ——— hebben, ——— heb-ber, to be wrong

ongelijkheid, on-HGer-**leyk-heyt,** c., inequality

ongelofelijk, on-HGer-**loh-fer-luck,** a. & adv., incredible

ongelovige, on-HGer-**loh-ver-HGer,** c., unbeliever

ongeluk, on-HGer-**lerk,** n., misfortune; unhappiness; mishap   [happy, unlucky

ongelukkig, on-HGer-**lerk-kerHG,** a. & adv., un-

ongemak, on-HGer-**mak,** n., inconvenience

ongemakkelijk, on-HGer-**mak-ker-luck,** a. & adv., difficult   [nerly

ongemanierd, on-HGer-**mah-neert,** a., unman-

ongemerkt, on-HGer-**mayrkt,** a. & adv., imperceptible

ongemoeid, on-HGer-**moo'it,** a., undisturbed

ongenaakbaar, on-HGer-**nahk-bahr,** a., unapproachable

ongenade, on-HGer-nah-der, c., disgrace

ongenadig, on-HGer-nah-derHG, a. & adv., merciless

ongeneeslijk, on-HGer-**nay**-ser-luck, a., incurable

ongenegen, on-HGer-nay-HGer, a., unwilling

ongenoegen, on-HGer-noo-HGer, n., displeasure

ongenood, on-HGer-noht, a., uninvited

ongeoorloofd, on-HGer-ohr-lohft, a., unlawful

ongepast, on-HGer-**past**, a. & adv., improper

ongeregeld, on-HGer-ray-HGerlt, a. & adv., irregular [c. pl., riots

ongeregeldheden, on-HGer-ray-HGerlt-hay-der, irregular

ongerept, on-HGer-rept, a., intact; (fig.) pure

ongeriefelijk, on-HGer-ree-fer-luck, a., inconvenient [absurd

ongerijmd, on-HGer-reymt, a., preposterous,

ongerust, on-HGer-rerst, a., uneasy, worried

ongerustheid, on-HGer-rerst-heyt, c., uneasiness

ongeschikt, on-HGer-sHGikt, a., unfit, unsuited, inapt [ated

ongeschonden, on-HGer-sHGon-der, a., unviol-

ongeschoold, on-HGer-sHGohlt, a., untrained

ongesteld, on-HGer-stelt, a., unwell, indisposed

ongestoord, on-HGer-stohrt, a. & adv., undisturbed [with impunity

ongestraft, on-HGer-**straft**, a., unpunished. adv.,

ongetwijfeld, on-HGer-tvey-ferlt, adv., undoubtedly

ongevaarlijk, on-HGer-vahr-luck, a., harmless

ongeval, on-HGer-val, n., mishap, accident

ongeveer, on-HGer-vayr, adv., about, nearly

ongeveinsd, on-HGer-veynst, a. & adv., unfeigned, sincere [feeling

ongevoelig, on-HGer-voo-lerHG, a. & adv., un-

ongewapend, on-HGer-vah-pent, a., unarmed

ongewoon, on-HGer-vohn, a., unusual, uncommon

ongezellig, on-HGer-zel-lerHG, a., unsociable

ongezond, on-HGer-zont, a., unhealthy

ongezouten, on-HGer-zow-ter, a., unsalted, fresh

ongodsdienstig, on-HGots-deen-sterHG, a. & adv., irreligious [able

ongunstig, on-HGern-sterHG, a. & adv., unfavour-

onguur, on-HGEEr, a., rough, inclement (weather)
onhandelbaar, on-hɑn-derl-bahr, a., intractable
onhandig, on-hɑn-derHG, a. & adv., clumsy
onhebbelijk, on-heb-ber-luck, a., unmannerly
onheil, on-heyl, n., disaster, calamity
onheilspellend, on-heyl-spel-lent, a., ominous
onherbergzaam, on-hayr-bayrHG-sahm, a., in-hospitable [nizable
onherkenbaar, on-hayr-ken-bahr, a., unrecog-
onherroepelijk, on-hayr-roo-per-luck, a. & adv., irrevocable
onherstelbaar, on-hayr-stel-bahr, a., irreparable
onheuglijk, on-herHG-luck, a., immemorial
onheus, on-herss, a. & adv., ungracious, unkind
onhoudbaar, on-howt-bahr, a., untenable
onjuist, on-yowst, a. & adv., incorrect
onkies, on-keess, a. & adv., immodest, indelicate
onkosten, on-kos-ter, c. pl., charges, expenses
onkreukbaar, on-krerk-bahr, a., unimpeachable
onkruid, on-krowt, n., weeds
onkuis, on-kowss, a. & adv., impure
onkunde, on-kern-der, c., ignorance
onkwetsbaar, on-kvets-bahr, a., invulnerable
onlangs, on-lɑngs, adv., the other day
onleesbaar, on-lays-bahr, a. & adv., illegible
onlesbaar, on-less-bahr, a., unquenchable
onloochenbaar, on-loh-HGen-bahr, a., undeni- [able
onlusten, on-lerss-ter, c. pl., disturbances
onmacht, on-mɑHGt, c., impotence; fainting fit
onmatig, on-mah-terHG, a. & adv., immoderate
onmeetbaar, on-mayt-bahr, a., immeasurable
onmens, on-menss, n., monster, brute
onmenselijk, on-men-ser-luck, a. & adv., brutal
onmetelijk, on-may-ter-luck, a. & adv., immense
onmiddelijk, on-mid-der-luck, a. & adv., imme- [diate
onmin, on-min, c., discord, dissension
onmisbaar, on-miss-bahr, a., indispensable
onmogelijk, on-moh-HGer-luck, a., impossible. adv., not possibly
onmogelijkheid, on-moh-HGer-luck-heyt, c., impossibility
onmondig, on-mon-derHG, a., under age

onnadenkend, on-nah-**den**-kent, a. & adv., thoughtless [unnatural

onnatuurlijk, on-nah-**t**EEr-luck, a. & adv.,

onnauwkeurigheid, on-now-ker-rerHG-heyt, c., inaccuracy [able

onnoemelijk, on-**noo**-mer-luck, a., unmention-

onnodig, on-**noh**-derHG, a. & adv., unnecessary

onnozel, on-**noh**-zerl, a. & adv., silly [tible

onomkoopbaar, on-om-**kohp**-bahr, a., incorrup-

onomstotelijk, on-om-**stoh**-ter-luck, a., irrefutable [plain

onomwonden, on-om-**von**-der, a. & adv., frank,

onontbeerlijk, on-ont-**bayr**-luck, a., indispensable

onontwikkeld, on-ont-**vick**-kerlt, a., undeveloped

onooglijk, on-**oh**-HGer-luck, a., ungraceful

onophoudelijk, on-op-**how**-der-luck, a. & adv., incessant

onoplettend, on-op-**let**-tent, a. & adv., inattentive

onoplosbaar, on-op-**loss**-bahr, a., insoluble

onoprecht, on-op-**re**HGt, a. & adv., insincere

onopzettelijk, on-op-**set**-ter-luck, a. & adv., un-

onordelijk, on-**or**-der-luck, a., unruly [intentional

onoverkomelijk, on-oh-ver-**koh**-mer-luck, a., insurmountable [invincible

onoverwinnelijk, on-oh-ver-**vin**-ner-luck, a.,

onpartijdig, on-par-**tey**-derHG, a. & adv., impartial

onpasselijk, on-**pas**-ser-luck, a., indisposed

onplezierig, on-pler-**zee**-rerHG, a., unpleasant

onraad, on-raht, n., danger, trouble

onrecht, on-reHGt, n., injustice [unlawful

onrechtmatig, on-reHGt-**mah**-terHG, a. & adv.,

onrechtvaardig, on-reHGt-**fahr**-derHG, a. & adv., unjust [c., injustice

onrechtvaardigheid, on-reHGt-**fahr**-derHG-heyt,

onredelijk, on-**ray**-der-luck, a. & adv., unreasonable [adv., irregular

onregelmatig, on-ray-HGel-**mah**-terHG, a. &

onrein, on-reyn, a., impure, unclean

onrijp, on-reyp, a., unripe, immature

onroerend, on-**roo**-rent, a., immovable

onrust, on-rerst, c., unrest, commotion

onrustig, on-rerss-terHG, a. & adv., restless

onruststoker, on-rerst-stoh-ker, c., agitator

ons, onss, pron., us; our. n., ounce [coherent

onsamenhangend, on-sah-men-h**a**ng-ent, a., in-

onschadelijk, on-sHGah-der-luck, a., harmless

onschatbaar, on-sHG**a**t-bahr, a., invaluable

onschuld, on-sHGerlt, c., innocence

onschuldig, on-sHGerl-derHG, a. & adv., innocent; harmless

onsmakelijk, on-smah-ker-luck, a., unsavoury

onsterfelijk, on-stayr-fer-luck, a., immortal

onstoffelijk, on-stof-fer-luck, a., immaterial

onstuimig, on-stow-merHG, a. & adv., boisterous

onsympathiek, on-sim-pah-teek, a., uncongenial

ontaard, ont-ahrt, a., degenerate

ontberen, ont-bay-rer, v., to be in want of

ontbering, ont-bay-ring, c., privation, hardship

ontbieden, ont-bee-der, v., to send for

ontbijt, ont-beyt, n., breakfast

ontbijten, ont-bey-ter, v., to breakfast

ontbinden, ont-bin-der, v., to untie; to disband

ontbrandbaar, ont-br**a**nt-bahr, a., inflammable

ontbreken, ont-bray-ker, v., to be missing

ontcijferen, ont-sey-fer-rer, v., to decipher

ontdaan, on-dahn, a., disconcerted

ontdekken, on-deck-ker, v., to discover

ontdekking, on-deck-king, c., discovery

ontduiken, on-dow-ker, v., to dodge; to elude

onteigenen, ont-ey-HGer-ner, v., to expropriate

ontelbaar, on-tel-bahr, a. & adv., innumerable

ontembaar, on-tem-bahr, a., indomitable

onteren, ont-ay-rer, v., to dishonour; to desecrate

onterven, ont-ayr-ver, v., to disinherit

ontevreden, on-ter-vray-der, a., discontented

ontfermen, ont-fayr-mer, zich —— over, ziHG
—— oh-ver, v., to take pity on

ontginnen, ont-HGin-ner, v., to reclaim (land); to
exploit [sionment

ontgoocheling, ont-HGoh-HGer-ling, c., disillu-

onthaal, ont-hahl, n., entertainment [(from)

ontheffen (van), ont-hef-fer (f**a**n), v., to free

onthelligen, ont-hey-ler-HGer, v., to profane
onthoofden, ont-hohf-der, v., to behead
onthouden, ont-how-der, v., to withhold
onthouding, ont-how-ding, c., abstinence; abstention
onthullen, ont-herl-ler, v., to unveil; to reveal
onthutst, ont-hertst, a., dismayed, upset
ontijdig, on-tey-derHG, a. & adv., untimely
ontkennen, ont-ken-ner, v., to deny
ontkiemen, ont-kee-mer, v., to germinate
ontknoping, ont-k'noh-ping, c., unravelling
ontkomen, ont-koh-mer, v., to escape
ontlasting, ont-lass-ting, c., discharge, relief
ontleden, ont-lay-der, v., to analyse; to dissect
ontlopen, ont-loh-per, v., to escape, to avoid
ontmaskeren, ont-mass-ker-rer, v., to unmask
ontmoedigen, ont-moo-der-HGer, v., to discourage
ontmoeten, ont-moo-ter, v., to meet (with)
ontnemen, ont-nay-mer, v., to deprive of
ontnuchteren, ont-nerHG-ter-rer, v., to sober
ontoegankelijk, on-too-HGan-ker-luck, a., inaccessible
ontoelaatbaar, on-too-laht-bahr, a., inadmissible
ontoereikend, on-too-rey-kent, a., insufficient
ontoerekenbaar, on-too-ray-ken-bahr, a., of unsound mind
ontoonbaar, on-tohn-bahr, a., not presentable
ontploffen, ont-plof-fer, v., to explode
ontploffing, ont-plof-fing, c., detonation, explosion
ontplooien, ont-ploh-yer, v., to unfurl [sion
ontraden, ont-rah-der, v., to dissuade
ontroeren, ont-roo-rer, v., to move, to affect
ontroering, ont-roo-ring, c., emotion
ontroostbaar, on-trohst-bahr, a., inconsolable
ontrouw, on-trow, a. & adv., unfaithful
ontruimen, ont-row-mer, v., to evacuate, to clear
ontschepen, ont-sHGay-per, v., to disembark
ontsieren, ont-see-rer, v., to deface
ontslaan, ont-slahn, v., to discharge
ontslag, ont-slaHG, n., discharge; resignation
ontsluiten, ont-slow-ter, v., to unlock; to open

ontsmetten, ont-smet-ter, v., to disinfect
ontsnappen, ont-snap-per, v., to escape
ontspannen, ont-span-ner, v., to unbend
ontspanning, ont-span-ning, c., relaxation
ontsporen, ont-spoh-rer, v., to be derailed
ontstaan, ont-stahn, v., to arise, to originate
ontsteken, ont-stay-ker, v., to light, to kindle
ontsteld, ont-stelt, a., alarmed
onstemd, ont-stemt, a., displeased, vexed
ontstemming, ont-stem-ming, c., resentment
ontstoken, ont-stoh-ker, a., inflamed (wound)
onttrekken, ont-treck-ker, v., to withdraw
ontuchtig, on-terHG-terHG, a. & adv., lewd
ontvangbewijs, ont-*fang*-ber-veyss, n., receipt
ontvangen, ont-*fang*-er, v., to receive   [tor
ontvanger, ont-*fang*-er, c., receiver; (tax) collec-
ontvangst, ont-*fangst*, c., reception; receipt
ontvankelijk, ont-*fan*-ker-luck, a., susceptible
ontveinzen, ont-feyn-zer, v., to disguise
ontvlammen, ont-flam-mer, v., to inflame
ontvluchten, ont-flerHG-ter, v., to fly; to flee
ontvoeren, ont-foo-rer, v., to kidnap, to abduct
ontvolken, ont-fol-ker, v., to depopulate
ontvouwen, ont-fow-er, v., to unfold
ontvreemden, ont-fraym-der, v., to steal
ontwaken, ont-vah-ker, v., to awake
ontwapenen, ont-vah-per-ner, v., to disarm
ontwapening, ont-vah-per-ning, c., disarmament
ontwerp, ont-vayrp, n., plan, project, design
ontwerpen, ont-vayr-per, v., to plan, to draft
ontwijden, ont-vey-der, v., to profane, to defile
ontwijken, ont-vey-ker, v., to dodge, to evade
ontwikkeld, ont-vik-kelt, a., educated; developed
ontwrichten, ont-vriHG-ter, v., to dislocate
ontzag, ont-saHG, n., awe, respect
ontzaglijk, ont-*sa*-HGer-luck, a. & adv., awful,
    immense
ontzeggen, ont-seHG-er, v., to deny; to refuse
ontzettend, ont-set-tent, a. & adv., appalling
ontzetting, ont-set-ting, c., relief, rescue; horror
ontzield, ont-seelt, a., inanimate
ontzien, ont-seen, v., to respect; to spare; to save

onuitputtelijk, on-owt-**pert**-ter-luck, a., inexhaustible [bearable

onuitstaanbaar, on-owt-**stahn**-bahr, a., un-

onuitvoerbaar, on-owt-**foor**-bahr, a., impracticable

onvast, on-*fast*, a., unsteady, shaky [ticable

onveilig, on-fey-lerHG, a., unsafe

onveranderlijk, on-fer-*an*-der-luck, a., invariable

onverantwoordelijk, on-fer-*ant*-**vohr**-der-luck, a., unaccountable [rigible

onverbeterlijk, on-fer-**bay**-ter-luck, a., incor-

onverbiddelijk, on-fer-**bid**-der-luck, a., inexorable

onverdraagzaam, on-fer-**drah**HG-sahm, a., intolerant [compatible

onverenigbaar, on-fer-ay-nerHG-bahr, a., in-

onverflauwd, on-fer-**flowt**, a., undiminished

onvergankelijk, on-fer-HG*an*-ker-luck, a., imperishable [donable

onvergeeflijk, on-fer-HG**ay**-fer-luck, a., unpar-

onvergelijkelijk, on-fayr-HG**er**-ley-ker-luck, a. & adv., matchless [gettable

onvergetelijk, on-fayr-HG**ay**-ter-luck, a., unfor-

onverklaarbaar, on-fer-**klahr**-bahr, a., inexplicable [inevitable

onvermijdelijk, on-fer-**mey**-der-luck, a. & adv.,

onvermoeid, on-fer-**moo**-it, a., untired

onvermogen, on-fer-moh-HGer, n., impotence

onvermurwbaar, on-fer-**merrv**-bahr, a., unrelenting

onversaagd, on-fer-**sah**HGt, a. & adv., undaunted

onverschillig, on-fer-**s**HGil-lerHG, a. & adv., indifferent [unflinching

onverschrokken, on-fer-**srock**-ker, a. & adv.,

onverstaanbaar, on-fer-**stahn**-bahr, a., unintelligible [unwise

onverstandig, on-fer-**stan**-derHG, a. & adv.,

onverstoorbaar, on-fer-**stohr**-bahr, a. & adv., imperturbable [table

onvertaalbaar, on-fer-**tahl**-bahr, a., untranslatable

onverteerbaar, on-fer-**tayr**-bahr, a., indigestible

onvervalst, on-fer-**valst**, a., genuine

onverwacht, on-fer-**va**HGt, a., unexpected

onverwachts, on-fer-v*a*HGts, adv., unexpectedly

onverwijld, on-fer-veylt, adv., immediately

onverzettelijk, on-fer-zet-ter-luck, a., stubborn

onverzoenlijk, on-fer-zoon-luck, a., implacable

onverzwakt, on-fer-zv*a*kt, a., unweakened

onvoldaan, on-fol-dahn, a., unsatisfied

onvoldoende, on-fol-**doon**-der, a. & adv., in- [plete
sufficient

onvolledig, on-fol-lay-derHG, a. & adv., incom-

onvolmaaktheid, on-fol-**mahkt**-heyt, c., imper-

onvoltooid, on-fol-toh-it, a., unfinished [fection

onvoorbereid, on-fohr-ber-reyt, a., unprepared

onvoordelig, on-fohr-**day**-lerHG, a., unprofitable

onvoorwaardelijk, on-fohr-**vahr**-der-luck, a. &
adv., unconditional [imprudent

onvoorzichtig, on-fohr-ziHG-terHG, a. & adv.,

onvoorzien, on-fohr-zeen, a., unforeseen [kind

onvriendelijk, on-freen-der-luck, a. & adv., un-

onvruchtbaar, on-frerHGt-bahr, a., infertile

onwaardig, on-vahr-derHG, a., unworthy

onwaarheid, on-vahr-heyt, c., lie, untruth

onwaarschijnlijk, on-vahr-sHGeyn-luck, a., improbable

onwankelbaar, on-v*a*n-kerl-bahr, a., unshakable

onweer, on-vayr, n., thunder-storm [table

onweerlegbaar, on-vayr-leHG-bahr, a., irrefu-

onweerstaanbaar, on-vayr-stahn-bahr, a., irre-

onwel, on-vel, a., unwell, indisposed [sistible

onwetend, on-vay-tent, a., ignorant

onwettelijk, on-vet-ter-luck, a., illegal

onwijs, on-veyss, a. & adv., unwise, foolish

onwillekeurig, on-vil-ler-**ker**-rerHG, a. & adv.,
involuntary

onwillig, on-vil-lerHG, a. & adv., unwilling

onwrikbaar, on-vrick-bahr, a., immovable

onze, on-zer, pron., our. de ——, der ——, ours

onzedelijk, on-zay-der-luck, a. & adv., immoral

onzedig, on-zay-derHG, a. & adv., immodest

onzekerheid, on-zay-ker-heyt, c., uncertainty

onzelfzuchtig, on-zelf-serHG-terHG, a. & adv.,
unselfish

onzichtbaar, on-ziHGt-bahr, a. & adv., invisible

onzijdig, on-zey-derHG, a., neutral

onzin, on-zin, c., nonsense

onzindelijk, on-zin-der-luck, a., unclean, dirty

onzinnig, on-zin-nerHG, a. & adv., absurd

onzuiver, on-zow-ver, a., impure; (mus.) out of tune

oog, ohHG, n., eye; spot. **met het —— op,** in view of [het —— op, in view of tune

oogappel, ohHG-ap-perl, c., eye-ball

oogarts, ohHG-arts, c., oculist

ooggetuige, ohHG-HGer-tow-HGer, c., eye-witness

ooghaartje, ohHG-hahrt-yer, n., eyelash

oogopslag, ohHG-op-slaHG, c., look, glance

oogst, ohHGst, c., harvest, crop(s)

oogsten, ohHG-ster, v., to harvest, to reap

oogwenk, ohHG-venk, c., wink. **in een ——,** in ayn ——, in a moment [ayn ——, in a moment

ooi, oh'ee, c., ewe

ooievaar, oh-yer-vahr, c., stork

ooit, oh-it, adv., ever

ook, ohk, adv., too, also, as well

oom, ohm, c., uncle

oor, ohr, n., ear; handle; dog's ear (books)

oorbelletje, ohr-bel-lert-yer, n., ear-drop

oord, ohrt, n., place, region [opinion

oordeel, ohr-dayl, n., judgment; sentence; [opinion

oordelen, ohr-day-ler, v., to judge; to deem

oorkonde, ohr-kon-der, c., deed, charter, document [ment

oorkussen, ohr-kers-ser, n., pillow [ment

oorlog, ohr-loHG, c., war, warfare

oorlogvoerend, ohr-loHG-foo-rent, a., at war

oorlogzuchtig, ohr-loHG-serHG-terHG, a., warlike

oorpijn, ohr-peyn, c., ear-ache

oorsprong, ohr-sprong, c., origin, source

oorspronkelijk, ohr-spron-ker-luck, a. & adv., original

oorverdovend, ohr-fer-doh-vent, a., deafening

oorvijg, ohr-feyHG, c., box on the ear

oorworm, ohr-vorm, c., earwig

oorzaak, ohr-zahk, c., cause, origin

oostelijk, ohs-ter-luck, a., eastern, easterly

oosten, ohs-ter, n., East, Orient

oosters, ohs-terss, a., eastern, oriental

ootmoedig, oht-moo-der_HG_, a. & adv., humble

op, op, prep., on, upon; in; at. adv., up

opa, oh-pah, c., (pop.) grandfather

opbellen, op-bel-ler, v., to ring up, to phone up

opbergen, op-bayr-_HG_er, v., to put away

opbeuren, op-ber-rer, v., to lift up; to cheer (up)

opblazen, op-blah-zer, v., to inflate; to blow up

opbloei, op-bloo'ee, c., revival; flourishing

opbouw, op-bow, c., erection, construction

opbrengen, op-breng-er, v., to yield; to pay

opbrengst, op-brengst, c., yield, output, produce

opbruisen, op-brow-ser, v., to bubble up

opdat, op-_dat_, conj., that. —— **niet,** —— neet, conj., that. [lest

opdienen, op-dee-ner, v., to serve (up)

opdirken op-dir-ker, v., to trick out; to dress up

opdoeken, op-doo-ker, v., to do away with

opdoen, op-doon, v., to bring in; to obtain; to lay in [etc.)

opdraaien, op-drah-yer, v., to wind up (a watch,

opdracht, op-dra_HG_t, c., charge, commission

opdragen, op-drah-_HG_er, v., to dedicate; to charge

opdrijven, op-drey-ver, v., to force up (prices)

opdringen, op-dring-er, v., to thrust upon; to press on

opdrinken, op-drin-ker, v., to drink up, to empty

opdrogen, op-droh-_HG_er, v., to dry up

opdweilen, op-dvey-ler, v., to mop up

opeen, op-ayn, adv., together; one upon another

opeenhopen, op-ayn-hoh-per, v., to heap up

opeisen, op-ey-ser, v., to claim; to demand

open, oh-per, a. & adv., open; vacant

openbaar, oh-pen-bahr, a. & adv., public

openbaarmaking, oh-pen-**bahr**-mah-king, c., publication

openbaren, oh-pen-**bah**-rer, v., to reveal

openbreken, oh-per-bray-ker, v., to break open

openen, oh-per-ner, v., to open

openhartig, oh-pen-**har**-ter_HG_, a. & adv., frank

opening, oh-per-ning, c., opening; gap

openlijk, oh-per-luck, a. & adv., public, open

openrukken, oh-per-rerk-ker, v., to tear open

opereren, oh-per-**ray**-rer, v., to operate

opeten, op-ay-ter, v., to eat (up)

opfokken, op-fock-ker, v., to rear, to breed

opfrissen, op-fris-ser, v., to refresh

opgaan, op-HGahn, v., to rise; to go up; to mount

opgang, op-HGang, c., rise; growth; success

opgave, op-HGah-ver, c., task; exercise; statement

opgeruimd, op-HGer-rowmt, a. & adv., cheerful

opgetogen, op-HGer-toh-HGer, a., elated, ravished

opgeven, op-HGay-ver, v., to give up; to state; to set (a task)

opgewekt, op-HGer-veckt, a. & adv., cheerful

opgewonden, op-HGer-von-der, a., excited

opgraven, op-HGrah-ver, v., to dig up; to exhume

opgraving, op-HGrah-ving, c., excavation

ophaalbrug, op-hahl-brerHG, c., drawbridge

ophalen, op-hah-ler, v., to pull up; to shrug; to collect   [suspend

ophangen, op-hang-er, v., to hang (up), to

opheffen, op-hef-fer, v., to raise, to lift up

ophelderen, op-hel-der-rer, v., to clear up

ophijsen, op-hey-ser, v., to hoist (up)

ophitsen, op-hit-ser, v., to set on, to incite

ophogen, op-hoh-HGer, v., to raise

ophoping, op-hoh-ping, c., accumulation

ophouden, op-how-der, v., to hold up (out); to uphold; to cease

opkijken, op-key-ker, v., to look up

opklapbed, op-klap-bet, n., folding bed

opklaren, op-klah-rer, v., to clear up

opklimmen, op-klim-mer, v., to ascend, to mount

opknabbelen, op-k'nab-ber-ler, v., to munch

opknappen, op-k'nap-per, v., to tidy up; to recuperate

opkomen, op-koh-mer, v., to come up; to come on

opkomst, op-komst, c., origin; attendance

opkopen, op-koh-per, v., to buy up

opkweken, op-kvay-ker, v., to rear, to nurse

oplaag, op-lahHG, c., edition; circulation (news-

oplaaien, op-lah-yer, v., to flare up   [papers)

opleggen, op-leHG-er, v., to impose; to lay on

opleiden, op-ley-der, v., to train, to educate

opletten, op-let-ter, v., to pay attention; to attend

oplettendheid, op-let-tent-heyt, c., attention
opleveren, op-lay-ver-rer, v., to yield; to deliver
opleving, op-lay-ving, c., revival [(up)
oplichter, op-liнg-ter, c., swindler, crook
oploop, op-lohp, c., tumult; crowd
oplopen, op-loh-per, v., to mount (up), to rise
oplosbaar, op-loss-bahr, a., soluble; solvable
oplossen, op-los-ser, v., to dissolve; to solve
oplossing, op-los-sing, c., solution
opluchting, op-lerнg-ting, c., relief
opluisteren, op-lowss-ter-rer, v., to adorn
opmaken, op-mah-ker, v., to spend; to make (bed); to dress (hair)
opmars, op-marss, c., advance, march on (to)
opmerkelijk, op-**mayr**-ker-luck, a. & adv., remarkable
opmerken, op-mayr-ker, v., to notice; to remark
opmerking, op-mayr-king, c., observation, remark
opmerkzaam, op-mayrk-sahm, a. & adv., attentive. —— **maken op**, —— mah-ker op, to draw attention to
opmeten, op-may-ter, v., to measure; to survey
opmonteren, op-mon-ter-rer, v., to cheer up
opname, op-nah-mer, c., record; photo, view
opnemen, op-nay-mer, v., to take up; to insert
opnieuw, op-nee'oo, adv., again, once more
opnoemen, op-noo-mer, v., to enumerate; to name
opoe, oh-poo, c., granny [name
opofferen, op-of-fer-rer, v., to sacrifice
oponthoud, op-ont-howt, c., delay; halt; stay
oppakken, op-pak-ker, v., to pick up
oppassen, op-pas-ser, v., to take care of
oppassend, op-pas-sent, a., well-behaved
oppasser, op-pas-ser, c., (mil.) batman; keeper (zoo) [mand
opperbevel, op-per-ber-vel, n., supreme command
opperhoofd, op-per-hohft, n., chief(tain), head
oppermachtig, op-per-maнg-terнg, a., supreme
oppervlakkig, op-per-flak-kerнg, a. & adv., superficial
oppervlakte, op-per-flak-ter, c., surface

oppoetsen, op-poot-ser, v., to polish
oppompen, op-pom-per, v., to pump up
oppotten, op-pot-ter, v., to save up
oprakelen, op-rah-ker-ler, v., to stir up
opraken, op-rah-ker, v., to run out (low)
oprapen, op-rah-per, v., to pick (take) up
oprecht, op-reHGt, a. & adv., sincere, genuine
oprechtheid, op-reHGt-heyt, c., sincerity
oprichten, op-riHG-ter, v., to establish, to found
oprichting, op-riHG-ting, c., erection; foundation
oprijlaan, op-rey-lahn, c., (carriage) drive
oprijzen, op-rey-zer, v., to rise, to get up
oproep, op-roop, c., summons; call
oproepen, op-roo-per, v., to call up
oproer, op-roor, n., revolt, rebellion
oproerig, op-roo-rerHG, a. & adv., rebellious
oprollen, op-rol-ler, v., to roll (coil) up
opruien, op-row-er, v., to incite, to stir up
opruier, op-row-er, c., agitator
opruimen, op-row-mer, v., to clear away
oprukken, op-rerk-ker, v., to advance
opscheppen, op-sHGep-per, v., to brag
opschepper, op-sHGep-per, c., braggart
opschieten, op-sHGee-ter, v., to get on, to proceed
opschik, op-sHGik, c., finery
opschilderen, op-sHGil-der-rer, v., to paint up
opschorten, op-sHGor-ter, v., to defer, to adjourn
opschrift, op-srift, n., inscription; heading
opschrijven, op-srey-ver, v., to write down
opschudding, op-sHGerd-ding, c., commotion
opsieren, op-see-rer, v., to adorn, to embellish
opslaan, op-slahn, v., to raise; to turn up; to lay in
opslag, op-slaHG, c., rise (prices); storage
opslokken, op-slock-ker, v., to swallow
opslorpen, op-slor-per, v., to sip (lap) up
opsluiten, op-slow-ter, v., to lock up (in)
opsnuiven, op-snow-ver, v., to inhale, to sniff
opsommen, op-som-mer, v., to enumerate
opsporen, op-spoh-rer, v., to track, to trace
opspraak, op-sprahk, c., scandal
opspringen, op-spring-er, v., to leap (jump) up
opstaan, op-stahn, v., to get up; to rebel

opstand, op-st**a**nt, c., revolt, uprising

opstandeling, op-st**a**n-der-ling, c., rebel

opstandig, op-st**a**n-derHG, a., revolting

opstapelen, op-st**a**h-per-ler, v., to pile up

opsteken, op-st**a**y-ker, v., to lift; to light

opstel, op-stel, n., essay, theme

opstellen, op-st**e**l-ler, v., to draft; to mount

opstijgen, op-st**e**y-HGer, v., to rise, to go up

opstoken, op-st**o**h-ker, v., to burn; to stir up

opstootje, op-st**o**ht-yer, n., riot, disturbance

opstopping, op-st**o**p-ping, c., (traffic) block

opstropen, op-str**o**h-per, v., to roll (tuck) up

optekenen, op-t**a**y-ker-ner, v., to write down

optellen, op-t**e**l-ler, v., to add (count) up

optillen, op-t**i**l-ler, v., to lift up

optocht, op-toHGt, c., procession

optreden, op-tr**a**y-der, v., to appear. —— **tegen**, —— t**a**y-HGer, to take action against

optrekken, op-tr**e**ck-ker, v., to pull (draw) up

opvallend, op-f**a**l-lent, a. & adv., striking

opvatten, op-f**a**t-ter, v., to take up; to conceive

opvatting, op-f**a**t-ting, c., conception, view

opvegen, op-f**a**y-HGer, v., to sweep (up)

opvlammen, op-fl**a**m-mer, v., to flame (flare) up

opvliegend, op-fl**ee**-HGent, a., quick-tempered

opvoeden, op-f**oo**-der, v., to educate; to rear

opvoeding, op-f**oo**-ding, c., education [gogic

opvoedkundig, op-f**oo**t-k**e**rn-derHG, a., peda-

opvoeren, op-f**oo**-rer, v., to speed up; to perform

opvoering, op-f**oo**-ring, c., performance

opvolgen, op-f**o**l-HGer, v., to succeed; to act upon

opvolger, op-f**o**l-HGer, c., successor

opvorderen, op-f**o**r-der-rer, v., to claim

opvouwen, op-f**ow**-er, v., to fold up

opvrolijken, op-fr**o**h-ler-ker, v., to brighten

opvullen, op-f**e**rl-ler, v., to fill up; to pad

opwaarts, op-v**ah**rts, a. & adv., upward

opwachten, op-v**a**HGt-ter, v., to wait for

opwarmen, op-v**a**r-mer, v., to warm up

opwekken, op-v**e**ck-ker, v., to rouse, to awake

opwelling, op-v**e**l-ling, c., outburst; access

opwinden, op-v**i**n-der, v., to wind up; to excite

opwinding, op-vin-ding, c., excitement, commotion [withdraw

opzeggen, op-seHG-er, v., to say, to recite; to

opzenden, op-sen-der, v., to send, to forward

opzet, op-set, n., intention. met ——, met ——, purposely

opzettelijk, op-set-ter-luck, a. & adv., intentional

opzetten, op-set-ter, v., to put on (up); to stuff

opzicht, op-siHGt, n., supervision. in dit ——, in dit ——, in this respect

opzichter, op-siHG-ter, c., overseer

opzichtig, op-siHG-terHG, a. & adv., gaudy, showy

opzien, op-seen, v., to look up

opzienbarend, op-seen-bah-rent, a., sensational

opzoeken, op-soo-ker, v., to seek; to call on

opzuigen, op-sow-HGer, v., to suck in (up)

opzwellen, op-svel-ler, v., to swell

orde, or-der, c., order [order

ordelijk, or-der-luck, a., orderly. adv., in good

ordeloos, or-der-lohss, a., disorderly

order, or-der, c., command, order

ordeteken, or-der-tay-ker, n., badge

ordinair, or-dee-nayr, a. & adv., vulgar, common

ordonnans, or-don-anss, c., orderly

orgel, or-HGerl, n., (mus.) organ

oriënteren(zich), oh-ree-en-tay-rer(ziHG), v., to take one's bearings

origineel, oh-ree-HGee-nayl, n., a. & adv., original

orkaan, or-kahn, c., hurricane

os, oss, c., ox

oud, owt, a., old; stale; ancient

oudbakken, owt-bak-ker, a., stale

oudejaarsavond, ow-der-yahrs-ah-vont, c., New [Year's Eve

ouder, ow-der, a., older, elder

ouderlijk, ow-der-luck, a., parental

ouders, ow-derss, c. pl., parents

ouderwets, ow-der-vets, a. & adv., old-fashioned

oudheid, owt-heyt, c., antiquity

oudje, owt-yer, n., old man or woman

oudoom, owt-ohm, c., great-uncle

oudst, owtst, a., oldest, eldest

oudstrijder, owt-strey-der, c., veteran

oudtante, owt-tan-ter, c., great-aunt

ouwelijk, ow-er-luck, a., oldish, elderly

oven, oh-ver, c., oven; furnace; kiln

over, oh-ver, prep., over, across; beyond; via

overal, oh-ver-al, adv., everywhere

overbevolkt, oh-ver-ber-volkt, a., over-populated

overblijfsel, oh-ver-bleyf-serl, n., remainder

overblijven, oh-ver-bley-ver, v., to be left

overbluffen, oh-ver-blerf-fer, v., to bluff

overbodig, oh-ver-boh-derHG, a., superfluous

overboord, oh-ver-bohrt, adv., overboard

overbrengen, oh-ver-breng-er, v., to transport

overbuur, oh-ver-beer, c., opposite neighbour

overdaad, oh-ver-daht, c., excess

overdadig, oh-ver-dah-derHG, a. & adv., excessive

overdag, oh-ver-daHG, adv., in the day-time

overdenking, oh-ver-den-king, c., consideration

overdoen, oh-ver-doon, v., to do over again

overdreven, oh-ver-dray-ver, a., exaggerated

overdrijven, oh-ver-drey-ver, v., to exaggerate

overeenkomen, oh-ver-ayn-koh-mer, v., to agree

overeenkomst, oh-ver-ayn-komst, c., resemblance
 [adv., corresponding

overeenkomstig, oh-ver-ayn-koms-terHG, a. &

overeenstemmen, oh-ver-ayn-stem-mer, v., to agree
 [harmony

overeenstemming, oh-ver-ayn-stem-ming, c.,

overeind, oh-ver-eynt, adv., upright, erect

overgaan, oh-ver-HGahn, v., to go; to pass off; to be removed

overgang, oh-ver-HGang, c., transition

overgave, oh-ver-HGah-ver, c., handing over

overgeven, oh-ver-HGay-ver, v., to hand over

overgrootmoeder, oh-ver-HGroht-moo-der, c.,
 great-grandmother
 [grandfather

overgrootvader, oh-ver-HGroht-fah-der, c., great-

overhaast, oh-ver-hahst, a. & adv., hasty

overhaasten(zich), oh-ver-hah-ster(ziHG), v., to hurry
 [persuade

overhalen, oh-ver-hah-ler, v., to fetch over; to

overhandigen, oh-ver-han-der-HGer, v., to deliver

overhebben, oh-ver-heb-ber, v., to have left

overheen, oh-ver-hayn, adv., across, over
overheerlijk, oh-ver-hayr-luck, a., exquisite
overheersen, oh-ver-hayr-ser, v., to dominate
overheersend, oh-ver-hayr-sent, a., (pre)dominant
overheerser, oh-ver-hayr-ser, c., tyrant, despot
overhellen, oh-ver-hel-ler, v., to lean over
overhemd, oh-ver-hemt, n., shirt
overhoop, oh-ver-hohp, adv., in a heap
overhouden, oh-ver-how-der, v., to save
overig, oh-ver-rerHG, a., remaining
overigens, oh-ver-rer-HGens, adv., for the rest
overijling, oh-ver-ey-ling, c., precipitation
overjas, oh-ver-yass, c., overcoat
overkant, oh-ver-kant, c., opposite side
overkomen, oh-ver-koh-mer, v., to come over
overkomen, oh-ver-koh-mer, v., to befall
overkomst, oh-ver-komst, c., visit   [reload
overladen, oh-ver-lah-der, v., to transfer; to
overladen, oh-ver-lah-der, v., to overburden
overland, oh-ver-lant, adv., by land
overlast, oh-ver-last, c., inconvenience
overlaten, oh-ver-lah-ter, v., to leave
overleden, oh-ver-lay-der, p.p., deceased
overleg, oh-ver-leHG, n., deliberation
overleggen, oh-ver-leHG-ger, v., to deliberate
overleven, oh-ver-lay-ver, v., to survive
overleveren, oh-ver-lay-ver-rer, v., to hand down
overlevering, oh-ver-lay-ver-ring, c., tradition
overlijden, oh-ver-ley-der, v., to die
overlopen, oh-ver-loh-per, v., to overflow; to
overloper, oh-ver-loh-per, c., deserter   [desert
overluid, oh-ver-lowt, adv., aloud
overmaat, oh-ver-maht, c., excess
overmacht, oh-ver-maHGt, c., superior power
overmaken, oh-ver-mah-ker, v., to do over again
overmeesteren, oh-ver-mays-ter-rer, v., to overpower   [less
overmoedig, oh-ver-moo-derHG, a. & adv., reck-
overmorgen, oh-ver-mor-HGer, adv., the day after to-morrow   [night
overnachten, oh-ver-naHG-ter, v., to stay the

overnemen, oh-ver-**nay**-mer, v., to take over

overpeinzing, oh-ver-**peyn**-zing, c., meditation

overplaatsen, oh-ver-**plaht**-ser, v., to remove

overplanten, oh-ver-**plan**-ter, v., to transplant

overreden, oh-ver-**ray**-der, v., to persuade

overreiken, oh-ver-**rey**-ker, v., to pass, to hand

overrijden, oh-ver-**rey**-der, v., to run over

overrompelen, oh-ver-**rom**-per-ler, v., to surprise   [switch over

overschakelen, oh-ver-sHGah-ker-ler, v., to

overschatten, oh-ver-sHG**at**-ter, v., to overrate

overschieten, oh-ver-sHG**ee**-ter, v., to remain

overschoen, oh-ver-sHG**oo**n, c., overshoe, golosh

overschot, oh-ver-sHG**ot**, n., rest, remainder

overschrijden, oh-ver-**srey**-der, v., to step across; (fig.) to exceed

overschrijven, oh-ver-**srey**-ver, v., to write out

overslaan, oh-ver-**slahn**, v., to omit; to pass over

overspannen, oh-ver-**span**-ner, a., overstrung

overspel, oh-ver-**spel**, n., adultery

overstappen, oh-ver-**stap**-per, v., to cross; to change (trains)

oversteken, oh-ver-**stay**-ker, v., to cross (over)

overstelpen, oh-ver-**stel**-per, v., to overwhelm

overstroming, oh-ver-**stroh**-ming, c., flood

overtocht, oh-ver-toHG**t**, c., passage, crossing

overtollig, oh-ver-tol-lerHG, a. & adv., superfluous

overtreden, oh-ver-**trey**-der, v., to transgress

overtreffen, oh-ver-**tref**-fer, v., to outdo, to surpass   [trace

overtrekken, oh-ver-**treck**-ker, v., to cross; to

overtuigen, oh-ver-**tow**-HGent, v., to convince

overtuiging, oh-ver-**tow**-HGing, c., conviction

overuren, oh-ver-EE-rer, n. pl., overtime

overval, oh-ver-**fal**, c., raid; surprise (attack)

overvaren, oh-ver-**fah**-rer, v., to cross (over)

overvleugelen, oh-ver-**fler**-HGer-ler, v., to surpass

overvloed, oh-ver-**floot**, c., abundance

overvloedig, oh-ver-**floo**-derHG, a. & adv., abundant

overvol, oh-ver-**fol**, a., crowded   [abundant

overweg, oh-ver-veHG, c., level crossing

overwegen, oh-ver-**vay**-HGer, v., to consider

overweging, oh-ver-vay-HGing, c., consideration.
in ——— **geven**, in ——— HGay-ver, to suggest
overweldigen, oh-ver-vel-der-HGer, v., to overpower [whelming
overweldigend, oh-ver-vel-der-HGent, a., over-
overwerken, oh-ver-vayr-ker, v., to do overtime
overwicht, oh-ver-viHGt, n., preponderance
overwinnaar, oh-ver-vin-nahr, c., conqueror
overwinnen, oh-ver-vin-ner, v., to conquer
overwinning, oh-ver-vin-ning, c., victory
overzees, oh-ver-zayss, a., oversea(s)
overzenden, oh-ver-zen-der, v., to send
overzetten, oh-ver-zet-ter, v., to ferry over
overzicht, oh-ver-ziHGt, n., survey
overzichtelijk, oh-ver-ziHG-ter-luck, a., clear
overzien, oh-ver-zeen, v., to survey [across
overzwemmen, oh-ver-zvem-mer, v., to swim

paadje, paht-yer, n., foot-path
paaien, pah-yer, v., to soothe, to appease
paal, pahl, c., pole, post, stake
paar, pahr, n., pair, brace
paard, pahrt, n., horse; knight (at chess). **te** ———,
ter ———, on horseback
paardekracht, pahr-der-kraHGt, c., horse-power
paardenbloem, pahr-der-bloom, c., dandelion
paardenfokkerij, pahr-der-fock-ker-rey, c.,
horse-breeding; stud
paardenhorzel, pahr-der-hor-zerl, c., horse-fly
paardenstal, pahr-der-stal, c., horse-stable
paardrijden, pahrt-rey-der, n., horse-riding
paarlemoer, pahr-ler-moor, n., mother of pearl
paars, pahrss, n. & a., purple
paartje, pahrt-yer, n., couple (of lovers)
paasbloem, pahss-bloom, c., primrose
Paasdag, pahss-daHG, c., Easter Day
Paasfeest, pahss-fayst, n., Easter; Passover
Paasvacantie, pahss-fah-kan-see, c., Easter
pacht, paHGt, c., lease; rent [holidays
pachtboer, paHGt-boor, c., tenant-farmer
pachten, paHG-ter, v., to farm; to rent
pachter, paHG-ter, c., tenant(-farmer); lessee

pad, p*a*t, n., path; gangway. c., toad [room
paddenstoel, p*a*d-der-stool, c., toadstool; mush-
padvinder, p*a*t-fin-der, c., Boy Scout [ment
padvinderij, p*a*t-fin-der-rey, c., boy-scout move-
padvindster, p*a*t-fint-ster, c., Girl Guide
pafferig, p*a*f-fer-rerHG, a., bloated, puffy, flabby
pagaaien, pah-HGah-yer, v., to paddle
pagina, pah-HGee-nah, c., page (of a book)
pak, p*a*k, n., suit (of clothes); parcel; pack
pakhuis, p*a*k-howss, n., warehouse
pakken, p*a*k-ker, v., to pack; to seize; to hug
pakkend, p*a*k-kent, a., gripping; catchy; fetching
pakpapier, p*a*k-pah-peer, n., packing-paper
pal, p*a*l, c., catch, click. a. & adv., firm
paleis, pah-leyss, n., palace
paling, pah-ling, c., eel
paljas, p*a*l-y*a*ss, c., buffoon, clown; pallet
palm, p*a*lm, c., palm (tree and hand)
pamflet, p*a*m-flet, n., lampoon, libel; pamphlet
pan, p*a*n, c., (frying-)pan; tile; (pop.) row
pand, p*a*nt, n., pledge; flap (of coat); premises
pandgever, p*a*nt-HGay-ver, c., pawner
pandhouder, p*a*nt-how-der, c., pawnee
paniek, pah-neek, c., panic, scare
pannekoek, p*a*n-ner-kook, c., pancake [works
pannenbakkerij, p*a*n-ner-b*a*k-ker-rey, c., tile-
pantalon, p*a*n-tah-lon, c., trousers; (ladies')
panter, p*a*n-ter, c., panther [knickers
pantoffel, p*a*n-tof-ferl, c., slipper [husband
pantoffelheld, p*a*n-tof-ferl-helt, c., henpecked
pantser, p*a*nt-ser, n., cuirass; armour-plating
pantserafweergeschut, p*a*nt-ser-*a*f-vayr-HGer-
sHGert, n., anti-tank guns
pantserwagen, p*a*nt-ser-vah-HGer, c., armoured
pap, p*a*p, c., porridge, pap; poultice [car
papaver, pah-pah-ver, c., poppy
papegaai, pah-per-HGah'ee, c., parrot
paperassen, pah-per-r*a*s-ser, c. pl., papers; waste
papier, pah-peer, n., paper [paper
papierfabriek, pah-peer-fah-breek, n., paper-
paraat, pah-raht, a., ready, prepared [mill
parabel, pah-rah-berl, c., parable

parachutetroepen, pah-rah-sh*EE*t-troo-per, c. pl., paratroops

paradijs, pah-rah-d*eyss*, n., paradise

paraplu, pah-rah-pl*EE*, c., umbrella

parasol, pah-rah-sol, c., sunshade, porasol

pardon! p*a*r-don, interj., (so) sorry!

parel, p*a*h-rerl, c., pearl

parelen, p*a*h-rer-ler, v., to pearl; to sparkle

paren, p*a*h-rer, v., to pair, to couple

parfum, p*a*r-ferm, n., scent, perfume

parkeerterrein, p*a*r-kayr-tayr-reyn, n., car park

parkeren, p*a*r-kay-rer, v., to park

parketvloer, p*a*r-ket-floor, c., parquet floor

parkiet, p*a*r-keet, c., parakeet; budgerigar

parlement, p*a*r-ler-ment, n., parliament

parmantig, p*a*r-man-terHG, a. & adv., pert, smart

parochiaan, p*a*-roHG-ee-ahn, c., parishioner

parochie, p*a*-roHG-ee, c., parish

parodie, pah-roh-dee, c., parody, travesty

parool, pah-rohl, n., parole; password; slogan

part, part, n., part, portion   [floor

parterre, p*a*r-tayr-rer, n., pit (theatre); ground-

particulier, p*a*r-tee-k*EE*-leer, a., private. c., private person

partij, p*a*r-t*ey*, c., party; parcel; game; (mus.) part. —— **kiezen voor,** —— kee-zer vohr, to take part with

partijdig, p*a*r-tey-derHG, a. & adv., partial

partijleider, p*a*r-tey-ley-der, c., party leader

partijzuchtig, p*a*r-tey-zerHG-terHG, a., factious

parvenu, p*a*r-ver-n*EE*, c., parvenu, upstart

pas, pass, c., pace; step; passport; pass, defile

pas, pass, adv., hardly, scarcely; just (now), newly

Pasen, pah-ser, c., Easter; Passover

pasfoto, p*a*ss-foh-toh, c., passport photo

paspoort, p*a*ss-pohrt, n., passport

passagier, p*a*s-sah-zheer, c., passenger

passen, p*a*s-ser, v., to fit (on); to become, to befit

passend, p*a*s-sent, a., fitting; suitable

passer, p*a*s-ser, c., (pair of) compasses

passeren, p*a*s-say-rer, v., to pass (by); to occur

passie, p*a*s-see, c., passion

passiespel, pas, pas-see-spel, n., passion-play
pastei, pas-tey, c., pie; pasty
pastoor, pas-tohr, c., priest; rector
pastorie, pas-toh-**ree**, c., presbytery; rectory
patent, pah-tent, n., patent, licence. a., first-rate
patiënt, pah-see-ent, c., patient
patrijs, pah-treyss, c., partridge
patrijshond, pah-treyss-hont, c., spaniel
patrijspoort, pah-treyss-pohrt, c., port-hole
patroon, pah-trohn, c., employer, master; patron
saint; cartridge; pattern, design
patrouille, pah-trool-yer, c., patrol
pats, pats, c., smack. interj., bang! slap!
paus, powss, c., pope
pauselijk, pow-ser-luck, a., pontifical, papal
pauseren, pow-zay-rer, v., to pause, to stop
pauw, pow, c., peacock
pauze, pow-zer, c., pause; interval; (mus.) rest
paviljoen, pah-vil-yoon, c., pavilion, tent
pech, peнG, n., bad luck, hard luck
pechvogel, peнG-foh-нGerl, c., unlucky fellow
pedaal, per-dahl, n., pedal (bicycle, piano, etc.)
peddelen, ped-der-ler, v., to pedal; to paddle
peen, payn, c., carrot
peer, payr, c., pear; (electric) bulb
pees, payss, c., tendon; string
peetoom, pay-tohm, c., godfather
peettante, payt-tan-ter, c., godmother
peil, peyl, n., gauge; (fig.) standard
peilen, pey-ler, v., to gauge; to sound, to fathom
peinzen, peyn-zen, v., to meditate
pekel, pay-kerl, c., brine, pickle, souse
pelgrim, pel-нGrim, c., pilgrim
pelikaan, pay-lee-kahn, c., pelican
pellen, pel-ler, v., to peel, to shell
pels, pelss, c., fur; fur coat
pelsdier, pelss-deer, n., furred animal
pelsmantel, pelss-man-terl, c., fur coat
peluw, pay-lee, c., bolster
pen, pen, c., pen; nib; feather; peg
pendule, pen-dee-ler, c., mantelpiece clock
penhouder, pen-how-der, c., penholder

penningmeester, pen-ning-mays-ter, c., treasurer   [urer
pens, penss, c., paunch; tripe
penseel, pen-sayl, n., (artist's paint-) brush, pencil
pensioen, pen-see-**oon**, n., (retiring) pension
pensionaat, pen-see-oh-naht, n., boarding-school
peper, pay-per, c., pepper
peperduur, pay-per-dEEr, a., very expensive
peperkoek, pay-per-kook, c., gingerbread
pepermuntje, pay-per-**mernt**-yer, n., peppermint lozenge   [mint lozenge
per, payr, prep., by; per; to
perceel, payr-sayl, n., plot (ground); premises
pereboom, pay-rer-bohm, c., pear-tree
periode, pay-ree-oh-der, c., period; stage; spell (of rain)
perk, payrk, n., (flower-)bed; limit, bound
perkament, per-kah-ment, n., parchment
permissie, payr-mis-see, c., permission; (mil.)
perron, payr-ron, n., platform
perronkaartje, payr-ron-kahrt-yer, n., platform-ticket   [ticket
pers, payrss, c., press
per se, payr say, adv., of necessity; by all means
persen, payr-ser, v., to press, to squeeze
personeel, payr-soh-nayl, n., staff; servants. a., personal
persoon, payr-sohn, c., person
persoonlijk, payr-sohn-luck, a. & adv., personal
persoonsbewijs, payr-**sohns**-ber-veys, n., identity card
pertinent, payr-tee-**nent**, a. & adv., categorical
perzik, payr-zick, c., peach
pest, pest, c., plague; (fig.) pest
pesten, pess-ter, v., (pop.) to badger, to nag
pet, pet, c., cap
petekind, pay-ter-kint, n., god-child
peterselie, pay-ter-say-lee, c., parsley
petroleumlamp, pay-**troh**-lay-erm-lamp, c., paraffin-lamp
peukje, perk-yer, n., end (cigar, etc.)
peultjes, perlt-yess, n. pl., podded peas
peuter, per-ter, c., pipe-cleaner; tiny tot
peuteren, per-ter-rer, v., to potter, to fumble
peuzelen, per-zer-ler, v., to munch; to peck

pianobegeleiding, pee-ah-no-ber-HGer-ley-ding, c., piano accompaniment

pianokrukje, pee-ah-no-krerk-yer, n., piano-stool

pianostemmer, pee-ah-no-stem-mer, c., piano-tuner

picknicken, pick-nick-er, v., to picnic

piekeren, pee-ker-rer, v., to brood, to worry

piekfijn, peek-feyn, a. & adv., spruce, smart

pienter, peen-ter, a. & adv., clever, sharp

piepen, pee-per, v., to squeak; to chirp; to creak

piepjong, peep-yong, a., very young

pier, peer, c., jetty, pier; earthworm

pijl, peyl, c., arrow; dart

pijler, pey-ler, c., pillar; pier (of bridge)

pijlsnel, peyl-snel, a., swift as an arrow

pijn, peyn, c., pain; pine(-tree)

pijnappel, peyn-ap-perl, c., fir-cone

pijnigen, pey-ner-HGer, v., to torture

pijnlijk, peyn-luck, a. & adv., painful

pijnstillend, peyn-stil-lent, a., soothing

pijp, peyp, c., pipe (for smoking, organ, etc.); tube; leg (of trousers)

pijpenrek, pey-per-reck, n., pipe-rack

pik, pick, c., pickaxe; peck; grudge, spite

pikant, pee-kant, a., piquant, pungent, spicy

pikdonker, pick-don-ker, n., pitch darkness

pikken, pick-ker, v., to pick; to peck

pil, pil, c., pill

pilaar, pee-lahr, c., pillar, column, post

piloot, pee-loht, c., (air-)pilot

pimpelen, pim-per-ler, v., (pop.) to tipple, to bib

pin, pin, c., peg, pin

pincet, pin-set, n., tweezers

pindakaas, pin-dah-kahss, c., pea-nut butter

pingelen, ping-er-ler, v., to haggle, to higgle

pink, pink, c., little finger   [flower

pinksterbloem, pink-ster-bloom, c., cuckoo-

Pinksteren, pink-ster-rer, c., Whitsuntide

pioenroos, pee-oon-rohss, c., peony

pionier, pee-oh-neer, c., pioneer

pisang, pee-zang, c., banana

pissebed, pis-ser-bet, c., dandelion

piston, pis-ton, c., (mus.) cornet
pistool, pis-tohl, n., pistol
pit, pit, c., kernel; pip; wick; burner; (fig.) spirit
pittig, pit-terHG, a. & adv., pithy, racy, lively
plaag, plahHG, c., plague, nuisance, bore, pest
plaaggeest, plahHG-HGayst, c., teaser
plaagziek, plahHG-seek, a., (fond of) teasing
plaat, plaht, c., plate; slab; sheet (of iron); picture
plaats, plahts, c., place; seat; room; court. **in —
van**, in — fan, instead of
plaatsbespreking, plahts-ber-spray-king, c.,
(advance) booking
plaatsbewijs, plahts-ber-veyss, n., ticket
plaatselijk, plaht-ser-luck, a. & adv., local
plaatsen, plaht-ser, v., to put; to set up; to insert; to invest
plaatshebben, plahts-heb-ber, v., to take place
plaatsing, plaht-sing, c., placing; insertion; investment   [tute
plaatsvervanger, plahts-fer-vang-er, c., substi-
plafond, plah-fon, n., ceiling
plagen, plah-HGer, v., to tease, to vex, to nag
plagerij, plak-HGer-rey, c., teasing, nagging
plakband, plack-bant, c., gummed paper
plakkaat, plack-kaht, n., placard, poster
plakken, plack-ker, v., to paste; to stick
plakkerig, plack-ker-rerHG, a., sticky
plakzegel, plack-say-HGerl, n., receipt-stamp
plan, plan, n., plan, project, intention
planeet, plah-nayt, c., planet
plank, plank, c., plank, board, shelf
plantaardig, plan-tahr-derHG, a., vegetable
planten, plan-ter, v., to plant
plantengroei, plan-ter-HGroo'ee, c., vegetation
plantkunde, plant-kern-der, c., botany
plantsoen, plant-soon, n., pleasure-grounds,
plas, plass, c., pool, puddle; lake   [park
plassen, plass-ser, v., to splash
plastiek, plass-teek, c., plastic; plastic art
plat, plat, a., flat; level; (fig.) low, vulgar
plataan, plah-tahn, c., plane-tree
platdrukken, plat-drerk-ker, v., to squeeze flat

plattegrond, plat-ter-HGront, c., ground-plan; map   [ner, c., countryman

plattelandsbewoner, plat-ter-lants-ber-voh-

platvoet, plat-foot, c., flat-foot (of person)

plaveisel, plah-vey-serl, n., pavement

plechtig, pleHG-terHG, a. & adv., solemn

pleegkind, playHG-kint, n., foster-child

pleegouders, playHG-ow-derss, c. pl., foster-parents

plegen, play-HGer, v., to commit, to perpetrate

pleidooi, pley-doh'ee, n., pleading, defence

plein, pleyn, n., square   [plaster, stucco

pleister, pleys-ter, n., plaster (on a wound). c.,

pleit, pleyt, n., (law)suit; plea

pleiten, pley-ter, v., to plead; to argue

plek, pleck, c., spot, place; stain

pleuris, pler-riss, c., pleurisy

plezier, pler-zeer, n., pleasure. **veel** ——! fayl —— , enjoy yourself!   [amusing

plezierig, pler-zee-rerHG, a. & adv., pleasant,

plicht, pliHGt, c., duty

plichtgetrouw, pliHGt-HGer-trow, a. & adv., dutiful   [ment

plichtpleging, pliHGt-play-HGing, c., compli-

plichtsbesef, pliHGts-ber-sef, n., sense of duty

ploeg, plooHG, c., plough; gang (of workmen);

ploegbaas, plooHG-bahss, c., foreman   [team

ploegen, plooHG-er, v., to plough

ploert, ploort, c. (pop.) cad; snob

ploeteren, ploo-ter-rer, v., to drudge   [(teeth)

plomberen, plom-bay-rer, v., to stop, to fill

plomp, plomp, a. & adv., clumsy; coarse

plonzen, plon-zer, v., to flop; to splash

plooi, ploh-ee, c., fold; crease; wrinkle

plooien, ploh-yer, v., to fold; to crease; to wrinkle

plotseling, plot-ser-ling, adv., suddenly

pluche, plEEsh, c., plush

pluim, plowm, c., plume, feather

pluimpje, plowmp-yer, n., little feather; compli-

pluimvee, plowm-fay, n., poultry   [ment

pluisje, plowsh-yer, n., fluff   [(birds)

plukken, plerk-ker, v., to pick (flowers); to pluck

plumeau, plEE-moh, c., feather-duster
plunderen, plern-der-rer, v., to plunder, to loot
plundering, plern-der-ring, c., pillage, looting
plunje, plern-yer, c., (pop.) togs, duds, rig-out
pochen, po-HGer, v., to brag, to boast
podium, poh-dee-erm, n., platform; dais
poedel, poo-derl, c., poodle
poeder, poo-der, n., powder
poel, pool, c., puddle, pool
poelier, poo-leer, c., poulterer
poes, pooss, c., cat, puss(y)
poeslief, pooss-leef, a., suave, bland
poets, poots, c., trick, practical joke
poetsdoek, poots-dook, c., polishing cloth
poetsen, poot-ser, v., to polish, to clean
poezelig, poo-zer-lerHG, a., chubby, plump
pofbroek, pof-brook, c., knickerbockers
pogen, poh-HGer, v., to try, to endeavour
poging, poh-HGing, c., effort, endeavour
pokken, pok-ker, c., pl., smallpox
polijsten, poh-leys-ter, v., to polish, to burnish
polis, poh-liss, c., (insurance) policy
politie, poh-lee-see, c., police
politieagent, poh-lee-see-ah-HGent, c., policeman
politiebureau, poh-lee-see-bEE-roh, n., police-
   station
                                 [policy
politiek, poh-lee-teek, a., political. c., politics;
polkahaar, pol-kah-hahr, n., bobbed hair
pols, pols, c., pulse; wrist; leaping-pole
polshorloge, pols-hor-loh-zher, n., wrist-watch
polsslag, pols-slaHG, c., pulsation, pulse
pomp, pomp, c., pump
pompoen, pom-poon, c., pumpkin
pont, pont, c., ferry-boat
pontonbrug, pon-ton-brerHG, c., pontoon-bridge
pook, pohk, c., poker
poolcirkel, pohl-seer-kerl, c., polar circle
poort, pohrt, c., doorway
poos, pohss, c., interval, time
poot, poht, c., leg, paw, foot
pop, pop, c., doll, puppet; (tailor's) dummy
popelen, poh-per-ler, v., to throb

populair, poh-pEE-layr, a. & adv., popular

populier, poh-pEE-leer, c., poplar

porren, por-rer, v., to poke, to stir; to spur on

porselein, por-ser-leyn, n., china, china-ware

port, port, n., postage. c., port(-wine)

portaal, por-tahl, n., porch; hall; landing (stairs)

portefeuille, por-ter-fer-yer, c., wallet; portfolio

portemonnaie, por-ter-mon-nay, c., purse

portie, por-see, c., portion   [carriage-door

portier, por-teer, c., doorkeeper; hall-porter. n.,

portret, por-tret, n., portrait, photo; likeness

poseren, poh-zay-rer, v., to sit (to an artist); to

positie, poh-zee-see, c., position; situation [pose

post, post, c., mail; post-office; post; place; sentry

postbode, post-boh-der, c., postman

postdirecteur, post-dee-reck-terr, c., postmaster

postduif, post-dowf, c., carrier-pigeon

postkantoor, post-kan-tohr, n., post-office

postspaarbank, post-spahr-bank, c., post-office
  savings-bank

posttarief, post-tah-reef, n., postal rate

postwissel, post-vis-serl, c., post-office order

postzegel, post-say-HGerl, c., (postage) stamp

pot, pot, c., pot; jar; stakes, pool

potdicht, pot-diHGt, a., perfectly closed

poten, poh-ter, v., to plant

potig, poh-terHG, a., robust, strong-limbed

potlood, pot-loht, n., (lead-)pencil   [grotesque

potsierlijk, pot-seer-luck, a. & adv., droll,

potten, pot-ter, v., to pot (plants); to hoard

pover, poh-ver, a., poor, shabby; meagre

praal, prahl, c., pomp, magnificence

praat, praht, c., talk, tattle

praatjesmaker, praht-yers-mah-ker, c., brag-

praatziek, praht-seek, a., talkative   [gart

prachtig, praHG-terHG, a. & adv., splendid

practijk, prak-teyk, c., practice

practisch, prak-teess, a. & adv., practical

pralen, prah-ler, v., to shine; to show off

praten, prah-ter, v., to chat, to talk

precies, pray-seess, a. & adv., precise   [man

predikant, pray-dee-kant, c., preacher; clergy-

preek, prayk, c., sermon
preekstoel, prayk-stool, c., pulpit
prei, prey, c., leek
prentbriefkaart, prent-breef-kahrt, c., picture [postcard
presenteerblad, prer-sen-tayr-blat, n., salver
president, pray-zee-dent, c., chairman; foreman
prestatie, pres-tah-see, c., performance, feat
pret, pret, c., fun, pleasure
pretje, pret-yer, n., lark, frolic, jollification
prettig, pret-terHG, a. & adv., amusing, nice
preuts, prerts, a. & adv., prudish, demure
prevelen, pray-ver-ler, v., to mutter, to mumble
prieel, pree-ayl, n., arbour, summer-house
priester, prees-ter, c., priest
priesterwijding, prees-ter-vey-ding, c., ordina- [tion
prijken, prey-ker, v., to glitter, to shine
prijs, preyss, c., price; prize
prijscourant, preyss-koo-rant, c., price-list
prijsgeven, preyss-HGay-ver, v., to abandon
prijzen, prey-zer, v., to praise
prijzenswaardig, prey-zerns-vahr-derHG, a., [praiseworthy
prik, prick, c., sting, prick, stab
prikkel, prick-kerl, c., goad; sting; (fig.) incentive
prikkelbaar, prick-kerl-bahr, a., irritable
prikkeldraad, prick-kerl-draht, c., barbed wire
prikkelen, prick-ker-ler, v., to prickle; to tickle
principieel, prin-see-pee-ayl, a. & adv., funda- [mental
prins, prins, c., prince
prinses, prin-sess, c., princess
prins-gemaal, prins-HGer-mahl, c., Prince Con- [sort
privaat, pree-vaht, a., private. n., lavatory
proberen, proh-bay-rer, v., to try; to attempt
probleem, proh-blaym, n., problem
proces, proh-sess, n., process; lawsuit
processie, proh-ses-see, c., procession [report
proces-verbaal, proh-ses-fer-bahl, n., warrant;
productie, proh-derk-see, c., production; output
proef, proof, c., trial, experiment; proof; sample
proefneming, proof-nay-ming, c., experiment- [ation
proefschrift, proof-srift, n., thesis (for a doctor-
proeftijd, proof-teyt, c., (time of) probation

proefvlucht, proof-flerHGt, c., test-flight
proefwerk, proof-vayrk, n., test, test-paper
proesten, proos-ter, v., to sneeze
proeven, proo-ver, v., to taste
profeet, proh-fayt, c., prophet
profijt, proh-feyt, n., profit, gain   [tage of
profiteren, proh-fee-tay-rer, v., to take advan-
program(ma), proh-gram(mah), n., programme;
    curriculum, syllabus   [c., projector
projectielantaarn,   proh-yeck-see-lan-tahr-er,
promotie, proh-moh-see, c., promotion, ad-
    vancement
prompt, prompt, a. & adv., prompt, ready
pronken, pron-ker, v., to show off
pronkerig, pron-ker-rerHG, a. & adv., showy
prooi, proh'ee, c., prey
prop, prop, c., plug; wad; stopper; gag
proper, proh-per, a., clean, neat
propvol, prop-fol, a., crammed   [protest
protesteren, proh-tess-tay-rer, v., to (make a)
proviand, proh-vee-ant, c., provisions, victuals
provincie, proh-vin-see, c., province
provisiekamer, proh-vee-zee-kah-mer, c., larder
prozaschrijver, proh-zah-srey-ver, c., prose-
pruik, prowk, c., wig   [writer
pruilen, prow-ler, v., to pout, to sulk
pruim, prowm, c., plum; prune; quid (of tobacco)
pruimtabak, prowm-tah-bak, c., chewing-
    tobacco
prul, prerl, n., rag; bauble; trash   [basket
prullenmand, prerl-ler-mant, c., waste-paper
prutser, prert-ser, c., potterer, fumbler
pruttelen, prert-ter-ler, v., to grumble; to simmer
pseudoniem, pser-doh-neem, n., pen-name
psychiater, psee-HGee-ah-ter, c., psychiatrist
publiceren, pEE-blee-say-rer, v., to publish
publiek, pEE-bleek, a. & adv., public. n., public.
    het grote ——, het HGroh-ter ——, the
    general public
puik, powk, a., excellent, first-rate
puilen, pow-ler, v., to protrude
puimsteen, powm-stayn, c., pumice-stone

puin, pown, n., ruins, rubbish, debris

puinhoop, **pown**-hohp, c., rubbish-heap; (heap [of] ruins

puist, powst, c., tumour; pimple

puistig, pows-terHG, a., covered with pimples

pummel, perm-merl, c., boor, lout

punaise, pEE-nay-zer, c., drawing-pin

punt, pernt, c., point, tip; dot; full stop. n., point, item. **op het —— staan**, op het —— stahn, to be about to

puntdicht, pernt-diHGt, n., epigram

puntgevel, pernt-HGay-verl, c., gable

puntig, pern-terHG, a., pointed, sharp

pupil, pEE-**pil**, c., ward, pupil; pupil of the eye

purper, perr-per, n., purple

put, pert, c., well; pit

putten, pert-ter, v., to draw (water)

puur, pEer, a., pure, sheer; neat, raw (spirits)

(See also **kw.**)

qualiteit, kvah-lee-teyt, c., quality

quantiteit, kvan-tee-teyt, c., quantity

quarantaine, kah-ran-tay-ner, c., quarantine

quitte, keet, a., quits

raad, raht, c., advice; counsel

raadgeving, raht-HGay-ving, c., advice

raadhuis, raht-howss, n., town hall

raadplegen, raht-play-HGer, v., to consult

raadsbesluit, rahts-ber-slowt, n., decision; decree

raadsel, raht-serl, n., riddle, puzzle

raadselachtig, raht-serl-aHG-terHG, a., puzzling

raadslid, rahts-lit, n., councillor

raadzaam, raht-sahm, a., advisable

raaf, rahf, c., raven

raam, rahm, n., window; frame

raap, rahp, c., turnip; rape (for animals)

raar, rahr, a. & adv., strange, odd

raaskallen, rahss-kal-ler, v., to talk nonsense

rabarber, rah-bar-ber, c., rhubarb

rad, rat, n., wheel. a., swift, nimble

raddraaier, rad-drah-yer, c., ring-leader

radeloos, rah-der-lohss, a., desperate, distracted

raden, rah-der, v., to guess; to advise [thorough
radicaal, rah-dee-kahl, a. & adv., radical;
radijs, ra-deyss, c., radish [less station
radiostation, rah-dee-oh-stah-see'on, n., wire-
radiotoestel, rah-dee-oh-toos-tel, n., wireless set
rafelen, rah-fer-ler, v., to unravel
raffinaderij, raf-fee-nah-der-rey, c., refinery
rakelen, rah-ker-ler, v., to rake
raken, rah-ker, v., to touch; to hit; to concern
rakker, rak-ker, c., rascal, rogue
ram, ram, c., ram; (battering-)ram
ramen, rah-mer, v., to estimate
rammelen, ram-mer-ler, v., to rattle, to clank
ramp, ramp, c., disaster, calamity
rampzalig, ramp-sah-lerHG, a. & adv., wretched
rand, rant, c., brim; margin; edge; border
rang, rang, c., rank, grade, degree
rangschikken, rang-sHGik-ker, v., to (ar)range
rank, rank, c., tendril. a., slender, slim
ransel, ran-serl, c., knapsack, rucksack
ranselen, ran-ser-ler, v. (pop.) to thrash, to whop
ransig, ran-serHG, a., rancid
rantsoen, rant-soon, n., ration, allowance
rap, rap, a. & adv., quick, agile
rapen, rah-per, v., to pick up, to gather
rapport, rap-port, n., report, statement
ras, rass, n., race, breed. a. & adv., quick
ratelslang, rah-terl-slang, c., rattlesnake
rauw, row, a., raw, uncooked; hoarse
ravijn, rah-veyn, n., ravine; gully
ravotten, rah-vot-ter, v., to romp
razen, rah-zer, v., to rage; to bluster
razend, rah-zernt, a., furious, raving, **mad**
reactie, ray-ak-see, c., reaction
reageerbuis, ray-ah-HGayr-bowss, c., test-tube
recensie, rer-sen-see, c., review, criticism
recept, rer-sept, n., recipe; prescription
recherche, rer-shayr-sher, c., detective force
rechercheur, rer-shayr-sherr, c., detective
recht, reHGt, a. & adv., straight, right. n., right,
   claim; justice; law; duties. —— **hebben op**,
  —— **heb-ber op, to be entitled to**

rechter, reHG-ter, c., judge. a., right(-hand)

rechtmatig, reHGt-**mah**-terHG, a., lawful

rechtop, reHGt-op, adv., upright, erect

rechts, reHGts, a., right(-handed). adv., to the right

rechtschapen, reHGt-sHGah-per, a. & adv., honest

rechtsgeding, reHGts-HGer-ding, n., lawsuit

rechtsgeleerde, reHGts-HGer-layr-der, c., lawyer, jurist

rechtsom, reHGts-om, adv., to the right

rechtstreeks, reHGt-strayks, a. & adv., direct

rechtuit, reHGt-**owt**, adv., straight on; (fig.) frankly

rechtvaardig, reHGt-fahr-derHG, a. & adv., just

reclame, rer-klah-mer, c., advertising

reclameren, rer-klah-may-rer, v., to claim

recreatie, ray-kray-ah-see, c., recreation

recruut, rer-krEEt, c., recruit

rector, reck-tor, c., headmaster; rector

reçu, rer-sEE, n., (luggage-)ticket; receipt

redacteur, rer-dak-terr, c., editor

redactie, rer-dak-see, c., editorial staff

reddeloos, red-der-lohss, a. & adv., past recovery

redden, red-der, v., to save, to rescue

redding, red-ding, c., rescue; salvation

reddingsboot, red-dings-boht, c., lifeboat

reddingsgordel, red-dings-HGor-derl, c., lifebelt

rede, ray-der, c., reason; speech; (naut.) roads

redelijk, ray-der-luck, a. & adv., rational; reasonable [able

redeloos, ray-der-lohss, a., irrational

reden, ray-der, c., reason, ground, motive

redenaar, ray-der-nahr, c., orator

redeneren, ray-der-nay-rer, v., to reason, to argue

reder, ray-der, c., (naut.) (ship-)owner

redetwisten, ray-der-tvis-ter, v., to dispute

redevoering, ray-der-foo-ring, c., speech, address

redmiddel, ret-mid-derl, n., remedy

ree, ray, c., roe, hind, doe

reeds, raytss, adv., already

reeks, raykss, c., series; train (of things)

reep, rayp, c., rope, line; bar (soap, etc.)

reet, rayt, c., cleft, chink, crevice

---

refrein, rer-freyn, n., refrain, chorus

refter, ref-ter, c., refectory   [———, as a rule

regel, ray-HGerl, c., line; rule. **in de** ———, in der

regelen, ray-HGer-ler, v., to arrange; to adjust

regeling, ray-HGer-ling, c., arrangement; regulation   [regular

regelmatig, ray-HGerl-mah-terHG, a. & adv.,

regelrecht, ray-HGerl-reHGt, adv., straight, right

regen, ray-HGer, c., rain

regenachtig, ray-HGer-aHG-terHG, a., rainy, wet

regenboog, ray-HGer-bohHG, c., rainbow

regenbui, ray-HGer-bow, c., shower of rain

regenen, ray-HGer-ner, v., to rain

regenjas, ray-HGer-yass, c., rain-coat

regeren, rer-HGay-rer, v., to rule, to reign over

regering, rer-HGay-ring, c., government; reign

regie, ray-zhee, c., stage-management; direction

reglement, ray-HGler-ment, n., rules, regulations

reiger, rey-HGer, c., heron

reiken, rey-ker, v., to reach; to stretch

reikhalzen(naar), reyk-hal-zer(nahr), v., to long

rein, reyn, a. & adv., clean, pure   [(for)

reinigen, rey-ner-HGer, v., to clean, to purify

reis, reyss, c., journey, trip

reisbureau, reyss-BEE-roh, n., travel agency

reisgids, reyss-HGits, c., guide(-book); time-table

reiskosten, reyss-koss-ter, c. pl., travelling-
expenses

reisvaardig, reyss-fahr-derHG, a., ready to set

reizen, rey-zer, v., to travel   [out

reiziger, rey-zer-HGer, c., (commercial) traveller

rek, reck, n., rack; clothes-horse

rekbaar, reck-bahr, a., elastic

rekenen, ray-ker-ner, v., to count; to cipher

rekening, ray-ker-ning, c., account; calculation

rekenschap, ray-ken-sHGap, c., account

rekken, reck-ker, v., to draw out; to stretch

rekstok, reck-stock, c., horizontal bar

relaas, rer-lahss, n., account, tale, story

relletje, rel-let-yer, n., row, disturbance

rem, rem, c., brake; (fig.) check

remise, rer-mee-zer, c., remittance; drawn game

remmen, rem-mer, v., to brake; (fig.) to keep in [check
ren, ren, c., chicken-run; race, trot
renbaan, ren-bahn, c., race-course, **race-track**
rendier, ren-deer, n., reindeer
rennen, ren-ner, v., to run, to race
renpaard, ren-pahrt, n., race-horse
rente, ren-ter, c., interest [means
rentenier, ren-ter-**neer,** c., man of independent
rentmeester, rent-mays-ter, c., (estate-)steward, (land-)agent
reparatie, ray-pah-**rah**-see, c., repair(s)
repareren, ray-pah-**ray**-rer, v., to repair
repeteren, ray-per-**tay**-rer, v., to repeat; to revise; to rehearse [parts
reservedelen, rer-**zayr**-ver-day-ler, n. pl., spare
residentie, ray-zee-**den**-see, c., royal residence
rest, rest, c., rest, remainder
restauratie, res-toh-**rah**-see, c., refreshment room; restoration [dining-car
restauratiewagen, res-toh-rah-see-vah-HGer, c.,
resultaat, ray-zerl-**taht,** n., outcome, result
retourkaartje, rer-**toor**-kahrt-yer, n., return-[ticket
reuk, rerk, c., smell, scent
reumatiek, rer-mah-**teek,** c., rheumatism
reus, rerss, c., giant
reusachtig, rer-**zaHG**-terHG, a. & adv., gigantic
reutelen, rer-ter-ler, v., to rattle (in the throat)
revolutie, ray-voh-**lee**-see, c., revolution
revue, rer-**vee,** c., review; revue (on the stage)
richel, riHG-erl, c., border, ledge
richten, riHG-ter, v., to direct, to point
richting, riHG-ting, c., direction, trend
richtlijn, riHGt-leyn, c., directive
ridder, rid-der, c., knight
riem, reem, c., belt, girdle; strap, thong; oar; ream
riet, reet, n., reed; thatch; rush
rietsuiker, reet-sow-ker, c., cane-sugar
rif, rif, n., carcass; reef
rij, rey, c., queue; file, row, series, line. **in de ——** **staan, in der —— stahn,** to queue
rijbewijs, rey-ber-veyss, n., driving licence
rijbroek, rey-brook, c., riding-breeches

rijden, rey-der, v., to ride; to drive
rijgen, rey-HGer, v., to tack; to lace; to string
rijk, reyk, n., empire, kingdom. a., rich
rijkdom, reyk-dom, c., wealth
rijkelijk, rey-ker-luck, adv., richly, abundantly
rijksmuseum, reykss-mEE-zay-erm, n., national
rijkunst, rey-kernst, c., horsemanship   [museum
rijlaars, rey-lahrss, c., riding-boot
rijles, rey-less, c., riding-lesson; driving-lesson
rijm, reym, n., rhyme. c., hoar-frost
rijmen, rey-mer, v., to rhyme; (fig.) to tally
rijp, reyp, c., hoar-frost. a., ripe
rijpaard, rey-pahrt, n., riding-horse
rijs, reyss, n., sprig, twig
rijst, reyst, c., rice
rijstepap, reyss-ter-pap, c., rice-milk
rijstveld, reyst-felt, n., paddy-field
rijtuig, rey-towHG, n., carriage; cab
rijweg, rey-veHG, c., carriage-way
rijwiel, rey-veel, n., cycle, bicycle   [repairer
rijwielhersteller, rey-veel-hayr-stel-ler, c., cycle
rijwielpad, rey-veel-pat, n., cycle-track
rijzen, rey-zer, v., to rise; to go up
rijzweep, rey-zvayp, c., riding-whip
rillen, ril-ler, v., to shiver, to shudder
rilling, ril-ling, c., shiver, shudder
rimpel, rim-perl, c., wrinkle; rumple
rinkelen, rin-ker-ler, v., to jingle
riool, ree-'ohl, n., drain, sewer
rioolwater, ree'ohl-vah-ter, n., sewage
risico, ree-zee-koh, n., risk
riskeren, riss-kay-rer, v., to risk, to venture
ritje, rit-yer, n., drive, ride
ritmeester, rit-mays-ter, c., cavalry captain
ritselen, rit-ser-ler, v., to rustle
ritssluiting, rits-slow-ting, c., zip-fastener
rivier, ree-veer, c., river
riviermond, ree-veer-mont, c., mouth of a river
rivieroever, ree-veer-oo-ver, c., riverside
robbedoes, rob-ber-dooss, c., (pop.) tomboy,
robijn, roh-beyn, a., ruby   [romper
roddelen, rod-der-ler, v., (pop.) to gossip

roede, roo-der, c., rod; birch; wand

roeiboot, roo'ee-boht, c., rowing-boat

roeien, roo'yer, v., to row, to pull

roeiriem, roo'ee-reem, c., oar; scull

roeiwedstrijd, roo'ee-vet-streyt, c., boat-race

roek, rook, c., rook

roekeloos, roo-ker-lohss, a. & adv., reckless

roem, room, c., glory, fame [to boast of

roemen, roo-mer, v., to praise. —— op, —— op,

roemrijk, room-reyk, a., glorious, renowned

roep, roop, c., call; publication of banns

roepen, roo-per, v., to call, to cry, to shout

roeping, roo-ping, c., call(ing), vocation

roer, roor, n., rudder; helm; stem (of a pipe)

roeren, roo-rer, v., to stir; (fig.) to move

roerend, roo-rernt, a., moving, touching, thrilling

roerloos, roor-lohss, a., rudderless; motionless

roes, rooss, c., drunken fit, intoxication

roest, roost, n., rust; smut

roesten, rooss-ter, v., to rust; to perch (of birds)

roestvrij, roost-frey, a., stainless, rust-proof

roet, root, n., soot

roetzwart, root-svart, a., (as) black as soot

roffel, rof-ferl, c., roll of drums

rogge, roHG-er, c., rye

rok, rock, c., dress-coat; skirt

roken, roh-ker, v., to smoke

rol, rol, c., roll; scroll; roller; part (of an actor)

rollen, rol-ler, v., to roll; to tumble

rolschaats, rol-sHGahts, c., roller-skate

rolstoel, rol-stool, c., wheel-chair

roltrap, rol-trap, c., escalator

roman, roh-man, c., novel

romanschrijver, roh-man-srey-ver, c., novelist

rommel, rom-merl, c., rubbish, lumber, litter

rommelig, rom-mer-lerHG, a., untidy

romp, romp, c., trunk (body); hull; fuselage

rompslomp, romp-slomp, c., (fuss and) bother,

rond, ront, a., n., prep., round [ado

rondborstig, ront-borss-terHG, a. & adv., frank

ronddwalen, ront-dvah-ler, v., to wander [man)

ronde, ron-der, c., round; tour; beat (of police-

rondom, ron-dom, adv., & prep., round about
rondschrijven, ront-srey-ver, n., circular letter
rondtrekken, ront-treck-ker, v., to wander about
ronduit, ront-owt, adv., frankly, plainly
rondwentelen, ront-ven-ter-ler, v., to revolve
ronken, ron-ker, v., to snore; to snort; to drone
röntgenonderzoek, rernt-HGen-on-der-zook, n.,
rood, roht, a. & n., red   [X-ray examination
roodborstje, roht-bor-sher, n., (robin) redbreast
roodbruin, roht-brown, a., russet
roodharig, roht-hah-rerHG, a., red-haired
roodhuid, roht-howt, c., redskin
roodvonk, roht-fonk, c., scarlet fever
roof, rohf, c., robbery; scab
roofdier, rohf-deer, n., beast of prey
roofvogel, rohf-foh-HGerl, c., bird of prey   [cious
roofzuchtig, rohf-serHG-terHG, a. & adv., rapa-
rooien, roh-yer, v., to dig up; to pull up (trees)
rook, rohk, c., smoke
rooklucht, rohk-lerHGt, c., smell of smoke
rooktabak, rohk-tah-bak, c., pipe-tobacco
rookvlees, rohk-flayss, n., smoked beef
rookwolk, rohk-volk, c., cloud of smoke
room, rohm, c., cream
roomijs, rohm-eyss, n., ice-cream   [(target)
roos, rohss, c., rose; scurf, dandruff; bull's-eye
rooskleurig, rohss-kler-terHG, a., rose-coloured;
rooster, rohss-ter, n., grate; grill   [(fig.) bright
roosteren, rohss-ter-rer, v., to toast; to roast
rossig, ros-serHG, a., reddish, ruddy
rot, rot, a., rotten, putrid
rots, rotss, c., rock; cliff; crag
rotsachtig, rotss-aHG-terHG, a., rocky
rotsblok, rotss-block, n., boulder, piece of rock
rotsvast, rotss-fast, a., firm as a rock
rotten, rot-ter, v., to rot, to decay
rotting, rot-ting, c., cane; decay, putrefaction
rouw, row, c., mourning
rouwbeklag, row-ber-klaHG, n., condolence
rouwbrief, row-breef, c., notification of death
rouwen, row-er, v., to be in mourning
roven, roh-ver, v., to rob, to pillage

rover, roh-ver, c., robber, brigand   [bers
roversbende, roh-vers-ben-der, c., gang of rob-
royaal, roh-yahl, a. & adv., liberal, free-handed
royeren, roh-yay-rer, v., to expel; to cancel
rozengeur, roh-zer-HGerr, c., perfume of roses
rozet, roh-zet, c., rosette
rozijn, roh-zeyn, c., raisin
rubberboot, rerb-ber-boht, c., (rubber) dinghy
rubriek, REE-breek, c., head(ing); column, sec-
    tion (of a paper)
rug, rerHG, c., back; ridge (of mountains)
ruggegraat, rerHG-er-HGraht, c., backbone
ruggesteun, rerHG-er-stern, c., backing
rugleuning, rerHG-ler-ning, c., back (of a chair)
rugzak, rerHG-sak, c., rucksack
rui, row, c., moulting
ruig, rowHG, a., shaggy; rough
ruiken, row-ker, v., to smell, to scent
ruiker, row-ker, c., nosegay
ruilen, row-ler, v., to exchange, to barter
ruim, rowm, a. & adv., large; ample. n., (naut.)
ruimen, row-mer, v., to empty; to clear   [hold
ruimschoots, rowm-sHGohts, adv., amply, abun-
ruimte, rowm- ter, c., room, space   [dantly
ruïne, REE-ee-ner, c., ruins; (fig.) wreck
ruisen, row-ser, v., to rustle; to purl; to murmur
ruit, rowt, c., pane (of glass); diamond; lozenge
ruitenwisser, row-ter-vis-ser, c., windscreen
ruiter, row-ter, c., horseman   [wiper
ruiterij, row-ter-rey, c., cavalry
ruiterlijk, row-ter-luck, a. & adv., frank, plain
ruk, rerk, c., pull, jerk
rukken, rerk-ker, v., to pull, to jerk, to snatch
rukwind, rerk-vint, c., gust of wind
rumoer, REE-moor, n., noise, clamour, uproar
rumoerig, REE-moo-rerHG, a., noisy, tumultuous
rund, rernt, n., cow, bull, ox
rundvee, rernt-fay, n., horned cattle
rundvlees, rernt-flayss, n., beef
rups, rerpss, c., caterpillar
rust, rerst, c., rest, quiet, calm
rusteloos, rerss-ter-lohss, a. & adv., restless

rusten, rerss-ter, v., to rest
rustig, rerss-terHG, a. & adv., quiet, calm, still
ruw, rEE, a. & adv., rough; raw; crude; (fig.) rude
ruzie, rEE-zee, c., quarrel, row, squabble, brawl
ruziemaker, rEE-zee-mah-ker, c., quarrelsome
  person

saai, sah'ee, a. & adv., dull, drab, tedious, slow
saamhorigheid, sahm-hoh-terHG-heyt, c., solid-
sabel, sah-berl, c., sword, sabre. n., sable   [arity
saboteren, sah-boh-tay-rer, v., to sabotage
sacristie, sah-kriss-tee, c., sacristy, vestry
sage, sah-HGer, c., legend, tradition
salaris, sah-lah-riss, n., salary
saldo, sal-doh, n., balance. **batig ——,** bah-terHG
  ——, credit balance   [dresser's]
salon, sah-lon, c., drawing-room; saloon (hair-
salueren, sah-lEE-ay-rer, v., to (give a) salute
salvo, sal-voh, n., volley, salvo
samen, sah-mer, adv., together   [together
samendrukken, sah-mer-drerk-ker, v., to press
samengaan, sah-mer-HGahn, v., to go together;
  to tally   [complex; compound
samengesteld, sah-mer-HGer-stelt, a. & p.p.,
samenhang, sah-mer-hang, c., context; coherence   [together
samenkomen, sah-mer-koh-mer, v., to come
samenleving, sah-mer-lay-ving, c., society
samenloop, sah-mer-lohp, c., coincidence; concourse
samenscholing, sah-mer-sHGoh-ling, c., riot
samenschrapen, sah-mer-srah-per, v., to scrape
  together   [together
samensmelten, sah-mer-smel-ter, v., to melt
samenspannen, sah-mer-span-ner, v., to conspire
samenspanning, sah-mer-span-ning, c., conspiracy
samenspel, sah-mer-spel, n., team-work; com-
  bined action
samenspraak, sah-mer-sprahk, c., conversation
samenstellen, sah-mer-stel-ler, v., to compose

samenstelling, sah-mer-stel-ling, c., composition

samenstromen, sah-mer-stroh-mer, v., to flow together [traction

samentrekking, sah-mer-treck-king, c., con-

samenvallen, sah-mer-fal-ler, v., to coincide

samenvatting, sah-mer-fat-ting, c., summary

samenvoegen, sah-mer-foo-HGer, v., to join

samenwerken, sah-mer-vayr-ker, v., to co-operate [together

samenwonen, sah-mer-voh-ner, v., to live

samenzweren, sah-mer-zvay-rer, v., to conspire

sanctie, sænk-see, c., sanction

sandaal, san-dahl, c., sandal

saneren, sah-nay-rer, v., to reorganize (finances)

sap, sap, n., sap; juice; fluid

sapperloot! sap-per-loht, interj., by Jove!

sappig, sap-perHG, a., sappy; juicy

sarcastisch, sar-kass-teess, a. & adv., sarcastic

sardientje, sar-deent-yer, n., sardine

sarren, sar-rer, v., to tease, to nag, to badger

satanisch, sah-tah-neess, a. & adv., satanic

satijnen, sah-tey-ner, a., satin

saus, sowss, c., sauce; gravy

sauskom, sowss-kom, c., sauceboat

savoyekool, sah-voh-yer-kohl, c., savoy (cabbage)

scalperen, skal-pay-rer, v., to scalp

schaakbord, sHGahk-bort, n., chess-board [men

schaakspel, sHGahk-spel, n., chess; set of chess-

schaal, sHGahl, c., scale(s); shell; dish; plate. **op grote ——, op** HGroh-ter **——,** on a large scale

schaamte, sHGahm-ter, c., shame [scale

schaamteloos, sHGahm-ter-lohss, a. & adv., shameless

schaap, sHGahp, n., sheep [shameless

schaapherder, sHGahp-hayr-der, c., shepherd

schaapskooi, sHGahps-koh'ee, c., sheep-fold

schaar, sHGahr, c., scissors; shears

schaars, sHGahrss, a. & adv., scarce, scanty

schaarste, sHGahrss-ter, c., scarcity, shortage

schaats, sHGahtss, c., skate

schaatsenrijden, sHGaht-ser-rey-der, v., to skate

schade, sHGah-der, c., damage; detriment

schadelijk, sHGah-der-luck, a., harmful, injurious

schadeloosstelling, SHGah-der-lohss-stel-ling, c., compensation

schaden, SHGah-der, v., to damage, to hurt

schadepost, SHGah-der-post, c., loss

schadevergoeding, SHGah-der-fer-HGoo-ding, c., indemnification

schaduw, SHGah-dEE, c., shade, shadow

schaduwbeeld, SHGah-dEE-baylt, n., silhouette

schaduwrijk, SHGah-dEE-reyk, a., shady

schaduwzijde, SHGah-dEE-zey-der, c., shady side

schakel, SHGah-kerl, c., link

schakelaar, SHGah-ker-lahr, c., switch

schakelbord, SHGah-kerl-bort, n., switch-board

schaken, SHGah-ker, v., to play chess; to abduct

schakering, SHGah-kay-ring, c., nuance, shade

schalk, SHGalk, c., wag, rogue

schalks, SHGalkss, a. & adv., waggish, roguish

schallen, SHGal-ler, v., to (re)sound

schamel, SHGah-merl, a. & adv., poor   [ashamed

schamen (zich), SHGah-mer (ziHG), v., to be

schamper, SHGam-per, a. & adv., scornful

schandaal, SHGan-dahl, n., scandal, shame

schandalig, SHGan-dah-lerHG, a., disgraceful

schanddaad, SHGand-daht, c., outrage

schande, SHGan-der, c., shame, disgrace

schandelijk, SHGan-der-luck, a. & adv., shameful

schandvlek, SHGant-fleck, c., stain, blemish

schapebout, SHGah-per-bowt, c., leg of mutton

schapenvlees, SHGah-per-flayss, n., mutton

schappelijk, SHGap-per-luck, a. & adv., fair, moderate

scharlaken, SHGar-lah-ker, n. & a., scarlet

scharnier, SHGar-neer, n., hinge   [fumble

scharrelen, SHGar-rer-ler, v., to muddle; to

schat, SHGat, c., treasure; (fig.) darling   [ter]

schateren, SHGah-ter-rer, v., to roar (with laugh-

schaterlach, SHGah-ter-laHG, c., loud laughter

schatkist, SHGat-kist, c., (public) treasury

schatplichtig, SHGat-pliHG-terHG, a., tributary

schatrijk, SHGat-reyk, a., wealthy

schatten, SHGat-ter, v., to value; to estimate

schatting, SHGat-ting, c., tribute; estimation

schavot, SHGah-vot, n., scaffold
schavuit, SHGah-vowt, c., rascal
schede, SHGay-der, c., sheath
schedel, SHGay-derl, c., skull
scheef, SHGayf, a., oblique; on one side; wry
scheel, SHGayl, a., squinting
scheen, SHGayn, c., shin
scheep gaan, SHGayp HGahn, v., to go on board
scheepsbemanning, SHGayps-ber-man-ning, c.,
    ship's crew
scheepsjongen, SHGayps-yong-er, c., cabin-boy
scheepslading, SHGayps-lah-ding, c., cargo
scheepsruim, SHGayps-rowm, n., ship's hold
scheepsruimte, SHGayps-rowm-ter, c., tonnage
scheepstimmerwerf, SHGayps-tim-mer-vayrf,
    c., ship-yard
scheepvaart, SHGayp-fahrt, c., shipping
scheepvaartmaatschappij, SHGayp-fahrt-maht-
    SHGap-pey, c., shipping company   [razor
scheerapparaat, SHGayr-ap-pah-raht, n., safety-
scheergerei, SHGayr-HGer-rey, c., shaving-tackle
scheerkwast, SHGayr-k'vast, c., shaving-brush
scheermes, SHGayr-mess, n., razor
scheermesje, SHGayr-mess-sher, n., razor-blade
scheerzeep, SHGayr-zayp, c., shaving-soap
scheiden, SHGey-der, v., to separate; to divorce
scheiding, SHGey-ding, c., separation; parting;
    divorce   [referee
scheidsrechter, SHGeyts-reHG-ter, c., arbiter;
scheikunde, SHGey-kern-der, c., chemistry
schel, SHGel, c., bell. a. & adv., shrill
schelden, SHGel-der, v., to call names
scheldnaam, SHGelt-nahm, c., nickname
scheldwoord, SHGelt-vohrt, c., abusive word
schelen, SHGay-ler, v., to differ; to want. wat
    kan dat ——? vat kan dat ——, what does
    it matter?
schelm, SHGelm, c., rascal, rogue
schelms, SHGelmss, a. & adv., roguish, knavish
schelp, SHGelp, c., shell; scallop
schelvis, SHGel-viss, c., haddock
schema, SHGay-mah, n., outline, sketch, skeleton

schemerachtig, SHGay-mer-*a*HG-terHG, a., dusky
schemering, SHGay-mer-ring, c., twilight, dusk
schemerlamp, SHGay-mer-lamp, c., shaded lamp
schemerlicht, SHGay-mer-liHGt, n., twilight
schenden, SHGen-der, v., to disfigure; (fig.) to
schenkblad, SHGenk-bl*a*t, n., tray   [violate
schenken, SHGen-ker, v., to pour (out); to grant
schenking, SHGen-king, c., gift, grant, donation
schep, SHGep, c., scoop; spoonful
scheppen, SHGep-per, v., to create; to scoop
schepper, SHGep-per, c., creator; scoop
schepping, SHGep-ping, c., creation
schepsel, SHGep-serl, n., creature
schepter, SHGep-ter, c., sceptre
scheren, SHGay-rer, v., to shave; to shear; to trim
scherf, SHGerf, c., fragment, splinter
scherm, SHGayrm, n., screen; curtain; awning
schermen, SHGayr-mer, v., to fence
schermkunst, SHGayrm-kernst, c., art of fencing
schermutseling, SHGayr-**mert**-ser-ling, c., skirmish
scherp, SHGayrp, a. & adv., sharp; keen; severe
scherpen, SHGayr-per, v., to sharpen; to whet
scherpschutter, SHGayrp-SHGert-ter, c., sharp-shooter; sniper
scherpziend, SHGayrp-seent, a., keen-sighted
scherpzinnig, SHGayrp-sin-nerHG, a. & adv., acute
scherts, SHGayrtss, c., joke, raillery
schertsen, SHGayrt-ser, v., to joke, to jest
schets, SHGets, c., sketch, outline
schetsen, SHGet-ser, v., to sketch, to draw
schetteren, SHGet-ter-rer, v., to blare; to brag
scheur, SHGerr, c., crack, tear, slit
scheuren, SHGer-rer, v., to tear (up), to rend
scheuring, SHGer-ring, c., (fig.) rupture, schism
scheut, SHGert, c., shoot, sprig; dash (of brandy)
schichtig, SHGiHG-terHG, a. & adv., skittish, shy
schielijk, SHGee-luck, a. & adv., sudden, quick
schiereiland, SHGeer-ey-l*a*nt, n., peninsula
schieten, SHGee-ter, v., to shoot; to fire
schietoefeningen, SHGeet-oo-fer-ning-er, c. pl., target-practice

schiften, SHGif-ter, v., to sort (out); to curdle

schijfje, SHGeyf-yer, n., thin slice

schijn, SHGeyn, c., glimmer; (fig.) appearance. de —— redden, der —— red-der, to keep up appearances

schijnbaar, SHGeyn-bahr, a. & adv., apparent

schijnen, SHGeyf-ner, v., to shine; to seem

schijnheilig, SHGeyn-**hey**-lerHG, a. & adv., hypocritical

schijnsel, SHGeyn-serl, n., glimmer, glow, sheen

schijnwerper, SHGeyn-vayr-per, c., searchlight; floodlight [oneself

schik hebben, SHGick heb-ber, v., to amuse

schikken, SHGick-ker, v., to arrange; to settle

schikking, SHGick-king, c., arrangement, settle-

schil, SHGil, c., rind; peel, skin [ment

schild, SHGilt, n., shield [painter

schilder, SHGil-der, c., painter, artist; (house-)

schilderachtig, SHGil-der-aHG-terHG, a. & adv., picturesque [picture

schilderen, SHGil-der-rer, v., to paint; (fig.) to

schilderij, SHGil-der-rey, c., picture, painting

schilderkunst, SHGil-der-kernst, c., (art of) painting [ing

schilderstuk, SHGil-der-sterk, n., picture, paint-

schildpad, SHGilt-pat, c., tortoise; turtle

schilfer, SHGil-fer, c., scale; dandruff; flake

schillen, SHGil-ler, v., to peel

schim, SHGim, c., shadow; ghost, spectre [mildew

schimmel, SHGim-merl, c., grey horse; mould;

schimpen, SHGim-per, v., to scoff, to gibe, to rail

schimpscheut, SHGimp-sHGert, c., gibe, jeer

schip, SHGip, n., ship; nave (of a church)

schipbreuk, SHGip-brerk, c., shipwreck. —— lijden, —— ley-der, to be shipwrecked

schipbreukeling, SHGip-brer-ker-ling, c., shipwrecked person

schipbrug, SHGip-brerHG, c., bridge of boats

schipper, SHGip-per, c., boatman; skipper

schitteren, SHGit-ter-rer, v., to glitter, to shine

schitterend, SHGit-ter-rernt, a. & adv., (fig.) [brilliant

schminken, shmin-ker, v., to make up [brilliant

schobbejak, sHGob-ber-yak, c., rogue, scamp

schoeisel, sHGoo-ee-serl, n., foot-wear, shoes

schoen, sHGoon, c., shoe; boot

schoenborstel, sHGoon-bor-sterl, c., shoe-brush

schoenlepel, sHGoon-lay-perl, c., shoe-horn

schoenpoetser, sHGoon-poot-ser, c., shoe-black

schoensmeer, sHGoon-smayr, n., boot-polish

schoenveter, sHGoon-fay-ter, c., boot-lace

schoffelen, sHGof-fer-ler, v., to hoe

schoft, sHGoft, c., scoundrel, scamp

schok, sHGock, c., jerk; shock; concussion

schokken, sHGock-ker, v., to shake, to jerk

schol, sHGol, c., floe (of ice); plaice

scholier, sHGoh-leer, c., schoolboy, schoolgirl

scholing, sHGoh-ling, c., schooling, training

schommel, sHGom-merl, c., swing

schommelen, sHGom-mer-ler, v., to swing; to rock; to roll

schommelstoel, sHGom-merl-stool, c., rocking-chair [chair

schoof, sHGohf, c., sheaf

schooien, sHGoh-yer, v., to beg

schooier, sHGoh-yer, c., beggar; tramp

school, sHGohl, c., school; college; shoal (of fish)

schoolbank, sHGohl-bank, c., form, desk (at school) [school]

schoolbord, sHGohl-bort, n., blackboard [school]

schooljongen, sHGohl-yong-er, c., schoolboy

schoollokaal, sHGohl-loh-kahl, n., class-room

schoolmakker, sHGohl-mak-ker, c., schoolmate

schoolmeester, sHGohl-mays-ter, c., school-master; (fig.) pedant

schoolmeisje, sHGohl-mey-sher, n., schoolgirl

schooltas, sHGohl-tass, c., satchel

schoon, sHGohn, a. & adv., beautiful; clean; pure

schoonbroer, sHGohn-broor, c., brother-in-law

schoonheid, sHGohn-heyt, c., beauty

schoonmaak, sHGohn-mahk, c., house-cleaning

schoonmoeder, sHGohn-moo-der, c., mother-in-law [in-law

schoonouders, sHGohn-ow-derss, c. pl., parents-

schoonvader, sHGohn-fah-der, c., father-in-law

schoonvegen, sHGohn-fay-HGer, v., to sweep

schoonzoon, sHGohn-zohn, c., son-in-law [clean

schoonzuster, SHGohn-zers-ter, c., sister-in-law
schoorsteen, SHGohr-stayn, c., chimney; funnel
schoorsteenmantel, SHGohr-stayn-man-terl, c.,
   mantelpiece   [chimney-sweep
schoorsteenveger, SHGohr-stayn-fay-HGer, c.,
schoorvoetend, SHGohr-foo-tent, adv., reluctantly
schoot, SHGoht, c., lap; (fig.) womb
schoothondje, SHGoht-hont-yer, n., lap-dog
schop, SHGop, c., kick; spade, shovel; scoop
schoppen, SHGop-per, v., to kick
schoppen-vrouw, SHGop-per-frow, c., queen of
                                              [spades
schor, SHGor, a., hoarse, husky
schorpioen, SHGor-pee-oon, c., scorpion
schors, SHGorss, c., bark; rind
schorsen, SHGor-ser, v., to suspend; to adjourn
                                          [(a meeting)
schort, SHGort, c., apron; pinafore
schot, SHGot, n., shot, report; partition (in a room)
schotel, SHGoh-terl, c., dish
schoteltje, SHGoh-telt-yer, n., saucer; dish
schots, SHGotss, adv., rudely, c., floe (of ice)
schotschrift, SHGot-srift, n., lampoon, libel
schouder, SHGow-der, c., shoulder
                                              [blade
schouderblad, SHGow-der-blat, n., shoulder-
schouderophalen, SHGow-der-op-hah-ler, n.,
   shrug of the shoulders
schouw, SHGow, c., fireplace, chimney; inspection
schouwburg, SHGow-berrHG, c., theatre
schouwspel, SHGow-spel, n., spectacle, sight
schraag, srahHG, c., trestle
schraal, srahl, a., poor; slender; lean; thin
schraapzucht, srahp-serHGt, c., stinginess
schragen, srah-HGer, v., to support, to prop (up)
schram, sram, c., scratch
                                              [smart
schrander, sran-der, a. & adv., clever, bright,
schransen, sran-ser, v., to gormandize
schrapen, srah-per, v., to scrape
schraperig, srah-per-rerHG, a., stingy, covetous
schrappen, srap-per, v., to cross out; to scrape
schrede, sray-der, c., step, pace
schreeuw, sray'oo, c., shout, cry, scream
schreeuwen, sray-ver, v., to cry, to shout, to
schreien, srey-er, v., to weep
                                              [shriek

schriel, sreel, a. & adv., stingy, mean

schrift, srift, n., copy-book; writing

schriftelijk, srif-ter-luck, a. & adv., in writing

schrijfbehoeften, sreyf-ber-hoof-ter, c. pl., stationery

schrijffout, sreyf-fowt, c., slip of the pen [writer

schrijfmachine, sreyf-mah-shee-ner, c., type-

schrijftaal, sreyf-tahl, c., written language

schrijftafel, sreyf-tah-ferl, c., writing-table

schrijlings, srey-lings, adv., astride

schrijnwerker, sreyn-vayr-ker, c., joiner, cab-

schrijven, srey-ver, v., to write [inet-maker

schrijver, srey-ver, c., writer; author; clerk

schrik, srick, c., fright; alarm. **iemand ——
aanjagen,** ee-mant —— **ahn-yah-HGer,** to
give someone a fright [ened

schrikachtig, srick-αHG-terHG, a., easily fright-

schrikbarend, srick-bah-rernt, a.&adv., appalling

schrikkelijk, srick-ker-luck, a., dreadful

schrikkeljaar, srick-kerl-yahr, n., leap year

schrikken, srick-ker, v., to be frightened

schril, sril, a. & adv., shrill; glaring; violent

schrobben, srob-ber, v., to scrub

schroef, sroof, c., screw; propeller

schroeien, sroo-yer, v., to singe; to scorch

schroevedraaier, sroo-ver-drah-yer, c., screw-

schrokkig, srock-kerHG, a., greedy [driver

schromelijk, sroh-mer-luck, a. & adv., terrible

schroom, srohm, c., diffidence; fear

schroot, sroht, n., scrap-iron; grape-shot

schub, sHGerp, c., scale (of a fish)

schuchter, sHGerHG-ter, a. & adv., shy, timid

schudden, sHGerd-der, v., to shake; to shuffle

schuier, sHGow-er, c., brush; (carpet-)sweeper

schuif, sHGowf, c., slide; bolt

schuifdeur, sHGowf-dert, c., sliding-door

schuifelen, sHGow-fer-ler, v., to shuffle [der

schuifladder, sHGowf-lad-der, c., extension-lad-

schuifraam, sHGowf-rahm, n., sash-window

schuilen, sHGow-ler, v., to (take) shelter; to hide

schuilkelder, sHGowl-kel-der, c., underground
shelter

schuilnaam, SHGowl-nahm, c., pen-name

schuilplaats, SHGowl-plahtss, c., hiding-place;

schuim, SHGowm, n., foam; froth; lather [shelter

schuimspaan, SHGowm-spahn, c., skimmer

schuin(s), SHGown(ss), a. & adv., slanting; (fig.)

schuit, SHGowt, c., barge, boat [obscene

schuiven, SHGOW-ver, v., to push; to slip

schuld, SHGerlt, c., debt; guilt

schuldbekentenis, SHGerlt-ber-ken-ter-niss, c., confession of guilt; IOU

schuldbewust, SHGerlt-ber-verst, a., guilty

schuldeiser, SHGerlt-ey-ser, c., creditor

schuldenaar, SHGerl-der-nahr, c., debtor

schuldig, SHGerl-derHG, a., guilty. —— zijn, —— zeyn, to owe [shabby, mean

schunnig, SHGern-nerHG, a. & adv., scurrilous

schuren, SHGEE-rer, v., to scour; to scrub

schurft, SHGerrft, c., itch, scabies; mange; scab

schurftig, SHGerrf-terHG, a., scabby

schurk, SHGerrk, c., scoundrel, rogue, villain

schutting, SHGert-ting, c., fence; hoarding

schuur, SHGEEr, c., barn; shed [sand-paper

schuurpapier, SHGEEr-pah-peer, n., emery-paper,

schuw, SHGEE, a. & adv., shy, timid

schuwen, SHGEE-ver, v., to shun

secretaris, sik-rer-tah-riss, c., secretary; town

sectie, seck-see, c., section; post-mortem [clerk

secuur, ser-KEEr, a. & adv., accurate

sedert, say-dert, prep. & adv., since

sein, seyn, n., signal

seinen, sey-ner, v., to signal; to telegraph

seinhuisje, seyn-how-sher, n., signal-box

seizoen, sey-zoon, n., season

sensatie, sen-sah-see, c., sensation; thrill

september, sep-tem-ber, c., September

sering, ser-ring, c., lilac

serre, sayr-rer, c., conservatory; greenhouse

servet, sayr-vet, n., napkin, serviette

servies, sayr-veess, n., tea-set; dinner-set

sfeer, sfayr, c., sphere; (fig.) province, domain

sidderen, sid-der-rer, v., to tremble, to shake

sieraad, see-raht, n., ornament

sierlijk, seer-luck, a. & adv., elegant
sigaar, see-HGahr, c., cigar   [holder
sigarenpijpje, see-HGah-rer-peyp-yer, n., cigar-
signaal, see-n'yahl, n., signal; (mil.) bugle-call
signalement, see-n'yah-ler-ment, n., description
sijpelen, sey-per-ler, v., to trickle
sik, sick, c., goat; goat's beard; goatee
sikkel, sick-kerl, c., sickle
simpel, sim-perl, a., simple; silly
sinaasappel, see-nahss-*a*p-perl, c., orange
sinds, sints, prep. & adv., since
singel, sing-erl, c., moat; girdle; girth
sinjeur, see-n'yerr, c., (strange) fellow
sintels, sin-terlss, c. pl., cinders
sissen, sis-ser, v., to hiss; to sizzle, to frizzle
sjaal, shahl, c., shawl, wrap; scarf
sjacheraar, sh*a*-HGer-rahr, c., barterer
sjees, shayss, c., gig
sjerp, shayrp, c., sash, scarf
sjofel, shoh-ferl, a., shabby
sjokken, shock-ker, v., to trudge, to jog
sjouwer, show-er, c., porter
skilopen, skee-loh-per, v., to ski
sla, slah, c., salad; lettuce
slaaf, slahf, c., slave, bondman   [blows
slaags raken, slahHGs rah-ker, v., to come to
slaan, slahn, v., to strike; to beat; to slap
slaap, slahp, c., sleep   [with sleep
slaapdronken, slahp-dron-ker, a., overcome
slaapkamer, slahp-kah-mer, c., bedroom
slaapwandelaar, slahp-v*a*n-der-lahr, c., sleep-
slaapzaal, slahp-sahl, c., dormitory   [walker
slachten, sl*a*HG-ter, v., to slaughter
slachtoffer, sl*a*HGt-of-fer, n., victim
slag, sl*a*HG, c., blow; stroke; slap; beat; clap;
slag, sl*a*HG, n., sort, kind   [warble
slagader, sl*a*HG-ah-der, c., artery
slagboom, sl*a*HG-bohm, c., barrier
slagen, slah-HGer, v., to succeed; to pass (exam-
slager, slah-HGer, c., butcher   [ination]
slagerij, slah-HGer-rey, c., butcher's shop
slagregen, sl*a*HG-ray-HGer, c., downpour

slagroom, sl*a*HG-rohm, c., whipped cream
slagschip, sl*a*HG-sHGip, n., battleship
slagtand, sl*a*HG-t*a*nt, c., fang; tusk
slagvaardig, sl*a*HG-fahr-derHG, a., (fig.) quick [witted
slagveld, sl*a*HG-felt, n., battlefield
slagzin, sl*a*HG-sin, c., slogan
slak, sl*a*k, c., snail; slug
slakkenhuisje, sl*a*k-ker-how-sher, n., snail-shell
slang, sl*a*ng, c., snake; tube, hose
slangegif, sl*a*ng-er-HGif, n., snake-poison
slangenbezweerder, sl*a*ng-er-ber-zvayr-der, c., [snake-charmer
slank, sl*a*nk, a. & adv., slender
slaolie, slah-oh-lee, c., salad oil [(fig.) lax
slap, sl*a*p, a., slack; soft; limp; supple; flabby;
slapeloosheid, slah-per-lohss-heyt, c., sleepless- [ness
slapen, slah-per, v., to sleep
slaperig, slah-per-rerHG, a., sleepy
slavernij, slah-ver-ney, c., slavery, servitude
slecht, sleHGt, a. & adv., bad; wicked
slechten, sleHG-ter, v., to level; to demolish
slechts, sleHGtss, adv., only, merely, but
slede, slay-der, c., sledge, sleigh
sleepboot, slayp-boht, c., tug(-boat)
sleeptouw, slayp-tow, n., tow-rope
slemppartij, slemp-p*a*r-tey, c., carousal
slenteren, slen-ter-rer, v., to lounge, to saunter
slepen, slay-per, v., to drag; to trail; (naut.) to [tow
sleuf, slerf, c., slot, groove, notch
sleur, slerr, c., rut, routine
sleuren, sler-rer, v., to drag
sleutel, sler-terl, c., key; (mus.) clef
sleutelbeen, sler-terl-bayn, n., collar bone
sleutelbloem, sler-terl-bloom, c., cowslip; prim- [rose
sleutelgat, sler-terl-HG*a*t, n., keyhole
slib, slip, c., mire, ooze, mud, slime
slibberen, slib-ber-rer, v., to slip; to slide
slibberig, slib-ber-rerHG, a., slippery
slijk, sleyk, n., mud, slime, mire
slijm, sleym, n., slime; phlegm
slijpen, sley-per, v., to grind, to whet; to polish [(diamonds)
slijpsteen, sleyp-stayn, c., grindstone
slijtage, sley-tah-zher, c., wear and tear

slijten, sley-ter, v., to wear out; to retail
slijter, sley-ter, c., retailer; licensed victualler
slikken, slick-ker, v., to swallow
slim, slim, a. & adv., sly, artful
slinger, sling-er, c., handle; pendulum
slingeren, sling-er-rer, v., to swing; to roll
slinken, slin-ker, v., to shrink; to boil down
slinks, slinkss, a. & adv., cunning
slip, slip, c., flap, tail (of a coat); lappet
slippen, slip-per, v., to skid; to slip
slobkous, slop-kowss, c., gaiter; spat
sloep, sloop, c., sloop, shallop
sloffen, slof-fer, v., to shuffle
slok, slock, c., draught (of water)
slokken, slock-ker, v., to swallow
slonzig, slon-zerHG, a., slovenly, dowdy
sloop, slohp, c., pillow-case
sloot, sloht, c., ditch
slop, slop, n., slum   [mine
slopen, sloh-per, v., to pull down; (fig.) to under-
slordig, slor-derHG, a. & adv., careless, slovenly
slot, slot, n., lock; clasp; castle; conclusion.
  achter —— en grendel, aHG-ter —— en
  HGren-derl, under lock and key
slotenmaker, sloh-ter-mah-ker, c., locksmith
slotnummer, slot-nerm-mer, n., last item
slotsom, slot-som, c., result
sluier, slow-er, c., veil
sluikhandel, slowk-han-derl, c., smuggling
sluimering, slow-mer-ring, c., doze, slumber
sluipen, slow-per, v., to steal; to slip (out)
sluipmoord, slowp-mohrt, c., assassination
sluis, slowss, c., sluice
sluitboom, slowt-bohm, c., (railway) gate; bar
sluiten, slow-ter, v., to shut; to close; to lock
sluiting, slow-ting, c., fastening(s); closing
slurf, slerrf, c., trunk (of an elephant)
slurpen, slerr-per, v., to sip, to lap; to suck
sluw, slEE, a. & adv., crafty, astute, foxy
smaad, smaht, c., revilement, opprobrium
smaadschrift, smaht-srift, n., libel
smaak, smahk, c., taste; liking

smaakvol, smak-fol, a. & adv., in good taste
smachten, smaHG**-ter,** v., to languish, to yearn for
smaden, smah-der, v., to defame, to revile
smakelijk, smah-ker-luck, a. & adv., tasty
smakeloos, smah-ker-lohss, a. & adv., tasteless
smaken, smah-ker, v., to taste
smal, smal, a. & adv., narrow
smalen, smah-ler, v., to rail
smalfilm, smal-film, c., miniature film
smaragd, smah-raHGt**,** n., emerald
smart, smart, c., sorrow, grief, affliction
smartelijk, smar-ter-luck, a. & adv., grievous,
smeden, smay-der, v., to forge   [painful
smederij, smay-der-rey, c., smithy
smeedijzer, smayt-ey-zer, n., wrought iron
smeekbede, smayk-bay-der, c., supplication
smeer, smayr, c., grease, fat; stain, spot
smeerlap, smayr-lap, c., (fig.) blackguard
smeken, smay-ker, v., to beseech, to entreat
smelten, smel-ter, v., to melt
smeitkroes, smelt-krooss, c., melting-pot
smeren, smay-rer, v., to oil; to lubricate
smerig, smay-rerHG**,** a. & adv., dirty, filthy,
smet, smet, c., stain, spot; slur, blemish   [greasy
smetteloos, smet-ter-lohss, a., stainless
smeulen, smer-ler, v., to smoulder
smid, smit, c., (black)smith
smidse, smit-ser, c., smithy
smijten, smey-ter, v., to fling, to hurl, to throw
smoesje, smoo-sher, n., (pop.) poor excuse
smokkelaar, smock-ker-lahr, c., smuggler
smokkeien, smock-ker-ler, v., to smuggle
smoren, smoh-rer, v., to smother; to strangle;
   (fig.) to stifle
smullen, smerl-ler, v., to feast
smulpartij, smerl-par-tey, c., banquet
snaak, snahk, c., wag
snaar, snahr, c., chord, string   [(for)
snakken (naar), snack-ker (nahr), v., to yearn
snappen, snap-per, v., to snatch; to catch; to
   understand
snateren, snah-ter-rer, v., to chatter, to cackle

snauwen, snow-er, v., to snarl; to snap
snavel, sneb, snah-verl, snep, c., bill, beak
snede, snay-der, c., slice; rasher; cut; edge (knife,
snedig, snay-derHG, a., witty, smart   [etc.]
sneeuw, snay'oo, c., snow
sneeuwbal, snay'oo-bal, c., snowball
sneeuwen, snay-ver, v., to snow   [snowdrift
sneeuwjacht, snay'oo-yaHGt, c., snowstorm,
sneeuwklokje, snay'oo-klock-yer, n., snowdrop
sneeuwvlok, snay'oo-flock, c., snowflake
snel, snel, a. & adv., quick, fast, rapid, speedy
snelheid, snel-heyt, c., velocity, speed, swiftness
snellen, snel-ler, v., to hurry, to hasten
sneltrein, snel-treyn, c., fast train, express
snerpend, snayr-pernt, a.,biting, piercing, cutting
snert, snayrt, c., pea-soup; (fig.) trash
sneuvelen, sner-ver-ler, v., to be killed (in action)
snibbig, snib-berHG, a. & adv., snappish, snappy
snijboon, sney-bohn, c., French bean; (fig.) queer
snijden, sney-der, v., to cut (up); to carve   [fish
snik, snick, c., sob, gasp
snikheet, snick-hayt, a., stifling
snikken, snick-ker, v., to sob
snipper, snip-per, c., cutting; scrap
snoeien, snoo-yer, v., to lop; to prune
snoeimes, snoo'ee-mess, n., pruning-knife
snoek, snook, c., pike (fish)
snoep, snoop, c., sweets
snoepachtig, snoop-aHG-terHG, a., fond of sweets
snoepen, snoo-per, v., to eat sweets
snoer, snoor, n., string; cord; flex
snoet, snoot, c., muzzle, snout
snoever, snoo-ver, c., boaster, braggart
snoezig, snoo-zerHG, a. & adv., sweet, lovely
snoodaard, snoh-dahrt, c., villain
snor, snor, c., moustache; whiskers (of a cat)
snorken, snor-ker, v., to snore
snorren, snor-rer, v., to drone; to purr; to whiz
snuffelen, snerf-fer-ler, v., to nose, to ferret
snugger, snerHG-er, a. & adv., (pop.) clever; bright
snuifdoos, snowf-dohss, c., snuff-box
snuifje, snowf-yer, n., pinch of snuff

snuisterijen, snows-ter-rey-er, c. pl., knick-knacks, trinkets [elephant)

snuit, snowt, c., muzzle, snout; trunk (of an

snuiven, snow-ver, v., to sniff; to take snuff

sober, soh-ber, a. & adv., sober; scanty

sociëteit, soh-see-teyt, c., club(-house); society

soep, soop, c., soup; broth

soepel, soo-perl, a., flexible

soes, sooss, c., doze; puffed cake

soezen, soo-zer, v., to doze

sok, sock, c., sock; (fig.) mug, fogey

sokophouder, sock-op-how-der, c., sock-sus-

soldaat, sol-daht, c., soldier [pender

solderen, sol-day-rer, v., to solder, to braze

soldij, sol-dey, c., (mil.) pay

solist, soh-list, c., soloist

sollicitant, sol-lee-see-tant, c., candidate

solliciteren (naar), sol-lee-see-tay-rer (nahr),

som, som, c., sum; problem [v., to apply (for)

somber, som-ber, a. & adv., gloomy, dreary, sad

sommige, som-mer-HGer, a., some [perhaps

soms, soms, adv., sometimes, now and then;

soort, sohrt, c., sort, species; brand

soortgelijk, sohrt-HGer-leyk, a., similar

sop, sop, n., broth. **het ruime ——, het row-mer ——,** the open sea

soppen, sop-per, v., to sop, to steep; to dip

sopraan, soh-prahn, c., (mus.) treble, soprano

sorteren, sor-tay-rer, v., to sort, to assort

souperen, soo-pay-rer, v., to have supper

spaak, spahk, c., spoke; rung (of a chair)

spaarbank, spahr-bank, c., savings-bank

spaarpot, spahr-pot, c., money-box [thrifty

spaarzaam, spahr-zahm, a. & adv., saving,

span, span, n., span; team; pair [strain

spannen, span-ner, v., to tighten, to stretch, to

spannend, span-nernt, a., tight; thrilling

spanning, span-ning, c., tension, strain

spar, spar, c., rafter

sparen, spah-rer, v., to save; to spare

spartelen, spar-ter-ler, v., to flounder

spat, spat, c., stain, speck

spatader, spɑt-ah-der, c., varicose vein
spatbord, spɑt-bort, n., mud-guard; splash-
spatten, spɑt-ter, v., to splash   [board
specerij, spay-ser-rey, c., spice
specht, speHGt, c., woodpecker
speeksel, spayk-serl, n., saliva, spittle
speelbal, spayl-bɑl, c., (playing) ball; (fig.) play-
speelgoed, spayl-HGoot, n., toys   [thing
speelplaats, spayl-plahtss, c., playground
speels, spaylss, a., sportive
speeltuin, spayl-town, c., recreation-ground
speer, spayr, c., spear; javelin
spek, speck, n., pork; bacon
spektakel, speck-tah-kerl, n., uproar; racket
spel, spel, n., play; gambling; game; pack (of
spelbreker, spel-bray-ker, c., kill-joy   [cards]
speld, spelt, c., pin
spelen, spay-ler, v., to play; to gamble
speler, spay-ler, c., player; gambler; musician;
spellen, spel-ler, v., to spell   [actor
spelletje, spel-let-yer, n., game
spelonk, sper-lonk, c., cave, grotto
spelregel, spel-ray-HGerl, c., rule of the game
spervuur, spayr-VEEr, n., (mil.) barrage
sperwer, spayr-ver, c., sparrow-hawk
speuren, sper-rer, v., to trace
spichtig, spiHG-terHG, a., weedy, lank
spie, spee, c., (mech.) wedge, pin, peg
spiegel, spee-HGerl, c., mirror; level (of the sea)
spiegelei, spee-HGerl-ey, n., fried egg
spier, speer, c., muscle; (naut.) boom
spierkracht, speer-krɑHGt, c., muscular strength
spiernaakt, speer-nahkt, a., stark naked
spierwit, speer-vit, a., snow-white
spies, speess, c., spear, dart, javelin
spijbelen, spey-ber-ler, v., to play truant
spijker, spey-ker, c., nail; tack
spijs, speyss, c., food, fare
spijskaart, speyss-kahrt, c., bill of fare
spijsvertering, speyss-fer-tay-ring, c., digestion
spijt, speyt, c., regret   [mer, I am sorry
spijten, spey-ter. —— **het spijt me, het speyt**

spijzigen, spey-zer-HGer, v., to feed
spikkel, spick-kerl, c., spot, speckle, speck
spil, spil, c., axis, axle; (mech.) spindle
spin, spin, c., spider
spinazie, spee-**nah**-zee, c., spinach
spinnen, spin-ner, v., to spin; to purr (of a cat)
spinneweb, spin-ner-vep, n., cobweb
spinnewiel, spin-ner-veel, n., spinning-wheel
spion, spee-on, c., spy
spionnage, spee-on-nah-zher, c., espionage
spiritisme, spee-ree-tiss-mer, c., spiritualism
spiritus, spee-ree-terss, c., spirit(s)
spit, spit, n., spit; lumbago   [pointed
spits, spitss, c., point; spire; top, peak. a., sharp,
spitsboef, spitss-boof, c., scoundrel, rascal
spitsuren, spitss-EE-rer, n. pl., rush hours
spitsvondig, spitss-fon-derHG, a. & adv., subtle
spitten, spit-ter, v., to dig
spleet, splayt, c., cleft, crevice, chink
splijten, spley-ter, v., to split, to cleave
splinternieuw, splin-ter-nee'oo, a., brand-new
split, split, n., slit, slash
splitsen, split-ser, v., to split (up); to divide
splitsing, split-sing, c., splitting (up); fission (of
spoed, spoot, c., speed, haste   [the atom)
spoedbestelling, spoot-ber-stel-ling, c., express
     delivery
spoedig, spoo-derHG, a., speedy. adv., quickly
spoel, spool, c., bobbin, spool
spoelen, spoo-ler, v., to rinse, to wash; to spool
spoken, spoh-ker, v., to haunt
spons, sponss, c., sponge
spontaan, spon-tahn, a. & adv., spontaneous
spook, spohk, n., phantom, ghost
spookhuis, spohk-howss, n., haunted house
spoor, spohr, c., spur. n., foot-print, trace; scent;
     rut, track; railway   [table
spoorboekje, spohr-book-yer, n., (railway) time-
spoorloos, spohr-lohss, adv., without a trace
spoorwegbeambte,   spohr-veHG-ber-**a**m-ter,
     c., railway-employee
spoorwegnet, spohr-veHG-net, n., railway system

sport, sport, c., sport; rung (of a ladder)
sportief, spor-**teef**, a., sportsmanlike
sportterrein, sport-tayr-reyn, c., sports ground
spot, spot, c., mockery, derision
spotachtig, spot-*a*HG-terHG, a., mocking   [cheap
spotgoedkoop, spot-HGoot-kohp, a. & adv., very
spotlach, spot-la*HG, c., jeer, sneer, mocking
spotprent, spot-prent, c., caricature   [laugh
spotprijs, spot-preyss, c., ridiculously low price
spotten, spot-ter, v., to mock, to sneer. —— **met,** —— met, to scoff at
spotternij, spot-ter-**ney,** c., taunt, mockery
spotvogel, spot-foh-HGerl, c., mocking-bird
spraak, sprahk, c., language, speech
spraakkunst, sprahk-kernst, c., grammar
spraakzaam, sprahk-sahm, a., talkative
sprakeloos, sprah-ker-lohss, a., speechless
sprankje, spr*a*nk-yer, n., spark
spreekbuis, sprayk-bowss, c., (fig.) mouth-piece
spreekfout, sprayk-fowt, c., slip of the tongue
spreekkamer, sprayk-kah-mer, c., consulting-room; parlour
spreektaal, sprayk-tahl, c., spoken language
spreekuur, sprayk-EEr, n., consulting hour
spreekwijze, sprayk-vey-zer, c., locution
spreekwoord, sprayk-vohrt, n., proverb
spreeuw, spray'oo, c., starling
sprei, sprey, c., bedspread, coverlet   [bed]
spreiden, sprey-der, v., to spread; to make (a
spreken, spray-ker, v., to speak, to talk, to say
spreker, spray-ker, c., speaker; lecturer; orator
sprenkelen, spren-ker-ler, v., to sprinkle
spreuk, sprerk, c., motto; maxim   [insect]
spriet, spreet, c., blade (of grass); feeler (of an
springen, spring-er, v., to jump; to skip; to chap; to burst
springlevend, spring-lay-vernt, a., fully alive
springstof, spring-stof, c., explosive
springstok, spring-stock, c., leaping-pole
springtouw, spring-tow, n., skipping-rope
sprinkhaan, sprink-hahn, c., grasshopper
sproeien, sproo-yer, v., to sprinkle; to spray

sproet, sproot, c., freckle [wood
sprokkelen, sprock-ker-ler, v., to gather dead
sprong, sprong, c., jump, bound, caper
sprookje, sprohk-yer, n., fairy-tale
spruit, sprowt, c., sprout, sprig
spruitjes, sprowt-yess, n. pl., (Brussels) sprouts
spuien, spow-er, v., to sluice; to let in fresh air
spuit, spowt, c., syringe; fire-engine; sprayer
spuiten, spow-ter, v., to spout, to spirt; to spray
spuitwater, spowt-vah-ter, n., soda-water
spul, sperl, n., stuff; booth. **spullen**, sperl-ler,
    duds, togs
spulletjes, sperl-let-yess, n. pl. (pop.) duds
spuwen, spEE-ver, v., to spit; to squirt; to vomit
staaf, stahf, c., bar; stave; ingot
staak, stahk, c., stake, (bean-)pole, stick
staal, stahl, n., steel; sample
staalfabriek, stahl-fah-breek, c., steel-works
staaltje, stahlt-yer, n., sample
staan, stahn, v., to stand, to be; to become
staand, stahnt, a., standing; upright
staart, stahrt, c., tail; pigtail
staat, staht, c., state; rank; list. **in —— zijn om
    . . .**, in —— zeyn om . . ., to be able to . . .
staathuishoudkunde, staht-hows-howt-kern-
    der, c., political economy [manship
staatkunde, staht-kern-der, c., politics; states-
staatsexamen, stahts-ayk-sah-mer, n., = Gen-
    eral Certificate of Education
staatsie, staht-see, c., pomp, ceremony
stad, stat, c., town, city
stadgenoot, stat-HGer-noht, c., fellow-townsman
stadhuis, stat-howss, n., town hall, city hall
stadion, stah-dee-on, n., stadium
stadium, stah-dee-erm, n., phase, stage
stadsbestuur, stats-ber-stEEr, n., municipality
stadsmensen, stats-men-ser, c. pl., townsfolk
staf, staf, c., staff; mace; crosier
staken, stah-ker, v., to stop; to go on strike
staker, stah-ker, c., striker
staking, stah-king, c., strike, stoppage
stakker, stak-ker, c., (pop.) poor thing

stal, stal, c., stable; (pig-)sty; cow-house
stalen, stah-ler, a., steel; (fig.) iron
stallen, stal-ler, v., to stable; to put up (vehicles)
stam, stam, c., stem; trunk; stock, race
stamboom, stam-bohm, c., pedigree; family tree
stamelen, stah-mer-ler, v., to stammer
stamhoofd, stam-hohft, n., chieftain
stampen, stam-per, v., to stamp (one's feet);
stamper, stam-per, c., pistil   [(naut.) to pitch
stampvol, stamp-fol, a., packed, crammed
stamvader, stam-fah-der, c., ancestor
stand, stant, c., rank, standing; attitude; position;
standaard, stan-dahrt, c., standard [height; score
standbeeld, stant-baylt, n., statue
standhouden, stant-how-der, v., to stand firm
standje, stant-yer, n., scolding; row
standplaats, stant-plahtss, c., stand, standing-
                                  place; station
standpunt, stant-pernt, n., point of view
standvastig, stant-fass-terHG, a. & adv., constant
stang, stang, c., (mech.) rod, bar, pole
stank, stank, c., stench, nasty smell
stap, stap, c., pace, stride, step
stapel, stah-perl, c., stack, pile; (naut.) stocks
stapelgek, stah-perl-HGeck, a., raving mad
stappen, stap-per, v., to step, to stride
stapvoets, stap-footss, adv., at walking pace
star, star, a., rigid, fixed
staren, stah-rer, v., to stare
startbaan, start-bahn, c., runway, starting-track
statig, stah-terHG, a. & adv., stately, solemn
station, stah-see'on, n., (railway) station
stationschef, stah-see'ons-shef, c., station-master
statistiek, stah-tiss-teek, c., statistics
staven, stah-ver, v., to confirm, to substantiate
stedelijk, stay-der-luck, a., urban, municipal
steeds, staytss, adv., always. —— **hoger**, ——
          hoh-HGer, higher and higher
steeg, stayHG, c., alley, lane
steek, stayk, c., stitch; stab   [valid
steekhoudend, stayk-how-dernt, a., sound, solid,
steel, stayl, c., handle (of a tool); stem, stalk

steen, stayn, c., stone; brick; piece (at draughts)
steenachtig, stayn-*a*HG-terHG, a., stony
steenbakkerij, stayn-bak-ker-rey, c., brick-works
steendruk, stayn-drerk, c., lithography
steengroeve, stayn-HGroo-ver, c., quarry
steenhouwer, stayn-how-er, c., stone-mason
steenkool, stayn-kohl, c., (pit-)coal
steenpuist, stayn-powst, c., boil
steentje, staynt-yer, n., pebble
steenweg, stayn-veHG, c., paved road
steiger, stey-HGer, c., scaffolding; pier
steigeren, stey-HGer-rer, v., to prance
steil, steyl, a., steep; precipitous
steilte, steyl-ter, c., steepness; precipice
stek, steck, c., cutting, slip (of a plant)
stekeblind, stay-ker-blint, a., totally blind
stekelig, stay-ker-lerHG, a., prickly, thorny
stekelvarken, stay-kerl-far-ker, n., porcupine
steken, stay-ker, v., to prick; to sting; to smart
stekker, steck-ker, c., (wall-)plug
stel, stel, n., set; lot; kit
stelen, stay-ler, v., to steal; to pilfer
stellage, stel-lah-zher, c., scaffolding
stellen, stel-ler, v., to put; to adjust; **to suppose**
stellig, stel-lerHG, a. & adv., positive
stelling, stel-ling, c., thesis; proposition; (mil.)
stelregel, stel-ray-HGerl, c., maxim   [position
stelsel, stel-serl, n., system
stelt, stelt, c., stilt
stem, stem, c., voice; vote; (mus.) part
stembiljet, stem-bil-yet, n., voting-paper
stembus, stem-berss, c., ballot-box; poll
stemmen, stem-mer, v., to vote; (mus.) to tune
stemmig, stem-merHG, a. & adv., grave, sober
stemming, stem-ming, c., voting; mood, feeling
stempel, stem-perl, c., stamp; (fig.) imprint
stempelen, stem-per-ler, v., to stamp
stemplicht, stem-pliHGt, c., compulsory voting
stemvork, stem-fork, c., tuning-fork
stenen, stay-ner, a., of stone. v., to groan
stenigen, stay-ner-HGer, v., to stone (to death)
stenograaf, stay-noh-HGrahf, c., shorthand writer

ster, stayr, c., star
sterfbed, stayrf-bet, n., death-bed
sterfelijk, stayr-fer-luck, a., mortal
sterfgeval, stayrf-HGer-val, n., death
sterftecijfer, stayrf-ter-sey-fer, n., death-rate
sterk, stayrk, a. & adv., strong, robust
sterken, stayr-ker, v., to fortify
sterkte, stayrk-ter, c., strength; stronghold
sterrenkunde, stayr-rer-kern-der, c., astronomy
sterrenwacht, stayr-rer-vaHGt, c., observatory
sterrenwichelaar, stayr-rer-viHG-er-lahr, c., astrologer
sterretje, stayr-rert-yer, n., asterisk; little star
sterveling, stayr-ver-ling, c., mortal
sterven, stayr-ver, v., to die. op —— liggen, op —— liHG-er, to be dying
steun, stern, c., support; help
steunen, ster-ner, v., to support; to lean; to groan
steur, sterr, c., sturgeon
steven, stay-ver, c., prow
stevig, stay-verHG, a. & adv., solid, strong, firm
stichtelijk, stiHG-ter-luck, a. & adv., edifying
stichten, stiHG-ter, v., to found; to establish
stichting, stiHG-ting, c., institution; foundation
stiefbroeder, steef-broo-der, c., stepbrother
stiefmoeder, steef-moo-der, c., stepmother
stiefvader, steef-fah-der, c., stepfather
stiefzoon, steef-sohn, c., stepson
stiefzuster, steef-serss-ter, c., stepsister
stiekem, stee-kem, adv., on the quiet
stier, steer, c., bull
stift, stift, c., peg; pin; point
stijf, steyf, a. & adv., stiff
stijfkop, steyf-kop, c., headstrong person
stijfsel, steyf-serl, n., starch; paste
stijgbeugel, steyHG-ber-HGerl, c., stirrup
stijgen, stey-HGer, v., to rise, to mount
stijl, steyl, c., (door-)post
stijven, stey-ver, v., to starch; to stiffen
stikdonker, stick-don-ker, a., pitch-dark
stikken, stick-ker, v., to stitch; to stifle; to choke
stikstof, stick-stof, c., nitrogen

stil, stil, a. & adv., still, silent
stilhouden, stil-how-der, v., to (come to a) stop. zich ——, ziHG ——, to keep quiet
stillen, stil-ler, v., to hush, to quiet; to allay
stilletjes, stil-let-yerss, adv., secretly, stealthily
stilleven, stil-lay-ver, n., still life
stilliggen, stil-liHG-er, v., to lie quiet; to lie idle
stilstand, stil-stant, c., standstill; stagnation
stilte, stil-ter, c., silence, stillness
stilzwijgend, stil-zvey-HGernt, a. & adv., silent
stinken, stin-ker, v., to stink
stippellijn, stip-perl-leyn, c., dotted line
stipt, stipt, a. & adv., punctual
stoeien, stoo-yer, v., to romp
stoel, stool, c., chair
stoelendans, stoo-ler-dans, c., musical chairs
stoep, stoop, c., steps; pavement
stoer, stoor, a., stalwart, sturdy, hefty
stoet, stoot, c., train, retinue; procession
stoeterij, stoo-ter-rey, c., stud; stud-farm
stof, stof, c., matter; material; theme. n., powder, [dust
stofbril, stof-bril, c., goggles
stofdoek, stof-dook, c., duster
stoffeerder, stof-fayr-der, c., upholsterer
stoffelijk, stof-fer-luck, a., material. —— overschot, —— oh-ver-sHGot, n., mortal remains
stofferen, stof-fay-rer, v., to upholster
stoffig, stof-ferHG, a., dusty
stofvrij, stof-frey, a., dust-proof
stofwolk, stof-volk, c., cloud of dust
stofzuiger, stof-sow-HGer, c., vacuum cleaner
stoïcijns, stoh-ee-seynss, a. & adv., stoic(al)
stok, stock, c., (walking-)stick, cane; pole; roost
stokdoof, stock-dohf, a., stone-deaf
stoken, stoh-ker, v., to burn; to distil
stoker, stoh-ker, c., fireman, stoker; distiller
stokoud, stock-owt, a., very old [(fig.) hobby
stokpaardje, stock-pahrt-yer, n., hobby-horse;
stokvis, stock-fiss, c., stockfish
stollen, stol-ler, v., to curdle, to clot, to congeal
stolp, stolp, c., cover, glass-shade, glass-bell
stom, stom, a. & adv., dumb; stupid

stomen, stoh-mer v., to steam

stommelen, stom-mer-ler, v., to clatter, to clump

stommerik, stom-mer-rick, c., (pop.) blockhead

stomp, stomp, a., blunt, dull. c., stump; punch

stompzinnig, stomp-sin-nerHG, a., obtuse, dull

stoof, stohf, c., foot-warmer

stookolie, stohk-oh-lee, c., liquid fuel

stoom, stohm, c., steam

stoomboot, stohm-boht, c., steamer

stoomketel, stohm-kay-terl, c., (steam-)boiler

stoomwals, stohm-v𝑎lss, c., steam-roller

stoornis, stohr-niss, c., disorder

stoot, stoht, c., push; punch; thrust; stab; stroke

stoottroepen, stoht-troo-per, c. pl., shock-troops

stop, stop, c., plug; stopper; darn (in a sock)

stopcontact, stop-kon-t𝑎kt, n., plug connection

stopnaald, stop-nahlt, c., darning-needle

stoppel, stop-perl, c., stubble

stoppen, stop-per, v., to darn; to stop; to fill

stopplaats, stop-plahtss, c., halting-place, (bus-)

stopverf, stop-fayrf, c., putty   [stop

storen, stoh-rer, v., to disturb; to jam

storing, stoh-ring, c., disturbance; jamming
(wireless)

storm, storm, c., storm, blast, gale   [stormy

stormachtig, storm-𝑎HG-terHG, a. & adv.,

stormen, stor-mer, v., to storm. **het stormt,** het
stormt, it is blowing a gale   [by storm

stormenderhand, stor-mer-der-h𝑎nt, adv.,(mil.)

stormlamp, storm-lamp, c., hurricane lantern

stormloop, storm-lohp, c., (mil.) assault; rush

stortbad, stort-b𝑎t, n., shower-bath

stortbui, stort-bow, c., downpour

storten, stor-ter, v., to shed; to spill; to dump

stortregen, stort-ray-HGer, c., torrential rain

stoten, stoh-ter v., to bump; to push; to butt

stotteren, stot-ter-rer, v., to stammer

stout, stowt, a. & adv., naughty; daring, bold

stoutmoedigheid, stowt-moo-derHG-heyt, c.,
boldness, daring

stoven, stoh-ver, v., to stew

straal, strahl, c., ray; flash; radius; jet, spout

straalaandrijving, strahl-ahn-drey-ving, c., jet propulsion

straaljager, strahl-yah-HGer, c., jet fighter

straalkachel, strahl-ka*H*G-erl, c., electric radia-

straat, straht, c., street, road; strait(s) [tor

straatarm, straht-*a*rm, a., very poor

straf, straf, c., penalty. a. & adv., severe

strafbaar, straf-bahr, a., punishable

straffeloos, straf-fer-lohss, adv., with impunity

straffen, straf-fer, v., to punish

strafrecht, straf-re*H*Gt, n., criminal law

strafschop, straf-s*H*Gop, c., penalty kick

strafwerk, straf-vayrk, n., detention work

strak, stra*k*, a. & adv., stiff, tight, fixed, intent

straks, straks*s*, adv., presently

stralen, strah-ler, v., to shine, to beam

stram, stra*m*, a., rigid

strand, stra*nt*, n., beach, sands, shore

stranden, stran-der, v., to strand

strandjutter, strant-yert-ter, c., beachcomber

strandstoel, stra*nt*-stool, c., beach chair

streek, strayk, c., trick; stroke (with the pen); region. een —— uithalen, ayn —— owt-hah-ler, to play a trick

streep, strayp, c., line, stripe, streak

streepje, strayp-yer, n., dash; hyphen

strekken, streck-ker, v., to extend, to stretch

strekking, streck-king, c., purport, tendency

strelen, stray-ler, v., to caress, to stroke

stremmen, strem-mer, v., to curdle; to obstruct

streng, streng, a. & adv., severe, stern, rigid

strengelen, streng-er-ler, v., to twist

streven (naar), stray-ver (nahr), v., to strive

striem, streem, c., stripe, wale [(after)

strijd, streyt, c., fight, struggle

strijdbaar, streyt-bahr, a., able-bodied

strijden, strey-der, v., to fight, to struggle

strijdig, strey-der*H*G, a., incompatible

strijdvraag, streyt-frah*H*G, c., question at issue

strijken, strey-ker, v., to iron; to smooth

strijkijzer, streyk-ey-zer, n., flat-iron

strijkplank, streyk-pl*a*nk, c., ironing-board

strijkstok, streyk-stock, c., (mus.) bow
strik, strick, c., (bow-)tie; knot (of ribbons); snare
strikt, strickt, a. & adv., strict, precise
strikvraag, strick-fraHG, c., catch question
stro, stroh, n., straw
stroef, stroof, a. & adv., stiff, harsh, rough
stromen, stroh-mer, v., to flow; to pour   [totter
strompelen, strom-per-ler, v., to stumble, to
stronk, stronk, c., stalk; stump
strooibiljet, stroh-ee-bil-yet, n., handbill
strooien, stroh-yer, v., to strew, to sprinkle. a.,
strook, strohk, c., strip; slip; counterfoil   [straw
stroom, strohm, c., stream; current; river
stroomaf, strohm-af, adv., down the river
stroomop, strohm-op, adv., up the river
stroop, strohp, c., syrup; treacle
strooplikker, strohp-lick-ker, c., (pop.) toady
strooptocht, strohp-toHGt, c., raid, depredation
strop, strop, c., (hangman's) rope; strap; snare
stropen, stroh-per, v., to poach; to skin; to pillage
stroper, stroh-per, c., poacher; raider
stropop, stroh-pop, c., dummy
strot, strot, c., throat
strottenhoofd, strot-ter-hohft, n., larynx
strozak, stroh-zak, c., straw mattress
struik, strowk, c., shrub, bush   [block
struikelblok, strow-kerl-block, n., stumbling-
struikelen, strow-ker-ler, v., to stumble   [bushes
struikgewas, strowk-HGer-vass, n., brushwood,
struikrover, strowk-roh-ver, c., highwayman
struisvogel, strowss-foh-HGerl, c., ostrich
studeren, stEE**-day-rer,** v., to study
studiebeurs, stEE**-dee-berrss,** c., scholarship
studieboek, stEE**-dee-book,** n., text-book
stug, sterHG, a. & adv., stiff; gruff, surly
stuifmeel, stowf-mayl, n., pollen
stuip, stowp, c., convulsion; whim, freak   [vulsions
stuiptrekken, stowp-treck-ker, v., to be in con-
stuiten, stow-ter, v., to bounce; to stem
stuiven, stow-ver, v., to be dusty; to rush
stuk, sterk, n., piece; article; document. a., broken.
   —— **voor** ——, —— **fohr** ——, one by one

stukadoor, stEE-kah-**dohr**, c., plasterer
stukgaan, sterk-HGahn, v., to go to pieces
stumper, **sterm**-per, c., bungler, duffer　[shaky
stuntelig, **stern**-ter-lerHG, a. & adv., clumsy;
sturen, stEE-rer, v., to drive; to steer; to send
stut, stert, c., support, prop
stuur, stEEr, n., wheel; handlebar; helm
stuurboord, stEEr-bohrt, n., starboard　[gear
stuurinrichting, stEEr-in-riHG-ting, c., steering-
stuurloos, stEEr-lohss, a. & adv., out of control
stuurman, stEEr-*man*, c., coxswain
stuurs, stEErss, a., surly, gruff, sullen
stuw, stEE, c., dam, weir
stuwen, stEE-er, v., to propel; (naut.) to stow
subsidie, serp-see-dee, c., subsidy, grant
succes, serk-sess, n., success. **veel ——**! fayl ——,
　　good luck!
successierechten, serk-ses-see-reHG-ter, n. pl.,
　　death-duties
suf, serf, a., dull, sleepy; dazed
suffen, serf-fer, v., to doze
suiker, sow-ker, c., sugar
suikerbakker, sow-ker-bak-ker, c., confectioner
suikergoed, sow-ker-HGoot, n., confectionery
suikerpot, sow-ker-pot, c., sugar-basin
suikerriet, sow-ker-reet, n., sugar-cane
suikerziekte, sow-ker-zeek-ter, c., diabetes
suizen, sow-zer, v., to buzz; to whizz
sukade, sEE-kah-der, c., candied lemon-peel
sukkel, serk-kerl, c., crock; invalid
sukkelen, serk-ker-ler, v., to be ailing
sul, serl, c., noodle, soft Johnny, mug
surrogaat, serrt-roh-HGaht, n., substitute　[tor
surveillant, sEEr-vey-*ant*, c., overseer; invigila-
sussen, sers-ser, v., to hush, to soothe, to ease
symbool, sim-bohl, n., symbol, emblem
sympathiek, sim-pah-teek, a. & adv., congenial

taai, tah-ee, a., tough; tedious, dull
taai-taai, tah-ee-tah-ee, c., tough gingerbread
taak, tahk, c., task, job; homework
taal, tahl, c., language, speech

taaleigen, tahl-ey-HGer, n., idiom [matical
taalkundig, tahl-kern-derHG, a. & adv., gram-
taaltje, tahlt-yer, n., lingo, jargon, jabber
taankleurig, tahn-kler-rerHG, a., tawny
taart, tahrt, c., tart; cake; pie
taartje, tahrt-yer, n., tartlet
tabak, tah-*bak*, c., tobacco
tabberd, *tab*-bert, c., robe, gown
tabel, tah-bel, c., table, list, index
tablet, tah-blet, n., tablet; slab; lozenge
tachtig, t*a*HG-terHG, a., eighty
tachtigste, t*a*HG-terHG-ster, a., eightieth
tactiek, tak-teek, c., tactics
tafel, tah-*ferl*, c., table
tafelbediende, tah-ferl-ber-deen-der, c., attendant at table
tafelkleed, tah-ferl-klayt, n., table-cover
tafelzilver, tah-ferl-zil-ver, n., silverware
tafereel, t*a*-fer-rayl, n., scene, picture
taille, t*a*-yer, c., waist; waist-line; bodice
tak, t*ak*, c., branch; bough
takel, tah-kerl, c., pulley
takelen, tah-ker-ler, v., to hoist up; (naut.) to rig
takje, t*ak*-yer, n., twig, sprig (of heather)
takkenbos, t*ak*-ker-boss, c., faggot
tal, t*al*, n., number. —— van, —— f*an*, a great
talentvol, tah-lent-fol, a., gifted [number of
talk, t*alk*, c., tallow; talc
talloos, t*al*-lohss, a., countless
talmen, t*al*-mer, v., to delay, to loiter
talrijk, t*al*-reyk, a., numerous
tam, t*am*, a. & adv., tame, domesticated
tamboer, t*am*-boor, c., (mil.) drummer
tamelijk, tah-mer-luck, a. & adv., fair, tolerable
tand, t*ant*, c., tooth; cog; prong
tandarts, t*ant*-*a*rts, c., dentist
tandenborstel, t*an*-der-bor-sterl, c., tooth-brush
tandenstoker, t*an*-der-stoh-ker, c., tooth-pick
tandheelkunde, t*ant*-hayl-kern-der, c., dentistry
tandpasta, t*ant*-*pass*-tah, c., tooth-paste
tandpijn, t*ant*-peyn, c., toothache
tanen, tah-ner, v., to tan; (fig.) to fade

tang, tang, c., pincers; (fire-)tongs
tanken, ten-ker, v., to fill up; to refuel
tante, tan-ter, c., aunt
tapijt, tah-peyt, n., carpet
tappen, tap-per, v., to tap; to crack (jokes)
taptemelk, tap-ter-melk, c., skimmed milk
tapverbod, tap-fer-bot, n., prohibition
tarief, tah-reef, n., tariff, rate
tarten, tar-ter, v., to challenge; to dare
tarwe, tar-ver, c., wheat
tas, tass, c., cup; heap; bag; satchel
tastbaar, tast-bahr, a., tangible
tasten, tas-ter, v., to feel, to touch; to grope
tatoueren, tah-too-ay-rer, v., to tattoo
taxeren, tak-say-rer, v., to value, to appraise
te, ter, prep., at, in, to. adv., too
techniek, tayHG-neek, c., technical science
teder, tay-der, a. & adv., tender, delicate
teef, tayf, c., female dog
teelt, taylt, c., cultivation; breeding
teen, tayn, c., toe; osier(-twig)
teer, tayr n., tar. a. & adv., see **teder**
teergevoelig, tayr-HGer-voo-lerHG, a. & adv.,
    tender
tegel, tay-HGerl, c., tile   [the same time
tegelijk(ertijd), ter-HGer-leyk(er-teyt), adv., at
tegemoetgaan, ter-HGer-moot-HGahn, v., to go
    to meet   [come to meet
tegemoetkomen, ter-HGer-moot-koh-mer, v., to
tegemoetkoming, ter-HGer-moot-koh-ming, c.,
    concession   [to. adv., against
tegen, tay-HGer, prep., against, by, towards, at,
tegenaanval, tay-HGen-ahn-val, c., counter-
    attack   [the contrary
tegenbericht, tay-HGen-ber-riHGt, n., message to
tegenbezoek, tay-HGen-ber-zook, n., return visit
tegendeel, tay-HGen-dayl, n., reverse, contrary
tegengif(t), tay-HGen-HGif(t), n., antidote
tegenhanger, tay-HGen-hang-er, c., counterpart
tegenhouden, tay-HGen-how-der, v., to hold up
tegenkomen, tay-HGen-koh-mer, v., to meet
tegenover, tay-HGen-oh-ver, prep., opposite

tegenovergesteld, tay-HGen-oh-ver-HGer-stelt, a., opposite

tegenpartij, tay-HGen-par-tey, c., opponent

tegenslag, tay-HGen-slaHG, c., set-back

tegenspartelen, tay-HGen-spar-ter-ler, v., to resist; (fig.) to jib

tegenspoed, tay-HGen-spoot, c., ill-luck, adversity

tegenspreken, tay-HGen-spray-ker, v., to contradict [mutter objections

tegensputteren, tay-HGen-spert-ter-rer, v., to

tegenstand, tay-HGen-stant, c., resistance

tegenstander, tay-HGen-stan-der, c., opponent

tegenstelling, tay-HGen-stel-ling, c., contrast

tegenstrijdig, tay-HGen-**strey**-derHG, a., contradictory [appointing

tegenvallen, tay-HGen-fal-ler, v., to be disappointment

tegenvaller, tay-HGen-fal-ler, c., disappointment

tegenvoeter, tay-HGen-foo-ter, c., antipode

tegenwerking, tay-HGen-vayr-king, c., opposition

tegenwicht, tay-HGen-viHGt, n., counterpoise

tegenwind, tay-HGen-vint, c., adverse wind

tegenwoordig, tay-HGen-**vohr**-derHG, a., present (-day). adv., at present. —— zijn bij, —— zeyn bey, to be present at

tegenzin, tay-HGen-zin, c., dislike, aversion

tegoed, ter-HGoot, n., (bank) balance

tehuis, ter-howss, n., home. adv., at home

teisteren, tey-ster-rer, v., to harass; to infest

teken, tay-ker, n., sign, mark; indication; signal

tekenaar, tay-ker-nahr, c., draughtsman, designer

tekenen, tay-ker-ner, v., to draw, to sketch; to sign; to mark

tekenfilm, tay-ken-film, c., cartoon (film, etc.)

tekening, tay-ker-ning, c., drawing, sketch; design

tekort, ter-kort, n., shortage, deficiency [ing

tekortkoming, ter-kort-koh-ming, c., shortcoming

tekst, teckst, c., text; context; script; letterpress

tel, tel, c., count. de —— kwijt zijn, der —— kveyt zeyn, to have lost count

telefoonboek, tay-ler-fohn-book, n., telephone directory

telefooncel, tay-ler-fohn-sel, c., call-box

telefooncentrale, tay-ler-fohn-sen-trah-ler, c., telephone exchange

telegraaf, tay-ler-HGrahf, c., telegraph

telegraferen, tay-ler-HGrah-**fay**-rer, v., to cable

telen, tay-ler, v., to cultivate; to breed

teleurstellen, ter-**lerr**-stel-ler, v., to disappoint

televisie, tay-ler-**vee**-zee, c., television

telkens, tel-kenss, adv., again and again. —— **wanneer,** —— van-nayr, whenever

tellen, tel-ler, v., to count; to number

temmen, tem-mer, v., to tame, to subdue

tempel, tem-perl, c., temple   [temperament

temperament, tem-per-rah-**ment,** n., temper,

temperatuur, tem-per-rah-**tEER,** c., temperature

tempo, tem-poh, n., pace, rate; (mus.) movement

ten, ten, prep., at, to. —— **eerste,** —— **ayr**-ster, adv., first(ly)

tenger, teng-er, a., slender, slim

tengevolge (van), ten-HGer-vol-HGer (fan), prep., owing (to)

tenminste, ten-**minss**-ter, adv., at least

tennisbaan, ten-niss-bahn, c., tennis-court

tent, tent, c., tent; booth; (naut.) awning

tentamen, ten-**tah**-mer, n., preliminary examination

tentoonstelling, ten-**tohn**-stel-ling, c., exhibition

tenue, ter-**nEE,** n., (mil.) uniform

tenzij, ten-zey, conj., unless

terdege, tayr-**day**-HGer, adv., thoroughly

terecht, ter-reHGt, adv., rightly

terechtstaan, ter-reHGt-stahn, v., to be committed for trial

terechtstelling, ter-reHGt-stel-ling, c., trial

terechtwijzing, ter-reHGt-vey-zing, c., reprimand   [live on

teren, tay-rer, v., to tar. —— **op,** —— op, v., to

tergen, tayr-**HGer,** v., to provoke

tering, tay-ring, c., consumption (of the lungs)

terloops, tayr-**lohpss,** adv., incidentally

termijn, tayr-**meyn,** c., term, time; instalment

ternauwernood, tayr-**now**-er-noht, adv., scarcely

terpentijn, tayr-**pen**-teyn, c., turpentine

terras, tayr-rass, n., terrace
terrein, tayr-reyn, n., ground; site; (fig.) field
terstond, tayr-stont, adv., at once, directly
terug, ter-rerHG, adv., back, backward [back
terugbetalen, ter-rerHG-ber-tah-ler, v., to pay
terughoudend, ter-rerHG-how-dent, a., reserved,
terugkeer, ter-rerHG-kayr, c., return [aloof
terugschrikken, ter-rerHG-srick-ker, v., to recoil
terugtocht, ter-rerHG-toHGt, c., retreat
terugweg, ter-rerHG-veHG, c., way back
terugwinnen, ter-rerHG-vin-ner, v., to regain
terwijl, ter-veyl, conj., while; whereas. adv.,
terzijde, tayr-zey-der, adv., aside [meanwhile
teugel, ter-HGerl, c., bridle, rein
teugelloos, ter-HGerl-lohss, a., unrestrained
teveel, ter-fayl, n., surplus. a. & adv., too much
tevens, tay-vens, adv., at the same time [(many)
tevergeefs, ter-fer-HGayfs, adv., in vain
tevreden, ter-vray-der, a. & adv., content(ed)
tevredenstellen, ter-vray-den-stel-ler, v., to
content [(ing)
tewaterlating, ter-vah-ter-lah-ting, c., launch-
thans, tans, adv., now, at present, by this time
thee, tay, c., tea. —— **drinken,** —— **drin-ker,**
v., to have tea
theeservies, tay-sayr-viss, n., tea-set
thema, tay-mah, c., exercise. n., theme, subject
theoloog, tay-oh-lohHG, c., theologian; clerical
thuis, towss, adv., at home. n., home [student
thuisbrengen, towss-breng-er, v., to see (a person) home
thuiskomst, towss-komst, c., home-coming
tien, teen, a., ten
tiende, teen-der, a., tenth. n., tithe
tieren, tee-rer, v., to rage; to thrive
tijd, teyt, c., time; season; period
tijdelijk, tey-der-luck, a. & adv., temporary
tijdens, tey-derns, prep., during
tijdgenoot, teyt-HGer-noht, c., contemporary
tijdig, tey-derHG, a., timely. adv., in good time
tijding, tey-ding, c., news, tidings
tijdje, teyt-yer, n., while

tijdperk, teyt-payrk, n., period
tijdschrift, teyt-srift, n., magazine, periodical
tijdstip, teyt-stip, n., date; moment
tijdverdrijf, teyt-fer-dreyf, n., pastime
tijdverspilling, teyt-fer-spil-ling, c., waste of time
tijger, tey-HGer, c., tiger   [time
tikje, tick-yer, n., pat; bit; (fig.) touch, dash
tikken, tick-ker, v., to tick; to click; to touch
tillen, til-ler, v., to lift, to raise
timmeren, tim-mer-rer, v., to carpenter; to build
timmerhout, tim-mer-howt, n., timber
timmerman, tim-mer-man, c., carpenter
tingelen, ting-er-ler, v., to tinkle
tinmijn, tin-meyn, c., tin-mine
tintelen, tin-ter-ler, v., to twinkle
tintje, tint-yer, n., tinge
tip, tip, c., tip; corner
tippelen, tip-per-ler, v., (pop.) to trot, to toddle
tiran, tee-ran, c., tyrant
titel, tee-terl, c., title; heading
tjilpen, tyeel-per, v., to chirp, to twitter
tobbe, tob-ber, c., tub
tobben, tob-ber, v., to drudge; to worry
toch, toHG, adv., yet, still, after all; surely
tocht, toHGt, c., draught; march, journey
tochtdeur, toHGt-derr, c., swing-door
tochtig, toHG-terHG, a., draughty
tochtje, toHGt-yer, n., excursion
tochtscherm, toHGt-sHGayrm, n., draught-screen
toe, too, a., shut. adv., to, towards
toebehoren, too-ber-hoh-rer, v., to belong to
toebereidsel, too-ber-reyt-serl, n., preparation
toebrengen, too-breng-er, v., to inflict
toedienen, too-dee-ner, v., to administer
toedoen, too-doon, v., to close, to shut
toeëigenen (zich), too-ay-HGer-ner (ziHG), v., to appropriate
toegang, too-HGang, c., admission; entry; entrance
toegankelijk, too-HGan-ker-luck, a., accessible
toegeeflijk, too-HGay-fer-luck, a. & adv., indulgent
toegenegen, too-HGer-nay-HGer, a., affectionate
toegespen, too-HGess-per, v., to buckle (up)

toegeven, too-HGay-ver, v., to grant, to admit
toegevend, too-HGay-vernt, a., indulgent
toegift, too-HGift, c., extra
toehoorder, too-hohr-der, c., listener, hearer
toejuichen, too-yow-HGer, v., to applaud
toekennen, too-ken-ner, v., to award
toekijken, too-key-ker, v., to look on
toeknopen, too-k'noh-per, v., to button up
toekomst, too-komst, c., future
toekomstig, too-kom-sterHG, a., future
toelachen, too-laHG-er, v., to smile at
toelage, too-lah-HGer, c., allowance, grant
toelaten, too-lah-ter, v., to admit; to permit
toeleg, too-leHG, c., design, intention, attempt
toelichten, too-liHG-ter, v., to elucidate
toeloop, too-lohp, c., concourse, run, rush
toemaken, too-mah-ker, v., to close; to fasten
toen, toon, conj., when, as. adv., then, at that time
toenaaien, too-nah-yer, v., to sew up
toenadering, too-nah-der-ring, c., approach
toenemen, too-nay-mer, v., to increase
toenmalig, toon-**mah**-lerHG, a., of the (that) time, then   [time
toentertijd, toon-tayr-**teyt**, adv., at the (that)
toepasselijk, too-p*as*-ser-luck, a., appropriate
toepassen, too-p*as*-ser, v., to apply, to practise
toer, toor, c., tour, trip; turn; feat, trick. **een hele**
——, ayn hay-ler ——, quite a job
toereikend, too-rey-kernt, a., adequate, enough
toerekenbaar, too-ray-ker-bahr, a., responsible
toeren, too-rer, v., to take a drive (ride)
toernooi, toor-noh'ee, n., tournament
toeroepen, too-roo-per, v., to call (out) to
toerusten, too-rers-ter, v., to equip
toeschouwer, too-sHGow-er, c., spectator
toeschrijven, too-srey-ver, v., to ascribe
toeslaan, too-slahn, v., to bang; to shut
toeslag, too-slaHG, c., extra allowance; extra fare
toesnauwen, too-snow-er, v., to snarl at
toespeling, too-spay-ling, c., hint
toespraak, too-sprahk, c., address, speech
toestaan, too-stahn, v., to allow; to grant

toestand, too-*stant*, c., situation
toestel, too-*stel*, n., apparatus, appliance
toestemming, too-*stem*-ming, c., consent
toeter, too-*ter*, c., hooter
toetreden, too-*tray*-der, v., to join; to walk up to
toets, tootss, c., key (piano, etc.); test; touch
toetsen, toot-*ser*, v., to test, to try
toeval, too-*fal*, n., chance; (epileptic) fit
toevallig, too-*fal*-lerHG, a. & adv., accidental
toevertrouwen, too-*fayr*-trow-er, v., to entrust
toevlucht, too-flerHGt, c., recourse, refuge
toevluchtsoord, too-flerHGt-sohrt, n., asylum,
toevoegen, too-foo-HGer, v., to add [shelter
toevoer, too-foor, c., supply; flow (of air)
toewenken, too-*ven*-ker, v., to beckon to
toewensen, too-*ven*-ser, v., to wish
toewerpen, too-*vayr*-per, v., to throw to; to slam
toewijden, too-*vey*-der, v., to dedicate; to devote
toewijzen, too-*vey*-zer, v., to allot
toewuiven, too-*vow*-ver, v., to wave (one's hat) to
toezegging, too-*zayHG*-ing, c., promise
toezenden, too-*zen*-der, v., to send; to remit
toezicht, too-ziHGt, n., supervision [money]
toezien, too-zeen, v., to look on; to be careful
toilet, tva-*let*, n., dressing-table; lavatory
tol, toll, c., tribute; duties; top (toy)
tolk, tollk, c., interpreter
tomaat, toh-*maht*, c., tomato
tomeloos, toh-*mer*-lohss, a., unrestrained
tomen, toh-*mer*, v., to curb
ton, ton, c., cask; ton
toneel, toh-*nayl*, n., stage; scene; theatre
toneelkijker, toh-*nayl*-key-ker, c., opera-glasses
toneelschrijver, toh-*nayl*-srey-ver, c., playwright
toneelspeler, toh-*nayl*-spay-ler, c., actor
toneelstuk, toh-*nayl*-sterk, n., (stage-)play
tonen, toh-ner, v., to show
tong, tong, c., tongue; sole (fish)
tongval, tong-*fal*, c., accent; dialect
toog, tohHG, c., cassock
tooien, toh-*yer*, v., to decorate
toom, tohm, c., bridle

toon, tohn, c., tone; sound; pitch; stress, accent
toonbaar, toonbaar, tohn-bahr, a., presentable
toonbank, tohn-bank, c., counter
toonbeeld, tohn-baylt, n., pattern, model
toonhoogte, tohn-hohHG-ter, c., (mus.) pitch
toonkunstenaar, tohn-kern-ster-nahr, c., musi-
toonladder, tohn-lad-der, c., (mus.) scale [cian
toorn, tohrn, c., anger, wrath
toorts, tohrts, c., torch
top, top, c., summit; tip; apex. **van —— tot teen**,
    fan —— tot tayn, from top to toe
toppunt, top-pernt, n., see **top**; (fig.) climax
tor, tor, c., beetle
toren, toh-rer, c., tower; steeple; belfry; turret
torenklok, toh-rer-klock, c., church-bell; church-
torenspits, toh-rer-spits, c., spire [clock
tornen, tor-ner, v., to rip (open)
torpederen, tor-pay-day-rer, v., to torpedo
torpedojager, tor-pay-doh-yah-HGer, c., de-
torsen, tor-ser, v., to bear, to carry [stroyer
tortelduif, tor-terl-dowf, c., turtle-dove
tot, tot, conj., until, till. prep., as far as, to
totaal, toh-tahl, n., total. a. & adv., total, entire
totdat, tot-dat, conj., until, till
totstandkoming, tot-stant-koh-ming, c., realiza-
touw, tow, n., rope; cord; string, twine [tion
touwslager, tow-slah-HGer, c., rope-maker
touwtrekken, tow-treck-ker, n., tug-of-war
tovenaar, toh-ver-nahr, c., magician
toveren, toh-ver-rer, v., to conjure
toverkracht, toh-ver-kraHGt, c., witchcraft
toverspreuk, toh-ver-sprerk, c., incantation
traag, trahHG, a. & adv., slow, inert, sluggish
traan, trahn, c., tear
traangas, trahn-HGass, n., tear-gas
trachten, traHG-ter, v., to attempt, to try
traject, trah-yecht, n., stretch, distance
traktement, trak-ter-ment, n., pay, salary
trakteren, trak-tay-rer, v., to treat, to regale
tralies, trah-leess, c. pl., grating; trellis
tramhalte, trem-hal-ter, c., tram-stop
transpireren, trans-pee-ray-rer, v., to perspire

transportfiets, trans-port-feets, c., carrier cycle
trant, trant, c., way, manner, method
trap, trap, c., kick; step; stairs; (fig.) degree
trapleuning, trap-ler-ning, c., banisters
trappelen, trap-per-ler, v., to trample
trappen, trap-per, v., to tread; to kick
trapper, trap-per, c., pedal
trapsgewijze, traps-HGer-vey-zer, adv., gradually
trechter, trayHG-ter, c., funnel; crater; shell-hole
trede, tray-der, c., pace, step; rung (of a ladder)
treden, tray-der, v., to step, to tread
treeplank, tray-plank, c., footboard, running-
[board
treffen, tref-fer, v., to hit, to strike
treffend, tref-fent, a. & adv., striking, moving
treiler, trey-ler, c., trawler
trein, treyn, c., train; suite, retinue
treiteren, trey-ter-rer, v., to nag, to tease
trek, treck, c., pull; draught; stroke; feature;
inclination
[to go
trekken, treck-ker, v., to draw, to drag; to attract;
trekpaard, treck-pahrt, n., draught-horse
trekschuit, treck-sHGowt, c., tow-boat
trekvogel, treck-foh-HGerl, c., bird of passage
treuren, trer-rer, v., to mourn, to grieve
treurig, trer-rerHG, a. & adv., sad, mournful
treurmars, trerr-marss, c., funeral march
treurspel, trerr-spel, n., tragedy
treurwilg, trerr-vilHG, c., weeping willow
treuzelachtig, trer-zer-laHG-terHG, a., dawdling
treuzelen, trer-zer-ler, v., to dawdle, to linger
tribune, tree-bEE-ner, c., platform; stand; gallery
triestig, treess-terHG, a., dismal, dejected, gloomy
trillen, tril-ler, v., to tremble, to quiver
trilling, tril-ling, c., quiver(ing), vibration
trimester, tree-mess-ter, n., three months' term
triomfantelijk, tree-om-fan-ter-luck, a. & adv.,
triumphant
[procession
triomftocht, tree-omf-toHGt, c., triumphal
triplexhout, tree-plecks-howt, n., three-ply wood
trippelen, trip-per-ler, v., to trip
troebel, troo-berl, a., turbid, muddy, troubled
troef, troof, c., trump(s)

troep, troop, c., crowd, troop, body, pack, band
troetelkind, troo-terl-kint, n., pet, spoiled child
troeven, troo-ver, v., to trump
troffel, trof-ferl, c., trowel
trog, troHG, c., trough
trommel, trom-merl, c., drum; box, tin, case
tronie, troh-nee, c., face, visage
troon, trohn, c., throne   [throne
troonopvolger, trohn-op-fol-HGer, c., heir to the
troost, trohst, c., consolation, comfort
troosteloos, troh-ster-lohss, a., disconsolate
troosten, troh-ster, v., to console, to comfort
tropen, troh-per, c. pl., tropics
tros, tross, c., cluster, bunch; (naut.) hawser
trots, trots, c., pride. a. & adv., proud
trotsaard, trot-sahrt, c., proud person   [face
trotseren, trot-say-rer, v., to defy, to brave, to
trottoir, trot-to'ahr, n., footway, pavement
trouw, trow, a. & adv., faithful, true, loyal. c.,
       fidelity, loyalty; marriage
trouwakte, trow-ak-ter, c., marriage certificate
trouwbreuk, trow-brerk, c., breach of faith
trouwdag, trow-daHG, c., wedding-day
trouweloos, trow-er-lohss, a. & adv., disloyal
trouwen, trow-er, v., to marry   [indeed
trouwens, trow-enss, adv., for that matter,
trui, trow, c., jersey, sweater
tucht, terHGt, c., discipline
tuchtigen, terHG-ter-HGer, v., to chastise
tuffen, terf-fer, v., to motor   [scum
tuig, towHG, n., tools; harness; (fig.) trash, rabble,
tuimelen, tow-mer-ler, v., to tumble, to topple
tuin, town, c., garden   [(over)
tuinarchitect, town-ar-shee-tect, c., landscape
tuinbouw, town-bow, c., horticulture   [gardener
tuinhuisje, town-how-sher, n., summer-house
tuinier, tow-neer, c., gardener
tuit, towt, c., nozzle, spout
tuiten, tow-ter, v., to tingle
tulband, terl-bant, c., turban; sponge-cake
tulp, terlp, c., tulip
tulpebol, terl-per-bol, c., tulip-bulb

tureluurs, tEE-rer-lEErss, a., mad, frantic, wild

turen, tEE-rer, v., to peer

turf, terrf, c., peat; turf

tussen, ters-ser, prep., between; among, amidst

tussenbeidekomen, ters-ser-bey-der-koh-mer, v., to intervene

tussenkomst, ters-ser-komst, c., intervention

tussenpersoon, ters-ser-per-sohn, c., intermediary

tussenschot, ters-ser-sHGot, n., partition

tussentijd, ters-ser-teyt, c., interval

tussenvoegsel, ters-ser-fooHG-serl, n., insertion

twaalf, tvahlf, a., twelve

twaalfde, tvahlf-der, a., twelfth

twee, tvay, a., two. —— aan ——, —— ahn ——, by twos

tweedaags, tvay-daHGs, a., of two days

tweede, tvay-der, a., second

tweedehands, tvay-der-hants, a., second-hand

tweedekker, tvay-deck-ker, c., biplane

tweedracht, tvay-draHGt, c., discord

tweeërlei, tvay-er-ley, a., of two kinds

tweegevecht, tvay-HGer-veHGt, n., duel

tweeling, tvay-ling, c., (pair of) twins [brother

tweelingbroeder, tvay-ling-broo-der, c., twin-

tweepersoons, tvay-per-sohnss, a., double, for two [voices

tweestemmig, tvay-stem-merHG, a., for two

tweetal, tvay-tal, n., pair, two

tweetalig, tvay-tah-lerHG, a., bilingual

tweevoudig, tvay-fow-derHG, a., twofold

twijfel, tvey-ferl, c., doubt [doubtful

twijfelachtig, tvey-ferl-aHG-terHG, a. & adv.,

twijfelen, tvey-fer-ler, v., to doubt

twijg, tveyHG, c., twig, spray; (fig.) scion

twintig, tvin-terHG, a., twenty

twintigste, tvin-terHG-ster, a., twentieth

twintigtal, tvin-terHG-tal, n., score, twenty

twist, tvist, c., quarrel, dispute, row

twisten, tvist-er, v., to quarrel, to wrangle

twistgesprek, tvist-HGer-spreck, n., dispute

twistvraag, tvist-frahHG, c., question at issue

twistziek, tvist-seek, a., quarrelsome

typen, tee-per, v., to type(write)
typhus, tee-ferss, c., typhoid fever; typhus fever
typisch, tee-peess, a. & adv., typical; quaint

U, EE, pron., you
ui, ow, c., onion; (fig.) joke
uil, owl, c., owl
uilskuiken, owls-kow-ker, n., noodle, ninny,
uit, owt, prep., out of, from. adv., out   [goose
uitademen, owt-ah-der-mer, v., to breathe out
uitbarsting, owt-bαr-sting, c., eruption; outburst
uitbetalen, owt-ber-tah-ler, v., to pay out   [off
uitblijven, owt-bley-ver, v., to stay away; to hold
uitblinken, owt-blin-ker, v., to shine, to excel
uitblussen, owt-blers-ser, v., to extinguish
uitbouw, owt-bow, c., annex, wing (of a building)
uitbrander, owt-brαn-der, c., (pop.) scolding
uitbreiden, owt-brey-der, v., to spread; to enlarge
uitbreiding, owt-brey-ding, c., extension
uitbroeden, owt-broo-der, v., to hatch
uitbuiten, owt-bow-ter, v., to exploit
uitbundig, owt-bern-derHG, a. & adv., exuberant
uitdagen, owt-dah-HGer, v., to challenge, to defy
uitdelen, owt-day-ler, v., to distribute
uitdoen, owt-doon, v., to put out; to take off
uitdossen, owt-dos-ser, v., to dress up
uitdoven, owt-doh-ver, v., to extinguish
uitdraaien, owt-drah-yer, v., to turn out
uitdrinken, owt-drin-ker, v., to empty (one's
uitdrogen, owt-droh-HGer, v., to dry up [glass)
uitdrukkelijk, owt-drerk-ker-luck, a. & adv.,
    express
uitdrukking, owt-drerk-king, c., expression
uiteen, owt-ayn, adv., apart
uiteendrijven, owt-ayn-drey-ver, v., to disperse
uiteenlopend, owt-ayn-loh-pernt, a., divergent
uiteenzetting, owt-ayn-zet-ting, c., explanation
uiteinde, owt-eyn-der, n., extremity, end
uiteindelijk, owt-eyn-der-luck, a. & adv., ultimate
uiten, ow-ter, v., to utter, to express
uiterlijk, ow-ter-luck, n., appearance, exterior.
    a., outward. adv., at the latest

uitermate, ow-ter-**mah**-ter, adv., exceedingly
uiterst, ow-terst, a. & adv., farthest, utmost
uiterste, ow-ter-ster, n., extreme, extremity
uitflappen, owt-**flap**-per, v., to blurt out
uitfluiten, owt-**flow**-ter, v., to catcall, to hiss
uitgaaf, owt-HGahf, c., publication; edition;
uitgaan, owt-HGahn, v., to go out   [expense
uitgang, owt-HGang, c., exit; ending   [point
uitgangspunt, owt-HGang-spernt, n., starting-
uitgave, owt-HGah-ver, c., see uitgaaf
uitgebreid, owt-HGer-breyt, a. & adv., wide
uitgelaten, owt-HGer-lah-ter, a., exultant
uitgelezen, owt-HGer-lay-zer, a., select
uitgeput, owt-HGer-pert, a. & p.p., exhausted
uitgeslapen, owt-HGer-slah-per, a., (fig.) shrewd
uitgestorven, owt-HGer-stor-ver, a. & p.p., extinct
uitgestrekt, owt-HGer-streckt, a., vast
uitgeven, owt-HGay-ver, v., to spend; to issue; to
    publish. **zich —— voor . . .,** ziHG —— fohr
    . . ., to give oneself out as . . .
uitgever, owt-HGay-ver, c., publisher   [business
uitgeverij, owt-HGay-ver-rey, c., publishing-
uitgewerkt, owt-HGer-vayrkt, a., elaborate
uitgezonderd, owt-HGer-zon-dert, prep., except
uitgifte, owt-HGif-ter, c., issue
uitgillen, owt-HGil-ler, v., to scream
uitglijden, owt-HGley-der, v., to slip   [(tricks)
uithalen, owt-hah-ler, v., to draw out; to play
uithangbord, owt-hang-bort, n., signboard
uithoek, owt-hook, c., out-of-the-way place
uithollen, owt-hol-ler, v., to hollow (out)
uithongeren, owt-hong-er-rer, v., to starve (out)
uithouden, owt-how-der, v., to suffer, to bear
uithouwen, owt-how-er, v., to carve (out)
uithuwelijken, owt-hEE-ver-luck-er, v., to give in
uiting, ow-ting, c., utterance   [marriage
uitjouwen, owt-yow-er, v., to hoot (at), to boo
uitkering, owt-kay-ring, c., payment; benefit
uitkiezen, owt-kee-zer, v., to choose
uitkijk, owt-keyk, c., look-out (man)
uitkleden, owt-klay-der, v., to undress
uitkloppen, owt-klop-per, v., to beat (carpets)

uitknijpen, owt-k'ney-per, v., to squeeze
uitknippen, owt-k'nip-per, v., to cut out
uitknipsel, owt-k'nip-serl, n., cutting, clipping
uitkomst, owt-komst, c., result; help; relief
uitlachen, owt-laHG-er, v., to laugh at
uitlaten, owt-lah-ter, v., to let out; to leave off
uitlating, owt-lah-ting, c., remark; omission
uitleg, owt-leHG, c., explanation
uitleggen, owt-leHG-er, v., to explain; to lay out
uitleveren, owt-lay-ver-rer, v., to deliver up
uitlezen, owt-lay-zer, v., to read through
uitlokken, owt-lock-ker, v., to provoke
uitloven, owt-loh-ver, v., to offer
uitmaken, owt-mah-ker, v., to finish; to put out;
   to form; to settle; to call names
uitmonding, owt-mon-ding, c., mouth, outlet
uitmuntend, owt-**mern**-tent, a. & adv., excellent
uitnemendheid, owt-**nay**-ment-heyt, c., excellence
uitnodigen, owt-noh-der-HGer, v., to invite
uitoefenen, owt-oo-fer-ner, v., to exercise, to practise
uitpakken, owt-pak-ker, v., to unpack   [practise
uitpersen, owt-payr-ser, v., to squeeze
uitpuilen, owt-pow-ler, v., to bulge
uitputting, owt-pert-ting, c., exhaustion
uitreiken, owt-rey-ker, v., to distribute
uitrekenen, owt-ray-ker-ner, v., to calculate
uitrekken, owt-reck-ker, v., to stretch out
uitroeien, owt-roo-yer, v., to exterminate
uitroep, owt-roop, c., cry
uitrukken, owt-rerk-ker, v., to tear out
uitrusten, owt-rerss-ter, v., to rest; to equip
uitrusting, owt-rerss-ting, c., equipment
uitschakelen, owt-sHGah-ker-ler, v., to switch off
uitscheiden, owt-sHGey-der, v., to leave off.
   schei uit! sHGey owt, stop it!
uitschelden, owt-sHGel-der, v., to call names
uitschot, owt-sHGot, n., refuse, rubbish, trash
uitslaan, owt-slahn, v., to beat out; to spread
uitslag, owt-slaHG, c., result; eruption, rash
uitsloven (zich), owt-sloh-ver (ziHG), v. to
   drudge

uitsluitend, owt-slow-ternt, a. & adv., exclusive
uitsmijter, owt-smey-ter, c., meat sandwich with
fried egg [unharness
uitspannen, owt-span-ner, v., to stretch; to
uitspansel, owt-span-serl, n., firmament, sky
uitsparen, owt-spah-rer, v., to save
uitspatting, owt-spat-ting, c., debauch(ery)
uitspraak, owt-sprahk, c., verdict
uitspreiden, owt-sprey-der, v., to spread out
uitspreken, owt-spray-ker, v., to pronounce
uitstaan, owt-stahn, v., to endure
uitstallen, owt-stal-ler, v., to display [play
uitstalling, owt-stal-ling, c., (shop-window) dis-
uitstapje, owt-stap-yer, n., excursion, tour
uitstappen, owt-stap-per, v., to alight
uitsteeksel, owt-stayk-serl, n., projection
uitsteken, owt-stay-ker, v., to hold out [ing out
uitstekend, owt-stay-kernt, a., protruding, stick-
uitstekend, owt-stay-kernt, a. & adv., excellent
uitstel, owt-stel, n., postponement
uitstellen, owt-stel-ler, v., to put off
uitstorten, owt-stor-ter, v., to pour out (forth)
uitstralen, owt-strah-ler, v., to radiate
uitstrekken, owt-streck-ker, v., to stretch out
uitstrooien, owt-stroh-yer, v., to strew
uitteren, owt-tay-rer, v., to pine away
uittocht, owt-toHGt, c., departure [off
uittrekken, owt-treck-ker, v., to pull out; to take
uittreksel, owt-treck-serl, c., extract; excerpt
uitvaagsel, owt-fahHG-serl, n., scum, riff-raff
uitvaardigen, owt-fahr-der-HGer, v., to promul-
uitvaart, owt-fahrt, c., funeral (service) [gate
uitval, owt-fal, c., (mil.) sally; (fig.) outburst
uitvaren, owt-fah-rer, v., to sail out; to fly out
uitverkocht, owt-fer-koHGt, c., sold out; out of
print
uitverkoop, owt-fer-kohp, c., clearance sale
uitverkoren, owt-fer-koh-rer, a., chosen
uitvinden, owt-fin-der, v., to invent
uitvinder, owt-fin-der, c., inventor
uitvlucht, owt-flerHGt, c., pretext
uitvoer, owt-foor, c., export

---

uitvoerbaar, owt-foor-bahr, a., feasible, workable
uitvoeren, owt-foo-rer, v., to carry out; to export
uitvoerig, owt-foo-rerHG, a. & adv., full, ample
uitvoering, owt-foo-ring, c., execution
uitvorsen, owt-for-ser, v., to find out
uitwas, owt-vass, n., outgrowth
uitwasemen, owt-vah-ser-mer, v., to exhale
uitweg, owt-veHG, c., escape, way out
uitweiden (over), owt-vey-der (oh-ver), v., to dwell (upon)
uitwendig, owt-ven-derHG, a. & adv., exterior
uitwerken, owt-vayr-ker, v., to work out; to effect
uitwerking, owt-vayr-king, c., effect
uitwijken, owt-vey-ker, v., to make room
uitwisselen, owt-vis-ser-ler, v., to exchange
uitzenden, owt-sen-der, v., to broadcast; to send
uitzet, owt-set, c., outfit; trousseau [out
uitzetten, owt-set-ter, v., to expand; to invest
uitzicht, owt-siHGt, n., outlook, prospect
uitzien, owt-seen, v., to look out; to be like
uitzoeken, owt-soo-ker, v., to pick out
uitzondering, owt-son-der-ring, c., exception
uitzuigen, owt-sow-HGer, v., to suck out
uitzuiger, owt-sow-HGer, c., extortioner
unie, EE-nee, c., union
uniek, EE-neek, a., unique, unparalleled
uur, EEr, n., hour. adv., o'clock
uurwerk, EEr-vayrk, n., timepiece; clockwork
uw, EE, pron., your
uwerzijds, EE-ver-zeyts, adv., on your part

vaag, fahHG, a. & adv., vague, faint, hazy
vaak, fahk, adv., frequently. c., sleepiness
vaal, fahl, a., sallow, faded
vaandel, fahn-derl, c., colours, standard, banner
vaandrig, fahn-drerHG, c., cornet
vaardig, fahr-derHG, a. & adv., skilled; fluent
vaart, fahrt, c., navigation; speed; canal. **in volle** ——, in fol-ler ——, at full speed
vaartuig, fahr-towHG, n., vessel
vaarwel, fahr-**vel**, n. & interj., farewell
vaas, fahss, c., vase

vaatje, faht-yer, n., small cask

vaatwerk, faht-vayrk, n., plates and dishes

vacantie, fah-kan-see, c., holiday(s), vacation

vacantieganger, fah-kan-see-HGang-er, c., holiday maker
[sort

vacantieoord, fah-kan-see-ohrt, n., holiday re-

vacature, fah-kah-TEE-rer, c., vacancy, vacant post

vacht, faHGt, c., fleece, pelt

vadem, fah-dem, c., fathom

vader, fah-der, c., father

vaderland, fah-der-lant, n., fatherland, (native)
[country

vaderlands, fah-der-lants, a., native; patriotic

vaderlandsliefde, fah-der-lants-leev-der, c.,
patriotism
[father

vaderlijk, fah-der-luck, a., paternal, like a

vadsig, fat-serHG, a. & adv., indolent, lazy

vagevuur, fah-HGer-fEEr, n., purgatory

vak, fak, n., subject, branch; trade, line; partition

vakkennis, fak-ken-niss, c., professional knowledge

vakvereniging, fak-fer-ray-nerHG-ing, c., trade-
val, fal, c., trap; fall
[union

valies, fah-lees, n., portmanteau, travelling-bag

valk, falk, c., falcon, hawk

vallei, fal-ley, c., valley, glen, dale

vallen, fal-ler, v., to fall

valluik, fal-lowk, n., trapdoor

vals, falss, a. & adv., false; vicious; forged

valscherm, fal-sHGayrm, n., parachute

valstrik, fal-strick, c., gin; trap; snare

valuta, fah-LEE-tah, c., value; currency

van, fan, prep., of, from, for, with

vanaf, fan-af, prep., since, from

vanavond, fan-ah-vont, adv., this evening

vandaag, fan-dahHG, adv., this day, to-day

vandaar, fan-dahr, adv., from there; hence

vaneen, fan-ayn, adv., apart

vangen, fang-er, v., to catch

vangst, fangst, c., catch, haul, capture

vannacht, fan-naHGt, adv., to-night; last night

vanouds, fan-owts, adv., of old
[behalf of

vanwege, fan-vay-HGer, adv., on account of; on

vanzelf, fan-zelf, adv., of its own accord

vanzelfsprekend, fan-zelf-spray-kernt, a., self-evident

varen, fah-rer, v., to sail. c., fern, bracken

variëren, fah-ree-ay-rer, v., to vary, to range

varken, far-ker, n., pig, swine

varkenshok, far-kers-hock, n., pigsty

varkensvlees, far-kers-flayss, n., pork

vast, fast, a. & adv., fast, fixed, steady

vastberaden, fast-ber-**rah**-der, a. & adv., resolute, firm

vastbinden, fast-bin-der, v., to fasten

vasteland, fast-er-lant, c., continent

vasten, fass-ter, v., to fast. c., Lent [Tuesday

vastenavond, fass-ten-ah-vont, c., Shrove-

vastgespen, fast-HGess-per, v., to buckle (up)

vastgrijpen, fast-HGrey-per, v., to catch hold of

vasthechten, fast-heHG-ter, v., to attach

vasthouden, fast-how-der, v., to hold (fast). —— **aan,** —— ahn, to stick to.

vasthoudend, fast-how-dernt, a., stingy; tenacious

vastleggen, fast-leHG-er, v., to fasten

vastmaken, fast-mah-ker, v., to fasten

vaststellen, fast-stel-ler, v., to fix; to establish

vastzitten, fast-sit-ter, v., to stick; to be stuck

vat, fat, n., barrel, vat, cask. c., grip, hold

vatbaar (voor), fat-bahr (fohr), a., capable of

vatten, vat-ter, v., to catch; to understand

vechten, feHG-ter, v., to fight

vechtersbaas, feHG-ters-bahss, c., fighter

vechtpartij, feHGt-par-tey, c., scuffle, tussle

vee, fay, n., cattle, live-stock

veearts, fay-arts, c., veterinary surgeon

veeboer, fay-boor, c., cattle-breeder

veeg, fayHG, c., wipe; whisk; slap

veel, fayl, a., much, many. adv., much

veelal, fay-lal, adv., often, as a rule, mostly

veelbelovend, fayl-ber-loh-vernt, a., promising

veelbetekenend, fayl-ber-tay-ker-nernt, a., sig-

veeleisend, fayl-ey-sernt, a., exacting [nificant

veelvuldig, fayl-ferl-derHG, a. & adv., frequent

veelwijverij, fayl-vey-ver-rey, c., polygamy

veelzijdig, fayl-zey-derHG, a., many-sided; wide

veen, fayn, n., peat

veepest, fay-pest, c., cattle-plague

veer, fayr, n., ferry. c., spring; feather

veerkracht, fayr-kraHGt, c., elasticity

veerman, fayr-man, c., ferryman

veertien, fayr-teen, a., fourteen

veertiende, fayr-teen-der, a., fourteenth

veertig, fayr-terHG, a., forty

veertigste, fayr-terHG-ster, a., fortieth

veestapel, fay-stah-perl, c., stock of cattle

veeteelt, fay-taylt, c., cattle-breeding

vegen, fay-HGer, v., to sweep; to brush; to wipe

veger, fay-HGer, c., (sweeping-)brush; wiper

veilen, fey-ler, v., to sell by auction

veilig, fey-lerHG, a. & adv., safe

veiligheid, fey-lerHG-heyt, c., safety [ity Council

Veiligheidsraad, fey-lerHG-heyts-raht, c., Secur-

veiligheidsspeld, fey-lerHG-heyts-spelt, c., [safety-pin

veiling, fey-ling, c., auction sale

veinzen, feyn-zer, v., to feign

veinzerij, feyn-zer-rey, c., hyprocrisy

vel, fel, n., skin; hide; sheet of paper

veld, felt, n., field

veldfles, felt-fless, c., (mil.) water-bottle

veldheer, felt-hayr, c., (mil.) general [marshal

veldmaarschalk, felt-mahr-sHGalk, c., field-

veldprediker, felt-pray-der-ker, c., army-chap-

veldslag, felt-slaHG, c., battle [lain

veldtocht, felt-toHGt, c., campaign

veldwachter, felt-vaHG-ter, c., village policeman

velerlei, fay-ler-ley, a., of many kinds

vellen, fel-ler, v., to cut down; to pass (judgment)

velletje, fel-let-yer, n., skin, film; sheet of paper

venijnig, fer-ney-nerHG, a. & adv., venomous; virulent

vennootschap, fen-noht-sHGap, c., partnership

venster, fen-ster, n., window

vensterbank, fen-ster-bank, c., window-sill

vensterruit, fen-ster-rowt, c., window-pane

vent, fent, c., fellow

venten, fen-ter, v., to hawk

venter, fen-ter, c., pedlar, hawker
ventiel, fen-teel, n., valve
ver, fayr, a., far, remote, distant
verachtelijk, fer-*a*HG-ter-luck, a., contemptuous
verachting, fer-*a*HG-ting, c., contempt
verademing, fer-ah-der-ming, c., relief
varafgelegen, fayr-af-HGer-leHG-er, a., distant
verafgoden, fer-*af*-HGoh-der, v., to idolize
verafschuwen, fer-*af*-SHGEE-ver, v., to loathe
veranderen, fer-*an*-der-rer, v., to alter
verandering, fer-*an*-der-ring, c., alteration
veranderlijk, fer-*an*-der-luck, a., changeable
verantwoordelijk, fer-ant-vohr-der-luck, a., responsible
verantwoorden, fer-*ant*-vohr-der, v., to justify
verbaasd, fer-*bahst*, a., astonished
verband, fer-*bant*, n., connection; bandage, dressing. in — met, in — met, in connection with
verbannen, fer-*ban*-ner, v., to exile
verbazen, fer-bah-zer, v., to astonish
verbazingwekkend, fer-bah-zing-**veck**-kernt, a., stupendous [conceit
verbeelding, fer-bayl-ding, c., imagination; verbergen, fer-bayr-HGer, v., to conceal
verbeteren, fer-bay-ter-rer, v., to improve
verbetering, fer-bay-ter-ring, c., improvement
verbeurdverklaren, fer-berrt-fer-klah-rer, v., to confiscate
verbieden, fer-bee-der, v., to forbid
verbijsterd, fer-bey-stert, a., bewildered
verbinden, fer-bin-der, v., to bandage; to link
verbinding, fer-bin-ding, c., connection; communication [tract
verbintenis, fer-bin-ter-niss, c., alliance; contract
verbitterd, fer-bit-tert, a., embittered
verbittering, fer-bit-ter-ring, c., bitterness
verbleken, fer-blay-ker, v., to (grow) pale; to fade
verblijden, fer-bley-der, v., to rejoice
verblijf, fer-bleyf, n., residence [expenses
verblijfkosten, fer-bleyf-kos-ter, c. pl., hotel
verblijfplaats, fer-bleyf-plahtss, c., residence

verblinden, fer-**blin**-der, v., to blind
verbloemen, fer-**bloo**-mer, v., to disguise
verbluft, fer-**blerft,** a., flabbergasted
verbod, fer-**bot,** n., interdiction
verbond, fer-**bont,** n., alliance; treaty
verborgen, fer-**bor**-HGer, a. & p.p., hidden,
   occult   [vate
verbouwen, fer-**bow**-er, v., to rebuild; to culti-
verbouwereerd, fer-**bow**-er-rayrt, a., dumb-
verbranden, fer-**bran**-der, v., to burn   [founded
verbrassen, fer-**bras**-ser, v., to squander
verbreden, fer-**bray**-der, v., to broaden
verbreiden, fer-**brey**-der, v., to spread
verbrijzelen, fer-**brey**-zer-ler, v., to smash
verbruik, fer-**browk,** n., consumption; wastage
verbruiken, fer-**browk**-er, v., to consume; to
verbruiker, fer-**browk**-er, c., consumer   [spend
verbuigen, fer-**bow**-HGer, v., to bend; to twist
verdacht, fer-**da**HGt, a. & adv., suspect(ed)
verdagen, fer-**da**HG-er, v., to adjourn
verdampen, fer-**dam**-per, v., to evaporate
verdedigen, fer-**day**-der-HGer, v., to defend
verdediging, fer-**day**-der-HGing, c., defence
verdeeldheid, fer-**daylt**-heyt, c., discord
verdelen, fer-**day**-ler, v., to divide; to distribute
verdelgen, fer-**del**-HGer, v., to destroy
verdenken, fer-**den**-ker, v., to suspect
verdenking, fer-**den**-king, c., suspicion
verder, fayr-der, a. & adv., farther
verderf, fer-**dayrf,** n., destruction
verderfelijk, fer-**dayr**-fer-luck, a., pernicious
verdicht, fer-**di**HGt, a., fictitious; condensed
verdichtsel, fer-**di**HGt-serl, n., fiction
verdienen, fer-**dee**-ner, v., to earn; to merit
verdienste, fer-**deen**-ster, c., wages; profit; merit
verdienstelijk, fer-**deen**-ster-luck, a., meritorious
verdieping, fer-**dee**-ping, c., floor, storey
verdiept, fer-**deept,** a. & p.p., absorbed
verdierlijken, fer-**deer**-luck-er, v., to grow brutal
verdikking, fer-**dick**-king, c., thickening
verdoemen, fer-**doo**-mer, v., to damn
verdoeming, fer-**doo**-ming, c., damnation

verdorren, fer-dor-rer, v., to wither
verdorven, fer-dor-ver, a., corrupt   [to stun
verdoven, fer-doh-ver, v., to deafen; to numb;
verdovingsmiddel, fer-doh-vings-mid-derl, n., anaesthetic
verdraagzaam, fer-drahG-sahm, a., tolerant
verdraaien, fer-drah-yer, v., to distort
verdrag, fer-draHG, n., pact, treaty
verdragen, fer-drah-HGer, v., to bear, to suffer
verdriet, fer-dreet, n., grief, sorrow
verdrietig, fer-dree-terHG, a., peevish, sullen
verdrijven, fer-drey-ver, v., to drive away; to dispel   [oust
verdringen, fer-dring-er, v., to push aside; to
verdrinken, fer-drink-er, v., to drown; to spend on drink   [wither
verdrogen, fer-droh-HGer, v., to dry up; to
verdronken, fer-dron-ker, a. & p.p., drowned
verdrukken, fer-drerk-ker, v., to oppress
verdubbelen, fer-derb-ber-ler, v., to (re)double
verduidelijken, fer-dow-der-luck-er, v., to explain   [embezzle
verduisteren, fer-dow-ster-rer, v., to darken; to
verduistering, fer-dow-ster-ring, c., eclipse
verdunnen, fer-dern-ner, v., to dilute
verduren, fer-dEE-rer, v., to endure
verdwaald, fer-dvahlt, a. & p.p., lost, stray
verdwalen, fer-dvah-ler, v., to lose one's way
verdwijnen, fer-dvey-ner, v., to disappear
veredelen, fer-ay-der-ler, v., to ennoble
vereelt, fer-aylt, a., callous   [simplify
vereenvoudigen, fer-ayn-fow-der-HGer, v., to
vereeuwigen, fer-ay-ver-HGer, v., to perpetuate
vereffenen, fer-ef-fer-ner, v., to settle
vereisen, fer-ey-ser, v., to demand
vereiste, fer-ey-ster, n., requirement
veren, fay-rer, a., a feather. v., to be springy
verenigen, fer-ay-ner-HGer, v., to unite. **zich** ——
met, ziHG —— met, to agree with
vereniging, fer-ay-ner-HGing, c., union; society; club
vereren, fer-ay-rer, v., to respect, to honour

verergeren, fer-ayr-HGer-rer, v., to become
verering, fer-ay-ring, c., veneration   [worse
verf, fayrf, c., paint; dye
verfijnen, fer-fey-ner, v., to refine
verfkwast, fayrf-kvast, c., paint-brush
verflauwen, fer-flow-er, v., to slacken
verfoeilijk, fer-foo'ee-luck, a., detestable
verfraaien, fer-frah-yer, v., to embellish
verfrissen, fer-fris-ser, v., to refresh   [colours
verfwaren, fayrf-vah-rer, c. pl., dye-stuffs,
vergaan, fer-HGahn, v., to perish; to be wrecked
vergaarbak, fer-HGahr-bak, c., receptacle
vergadering, fer-HGah-der-ring, c., meeting
vergallen, fer-HGal-ler, v., to embitter
vergankelijk, fer-HGan-ker-luck, a., transitory
vergaren, fer-HGah-rer, v., to collect, to hoard
vergassen, fer-HGas-ser, v., to gas
vergeeflijk, fer-HGay-fer-luck, a., pardonable
vergeefs, fer-HGayfss, a. & adv., useless
vergeetachtig, fer-HGayt-aHG-terHG, a., forgetful
vergeet-mij-nietje, fer-HGayt-mer-neet-yer, n.,
   forget-me-not
vergelden, fer-HGel-der, v., to repay
vergelijk, fayr-HGer-leyk, n., agreement
vergelijken, fayr-HGer-ley-ker, v., to compare.
   vergeleken met . . ., vayr-HGer-lay-ker met
   . . ., as compared with . . .
vergelijking, fayr-HGer-ley-king, c., comparison
vergemakkelijken, fayr-HGer-mak-ker-luck-er,
   v., to make easier
vergen, fayr-HGer, v., to demand
vergenoegd, fayr-HGer-nooHGt, a., satisfied
vergetelheid, fer-HGay-terl-heyt, c., oblivion
vergeten, fer-HGay-ter, v., to forget
vergeven, fer-HGay-ver, v., to pardon; to poison
vergevingsgezind, fer-HGay-vinHGs-HGer-zint,
   a., forgiving   [to ascertain
vergewissen (zich), fayr-HGer-viss-ser (ziHG), v.,
vergezellen, fayr-HGer-zel-ler, v., to accompany
vergezicht, fayr-HGer-ziHGt, n., prospect
vergezocht, fayr-HGer-zoHGt, a., far-fetched
vergieten, fer-HGee-ter, v., to shed; to spill

vergif, fer-HGif, n., poison
vergiffenis, fer-HGif-fer-niss, c., pardon
vergiftig, fer-HGif-terHG, a., poisonous
vergiftigen, fer-HGif-ter-HGer, v., to poison
vergissen (zich), fer-HGis-ser (ziHG), v., to be
vergissing, fer-HGis-sing, c., error [mistaken
vergoeden, fer-HGoo-der, v., to make good
vergoeding, fer-HGoo-ding, c., compensation
vergoelijken, fer-HGoo-luck-er, v., to smooth over
vergrijp, fer-HGreyp, n., offence [glass
vergrootglas, fer-HGroht-HGlass, n., magnifying-
vergroten, fer-HGroh-ter, v., to enlarge
vergulden, fer-HGerl-der, v., to gild
vergunning, fer-HGern-ning, c., permission
verhaal, fer-hahl, n., narrative
verhaasten, fer-hahss-ter, v., to hasten
verhalen, fer-hah-ler, v., to narrate
verhandeling, fer-han-der-ling, c., treatise
verhard, fer-hart, a. & p.p., hardened
verharen, fer-hah-rer, v., to lose one's hair
verheerlijken, fer-hayr-luck-er, v., to glorify
verheffen, fer-hef-fer, v., to lift up
verhelen, fer-hay-ler, v., to hide, to keep secret
verhemelte, fer-hay-merl-ter, n., palate; canopy
verheugd, fer-herHGt, a. & adv., pleased
verheugen, fer-her-HGer, v., to delight. zich
———, ziHG ———, to rejoice in, at
verheven, fer-hay-ver, a. & adv., elevated
verhinderen, fer-hin-der-rer, v., to prevent
verhindering, fer-hin-der-ring, c., prevention;
verhitten, fer-hit-ter, v., to heat [hindrance
verhogen, fer-hoh-HGer, v., to heighten
verhoging, fer-hoh-HGing, c., raising; dais
verhongeren, fer-hong-er-rer, v., to starve (to
verhoor, fer-hohr, n., hearing; trial [death]
verhoren, fer-hoh-rer, v., to hear; to try [tion
verhouding, fer-how-ding, c., relation; propor-
verhuiswagen, fer-howss-vah-HGer, c., removal
verhuizen, fer-how-zer, v., to remove [van
verhuren, fer-hee-rer, v., to let (out)
verhuurder, fer-heer-der, c., lessor, landlord
verijdelen, fer-ey-der-ler, v., to frustrate

verjaardag, fer-yahr-daHG, c., birthday; anniversary [versary

verjagen, fer-yah-HGer, v., to drive away

verjaren, fer-yah-rer, v., to celebrate one's birthday [day

verjongen, fer-yong-er, v., to rejuvenate

verkeer, fer-kayr, n., traffic; intercourse

verkeerd, fer-kayrt, a. & adv., wrong; false

verkeersbord, fer-kayrss-bort, n., road sign

verkeersongeval, fer-kayrss-on-HGer-val, n., street accident [passenger plane

verkeersvliegtuig, fer-kayrss-fleeHG-towHG, n.,

verkeersweg, fer-kayrss-veHG, c., thoroughfare

verkenner, fer-ken-ner, c., scout

verkering, fer-kay-ring, c., courtship

verkiesbaar, fer-keess-bahr, a., eligible

verkieslijk, fer-keess-luck, a., preferable

verkiezen, fer-kee-zer, v., to prefer; to elect

verkiezingen, fer-kee-zing-er, c. pl., elections

verklaarbaar, fer-klahr-bahr, a., explicable

verklappen, fer-klap-per, v., to blab

verklaren, fer-klah-rer, v., to explain; to declare

verklaring, fer-klah-ring, c., explanation; statement [one's clothes

verkleden (zich), fer-kley-der (ziHG), v., to change

verkleinen, fer-kley-ner, v., to reduce; to belittle

verkleumd, fer-klermt, a., numb, benumbed

verkleuren, fer-kler-rer, v., to fade, to lose colour

verklikker, fer-klick-ker, c., tell-tale

verknocht, fer-k'noHGt, a., devoted

verknoeien, fer-k'noo-yer, v., to spoil; to waste

verkondigen, fer-kon-der-HGer, v., to proclaim

verkoop, fayr-kohp, c., sale

verkoopprijs, fayr-kohp-preyss, c., selling price

verkopen, fer-koh-per, v., to sell, to dispose of

verkoper, fer-koh-per, c., seller; salesman

verkoping, fer-koh-ping, c., (public) sale, auction

verkorten, fer-kor-ter, v., to shorten

verkouden, fer-kow-der, a., having a cold

verkrachten, fer-kraHG-ter, v., to violate

verkrijgbaar, fer-kreyHG-bahr, a., obtainable

verkrijgen, fer-kreyHG-er, v., to obtain

verkroppen, fer-krop-per, v., (fig.) to swallow

verkwanselen, fer-kvan-ser-ler, v., to barter away

verkwikken, fer-kvick-ker, v., to refresh
verkwisten, fer-kviss-ter, v., to squander
verkwister, fer-kviss-ter, c., prodigal
verlagen, fer-lah-HGer, v., to lower; to debase
verlaging, fer-lah-HGing, c., reduction; debase-
verlamd, fer-lamt, a. & p.p., paralysed [ment
verlangen, fer-lang-er, v., to desire; to long. n., desire [ous (of)
verlangend (naar), fer-lang-ernt(nahr), a., desir-
verlaten, fer-lah-ter, a., lonely; deserted. v., to leave, to abandon. zich —— op, ziHG —— op, to rely upon
verleden, fer-lay-der, n., past. a., past, last
verlegen, fer-lay-HGer, a., timid; confused; shop-soiled
verlegenheid, fer-lay-HGer-heyt, c., shyness
verleidelijk, fer-ley-der-luck, a. & adv., tempting
verleiden, fer-ley-der, v., to tempt; to seduce
verleiding, fer-ley-ding, c., temptation
verlenen, fer-lay-ner, v., to grant; to confer
verlangen, fer-lang-er, v., to prolong
verleppen, fer-lep-per, v., to fade [liven
verlevendigen, fer-lay-ven-der-HGer, v., to en-
verlicht, fer-liHGt, a., (fig.) enlightened; relieved
verlichten, fer-liHG-ter, v., to light; to lighten
verlichting, fer-liHG-ting, c., illumination; relief
verliefd, fer-leeft, a., in love
verlies, fer-leess, n., loss; bereavement
verliezen, fer-lee-zer, v., to lose
verlof, fer-lof, n., leave; licence
verlokkelijk, fer-lock-ker-luck, a., tempting
verlokken, fer-lock-ker, v., to tempt
verloochenen, fer-lohHG-er-ner, v., to deny
verloofde, fer-lohv-der, c., betrothed
verloop, fer-lohp, n., lapse, course, progress
verlopen, fer-loh-per, v., to pass (away); to expire
verloren, fer-loh-rer, a. & p.p., lost
verlossen, fer-los-ser, v., to deliver
verlossing, fer-los-sing, c., deliverance
verloting, fer-loh-ting, c., lottery, draw
verloven (zich), fer-loh-ver (ziHG), v., to become
verloving, fer-loh-ving, c., betrothal [engaged

verluchting, fer-lerHG-ting, c., relief; illumina-
 [to delight in
verlustigen (zich), fer-lerss-ter-HGer (ziHG), v.,
vermaak, fer-mahk, n., pleasure, delight. **tot
—— van . . .,** tot **—— fan . . .,** to the amusement of . . .
vermaard, fer-mahrt, a., celebrated
vermageren, fer-mah-HGer-rer, v., to grow thin
vermakelijk, fer-mah-ker-luck, a., amusing
vermakelijkheid, fer-mah-ker-luck-heyt, c.,
 amusement [to bequeath
vermaken, fer-mah-ker, v., to amuse; to alter;
vermanen, fer-mah-ner, v., to warn
vermannen (zich), fer-man-ner (ziHG), v., to
 pull oneself together
vermeend, fer-maynt, a., fancied
vermeerderen, fer-mayr-der-rer, v., to increase
vermelden, fer-mel-der, v., to mention
vermengen, fer-meng-er, v., to mix
vermenigvuldigen, fer-may-nerHG-**ferl**-der-
 HGer, v., to multiply
vermetel, fer-may-terl, a. & adv., daring, reck-
vermijden, fer-mey-der, v., to avoid [less
verminderen, fer-min-der-rer, v., to diminish
verminkt, fer-minkt, a. & p.p., crippled
vermoedelijk, fer-moo-der-luck, a. & adv., pre-
 sumable [sume. n., suspicion; surmise
vermoeden, fer-moo-der, v., to suspect; to pre-
vermoeid, fer-moo'eet, a., tired, fatigued
vermoeidheid, fer-moo'eet-heyt, c., fatigue
vermoeien, fer-moo-yer, v., to fatigue, to tire
vermogen, fer-moh-HGer, n., wealth; power;
 capacity. v., to be able
vermolmen, fer-mol-mer, v., to moulder (away)
vermommen, fer-mom-mer, v., to disguise
vermoorden, fer-mohr-der, v., to murder
vermurwen, fer-merr-ver, v., to soften
vernedering, fer-nay-der-ring, c., humiliation
vernemen, fer-nay-mer, v., to learn, to hear
vernielen, fer-nee-ler, v., to destroy
vernieling, fer-nee-ling, c., destruction [nullify
vernietigen, fer-nee-ter-HGer, v., to destroy; to

vernieuwen, fer-**nee**-ver, v., to renew

vernis, fer-**niss,** n., varnish

vernuft, fer-**nerft,** n., ingenuity; wit

vernuftig, fer-**nerf**-terHG, a. & adv., ingenious; witty   [neglect

veronachtzamen, fer-on-*a*HGt-sah-mer, v., to

veronderstellen, fer-on-der-**stel**-ler, v., to suppose   [position

veronderstelling, fer-on-der-**stel**-ling, c., supposition

verongelijken, fer-on-ger-**ley**-ker, v., to wrong

verongelukken, fer-on-HGer-**lerk**-ker, v., to come to grief   [pollute

verontreinigen, fer-ont-rey-ner-HGer, v., to

verontrusten, fer-ont-**rerss**-ter, v., to alarm

verontschuldiging, fer-ont-sHGerl-der-HGing, c., excuse, apology. **ter** ——, tayr ——, by way of excuse   [dignant

verontwaardigd, fer-ont-**vahr**-derHGt, a., in-

verontwaardiging, fer-ont-**vahr**-der-HGing, c., indignation

veroordelen, fer-**ohr**-day-ler, v., to condemn

veroorloven, fer-ohr-**loh**-ver, v., to allow

veroorzaken, fer-ohr-**zah**-ker, v., to cause

verordenen, fer-or-der-ner, v., to order

verouderd, fer-**ow**-dert, a., obsolete

veroveraar, fer-oh-ver-rahr, c., conqueror

veroveren, fer-oh-**ver**-rer, v., to conquer

verpachten, fer-p*a*HG-ter, v., to lease

verpakken, fer-**pak**-ker, v., to pack; to wrap up

verpakking, fer-**pak**-king, c., packing

verpanden, fer-p*a*n-der, v., to pawn   [personify

verpersoonlijken, fer-per-**sohn**-luck-er, v., to

verpesten, fer-**pess**-ter, v., (fig.) to poison

verplaatsen, fer-**plaht**-ser, v., to move; to transfer

verplanten, fer-pl*a*n-ter, v., to transplant

verpleegster, fer-**play**HG-ster, c., nurse

verplegen, fer-**play**-HGer, v., to nurse   [tenance

verpleging, fer-**play**-HGing, c., nursing; main-

verpletteren, fer-**plet**-ter-rer, v., to crush

verplicht, fer-**pli**HGt, a., obliged; due; compulsory. **zeer** ——, zayr ——, much obliged

verplichten, fer-pliHG-ter, v., to force
verplichting, fer-pliHG-ting, c., obligation
verpozen (zich), fer-poh-zer (ziHG), v., to rest
verraad, fer-raht, n., treachery, treason
verraden, fer-rah-der, v., to betray
verrader, fer-rah-der, c., traitor
verraderlijk, fer-rah-der-luck, a., treacherous
verrassen, fer-ras-ser, v., to surprise
verrassing, fer-ras-sing, c., surprise
verre, fayr-rer, a., distant, far
verregaand, fayr-rer-HGahnt, a., excessive
verrekijker, fayr-rer-key-ker, c., telescope
verrekken, fer-reck-ker, v., to sprain; to strain
verreweg, fayr-rer-veHG, adv., by far
verrichten, fer-riHG-ter, v., to perform
verrijken, fer-rey-ker, v., to enrich
verrijzenis, fer-rey-zer-niss, c., resurrection
verroeren, fer-roo-rer, v., to stir
verroesten, fer-roo-ster, v., to rust
verrotten, fer-rot-ter, v., to rot
verruilen, fer-row-ler, v., to exchange
verruimen, fer-row-mer, v., to enlarge
verrukkelijk, fer-rerk-ker-luck, a., delightful
verrukking, fer-rerk-king, c., delight
vers, vayrss, n., verse; couplet; stanza. a. & adv., fresh, new(-laid)
versagen, fer-sah-HGer, v., to despair
verschaffen, fer-sHGaf-fer, v., to procure
verschalken, fer-sHGal-ker, v., to outwit   [ment
verschansing, fer-sHGan-sing, c., (mil.) entrench-
verscheiden, fer-sHGey-der, a., several; various
verscheidenheid, fer-sHGey-der-heyt, c., variety
verscheping, fer-sHGay-ping, c., shipment
verscheuren, fer-sHGer-rer, v., to tear
verschiet, fer-sHGeet, n., distance; (fig.) prospect
verschijnen, fer-sHGey-ner, v., to appear
verschijning, fer-sHGey-ning, c., appearance
verschijnsel, fer-sHGeyn-serl, n., phenomenon;
verschil, fer-sHGil, n., difference   [symptom
verschillend, fer-sHGil-lernt, a. & adv., different
verschoppeling, fer-sHGop-per-ling, c., outcast
verschoten, fer-sHGoh-ter, a. & p.p., faded

verschrikkelijk, fer-srick-ker-luck, a. & adv., terrible

verschrikken, fer-srick-ker, v., to frighten

verschrikking, fer-srick-king, c., fright; horror

verschroeien, fer-sroo-yer, v., to singe, to scorch

verschrompelen, fer-srom-per-ler, v., to shrivel

verschuilen (zich), fer-sнGow-ler (ziнG), v., to hide (oneself)   [postpone

verschuiven, fer-sнGow-ver, v., to shift; to

verschuldigd, fer-sнGerl-derнGt, a., indebted

versieren, fer-see-rer, v., to adorn

versiering, fer-see-ring, c., decoration

verslaafd (aan), fer-slahft (ahn), a., addicted (to)

verslaan, fer-slahn, v., to beat

verslag, fer-slaнG, n., report, account   [dismayed

verslagen, fer-slah-нGer, a. & adv., defeated;

verslaggever, fer-slaнG-нGay-ver, c., reporter

verslapen (zich), fer-slah-per (ziнG), v., to over-sleep (oneself)

verslappen, fer-slap-per, v., to slacken

versleten, fer-slay-ter, a., threadbare

verslijten, fer-sley-ter, v., to wear out

verslinden, fer-slin-der, v., to devour

versmaden, fer-smah-der, v., to scorn, to despise

versnapering, fer-snah-per-ring, c., dainty, bit

versnellen, fer-snel-ler, v., to accelerate   [bit

versnelling, fer-snel-ling, c., gear, speed

versnipperen, fer-snip-per-rer, v., to cut into bits

verspelen, fer-spay-ler, v., to lose (in playing)

versperren, fer-spayr-rer, v., to block; to bar

verspieder, fer-spee-der, c., scout, spy

verspillen, fer-spil-ler, v., to squander

verspreiden, fer-sprey-der, v., to spread

verstaan, fer-stahn, v., to understand, to know

verstaanbaar, fer-stahn-bahr, a. & adv., under-standable

verstand, fer-stant, n., understanding, reason

verstandhouding, fer-stant-how-ding, c., under-standing

verstandig, fer-stan-derнG, a. & adv., sensible

versteend, fer-staynt, a., petrified

verstekeling, fer-stay-ker-ling, c., stowaway

verstellen, fer-stel-ler, v., to mend; to adjust
versterken, fer-stayr-ker, v., to strengthen
verstijfd, fer-steyft, a. & p.p., stiff; numb
verstikken, fer-stick-ker, v., to stifle, to choke
verstoken, fer-stoh-ker, v., to burn. —— **van,** —— fan, a., devoid of
verstokt, fer-stockt, a., obdurate
verstommen, fer-stom-mer, v., to silence
verstoord, fer-stohrt, a. & p.p., disturbed; vexed
verstoppen, fer-stop-per, v., to hide; to stop up
verstoren, fer-stoh-rer, v., to disturb; to annoy
verstoten, fer-stoh-ter, v., to disown; to repudiate
verstrekken, fer-streck-ker, v., to provide
verstrijken, fer-strey-ker, v., to expire
verstrooid, fer-stroh-eet, a., absent-minded; scattered [mindedness
verstrooidheid, fer-stroh-eet-heyt, c., absent-
verstuiken, fer-stow-ker, v., to sprain
versuft, fer-serft, a. & p.p., dazed, stunned
vertakking, fer-tak-king, c., branching
vertalen, fer-tah-ler, v., to translate
vertaling, fer-tah-ling, c., translation
verte, fayr-ter, c., distance
verteerbaar, fer-tayr-bahr, a., digestible
vertegenwoordiger, fer - tay - HGer - vohr - der - HGer, c., representative
vertellen, fer-tel-ler, v., to relate
vertelling, fer-tel-ling, c., story, tale
verteren, fer-tay-rer, v., to spend; to digest
vertering, fer-tay-ring, c., expenses; digestion
vertoeven, fer-too-ver, v., to sojourn
vertolker, fer-tol-ker, c., interpreter
vertoning, fer-toh-ning, c., show; performance
vertoon, fer-tohn, n., show, display; ostentation
vertoornd, fer-tohrnt, a. & p.p., angry
vertraging, fer-trah-HGing, c., delay; slackening
vertrappen, fer-trap-per, v., to trample upon
vertrek, fer-treck, n., apartment, room; departure
vertrekken, fer-treck-ker, v., to leave
vertroetelen, fer-troo-ter-ler, v., to spoil
vertroosting, fer-trohss-ting, c., comfort
vertrouwd, fer-trowt, a., trusted

vertrouwelijk, fer-trow-er-luck, a., confidential
vertrouwen, fer-trow-er, v., to trust. n., trust
vertwijfeling, fer-tvey-fer-ling, c., despair
vervaardigen, fer-fahr-der-HGer, v., to manu- [facture
verval, fer-fal, n., decline
vervallen, fer-fal-ler, v., to decay; to expire. a., dilapidated; expired
vervalsen, fer-fal-ser, v., to forge; to falsify
vervangen, fer-fang-er, v., to replace; to relieve
vervelen, fer-fay-ler, v., to bore; to annoy
verven, fayr-ver, v., to paint; to dye
verversing, fer-fayr-sing, c., refreshment
vervliegen, fer-flee-HGer, v., to evaporate
vervloeken, fer-floo-ker, v., to curse
vervoer, fer-foor, n., transport; transit
vervoering, fer-foo-ring, c., rapture [ance
vervoermiddel, fer-foor-mid-derl, n., convey-
vervolg, fer-folHG, n., continuation. **in het ——,** in het ——, in future
vervolgen, fer-fol-HGer, c., to continue; to pursue
vervolgens, fer-fol-HGenss, adv., further, next
vervolging, fer-fol-HGing, c., persecution
vervreemden, fer-fraym-der, v., to alienate
vervullen, fer-ferl-ler, v., to carry out
vervulling, fer-ferl-ling, c., fulfilment
verwaand, fer-vahnt, a., arrogant, conceited
verwaardigen (zich), fer-vahr-der-HGer (ziHG), v., to deign to
verwaarlozen, fer-vahr-loh-zer, v., to neglect
verwachten, fer-vaHG-ter, v., to expect
verwachting, fer-vaHG-ting, c., expectation
verwant, fer-vant, a., related, allied
verwantschap, fer-vant-sHGap, c., kinship
verward, fer-vart, a. & adv., entangled, confused
verwarming, fer-var-ming, c., heating, warming
verwarren, fer-var-rer, v., to entangle, to confuse
verweerd, fer-vayrt, a., weather-beaten
verwekken, fer-veck-ker, v., to cause; to rouse
verwelken, fer-vel-ker, v., to wither, to fade
verwelkomen, fer-vel-koh-mer, v., to welcome
verwennen, fer-ven-ner, v., to spoil (a child)
verwensen, fer-ven-ser, v., to curse

verwerken, fer-*vayr*-ker, v., (fig.) to digest
verwerpen, fer-*vayr*-per, v., to reject
verwerven, fer-*vayr*-ver, v., to obtain
verwezenlijken, fer-*vay*-zer-luck-er, v., to realize
verwijden, fer-*vey*-der, v., to widen   [expel
verwijderen, fer-*vey*-der-rer, v., to remove, to
verwijdering, fer-*vey*-der-ring, c., removal; estrangement
verwijsd, fer-*veyft*, a. & adv., effeminate
verwijt, fer-*veyt*, n., reproach
verwijten, fer-*vey*-ter, v., to reproach
verwijzen, fer-*vey*-zer, v., to refer
verwikkeling, fer-*vick*-ker-ling, c., complication
verwilderd, fer-*vil*-dert, a., neglected, wild
verwisselen, fer-*vis*-ser-ler, v., to exchange
verwittigen, fer-*vit*-ter-HGer, v., to inform
verwoed, fer-*voot*, a. & adv., furious
verwoesten, fer-*vooss*-ter, v., to destroy
verwoesting, fer-*vooss*-ting, c., destruction
verwonden, fer-*von*-der, v., to wound; to hurt
verwonderen, fer-*von*-der-rer, v., to astonish
verwondering, fer-*von*-der-ring, c., surprise
verwonderlijk, fer-*von*-der-luck, a. & adv., surprising
verwringen, fer-*vring*-er, v., to distort, to twist
verzachten, fer-*za*HG-ter, v., to soften
verzadigen, fer-*zah*-der-HGer, v., to satisfy
verzaken, fer-*zah*-ker, v., to forsake
verzakken, fer-*zak*-ker, v., to sink
verzamelen, fer-*zah*-mer-ler, v., to collect
verzameling, fer-*zah*-mer-ling, v., collection
verzegelen, fer-*zay*-HGer-ler, v., to seal   [sure
verzekeren, fer-*zay*-ker-rer, v., to assure; to in-
verzekering, fer-*zay*-ker-ring, c., insurance
verzenden, fer-*zen*-der, v., to forward
verzengen, fer-*zeng*-er, v., to singe
verzet, fer-*zet*, n., resistance; recreation
verzetten, fer-*zet*-ter, v., to move. **zich** ——
tegen, ziHG —— tay-HGer, to oppose
verziend, fayr-*zeent*, a., long-sighted
verzinnen, fer-*zin*-ner, v., to invent
verzinsel, fer-*zin*-serl, n., invention

verzoek, fer-**zook**, n., request; petition
verzoeken, fer-**zoo**-ker, v., to request; to invite
verzoenen, fer-**zoo**-ner, v., to reconcile
verzorgen, fer-**zor**-HGer, v., to take care of
verzorging, fer-**zor**-HGing, c., provision; care
verzot (op), fer-**zot** (op), a., fond (of), keen (on)
verzuchting, fer-**zerHG**-ting, c., sigh; lamentation
verzuimen, fer-**zow**-mer, v., to neglect
verzwakken, fer-**zvak**-ker, v., to weaken
verzwelgen, fer-**zvel**-HGer, v., to swallow
verzwijgen, fer-**zvey**-HGer, v., to keep a secret
vest, fest, c., waistcoat
vestigen, fess-ter-HGer, v., to establish
vesting, fess-ting, c., fortress
vet, fet, n., fat; grease. a., fat; greasy
vete, fay-ter, c., enmity
veter, fay-ter, c., shoe-lace, boot-lace
vetmesten, fet-mes-ter, v., to fatten
vettig, fet-terHG, a., greasy
vetvlek, fet-fleck, c., grease spot
veulen, fer-ler, n., foal; colt; filly
vezel, fay-zerl, c., fibre, filament
vezelig, fay-zer-lerHG, a., fibrous; stringy
vier, feer, a., four
vierde, feer-der, a., fourth
vieren, fee-rer, v., to celebrate
vierkant, feer-kant, n. & a., square
viervoeter, feer-foo-ter, c., quadruped
viervoudig, feer-fow-derHG, a., fourfold
vies, feess, a., dirty; filthy; foul; fastidious
vijand, fey-ant, c., enemy
vijandelijk, fey-an-der-luck, a., hostile
vijandschap, fey-ant-sHGap, c., enmity
vijf, feyf, a., five
vijfde, feyf-der, a., fifth
vijftien, feyf-teen, a., fifteen
vijftiende, feyf-teen-der, a., fifteenth
vijftig, feyf-terHG, a., fifty
vijftigste, feyf-terHG-ster, a., fiftieth
vijg, feyHG, c., fig
vijl, feyl, c., file
vijlen, fey-ler, v., to file; (fig.) to polish

vijver, fey-ver, c., pond
vijzel, fey-zerl, c., jack-screw; mortar
villen, fil-ler, v., to fleece; (fig.) to rob
vilt, filt, n., felt
vin, fin, c., fin
vinden, fin-der, v., to find; to think
vindingrijk, fin-ding-reyk, a., resourceful
vinger, fing-er, c., finger
vingerafdruk, fing-er-af-drerk, c., finger-print
vingerhoed, fing-er-hoot, c., thimble
vink, fink, c., finch
vinnig, fin-nerHG, a. & adv., sharp, biting
viool, fee-ohl, c., violin; violet
viooltje, fee-ohlt-yer, n., violet; pansy
vis, fiss, c., fish
visite, fee-zee-ter, c., visit; visitors
vissen, fiss-ser, v., to fish
visser, fiss-ser, c., fisherman; angler
visserij, fiss-ser-rey, c., fishery, fishing-industry
vitrage, fee-trah-zher, c., lace curtain
vitten, fit-ter, v., to find fault
vitter, fit-ter, c., fault-finder
vla, flah, c., tart; custard
vlaag, flahHG, c., gust of wind, shower; (fig.) fit
vlag, flaHG, c., flag; standard
vlaggen, flaHG-er, v., to put out the flag
vlak, flak, n., level. a., flat, level. adv., flatly; close
vlakte, flak-ter, c., plain; level
vlam, flam, c., flame, blaze
vlammen, flam-mer, v., to be ablaze
vlas, flass, n., flax
vlashaar, flass-hahr, n., flaxen hair
vlecht, fleHGt, c., plait, braid
vlechten, fleHG-ter, v., to twist; to plait
vlechtwerk, fleHGt-vayrk, n., wicker-work
vleermuis, flayr-mowss, c., bat
vlees, flayss, n., meat; flesh; pulp (of fruit)
vleesgerecht, flayss-HGer-reHGt, n., meat-course
vlegel, flay-HGerl, c., flail; (fig.) boor
vlegelachtig, flay-HGerl-aHG-terHG, a., boorish
vleien, fley-er, v., to flatter
vleier, fley-er, c., flatterer

vleierig, fley-er-rerHG, a., coaxing
vlek, fleck, n., small market-town. c., stain
vlekkeloos, fleck-ker-lohss, a., stainless
vlekkenwater, fleck-ker-vah-ter, n., stain remover
vlerk, flayrk, c., wing; (pop.) boor
vleselijk, flay-ser-luck, a., carnal
vleugel, fler-HGerl, c., wing; grand piano
vleugeldeur, fler-HGerl-derr, c., folding-door(s)
vlezig, flay-zerHG, a., plump; meaty; pulpy (fruit)
vlieg, fleeHG, c., fly
vliegdekschip, fleeHG-deck-sHGip, n., aircraft
vliegen, flee-HGer, v., to fly   [carrier
vlieger, flee-HGer, c., airman; kite
vliegtuig, fleeHG-towHG, n., aeroplane
vliegtuigmoederschip, fleeHG-towHG-**moo**-der-sHGip, n., sea-plane carrier
vliegveld, fleeHG-felt, n., aerodrome, airfield
vliegwiel, fleeHG-veel, n., fly-wheel
vlier, fleer, c., elder
vliering, flee-ring, c., attic, loft
vlies, fleess, n., fleece; film; membrane
vlijen, fley-er, v., to lay down. **zich ——,** ziHG ——, to nestle
vlijt, fleyt, c., diligence, industry
vlijtig, fley-terHG, a., diligent, industrious
vlinder, flin-der, c., butterfly
vlo, floh, c., flea
vloed, floot, c., flood, tide; stream; (fig.) flood
vloeibaar, floo-ee-bahr, a., liquid
vloeien, floo-yer, v., to flow; to blot
vloeipapier, floo-ee-pah-peer, n., blotting-paper
vloeitje, floo-eet-yer, n., cigarette paper
vloek, flook, c., curse; swear-word
vloeken, floo-ker, v., to swear
vloer, floor, c., floor, flooring
vloerkleed, floor-klayt, n., carpet
vlok, flock, c., flake (snow); flock (cotton); tuft [(hair)
vloot, floht, c., fleet, navy
vlootbasis, floht-bah-ziss, c., naval base
vlot, flot, n., raft. a. & adv., afloat; smooth; fluent
vlotheid, flot-heyt, c., smoothness; fluency
vlucht, flerHGt, c., flight; escape; flock

vluchteling, flerHG-ter-ling, c., fugitive
vluchten, flerHG-ter, v., to fly, to flee
vluchtheuvel, flerHGt-her-verl, c., traffic island
vluchtig, flerHG-terHG, a. & adv., hasty
vlug, flerHG, a. & adv., quick; nimble; fledged
vlugschrift, flerHG-srift, n., pamphlet
vocht, foHGt, n., fluid; juice; moisture
vochtig, foHG-terHG, a., damp, moist
vod, fot, c., tatter; (fig.) rubbish
voeden, foo-der, v., to feed
voeder, foo-der, n., fodder. c., feeder
voeding, foo-ding, c., feeding; nourishment
voedsel, foot-serl, n., food, nourishment
voedzaam, foot-sahm, a., nourishing
voegen, fooHG-er, v., to add; to suit, to be proper.
  zich —— naar, ziHG —— nahr, to comply
  with
voelbaar, fool-bahr, a., perceptible; palpable
voelen, foo-ler, v., to feel
voeren, foo-rer, v., to feed; to convey; to lead; to
  bring; to line (a coat); to wage (war); to conduct (a campaign)
voering, foo-ring, c., lining   [waggoner
voerman, foor-man, c., coachman, driver;
voertuig, foor-towHG, n., vehicle, carriage
voet, foot, c., foot
voetbal, foot-bal, c., football
voetballen, foot-bal-ler, v., to play football
voetballer, foot-bal-ler, c., footballer
voetbalveld, foot-bal-felt, n., football ground
voetbank, foot-bank, c., footstool
voetganger, foot-HGang-er, c., pedestrian
voetpad, foot-pat, n., pathway, footpath
voetstap, foot-stap, c., footstep; footprint
voetstuk, foot-sterk, n., pedestal, foot
vogel, foh-HGerl, c., bird
vogelkooi, foh-HGerl-koh-ee, c., birdcage
vogellijm, foh-HGerl-leym, c., mistletoe; bird-lime
vogelverschrikker, foh-HGerl-fer-srick-ker, c.,
  scarecrow
vogelvrij, foh-HGerl-frey, a., outlawed
vol, fol, a., full

volbloed, fol-**bloot,** a., thoroughbred
volbrengen, fol-**breng-**er, v., to fulfil
voldaan, fol-**dahn,** a. & p.p., satisfied; paid
voldoen, fol-**doon,** v., to satisfy; to pay
voldoende, fol-**doon-**der, a. & adv., sufficient
voldoening, fol-**doo-**ning, c., satisfaction
voleindigen, fol-eyn-der-HGer, v., to complete
volgeling, fol-HGer-ling, c., follower, adherent
volgen, fol-HGer, v., to follow (up); to attend (lectures)
volgend, fol-HGernt, a., following; succeeding
volgens, fol-HGernss, prep., according to; by
volgorde, folHG-or-der, c., sequence
volgzaam, folHG-sahm, a., docile
volharden, fol-**har-**der, v., to persevere
volharding, fol-**har-**ding, c., perseverance
volhouden, fol-**how-**der, v., to persist
volk, folk, n., nation, people
volkenrecht, fol-ker-reHGt, n., law of nations
volkomen, fol-**koh-**mer, a. & adv., perfect
volkrijk, folk-reyk, a., populous
volksfeest, folks-fayst, n., national feast   [health
volksgezondheid, folks-HGer-zont-heyt, c., public
volkslied, folks-leet, n., national anthem
volksstam, folks-stam, c., tribe, race
volkstaal, folks-tahl, c., popular language
volkstelling, folks-tel-ling, c., census
volledig, fol-lay-derHG, a. & adv., complete
volleerd, fol-layrt, a., finished
vollemaan, fol-ler-mahn, c., full moon
volmaakt, fol-**mahkt,** a. & adv., perfect
volmacht, fol-maHGt, c., full powers; proxy
volmondig, fol-**mon-**derHG, a. & adv., frank
volop, fol-op, adv., in abundance   [plete
volslagen, fol-slah-HGer, a. & adv., utter, com-
volstrekt, fol-streckt, a. & adv., absolute
voltallig, fol-tal-lerHG, a., full, complete
voltooien, fol-toh-yer, v., to complete
voltrekken, fol-treck-ker, v., to execute; to   [celebrate
voluit, fol-owt, adv., in full
volwassen, fol-vas-ser, a., grown-up
vondeling, fon-der-ling, c., foundling

vondst, fonst, c., find(ing), discovery

vonk, fonk, c., sparkle

vonnis, fon-niss, n., judgment

voogd, fohHGT, c., guardian

voogdij, fohHG-dey, c., guardianship

voor, fohr, c., furrow. prep., for; in front of. adv., in front. conj., before

vooraan, foh-rahn, adv., in front

vooraanstaand, foh-**rahn**-stahnt, a., leading

vooraf, foh-**raf,** adv., beforehand

voorafgaand, foh-**raf**-HGahnt, a., preceding

vooral, foh-**ral,** adv., above all   [preliminary

vooravond, fohr-ah-vont, c., eve

voorbarig, fohr-bah-rerHG, a. & adv., premature

voorbedacht, fohr-ber-daHGT, a., premeditated

voorbeeld, fohr-baylt, n., example. **een ——**
geven, ayn —— HGay-ver, to set an example

voorbeeldig, fohr-bayl-derHG, a., exemplary

voorbehoud, fohr-ber-howt, n., restriction

voorbereiden, fohr-ber-rey-der, v., to prepare

voorbereiding, fohr-ber-rey-ding, c., preparation

voorbeschikken, fohr-ber-sHGick-ker, v., to
predestine

voorbij, fohr-bey, prep., beyond. adv., past

voorbijgaan, fohr-bey-HGahn, v., to pass (by)

voorbijganger, fohr-bey-HGang-er, c., passer-by

voorbode, fohr-boh-der, c., forerunner

voordat, fohr-dat, conj., before

voordeel, fohr-dayl, n., advantage; gain, profit

voordelig, fohr-day-lerHG, a. & adv., profitable.

voordeur, fohr-derr, c., front door   [cheap

voordoen, fohr-doon, v., to put on; to show how to

voordracht, fohr-draHGT, c., discourse; recital;
diction   [recite

voordragen, fohr-drah-HGer, v., to propose; to

vooreerst, fohr-ayrst, adv., in the first place

voorgaan, fohr-HGahn, v., to precede   [pastor

voorganger, fohr-HGang-er, c., predecessor;

voorgevel, fohr-HGay-verl, c., forefront

voorgeven, fohr-HGay-ver, v., to pretend

voorgevoel, fohr-HGer-vool, n., presentiment

voorgrond, fohr-HGront, c., foreground

voorhanden, fohr-*han*-der, a., in stock
voorheen, fohr-*hayn*, adv., formerly
voorhoede, fohr-*hoo*-der, c., vanguard
voorhoofd, fohr-*hohft*, n., forehead
voorin, fohr-*in*, adv., in front
vooringenomen, fohr-in-HGer-noh-mer, a., pre- [judiced
voorjaar, fohr-*yahr*, n., spring
voorkamer, fohr-*kah*-mer, c., front room
voorkeur, fohr-*kerr*, c., preference
voorkomen, fohr-*koh*-mer, n., appearance. v., to
   get ahead; to appear (for trial); to be found;
   to occur; to seem to   [anticipate
voorkomen, fohr-*koh*-mer, v., to prevent; to
voorkomend, fohr-*koh*-mernt, a. & adv., obliging
voorlaatst, fohr-*lahtst*, a., last but one
voorleggen, fohr-*leHG*-er, v., to lay (put) before
voorlezen, fohr-*lay*-zer, v., to read out; to read to
voorlicht, fohr-*liHGt*, n., head-light
voorlichten, fohr-*liHG*-ter, v., to instruct, to
voorliefde, fohr-*leef*-der, c., predilection [advise
voorlopen, fohr-*loh*-per, v., to be fast; to go in
   front   [for the present
voorlopig, fohr-*loh*-perHG, a., provisional. adv.,
voormalig, fohr-*mah*-lerHG, a., late, former
voormiddag, fohr-mid-*daHG*, c., forenoon
voornaam, fohr-*nahm*, c., Christian name
voornaam, fohr-*nahm*, a., distinguished
voornaamste, fohr-*nahm*-ster, a., principal, chief
voornamelijk, fohr-*nah*-mer-luck, adv., chiefly,
   mainly   [tion
voornemen, fohr-*nay*-mer, n., intention; resolu-
voornoemd, fohr-*noomt*, a., above-mentioned
vooroordeel, fohr-*ohr*-dayl, n., prejudice
vooroorlogs, fohr-*ohr*-loHGs, a., pre-war
voorop, foh-*rop*, adv., in front
vooropgaan, foh-*rop*-HGahn, v., to lead the way
voorouders, fohr-*ow*-ders, c. pl., ancestors
voorover, foh-*roh*-ver, adv., (bending) forward
vooroverbukken, foh-*roh*-ver-berk-ker, v., to
   stoop   [head first
voorovervallen, foh-*roh*-ver-fal-ler, v., to fall
voorpoot, fohr-*poht*, c., foreleg

voorpost, fohr-post, c., outpost
voorproefje, fohr-proof-yer, n., (fore)taste
voorraad, fohr-raht, c., supply, store. **in ——,**
in ——, in stock
voorradig, fohr-rah-derHG, a., in stock [way
voorrang, fohr-rang, c., precedence; right of
voorrangsweg, fohr-rangs-veHG, c., major road
voorrecht, fohr-reHGt, n., privilege
voorrede, fohr-ray-der, c., preface [(money)
voorschieten, fohr-sHGee-ter, v., to advance
voorschoot, fohr-sHGoht, c., apron
voorschot, fohr-sHGot, n., loan [tion
voorschrift, fohr-srift, n., prescription; regula-
voorschrijven, fohr-srey-ver, v., to prescribe
voorslaan, fohr-slahn, v., to suggest
voorspel, fohr-spel, n., prelude [cast
voorspellen, fohr-spel-ler, v., to predict, to fore-
voorspelling, fohr-spel-ling, c., prophesy, forecast
voorspiegeling, fohr-spee-HGer-ling, c., delusion
voorspoed, fohr-spoot, c., prosperity
voorspoedig, fohr-spoo-derHG, a. & adv., success-
voorspraak, fohr-sprahk, c., intercession [ful
voorsprong, fohr-sprong, c., lead, start
voorstad, fohr-stat, c., suburb
voorstander, fohr-stan-der, c., supporter
voorste, fohr-ster, a., foremost, front, first
voorstel, fohr-stel, n., proposal; bill. **een ——**
doen, ayn —— doon, to make a proposal
voorstellen, fohr-stel-ler, v., to propose; to
represent; to introduce
voorstelling, fohr-stel-ling, c., idea, notion;
performance; introduction
voorsteven, fohr-stay-ver, c., (naut.) stem
voort, fohrt, adv., forward, on(wards); away, gone
voortaan, fohr-tahn, adv., in future
voortbrengen, fohrt-breng-er, v., to bring forth
voortbrengsel, fohrt-breng-serl, n., product(ion)
voortdurend, fohrt-dEE-rernt, a. & adv., continual
voortduwen, fohrt-dEE-ver, v., to push on
voorteken, fohr-tay-ker, n., indication, sign
voortgaan, fohrt-HGahn, v., to continue

voortgang, fohrt-HGang, c., progress

voortplanten, fohrt-plan-ter, v., to propagate

voortreffelijk, fohr-tref-fer-luck, a. & adv., excellent

voortrekken, fohrt-treck-ker, v., to favour

voortrukken, fohrt-rerk-ker, v., to march (press) [on

voorts, fohrts, adv., further, moreover

voortslepen, fohrt-slay-per, v., to drag along

voortsukkelen, fohrt-serk-ker-ler, v., to plod on

voortuin, fohr-town, c., front garden

voortvarend, fohrt-fah-rent, a. & adv., energetic

voortvluchtig, fohrt-flerHG-terHG, a., fugitive

voortzetten, fohrt-set-ter, v., to continue

vooruit, foh-rowt, adv., before(hand); forward

vooruitbetalen, foh-rowt-ber-tah-ler, v., to pay in advance

vooruitgang, foh-rowt-HGang, c., progress

vooruitkomen, foh-rowt-koh-mer, v., to get on

vooruitsteken, foh-rowt-stay-ker, v., to hold out

vooruitzicht, foh-rowt-siHGt, n., outlook

vooruitzien, foh-rowt-seen, v., to foresee

voorval, fohr-val, n., event

voorwaarde, fohr-vahr-der, c., condition

voorwaardelijk, fohr-vahr-der-luck, a. & adv., conditional

voorwaarts, fohr-vahrts, a. & adv., forward

voorwenden, fohr-ven-der, v., to pretend

voorwendsel, fohr-vent-serl, n., pretence, pretext

voorwerp, fohr-vayrp, n., object, thing [text

voorwiel, fohr-veel, n., front wheel

voorzichtig, fohr-ziHG-terHG, a. & adv., careful

voorzichtigheid, fohr-ziHG-terHG-heyt, c., prudence

voorzien, fohr-zeen, v., to foresee. —— **van,** —— fan, to provide with

voorzijde, fohr-zey-der, c., front side, face

voorzitter, fohr-zit-ter, c., chairman

voorzorg, fohr-zorHG, c., care, provision

voorzorgsmaatregel, fohr-zorHGs-maht-ray-HGerl, c., precaution

voos, fohss, a., woolly, spongy; (fig.) unsound

vorderen, for-der-rer, v., to demand; to advance

vordering, for-der-ring, c., claim; progress

vorig, foh-rerHG, a., former, preceding

vork, fork, c., fork

vorm, form, c., shape; formality; mould

vormelijk, for-mer-luck, a. & adv., formal

vormen, for-mer, v., to form, to shape; to constitute

vorming, for-ming, c., formation; education

vorst, forst, c., monarch, prince; frost

vorstelijk, for-ster-luck, a. & adv., royal

vorstenhuis, for-ster-howss, n., dynasty

vorstin, for-stin, c., queen, sovereign

vos, foss, fox

vouw, fow, c., fold; pleat, crease

vraag, frahHG, c., question; demand, request.—— **en aanbod,** —— **en ahn**-bot, supply and demand

vraaggesprek, frahHG-er-spreck, n., interview

vraagstuk, frahHG-sterk, n., problem, question

vraatzuchtig, fraht-serHG-terHG, a., gluttonous, [greedy

vracht, fraHGt, c., load; cargo [greedy

vrachtauto, fraHGt-oh-toh, c., motor-lorry

vrachtprijs, fraHGt-preyss, c., fare; carriage; freight [gon, van

vrachtwagen, fraHGt-vah-HGer, c., truck, wag-

vragen, frah-HGer, v., to ask; to require

vrede, fray-der, c., peace

vredelievend, fray-der-lee-vernt, a., peace-loving

vreedzaam, frayt-sahm, a. & adv., peaceful

vreemd, fraymt, a. & adv., strange; foreign; queer

vreemdeling, fraym-der-ling, c., stranger; [foreigner

vrees, frayss, c., fear, apprehension [foreigner

vreesachtig, frayss-aHG-terHG, a., timorous, timid

vrek, freck, c., miser

vrekkig, freck-kerHG, a., stingy

vreselijk, fray-ser-luck, a. & adv., dreadful

vreten, fray-ter, v., to feed (on); to gorge; to cram

vreugde, frerHG-der, c., gladness

vreugdevol, frerHG-der-fol, a., joyous

vrezen, fray-zer, v., to fear

vriend, freent, c., (boy) friend

vriendelijk, freen-der-luck, a. & adv., friendly

vriendin, freen-din, c., (lady) friend
vriendschap, freent-sHGap, c., friendship
vriendschappelijk, freent-sHGap-per-luck, a. &
    adv., friendly
vriespunt, frees-pernt, n., freezing-point
vriezen, free-zer, v., to freeze
vrij, frey, a., free. adv., freely; pretty, rather
vrijbuiter, frey-bow-ter, c., freebooter, privateer
vrijdag, frey-daHG, c., Friday
vrijdenker, frey-den-ker, c., free-thinker
vrijen, frey-er, v., to court; to make love
vrijer, frey-er, c., sweetheart, lover
vrijgeleide, frey-HGer-ley-der, n., safe-conduct
vrijgevig, frey-HGay-verHG, a. & adv., generous
vrijgezel, frey-HGer-zel, c., bachelor
vrijheid, frey-heyt, c., freedom
vrijlaten, frey-lah-ter, v., to set at liberty
vrijmetselarij, frey-met-ser-lah-rey, c., free-
    masonry   [bold
vrijmoedig, frey-**moo**-derHG, a. & adv., frank,
vrijpostig, frey-**poss**-terHG, a. & adv., bold, pert
vrijspraak, frey-sprahk, c., acquittal
vrijstelling, frey-stel-ling, c., exemption
vrijuit, frey-owt, adv., frankly, freely
vrijwaren (voor), frey-vah-rer (fohr), v., to
vrijwel, frey-vel, adv., pretty well   [guard (from)
vrijwillig, frey-vil-lerHG, a. & adv., voluntary
vrijwilliger, frey-vil-ler-HGer, c., volunteer
vroedvrouw, froot-frow, c., midwife
vroeg, frooHG, a. & adv., early. —— **of laat**, ——
    of laht, sooner or later   [earlier
vroeger, frooHG-er, a., former, previous. adv.,
vroegtijdig, frooHG-tey-derHG, a. & adv., pre-
vrolijk, froh-luck, a. & adv., gay, merry   [mature
vroom, frohm, a. & adv., pious
vroomheid, frohm-heyt, c., piety
vrouw, frow, c., woman; wife; queen (at cards)
vrouwelijk, frow-er-luck, a., female; womanly
vrucht, frerHGt, c., fruit
vruchtbaar, frerHGt-bahr, a., fruitful; fertile
vruchtboom, frerHGt-bohm, c., fruit-tree
vruchteloos, frerHG-ter-lohss, a. & adv., futile

vuil, fowl, a. & adv., dirty; soiled. n., dirt
vuiligheid, fow-lerHG-heyt, c., filth
vuilnis, fowl-niss, c., (house) refuse; dust; dirt
vuilnisbak, fowl-niss-bak, c., dustbin
vuilnisbelt, fowl-niss-belt, c., refuse dump
vuist, fowst, c., fist. **voor de ——,** fohr der
vulkaan, ferl-kahn, c., volcano [off-hand
vullen, ferl-ler, v., to fill; to stuff
vulpen, ferl-pen, c., fountain-pen
vulpotlood, ferl-pot-loht, n., propelling pencil
vunzig, fern-zerHG, a., musty
vuren, fEE-rer, v., to fire, to shoot
vurig, fEE-rerHG, a. & adv., fiery; fervent
vuur, fEEr, n., fire; dry rot; (fig.) ardour
vuurpijl, fEEr-peyl, c., rocket
vuurproef, fEEr-proof, c., (fig.) crucial test, ordeal
vuurrood, fEEr-roht, a., as red as fire
vuursteen, fEEr-stayn, c., flint
vuurtoren, fEEr-toh-rer, c., lighthouse
vuurvast, fEEr-fast, a., fire-proof
vuurvreter, fEEr-fray-ter, c., fire-eater
vuurwapen, fEEr-vah-per, n., fire-arm
vuurwerk, fEEr-vayrk, c., fireworks

waadbaar, vaht-bahr, a., fordable
waag, vahHG, c., balance
waaghals, vahHG-halss, c., reckless fellow
waagstuk, vahHG-sterk, n., risky thing
waaien, vah-yer, v., to blow; to flutter
waaier, vah-yer, c., fan
waakhond, vahk-hont, c., watch-dog
waakzaam, vahk-sahm, a., vigilant
waan, vahn, c., delusion
waanzin, vahn-zin, c., madness; frenzy
waanzinnig, vahn-zin-nerHG, a., insane, mad,
crazy [ware(s)
waar, vahr, a., true. adv., where. c., goods, stuff,
waaraan, vah-rahn, adv., to (of) what, on whom
(which) [(which)
waarachter, vah-raHG-ter, adv., behind whom
waarachtig, vah-raHG-terHG, a. & adv., true, real
waarbij, vahr-bey, adv., by (near) which (whom)

waarborg, vahr-borHG, c., warrant, guarantee

waarborgen, vahr-borHG-er, v., to guarantee

waarboven, vahr-boh-ver, adv., over (above) which (whom)

waard, vahrt, c., host, innkeeper. a., worth

waarde, vahr-der, c., worth. **van geen ——,** fan HGayn ——, of no value

waardeloos, vahr-der-lohss, a., worthless

waarderen, vahr-day-rer, v., to appreciate

waardering, vahr-day-ring, c., appreciation

waardevol, vahr-der-fol, a., of great value

waardig, vahr-derHG, a., worthy

waardigheid, vahr-derHG-heyt, c., dignity

waardoor, vahr-dohr, adv., through (by) which

waarheen, vahr-hayn, adv., where (to), to what

waarheid, vahr-heyt, c., truth [place

waarin, vah-rin, adv., in what; in which

waarlangs, vahr-langs, adv., past (along) which

waarlijk, vahr-luck, adv., truly, indeed

waarmee, vahr-may, adv., with which (whom)

waarna, vahr-nah, adv., whereupon, after which

waarnaar, vahr-nahr, adv., to (at) which

waarnaast, vahr-nahst, adv., beside which

waarnemen, vahr-nay-mer, v., to perceive

waarnemer, vahr-nay-mer, c., observer; deputy

waarom, vah-rom, adv. & conj., why. n., why

waaronder, vah-ron-der, adv., under which

waarop, vah-rop, adv., on what; upon which

waarover, vah-roh-ver, adv., across which

waarschijnlijk, vahr-sHGeyn-luck, a. & adv., probable

waarschuwen, vahr-sHGee-ver, v., to caution

waarschuwing, vahr-sHGee-ving, c., warning

waartoe, vahr-too, adv., for which [(whom)

waartussen, vahr-ters-ser, adv., between which

waaruit, vahr-owt, adv., from which (what)

waarvan, vahr-van, adv., of which (what) [whom)

waarvoor, vahr-vohr, adv., for what (which,

waarzegger, vahr-zeHG-er, c., fortune-teller

waas, vahss, n., haze, mist

wacht, vaHGt, c., watchman; watch [to wait for

wachten, vaHG-ter, v., to wait. **—— op, —— op,**

wachtkamer, va*HG*t-kah-mer, c., waiting-room

wachtmeester, va*HG*t-mayss-ter, c., sergeant

wachtwoord, va*HG*t-vohrt, n., password

waden, vah-der, v., to wade, to ford

wafel, vah-ferl, c., wafer

wagen, vah-*HG*er, c., carriage; vehicle; waggon; cart; car. v., to venture, to risk

wagenmaker, vah-*HG*er-mah-ker, c., cartwright

wagenspoor, vah-*HG*er-spohr, n., (wheel-)rut

wagenwijd, vah-*HG*er-veyt, adv., wide

waggelen, va*HG*-er-ler, v., to totter, to stagger

waken, vah-ker, v., to watch   [smart

wakker, va*k*-ker, a. & adv., awake; alert; brisk;

wal, va*l*, c., rampart; bank, coast; quay

walgen (van), va*l*-*HG*er (fan), v., to loathe

walglijk, va*l*-*HG*er-luck, a., loathsome, disgusting

walmen, va*l*-mer, v., to smoke

wals, va*l*ss, v., waltz; (mech.) roller

walvis, va*l*-viss, c., whale   [notion

wanbegrip, van-ber-*HG*rip, n., fallacy, false

wand, va*nt*, c., wall

wandelen, van-der-ler, v., to take a walk

wandeling, van-der-ling, c., stroll, walk   [cane

wandelstok, van-der*l*-stock, c., walking-stick

wanen, vah-ner, v., to fancy, to imagine

wang, va*ng*, c., cheek

wangedrag, van-*HG*er-dra*HG*, n., bad conduct

wanhoop, van-hohp, c., despair   [despair (of)

wanhopen (aan), van-hoh-per (ahn), v., to

wanhopig, van-hoh-per*HG*, a. & adv., desperate

wankel, van-ker*l*, a., unsteady, shaky

wankelen, van-ker-ler, v., to stagger

wanneer, van-nayr, adv., when. conj., when; if

wanorde, van-or-der, c., disorder

wanordelijk, van-or-der-luck, a., disorderly

wansmaak, van-smahk, c., bad taste   [ging

want, va*nt*, conj., for. c., mitten. n., (naut.) rig-

wantrouwen, van-trow-er, n., distrust. v., to distrust   [ful

wantrouwig, van-trow-er*HG*, a. & adv., distrust-

wapen, vah-per, n., weapon; (coat of) arms

wapenen, vah-per-ner, v., to arm

wapenstilstand, vah-per-stil-stant, c., armistice

wapperen, vap-per-rer, v., to wave, to flutter, to float   [confusion

war, var, c., disorder. in de ——, in der ——, in

warboel, var-bool, c., muddle, confusion

warenhuis, vah-rer-howss, n., department [store(s)

warm, varm, a., warm, hot

warmte, varm-ter, c., warmth, heat

was, vass, n., c., wax. c., washing, laundry; rise (of

wasbak, vass-bak, c., wash-bowl [a river]

wasdoek, vass-dook, n., oil-cloth

wasem, vah-serm, c., steam, vapour

wasgoed, vass-HGoot, n., wash, washing

waskaars, vass-kahrss, c., wax-candle; taper

waskom, vass-kom, c., wash-hand basin

wassen, vas-ser, v., to wash; to grow; to rise. a.,

wasserij, vas-ser-rey, c., laundry [wax(en)

wastafel, vas-tah-ferl, c., wash-hand stand

wasvrouw, vas-frow, c., laundress

wat, vat, pron., what; something; which; that.
    interj., what! —— is er? —— is ayr, what
    is the matter?

water, vah-ter, n., water

waterdicht, vah-ter-diHGt, a., waterproof

waterig, vah-ter-rerHG, a., watery

waterjuffer, vah-ter-yerf-fer, c., dragon-fly

waterkan, vah-ter-kan, c., jug, ewer

waterleiding, vah-ter-ley-ding, c., waterworks

waterpas, vah-ter-pass, n., water-level. a., level

waterplaats, vah-ter-plahtss, c., urinal [pox

waterpokken, vah-ter-pock-ker, c. pl., chicken-

watersnood, vah-ters-noht, c., inundation

waterspiegel, vah-ter-spee-HGerl, c., surface of
    the water

waterstof, vah-ter-stof, c., hydrogen

waterval, vah-ter-fal, c., waterfall

waterverf, vah-ter-fayrf, c., water-colour(s)

watervliegtuig, vah-ter-fleeHG-towHG, n., sea-
    plane   [water-supply

watervoorziening, vah-ter-fohr-zee-ning, c.,

watervrees, vah-ter-frayss, c., hydrophobia

wauwelen, vow-er-ler, v., to twaddle, to drivel

wazig, vah-zerHG, a., hazy, foggy

we, ver, pron., we

wecken, veck-er, v., to preserve

wedden, ved-der, v., to bet

weddenschap, ved-der-sHGap, c., bet [return

wederdienst, vay-der-deenst, c., service in

wederhelft, vay-der-helft, c., better half

wederkerig, vay-der-kay-rerHG, a. & adv., mutual

wederliefde, vay-der-leev-der, c., love in return

wederopbouw, vay-der-op-bow, c., rebuilding

wedervergelding, vay-der-fer-HGel-ding, c., retaliation

wederzijds, vay-der-zeytss, a. & adv., mutual

wedijver, vet-ey-ver, c., competition

wedijveren, vet-ey-ver-rer, v., to compete

wedstrijd, vet-streyt, c., contest, competition

weduwe, vay-dEE-er, c., widow

weduwnaar, vay-dEE-nahr, c., widower

wee, vay, n. & interj., woe. a., sickly

weefgetouw, vayf-HGer-tow, n., weaving-loom

weefsel, vayf-serl, n., tissue, fabric

weegschaal, vayHG-sHGahl, c., balance, scales

week, vayk, c., week. a., tender, soft

weekblad, vayk-blat, n., weekly paper

weekdier, vayk-deer, n., mollusc

weekhartig, vayk-har-terHG, a., soft-hearted

weeklagen, vay-klah-HGer, v., to wail

weekloon, vayk-lohn, n., weekly wages

weelde, vayl-der, c., luxury; profusion [tuous

weelderig, vayl-der-rerHG, a., luxurious, sump-

weemoedig, vay-moo-derHG, a. & adv., sad

weer, vayr, n., weather. c., defence. adv., again.

    in de ―― zijn, in der ―― zeyn, to be busy

weerbaar, vayr-bahr, a., able-bodied; defensible

weerbarstig, vayr-bars-terHG, a., unruly

weerbericht, vayr-ber-riHGt, n., weather-report

weergalmen, vayr-HGal-mer, v., to resound

weergaloos, vayr-HGah-lohss, a., matchless

weerhouden, vayr-how-der, v., to restrain

weerkaatsen, vayr-kaht-ser, v., to reflect

weerleggen, vayr-leHG-er, v., to refute

weerlichten, vayr-liHG-ter, v., to lighten

weerloos, vayr-lohss, a., defenceless

weerschijn, vayr-sнGeyn, c., reflection; lustre

weersgesteldheid, vayr-sнGer-stelt-heyt, c., weather conditions

weerspannig, vayr-span-nerнG, a., refractory

weerstand, vayr-stant, c., resistance

weervoorspelling, vayr-fohr-spel-ling, c., weather-forecast

weerzien, vayr-zeen, v., to see again. **tot weer-ziens,** tot vayr-zeens, till we meet again

weerzin, vayr-zin, c., repugnance [nant

weerzinwekkend, vayr-zin-veck-kernt, a., repug-

wees, vayss, c., orphan

weeshuis, vayss-howss, n., orphanage

weetgierig, vayt-нGee-rerнG, a., eager to learn

weg, veнG, c., road, way; path. adv., away; lost, gone [to see off

wegbrengen, veнG-breng-er, v., to take away;

wegduwen, veнG-dEE-er, v., to push aside

wegen, vay-нGer, v., to weigh

wegens, vay-нGernss, prep., on account of

weggaan, veнG-нGahn, v., to go away

wegkwijnen, veнG-k'vey-ner, v., to languish

weglaten, veнG-lah-ter, v., to omit

wegnemen, veнG-nay-mer, v., to take away; to

wegraken, veнG-rah-ker, v., to get lost [pilfer

wegruimen, veнG-row-mer, v., to clear away

wegstoppen, veнG-stop-per, v., to hide

wegwijzer, veнG-vey-zer, c., guide; signpost

wegzakken, veнG-sak-ker, v., to sink; to fade

wei, vey, c., meadow [(of wireless)

weide, vey-der, c., meadow, pasture

weiden, vey-der, v., to graze, to feed

weifelen, vey-fer-ler, v., to hesitate

weigeren, vey-нGer-rer, v., to refuse

weigering, vey-нGer-ring, c., refusal

weiland, vey-lant, n., pasture

weinig, vey-nerнG, a., little; few. adv., little

wekelijks, vay-ker-lucks, a. & adv., weekly

weken, vay-ker, v., to soften; to soak

wekken, veck-ker, v., to awake; to cause

wekker, veck-ker, c., alarm-clock; caller

wel, vel, c., spring, fountain. a., well. adv., well; very; indeed

welbehagen, **vel-ber-hah-**HGer, n., pleasure

welbespraakt, **vel-ber-sprahkt**, a., fluent

weldaad, **vel-**daht, c., benefit   [lence

weldadigheid, **vel-dah-**derHG-heyt, c., benevo-

weldoener, **vel-doo-**ner, c., benefactor

weldra, **vel-**drah, adv., shortly, before long

weleer, **vel-**ayr, adv., formerly

weleerwaarde, **vel-ayr-vahr-**der, a., reverend

welgedaan, **vel-**HGer-dahn, a., well-fed, plump

welgesteld, **vel-**HGer-stelt, a., well off

welgevallen, **vel-**HGer-val-ler, n., pleasure

welig, **vay-**lerHG, a., luxuriant

weliswaar, **vel-iss-vahr**, adv., indeed, it is true

welk, velk, a. & pron., what; which; who, that, [which

welkom, **vel-**kom, n. & a., welcome

wellevend, **vel-lay-**vernt, a., courteous, well-bred

wellicht, **vel-**liHGt, adv., perhaps

welluidend, **vel-low-**dernt, a., harmonious

wellustig, **vel-lerss-**terHG, a. & adv., sensual

welnu, **vel-nEE**, interj., well then, well

welp, velp, n., cub   [quence

welsprekendheid, **vel-spray-**kernt-heyt, c., elo-

welstand, **vel-**stant, c., welfare. in —— **leven**, in —— **lay**-ver, to be well off

welvaart, **vel-**fahrt, c., prosperity

welvarend, **vel-fah-**rernt, a., prosperous; healthy

welving, **vel-**ving, c., vault

welvoeglijk, **vel-foo-**HGer-luck, a., becoming

welwillend, **vel-vil-**lernt, a. & adv., kind

welzijn, **vel-**zeyn, n., welfare   [(with)

wemelen (van), **vay-mer-**ler (fan), v., to swarm

wenden, **ven-**der, v., to turn

wending, **ven-**ding, c., turn, swing

wenen, **vay-**ner, v., to weep

wenk, venk, c., hint, nod, tip

wenkbrauw, **venk-**brow, c., eyebrow

wenken, **ven-**ker, v., to beckon

wennen, **ven-**ner, v., to accustom

wens, venss, c., desire

wenselijk, **ven-ser-**luck, a., desirable

wensen, ven-ser, v., to wish, to desire

wentelen, ven-ter-ler, v., to roll; to revolve

wenteltrap, ven-terl-tra*p*, c., winding staircase

wereld, vay-rerlt, c., universe

werelddeel, vay-rerlt-dayl, n., continent

wereldlijk, vay-rerlt-luck, a., worldly

werelds, vay-rerlts, a., worldly; secular

wereldstad, vay-rerlt-sta*t*, c., metropolis

weren, vay-rer, v., to avert; to keep out

werf, vayrf, c., shipyard; dockyard; quay

werk, vayrk, n., work, labour; job

werkdadig, vayrk-dah-derHG, a., effective

werkdag, vayrk-da*HG*, c., working-day, week-day [day]

werkelijk, vayr-ker-luck, a. & adv., real

werkelijkheid, vayr-ker-luck-heyt, c., reality

werkeloos, vayr-ker-lohss, a., inactive; out of work [work]

werken, vayr-ker, v., to work; to act

werkgever, vayrk-HGay-ver, c., employer

werking, vayr-king, c., action; effect [study]

werkkamer, vayrk-kah-mer, c., working-room,

werkkracht, vayrk-kra*HG*t, c., energy; workman

werklieden, vayrk-lee-der, c. pl., workmen,

werkloon, vayrk-lohn, n., wage(s) [labourers]

werkloos, vayr-ker-lohss, a., unemployed

werklust, vayrk-lerst, c., zest for work

werkman, vayrk-ma*n*, c., workman; artisan

werknemer, vayrk-nay-mer, c., employee

werkplaats, vayrk-plahtss, c., workshop

werkster, vayrk-ster, c., charwoman; (girl) worker

werktuig, vayrk-towHG, n., tool, instrument

werktuigkunde, vayrk-towHG-kern-der, c., mechanics [mechanical]

werktuiglijk, vayrk-towHG-er-luck, a. & adv.,

werkzaam, vayrk-sahm, a. & adv., industrious

werkzaamheden, vayrk-sahm-hay-der, c. pl., activities

werpen, vayr-per, v., to throw, to cast

wervelwind, vayr-verl-vint, c., whirlwind

werven, vayr-ver, v., to recruit; to canvass for

wesp, vesp, c., wasp

wespennest, vess-per-nest, c., (fig.) hornet's nest

westelijk, vess-ter-luck, a., westerly

westen, vess-ter, n., west

westers, vess-terss, a., western

wet, vet, c., law; act

wetboek, vet-book, n., code (of law)

weten, vay-ter, v., to be acquainted with, to know

wetenschap, vay-ter-SHGap, c., science; knowledge [adv., scientific

wetenschappelijk, vay-ter-SHGap-per-luck, a. &

wetenswaardig, vay-terns-vahr-derHG, a., worth

wetgever, vet-HGay-ver, c., legislator [knowing

wetgeving, vet-HGay-ving, c., legislation

wethouder, vet-how-der, c., alderman

wetsvoorstel, vets-fohr-stel, n., bill

wettelijk, vet-ter-luck, a. & adv., legal

wetteloos, vet-ter-lohss, a., lawless

wetten, vet-ter, v., to sharpen

wettig, vet-terHG, a. & adv., lawful

wettigen, vet-ter-HGer, v., to legitimate; to justify

weven, vay-ver, v., to weave

weverij, vay-ver-rey, c., weaving; weaving-mill

wezel, vay-zerl, c., weasel

wezen, vay-zer, v., to be. n., being; nature

wezenlijk, vay-zer-luck, a. & adv., real; essential

wezenloos, vay-zer-lohss, a., blank

wicht, viHGt, n., baby, child

wie, vee, pron., who

wieden, vee-der, v., to weed

wieg, veeHG, c., cradle

wiegelied, veeHG-er-leet, n., lullaby

wiek, veek, c., wing; sail (of a mill)

wiel, veel, n., wheel; pool

wielrenner, veel-ren-ner, c., racing cyclist

wielrijder, veel-rey-der, c., cyclist

wier, veer, n., sea-weed. pron., whose

wierook, vee-rohk, c., incense

wig, viHG, c., wedge; (mech.) key

wij, vey, pron., we

wijd, veyt, a. & adv., wide, spacious, large. —— **en zijd** —— en zeyt, far and wide

wijden, vey-der, v., to consecrate; to ordain

wijdlopig, veyt-loh-perHG, a., prolix

wijdte, veyt-ter, c., width; gauge (of a railway)

wijf, veyf, n., woman, vixen, shrew

wijfje, veyf-yer, n., (female (of animals)

wijk, veyk, c., district; quarter; round; beat

wijken, veyk-er, v., to yield, to give way

wijkverpleegster, veyk-fer-playHG-ster, c., district nurse

wijl, veyl, c., (short) time, while. conj., as, since

wijn, veyn, c., wine

wijngaard, veyn-HGahrt, c., vineyard   [shop

wijnhandel, veyn-han-derl, c., wine-trade; wine-

wijnoogst, veyn-ohHGst, c., vintage

wijnstok, veyn-stock, c., vine   [tune

wijs, veyss, a. & adv., wise. c., manner; melody;

wijsbegeerte, veyss-ber-HGayr-ter, c., philosophy

wijsgeer, veyss-HGayr, c., philosopher

wijsheid, veyss-heyt, c., wisdom

wijsvinger, veyss-fing-er, c., forefinger

wijwater, vey-vah-ter, n., holy water

wijze, vey-zer, c., wise man

wijzen, vey-zer, v., to point out

wijzer, vey-zer, c., hand (of a clock); pointer

wijzerplaat, vey-zer-plaht, c., dial, face (of a

wijzigen, vey-zer-HGer, v., to change   [clock)

wijziging, vey-zer-HGing, c., change, alteration

wikkelen, vick-ker-ler, v., to wrap (up)

wil, vil, c., will, wish. **ter wille van,** tayr **vil**-ler

fan, for the sake of   [fierce

wild, vilt, n., game. a. & adv., wild; savage; unruly;

wildernis, vil-der-niss, c., wilderness

wilgeboom, vil-HGer-bohm, c., willow-tree

willekeurig, vil-ler-ker-rerHG, a. & adv., arbitrary

willen, vil-ler, v., to wish, to want; to choose; to

intend

wilsbeschikking, vils-ber-sHGick-king, c., last

wilskracht, vils-kraHGt, c., will-power   [will

wimpel, vim-perl, c., pennant, pennon, streamer

wimper, vim-per, c., eyelash

windbuks, vint-berks, c., air-gun

winden, vin-der, v., to wind (up), to twist

winderig, vin-der-rerHG, a., windy, blowy

windhond, vint-hont, c., greyhound

windhoos, vint-hohss, c., whirlwind
windkussen, vint-kers-ser, n., air-cushion
windmolen, vint-moh-ler, c., windmill
windsel, vint-serl, n., bandage
windstilte, vint-stil-ter, c., calm
windstreek, vint-strayk, c., point of the compass
windvlaag, vint-flahHG, c., gust of wind
windwijzer, vint-vey-zer, c., weathercock
winkel, vin-kerl, c., shop; workshop [assistant
winkelbediende, vin-kerl-ber-deen-der, c., shop-
winkelier, vin-ker-leer, c., shopkeeper
winkeljuffrouw, vin-kerl-yerf-frow, c., shop-girl
winkelprijs, vin-kerl-preyss, c., retail price
winkelsluiting, vin-kerl-slow-ting, c., closing of
winkelwaar, vin-kerl-vahr, c., shop-wares [shops
winnaar, vin-nahr, c., winner, victor
winnen, vin-ner, v., to win, to gain; to harvest, to
winst, vinst, c., gain, benefit, profit [gather
winstgevend, vinst-HGay-vernt, a., lucrative
winter, vin-ter, c., winter; chilblain
wintergoed, vin-ter-HGoot, n., winter-clothes
winterkoninkje, vin-ter-koh-nink-yer, n., wren
wip, vip, c., see-saw; skip
wipneus, vip-nerss, c., turned-up nose
wippen, vip-per, v., to see-saw; to whip, to skip
wirwar, vir-var, c., tangle, muddle; maze
wiskunde, viss-kern-der, c., mathematics
wispelturig, viss-perl-tEE-rerHG, a. & adv.,
wissel, viss-serl, c., bill of exchange [inconstant
wisselbeker, viss-serl-bay-ker, c., challenge cup
wisselen, viss-ser-ler, v., to change (money)
wisselkantoor, viss-serl-kan-tohr, n., exchange-
office
wisselkoers, viss-serl-koorss, c., rate of exchange
wisselvallig, viss-serl-val-lerHG, a., uncertain
wisselwachter, viss-serl-vaHG-ter, c., pointsman,
switchman
wit, vit, a., white. **Witte Donderdag, vit-ter
don-der-daHG,** Maundy Thursday
witkalk, vit-kalk, c., whitewash
witkiel, vit-keel, c., railway-porter
wittebrood, vit-ter-broht, n., white bread

wittebroodsweken, vit-ter-brohts-vay-ker, c. pl.,
witten, vit-ter, v., to whitewash   [honeymoon
woede, voo-der, c., fury, rage
woedend, voo-dernt, a. & adv., furious. **zich ——**
   maken, ziHG —— mah-ker, to get into a rage
woeker, voo-ker, c., usury
woekeraar, voo-ker-rahr, c., usurer
woekeren, voo-ker-rer, v., to practise usury
woelen, voo-ler, v., to toss about; to grub, to root
woelig, voo-lerHG, a., turbulent, restless
woensdag, voons-daHG, c., Wednesday
woerd, voort, c., drake
woest, voost, a. & adv., waste; desert; wild; reck-
woesteling, vooss-ter-ling, c., brute   [less
woestenij, vooss-ter-ney, c., wilderness
woestijn, vooss-teyn, c., desert
wol, vol, c., wool
wolf, volf, c., wolf; weevil
wolk, volk, c., cloud
wolkbreuk, volk-brerk, c., cloud-burst
wolkenkrabber, vol-ker-krab-ber, c., sky-scraper
wolkenloos, vol-ker-lohss, a., cloudless
wollen, vol-ler, a., woollen
wollig, vol-lerHG, a., woolly, downy
wond, wonde, vont, von-der, c., wound, injury
wonder, von-der, n., wonder, marvel
wonderbaar, von-der-bahr, a., wonderful
wonderdadig, von-der-dah-derHG, a., miraculous
wonderlijk, von-der-luck, a. & adv., strange
wonderolie, von-der-oh-lee, c., castor-oil
wonen, voh-ner, v., to reside, to live
woning, voh-ning, c., house, dwelling
woonachtig, vohn-aHG-terHG, a., living
woonkamer, vohn-kah-mer, c., sitting-room
woonplaats, vohn-plahts, c., residence, home
woonwagen, vohn-vah-HGer, c., caravan
woord, vohrt, n., word, term
woordbreuk, vohrt-brerk, c., breach of faith
woordelijk, vohr-der-luck, a. & adv., verbal
woordenboek, vohr-der-book, n., dictionary
woordenlijst, vohr-der-leyst, c., vocabulary
woordenrijk, vohr-der-reyk, a., rich in words

woordentwist, vohr-der-tvist, c., dispute

woordenwisseling, vohr-der-vis-ser-ling, c., altercation

woordspeling, vohrt-spay-ling, c., pun

woordvoerder, vohrt-foor-der, c., spokesman

worden, vor-der, v., to become, to grow, to get

wording, vor-ding, c., birth, origin

worgen, vor-HGer, v., to strangle

worm, vorm, c., worm; maggot, grub

wormstekig, vorm-stay-kerHG, a., worm-eaten

worst, vorst, c., sausage

worstelaar, vor-ster-lahr, c., wrestler [struggle

worstelen, vor-ster-ler, v., to wrestle; (fig.) to

worsteling, vor-ster-ling, c., wrestling, struggle

wortel, vor-terl, c., root; carrot

woud, vowt, n., forest, wood

wouw, vow, c., kite (bird)

wraak, vrahk, c., revenge

wraakzucht, vrahk-serHGt, c., thirst for revenge

wrak, vrak, n., wreck. a., rickety, shaky

wrakhout, vrak-howt, n., wreckage

wrang, vrang, a., acid, sour, tart

wrat, vrat, c., wart

wreed, vrayt, a. & adv., cruel

wreedaard, vray-dahrt, c., brute, cruel man

wreedheid, vrayt-heyt, c., cruelty

wreef, vrayf, c., instep

wreken, vray-ker, v., to avenge; to revenge

wrevelig, vray-ver-lerHG, a. & adv., peevish

wrijven, vrey-ver, v., to rub

wrijving, vrey-ving, c., friction; rubbing

wringen, vring-er, v., to wring (out)

wroeging, vrooHG-ing, c., remorse

wroeten, vroo-ter, v., to root, to grub

wrok, vrock, c., grudge, resentment. **geen ——
koesteren**, HGayn —— koo-ster-rer, to bear
no malice

wrong, vrong, c., roll; wreath; turban

wuft, verft, a. & adv., frivolous

wuiven, vow-fer, v., to wave

wulps, verlps, a. & adv., lascivious, lewd

wurgen, verHG-er, v., to strangle

x-benen, icks-bay-ner, n. pl., turned-in legs
x-stralen, icks-strah-ler, c. pl., X-rays

yack, yak, c., yak
yen, yen, c., yen
yoghurt, yoHG-ert, c., yoghourt

zaad, zaht, n., seed
zaag, zahHG, c., saw; (fig.) bore
zaagmeel, zahHG-mayl, n., sawdust
zaaien, zah-yer, v., to sow
zaak, zahk, c., affair; case; thing; business
zaakgelastigde, zahk-HGer-las-terHG-der, c., proxy
zaakwaarnemer, zahk-vahr-nay-mer, c., solicitor
zaal, zahl, c., hall; ward (in a hospital)
zacht, zaHGt, a. & adv., soft; mild; gentle; smooth
zachtheid, zaHGt-heyt, c., softness, mildness
zachtjes, zaHGt-yess, adv., softly
zachtmoedig, zaHGt-moo-derHG, a. & adv., [gentle
zadel, zah-derl, c., saddle
zadelmaker, zah-derl-mah-ker, c., saddler
zagen, zah-HGer, v., to saw
zak, zak, c., bag; pocket; pouch
zakboekje, zak-book-yer, n., note-book
zakdoek, zak-dook, c., handkerchief
zakelijk, zah-ker-luck, a., real, essential
zakenman, zah-ker-man, c., business-man
zakformaat, zak-for-maht, n., pocket-size
zakgeld, zak-HGelt, n., pocket-money
zakken, zak-ker, v., to sink; to fall; to fail
zakkenroller, zak-ker-rol-ler, c., pickpocket
zaklantaarn, zak-lan-tah-rer, c., pocket-torch
zakmes, zak-mess, n., pocket-knife
zakwoordenboek, zak-vohr-der-book, n., pocket-
zalf, zalf, c., ointment [dictionary
zalig, zah-lerHG, a., blessed; heavenly, glorious
zaligheid, zah-lerHG-heyt, c., bliss
zalm, zalm, c., salmon
zalvend, zal-vernt, a. & adv., unctuous
zand, zant, n., sand
zandgrond, zant-HGront, c., sandy soil

zandloper, zant-loh-per, c., sand-glass

zang, zang, c., singing; song

zanger, zang-er, c., singer; poet

zangkoor, zang-kohr, n., choir   [concert

zanguitvoering, zang-owt-foo-ring, c., vocal

zangvereniging, zang-fer-ay-ner-HGing, c., choral society

zangvogel, zang-foh-HGerl, c., singing-bird

zaniken, zah-ner-ker, v., to bother

zat, zat, a., satiated; drunk

zaterdag, zah-ter-daHG, c., Saturday

ze, zer, pron., she, her; they, them

zedelijk, zay-der-luck, a. & adv., moral

zedeloos, zay-der-lohss, a. & adv., immoral

zeden, zay-der, c. pl., morals

zedenleer, zay-der-layr, c., morality

zedenwet, zay-der-vet, c., moral law

zedig, zay-derHG, a. & adv., modest, coy, demure

zee, zay, c., sea, ocean

zeeëngte, zay-eng-ter, c., strait(s)

zeef, zayf, c., sieve, strainer

zeehond, zay-hont, c., seal

zeekreeft, zay-krayft, c., lobster

zeelieden, zay-lee-der, c. pl., seamen

zeemacht, zay-maHGt, c., naval forces

zeeman, zay-man, c., seaman

zeemanshuis, zay-mans-howss, n., sailors' home

zeemeeuw, zay-may'oo, c., (sea-)gull

zeemleer, zaym-layr, n., shammy   [power

zeemogendheid, zay-moh-HGent-heyt, c., naval

zeep, zayp, c., soap. **groene ——,** HGroo-ner ——, soft soap

zeepbakje, zayp-bak-yer, n., soap-dish

zeer, zayr, adv., very, much, greatly. n. & a., sore

zeereis, zay-reyss, c., sea-voyage

zeerover, zay-roh-ver, c., pirate

zeespiegel, zay-spee-HGerl, c., surface of the sea

zeestraat, zay-straht, c., strait(s)

zeevaart, zay-fahrt, c., navigation

zeewier, zay-veer, n., seaweed

zeeziek, zay-zeek, a., seasick

zegel, zay-HGerl, c., seal; stamp

zegellak, zay-HGerl-lak, c., sealing-wax
zegelrecht, zay-HGerl-reHGt, n., stamp-duty
zegen, zay-HGer, c., blessing
zegenen, zay-HGer-ner, v., to bless
zegepraal, zay-HGer-prahl, c., triumph
zegevieren, zay-HGer-fee-rer, v., to triumph
zeggen, zeHG-er, v., to say, to tell
zegsman, zeHGs-man, c., informant
zeil, zeyl, n., sail; floor-cloth; tarpaulin
zeilboot, zeyl-boht, c., sailing-boat
zeildoek, zeyl-dook, n., oilcloth; canvas
zeilen, zey-ler, v., to sail
zeilschip, zeyl-sHGip, n., sailing-vessel
zeis, zeyss, c., scythe
zeker, zay-ker, a. & adv., certain. —— weten,
     —— vay-ter, to know for sure
zekerheid, zay-ker-heyt, c., certainty
zekering, zay-ker-ring, c., fuse
zelden, zel-der, adv., seldom
zeldzaam, zelt-sahm, a. & adv., rare, scarce
zelf, zelf, pron., self. **hij** ——, hey ——, he himself
zelfbeheersing, zelf-ber-hayr-sing, c., self-control
zelfbehoud, zelf-ber-howt, n., self-preservation
zelfbewust, zelf-ber-verst, a., self-confident
zelfde, zelf-der, a., same, similar
zelfmoord, zelf-mohrt, c., suicide
zelfs, zelfs, adv., even   [pendent
zelfstandig, zelf-stan-derHG, a. & adv., inde-
zelfverdediging, zelf-fer-day-derHG-ing, c., self-
     defence   [self-denial
zelfverloochening, zelf-fer-loh-HGer-ning, c.,
zelfvertrouwen, zelf-fer-trow-er, n., self-con-
zelfzucht, zelf-serHGt, c., selfishness   [fidence
zemelen, zay-mer-ler, c. pl., bran
zendeling, zen-der-ling, c., missionary
zenden, zen-der, v., to send; to dispatch
zender, zen-der, c., sender; (radio-)transmitter
zending, zen-ding, c., sending; consignment
zenuw, zay-nEE, c., nerve   [nervous
zenuwachtig, zay-nEE-aHG-terHG, a. & adv.,
zenuwlijder, zay-nEE-ley-der, c., nerve-sufferer

zenuwslopend, zay-NEE-sloh-pernt, a., nerve-racking [ease

zenuwziekte, zay-NEE-zeek-ter, c., nervous disease

zerk, zayrk, c., slab (of stone); tombstone

zes, zess, a., six

zesde, zess-der, a., sixth

zestien, zess-teen, a., sixteen

zestiende, zess-teen-der, a., sixteenth

zestig, zess-terHG, a., sixty

zestigste, zess-terHG-ster, a., sixtieth

zet, zet, c., leap; shove; move

zetel, zay-terl, c., seat, chair

zetfout, zet-fowt, c., misprint, (printer's) error

zetmeel, zet-mayl, n., starch

zetten, zet-ter, v., to place, to set, to put; to make

zeug, zerHG, c., sow [(tea)

zeuren, zer-rer, v., to worry; to tease

zeurkous, zerr-kowss, c., bore

zeven, zay-ver, v., to sift, a., seven

zevende, zay-ven-der, a., seventh

zeventien, zay-ven-teen, a., seventeen

zeventiende, zay-ven-teen-der, a., seventeenth

zeventig, zay-ven-terHG, a., seventy

zeventigste, zay-ven-terHG-ster, a., seventieth

zever, zay-ver, c., slaver

zich, ziHG, pron., one (him, her, it)self, themselves

zicht, ziHGt, c., sickle. n., sight; visibility

zichtbaar, ziHGt-bahr, a. & adv., visible

zichzelf, ziHG-self, pron., one (him, her, it)self,

zieden, zee-der, v., to seethe [themselves

ziek, zeek, a., ill, diseased

ziekelijk, zee-ker-luck, a., ailing; morbid

ziekenhuis, zee-ker-howss, n., hospital

ziekenoppasser, zee-ker-op-pas-ser, c., hospital attendant

ziekenwagen, zee-ker-vah-HGer, c., ambulance

ziekenzaal, zee-ker-zahl, c., hospital ward

ziekte, zeek-ter, c., illness; complaint

ziel, zeel, c., soul; mind, spirit

zielig, zee-lerHG, a., pitiful

zielkunde, zeel-kern-der, c., psychology

zielloos, zeel-lohss, a., soulless; inanimate

zielsbedroefd, zeels-ber-drooft, a., broken-
zielsblij, zeels-bley, a., overjoyed   [hearted
zielzieke, zeels-see-ker, c., mental patient
zieltogen, zeel-toh-HGer, v., to be dying
zien, zeen, v., to see, to notice. **tot ziens!** tot
   zeens, so long!
zienderogen, zeen-der-roh-HGer, adv., visibly
zienswijze, zeens-vey-zer, c., view, opinion
ziften, zif-ter, v., to sift
zigeuner, zee-HGer-ner, c., gipsy
zij, zey, pron., she; they. c., side; silk
zijde, zey-der, c., side; silk
zijdelings, zey-der-lings, a. & adv., sidelong
zijden, zey-der, a., silk; silken
zijdeur, zey-derr, c., side-door
zijn, zeyn, v., to be. pron., his, its, one's
zijrivier, zey-ree-veer, c., tributary
zijspan, zey-span, n., side-car
zijwaarts, zey-vahrts, a., lateral. adv., sideways
zilt, zilt, a., salty, briny
zilver, zil-ver, n., silver; (silver) plate
zilverwerk, zil-ver-vayrk, n., silverware
zin, zin, c., meaning; mind, desire; sentence
zindelijk, zin-der-luck, a., tidy, neat
zingen, zing-er, v., to sing; to warble
zink, zink, n., zinc
zinken, zin-ker, v., to sink. a., zinc
zinkzalf, zink-salf, c., zinc-ointment
zinnebeeld, zin-ner-baylt, n., symbol
zinnelijk, zin-ner-luck, a., sensual
zinnen, zin-ner, v., to ponder   [delusion
zinsbegoocheling, zins-ber-HGoh-HGer-ling, c.,
zinspelen (op), zin-spay-ler (op), v., to hint (at)
zinspeling, zin-spay-ling, c., hint
zinspreuk, zin-sprerk, c., motto
zinsverband, zins-fer-bant, n., context
zitplaats, zit-plahtss, c., seat
zitten, zit-ter, v., to sit; to fit (of clothes)
zittend, zit-ternt, a., sitting, seated; sedentary
zitting, zit-ting, c., seat; session
zo, zoh, adv., thus; presently. conj., as; if
zoals, zoh-alss, conj., as, such as, like

zodanig, zoh-*dah*-nerHG, a., such. adv., so, in
zodat, zoh-*dat*, conj., so that   [such a manner
zode, zoh-der, c., turf, sod
zodra, zoh-*drah*, conj., as soon as
zoeken, zoo-ker, v., to look for
zoeklicht, zook-lihGt, n., searchlight
zoel, zool, a., mild, balmy
zoemen, zoo-mer, v., to drone, to buzz
zoen, zoon, c., kiss; atonement
zoenen, zoo-ner, v., to kiss
zoet, zoot, a., sweet; good (child)
zoetigheid, zoo-terHG-heyt, c., sweetness; sweets
zoetjesaan, zoot-yer-sahn, adv., gently; gradu-
    ally
zoëven, zoh-ay-ver, adv., a moment ago, just now
zog, zoHG, n., wake (of a ship)
zogen, zoh-HGer, v., to suckle, to nurse
zogenaamd, zoh-HGer-nahmt, a., so-called.
    adv., on the pretext
zolang, zoh-*lang*, conj., so long as. adv., mean-
zolder, zol-der, c., loft; ceiling   [while
zolderkamertje, zol-der-kah-mert-yer, n., attic
zomen, zoh-mer, v., to hem (a dress)
zomer, zoh-mer, c., summer
zomerkleren, zoh-mer-klay-rer, c. pl., summer-
    clothes   [freckles
zomersproeten, zoh-mer-sproo-ter, c. pl.,
zo'n, zohn, a., such, such a
zon, zon, c., sun
zondaar, zon-dahr, c., sinner
zondag, zon-daHG, c., Sunday   [it's a pity
zonde, zon-der, c., sin. het is ——, het is ——,
zondenbok, zon-der-bock, c., scapegoat
zonder, zon-der, prep., without; but for
zonderling, zon-der-ling, a. & adv., queer. c.,
    original, freak
zondig, zon-derHG, a. & adv., sinful
zondigen, zon-der-HGer, v., to sin
zondvloed, zont-floot, c., deluge, flood
zonnebad, zon-ner-bat, n., sun-bath
zonnebril, zon-ner-bril, c., sun-spectacles
zonneklaar, zon-ner-klahr, a., as clear as daylight

zonnescherm, zon-ner-sHGayrm, n., sunshade; sunblind

zonneschijn, zon-ner-sHGeyn, c., sunshine

zonnesteek, zon-ner-stayk, c., sunstroke

zonnewijzer, zon-ner-vey-zer, c., sundial

zonnig, zon-nerHG, a., sunny

zonsondergang, zons-on-der-HGang, c., sunset

zonsopgang, zons-op-HGang, c., sunrise

zonsverduistering, zons-fer-dows-ter-ring, c., [solar eclipse

zoogdier, zohHG-deer, n., mammal

zool, zohl, c., sole (of a shoe)

zoom, zohm, c., hem; edge; fringe; bank

zoon, zohn, c., son

zorg, zorHG, c., care; anxiety; trouble; easy chair

zorgeloos, zor-HGer-lohss, a., careless; care-free

zorgen (voor), zor-HGer (fohr), v., to take care (of)

zorgvuldig, zorHG-ferl-derHG, a. & adv., careful

zorgwekkend, zorHG-veck-kernt, a., alarming

zot, zot, a. & adv., foolish. c., fool

zout, zowt, n., salt. a., salt, briny

zouteloos, zow-ter-lohss, a., saltless; insipid

zoutmijn, zowt-meyn, c., salt-mine

zoutvaatje, zowt-faht-yer, n., salt-cellar

zoveel, zoh-fayl, a., so much, so many

zover, zoh-fayr, adv., so far

zowat, zoh-vat, adv., about

zucht, zerHGt, c., sigh; desire; craving

zuchten, zerHG-ter, v., to sigh

zuidelijk, zow-der-luck, a., southern

zuiden, zow-der, n., south

zuidpool, zowt-pohl, c., south pole

zuigeling, zow-HGer-ling, c., baby

zuigen, zow-HGer, v., to suck

zuigfles, zowHG-fless, c., feeding-bottle

zuil, zowl, c., column, pillar

zuinig, zow-nerHG, a. & adv., thrifty, frugal

zuinigheid, zow-nerHG-heyt, c., economy, thrift

zuivel, zow-verl, n., dairy-produce

zuiver, zow-ver, a. & adv., pure; clean

zuiveren, zow-ver-rer, v., to clean

zuiverheid, zow-ver-heyt, c., cleanness

zulk, zerlk, pron. & a., such

zult, zerlt, c., brawn

zus, zerss, c., sister. adv., thus. —— of zo, ——
  of zoh, touch and go

zuster, zerss-ter, c., sister; nurse

zusterschool, zerss-ter-sHGohl, c., convent school

zuur, zeer, a. & adv., sour; tart

zuurkool, zeer-kohl, c., sauerkraut

zuurstof, zeer-stof, c., oxygen

zuurtjes, zeert-yerss, n. pl., acid drops; pickles

zwaaien, zvah-yer, v., to swing, to wield

zwaan, zvahn, c., swan

zwaar, zvahr, a. & adv., heavy; bulky; stout

zwaard, zvahrt, n., sword

zwaarlijvig, zvahr-ley-verHG, a., corpulent

zwaarmoedig, zvahr-moo-derHG, a., melancholic

zwaarte, zvahr-ter, c., weight   [gravity

zwaartepunt, zvahr-ter-pernt, n., centre of

zwaartillend, zvahr-til-lernt, a., pessimistic

zwaarwichtig, zvahr-viHG-terHG, a., weighty

zwabber, zvab-ber, c., mop, swab

zwachtel, zvaHG-terl, c., bandage

zwager, zvah-HGer, c., brother-in-law

zwak, zvak, a. & adv., weak; delicate; frail. n.,

zwakheid, zvak-heyt, c., weakness   [weak point

zwakkeling, zvak-ker-ling, c., weakling

zwakzinnig, zvak-sin-nerHG, a., mentally defec-

zwaluw, zvah-lee, c., swallow   [tive

zwammen, zvam-mer, v., (pop.) to jaw

zwanger, zvang-er, a., pregnant

zwangerschap, zvang-er-sHGap, c., pregnancy

zwarigheid, zvah-rerHG-heyt, c., difficulty;

zwart, zvart, a., black   [scruple

zwartgallig, zvart-HGal-lerHG, a., melancholy

zwartmaken, zvart-mah-ker, v., to blacken

zwavel, zvah-verl, c., sulphur

zweefbaan, zvayf-bahn, c., overhead railway

zweefmolen, zvayf-moh-ler, c., giant's stride

zweefvlieger, zvayf-flee-HGer, c., glider-pilot

zweefvliegtuig, zvayf-fleeHG-towHG, n., glider

zweem, zvaym, c., semblance; trace; shade, touch

zweep, svayp, c., whip

zweer, svayr, c., ulcer, boil; tumour

zweet, svayt, n., perspiration

zweetdroppel, svayt-drop-perl, c., bead of per- [spiration

zwelgen, zvel-HGer, v., to guzzle

zwelgpartij, zvelHG-par-tey, c., revelry

zwellen, zvel-ler, v., to expand

zwembad, zvem-bat, n., swimming-bath

zweminrichting, zvem-in-riHG-ting, c., public [baths

zwemmen, zvem-mer, v., to swim

zwendelaar, zven-der-lahr, c., swindler

zwenking, zven-king, c., turn, swerve

zwepen, zvay-per, v., to whip, to lash

zweren, zvay-rer, v., to swear; to fester

zwerftocht, zvayrf-toHGt, c., wandering

zwerm, zvayrm, c., swarm; cluster

zwerven, zvayr-ver, v., to wander

zwerver, zvayr-ver, c., wanderer, tramp

zweten, zvay-ter, v., to perspire

zwetsen, zvet-ser, v., to brag, to boast

zwetser, zvet-ser, c., braggart, boaster

zweven, zvay-ver, v., to float; to hover; to glide

zwichten, zviHG-ter, v., to give in

zwier, zveer, c., flourish; elegance; jauntiness

zwieren, zvee-rer, v., to reel; to glide

zwierig, zvee-rerHG, a. & adv., stylish, smart

zwijgen, zvey-HGer, v., to be silent

zwijgend, zvey-HGernt, a. & adv., silent

zwijm, zveym, c., fainting fit, swoon. in —— vallen, in —— fal-ler, to faint

zwijn, zveyn, n., pig; (fig.) swine

zwijnenboel, zvey-ner-bool, c., mess, piggery

zwijnerij, zvey-ner-rey, c., dirt, filth

zwoegen, zvoo-HGer, v., to drudge, to toil

zwoel, zvool, a., sultry, close, muggy

zwoerd, zvoort, n., bacon-rind

ENGELS-NEDERLANDS

WOORDENBOEK

(ENGLISH-DUTCH DICTIONARY)

(Men leze zorgvuldig de verklaring van de
nagebootste uitspraak op blz. x)

a, ee, art., een

abaft, e-baaft, adv., achter, naar achter

abandon, e-ben-d'n, v., verlaten, opgeven

abase, e-bees, v., vernederen, verlagen

abash, e-besj, v., beschamen

abate, e-beet, v., verzachten; verminderen

abbot, eb-but, s., abt c.

abbreviate, e-brie-vi-eet, v., afkorten

abdicate, eb-di-keet, v., afstand doen

abdomen, eb-do-men, s., buik c., onderbuik c.

abduction, eb-dak-sjun, s., ontvoering c.

abet, e-bet, v., aanhitsen; (help) steunen

abeyance, e-bee-'ns, s., tijdelijke opschorting c.

abhor, eb-hoar, v., verafschuwen, verfoeien

abhorrent, eb-hoar-'nt, a., weerzinwekkend

abide, e-baid, v., (endure) doorstaan; (await)
afwachten; —— by, vasthouden aan

ability, e-bil-li-ti, s., bekwaamheid c., vermogen [n.

abject, eb-dzjekt, a., laag, verachtelijk

ablaze, e-bleez, a. & adv., brandend; gloeiend

able, ee-b'l, a., knap, bevoegd. **to be** ——,
kunnen

ably, ee-bli, adv., bekwaam, handig

abnormal, eb-noar-m'l, a., abnormaal

aboard, e-board, adv., aan boord [n.

abode, e-bood, s., woonplaats c.; (house) verblijf

abolish, e-bol-lisj, v., afschaffen

abominable, e-bom-mi-ne-b'l, a., afschuwelijk

aboriginal, ab-e-rid-zji-n'l, a., inheems. s., inboorling c.

abortion, e-boar-sjun, s., miskraam c.

abound, e-baund, v., overvloedig zijn

about, e-baut, adv., ongeveer; (around) rondom

above, e-bav, adv. & prep., boven

abrasion, e-bree-sjun, s., afschaving c., afschuring c.

abreast, e-brest, adv., naast elkaar

abridge, e-bridzj, v., verkorten, bekorten

abroad, e-broad, adv., buiten; in het buitenland

abrupt, e-brapt, a., onverwacht; (steep) steil

abscess, eb-sis, s., ettergezwel n., abces n.

abscond, eb-skond, v., zich schuil houden

absence, eb-s'ns, s., afwezigheid c.

absent, eb-s'nt, a., afwezig. v., (—— oneself) wegblijven; —— ee, s., afwezige c.; —— minded, a., verstrooid

absolute, eb-s'l-joet, a., volstrekt; onbeperkt

absolve, eb-solv, v., vrijspreken; —— from, ontslaan van

absorb, eb-soarb, v., opzuigen; (fig.) geheel in beslag nemen

abstain, eb-steen, v., zich onthouden

abstainer, eb-stee-n'r, s., geheelonthouder c.

abstemious, eb-stie-mjus, a., matig, onthoudend

abstinence, eb-sti-n'ns, s., onthouding c.

abstract, eb-strekt, v., onttrekken; afleiden

abstract, eb-strekt, s., uittreksel n. a., abstrakt

absurd, eb-seurd, a., dwaas, onzinnig

abundant, e-ban-d'nt, a., overvloedig

abuse, e-bjoes, s., misbruik n.; belediging c.

abuse, e-bjoez, v., misbruiken; uitschelden

abusive, e-bjoe-siv, a., verkeerd; beledigend

abyss, e-bis, s., afgrond c.; hel c.

acacia, e-kee-sji-a, s., acacia c.

academy, e-ked-de-mi, s., academie c.

accede, ek-sied, v., instemmen; (throne) bestijgen

accelerate, ek-sel-le-reet, v., bespoedigen

accent, ek-s'nt, s., klemtoon c., nadruk c.

accent, ek-sent, v., de nadruk leggen op

accentuate, ek-sen-tjoe-eet, v., scherp doen uitkomen

accept, ek-sept, v., aannemen, aanvaarden; —— ance, s., aanneming c.; —— or, aannemer c.; (commercial) acceptant

access, ek-ses, s., toegang c.; aanval c., vlaag c.

accession, ek-ses-sjun, s., toetreding c.; troons-bestijging c.

accessory, ek-ses-se-ri, s., bijzaak c.; medeplichtige c.

accident, ek-si-d'nt, s., toeval n.; ongeluk n.

accidental, ek-si-den-t'l, a., toevallig; bijkomstig

acclaim, e-kleem, v., toejuicen .s., toejuiching c.

accommodate, e-kom-me-deet, v., aanpassen; (lodge) herbergen; —— with, voorzien van

accommodation, e-kom-me-dee-sjun, s., aanpassing c.; (lodging, shelter) onderdak n., logies n.

accompaniment, e-kam-pe-ni-m'nt, s., begeleiding c.

accompanist, e-kam-pe-nist, s., begeleider c.

accompany, e-kam-pe-ni, v., begeleiden

accomplice, e-kam-plis, s., medeplichtige c.

accomplish, e-kam-plisj, v., tot stand brengen; bereiken; —— ment, s., vervulling c.; voltooiing c.; —— ments, talenten n.pl.

accord, e-koard, s., overeenstemming c. v., overeenstemmen; in —— ance with, overeenkomstig; of one's own ——, uit eigen beweging; —— ing to, prep., volgens; naar gelang dat; —— ingly, adv., dienovereenkomstig

accordion, e-koar-di-'n, s., harmonica c.

accost, e-kost, v., aanspreken, aanklampen

account, e-kaunt, s., rekening c.; rekenschap c.; on ——, op afbetaling; on no ——, in geen geval; —— for, v., rekenschap afleggen van; —— able, a., verantwoordelijk; —— ant, s., boekhouder c.

accrue, e-kroe, v., aangroeien; voortspruiten

accumulate, e-kjoe-mjoe-leet, v., (gather) bijeenbrengen; (hoard) opeenhopen

accuracy, ek-joe-re-si, s., nauwkeurigheid c.

accurate, ek-joe-rit, a., nauwkeurig, stipt

accursed, e-keurst, a., vervloekt

accuse, e-kjoez, v., aanklagen, beschuldigen

accustom, e-kas-tum, v., gewennen

ace, ees, s., aas, n. & c.; (at games) één c.

ache, eek, s., pijn c. v., pijn doen; pijn lijden

achieve, e-tsjiev, v., volbrengen; verwerven; ——ment, s., volbrenging c.; prestatie c.; succes n.

acid, es-sid, a., zuur. s., zuur n.

acidity, es-sid-i-ti, s., zuurheid c.

acknowledge, ek-nol-lidzj, v., erkennen; bekennen; (receipt) nota nemen van

acknowledgement, ek-nol-lidzj-m'nt, s., erkenning c., bekentenis c.; (receipt) bericht van ontvangst n.

acme, ek-mi, s., toppunt n.

acorn, ee-koarn, s., eikel c. [c.

acoustics, e-koes-tiks, s., geluidsleer c.; acoustiek

acquaint, e-kweent, v., in kennis stellen; ——ance s., bekendheid c.; kennismaking c.; (person) kennis c.

acquiesce, ek-kwi-es, v., instemmen, berusten

acquiescence, ek-kwi-es-s'ns, s., berusting c.

acquire, e-kwair, v., verkrijgen, verwerven

acquisition, ek-kwi-zis-sjun, s., verwerving c.; (advantage) aanwinst c.

acquit, e-kwit, v., vrijspreken; ontslaan

acquittal, e-kwit-t'l, s., vrijspraak c.

acre, ee-k'r, s., acre c.

acrid, ek-krid, a., scherp, bijtend

across, e-kros, adv., erover; overdwars. prep., dwars over; door; aan de overkant van

act, ekt, s., daad c.; (of a play) bedrijf n.; (law) wet c. v., handelen; (in theatre) opvoeren, spelen

action, ek-sjun, s., handeling c., daad c.; (law) proces n.; (war) gevecht n.

active, ek-tiv, a., werkzaam, bedrijvig

activity, ek-ti-vi-ti, s., bedrijvigheid c.

actor, ek-t'r s., toneelspeler c., acteur c.

actress, ek-tris, s., toneelspeelster c., actrice c.

actual, ek-tjoe-ul, a., feitelijk; werkelijk

actuate, ek-tjoe-eet, v., in beweging brengen

acumen, e-kjoe-men, s., scherpzinnigheid c.

acute, e-kjoet, a., scherp; (pain) hevig, intens; (senses) scherpzinnig; (med.) acuut

acuteness, e-kjoet-nis, s., scherpte c.; scherpzinnigheid c.

adage, ed-didzj, s., spreekwoord n., gezegde n.

adamant, ed-de-m'nt, a., onvermurwbaar

adapt, e-dept, v., aanpassen, toepassen

adaptation, e-dept-ee-sjun, s., aanpassing c.; (plays, etc.) bewerking c.

add, ed, v., toevoegen, bijvoegen, optellen

adder, ed-d'r, s., adder c.

addicted, ed-dik-tid, a., verslaafd

addition, e-dis-sjun, s., toevoeging c., optelling c.

additional, e-dis-sjun-'l, a., aanvullend, extra

addled, ed-d'ld, a., bedorven, ledig; (brain) verward

address, e-dres, s., adres n.; toespraak c.; behendigheid c. v., adresseren; (orally) zich richten tot

adduce, e-djoes, v., aanvoeren, aanhalen

adequacy, ed-di-kwe-si, s., evenredigheid c.

adequate, ed-di-kwit, a., voldoende; geschikt

adhere, ed-hier, v., aankleven; aanhangen

adherence, ed-hier-'ns, s., aankleven n.; aanhangen n.; (loyalty) aanhankelijkheid c.

adherent, ed-hier-'nt, s., aanhanger c.

adhesive, ed-hie-siv, a., kleverig; gegomd

adjacent, e-dzjee-s'nt, a., aangrenzend

adjoin, e-dzjoin, v., grenzen aan; bijvoegen

adjoining, e-dzjoi-ning, a., aangrenzend

adjourn, e-dzjeurn, v., verdagen, uitstellen

adjournment, e-dzjeurn-m'nt, s., uitstel n.

adjudge, e-dzjadzj, v., toewijzen

adjunct, e-dzjankt, a., toegevoegd. s., aanhangsel n.

adjust, e-dzjast, v., regelen, in orde brengen

adjustment, e-dzjast-m'nt, s., regeling c., vereffening c.; (mech.) instelling c.

adjutant, ed-dzoe-t'nt, s., adjudant c.

administer, ed-mi-nis-t'r, v., beheren, besturen

administration, ed-mi-nis-tree-sjun, s., beheer n., bestuur n.; toepassing c.; toediening c.

admirable, ed-mi-re-b'l, a., bewonderenswaardig

admiral, ed-mi-r'l, s., admiraal c.

admire, ed-mair, v., bewonderen
admission, ed-mis-sjun, s., toegangsprijs c.; toelating c.; (confession) erkenning c.
admit, ed-mit, v., toelaten; (concede) toegeven
admittance, ed-mit-t'ns, s., toegang c.
admonish, ed-mon-nisj, v., vermanen; berispen
admonition, ed-me-nis-sjun, s., vermaning c.; (reproof) berisping c.
ado, e-doe, s., drukte c., ophef c., moeite c.
adopt, e-dopt, v., adopteren, aannemen
adore, e-doar, v., aanbidden
adorn, e-doarn, v., versieren, verfraaien
adornment, e-doarn-m'nt, s., versiering c.
adrift, e-drift, adv., (sea) drijvend; (lost) verloren
adroit, e-droit, a., handig, behendig
adulate, ed-joe-leet, v., pluimstrijken
adulation, ed-joe-lee-sjun, s., vleierij c.
adult, e-dalt, a., volwassen. s., volwassene c.
adulterate, e-dal-te-reet, v., vervalsen
adultery, e-dal-te-ri, s., overspel n.
advance, ed-vaans, v., (to lead) vooruitgaan; (press forward) voortrukken; (price) verhogen; (lend) voorschieten. s., (progress) vooruitgang c.; (money) voorschot n.; (price) verhoging c.; **in** ——, vooruit, bij voorbaat; ——**ment**, s., vooruitgang c.
advantage, ed-vaan-tidzj, s., voordeel n.
advantageous, ed-vaan-tee-dzjus, a., voordelig
advent, ed-v'nt, s., komst c.; advent c.
adventitious, ed-v'n-tis-sjus, a., bijkomstig
adventure, ed-vent-sjur, s., avontuur n.
adventurer, ed-vent-sjur-'r, s., avonturier c.
adventurous, ed-vent-sjur-us, a., avontuurlijk; (bold) vermetel, gewaagd
adversary, ed-veur-se-ri, s, tegenstander c.
adverse, ed-veurs, a., nadelig; ongunstig
advert (to), ed-veurt (toe), v., wijzen (op), verwijzen (naar)
advertise, ed-veur-taiz, v., bekend maken; reclame maken
advertisement, ed-veur-tis-m'nt, s., advertentie c.
advertiser, ed-veur-tai-z'r, s., adverteerder c. [c.

advice, ed-vais, s., raad c.; bericht n.
advisability, ed-vai-ze-bi-li-ti, s., raadzaamheid
advisable, ed-vai-ze-b'l, a., raadzaam [c.
advise, ed-vaiz, v., aanraden; (inform) berichten;
ill ——d, a., onoverlegd; well ——d, a.,
weldoordacht
adviser, ed-vai-z'r, s., raadsman c.
advocacy, ed-ve-ke-si, s., voorspraak c. [c.
advocate, ed-ve-kit, s., voorstander c., verdediger
aerated, è-e-ree-tid, a., koolzuurhoudend
aerial, èr-ri-'l, s., (radio) antenne c. a., lucht ...
aerodrome, èr-re-droom, s., vliegveld n.
aeroplane, èr-re-pleen, s., vliegmachine c.
afar, e-faar, adv., ver, in de verte
affable, ef-fe-b'l, a., vriendelijk, minzaam
affably, ef-fe-bli, adv., op een vriendelijke manier
affair, e-fèr, s., aangelegenheid c., zaak c.
affect, e-fekt, v., aantasten; betreffen; (move)
treffen; ——ed, a., gemaakt; (moved) aangedaan; ——ion, s., genegenheid c., liefde
c.; (ailment) aandoening c.
affectionate, e-fek-sjun-it, a., hartelijk
affianced, e-fai-'nst, s., verloofde c.
affidavit, ef-fi-dei-vit, s., beëdigde verklaring c.
affiliate, e-fil-li-eet, v., als lid opnemen
affinity, e-fin-ni-ti, s., verwantschap c.
affirm, e-feurm, v., verzekeren, bevestigen
affirmation, e-feurm-ee-sjun, s., verzekering c.,
bevestiging c.
affirmative, e-feur-me-tiv, a., bevestigend. s.,
bevestiging c.
affix, e-fiks, v., vasthechten, toevoegen
afflict, e-flikt, v., bedroeven; teisteren
affliction, e-flik-sjun, s., droefheid c.; ramp c.
affluence, ef-floe-'ns, s., overvloed c., rijkdom c.
affluent, ef-floe-'nt, a., rijk, overvloedig
afford, e-foard, v., (means) opleveren; (grant)
verschaffen; (pay) betalen
affray, e-free, s., vechtpartij c.
affright, e-frait, v., schrik aanjagen
affront, e-frŏnt, v., beledigen. s., belediging c.
aflame, e-fleem, a., vlammend, in vuur

afloat, e-**floot,** a. & adv., vlot; drijvend
aforesaid, e-**foar-**sed, a., voornoemd
afraid, e-**freed,** a., bang; **to be —— of,** bang
    zijn voor
afresh, e-**fresj,** adv., opnieuw, weer
aft, aaft, a. & adv., achter, naar achter
after, aaf-t'r, prep., achter; na. adv., daarna.
    conj., nadat; ——**noon,** s., namiddag c.;
    ——**thought,** later invallende gedachte c.;
    ——**wards,** adv., later, naderhand
again, e-**Geen,** adv., weer, opnieuw; bovendien
against, e-**Geenst,** prep., tegen, tegenover
age, eedzj, s., leeftijd c.; ouderdom c.; (period)
    eeuw c.; **to be of ——,** meerderjarig zijn;
    ——**d,** a., oud, bejaard
agency, ee-dzj'n-si, s., agentschap n.; bemidde-
    ling c.; vertegenwoordiging c.
agent, ee-dzj'nt, s., zaakwaarnemer c.; agent c.
aggravate, eG-Gre-veet, v., verergeren; verbitteren
aggregate, eG-Gri-Geet, v., verzamelen. a., geza-
    melijk. s., verzameling c., ophoping c.   [c.
aggression, e-Gres-sjun, s., aanval c., aanranding
aggressive, e-Gres-siv, a., aanvallend; strijdlustig
aggrieve, e-**Griev,** v., bedroeven; benadelen
aghast, e-**Gaast,** a., ontzet, verslagen
agile, ed-zjail, a., vlug, behendig
agitate, ed-zji-teet, v., (shake) schudden; (men-
    tal) opwinden; (stir up strife) opruien
agitation, ed-zji-**tee-**sjun, s., (mental) opwinding
    c.; (strife) opschudding c., onrust c.
ago, e-Go, adv., geleden; **long ——,** lang geleden
agonize, eG-Ge-naiz, v., kwellen, martelen
agony, eG-Ge-ni, s., folterende pijn c.; foltering c.
agree, e-**Grie,** v., overeenstemmen, het eens zijn;
    ——**to,** akkoord gaan met; ——**able,** a.,
    aangenaam; ——**ment,** s., overeenstemming
    c.; (contract) contract n., overeenkomst c.
agricultural, eG-Gri-ka̱lt-sjur-'l, a., landbouw ...
agriculture, eG-Gri-ka̱lt-sjur, s., landbouw c.
aground, e-**Graund,** adv., aan de grond
ague, ee-Gjoe, s., koortsrilling c.
ahead, e-**hed,** adv., vooruit, voorwaarts, vooraan

aid, eed, s., hulp c., bijstand c. v., helpen

aigret, ee-Grit, s., egret c., kleine witte reiger c.

ail, eel, v., schelen; ——ing, a., sukkelend

ailment, eel-m'nt, s., ongesteldheid c., ziekte c.

aim, eem, s., doel n.; mikpunt n. v., mikken

aimless, eem-lis, a., doelloos

air, èr, s., lucht c.; (mien) voorkomen n., houding c.; (tune) wijsje n. v., luchten, ventileren; ————conditioning, s., kunstmatige lucht-verversing en luchtontsmetting c.; ——gun, windbuks c.; ——(il)y, a., (adv.) luchtig; (fig.) ijl, nietig; ——ing, s., luchten n.; ——port, vlieghaven c.; ——ship, lucht-schip n.; ——tight, a., luchtdicht

aisle, eel, s., zijbeuk c.; (between pews) pad n.

ajar, e-dzjaar, a., op een kier, half open

akimbo, e-kim-bo, adv., in de zij

akin, e-kin, a., verwant

alabaster, el-le-baas-t'r, s., albast c.

alacrity, e-lek-kri-ti, s., bereidwilligheid c.

alarm, e-laarm, v., verontrusten. s., alarm n.; ——clock, wekker c.; ——ing, a., veront-rustend

album, el-bum, s., album c.

alcohol, el-ke-hol, s., alcohol c.

alert, e-leurt, a., waakzaam; **on the** ——, op zijn hoede; ——ness, s., waakzaamheid c.; (nimbleness) vlugheid c.

alias, ee-li-es, adv., alias, anders genoemd

alien, eel-jun, s., vreemdeling c., buitenlander c. a., vreemd, buitenlands

alienate, eel-jun-eet, v., vervreemden

alight, e-lait, v., uitstappen, afstappen. a., brand-end, verlicht; schitterend

alike, e-laik, a., gelijk. adv., evengoed, evenzeer

alive, e-laiv, a. & adv., levend; levendig

all, oal, a., alle, geheel, gans. adv., helemaal, geheel; ——along, aldoor, steeds; ——right, in orde; goed zo; —— the more, des te meer; not at ——, helemaal niet

allay, e-lee, v., tot bedaren brengen; stillen

allege, e-ledzj, v., beweren; aanvoeren

alleged, e-ledzj-'d, a., zogenaamd

allegiance, e-lie-dzj'ns, s., trouw c.

alleviate, e-lie-vi-eet, v., verlichten, verzachten

alley, el-li, s., steeg c.; **blind ——,** slop n.

alliance, e-lai-'ns, s., verbond n., verbintenis c.

allied, e-laid, a., verbonden, geallieerd

allot, e-lot, v., toewijzen, toedelen

allotment, e-lot-m'nt, s., aandeel n.; (ground) perceel n.; volkstuintje n.

allow, e-lau, v., (permit) toestaan; (agree) toegeven; **——ance,** s., vergunning c.; (monetary) toelage c., zakgeld n.; (rebate) korting c.; **to make ——ance for,** in aanmerking nemen

alloy, e-loi, s., allooi n.; mengsel n.

allude (to), e-ljoed (toe), v., zinspelen (op)

allure, e-ljoer, v., aanlokken; verlokken

alluring, e-ljoe-ring, a., aanlokkelijk; verleidelijk

allusion, e-ljoe-zjun, s., toespeling c.

ally, e-lai, s., bondgenoot c. v., verbinden

Almighty, oal-mai-ti, s., Almachtige c.

almond, a-m'nd, s., amandel c.

almost, oal-moost, adv., bijna, nagenoeg

alms, aams, s., aalmoes n.; **——house,** armenhuis n.

aloft, e-loft, adv., omhoog, hemelwaarts

alone, e-loon, a., alleen, eenzaam

along, e-long, adv., voort, verder. prep., langs

alongside, e-long-said, adv., langszij

aloof, e-loef, adv., op een afstand, ver; **keep ——,** zich op een afstand houden

aloud, e-laud, adv., luid, hardop

already, oal-red-di, adv., al, reeds

also, oal-so, adv., ook, eveneens; bovendien

altar, oal-t'r, s., altaar n.

alter, oal-t'r, v., veranderen

alteration, oal-te-ree-sjun, s., verandering c.

alternate, oal-teur-nit, a., afwisselend, verwisselend; **on —— days,** om de andere dag

alternative, oal-teur-ne-tiv, s., keus c., alternatief n. a., alternatief, ander

although, oal-dho, conj., hoewel, ofschoon
altitude, el-ti-tjoed, s., hoogte c.; hoogtepunt n.
altogether, oal-te-Gedh-'r, adv., over het geheel
alum, el-lum, s., aluin c.
aluminium, el-joe-min-jum, s., aluminium n.
always, oal-weez, adv., altijd, steeds
amass, e-mes, v., opeenhopen, vergaren
amateur, em-me-tjoer, s., amateur c.
amaze, e-meez, v., verbazen
amazement, e-meez-m'nt, s., verbazing c.
ambassador, em-bes-se-d'r, s., ambassadeur c.
amber, em-b'r, s., barnsteen n.   [c.
ambiguity, em-bi-Gjoe-i-ti, s., dubbelzinnigheid
ambiguous, em-bi-Gjoe-us, a., dubbelzinnig
ambition, em-bis-sjun, s., eerzucht c.
ambitious, em-bis-sjus, a., eerzuchtig
ambulance, em-bjoe-l'ns, s., ziekenwagen c.
ambuscade, em-bus-keed, s., hinderlaag c.
ambush, em-boesj, s., hinderlaag c.
ameliorate, e-miel-je-reet, v., verbeteren
amenable, e-mie-ne-b'l, a., gedwee, handelbaar
amend, e-mend, v., verbeteren; beter worden
amendment, e-mend-m'nt, s., verbetering c.,
beterschap c.
amends, e-mendz, make ——, v., het weer
goedmaken
amethyst, em-mi-thist, s., amethist n.
amiable, eem-je-b'l, a., lief, vriendelijk
amicable, em-mi-ke-b'l, a., vriendschappelijk
amid(st), e-mid(st), prep., te midden van
amidships, e-mid-sjips, adv., midscheeps
amiss, e-mis, adv. & a., verkeerd; te onpas; mis;
take ——, v., kwalijk nemen
amity, em-mi-ti, s., vriendschap c.
ammonia, e-moon-ja, s., ammonia c.
ammunition, em-mjoe-nis-sjun, s., munitie c.
amnesty, em-nis-ti, s., amnestie c., vergiffenis c.
among(st), e-mong(st), prep., onder, tussen
amorous, em-me-rus, a., verliefd; liefdes . . .
amount, e-maunt, v., bedragen, s., bedrag n.
ample, em-pul, a., ruim; overvloedig
amplify, em-pli-fai, v., vergroten; versterken

amputate, em-pjoe-teet, v., amputeren, afzetten

amuck, e-m*a*k, run ——, v., dol worden, amok gaan

amuse, e-mjoez, v., vermaken, amuseren

amusement, e-mjoez-m'nt, s., vermaak n.

amusing, e-mjoe-zing, a., vermakelijk, amusant

an, un, art., een

anæmia, e-niem-ja, s., bloedarmoede c.

anæsthetic, en-ies-thet-tik, a., pijnverdovend

analogous, e-nel-le-Gus, a., overeenkomstig

analyse, en-ne-laiz, v., ontleden, ontbinden

analysis, e-nel-li-sis, s., analyse c., ontleding c.

anarchy, en-ne-ki, s., anarchie c.

ancestor, en-sis-t'r, s., stamvader c., voorvader c.

ancestry, en-sis-tri, s., voorouders c.pl.; afstamming c., geboorte c.

anchor, eng-k'r, s., anker n. v., ankeren

anchorage, eng-ke-ridzj, s., ankergrond c.

anchovy, en-tsjo-vi, s., ansjovis c.

ancient, een-sjunt, a., oud

and, end, conj., en

anew, e-njoe, adv., opnieuw; anders

angel, een-dzjul, s., engel c.

anger, en-Gur, s., toorn c., boosheid c. v., vertoornen

angina, en-dzjai-ne, s., angina c.

angle, eng-Gul, s., hoek c. v., hengelen

angler, eng-Glur, s., hengelaar c.

angling, eng-Gling, s., hengelen n.

angry, eng-Gri, a., boos; (enraged) toornig

anguish, eng-Gwisj, s., angst c., smart c.

animal, en-ni-m'l, s., dier n. a., dierlijk

animate, en-ni-meet, v., bezielen; leven geven

animated, en-ni-mee-tid, a., levendig, levend

animation, en-ni-mee-sjun, s., levendigheid c.

animosity, en-ni-mos-si-ti, s., verbittering c.

aniseed, en-ni-sied, s., anijszaad n.

ankle, eng-k'l, s., enkel c.   [n.pl.

annals, en-nulz, s.pl., annalen c.pl., jaarboeken

annex, c-neks, s., aanhangsel n. v., toevoegen

annihilate, e-nai-hi-leet, v., vernietigen

anniversary, en-ni-veur-se-ri, s., jaarfeest n.

annotate, en-no-teet, v., aantekeningen maken

announce, e-nauns, v., aankondigen   [c.

announcement, e-nauns-m'nt, s., aankondiging

announcer, e-naun-s'r, s., aankondiger c.; (radio) omroeper c.

annoy, e-noi, v., ergeren; (molest) lastig vallen; ——ance, s., last c., hinder c.; ——ing, a., vervelend

annual, en-njoe-ul, a., jaarlijks. s., jaarboek n.

annuity, e-njoe-i-ti, s., jaargeld n.

annul, e-nal, v., vernietigen, te niet doen

annulment, e-nal-m'nt, s., vernietiging c.

anoint, e-noint, v., zalven; inwrijven

anomalous, e-nom-me-lus, a., afwijkend

anonymous, e-non-ni-mus, a., anoniem   [een

another, e-nadh-'r, a. & pron., een ander; nog

answer, aan-sur, s., antwoord n. v., antwoorden

answerable, aan-se-re-b'l, a., verantwoordelijk

ant, ent, s., mier c.

antagonist, en-teG-Ge-nist, s., tegenstander c.

antecedent, en-ti-sie-d'nt, a., voorafgaand

antecedents, en-ti-sie-d'ntz, s.pl., verleden n.

antedate, en-ti-deet, v., te vroeg dateren

antediluvian, en-ti-di-loe-vi-'n, a., ouderwets

antelope, en-ti-loop, s., antilope c.

anterior, en-tie-ri-'r, a., voorste; (time) vroeger

anteroom, en-ti-roem, s., voorkamer c.

anthem, en-thum, s., lofzang c. **national** ——, volkslied n.

anthracite, en-thre-sait, s., antraciet c.

anthrax, en-threks, s., bloedzweer c.

anticipate, en-tis-si-peet, v., voorkomen; een voorgevoel hebben van; voorzien

anticipation, en-tis-si-pee-sjun, s., voorgevoel n.; vooruitbetaling c.; voorkomen n. **in** ——, bij voorbaat

antics, en-tiks, s.pl., dolle sprongen c.pl.

antidote, en-ti-doot, s., tegengift n.

antipathy, en-tip-pe-thi, s., antipathie c.   [c.pl.

Antipodes, en-tip-pe-diez, s.pl., tegenvoeters

antiquarian, en-ti-kwèr-jun, a., oudheidkundig

antiquated, en-ti-kwee-tid, a., verouderd

antique, en-tiek, a., ouderwets, antiek
antiseptic, en-ti-sep-tik, a., antiseptisch
antlers, ent-l'rz, s. pl., gewei n.
anvil, en-vil, s., aanbeeld n.   [c.
anxiety, eng-zai-e-ti, s., bezorgdheid c.; begeerte
anxious, engk-sjus, a., ongerust; verlangend
any, en-ni, a., (any one) een, welk . . . ook; (some)
    iets, enig; (every) ieder, elk; not ——, geen
anybody, en-ni-bod-di, pron., iemand; iedereen
anyhow, en-ni-hau, adv., hoe dan ook; in ieder
    geval
anything, en-ni-thing, pron., iets; van alles
anyway, en-ni-wee, adv., op de een of andere
    manier
anywhere, en-ni-wèr, adv., ergens; overal
apart, e-paart, adv., afzonderlijk; terzijde
apartment, e-paart-m'nt, s., vertrek n.
apartments, e-paart-m'ntz, s.pl., woning c.
apathy, ep-pe-thi, s., gevoelloosheid c., apathie c.
ape, eep, s., aap c.   v., naäpen
aperient, e-pie-ri-'nt, s., laxeermiddel n.
aperture, ep-pe-tsjur, s., opening c.; spleet c.
apex, ee-peks, s., top c., toppunt n.
apiece, e-pies, adv., per stuk, elk
apish, ee-pisj, a., aapachtig; dwaas
apologize, e-pol-le-dzjaiz, v., zich verontschul-
    digen
apology, e-pol-le-dzji, s., verontschuldiging c.
apoplexy, ep-pe-plek-si, s., beroerte c.
apostle, e-pos-'l, s., apostel c.
apostrophe, e-pos-tre-fi, s., (gram.) afkappings-
    teken n.
apothecary, e-poth-i-ke-ri, s., apotheker c.
appal, e-poal, v., ontzetten, doen schrikken
appalling, e-poal-ing, a., verschrikkelijk   [n.
apparatus, ep-pe-ree-tus, s., apparaat n., toestel
apparel, e-per-'l, s., kleding c.; tooi c.
apparent, e-per-'nt, a., blijkbaar; schijnbaar
apparition, ep-pe-ris-sjun, s., verschijning c.
appeal, e-piel, s., smeekbede c.; (law) hoger
    beroep n.   v., een beroep doen op; smeken;
    (law) in beroep gaan

appear, e-pier, v., verschijnen; (seem) schijnen

appearance, e-pier-'ns, s., verschijning c.; (in public) optreden n.; (looks, figure) voorkomen n.

appease, e-piez, v., stillen, bevredigen

appellant, e-pel-'nt, s., (law) appellant c.

append, e-pend, v., aanhechten, bijvoegen

appendage, e-pen-didzj, s., aanhangsel n.

appendicitis, e-pen-di-sai-tis, s., blinde darmontsteking c.

appendix, e-pen-diks, s., (books) aanhangsel n.; (med.) blinde darm c.

appertain (to), ep-pe-teen (toe), v., toebehoren

appetite, ep-pe-tait, s., eetlust c., trek c. [(aan)

appetizer, ep-pe-tai-z'r, s., aperitief n.

appetizing, ep-pe-tai-zing, a., appetijtelijk

applaud, e-pload, v., toejuichen

applause, e-ploaz, s., toejuiching c., applaus n.

apple, ep-p'l, s., appel c.; ——-tree, appelboom c.

appliance, e-plai-'ns, s., (instrument) toestel n.

applicant, e-pli-k'nt, s., (candidate) sollicitant c.; (petitioner) aanvrager c.

application, ep-pli-kee-sjun, s., aanwending c.; toewijding c.; (request) aanvraag c.

apply, e-plai, v., (employ) aanwenden; (as candidate) solliciteren; (lay on) aanbrengen; ——to, (turn to) zich wenden tot

appoint, e-point, v., vaststellen; benoemen

appointment, e-point-m'nt, s., aanstelling c.; (meeting) afspraak c.; (post) functie c., ambt n.

apportion, e-poar-sjun, v., toebedelen; verdelen

apportionment, e-poar-sjun-m'nt, s., toebedeling c.

apposite, ep-pe-zit, a., geschikt, passend

appraise, e-preez, v., schatten, taxeren

appraisement, e-preez-m'nt, s., schatting c.

appraiser, e-pree-z'r, s., schatter c., taxateur c.

appreciable, e-prie-sje-b'l, a., merkbaar

appreciate, e-prie-sji-eet, v., waarderen; aanvoelen; op prijs stellen; (price) verhogen

appreciation, e-prie-sji-**ee**-sjun, s., waardering c.; begrip n., besef n.; (price) stijging c.

apprehend, ep-pri-hend, v., (fear) vrezen; (seize) vatten; (understand) begrijpen

apprehension, ep-pri-hen-sjun, s., (fear) vrees c.; (arrest) inhechtenisneming c.; (ideas) begrip n.

apprehensive, ep-pri-hen-siv, a., bezorgd

apprentice, e-pren-tis, s., leerjongen c.; —— ship, leertijd c., leerjaren n.pl.

apprise, e-praiz, v., in kennis stellen

approach, e-prootsj, v., naderen

approbation, ep-pre-bee-sjun, s., goedkeuring c.

appropriate, e-pro-pri-eet, v., zich toeëigenen. a., geschikt, passend; bevoegd

appropriateness, e-pro-pri-eet-nes, s., geschiktheid c.

approval, e-proe-vul, s., goedkeuring c., bijval c.

approve, e-proev, v., goedkeuren; bevestigen

approximate, e-prok-si-mit, a., bij benadering, ongeveer. v., benaderen; nader brengen

appurtenance, e-peur-ti-n'ns, s., bijvoegsel n.

apricot, ee-pri-kot, s., abrikoos c.

April, ee-pril, s., april c.

apron, ee-prun, s., schort c.; schootsvel n.

apse, (apsis), eps, (**ep**-sis), s., absis c.; apsis c.

apt, ept, a., (fit) geschikt; (inclined) geneigd; (capable) bekwaam; ——itude, s., geschiktheid c.; (inclination) neiging c.

aqueduct, ek-kwi-dakt, v., waterleiding c.

aqueous, ee-kwie-us, a., waterig, water . . .

aquiline, ek-kwi-lain, a., arends . . .

arable, er-re-b'l, a., bebouwbaar, bouw . . .

arbiter, aar-bi-t'r, s., scheidsrechter c.

arbitrary, aar-bi-tre-ri, a., willekeurig

arbitrate, aar-bi-treet, v., beslissen; als scheidsrechter optreden

arbitration, aar-bi-**tree**-sjun, s., arbitrage c.

arbour, aar-b'r, s., prieel n.

arc, aark, s., boog c.; ——**lamp,** booglamp c.

arcade, aar-keed, s., winkelgalerij c.

arch, aartsj, s., boog c., gewelf n.

archbishop, aartsj-bisj-up, s., aartsbisschop c.

archdeacon, aartsj-die-kun, s., aartsdeken c.

archduke, aartsj-djoek, s., aartshertog c.

archer, aart-sjur, s., boogschutter c.

archetype, aar-ki-taip, s., oertype n., model n.

architect, aar-ki-tekt, s., architect c., bouwmeester c.

archives, aar-kaivz, s.pl., archieven n.pl., archief c.

archway, aartsj-wee, s., gewelfde gang c.   [n.

arctic, aark-tik, a., noordelijk; noordpool ...

ardent, aar-d'nt, a., brandend, vurig

ardour, aar-d'r, s., hitte c.; (zest) vuur n.

arduous, aar-djoe-us, a., steil; moeilijk

area, èr-ri-a, s., (open) ruimte c.; (measure) oppervlakte c.

arena, e-rie-na, s., arena c., strijdperk n.

argue, aar-Gjoe, v., redetwisten; (discuss) beredeneren

argument, aar-Gjoe-m'nt, s., bewijs n.; redenering c.

aright, e-rait, adv., juist, goed

arise, e-raiz, v., (occur) zich voordoen; (revolt) opstaan; (originate) voortkomen, ontstaan

aristocracy, er-is-tok-kre-si, s., aristocratie c.

aristocratic, er-is-te-kret-tik, a., aristocratisch

arithmetic, e-rith-me-tik, s., rekenkunde c.

ark, aark, s., ark c.; Noah's ——, Ark van Noë c.

arm, aarm, s., arm c.; (weapon) wapen n. v., zich wapenen; pantseren

armament, aar-me-m'nt, s., krijgstoerusting c.

armchair, aarm-tsjèr, s., leuningstoel c.

armistice, aar-mis-tis, s., wapenstilstand c.

armlet, aarm-lit, s., armband c.

armour, aar-mur, s., wapenrusting c. v., pantseren

armoured, aar-murd, a., gepantserd, pantser ...

armoury, aar-me-ri, s., wapenkamer c.

armpit, aarm-pit, s., oksel c.

arms, aarmz, s.pl., wapenen n.pl.; **coat of ——,** familiewapen c.

army, aar-mi, s., leger n.; menigte c.

aromatic, er-re-met-tik, a., geurig, aromatisch

around, e-raund, adv. & prep., rondom, rond, om
arouse, e-rauz, v., opwekken, aanporren
arrange, e-reendzj, v., rangschikken; regelen
arrant, er-r'nt, a., doortrapt, aarts . . .
array, e-ree, v., uitdossen. s., (mil.) slagorde c.;
  (dress) kledij c.; (arrangement) rangschikking
arrears, e-rierz, s., achterstand c. [c.
arrest, e-rest, v., arresteren; (stop) tegenhouden.
  s., arrestatie c., arrest n.
arrival, e-rai-v'l, s., aankomst c.; (person)
  aangekomene c.
arrive, e-raiv, v., aankomen; (occur) gebeuren;
  (aim) bereiken
arrogance, er-re-G'ns, s., aanmatiging c.
arrogant, er-re-g'nt, a., aanmatigend
arrow, er-ro, s., pijl c.
arsenal, aar-se-n'l, s., arsenaal n., tuighuis n.
arsenic, aars-nik, s., rattekruid n.
arson, aar-s'n, s., brandstichting c.
art, aart, s., kunst c.; (cunning) list c.
arterial, aar-tier-jul, a., —— **road,** s., hoofdver-
  keersweg c.
artery, aar-te-ri, s., slagader c.
artful, aart-foel, a., (sly) geslepen, listig
artichoke, aar-ti-tsjok, s., artisjok c. [n.
article, aar-ti-k'l, s., artikel n.; (gram.) lidwoord
articulate, aar-tik-joe-leet, v., articuleren
artifice, aar-ti-fis, s., kunstgreep c.
artificial, aar-ti-fis-sjul, a., kunstmatig; kunst . . .
artillery, aar-til-le-ri, s., artillerie c.
artisan, aar-ti-zen, s., handwerksman c.
artist, aar-tist, s., kunstenaar c.; kunstschilder c.
artistic, aar-tist-ik, a., artistiek
as, ez, adv., zo, zoals, evenals, gelijk. conj., terwijl; toen; daar; naarmate; —— **for,** wat . . .
  betreft; —— **if,** —— **though,** alsof; ——
  soon ——, zodra; —— **to,** wat . . . betreft;
  —— **well,** ook, eveneens; —— **yet,** tot nog
  toe; voorlopig
asbestos, ez-bes-tus, s., asbest n., steenvlas n.
ascend, es-send, v., omhooggaan, stijgen
ascent, es-sent, s., beklimming c.; opgang c.

ascertain, es-se-teen, v., zich vergewissen van

ascribe, es-skraib, v., toeschrijven, toekennen

ash, esj, s., as c.; (tree) es c.; ———-pan, asbak c.; ———-tray, asbakje n.

ashamed, e-sjeemd, a., beschaamd

ashore, e-sjoar, adv., aan land; gestrand

aside, e-said, adv., ter zijde, op zij

ask, aask, v., (question) vragen; (demand) eisen; (beg) verzoeken; (invite) uitnodigen

askew, e-skjoe, adv., schuin, scheef

asleep, e-sliep, a., in slaap; **to be** ———, v., slapen; **to fall** ———, in slaap vallen

asparagus, es-sper-re-Gus, s., asperge c.

aspect, es-pekt, s., aanzien n.; voorkomen n.

aspen, es-p'n, s., esp c. a., espen . . .

aspersion, es-peur-sjun, s., besprenkeling c.; laster c.

asphyxia, es-fiks-ja, s., verstikking c.

aspirate, es-pi-reet, v., aspireren

aspire, es-spair, v., streven, trachten

ass, es, s., ezel c.

assail, es-seel, v., aanranden, aanvallen

assailant, es-seel-l'nt, s., aanrander c.

assassinate, es-ses-si-neet, v., vermoorden

assault, es-soalt, s., aanval c., bestorming c. v., aanranden, aanvallen; bestormen

assay, es-see, v., toetsen, keuren. s., toets c.

assemble, es-sem-b'l, v., verzamelen

assembly, es-sem-bli, s., bijeenkomst c.; vergadering c.

assent, es-sent, s., goedkeuring c. v., toestemmen

assert, es-seurt, v., beweren

assertion, es-seurt-sjun, s., bewering c.

assess, es-ses, v., belasten, aanslaan

assessment, es-ses-m'nt, s., aanslag c., belasting c.

assets, es-sets, s., activa n.pl., actief n.

assiduous, es-sid-djoe-us, a., ijverig, volhardend

assign, es-sain, v., toewijzen; overdragen. s., rechtverkrijgende c.; ———ment, toewijzing c.; taak c.

assignee, es-si-nie, s., gevolmachtigde c.

assist, es-sist, v., helpen; ——**ance**, s., hulp c.; ——**ant**, helper c., assistent c.; (shop) winkelbediende c.

assize, es-saiz, s., rechtszitting c.

associate, es-so-sji-eet, v., verenigen; omgaan. s., metgezel c.; deelgenoot c.

association, es-so-si-ee-sjun, s., genootschap n.

assort, es-soart, v., sorteren; omgaan

assortment, es-soart-m'nt, s., sortering c.; collectie c.

assuage, es-sweedzj, v., lenigen, bevredigen

assume, es-sjoem, v., aannemen; op zich nemen

assuming, es-sjoe-ming, a., aanmatigend

assumption, es-samp-sjun, s., veronderstelling

assurance, es-sjoe-r'ns, s., verzekering c.   [c.

assure, es-sjoer, v., verzekeren; overtuigen

asterisk, es-te-risk, s., sterretje n.

astern, e-steurn, adv., (naut.) achteruit

asthma, est-ma, s., astma n.

astir, e-steur, adv., in beweging, op de been

astonish, e-ston-nisj, v., verbazen

astound, e-staund, v., ontzetten

astray, e-stree, to go ——, v., verdwalen

astride, e-straid, adv., schrijlings

astronomer, es-tron-ne-m'r, s., sterrenkundige

astute, es-tjoet, a., slim, sluw, geslepen   [c.

astuteness, es-tjoet-nis, s., slimheid c., sluwheid

asunder, e-san-d'r, adv., uiteen, in stukken   [c.

asylum, e-sai-lum, s., schuilplaats c.; (mental) gekkenhuis n.

at, et, prep., aan, op, in, van, bij, om; —— **home**, thuis; —— **once**, dadelijk; tegelijk; —— **times**, nu en dan

athlete, eth-liet, s., atleet c.   [over

athwart, e-thwoart, adv. & prep., dwars, dwars

atom, et-tum, s., atoom n.; (fig.) greintje n.

atone, e-toon, v., boeten; ——**ment**, s., boete c.

atrocious, e-tro-sjus, a., afgrijselijk

atrophy, et-tre-fi, s., verkwijning c.

attach, e-tetsj, v., vastmaken; vasthechten; ——**able**, a., hechtbaar; ——**ment**, s., aanhankelijkheid c.

attack, e-tek, v., aanvallen. s., aanval c.

attain, e-teen, v., bereiken, verkrijgen; —— ment, s., bereiking c.; ——ments, s.pl., talenten n.pl.

attempt, e-tempt, v., pogen; ondernemen. s., poging c.; (attack) aanslag c.

attend, e-tend, v., (serve) bedienen; (nurse) verplegen; (escort) begeleiden; —— to, zorgen voor; ——ance, s., bediening c.

attendant, e-ten-d'nt, s., (servant, waiter) bediende c.; (keeper) oppasser c.; (escort, companion) begeleider c.

attention, e-ten-sjun, s., aandacht c.

attest, e-test, v., verklaren, bevestigen

attic, et-tik, s., dakkamertje n.; vliering c.

attire, e-tair, v., kleden, tooien. s., kleding c.

attitude, et-ti-tjoed, s., houding c.; standpunt n.

attorney, e-toar-ni, s., procureur c.; power of ——, volmacht c.

attract, e-trekt, v., aantrekken; ——ion, s., aantrekking c.; (personal) aantrekkelijkheid c.; ——ive, a., aantrekkelijk

attribute, e-trib-joet, v., toeschrijven. s., eigenschap c.

auburn, oa-b'n, a., kastanjebruin, roodbruin

auction, oak-sjun, v., veilen. s., veiling c.; ——eer, afslager c.

audacious, oa-dee-sjus, a., vermetel; brutaal

audacity, oa-des-si-ti, s., vermetelheid c.

audible, oa-di-b'l, a., hoorbaar [c.pl.

audience, oa-di-'ns, s., gehoor n.; toehoorders

audit, oa-dit, v., nazien. s., nazien der rekeningen n.; ——or, accountant c.; (hearer) toehoorder c.

augment, oaG-ment, v., vermeerderen, vergroten

augur, oa-Gur, s., voorspeller c. v., voorspellen

August, oa-Gust, s., augustus c.

august, oa-Gust, a., groots, verheven

aunt, aant, s., tante c.

auspicious, oa-spis-sjus, a., gunstig

austere, oa-stier, a., streng; stuurs; strikt

authentic, oa-then-tik, a., authentiek, echt

author, oa-thur, s., dader c.; schrijver c.
authoritative, oa-**thor**-ri-tee-tiv, a., gebiedend
authority, oa-**thor**-ri-ti, s., autoriteit c.; gezag n.
authorize, oa-the-raiz, v., machtigen; wettigen
autocar, oa-to-kaar, s., automobiel c.
automatic, oa-te-**met**-tik, a., automatisch
autumn, oa-tum, s., herfst c.
auxiliary, oag-zil-li-e-ri, s., hulp c.; helper c.
avail, e-veel, v., baten; —— oneself of, benutten. s., baat c., nut n.
available, e-veel-e-b'l, a., beschikbaar; geldig
avalanche, ev-ve-laansj, s., lawine c.
avaricious, ev-ve-**ris**-sjus, a., gierig, hebzuchtig
avenge, e-vendzj, v., wreken
avenue, ev-vi-njoe, s., laan c.; toegang c.
average, ev-ve-ridzj, s., gemiddelde n. a., gemiddeld
averse, e-veurs, a., afkerig
aversion, e-veur-sjun, s., afkeer c., tegenzin c.
avert, e-veurt, v., afwenden, afkeren
aviary, ee-vi-e-ri, s., volière c.
aviation, ee-vi-ee-sjun, s., luchtvaart c.
avidity, e-vid-di-ti, s., begeerte c., hebzucht c.
avocation, ev-ve-kee-sjun, s., beroep n.; werk n.
avoid, e-void, v., vermijden; uitwijken voor
avoidance, e-void-'ns, s., vermijding c.
avow, e-vau, v., erkennen; bekennen
avowal, e-vau-'l, s., belijdenis c.; bekentenis c.
await, e-weet, v., afwachten; wachten op
awake(n), e-week(-'n), v., ontwaken; (arouse)
   wekken. a., wakker
awakening, e-wee-ke-ning, s., ontwaken n.
award, e-woard, s., beslissing c. v., toekennen
aware, e-wèr, a., zich bewust, gewaar
away, e-wee, adv., weg, voort; far ——, ver weg
awe, oa, s., eerbied c., ontzag n., vrees c.
awful, oa-foel, a., ontzaglijk; ontzagwekkend
awhile, e-wail, adv., voor enige tijd
awkward, oa-kwurd, a., onaangenaam; (clumsy)
   onhandig; ——ness, s., onhandigheid c.
awl, oal, s., els c., priem c.
awning, oa-ning, s., dekzeil n.; zonnescherm n.

awry, e-rai, a. & adv., scheef, schuin; verkeerd
axe, eks, s., bijl c.
azure, ee-zjur, s., hemelsblauw n. a., hemelsblauw

babble, beb-b'l, v., babbelen; wauwelen
baby, bee-bi, s., kindje n., kleintje n.
bachelor, bet-sje-l'r, s., vrijgezel c.
back, bek, s., rug c.; achterkant c. v., (support)
    ondersteunen; (bet) wedden op. adv., ach-
    teruit; (return) terug
backbone, bek-boon, s., (anatomy) ruggegraat c.;
    (fig.) karaktervastheid c.
background, bek-graund, s., achtergrond c.
backseat, bek-siet, s., achterbank c.
backslide, bek-slaid, v., afvallig worden
backward, bek-wurd, a., achterlijk
backwards, bek-wurds, adv., achteruit
backwater, bek-woa-ter, s., dood water n.
bacon, bee-k'n, s., spek n.   [slechtheid c.
bad, bed, a., slecht; bedorven; —— ness, s.,
badge, bedzj, s., insigne n.; ordeteken n.
badger, bed-zjur, s., das c. v., sarren
baffle, bef-f'l, v., verbijsteren; verijdelen
bag, baG, s., zak c., baal c.; vangst c.; buidel c.
baggage, beG-Gidzj, s., (mil.) bagage c.
bagpipe, beG-paip, s., doedelzak c.
bail, beel, s., borg c.; —— out, v., borg stellen
bailiff, bee-lif, s., deurwaarder c.
bait, beet, s., aas n. v., verlokken
baize, beez, s., baai c.; groen laken n.
bake, beek, v., bakken; braden
bakelite, bee-ki-lait, s., bakeliet n.
baker, bee-ker, s., bakker c.
bakery, bee-ke-ri, s., bakkerij c.
balance, bel-l'ns, s., evenwicht n.; (scales) weeg-
    schaal c.; (commercial) saldo n. v., wegen;
    vereffenen; ——sheet, s., balans c.
balcony, bel-ke-ni, s., balkon n.
bald, boald, a., kaal; (fig.) onopgesmukt
baldness, boald-nis, s., kaalheid c.
bale, beel, s., baal c. v., in balen pakken
baleful, beel-foel, a., verderfelijk, noodlottig

balk, boak, v., verijdelen. s., balk c.
ball, boal, s., bal c.; (dance) bal n.; (bullet) kogel c.
ballast, bel-lust, s., ballast c. v., ballasten
ballet, bel-lee, s., ballet n.
balloon, be-loen, s., ballon c., luchtballon c.
ballot, bel-lut, s., stembriefje n.; loting c.
balm, baam, s., balsem c.; balsemgeur c.
balsam, boal-sum, s., balsem c.; springzaad n.
baluster, bel-le-st'r, s., baluster c., spijl c.
bamboo, bem-boe, s., bamboe n. & c.
bamboozle, bem-boe-zul, v., beetnemen
ban, ben, s., banvloek c. v., verbannen
banana, be-na-na, s., banaan c., pisang c.
band, bend, s., band c., snoer n.; (music) muziek-
corps n.; (gang) bende c.; troep c.
bandage, ben-didzj, s., verband n. v., verbinden
bandbox, bend-boks, s., hoededoos c.
bandmaster, bend-maas-t'r, s., kapelmeester c.
bandy(-legged), ben-di(-leGd), a., met o-benen
bane, been, s., verderf n.; ——ful, a., verderfelijk
bang, beng, s., bons c., knal c. v., knallen
banish, ben-nisj, v., verbannen
banister, ben-nis-t'r, s., trapspijl c.
banisters, ben-nis-t'rs, s. pl., trapleuning c.
bank, bengk, s., bank c.; (river) wal c., dijk c.
v., indammen; (money) deponeren
bank-book, bengk-boek, s., kassiersboekje n.
banker, beng-k'r, s., bankier c.; bankhouder c.
bank-holiday, bengk-hol-li-di, s., beursvacantie
bank-note, bengk-noot, s., bankbiljet n. [c.
bankrupt, bengk-rapt, a., bankroet, failliet
bankruptcy, bengk-rapt-si, s., faillissement n.
banner, ben-n'r, s., banier c., vaandel n.
banquet, beng-kwit, s., feestmaal n. v., smullen
banter, ben-t'r, s., scherts c. v., gekscheren
baptism, bep-tizm, s., doop c., doopsel n.
bar, baar, v., versperren. s., stang c., staaf c.;
(drinks) buffet n.; (chocolate) reep c.; (mus.)
maatstreep c.; (law) balie c.
barb, baarb, s., weerhaak c.; (fish) baard c.
barbarian, baar-bèr-jun, s., barbaar c. a., barbaars

barbarity, baar-ber-ri-ti, s., barbaarsheid c.

barbed, baar-b'd, —— wire, s., prikkeldraad c.

barber, baar-b'r, s., barbier c.

bard, baard, s., bard c., zanger c.

bare, bèr, a., naakt, bloot. v., ontbloten; ——
faced, a., onbeschaamd; ——footed, blootsvoets; ——headed, blootshoofds; ——ly,
adv., openlijk; nauwelijks; ——ness, s.,
naaktheid c.

bargain, baar-Gin, s., koop c., koopje n. v.,
afdingen

barge, baardzj, s., schuit c., aak c.

bark, baark, v., blaffen. s., geblaf n.; (tree) schors
[c.

barley, baar-li, s., gerst c.

barmaid, baar-meed, s., buffetjuffrouw c.

barn, baarn, s., schuur c.

barometer, be-rom-mi-t'r, s., barometer c.

baron, ber-run, s., baron c.

baroness, ber-re-nis, s., barones c.

barracks, ber-ruks, s.pl., kazerne c.

barrel, ber-rul, s., vat n., ton c.; (gun) loop c.

barren, ber-run, a., onvruchtbaar; dor

barrier, ber-ri-ur, s., slagboom c.; hinderpaal c.

barrister, ber-ris-t'r, s., advocaat c.

barrow, ber-ro, s., kruiwagen c., handwagen c.

barter, baar-tur, v., ruilen. s., ruilhandel c.

base, bees, v., baseren. s., basis c., grondslag c.;
(pedestal) voetstuk n. a., laag

baseless, bees-lis, a., ongegrond

basement, bees-m'nt, s., souterrain n.

baseness, bees-nis, s., laagheid c.

bashful, besj-foel, a., bedeesd, schuchter

bashfulness, besj-foel-nis, s., schuchterheid c.

basin, bee-s'n, s., schaal c., kom c.

basis, bee-sis, s., basis c., grondslag c.

bask, baask, v., zich koesteren

basket, baas-kit, s., mand c., korf c.

bass, bees, s., (mus.) bas c.; (fish) baars c.

bassoon, be-soen, s., (mus.) fagot c.

bastard, bes-turd, a., onecht. s., bastaard c.

baste, beest, v., met vet overgieten

bat, bet, s., vleermuis c.; knuppel c.

batch, betsj, s., troep c., partij c.
bath, baath, s., bad n.; ———**chair**, rolstoel c.; ———**room**, badkamer c.; **shower** ———, stortbad n., douche c.
bathe, beedh, v., baden; ———r, s., bader c.
batten, bet-t'n, s., lat c. v., zich vetmesten
batter, bet-t'r, s., beslag n. v., beuken
battle, bet-t'l, s., veldslag c.; strijd c.
battleship, bet-t'l-sjip, s., slagschip n.
bawl, boal, v., schreeuwen, bulken
bay, bee, s., (geographical) baai c.; (horse) vós c. v., blaffen; ———**tree**, s., laurierboom c.
bayonet, bee-e-nit, s., bajonet c.
be, bie, v., zijn; worden; gebeuren
beach, bietsj, s., strand n., kust c.
beacon, bie-k'n, s., baken n.
bead, bied, s., (glass) kraal c.; (fig.) parel c.
beadle, bied-d'l, s., pedel c.; bode c.
beagle, bieg-'l, s., brak c.; (fig.) speurhond c.
beak, biek, s., bek c., snavel c., sneb c.
beam, biem, s., balk c.; (light) straal c.
beaming, bie-ming, a., stralend
bean, bien, s., boon c.
bear, bèr, s., beer c.; (speculator) baissier c. v., dragen; (endure) verdragen, dulden; (produce) voortbrengen; ———**able**, a., te dragen; ———**er**, s., drager c.; (mech.) beer c.; ———**ing**, s., (behaviour) gedrag c.; (mech.) lager n. **take one's** ———**ings**, v., zich oriënteren
beard, bierd, s., baard c.; ———**ed**, a., gebaard
beardless, bierd-lis, a., baardeloos
beast, biest, s., beest n., dier n.; (fig.) beest n.
beastly, biest-li, adv. & a., beestig, gemeen
beat, biet, s., klap c.; (pulse) slag c.; (mus.) maat c. v., slaan; (thrash) afranselen; (conquer) verslaan
beautiful, bjoe-ti-foel, a., schoon, mooi
beautify, bjoe-ti-fai, v., verfraaien, versieren
beauty, bjoe-ti, s., schoonheid c.; ———**spot**, moesje n., schoonheidspleistertje n.
beaver, bie-v'r, s., bever c.; (fur) vilt c.
becalm, bi-kaam, v., stillen, bedaren

because, bi-koaz, conj., omdat; —— **of**, prep., wegens

beckon, bek-k'n, v., wenken, een wenk geven

become, bi-kam, v., worden; betamen

becoming, bi-kam-ming, a., (conduct) betamelijk; (dress) goed staand

bed, bed, s., bed n.; **flower** ——, bloembed n.; ——**ding**, beddegoed n.; ——**pan**, bedwarmer c.; ——**ridden**, a., bedlegerig; ——**room**, s., slaapkamer c.; ——**stead**, ledikant n.

bedeck, bi-dek, v., tooien, versieren

bedew, bi-djoe, v., bedauwen, bevochtigen

bee, bie, s., bij c.; ——**hive**, bijenkorf c.

beech, bietsj, s., beuk c.; beukenhout n.

beef, bief, s., rundvlees n.

beefsteak, bief-steek, s., runderlapje n.

beer, bier, s., bier n.

beet, biet, s., biet c.; ——**root**, beetwortel c.

beetle, biet-'l, s., tor c., kever c. v., stampen

befall, bi-foal, v., overkomen; gebeuren

befitting, bi-fit-ting, a., passend, voegzaam

before, bi-foar, prep., voor. adv., te voren

beforehand, bi-foar-hend, adv., van te voren

befoul, bi-faul, v., bevuilen

befriend, bi-frend, v., begunstigen

beg, beG, v., (request) vragen; (alms) bedelen; ——**gar**, s., bedelaar c.; ——**ging**, (alms) gebedel n.

beget, bi-Get, v., verwekken

begin, bi-Gin, v., beginnen, aanvangen; ——**ner**, s., beginneling c.; ——**ning**, begin n.

begone!, bi-Gon, interj., ga heen! ga weg!

begrime, bi-Graim, v., bemorsen

begrudge, bi-Gradzj, v., misgunnen

beguile, bi-Gail, v., bedriegen; bekoren

behalf, bi-haaf, on —— **of**, prep., uit naam van

behave, bi-heev, v., zich gedragen

behaviour, bi-heev-jur, s., gedrag n.

behead, bi-hed, v., onthoofden

behind, bi-haind, prep., achter. adv., van achter

behindhand, bi-haind-hend, a., achterstallig

behold, bi-hoold, v., aanschouwen. interj., ziedaar!

behove, bi-hoov, v., betamen

being, bie-ing, s., bestaan n.; (human) wezen n.

belabour, bi-lee-bur, v., (thrash) afrossen

belated, bi-lee-tid, a., verlaat, te laat

belch, beltsj, v., uitbraken; (pop.) boeren

beleaguer, bi-lie-Gur, v., belegeren

belfry, bel-fri, s., klokketoren c.

belie, bi-lai, v., logenstraffen

belief, bi-lief, s., geloof n.

believe, bi-liev, v., geloven

believer, bi-liev-ur, s., gelovige c.

belittle, bi-lit-'l, v., kleineren

bell, bel, s., bel c.; klok c.; schel c.

belligerent, bel-lid-zje-r'nt, a., strijdlustig

bellow, bel-lo, v., brullen, bulken. s., gebulk n.

bellows, bel-looz, s.pl., blaasbalg c.

belly, bel-li, s., buik c.; schoot c.

belong, bi-long, v., toebehoren

belongings, bi-long-ingz, s.pl., bezittingen c.pl.

beloved, be-lavd, a., geliefd, bemind

below, bi-lo, prep., onder. adv., naar beneden

belt, belt, s., gordel c., riem c.; (mil.) koppel c. v., omgorden

bemoan, bi-moon, v., bejammeren, bewenen

bench, bentsj, s., bank c.; (law) rechtbank c.

bend, bend, v., buigen. s., buiging c.; (road) bocht c.

beneath, bi-nieth, prep. & adv., beneden, onder

benediction, ben-ni-dik-sjun, s., zegen c.; lof n.

benefactor, ben-ni-fek-t'r, s., weldoener c.

benefice, ben-ni-fis, s., voorrecht n.

beneficence, bi-nef-fi-s'ns, s., weldadigheid c.

beneficial, ben-ni-fis-sjul, a., nuttig, voordelig

beneficiary, ben-ni-fis-sje-ri, s., begunstigde c.

benefit, ben-ni-fit, s., voordeel n.; nut n.

benevolence, bi-nev-ve-l'ns, s., welwillendheid c.

benevolent, bi-nev-ve-l'nt, a., welwillend

benign, bi-nain, a., goedaardig, vriendelijk

benignant, bi-niG-n'nt, a., genadig, gunstig

bent, bent, s., (fig.) neiging c., aanleg c.

benumb, bi-nam, v., verkleumen, verdoven

benzine, ben-zien, s., benzine c.

bequeath, bi-kwiedh, v., vermaken, nalaten

bequest, bi-kwest, s., legaat n.

bereave, bi-riev, v., beroven

bereavement, bi-riev-m'nt, s., beroving c.; verlies n.

berry, ber-ri, s., bes c.

berth, beurth, s., (cabin) kooi c., hut c.; (on a train) bed n.; (anchorage) ankerplaats c.; (position) baantje n. v., meren

beseech, bi-sietsj, v., smeken

beset, bi-set, v., omringen; aanvallen

beside, bi-said, prep., naast; buiten

besides, bi-saidz, adv., bovendien; behalve

besiege, bi-siedzj, v., belegeren; bestormen

besmear, bi-smier, v., besmeren, bezoedelen

besotted, bi-sot-tid, a., verdwaasd; dronken

bespangle, bi-speng-gul, v., bezaaien

bespatter, bi-spet-t'r, v., bespatten, besmeuren

bespeak, bi-spiek, v., bespreken, bestellen

besprinkle, bi-spring-k'l, v., besprenkelen

best, best, a., best. adv., het best. v., overtreffen

bestial, bes-ti-ul, a., dierlijk, beestachtig

bestir (oneself), bi-steur (wan-self), v., zich reppen

bestow, bi-sto, v., verlenen, schenken

bestowal, bi-sto-ul, s., schenking c., gift c.

bestrew, bi-stroe, v., bestrooien [den

bet, bet, s., weddenschap c. v., wedden, verwed-

betake (oneself), bi-teek (wan-self), v., zich begeven

betoken, bi-to-kun, v., aanduiden, voorspellen

betray, bi-tree, v., verraden; (seduce) verleiden

betrayal, bi-tree-ul, s., verraad n.; verleiding c.

betroth, bi-trodh, v., verloven

betrothal, bi-tro-dhul, s., verloving c.

better, bet-t'r, a. & adv., beter. v., verbeteren; beter worden

better, bettor, bet-t'r, s., wedder c.

betterment, bet-t'r-m'nt, s., verbetering c.

betting, bet-ting, s., wedden n.

between, bi-twïcn, prep., tussen; ——ourselves, onder ons gezegd. adv., er tussen in
bevel, bev-'l, a., schuin. s., helling c. v., afkanten
beverage, bev-ve-ridzj, s., drank c.
bevy, bev-vi, s., troep c., gezelschap n.
bewail, bi-weel, v., bewenen, bejammeren
beware, bi-wèr, v., oppassen, zich hoeden
bewilder, bi-wil-d'r, v., verbijsteren [c.
bewilderment, bi-wil-d'r-m'nt, s., verbijstering
bewitch, bi-witsj, v., beheksen, betoveren
beyond, bi-jond, prep. & adv., aan de andere zijde
bias, bai-us, s., vooroordeel n. v., bevooroordelen
bible, bai-b'l, s., bijbel c.
bibulous, bib-joe-lus, a., opslorpend; drank-
zuchtig
bicker, bik-k'r, v., kibbelen; kabbelen
bickering, bik-ke-ring, s., gekibbel n.
bicycle, bai-sik-'l, s., fiets c. v., fietsen
bid, bid, s., (at a sale) bod n. v., bieden; (order)
bevelen
bidder, bid-d'r, s., bieder c.
bidding, bid-ding, s., bieden n., bod n.; bevel n.
bide, baid, v., afwachten, wachten
bier, bier, s., lijkbaar c., baar c.
big, big, a., dik; groot; (important) voornaam
bigness, big-nis, s., grootte c.; dikte c.
bigot, big-Gut, s., dweper c.; (pious) kwezel c.
bigoted, big-Ge-tid, a., kwezelachtig
bilberry, bil-be-ri, s., blauwe bosbes c.
bile, bail, s., gal c.
bilious, bil-jus, a., galachtig; gal . . .
bilk, bilk, v., (pop.) bedotten, beetnemen
bill, bil, s., rekening c.; (of exchange) wissel c.;
(poster) aanplakbiljet n.; (parliament) wets-
ontwerp n.; (bird) snavel c.; ——of fare,
billet, bil-lit, s., kwartier n. [menu l.
billiards, bil-jurdz, s.pl., biljart n.
bin, bin, s., kist c., bak c.; (wine) wijnrek n.
bind, baind, v., binden; (books) inbinden; (vow)
verplichten; (fetter) vastbinden; ——up,
verbinden; ——ing, s., (books) band c. a.,
verplichtend

binocular(s), bai-**nok**-joe-l'r(z), s., veldkijker c.
biography, bai-**oG**-Gre-fi, s., levensbeschrijving c.
biplane, bai-pleen, s., tweedekker c.
birch, beurtsj, s., (tree) berk c.; (rod) roede c.
v. met de roede straffen
bird, beurd, s., vogel c.; —— of passage,
trekvogel c.; —— of prey, roofvogel c.
birth, beurth, s., geboorte c., afkomst c.
birthday, beurth-dee, s., verjaardag c.
birthmark, beurth-maark, s., moedervlek c.
birthplace, beurth-plees, s., geboorteplaats c.
birthrate, beurth-reet, s., geboortecijfer n.
biscuit, bis-kit, s., beschuit c., koekje n.
bishop, bis-sjup, s., bisschop c.; (chess) raads-
heer c.
bit, bit, s., beetje n., stukje n.; (horse) gebit n.
bitch, bitsj, s., teef c.
bite, bait, s., beet c., hap c. v., bijten
biting, bai-ting, a., bijtend; (wind) scherp
bitter, bit-t'r, a., bitter; ——ness, s., bitterheid c.
black, blek, s., zwart n. a., zwart; (gloomy)
donker. v., zwart maken; (shoes) poetsen
blackbeetle, blek-biet-'l, s., kakkerlak c.
blackberry, blek-be-ri, s., braambes c.
blackbird, blek-beurd, s., merel c.
black-currant, blek-**kar**-'nt, s., zwarte bes c.
blacken, blek-k'n, v., zwart maken
blackguard, bleG-Gaard, s., schurk c., ploert c.
blacking, blek-king, s., schoensmeer c.
blacklead, blek-led, s., potlood n.
blackleg, blek-leG, s., onderkruiper c.
blackmail, blek-meel, s., geldafdreiging c. v.,
geld afdreigen; ——er, s., chanteur c.
blacksmith, blek-smith, s., smid c.
blackthorn, blek-thoarn, s., sleedoorn c.
bladder, bled-d'r, s., blaas c.; blaar c.
blade, bled, s., kling c.; (grass) grasspriet c.;
(oar) blad n.; (razor) scheermesje n.
blame, bleem, s., blaam c. v., berispen
blameless, bleem-lis, a., onberispelijk
blanch, blaansj, v., bleken
bland, blend, a., zacht, vriendelijk

blandishment, blen-disj-m'nt, s., vleierij c.

blank, blengk, s., leegte c., leemte c. a., **(vacant)** leeg; (page) onbeschreven; (pure) zuiver

blanket, bleng-kit, s., deken c.

blare, blèr, s., geschal n. v., schallen

blaspheme, bles-fiem, v., lasteren, vloeken

blasphemy, bles-fi-mi, s., godslastering c.

blast, blaast, v., (explode) laten springen; (fig.) vernietigen. s., (gust) windstoot c.; (trumpet) stoot c.

blatant, blee-t'nt, a., schreeuwerig; opvallend

blaze, bleez, v., gloeien; opvlammen; schitteren. s., (glow) gloed c.; (flame) vlam c.

bleach, blietsj, v., bleken

bleak, bliek, a., (cold) guur; (bare) kaal

bleat, bliet, v., blaten. s., geblaat n.

bleed, blied, v., bloeden; aderlaten

bleeding, blie-ding, s., bloeding c.; aderlating c.

blemish, blem-misj, s., vlek c. v., bevlekken

blend, blend, v., mengen. s., mengsel n.

bless, bles, v., zegenen; ——**ed,** a., zalig

blessing, bles-sing, s., zegening c., zegen c.

blight, blait, s., (plant) meeldauw c. v., aantasten

blind, blaind, a., blind. v., verblinden. s., (window) rolgordijn n.; (Venetian) jalouzie c.; ——**fold,** v., blinddoeken; ——**man,** s., blinde c.; ——**ness,** blindheid c.

blink, blingk, v., knipogen; gluren [c.pl.]

blinkers, bling-kurz, s.pl., stofbril c.; oogkleppen

bliss, blis, s., zaligheid c.; ——**full,** a., zalig

blister, blis-t'r, s., blaar c. v., blaren

blithe, blaidh, a., blij, lustig

blizzard, bliz-zurd, s., koude sneeuwstorm c.

bloat, bloot, v., opzwellen

bloater, blo-t'r, s., verse bokking c.

block, blok, v., belemmeren, versperren. s., (wood) blok n.; (traffic) stremming c.; ——**ade, blokkade** c.; ——**head,** domkop c.

blood, blad, s., bloed n.; ——**hound,** bloedhond c.; ——**shed,** bloedbad n.; ——**shot,** a., met bloed belopen; ——**thirsty,** bloeddorstig; ——**y,** bloederig; (vulg.) donders

bloom, bloem, s., bloei c. v., bloeien

blooming, bloe-ming, a., bloeiend, stralend

blossom, blos-sum, s., bloesem c. v., bloeien

blot, blot, v., bezoedelen; (dry) vloeien. s., (ink) vlek c.; (blemish) smet c.; ——**ting-paper,** vloeipapier n.

blotch, blotsj, s., (boil) puist c.; (blot) klad c.

blouse, blauz, s., kiel c.; blouse c.

blow, blo, s., slag c.; (blast) windvlaag c. v., blazen; (wind) waaien; (nose) snuiten; —— **up,** (tyres) oppompen; (explode) in de lucht laten vliegen

blowpipe, blo-paip, s., blaaspijp c.

blubber, blab-b'r, s., walvisspek n. v., grienen

bludgeon, blad-zjun, s., knuppel c.

blue, bloe, s., blauw n.; blauwsel n. a., blauw; ——**bell,** s., grasklokje n.; ——**stocking** blauwkous c.

bluff, blaf, s., brutale grootspraak c.

bluish, bloe-isj, a., blauwachtig

blunder, blan-d'r, s., flater c., bok c.

blunt, blant, a., stomp; dom. v., afstompen

bluntness, blant-nis, s., botheid c.

blur, bleur, v., benevelen. s., klad c.

blurt (out), bleurt (aut), v., eruit flappen

blush, blasj, v., blozen. s., blos c.

bluster, blas-t'r, s., geraas c. v., razen; (boast) snoeven; ——**er,** s., opschepper c.; ——**ing,** a., tierend

boar, boar, s., beer c.; **wild** ——, wild zwijn n.

board, board, s., plank c.; (directors) raad c.; (food) kost c.; (naut.) boord n. v., beplanken; in de kost zijn; **notice**——, s., aanplakbord n.; ——**er,** kostganger c.; ——**ing-house,** kosthuis n.; ——**ing-school,** kostschool c.

boast, boost, v., bluffen, pochen. s., bluf c.

boaster, boos-t'r, s., snoever c., opschepper c.

boat, boot, s., boot c.; (rowing) schuit c.; **motor-**——, motorboot c.; **steam-**——, stoomboot c.

boat-hook, boot-hoek, s., bootshaak c. [c.

boating, boo-ting, s., bootjevaren n.

boatman, boot-m'n, s., botenverhuurder c.

boatswain, bo-s'n, s., bootsman c.

bob, bob, v., dobberen; (bow) knikken

bobbin, bob-bin, s., spoel c.; klos c.

bode, bood, v., voorspellen

bodice, bod-dis, s., lijfje n., keursje n.

bodily, bod-di-li, a. & adv., lichamelijk

bodkin, bod-kin, s., priem c., rijgpen c.

body, bod-di, s., lichaam n.; (corpse) lijk n.

bog, bog, s., moeras n.; —**gy,** a., moerassig

bogey (bogy), bo-Gi, s., (children's) boeman c.

bogie, bo-Gi, s., draaibaar onderstel n.

boil, boil, v., koken, zieden. s., steenpuist c.

boiler, boi-l'r, s., stoomketel c., waterketel c.

boisterous, bois-te-rus, a., onstuimig, rumoerig

bold, boold, a., moedig, stout; (vigorous) krachtig

boldness, boold-nis, s., stoutmoedigheid c.

bolster, bool-st'r, s., peluw c.; — **up,** v., steunen

bolt, boolt, v., grendelen; (horse) op hol gaan. s., grendel c.; (lightning) bliksemstraal c.

bomb, bom, s., bom c. v., bombarderen

bombard, bom-baard, v., bombarderen

bombastic, bom-bes-tik, a., bombastisch

bond, bond, s., (obligation) verplichting c.; (tie) band c.; (stock) schuldbekentenis c.; **in** —, (customs) in entrepot

bondage, bon-didzj, s., slavernij c.

bone, boon, s., been n., bot n.; (fish) graat c.

bonfire, bon-fair, s., vreugdevuur n.   [c.

bonnet, bon-nit, s., kapothoed c.; (car) motorkap

bonus, bo-nus, s., premie c.; bijslag c.

bony, bo-ni, a., benig; potig

book, boek, s., boek n. v., boeken, bespreken

bookbinder, boek-bain-d'r, s., boekbinder c.

book-case, boek-kees, s., boekenkast c.   [n.

booking-office, boe-king-of-fis, s., plaatsbureau

book-keeper, boek-kie-p'r, s., boekhouder c.

book-keeping, boek-kie-ping, s., boekhouden n.

book-mark, boek-maark, s., leeswijzer c.

bookseller, boek-sel-l'r, s., boekhandelaar c.

bookshop, boek-sjop, s., boekwinkel c.

bookstall, boek-stoal, s., boekenstalletje n.

bookworm, boek-weurm, s., boekenwurm c.

boom, boem, s., (commercial) prijsstijging c.; (spar) spier c.; (noise) gedreun n. v., (prices) in de hoogte gaan; (noise) dreunen

boon, boen, s., zegen c., weldaad c.

boor, boe-ur, s., lomperd c., boerenkinkel c.

boorish, boe-ur-isj, a., boers, pummelig

boot, boet, s., laars c.; hoge schoen c.

booth, boodh, s., kraam c., tent c.

booty, boe-ti, s., buit c., roof c.

border, boar-d'r, s., (ornamental edge) zoom c.; (frontier) grens c. v., omzomen; begrenzen

bordering, boar-de-ring, a., aangrenzend

bore, boar, v., doorboren; (weary) vervelen. s., (gun) ziel c.; (person) vervelende vent c.

born, boarn, a., geboren

borough, bar-re, s., stad c., stedelijke gemeente c.

borrow, bor-ro, v., lenen, ontlenen

bosom, boe-zum, s., boezem c., borst c.

botanist, bot-te-nist, s., plantkundige c.

both, booth, a., beide. conj., zowel . . . als

bother, bodh-'r, v., hinderen; zich zorgen maken

bottle, bot-tul, s., fles c. v., in flessen doen

bottom, bot-tum, s., bodem c.; grond c.; (seat) zitting c.; ——less, a., bodemloos

bough, bau, s., tak c.

bounce, bauns, v., springen. s., sprong c.

bound, baund, v., begrenzen; (jump) springen. s., sprong c.; ——ary, grens c.; —— for, a., op weg naar; —— to, (obliged) verplicht

bountiful, baun-ti-foel, a., mild; overvloedig

bounty, baun-ti, s., mildheid c.; premie c.

bout, baut, s., (turn) keer c.; (fit) aanval c.

bow, bo, s., (mus.) strijkstok c.; (curve) boog c.; (tie) strik c.

bow, bau, v., buigen; zich buigen. s., buiging c.; (ship) boeg c.

bowels, bau-ulz, s.pl., ingewanden n.pl.

bowl, bool, s., schaal c., kom. c.; (ball) kegelbal c. v., kegelen; bowlen; voortrollen

bowling-green, bo-ling-Grien, s., veld voor het balspel n.

BOX 348 **BRA**

box, boks, v., boksen. s., doos c., kist c., kistje n.; (theatre) loge c.; (on the ears) klap c., oorvijg c.; (tree) buksboom c.

boxing, bok-sing, s., boksen n.

boy, boi, s., jongen c., knaap c.; ——cott, v., boycotten. s., boycot c.; ——hood, jongens-jaren n.pl.

brace, brees, v., (tighten) spannen; (health) ver-sterken. s., (two) paar n.; (mech.) haak c.; ——s, pl., bretels c.pl.

bracelet, brees-lit, s., armband c.

bracing, bree-sing, a., versterkend, opfrissend

bracken, brek-k'n, s., adelaarsvaren c.

bracket, brek-kit, v., samenkoppelen. s., klamp c.; in ——s, tussen haakjes

brackish, brek-kisj, a., brak

brag, breg, v., bluffen; ——gart, s., bluffer c.

braid, breed, s., vlecht c.; haarlint n. v., vlechten

brain, breen, s., (mind) verstand n.; (substance) hersenen c.pl.

braise, breez, v., (meat) smoren

brake, breek, s., (mech.) rem c. v., remmen

bramble, brem-b'l, s., braamstruik c.

bran, bren, s., zemelen c.pl.

branch, brentsj, s., tak c.; (commercial) filiaal n.; —— off, v., zich vertakken

brand, brend, s., merk n., soort c.; (fire) brandend stuk hout n. v., brandmerken

brandish, bren-disj, v., zwaaien

brandy, bren-di, s., cognac c.; brandewijn c.

brass, braas, s., geel koper n. a., koperen

bravado, bre-va-do, s., grootspraak c.

brave, breev, a., moedig, dapper, flink

bravery, bree-ve-ri, s., dapperheid c., moed c.

bravo, bra-vo, interj., bravo! s., bravo c.

brawl, broal, v., kijven, razen. s., twist c.

brawn, broan, s., hoofdkaas c.; spierkracht c.

brawny, broa-ni, a., sterk, gespierd

bray, bree, v., (donkey) balken. s., gebalk n.

brazen, bree-z'n, a., (fig.) onbeschaamd

brazier, bree-zi-ur, s., koperslager c.; komfoor n.

brazil-nut, bre-zil-nøt, s., paranoot c.

breach, brietsj, s., breuk c.; schending c.

bread, bred, s., brood n.

breadth, bredth, s., breedte c.; strook c.

break, breek, v., breken; onderbreken; overtreden. s., breuk c.; onderbreking c.; pauze c.

breakage, bree-kidzj, s., breken n.

breakdown, breek-daun, s., defect n.; mislukking

breaker, bree-k'r, s., breker c. [c.

breakers, bree-k'rs, s.pl., branding c.

breakfast, brek-fust, s., ontbijt n. v., ontbijten

breakwater, breek-woa-t'r, s., golfbreker c.

bream, briem, s., brasem c.

breast, brest, s., borst c., boezem c.

breastbone, brest-boon, s., borstbeen n.

breastplate, brest-pleet, s., borstplaat c.

breath, breth, s., adem c.; zuchtje n.

breathe, briedh, v., ademen

breathless, breth-lis, a., buiten adem

bred, bred, a., opgevoed; opgefokt

breech, brietsj, s., (gun) stootbodem c.

breeches, briet-sjiz, s.pl., korte broek c.

breed, bried, v., opvoeden; opfokken. s., ras n.

breeder, brie-d'r, s., fokker c.

breeding, brie-ding, s., opvoeding c.

breeze, briez, s., bries c.; (fig.) ruzie c.

breezy, brie-zi, a., winderig; vrolijk, joviaal

brethren, bredh-rin, s.pl., broeders c.pl.

brevet, brev-vit, s., brevet n.

brevity, brev-vi-ti, s., kortheid c.

brew, broe, v., brouwen; (fig.) uitbroeden

brewer, broe-ur, s., brouwer c.

briar, brier, brai-ur, s., doornstruik c.

bribe, braib, v., omkopen. s., omkoopgeld n.

bribery, brai-be-ri, s., omkoperij c.

brick, brik, s., baksteen c.

bricklayer, brik-lee-ur, s., metselaar c.

bridal, brai-d'l, a., bruids . . ., huwelijks . . .

bride, braid, s., bruid c.; ——**groom,** bruidegom
c.; ——**smaid,** bruidsmeisje n.

bridge, bridzj, s., brug c. v., overbruggen

bridle, brai-d'l, s., teugel c. v., beteugelen

brief, brief, a., kort, beknopt. s., overzicht n.

brig, briG, s., brik c.

brigade, bri-Geed, s., brigade c.

brigadier, bri-Ge-dier, s., brigadecommandant c.

bright, brait, a., helder; (cheerful) opgewekt

brighten, brait-'n, v., opklaren

brightness, brait-nis, s., helderheid c.; (mind) pienterheid c.

brill, bril, s., griet c.

brilliancy, bril-jun-si, s., glans c., schittering c.

brilliant, bril-junt, a., schitterend, glansrijk

brim, brim, s., rand c. v., vol zijn; —— (over) with, overvloeien van

brimstone, brim-stoon, s., zwavel c.

brindled, brin-duld, a., gestreept

brine, brain, s., pekel c. v., pekelen

bring, bring, v., brengen; —— forward, (accounts) transporteren; —— in, (receipts) indienen; —— up, opvoeden

brink, bringk, s., rand c.

briny, brai-ni, a., pekelachtig, zout

brisk, brisk, a., (lively) levendig; (agile) vlug

brisket, bris-kit, s., borststuk n.

briskness, brisk-nis, s., levendigheid c.

bristle, bris-'l, s., borstelhaar n. v., de haren overeind zetten

bristling, bris-ling, a., opvliegend; borstelig

brittle, brit-'l, a., breekbaar, broos

brittleness, brit-'l-nis, s., broosheid c.

broach, brootsj, s., braadspit n.; (—— a subject) v., iets ter sprake brengen

broad, broad, a., breed, ruim, wijd

broadcast, broad-kaast, s., (radio) uitzending c. v., uitzenden, omroepen

broad-minded, broad-main-did, a., ruim van opvatting

brocade, bre-keed, s., brocaat n.

brogue, brooG, s., plat accent n.

broil, broil, v., roosteren. s., ruzie c.

broker, bro-k'r, s., makelaar c.; (second-hand furniture) uitdrager c.; **stock——**, effecten- makelaar c.; ——**age**, makelarij c.

bromide, bro-maid, s., bromide n.

bronchitis, brong-kai-tis, s., bronchitis c.

bronze, bronz, s., brons n. v., bronzen

brooch, brootsj, s., broche c., borstspeld c.

brood, broed, s., broedsel n. v., broeden

brook, broek, s., beek c. v., verdragen

broom, broem, s., bezem c.; (plant) brem c.

broth, broth, s., vleesnat n., bouillon c.

brothel, brodh-'l, s., bordeel n.

brother, brodh-'r, s., broer c.; ——**hood,** broederschap n.; ——**-in-law,** schoonbroer c.; ——**ly,** a., broederlijk

brow, brau, s., wenkbrauw c.; voorhoofd n.

browbeat, brau-biet, v., vrees aanjagen

brown, braun, a., bruin. v., bruinen

brownish, brau-nisj, a., bruinachtig

browse, brauz, v., afknabbelen, afgrazen

bruise, broez, s., kneuzing c., buil c. v., kneuzen

brunette, broe-net, s., brunette c.

brunt, brant, s., schok c.; geweld n.

brush, brasj, s., borstel c.; (painting) penseel n.; (thicket) kreupelhout n. v., afborstelen; (sweep) vegen

brushwood, brasj-woed, s., rijshout n.

brusque, brask, a., kortaf, brusk

Brussels sprouts, bras-'lz sprautz, s.pl., spruitjes n.pl.

brutal, broe-t'l, a., beestachtig; (cruel) wreed

brutality, broe-tel-li-ti, s., wreedheid c.; ruwheid

brutalize, broe-te-laiz, v., verdierlijken   [c.

brute, broet, s., wild dier n.; (fig.) onmens c.

bubble, bab-'l, s., bobbel c. v., pruttelen

buck, bak, s., (deer) reebok c.; mannetje n.

bucket, bak-kit, s., emmer c.

buckle, bak-'l, s., gesp c. v., vastgespen

buckskin, bak-skin, s., boksvel n.

buckwheat, bak-wiet, s., boekweit c.

bud, bad, s., knop c. v., uitkomen, ontluiken

budge, badzj, v., be:wegen, verroeren

budget, bad-zjit, s., begroting c.; (bag) zak c.

buff, baf, s., buffelleer n. a., lichtgeel

buffalo, baf-fe-lo, s., buffel c.

buffer, baf-f'r, s., (mech.) stootkussen n.

buffet, boe-fee, s., buffet n.

buffet, baf-fit, v., stoten, beuken

buffoon, baf-foen, s., potsenmaker c.

bug, baG, s., wandluis c.; ——bear, boeman c.

bugle, bjoe-Gul, s., (mil.) signaalhoorn c.

build, bild, v., bouwen. s., lichaamsbouw c.; ——er, bouwmeester c.; ——ing, gebouw n.

bulb, balb, s., bloembol c.; (lamp) peer c.

bulge, baldzj, v., uitpuilen. s., zwelling c.

bulk, balk, s., (volume) omvang c.; (cargo) lading c.; ——y, a., omvangrijk, lijvig

bull, boel, s., stier c.; (stock exchange) haussier c.; (papal) bul c.; ——dog, bulhond c.; ——dozer, graafmachine c.; ——finch, goudvink c.; ——ock, os c.; ——'s eye, (target) roos c.

bullet, boel-lit, s., kogel c.

bulletin, boel-li-tin, s., bulletin n.

bullion, boel-jun, s., ongemunt goud n.

bully, boel-li, s., bullebak c. v., pesten

bulrush, boel-rasj, s., lisdodde c.

bulwark, boel-wuk, s., (rampart) bolwerk n.; (naut.) verschansing c.; (fig.) bolwerk n.

bumble-bee, bam-b'l-bie, s., hommel c.

bump, bamp, s., bons c.; (swelling) buil c. v., stoten

bumper, bam-p'r, s., (glass) vol glas n.; (for motor-cars) buffer c., schokbreker c.

bumpkin, bamp-kin, s., boerenkinkel c.

bumptious, bamp-sjus, a., verwaand, opgeblazen

bunch, bantsj, v., aan bosjes binden. s., (fruits) tros c.; (keys) bos c.; —— of grapes, druiventros c.

bundle, band-'l, s., bundel c. v., samenbinden

bung, bang, s., spon c.; ——hole, spongat n.

bungalow, bang-Ge-lo, s., landhuisje n.

bungle, bang-Gul, v., knoeien. s., knoeiwerk n.

bungler, bang-Glur, s., knoeier c., prutser c.

bunion, ban-jun, s., eeltknobbel c.

bunker, bang-k'r, s., (naut.) kolenruim n.

bunkum, bang-kum, s., klets c., gezwam n.

bunting, ban-ting, s., vlaggedoek n.

buoy, boi, s., boei c.; **life——,** reddingsboei c.

buoyancy, boi-'n-si, s., drijfvermogen n.

buoyant, boi-'nt, a., drijvend; (fig.) opgewekt

burden, beur-d'n, s., last c., vracht c. v., belasten, bezwaren; **——some,** a., zwaar, drukkend

bureau, bjoe-ro, s., bureau n., schrijftafel c.

bureaucracy, bjoe-rok-kre-si, s., bureaucratie c.

burgess, beur-dzjis, s., burger c.

burgh, bar-re, see borough

burglar, beur-Glur, s., inbreker c.

burglary, beur-Gle-ri, s., inbraak c.

burial, ber-ri-'l, s., begrafenis c.

burial-ground, ber-ri-'l-graund, s., begraafplaats c.

burlesque, beur-lesk, a., koddig. s., klucht c.

burly, beur-li, a., groot, zwaar, dik

burn, beurn, v., branden; (destroy) verbranden; (food) aanbranden. s., brandwonde c.

burner, beur-n'r, s., brander c.

burnish, beur-nisj, v., polijsten, poetsen

burrow, bar-ro, v., graven, wroeten

bursar, beur-s'r, s., schatmeester c.

burst, beurst, v., doen barsten; openbarsten

bury, ber-ri, v., begraven; (conceal) verbergen

bus, bas, s., bus c.

bush, boesj, s., struik c.; (hair) haarbos c.

bushel, boesj-'l, s., schepel c.

bushy, boesj-i, a., ruig, gepluimd

business, biz-nis, s., bezigheid c.; zaak c.; beroep n.; **——like,** a., zakelijk; **——man,** s., zakenman c.

bust, bast, s., borstbeeld n., buste c.

bustle, bas-sul, s., gewoel n., drukte c. v., druk in de weer zijn, zich reppen

busy, biz-zi, a., bezig, druk. v., bezig houden

busybody, biz-zi-bod-di, s., bemoeial c.

but, bat, conj., maar. prep., zonder, behalve

butcher, boet-sjur, s., slager c. v., slachten

butler, bat-l'r, s., hoofdbediende c.

butt, bat, s., (target) mikpunt n.; (rifle) kolf c. v., stoten, botsen; **——s,** s.pl., schietbaan c.

butt-end, bat-end, s., uiteinde n.; kolf c.
butter, bat-t'r, s., boter c. v., smeren
buttercup, bat-t'r-**kap,** s., boterbloem c.
butter-dish, bat-t'r-disj, s., botervlootje n.
butterfly, bat-t'r-flai, s., vlinder c.
buttocks, bat-tuks, s.pl., achterste n.
button, bat-t'n, s., knoop c. v., vastknopen
button-hole, bat-t'n-hool, s., knoopsgat n.
buttress, bat-tris, s., stut c., steunpilaar c.
buxom, bak-sum, a., mollig, gezond en vrolijk
buy, bai, v., kopen; omkopen
buyer, bai-ur, s., koper c., inkoper c.
buzz, baz, v., gonzen. s., gegons n.
buzzard, baz-zurd, s., buizerd c.; (fig.) uil c.
by, bai, prep. bij; voorbij; langs; door; per;
   volgens; over. adv., nabij; erbij; voorbij
by-law, bai-loa, s., verordening c.
bystander, bai-sten-d'r, s., toeschouwer c.
byway, bai-wee, s., zijpad n., zijweg c.   [c.
byword, bai-weurd, s., spreekwoord n.; spotnaam

cab, keb, s., (motor) taxi c.; (horse) huurrijtuig n.
cabal, ke-bel, s., intrige c. v., samenspannen
cabbage, keb-bidzj, s., kool c.
cabin, keb-bin, s., hut c., kajuit c.
cabinet, keb-bi-nit, s., kastje n.; kabinet n.
cabinet-maker, keb-bi-nit-mee-k'r, s., schrijnwerker c.; kabinetsformateur c.
cable, kee-b'l, s., kabel c. v., telegraferen
cablegram, kee-b'l-Grem, s., kabeltelegram n.
cabman, keb-m'n, s., huurkoetsier c.; (taxi)
   chauffeur c.
cackle, kek-k'l, s., gekakel n. v., kakelen
cad, ked, s., ploert c., rotvent c.
caddy, ked-di, s., theekistje n.
cadge, kedzj, v., klaplopen; ——r, s., klaploper c.
cage, keedzj, s., kooi c.
cajole, ke-dzjool, v., vleien
cake, keek, s., koek c., gebak n.; (soap) stuk n.
calabash, kel-le-besj, s., kalebas c.
calamitous, ke-lem-mi-tus, a., noodlottig
calamity, ke-lem-mi-ti, s., onheil n., ramp c.

calcine, kel-sain, v., verkalken

calculate, kel-kjoe-leet, v., rekenen; berekenen

caldron, koal-dr'n, s., ketel c.

calendar, kel-lin-d'r, s., kalender c.

calf, kaaf, s., kalf n.; (leg) kuit c.

calico, kel-li-ko, s., calico n., katoen n.

call, koal, v., roepen; (name) noemen; (visit) bezoeken. s., geroep n.; (telephone) gesprek n.

callous, kel-lus, a. (fig.) ongevoelig

calm, kaam, s., kalmte c.; windstilte c. a., kalm, rustig. v., kalmeren, bedaren

calmness, kaam-nis, s., rust c., stilte c.

calumniate, ke-lum-ni-eet, v., belasteren

calumny, kel-lum-ni, s., laster c.

cambric, keem-brik, s., batist n.; zakdoek c.

camel, kem-'l, s., kameel c.

cameo, kem-mi-o, s., camee c.

camera, kem-me-ra, s., camera c.; in ——, met gesloten deuren

camisole, kem-mi-sool, s., onderlijfje n.

camomile, kem-me-mail, s., kamille c.

camp, kemp, v., kamperen. s., kamp n.; ——-bed, veldbed n.; ——-stool, vouwstoeltje n.

campaign, kem-peen, s., veldtocht c.

camphor, kem-f'r, s., kamfer c.

can, ken, s., kan c.; blik n. v., inmaken

can, ken, v., kunnen, vermogen

canal, ke-nel, s., kanaal n.

canary, ke-nèr-ri, s., kanarie c.

cancel, ken-s'l, v., doorhalen; vernietigen

cancer, ken-s'r, s., kanker c.

candid, ken-did, a., openhartig, eerlijk

candidate, ken-di-dit, s., kandidaat c.

candied, ken-did, a., met suiker ingelegd   [c.

candle, ken-d'l, s., kaars c.; ——-stick, kandelaar

candour, ken-d'r, s., oprechtheid c., eerlijkheid c.

candy, ken-di, s., kandij c.; v., met suiker inleggen

cane, keen, s., riet n.; rotting c. v., afrossen

canine, ken-nain, a., honds . . . s., hoektand c.

canister, ken-nis-t'r, s., bus c., trommel c.

canker, ken-k'r, s., mondkanker c.; (plants) kanker c.

cannibal, ken-ni-b'l, s., kannibaal c. [bole c.
cannon, ken-n'n, s., kanon n.; (billiards) caram-
canoe, ke-noe, s., kano c. v., kanoën
canon, ken-n'n, s., (mus.) canon c.; (church
   decree) kerkregel c.; (title) kanunnik c.
canopy, ken-ne-pi, s., baldakijn n., hemel c.
cant, kent, s., huicheltaal c. v., huichelen
cantankerous, ken-teng-ke-rus, a., twistziek
canteen, ken-tien, s., kantine c.
canter, ken-t'r, s., korte galop c.
canvas, ken-vus, s., zeildoek n.; linnen n.
canvass, ken-vus, v., (votes, etc.) werven
cap, kep, s., pet c., muts c.
capable, kee-pe-b'l, a., bekwaam; in staat
capacity, ke-pes-si-ti, s., (contents) inhoud c.;
   (ability) bekwaamheid c.; (position) bevoegdheid c.
cape, keep, s., kaap c.; (cover) cape c.
caper, kee-p'r, s., bokkesprong c. v., huppelen
capital, kep-pi-t'l, s., (money) kapitaal n.; (city)
   hoofdstad c.; (letter) hoofdletter c.
capitulate, ke-pit-joe-leet, v., capituleren
capon, kee-p'n, s., kapoen c.
capricious, ke-pris-sjus, a., grillig, nukkig
capsize, kep-saiz, v., omslaan; omwerpen
capstan, kep-stun, s., (naut.) kaapstander c.
capsule, kep-sjoel, s., capsule c.
captain, kep-tin, s., kapitein c. v., aanvoeren
captive, kep-tiv, a., gevangen. s., gevangene c.
captivity, kep-tiv-vi-ti, s., gevangenschap c.
capture, kept-sjur, s., vangst c.; gevangenneming
   c. v., gevangen nemen; veroveren
car, kaar, s., auto c.; wagen c.; (aero) gond c[.c.
caramel, ker-re-mel, s., karamel c.
carat, ker-rut, s., karaat n.
caravan, ker-re-ven, s., karavaan c.; woonwagen
caraway, ker-re-wee, s., (plant) karwij c. [c.
carbide, kaar-baid, s., carbid n.
carbine, kaar-bain, s., karabijn c.
carbolic, kaar-bol-lik, —— acid, s., carbol n.
carbon, kaar-b'n, s., koolstof c.; ——paper,**
   carbonpapier n.

carbuncle, kaar-bᴀng-k'l, s., (boil) puist c.; (gem) karbonkel c.

carburettor, kaar-bjoe-ret-t'r, s., carburateur c.

carcase, carcass, kaar-kus, s., lijk n.; wrak n.

card, kaard, s., kaart c., speelkaart c.; ——board, karton n.; ——board-box, kartonnen doos c.; ——case, visiteboekje n. [. . .

cardinal, kaar-di-n'l, s., kardinaal c. a., hoofd

care, kèr, s., (anxiety) bezorgdheid c.; (attention) zorg c.; (caution) voorzichtigheid c.; take ——!, interj., pas op! take —— of, v., zorgen voor; —— for, houden van, geven om; ——ful, a., zorgvuldig; voorzichtig; ——less, slordig; zorgeloos; ——lessness, s., slordigheid c.; c/o, per adres; ——taker, s., concierge c.

career, ke-rier, s., loopbaan c., carrière c.

caress, ke-res, v., liefkozen, s., liefkozing c.

cargo, kaar-ɢo, s., lading c.

caricature, ker-ri-ke-tjoer, s., karikatuur c.

carmine, kaar-main, s., karmijn n.

carnage, kaar-nidzj, s., bloedbad n., slachting c.

carnal, kaar-n'l, a., zinnelijk; vleselijk

carnation, kaar-nee-sjun, s., anjelier c.

carnival, kaar-ni-v'l, s., carnaval n., vastenavond

carol, ker-r'l, s., lied n., lofzang c. [c.

carp, kaarp, s., karper c. v., vitten

carpenter, kaar-pin-t'r, s., timmerman c.

carpet, kaar-pit, s., tapijt n., vloerkleed n.

carriage, ker-ridzj, s., rijtuig n.; (train) wagon c.; (freight) vracht c.; (deportment) gedrag n.

carrier, ker-ri-ur, s., vrachtrijder c.; (on bicycle) pakkendrager c.; ——pigeon, postduif c.

carrion, ker-ri-un, s., kreng n., aas n.

carrot, ker-r't, s., peen c., gele wortel c.

carry, ker-ri, v., dragen; —— on, doorgaan

cart, kaart, s., kar c., wagen c. v., vervoeren

cartage, kaar-tidzj, s., vervoer n.; (pay) sleep-loon n.

carter, kaar-t'r, s., voerman c., sleper c.

cartload, kaart-lood, s., karrevracht c.

cartoon, kaar-toen, s., spotprent c.; tekenfilm c.

cartridge, kaar-tridzj, s., patroon c.
carve, kaarv, v., kerven; (meat) voorsnijden
carving, kaar-ving, s., snijwerk n.
cascade, kes-keed, s., kleine waterval c.
case, kees, s., geval n.; (law) rechtszaak c.; (grammar) naamval c.; (box) kist c.; (cigarettes) étui n.; (violin) foedraal n.; (watch) kas c.; (books) boekenkast c.; **in** ——, ingeval
casement, kees-m'nt, s., openslaand venster n.
cash, kesj, s., kas c.; (ready money) contanten n.pl.; **in** ——, bij kas. v., verzilveren; innen
cash-book, kesj-boek, s., kasboek n.
cash-box, kesj-boks, s., geldkistje n.
cashier, kesj-ier, s., kassier c.
cashmere, kesj-mier, s., cachemir c., sjaal c.
cask, kaask, s., vat n., ton c.
casket, kaas-kit, s., kistje n., doos c.
cassock, kes-suk, s., toog c.
cast, kaast, s., worp c., gooi c.; (theatre) rolverdeling c.; (metal) vorm c. a., gegoten, giet . . . v., (throw) werpen; (metals) gieten; —— **-iron,** s., gietijzer n.
castanet, kes-te-net, s., castagnet c.
caste, kaast, s., kaste c.
castigate, kes-ti-Geet, v., tuchtigen, kastijden
castle, kaas-'l, s., kasteel n., slot n.
castor, kaas-t'r, s., (furniture bearings) rolletje n.
castor-oil, kaas-t'r-oil, s., wonderolie c.
casual, kez-joe-ul, a., toevallig; zonder plan
casualties, kez-joe-ul-teez, s.pl., slachtoffers n.pl.
casualty, kez-joe-ul-ti, s., ongeval n.
cat, ket, s., kat c.; **tom**——, kater c.
catalogue, ket-te-loG, s., catalogus c.
catarrh, ke-taar, s., catarre c.
catastrophe, ke-tes-tre-fi, s., ramp c., onheil n.
catch, ketsj, v., vangen; (seize) grijpen; —— **up,** inhalen. s., vangst c.; (trap) strikvraag c.; (profit) voordeel n.
catching, ket-sjing, a., aanstekelijk
catchword, ketsj-weurd, s., leus c.
category, ket-ti-Ge-ri, s., categorie c.
cater, kee-t'r, v., maaltijden verschaffen

caterer, kee-te-r'r, s., leverancier c.
caterpillar, kee-t'r-pil-l'r, s., rups c.
cathedral, ke-thie-dr'l, s., kathedraal c.
catholic, keth-e-lik, s., Katholiek c. a., Katholiek; algemeen; veelzijdig
cattle, ket-t'l, s., rundvee n., vee n.
cauliflower, kol-li-flau'r, s., bloemkool c.
caulk, koak, v., breeuwen, kalefateren
cause, koaz, s., oorzaak c., reden c. v., veroorzaken
causeway, koaz-wee, s., straatweg c.; dam c.
caustic, koas-tik, s., bijtmiddel n. a., bijtend, brandend; (fig.) sarcastisch
cauterize, koa-te-raiz, v., uitbranden
caution, koa-sjun, s., voorzichtigheid c. v., waarschuwen
cautious, koa-sjus, a., voorzichtig, omzichtig
cavalier, kev-ve-lier, s., ridder c., ruiter c.
cavalry, kev-v'l-ri, s., cavalerie c., ruiterij c.
cave, keev, s., hol n.; —— in, v., instorten
cavernous, kev-ve-nus, a., hol; vol spelonken
cavil, kev-vil, v., vitten. s., vitterij c.
cavity, kev-vi-ti, s., holte c.
caw, koa, v., krassen. s., gekras n. [peper c.
Cayenne pepper, kee-en pep-p'r, s., cayennecease, sies, v., ophouden, staken
ceaseless, sies-lis, a., onophoudelijk
cedar, sie-d'r, s., ceder c., cederboom c.
cede, sied, v., afstaan, opgeven
ceiling, sie-ling, s., plafond n., zoldering c.
celebrate, sel-li-breet, v., vieren; (extol) loven
celebrated, sel-li-bree-tid, a., beroemd
celerity, si-ler-ri-ti, s., snelheid c., spoed c.
celery, sel-le-ri, s., selderij c.
celestial, si-lest-jul, a., hemels
celibacy, sel-li-be-si, s., celibaat n.
cell, sel, s., cel c., kluis c.
cellar, sel-l'r, s., kelder c.
celluloid, sel-ljoe-loid, s., celluloid n.
cement, si-ment, s., cement n. v., cementeren
cemetery, sem-mi-tri, s., begraafplaats c.
censor, sen-s'r, s., censor c.; ——ship, censuur c.
census, sen-sus, s., volkstelling c.

cent, sent, s., honderd c.; (coin) cent c.
centenary, sen-tie-ne-ri, s., eeuwfeest n.
central, sen-tr'l, a., centraal, midden . . .; —— **heating,** s., centrale verwarming c.
centralize, sen-tre-laiz, v., centraliseren
centre, sen-t'r, s., middelpunt c., centrum n.
century, sent-sjoe-ri, s., eeuw c. [c.
ceramics, si-rem-miks, s.pl., pottenbakkerskunst
ceremonious, ser-ri-moon-jus, a., plechtstatig
ceremony, ser-ri-me-ni, s., ceremonie c.; (formality) formaliteit c.
certain(ly), seur-tin(li), a. & adv., zeker
certificate, seur-tif-fi-kit, s., getuigschrift n.
certify, seur-ti-fai, v., verklaren, verzekeren
certitude, seur-ti-tjoed, s., zekerheid c.
cessation, ses-see-sjun, s., ophouden n.
cession, ses-sjun, s., boedelafstand c., cessie c.
cesspool, ses-poel, s., zinkput c.; (fig.) poel c.
chafe, tsjeef, v., (rub) schuren; (fret) ergeren
chafing-dish, tsjee-fing-disj, s., komfoor n.
chaff, tsjaaf, s., kaf n.; plagerij c. v., plagen
chaffinch, tsjef-fintsj, s., boekvink c.
chain, tsjeen, s., ketting c. v., ketenen
chair, tsjèr, s., stoel c.
chairman, tsjèr-m'n, s., voorzitter c.
chaise, sjeez, s., sjees c.
chalice, tsjel-lis, s., kelk c.
chalk, tsjoak, s., krijt n. v., wit maken [dagen
challenge, tsjel-lindzj, s., uitdaging c. v., uit-
chalybeate, ke-lib-bi-it, a., ijzerhoudend
chamber, tsjeem-b'r, s., kamer c.; ——**pot,** nachtspiegel c.; ——**s,** (barrister) kantoor n.
chamberlain, tsjeem-b'r-lin, s., kamerheer c.
chambermaid, tsjeem-b'r-meed, s., kamer-meisje n.
chamois, sjem-wa, s., gems c.; (leather) zeem-leer n.
champagne, sjem-peen, s., champagne c.
champion, tsjem-pjun, s., kampioen c.
chance, tsjaans, s., (luck) toeval n.; (opportunity) gelegenheid c., kans c. a., toevallig. v., wagen

chancel, tsjaan-s'l, s., koor n.
chancellor, tsjaan-s'l-l'r, s., kanselier c.
chancery, tsjaan-se-ri, s., kanselarij c.
chandelier, sjen-de-lier, s., kroonluchter c.
change, tsjeendzj, s., (small money) kleingeld n.;
(alteration) verandering c.; (exchange) ver-
wisseling c. v., (alter) veranderen; (money)
wisselen; (trains) overstappen; (exchange)
verruilen
changeable, tsjeen-dzje-b'l, a., veranderlijk
changeless, tsjeendzj-lis, a., onveranderlijk
channel, tsjen-n'l, s., kanaal n. v., uithollen;
een kanaal graven
chant, tsjaant, s., gezang n. v., zingen
chaos, kee-os, s., chaos c., verwarring c.
chaotic, kee-ot-tik, a., chaotisch, verward
chap, tsjep, s., scheur c., spleet c.; (fellow) **vent** c.
v., scheuren, splijten
chapel, tsjep-p'l, s., kapel c.
chaperon, sjep-pe-roon, s., chaperon c.
chaplain, tsjep-lin, s., (mil.) aalmoezenier c.;
veldprediker c.
chaplet, tsjep-lit, s., krans c.; rozenhoedje n.
chapter, tsjep-t'r, s., hoofdstuk n.
char, tsjaar, v., verkolen, branden
character, ker-rik-t'r, s., karakter n.; letter c.
charcoal, tsjaar-kool, s., houtskool c.
charge, tsjaardzj, s., (load) last c.; (duty) taak c.;
(custody) hoede c.; (cost) kosten c.pl.;
(accusation) beschuldiging c.; (attack) aanval
c. v., (load) laden; (enjoin) bevelen; (accuse)
beschuldigen; (attack) aanvallen; (bill) in
rekening brengen
charily, tsjer-ri-li, adv., voorzichtig; zuinig
chariot, tsjer-ri-'t, s., strijdwagen c.
charitable, tsjer-ri-te-b'l, a., menslievend
charity, tsjer-ri-ti, s., liefde c.; liefdadigheid c.
charm, tsjaarm, s., tovermiddel n.; betovering c.
v., betoveren, bekoren
charming, tsjaar-ming, a., bekoorlijk; charmant
charnel-house, tsjaar-n'l-haus, s., knekelhuis n.
chart, tsjaart, s., tabel c.; (sea) zeekaart c.

charter, tsjaar-t'r, s., handvest n.; (privilege) voorrecht n. v., bevoorrechten; (ship) charteren

charwoman, tsjaar-woe-m'n, s., werkvrouw c.

chary, tsjèr-ri, a., voorzichtig; zuinig

chase, tsjees, s., jacht c. v., jagen; (pursue) achtervolgen

chasm, kezm, s., kloof c., afgrond c.

chaste, tsjeest, a., kuis, rein, zuiver

chasten, tsjees-t'n, v., zuiveren; (punish) kastijden

chastise, tsjes-taiz, v., kastijden, tuchtigen

chastity, tsjes-ti-ti, s., kuisheid c.

chasuble, tsjez-joe-b'l, s., kazuifel n.

chat, tsjet, v., keuvelen. s., gekeuvel n.

chattels, tsjet-t'lz, s.pl., bezitting c., goed n.

chatter, tsjet-t'r, s., gekakel n. v., kakelen; (teeth) klapperen; ——**box,** s., babbelkous c.

chauffeur, sjo-f'r, s., chauffeur c.

cheap, tsjiep, a., goedkoop; minderwaardig

cheapen, tsjiep-'n, v., (haggle) afdingen; in prijs verminderen

cheat, tsjiet, v., bedriegen. s., bedrog n.; (person) bedrieger c.

check, tsjèk, s., (restraint) belemmering c.; (chess) schaak n.; (control) contrôle c.; (identification) reçu n. v., belemmeren; (stop) tegenhouden; (verify) controleren; ——**mate,** s., schaakmat n. v., schaakmat zetten

cheek, tsjiek, s., wang c., kaak c.; (impudence) brutaliteit c. v., brutaal zijn

cheer, tsjier, s., (mood) stemming c.; (mirth) vrolijkheid c.; (applause) bijval c. v., opvrolijken; (applaud) toejuichen; (encourage) aanmoedigen; ——**ful,** a., blij, vrolijk; ——**less,** droevig, troosteloos

cheese, tsjiez, s., kaas c.

chemical, kem-mi-k'l, s., chemisch product n. a., chemisch

chemise, sji-miez, s., vrouwenhemd n.

chemist, kem-mist, s., scheikundige c.; (shop) apotheker c.

chemistry, kem-mis-tri, s., scheikunde c.
cheque, tsjek, s., cheque c.; ———**book**, cheque-boek n.
cherish, tsjer-risj, v., liefhebben; koesteren
cheroot, sje-roet, s., manillasigaar c.
cherry, tsjer-ri, s., kers c.
cherub, tsjer-rub, s., cherubijn c.
chess, tsjes, s., schaakspel n.
chest, tsjest, s., borst c.; (box) kist c.; (trunk) koffer c.; ——— **of drawers**, latafel c.
chestnut, tsjes-nat, s., kastanje c.
chew, tsjoe, v., kauwen; (fig.) overdenken
chicken, tsjik-kin, s., kuiken n.; (food) kip c.
chicken-pox, tsjik-kin-poks, s., waterpokken
chide, tsjaid, v., berispen, beknorren [c.pl.
chief, tsjief, s., hoofd n., leider c. a., voornaamste
chiefly, tsjief-li, adv., voornamelijk
chilblain, tsjil-bleen, s., winter c.
child, tsjaild, s., kind n.; ———**ish**, a., kinderachtig
childlike, tsjaild-laik, a., kinderlijk
chill, tsjil, a., kil. s., kilheid c. v., afkoelen
chilly, tsjil-li, a., kil, koel; huiverig
chime, tsjaim, s., klokkenspel n. v., luiden
chimney, tsjim-ni, s., schoorsteen c.
chimney-sweep, tsjim-ni-swiep, s., schoorsteenveger c.
chin, tsjin, s., kin c.
china, tsjai-ne, s., porselein n.
chink, tsjingk, s., spleet c., reet c. v., rinkelen
chintz, tsjints, s., sits n. a., sitsen
chip, tsjip, s., spaan c., splinter c. v., afschilferen
chips, tsjips, s.pl., patates frites c.pl.
chiropodist, kai-rop-pe-dist, s., pedicure c.
chirp, tsjeurp, v., tjilpen. s., getjilp n.
chisel, tsjiz-'l, s., beitel c. v., uitbeitelen
chivalrous, sjiv-v'l-rus, a., ridderlijk
chive, tsjaiv, s., bieslook n. & c.
chlorine, kloa-rain, s., chloor n.
chloroform, klor-re-foarm, s., chloroform c.
chocolate, tsjok-lit, s., chocolade c.
choice, tsjois, s., keus c.; voorkeur c. a., uitgelezen
choir, kwair, s., koor n.

choke, tsjook, v., smoren, **stikken;** —— **up,** verstoppen

choler, kol-l'r, s., gal c.; ——**ic**, a., opvliegend

cholera, kol-le-re, s., cholera c.

choose, tsjoez, v., kiezen, uitkiezen

chop, tsjop, s., karbonade c. v., kappen, kloven

chopper, tsjop-p'r, s., hakmes n.

choral, kor-r'l, a., koor . . .

chord, koard, s., snaar c.; (mus.) akkoord n.

chorister, kor-ris-t'r, s., koorzanger c.; koor-knaap c.

chorus, koa-rus, s., koor n.; (refrain) refrein n.

Christ, kraist, s., Christus c.

christen, kris-'n, v., dopen

christening, kris-ning, s., doop c.

Christianity, kris-ti-en-ni-ti, s., Christendom n.

Christmas, kris-mus, s., Kerstmis c.; ——**box,** Kerstgeschenk n.; ——**tree**, Kerstboom c.

chronic, kron-nik, a., chronisch

chronicle, kron-nik-k'l, s., kroniek c. v., boek-staven

chrysanthemum, kri-sen-the-mum, s., chrysant

chubby, tsjab-bi, a., mollig, poezelig [c.

chuck, tsjak, v., aaien. s., aai c.

chuckle, tsjak-k'l, v., gnuiven. s., gegnuif n.

chum, tsjam, s., kameraad c. v., samen wonen

chunk, tsjangk, s., brok c., homp c.

church, tsjeurtsj, s., kerk c.; ——**yard**, kerkhof n.

churl, tsjeurl, s., boerenkinkel c., vlegel c.

churlish, tsjeur-lisj, a., boers, lomp

churn, tsjeurn, s., karn c.; (milk can) melkbus c. v., karnen; (stir) omroeren

cider, sai-d'r, s., appelwijn c., cider c.

cigar, si-Gaar, s., sigaar c.; ——**case,** sigaren-koker c.

cigarette, si-Ge-ret, s., sigaret c.

cinder, sin-d'r, s., sintel c., slak c.

cinema, sin-ni-ma, s., bioscoop c., cinema c.

cinnamon, sin-ne-mun, s., kaneel n. & c.

cipher, sai-f'r, s., cijfer n.

circle, seur-k'l, s., cirkel c. v., draaien, rondgaan

circlet, seur-klit, s., cirkeltje n.; ring c.

circuit, seur-kit, s., omtrek c.; omweg c.

circuitous, seur-kjoe-i-tus, a., omslachtig

circular, seur-kjoe-l'r, s., circulaire c. a., rond

circulate, seur-kjoe-leet, v., circuleren; verspreiden [s., leesbibliotheek c.

circulating, seur-kjoe-lee-ting, —— library,

circumcise, seur-kum-saiz, v., besnijden

circumference, seur-**kam**-fe-r'ns, s., omtrek c.

circumscribe, seur-kum-skraib, v., omschrijven ; (to limit) beperken

circumspect, seur-kum-spekt, a., omzichtig

circumstance, seur-kum-st'ns, s., omstandigheid c.

circumstantial, seur-kum-**sten**-sjul, a., uitvoerig; (incidental) bijkomstig

circumvent, seur-kum-**vent**, v., misleiden

circus, seur-kus, s., circus n.; (place) rond plein

cistern, sis-t'n, s., waterreservoir n. [n.

citadel, sit-te-d'l, s., citadel c.

cite, sait, v., aanhalen; (summon) dagvaarden

citizen, sit-ti-z'n, s., burger c.

citizenship, sit-ti-z'n-sjip, s., burgerrecht n.

city, sit-ti, s., stad c.; grote stad c.

civil, siv-vil, a., civiel; (courteous) beleefd

civilian, si-vil-jun, s., burger c.

civility, si-**vil**-li-ti, s., beleefdheid c.

civilization, si-vi-lai-zee-sjun, s., beschaving c.

claim, kleem, s., eis c., aanspraak c.; (commercial) vordering c. v., eisen; (assert) **beweren**

claimant, kleem-'nt, s., eiser c.

clamber, klem-b'r, v., klauteren

clamorous, klem-me-rus, a., luidruchtig

clamour, klem-m'r, s., geschreeuw n., kreet c.

clamp, klemp, s., klamp c.; kram c. v., krammen

clan, klen, s., stam c., geslacht n.; (fig.) kliek c.

clandestine, klen-des-tin, a., heimelijk

clang, kleng, s., gekletter n. v., kletteren

clank, klengk, s., gerammel n. v., rammelen

clap, klep, v., klappen. s., slag c.; (thunder) donderslag c.; ——ping, applaus n.

clap-trap, klep-trep, s., knaleffect n.

claret, kler-r't, s., bordeauxwijn c.

clarify, kler-ri-fai, v., reinigen, verhelderen
clarinet, kler-ri-net, s., klarinet c.
clash, klesj, s., gekletter n.; (conflict) tegenstrijdigheid c. v., botsen; (colours) vloeken
clasp, klaasp, v., omarmen. s., haak c., gesp c.
class, klaas, s., klas c.; (status) stand c. v., indelen
classify, kles-si-fai, v., classificeren
clatter, klet-t'r, s., geklepper n. v., klepperen
clause, kloaz, s., clausule c.; (gram.) bijzin c.
claw, kloa, s., klauw c.; (birds) poot c.; (crab) schaar c. v., krabben, klauwen
clay, klee, s., klei c., leem n.; ——ey, a., kleiachtig
clean, klien, v., reinigen; (shoes) poetsen. a., schoon, zuiver; ——ing, s., schoonmaak c.
cleanliness, klien-li-nis, s., zindelijkheid c.
cleanse, klenz, v., reinigen, zuiveren
clear, klier, a., klaar; (obvious) duidelijk. v., zuiveren; (table) afnemen; (street) ontruimen
clearance, klie-r'ns, s., opruiming c.
clearness, klier-nis, s., klaarheid c.; duidelijkheid c.
cleave, kliev, v., kloven; (cling) aanhangen [c.
cleft, kleft, s., kloof c., spleet c.
clematis, klem-me-tis, s., clematis c.
clench, klentsj, v., (teeth) op elkaar klemmen; (fist) ballen
clergy, kleur-dzji, s., geestelijkheid c.
clergyman, kleur-dzji-m'n, s., geestelijke c.
clerical, kler-ri-k'l, a., schrijf . . .; (eccl.) geestelijk; ——error, s., schrijffout c.
clerk, klaark, s., klerk c.; secretaris c.
clever, klev-v'r, a., knap, handig, bekwaam
cleverness, klev-v'r-nes, s., knapheid c., bekwaamheid c.
click, klik, s., geklik n., getik n. v., tikken
client, klai-unt, s., klant c.; cliënt c.
clientele, kli-un-t'l, s., cliëntèle c.
cliff, klif, s., steile rots c.
climate, klai-mit, s., klimaat n., luchtstreek c.
climax, klai-meks, s., toppunt n.; hoogtepunt n.
climb, klaim, s., beklimming c. v., klimmen; (mountain) beklimmen; ——er, s., klimmer c.; (plant) klimplant c.

clinch, klintsj, s., greep c. v., vasthouden

cling, kling, v., kleven, zich vastklemmen

clink, klingk, s., gerinkel n. v., rinkelen

clip, klip, s., knijper c. v., afknippen; (sheep) scheren

cloak, klook, s., mantel c. v., bemantelen

cloak-room, klook-roem, s., garderobe c.

clock, klok, s., klok c.; **alarm** ———, wekker c.

clockwork, klok-weurk, s., uurwerk n.

clod, klod, s., aardkluit c., kluit c.

clog, klog, s., blok n.; klompschoen c. v., belemmeren; ——— up, verstoppen

cloister, klois-t'r, s., klooster n.; kloostergang c.

close, klooz, s., einde n. v., sluiten; (finish) besluiten. a., dicht; (near) dichtbij; (sultry) benauwd

closet, kloz-zit, s., privé vertrek n.; toilet n.

closure, klo-zjur, s., sluiting c.; slot n.

clot, klot, s., klonter c. v., klonteren

cloth, kloth, s., doek c.; (material) laken n.

clothe, kloodh, v., kleden

clothes, kloodhz, s.pl., kleren n.pl.; (bed) beddegoed n.; ———brush, kleerborstel c.

clothier, kloodh-i-ur, s., lakenhandelaar c.

clothing, kloodh-ing, s., kleding c.

cloud, klaud, s., wolk c. v., bewolken; (blur) benevelen; ———less, a., onbewolkt; ———y, bewolkt; (dim) vaag

clout, klaut, s., lap c., doek c. v., lappen

clove, kloov, s., kruidnagel c.; anjelier c.

cloven, klo-v'n, a., gespleten

clover, klo-v'r, s., klaver c.; **to be in** ———, een herenleventje hebben

clown, klaun, s., hansworst c.; (lout) lomperd c.

club, klab, s., club c.; (stick) knuppel c.; (cards) klaveren c.

cluck, klak, s., geklok n. v., klokken [klaveren c.

clue, kloe, s., leidraad c., sleutel c.

clump, klamp, s., klomp c.; (trees) groep c.

clumsiness, klam-zi-nis, s., onhandigheid c.

clumsy, klam-zi, a., onhandig, lomp

cluster, klas-t'r, s., tros c., bos c.; (group) groep c. v., zich groeperen

clutch, klatsj, s., greep c.; (motor) koppeling c. v., grijpen, pakken

coach, kootsj, s., koets c.; (tutor) repetitor c. v., in een koets rijden; trainen

coach-house, kootsj-haus, s., koetshuis n.

coachman, kootsj-m'n, s., koetsier c.

coagulate, ko-eG-joe-leet, v., stollen

coal, kool, s., steenkool c. v., van kolen voorzien; ——-pit, s., kolenmijn c.; ——-scuttle, kolennemmer c.

coalition, ko-e-lis-sjun, s., verbond n., coalitie c.

coarse, koars, a., grof, ruw; ——-ness, s., ruwheid c., grofheid c.

coast, koost, s., kust c. v., langs de kust varen

coast-guard, koost-Gaard, s., kustwacht c.

coat, koot, s., jas c.; (lady's) mantel c.; (animal) vacht c.; (paint) laag c. v., bekleden; (paint) verven; ——-ing, s., bekleding c.; ——- of arms, familiewapen n.

coax, kooks, v., vleien, flikflooien

cob, kob, s., (horse) hit c.; (coal) klomp c.; (maize) maïskolf c.

cobbler, kob-bl'r, s., schoenlapper c.; knoeier c.

cobweb, kob-web, s., spinneweb n.

cocaine, ko-keen, s., cocaïne c.

cochineal, kot-sji-niel, s., cochenille c.

cock, kok, s., (bird) haan c.; (tap) kraan c.; (hay) hooiopper c. v., (gun) spannen; (ears) spitsen; ——-ade, s., kokarde c.; ——-erel, jonge haan c.; ——-ney, geboren Londenaar c.; ——-roach, kakkerlak c.   [c.

cockle, kok-k'l, s., hartmossel c.; (corn) bolderik

cocoa, ko-ko, s., cacao c.; ——-nut, kokosnoot c.

cocoon, kok-koen, s., cocon c.   [traan c.

cod, kod, s., kabeljauw c.; ——-liver oil, lever-

coddle, kod-d'l, v., vertroetelen, verwennen

code, kood, s., (law) wetboek n.; telegramcode c.

codicil, kod-di-sil, s., aanhangsel n.

coerce, ko-eurs, v., dwingen, afdwingen

coffee, kof-fi, s., koffie c.; ——-pot, koffiepot c.

coffer, kof-f'r, s., geldkist c.; ——-s, pl., schatkist c.

coffin, kof-fin, s., doodskist c. v., kisten

cog, kog, s., tand c.; ——-wheel, tandrad n.

cogitate, kod-zjii-teet, v., overdenken, peinzen

cognac, kon-jek, s., cognac c.

cognate, koG-neet, a., verwant

cognizance, koG-ni-z'ns, s., kennisneming c.

cognizant, koG-ni-z'nt, a., kennend, wetend

cogwheel, koG-wiel, s., tandrad n., kamrad n.

coherence, ko-hier-'ns, s., samenhang c.

coherent, ko-hier-'nt, a., samenhangend

cohesion, ko-hie-zjun, s., samenhang c., cohesie

cohesive, ko-hie-siv, a., samenhangend [c.

coil, koil, s., tros c.; rol c. v., oprollen

coin, koin, s., munt c., geldstuk n. v., munten

coincide, ko-in-said, v., samenvallen

coke, kook, s., cokes c.pl. v., vercooksen

colander, kal-lun-d'r, s., vergiettest c.

cold, koold, s., kou c.; (catarrh) verkoudheid c. a., koud

colic, kol-lik, s., koliek c.

collaborate, ke-leb-be-reet, v., samenwerken

collapse, ke-leps, s., instorting c. v., instorten

collar, kol-l'r, s., boord c., kraag c.; (dog) hals-band c.

collar-bone, kol-l'r-boon, s., sleutelbeen n.

collate, kol-leet, v., vergelijken

collateral, kol-let-te-r'l, a., zijdelings; parallel

collation, kol-lee-sjun, s., vergelijking c.; (meal) lichte maaltijd c.

colleague, kol-lieG, s., collega c., ambtgenoot c.

collect, ke-lekt, v., verzamelen; collecteren

collected, ke-lek-tid, a., bedaard, zich zelf meester

collection, ke-lek-sjun, s., verzameling c.; (money) collecte c.; (postal) buslichting c.

collective, ke-lek-tiv, a., gemeenschappelijk

collector, ke-lek-t'r, s., verzamelaar c.; (revenue) ontvanger c.; (tickets) controleur c.

college, kol-lidzj, s., college n.; (school) inrich-ting voor middelbaar onderwijs c.; universi-teit c.

collide, ke-laid, v., botsen

collier, kol-j'r, s., mijnwerker c.; kolenschip n.

colliery, kol-je-ri, s., kolenmijn c.

collision, ke-li-zjun, s., aanvaring c., botsing c.

collop, kol-l'p, s., lapje vlees n.

colloquial, ke-lo-kwi-'l, a., alledaags   [ding c.

collusion, kel-joe-zjun, s., geheime verstandhou-

colon, ko-l'n, s., dubbele punt c.; dikke darm c.

colonel, keu-n'l, s., kolonel c.

colonist, kol-le-nist, s., kolonist c.

colonnade, kol-le-need, s., zuilenrij c.

colony, kol-le-ni, s., kolonie c., volksplanting c,

colossal, ke-los-s'l, a., reusachtig, kolossaal

colour, kal-l'r, s., kleur c. v., kleuren

colouring, kal-le-ring, s., kleursel n.; kleuring c.

colt, koolt, s., veulen n.; (fig.) robbedoes c.

column, kol-lum, s., zuil c., pilaar c.; (print)
kolom c.; (mil.) kolonne c.

coma, ko-ma, s., coma c.; slaapziekte c.

comb, koom, s., (hair, bird) kam c.; (honey) raat
c. v., kammen; (search) doorzoeken

combat, kom-b't, s., gevecht n. v., vechten;
——ant, s., strijder c.; ——ive, a., strijdlustig

combination, kom-bi-nee-sjun, s., combinatie c.;
verbinding c.; ——s, pl., hemdbroek c. [n.

combine, k'm-bain, v., verbinden. s., syndicaat

combustion, k'm-bast-sjun, s., verbranding c.

come, kam, v., komen; —— down, naar beneden
komen; —— in, binnen komen; —— off,
losgaan; —— out, buiten komen; —— up,
naar boven komen

comedian, ke-mie-djun, s., toneelspeler c.

comedy, kom-mi-di, s., blijspel n.

comet, kom-mit, s., komeet c.

comfort, kam-f'rt, s., (consolation) troost c.;
(ease) gemak n.; (relief) opbeuring c.; (well-
being) welstand c. v., troosten

comfortable, kam-f'rt-te-b'l, a., geriefelijk

comic, kom-mik, a., komisch, grappig

coming, kam-ming, a., toekomstig. s., komst c.

comma, kom-ma, s., komma c.

command, ke-maand, s., bevel n.; (mil.) com-
mando n.; (knowledge) beheersing c. v.,

bevelen; beheersen; ——er, s., bevelhebber c.; (mil.) commandant c.; (navy) kapitein-luitenant c.; ——ment, gebod n.

commemorate, ke-mem-me-reet, v., gedenken

commence, ke-mens, v., beginnen

commencement, ke-mens-m'nt, s., begin n.

commend, ke-mend, v., aanbevelen; prijzen [ling c.

commendation, ke-men-dee-sjun, s., aanbeve-

comment, kom-ment, v., commentaar geven, opmerken. s., opmerking c.; commentaar n.

commerce, kom-meurs, s., handel c.

commercial, ke-meur-sjul, a., commercieel, handels . . .

commiserate, ke-miz-ze-reet, v., beklagen

commission, ke-mis-sjun, s., (percentage) provisie c.; (order) opdracht c.; (mil.) aanstelling c.; (brokerage) commissie c. v., machtigen; opdracht geven

commissionaire, ke-mis-sjun-èr, s., portier c.

commit, ke-mit, v., (entrust) toevertrouwen; (crime) bedrijven; (fault) begaan; (bind) binden; (prison) gevangen zetten

committee, ke-mit-ti, s., comité c., bestuur n.

commodious, ke-mo-di-us, a., ruim, geriefelijk

commodity, ke-mod-di-ti, s., waar c., artikel n.

commodore, kom-me-doar, s., divisiecommandant c.

common, kom-m'n, a., (usual) gewoon; (universal) algemeen; (vulgar) vulgair. s., weide-recht n.; ——er, burger c.; ——place, gemeenplaats c.; ——wealth, gemenebest n.

Commons, kom-m'nz, House of ——, s., Lagerhuis n. [n.

commotion, ke-mo-sjun, s., beroering c., tumult

commune, ke-mjoen, v., zich onderhouden, spreken

communicate, ke-mjoe-ni-keet, v., in verbinding staan; (inform) mededelen

communication, ke-mjoe-ni-kee-sjun, s., mede-deling c.

Communion, ke-mjoe-ni-'n, s., Communie c.

community, ke-mjoe-ni-ti, s., gemeenschap c.
compact, kom-pekt, a., dicht, vast. s., verdrag n.
companion, k'm-pen-jun, s., kameraad c., makker c.; ——**ship,** gezelschap n.; kameraadschap c.
company, kam-pe-ni, s., gezelschap n.; (commercial) maatschappij c., vennootschap c.
comparative, k'm-per-re-tiv, a., vergelijkend
compare, k'm-pèr, v., vergelijken
comparison, k'm-per-ri-s'n, s., vergelijking c.
compartment, k'm-paart-m'nt, s., afdeling c.; (train) coupé c.
compass, kam-p's, s., (magnetic) kompas n.; (range) omtrek c.; (a pair of) ——**es,** pl., passer c.
compassionate, kem-pes-sje-nit, a., medelijdend
compel, kem-pel, v., dwingen, afdwingen
compensate, kom-pen-seet, v., vergoeden [c.
compensation, kem-pen-see-sjun, s., vergoeding
compete, k'm-peet, v., wedijveren, concurreren
competence, kom-pi-t'ns, s., bevoegdheid c.
competition, k'm-pi-tis-sjun, s., concurrentie c.; (games) wedstrijd c.
competitor, k'm-pet-ti-t'r, s., mededinger c.; (commercial) concurrent c.
compile, k'm-pail, v., samenstellen; verzamelen
complacent, k'm-plee-s'nt, a., zelfvoldaan
complain, k'm-pleen, v., klagen; zich beklagen
complaint, k'm-pleent, s., klacht c.; kwaal c.
complement, kom-pli-m'nt, s., aanvulling c.
complete, k'm-pliet, v., voltooien, afmaken. a., volledig; ——**ness,** s., volledigheid c.
completion, k'm-plie-sjun, s., voltooiing c. [steld
complex, kom-pleks, s., geheel n. a., samenge-
complexion, k'm-plek-sjun, s., gelaatskleur c.
compliance, k'm-plai-'ns, s., inwilliging c.
compliant, k'm-plai-'nt, a., inschikkelijk
complicate, kom-pli-keet, v., ingewikkeld maken
compliment, kom-pli-m'nt, v., gelukwensen. s., compliment n.
compliments, kom-pli-m'nts, s.pl., beleefde groeten c.pl.

comply, k'm-plai, v., zich schikken, berusten
component, k'm-po-n'nt, s., bestanddeel n.
compose, k'm-pooz, v., samenstellen; (mus.) componeren; (type) zetten
composer, k'm-po-z'r, s., componist c.
composite, kom-pe-zit, a., samengesteld
composition, kom-pe-**zis**-sjun, s., samenstelling c.; (essay) opstel n.; (mus.) componeren n.; (compound) mengsel n.
compositor, k'm-**poz**-zi-t'r, s., letterzetter c.
composure, k'm-po-zjur, s., kalmte c.; (self-control) bedaardheid c., bezadigdheid c.
compound, kom-paund, s., samenstelling c.; (enclosure) erf n. v., samenstellen, mengen. a., samengesteld; —— **fracture,** s., gecompliceerde breuk c.
comprehend, kom-pri-hend, v., begrijpen
comprehension, kom-pri-**hen**-sjun, s., begrip n.
compress, kom-press, s., compres n.
compress, k'm-pres, v., samendrukken
comprise, k'm-praiz, v., bevatten, omvatten
compromise, kom-pre-maiz, s., vergelijk n., schikking c. v., schikken; compromiteren
compulsion, k'm-**pal**-sjun, s., dwang c.
compulsory, k'm-**pal**-se-ri, a., gedwongen
compunction, k'm-**pangk**-sjun, s., wroeging c.
compute, k'm-pjoet, v., rekenen, berekenen
comrade, kom-rid, s., makker c., kameraad c.
concave, kon-keev, a., hol. s., holte c.
conceal, k'n-siel, v., verbergen; (keep secret) verzwijgen; —— **ment,** s., verberging c.; (place) schuilplaats c.
concede, k'n-sied, v., toegeven; toestaan
conceit, k'n-siet, s., verwaandheid c.
conceited, k'n-sie-tid, a., verwaand, eigenwijs
concentrate, kon-s'n-treet, v., concentreren
conception, k'n-sep-sjun, s., ontvangenis c.; (idea) begrip n.
concern, k'n-seurn, s., (affair, business) zaak c.; (anxiety) bezorgdheid c.; (importance) belang n. v., aangaan; **to be —— ed in,** betrokken zijn bij

concert, kon-surt, s., overeenstemming c.; concert n.

concession, k'n-ses-sjun, s., inwilliging c.

conciliate, k'n-sil-li-eet, v., verzoenen

concise, k'n-sais, a., beknopt, kort

conclude, k'n-kloed, v., eindigen; besluiten

conclusion, k'n-kloe-zjun, s., besluit n.; einde n.

conclusive, k'n-kloe-siv, a., beslissend

concoct, k'n-kokt, v., brouwen, verzinnen

concord, kong-koard, s., eendracht c., harmonie c.

concrete, k'n-kriet, s., beton n. a., concreet

concur, k'n-keur, v., overeenstemmen; —— rence, s., overeenstemming c.; samenloop c.

concussion, k'n-kas-sjun, s., schok c., botsing c.

condemn, k'n-dem, v., veroordelen; verdoemen

condense, k'n-dens, v., condenseren; samenpersen

condescend, kon-di-send, v., zich verwaardigen

condescension, kon-di-sen-sjun, s., minzaamheid c.

condiment, kon-di-m'nt, s., kruiderij c., toespijs c.

condition, k'n-dis-sjun, s., voorwaarde c.; (state) toestand c.; ——al, a., voorwaardelijk

condole, k'n-dool, v., condoleren

condolence, k'n-do-l'ns, s., rouwbeklag n.

condone, k'n-doon, v., vergeven

conducive, k'n-djoe-siv, a., bevorderlijk

conduct, kon-dukt, s., (behaviour) bedrag n.

conduct, k'n-dakt, v., leiden; —— oneself, zich gedragen; ——or, s., leider c.; (guide) gids c.; (bus) conducteur c.; (music) dirigent c.

conduit, kan-dit, s., leiding c., buis c.

cone, koon, s., kegel c.; (fir-tree) denappel c.

confectioner, k'n-fek-sje-n'r, s., suikerbakker c. banketbakker c.; ——y, (sweetmeats) suikergoed n.

confederate, k'n-fed-de-rit, s., bondgenoot c.

confederation, k'n-fed-de-ree-sjun, s., verbond n.

confer, k'n-feur, v., beraadslagen; (bestow) verlenen

confess, k'n-fes, v., bekennen; (eccl.) biechten

confession, k'n-fes-sjun, s., bekentenis c.; biecht c.

confide, k'n-faid, v., vertrouwen, toevertrouwen

confidence, kon-fi-d'ns, s., (trust) vertrouwen n.

confident, kon-fi-d'nt, a., overtuigd; vol vertrouwen

confidential, k'n-fi-den-sjul, a., vertrouwelijk

confine, k'n-fain, v., begrenzen; (imprison) opsluiten; ——ment, s., bevalling c.; (prison) arrest n.

confirm, k'n-feurm, v., bevestigen; (eccl.) vormen; ——ation, s., bevestiging c.; vormsel n.

confiscate, kon-fis-keet, v., verbeurd verklaren

conflagration, k'n-fle-Gree-sjun, s., brand c.

conflict, kon-flikt, s., conflict n.; (combat) strijd c. v., strijden, botsen

conflicting, k'n-flik-ting, a., tegenstrijdig

conform, k'n-foarm, v., schikken; —— to, zich aanpassen aan; ——able, a., overeenkomstig

confound, k'n-faund, v., verwarren

confront, k'n-frant, v., (oppose) het hoofd bieden; (face) staan tegenover

confuse, k'n-fjoez, v., verwarren, verbijsteren

confusion, k'n-fjoe-zjun, s., verwarring c.

confute, k'n-fjoet, v., weerleggen

congeal, k'n-dzjiel, v., stremmen, stollen

congenial, k'n-dzjie-ni-'l, a., sympathiek

congenital, kon-dzjen-ni't-l, a., aangeboren

congest, k'n-dzjest, v., ophopen; ——ed, a., overvol, verstopt; ——ion, s., (traffic) opstopping c.; (med.) congestie c.

congratulate, k'n-Gret-joe-leet, v., gelukwensen

congratulation, k'n-Gret-joe-lee-sjun, s., gelukwens c.

congregate, kong-Gri-Geet, v., zich verzamelen

congregation, kong-Gri-Gee-sjun, s., vergadering c.

congress, kong-Gres, s., congres n., vergadering c.

conjecture, k'n-dzjekt-sjur, v., vermoeden. s., vermoeden n.

conjugal, kon-dzjoe-Gul, a., echtelijk
conjunction, k'n-dzjangk-sjun, s., vereniging c.; (gram.) voegwoord n.
conjure, kan-dzjur, v., bezweren; goochelen
conjurer, kan-dzje-r'r, s., goochelaar c.
connect, ke-nekt, v., verbinden
connection, ke-nek-sjun, s., verbinding c.; (trains) aansluiting c.; ——s, pl., relaties c.pl.
connive (at), ke-naiv (et), v., oogluikend toelaten
connoisseur, kon-ni-seur, s., kunstkenner c.
conquer, kong-k'r, v., veroveren; overwinnen
conqueror, kong-ke-r'r, s., overwinnaar c.
conquest, kong-kwest, s., verovering c.; overwinning c.
conscience, kon-sjuns, s., geweten n.
conscientious, kon-sji-en-sjus, a., nauwgezet
conscious, kon-sjus, a., bewust, gewaar
consciousness, kon-sjus-nis, s., bewustzijn n.
conscript, kon-skript, s., dienstplichtige c.
conscription, kon-skrip-sjun, s., dienstplicht c.
consecrate, kon-si-kreet, v., wijden, inzegenen
consecutive, k'n-sek-joe-tiv, a., opeenvolgend
consent, k'n-sent, v., toestemmen. s., toestemming c.
consequence, kon-si-kw'ens, s., gevolg n.
consequential, kon-si-kwen-sjul, a., daaruit volgend; (affectation) gewichtig doend
consequently, kon-si-kw'nt-li, adv., bijgevolg
conservative, k'n-seur-ve-tiv, a., conservatief
conservatory, k'n-seur-ve-tri, s., broeikas c.
conserve, k'n-seurv, v., in stand houden
conserves, k'n-seurvs, s.pl., ingemaakte vruchten c.pl.
consider, k'n-sid-d'r, v., (reflect) overwegen; (view) beschouwen; ——able, a., aanzienlijk; ——ate, attent, kies; ——ation, s., (deliberation) beschouwing c.; (heed) attentie c.; ——ing, prep., in aanmerking genomen
consign, k'n-sain, v., zenden; overdragen
consignee, kon-sai-nee, s., geadresseerde c.
consignment, k'n-sain-m'nt, s., overdracht c.; (goods) zending c.

consignor, k'n-sai-n'r, s., afzender c.
consist (of), k'n-sist (ov), v., bestaan (uit)
consistency, k'n-sis-t'n-si, s., consequentie c.
consistent, k'n-sis-t'nt, a., consequent
consolation, kon-se-lee-sjun, s., troost c.
console, k'n-sool, v., troosten; ——r, s., trooster
consolidate, k'n-sol-li-deet, v., versterken [c.
consonant, kon-se-n'nt, s., medeklinker c.
consort, kon-soart, s., gemaal c.; gemalin c.
consort (with), k'n-soart (widh), v., omgaan (met)
conspicuous, k'n-spik-joe-us, a., (striking) opvallend; (distinguished) uitstekend
conspiracy, k'n-spir-re-si, s., samenzwering c.
conspirator, k'n-spir-re-t'r, s., samenzweerder c.
conspire, k'n-spair, v., samenzweren
constable, kan-ste-b'l, s., politieagent c.
constabulary, k'n-steb-joe-le-ri, s., politie c.
constancy, kon-st'n-si, s., standvastigheid c.
constant, kon-st'nt, a., (steadfast) standvastig; (faithful) trouw; (continuous) voortdurend
constipation, kon-sti-pee-sjun, s., verstopping c.
constituency, k'n-stit-joe-'n-si, s., kiesdistrict n.
constituent, k'n-stit-joe-'nt, s., bestanddeel n.; (voter) kiezer c.
constitute, kon-sti-tjoet, v., vormen; samenstellen
constitution, kon-sti-tjoe-sjun, s., samenstelling c.; (law) grondwet c.; (system) gestel n.
constrain, k'n-streen, v., dwingen, noodzaken
constraint, k'n-streent, s., dwang c.
constriction, k'n-strik-sjun, s., samentrekking c.
construct, k'n-strakt, v., bouwen; aanleggen
construction, k'n-strak-sjun, s., bouw c.; verklaring c.; (gram.) zinsbouw c.
construe, k'n-stroe, v., (gram.) ontleden; (interpret) verklaren [n.
consul, kon-sul, s., consul c.; ——ate, consulaat
consult, k'n-salt, v., raadplegen, consulteren
consultation, k'n-s'l-tee-sjun, s., raadpleging c.
consume, k'n-sjoem, v., verbruiken; (destroy) vernietigen; ——r, s., verbruiker c.

consummate, kon-se-meet, v., voltooien
consummation, kon-se-mee-sjun, s., voltooiing c.; voltrekking c.
consumption, k'n-samp-sjun, s., (use) verbruik n.; (med.) tering c.
consumptive, k'n-samp-tiv, a., teringachtig
contact, kon-tekt, s., contact n., aanraking c.
contagious, k'n-tee-dzjus, a., besmettelijk
contain, k'n-teen, v., bevatten, behelzen
contaminate, k'n-tem-mi-neet, v., besmetten; (corrupt) bederven
contemplate, kon-tem-pleet, v., beschouwen
contemporary, k'n-tem-pe-re-ri, a., gelijktijdig. s., tijdgenoot c.
contempt, k'n-tempt, s., minachting c.
contemptible, k'n-temp-ti-b'l, a., verachtelijk
contend, k'n-tend, v., twisten, strijden; (maintain) beweren
content, k'n-tent, a., tevreden. v., tevreden stellen; ——ment, s., tevredenheid c.
contention, k'n-ten-sjun, s., twist c.; bewering c.
contentious, k'n-ten-sjus, a., twistziek
contents, k'n-tents, s.pl., inhoud c.
contest, kon-test, v., betwisten. s., twist c., geschil n.; (sports) wedstrijd c.
contiguous, k'n-tig-joe-us, a., aangrenzend
continent, kon-ti-n'nt, s., vasteland n.
contingency, k'n-tin-dzjun-si, s., mogelijkheid c.
contingent, k'n-tin-dzjunt, a., mogelijk, onzeker
continual, k'n-tin-joe-ul, a., voortdurend
continuation, k'n-tin-joe-ee-sjun, s., voortzetting c., vervolg n.
continue, k'n-tin-joe, v., voortzetten, voortduren
continuous, k'n-tin-joe-us, a., onafgebroken
contortion, k'n-toar-sjun, s., verdraaiing c.
contraband, kon-tre-bend, s., smokkelhandel c.; (goods) smokkelwaar c.
contract, k'n-trekt, v., (shrink) inkrimpen; (disease) oplopen; (debts) aangaan; (marriage) sluiten; ——for, zich verbinden tot; ——ion, s., samentrekking c.; ——or, aannemer c.

contradict, k'n-tre-**dikt,** v., tegenspreken; ——**ion,** s., tegenspraak c.

contrary, kon-tre-ri, a., tegengesteld. s., tegendeel n.; on the ——, integendeel

contrast, kon-trest, s., tegenstelling c., contrast n.

contrast, k'n-**trest,** v., tegenover elkaar stellen

contravene, kon-tre-vien, v., indruisen tegen

contravention, kon-tre-ven-sjun, s., overtreding

contribute, k'n-**trib**-joet, v., bijdragen   [c.

contribution, kon-tri-bjoe-shun, s., bijdrage c.

contrite, kon-trait, a., berouwvol

contrivance, k'n-**trai**-v'ns, s., uitvinding c.

contrive, k'n-**traiv,** v., uitvinden, bedenken

control, k'n-**trool,** v., (curb) bedwingen; (guide) leiden. s., (authority) beheer n.; (supervision) toezicht n.; (restraint) beheersing c.

controller, k'n-**trool**-'r, s., controleur c.

controversial, kon-tre-**veur**-sjul, a., betwistbaar

controversy, kon-tre-veur-si, s., geschil n.

conundrum, ke-nan-drum, s., raadsel n.

convalescence, kon-ve-les-s'ns, s., herstel n.

convalescent, kon-ve-**les**-s'nt, a., herstellend

convenience, k'n-vien-juns, s., geschiktheid c.; (comfort) gemak n.; (lavatory) toilet n.

convenient, k'n-vien-junt, a., geschikt; gelegen

convent, kon-vunt, s., nonnenklooster n.

convention, k'n-ven-sjun, s., bijeenkomst c.; (agreement) overeenkomst c., verdrag n.

converge, k'n-**veurdzj,** v., convergeren

conversant, kon-veur-s'nt, a., bedreven, vertrouwd

conversation, kon-ve-see-sjun, s., conversatie c.

converse, k'n-**veurs,** v., spreken, zich onderhouden

conversion, k'n-veur-sjun, s., bekering c.

convert, kon-veurt, s., bekeerling c.

convert, k'n-veurt, v., veranderen; bekeren

convex, kon-veks, a., bol, convex

convey, k'n-**vee,** v., vervoeren; (impart) mededelen

conveyance, k'n-vee-'ns, s., vervoer n.; (vehicle) voertuig n.

convict, kon-vikt, s., dwangarbeider c.
convict, k'n-vikt, v., schuldig verklaren, veroordelen
conviction, k'n-vikt-sjun, s., veroordeling c.; (belief) overtuiging c.
convince, k'n-vins, v., overtuigen
convivial, k'n-viv-vi-ul, a., feestelijk, vrolijk
convoke, k'n-vook, v., bijeenroepen
convoy, kon-voi, s., konvooi n.; (mil.) escorte n.
convoy, kon-voi, v., begeleiden
convulse, k'n-vals, v., schokken; stuiptrekken
convulsion, k'n-val-sjun, s., stuip c.; schok c.
cony, ko-ni, s., konijn n.
coo, koe, v., kirren; ——ing, s., gekir n.
cook, koek, v., koken. s., kok c.; keukenmeid c.
cookery, koe-ke-ri, s., kookkunst c.
cool, koel, a., koel, fris; (calm) kalm. v., afkoelen
coolness, koel-nes, s., koelte c.; (nerve) koelbloedigheid c.
coop, koep, s., kippenmand c.; —— up, v., opsluiten
cooper, koe-p'r, s., kuiper c.
co-operate, ko-op-pe-reet, v., samenwerken
cope, koap, s., koorkap c.; —— with, v., verwerken, afkunnen
copious, koop-jus, a., ruim, overvloedig
copper, kop-p'r, s., koper n.; (coin) koperen munt c.; (boiler) ketel c. a., koperen
coppice, (copse,) kop-pis, (kops), s., kreupelhout n.
copy, kop-pi, s., afschrift n.; exemplaar n. v., afschrijven; ——book, s., schrift n.; ——right, kopijrecht n.
coquetry, ko-ki-tri, s., behaagzucht c.
coral, kor-rul, s., koraal n. a., koralen
cord, koard, s., koord n., touw n. v., binden
cordial, koar-di-ul, a., hartelijk. s., likeur c.
corduroy, koar-djoe-roi, s., manchester n., pilo n.
core, koar, s., binnenste n., kern c. v., uitboren
co-respondent, ko-ris-pon-d'nt, s., medeplichtige gedaagde c.
cork, koark, s., kurk c. a., kurken. v., kurken

corkscrew, koark-skroe, s., kurketrekker c.

cormorant, koar-me-r'nt, s., aalscholver c.

corn, koarn, s., koren n., graan n.; (foot) eksteroog

corner, koar-n'r, s., hoek c. [n.

cornflower, koarn-flau-ur, s., korenbloem c.

cornice, koar-nis, s., kroonlijst c., lijst c.

coronation, kor-re-nee-sjun, s., kroning c.

coroner, kor-re-n'r, s., lijkschouwer c.

coronet, kor-re-nit, s., kroontje n.; (wreath) krans c.

corporal, koar-pe-rul, s., korporaal c. a., lichamelijk

corporation, koar-pe-ree-sjun, s., corporatie c.; (municipality), gemeentebestuur n.

corps, koar, s., korps n., legerkorps n.

corpse, koarps, s., lijk n. [c.

corpulency, koar-pjoe-l'n-si, s., zwaarlijvigheid

corpulent, koar-pjoe-l'nt, a., corpulent, gezet

corpuscle, koar-pas-ul, s., bloedlichaampje n.

correct, ke-rekt, a., goed, correct. v., verbeteren; (reprove) berispen; ——**ive,** a., verbeterend. s., middel ter verbetering n.; ——**ness,** juistheid c.

correspond, kor-ris-pond, v., corresponderen; (agree) overeenkomen; ——**ence,** c., briefwisseling c.; ——**ent,** correspondent c.

corridor, kor-ri-doar, s., gang c., corridor c.; ——**train,** D-trein c., harmonicatrein c.

corroborate, ke-rob-be-reet, v., versterken

corroboration, ke-rob-be-ree-sjun, s., versterking c.

corrode, ke-rood, v., wegvreten; (rust) verroesten

corrosive, ke-ro-siv, a., bijtend, invretend

corrugate, kor-roe-Geet, v., rimpelen; ——**d iron,** s., gegolfd ijzer n.

corrupt, ke-rapt, v., bederven; (bribe) omkopen. a., bedorven; omkoopbaar; ——**ion,** s., bederf n.; (bribe) omkoping c.

corsair, koar-sèr, s., zeerover c.; kaperschip n.

corset, koar-sit, s., korset n.

cortege, koar-teedzj, s., stoet c., gevolg n.

cost, kost, s., prijs c.; (expense) kosten c.pl. v.,

kosten; ——ly, a., duur; (precious) kostbaar; ——s, s.pl., proceskosten c.pl.

costermonger, kos-te-mang-g'r, s., straatventer

costive, kos-tiv, a., hardlijvig [c.

costume, kos-tjoem, s., kostuum n.; klederdracht [c.

cosy, ko-zi, a., gezellig. s., theemuts c.

cot, kot, s., (child's) bedje n.; (naut.) kooi c.

cottage, kot-tidzj, s,. huisje n., hut c.

cotton, kot-t'n, s., katoen n.; (thread) katoengaren n.; ——wool, boomwol c.; watten c.pl.

couch, kautsj, s., rustbed n., divan c.

cough, kof, v., hoesten. s., hoest c.

council, kaun-sil, s., raad c.; ——lor, raadslid n.

counsel, kaun-sul, s., raadgeving c. v., aanraden

count, kaunt, s., graaf c.; telling c.; (total) aantal n. v., tellen; ——ing-house, s., kantoor n.; ——less, a., talloos

countenance, kaun-ti-n'ns, s., gezicht n., gelaat n. v., (favour) begunstigen; (tolerate) dulden

counter, kaun-t'r, s., toonbank c.; (games) legpenning c. adv., tegen; ——act, v., tegenwerken; (frustrate) verijdelen; ——balance, opwegen tegen; ——feit, s., namaak c. a., nagemaakt. v., namaken; (money) vervalsen; ——foil, s., strook c.; ——mand, v., herroepen; afbestellen; ——pane, s., beddesprei c.; ——part, tegenhanger c.; ——sign, v., medeondertekenen. s., geheim teken n.; (mil.) wachtwoord n.

countess, kaun-tis, s., gravin c.

country, kan-tri, s., land c.; ——man, buitenman c.; (compatriot) landgenoot c.

county, kaun-ti, s., graafschap n.

couple, kap-p'l, s., paar n. v., verenigen

courage, kar-ridzj, s., moed c.

courageous, ke-ree-dzjus, a., moedig.

course, koars, s., (direction) richting c.; (tuition) cursus c.; (race) renbaan c.; (ship) koers c.; (meals) gang c.; (river) loop c.; (succession) reeks c.; of ——, adv., natuurlijk

court, koart, s., (royal) hof n.; (law) gerechtshof n. v., het hof maken; ——ier, s., hoveling c.;

——-martial, krijgsraad c.; ——ship,
(wooing) vrijerij c.; ——yard, binnenplaats c.
courteous, koart-jus, a., hoffelijk
courtesy, keur-ti-si, s., vriendelijkheid c.
cousin, kaz-z'n, s., (male) neef c.; (female) nicht
cove, koov, s., (geology) inham c., kreek c.   [c.
covenant, kav-vi-n'nt, s., verdrag n., verbond n.
cover, kav-v'r, s., bedekking c.; (lid) deksel n.;
(shelter) dekking c. v., bedekken
covet, kav-vit, v., begeren   [sleutelbloem c.
cow, kau, s., koe c. v., bang maken; ——slip, s.,
coward, kau-urd, s., lafaard c.; ——ice, lafheid c.
cower, kau-ur, v., neerhurken   [steenkap c.
cowl, kaul, s., monnikspij c.; (chimney) schoor-
coxcomb, koks-koom, s., fat c., kwast c.
coxswain, kok-s'n, s., stuurman c.
coy, koi, a., (shy) schuchter; (modest) zedig
crab, kreb, s., krab c. v., krabben
crab-apple, kreb-ep-p'l, s., wilde appel c.
crack, krek, s., (chink) spleet c.; (burst) barst c.;
(noise) knal c. v., knallen; (fracture) breken;
(nuts) kraken; ——er, s., (firework) voet-
zoeker c.; (Xmas) knalbonbon n.; ——ers,
pl., notenkraker c.; ——le, v., knetteren
cradle, kree-d'l, s., (crib) wieg c.; (birthplace)
bakermat c.
craft, kraaft, s., (trade) ambacht n.; (naut.)
vaartuig n.; (cunning) list c.
craftsman, kraafts-m'n, s., vakman c.
crafty, kraaf-ti, a., listig, sluw
crag, kreG, s., steile rots c.; ——gy, a., rotsig
cram, krem, v., volstoppen; (coach) klaar stomen
cramp, kremp, s., kramp c. v., samenknellen
cranberry, kren-be-ri, s., veenbes c.
crane, kreen, s., kraanvogel c.; (hoist) kraan c.
crank, krengk, s., kruk c., zwengel c., slinger c.
crape, kreep, s., krip n., floers n.
crash, kresj, v., (collide) in botsing komen;
(break) verpletteren; (aero) neerstorten. s.,
(noise) gekraak n.; (collision) botsing c.;
(financial) krach c.   [ter c.
crater, kree-t'r, s., krater c.; (shell) granaattrech-

crave, kreev, v., smeken; —— for, verlangen naar
craving, kree-ving, s., hevig verlangen n.
crawl, kroal, v., kruipen, sluipen
crayfish, kree-fisj, s., rivierkreeft c.
crayon, kree-un, s., tekenkrijt n.
craze, kreez, s., manie c. v., gek maken
crazy, kree-zi, a., gek; (structure) bouwvallig
creak, kriek, v., knarsen, kraken
cream, kriem s., (milk) room c.; (ointment) crème c.
crease, kries, v., kreuken, vouwen. s., vouw c.
create, kri-eet, v., scheppen; voortbrengen
creature, kriet-sjur, s., schepsel n.
credentials, kri-den-sjulz, s.pl., geloofsbrieven
credible, kred-di-b'l, a., geloofwaardig   [c. pl.
credit, kred-dit, s., (belief) geloof n.; (honour) eer c.; ——able, a., eervol; ——or, s., schuldeiser c.
credulous, kred-joe-lus, a., lichtgelovig
creed, kried, s., geloofsbelijdenis c.; (faith) geloof
creek, kriek, s., kreek c., inham c.   [n.
creep, kriep, v., kruipen; (slip) sluipen
creeper, krie-p'r, s., (plant) kruipende plant c.
cremate, kri-meet, v., verbranden
cremation, kri-mee-sjun, s., lijkverbranding c.
Creole, kri-ool, s., Creool c.; Creoolse c.
crescent, kres-'nt, s., halve maan c.
cress, kres, s., waterkers c., tuinkers c.
crest, krest, s., (bird) kuif c.; (hill) top c.; (heraldry) helmteken n.
crestfallen, krest-foal-'n, a., terneergeslagen
crevice, krev-vis, s., scheur c., spleet c.
crew, kroe, s., (ship) bemanning c.; (workmen) ploeg c.   [rekken
crick, krik, s., kramp c.; (back) spit n. v., ver-
cricket, krik-kit, s., krekel c.; (game) cricket n.
crime, kraim, s., misdaad c.
criminal, krim-mi-n'l, s., misdadiger c. a., misdadig
crimson, krim-z'n, a., karmozijnrood
cringe (to), krindzj (toe), v., buigen (voor), kruipen (voor)

crinkle, kring-k'l, s., kronkel c. v., rimpelen
cripple, krip-p'l, s., kreupele c. v., verminken
crisis, krai-sis, s., crisis c.; keerpunt n.
crisp, krisp, a., (frizzy) gekruld; (brittle) bros
criterion, krai-tie-ri-un, s., toets c., maatstaf c.
critical, krit-ti-k'l, a., kritiek; (cavilling) critisch
criticism, krit-ti-sizm, s., kritiek c.
criticize, krit-ti-saiz, v., critiseren
croak, krook, v., (frog) kwaken; (crow) krassen
crochet, kro-sji, v., haken. s., haakwerk n.
crockery, krok-ke-ri, s., aardewerk n.
crocodile, krok-ke-dail, s., krokodil c.
crocus, kro-kus, s., krokus c.
crook, kroek, s., haak c.; (swindler) oplichter c.
crooked, kroe-kid, a., krom; (dishonest) oneerlijk
crop, krop, s., oogst c.; (craw) krop c. v., afknippen
cross, kros, s., kruis n. a., (vexed) boos. v.,
kruisen; (step) oversteken; —— out, door-
strepen; ——examination, s., kruisverhoor n.
crossing, kros-sing, s., kruispunt n.; overtocht c.
cross-road, kros-rood, s., zijweg c.
crotchet, krot-sjit, s., (music) kwartnoot c.
crouch, krautsj, v., ineenduiken
crow, kro, s., kraai c.; (cry) gekraai n. v., kraaien
crowbar, kro-baar, s., breekijzer n.
crowd, kraud, s., (quantity) menigte c.; (throng)
gedrang n. v., (throng) dringen; (press
together) opeendringen
crown, kraun, s., kroon c.; (wreath) krans c.;
(head) kruin c. v., kronen
crucible, kroe-si-b'l, s., smeltkroes c.
crucifix, kroe-si-fiks, s., kruisbeeld n.
crucify, kroe-si-fai, v., kruisigen
crude, kroed, a., (raw) rauw; (rough) ruw
cruel, kroe-ul, a., wreed; ——ty, s., wreedheid c.
cruet, kroe-it, s., flesje n.; (eccl.) ampul c.
cruise, kroez, s., kruistocht c. v., kruisen
cruiser, kroe-z'r, s., kruiser c.
crumb, kram, s., kruimel c. v., kruimelen
crumble, kram-b'l, v., verbrokkelen

crumple, kram-p'l, v., verfrommelen, kreuken

crunch, krantsj, v., vermalen; kauwen

crush, krasj, v., (press) samenpersen; (squeeze) uitpersen; (pound) verpletteren; (subdue) onderdrukken. s., gedrèng n.

crust, krast, s., korst c.

crusty, kras-ti, a., korstig; (surly) knorrig

crutch, kratsj, s., kruk c.; (support) steun c.

cry, krai, v., schreeuwen; (call) roepen; (weep) huilen. s., kreet c.; roep c.; gehuil n.

cryptic, krip-tik, a., geheim, verborgen

crystal, kris-t'l, s., kristal n. a., kristallen

cub, kab, s., jong n., welp n. v., jongen

cube, kjoeb, s., kubus c.; derde macht c.

cuckoo, koe-koe, s., koekoek c.

cucumber, kjoe-kum-b'r, s., komkommer c.

cuddle, kad-d'l, v., knuffelen, omhelzen

cudgel, kad-zjul, s., knuppel c. v., afrossen [c.

cue, kjoe, s., wenk c., aanwijzing c.; (billiard) keu

cuff, kaf, s., manchet c.; (blow) klap c. v., slaan

culinary, kjoe-li-ne-ri, a., keuken . . ., kook . . .

culminate, kal-mi-neet, v., culmineren

culpable, kal-pe-b'l, a., schuldig, misdadig

culprit, kal-prit, s., schuldige c.

cultivate, kal-ti-veet, v., (till) bebouwen; (grow) kweken

culture, kal-tsjur, s., cultuur c.

cumbersome, kam-b'r-sum, a., hinderlijk

cunning, kan-ning, a., listig, sluw. s., sluwheid c.

cup, kap, s., kop c., kopje n.; (trophy) beker c.

cupboard, kap-burd, s., kast c.

cupola, kjoe-pe-la, s., koepel c.

cur, keur, s., rekel c.; (fig.) schurk c.

curate, kjoe-rit, s., kapelaan c.

curb, keurb, s., kinketting c.; (fig.) toom c. v., bedwingen

curd, keurd, s., gestremde melk c.

curdle, keur-d'l, v., stremmen, stollen

cure, kjoer, s., kuur c.; (remedy) geneesmiddel n. v., genezen; (meat, etc.) verduurzamen

curfew, keur-fjoe, s., avondklok c.

curiosity, kjoe-ri-os-si-ti, s., nieuwsgierigheid c.

curious, kjoe-ri-us, a., (inquisitive) nieuwsgierig; (peculiar) zeldzaam

curl, keurl, s., krul c. v., krullen, kronkelen

currant, kar-r'nt, s., (dried) krent c.; **black ——,** zwarte bes c.; **——-bun,** krentenbroodje n.

currency, kar-r'n-si, s., circulatie c.; munt c.

current, kar-r'nt, s., stroom c. a., gangbaar

curse, keurs, s., vloek c. v., vloeken

cursory, keur-se-ri, a., vluchtig, haastig

curt, keurt, a., kort; (rude) kortaf

curtail, keur-teel, v., verkorten, beperken

curtailment, keur-teel-m'nt, s., vermindering c.

curtain, keur-tin, s., gordijn n.

curtsy, keurt-si, s., buiging c. v., een buiging maken

curve, keurv, s., kromming c. v., ombuigen

cushion, koe-sjun, s., kussen n.; (billiard) band c.

custard, kas-turd, s., vla c.; pudding c.

custody, kas-te-di, s., hechtenis c.; (care) zorg c.

custom, kas-tum, s., (habit) gewoonte c.; (trade) klandizie c.; **——ary,** a., gebruikelijk; **——er,** s., klant c.; **——house,** douanekantoor n.; **——s duties,** pl., invoer en uitvoerrechten n.pl.

cut, kat, v., snijden; (grass) maaien; (cards) afnemen; (gems) slijpen; (ignore) negeren. s., snede c.; (slash) houw c.; **——ler,** messenmaker c.; **——lery,** messenmakerij c.; **——let,** karbonade c.; **——off,** v., afsnijden; **——ter,** s., snijder c.; (knife) mes n.; (ship) kotter c.

cuticle, kjoe-ti-k'l, s., opperhuid c.

cuttle-fish, kat-t'l-fisj, s., inktvis c.

cyclamen, sik-kle-men, s., alpenviooltje n.

cycle, sai-k'l, s., fiets c.; (time) kringloop c.

cylinder, sil-lin-d'r, s., cylinder c.; (roller) wals c.

cynical, sin-ni-k'l, a., cynisch

cypress, sai-pris, s., cypres c.

dabble, deb-b'l, v., knoeien; **——r,** s., knoeier c.

daffodil, def-fe-dil, s., gele narcis c.

dagger, deG-G'r, s., dolk c.

dahlia, deel-ja, s., dahlia c.

daily, dee-li, a., dagelijks. s., dagblad n.

dainty, deen-ti, a., lekker. s., lekkernij c.

dairy, dèr-ri, s., melkinrichting c.

daisy, dee-zi, s., madeliefje n.

dale, deel, s., dal n.

dally, del-li, v., talmen; (play) dartelen   [ken

dam, dem, s., dam c.; (animal) moer c. v., indij-

damage, dem-midzj, s., schade c. v., beschadigen

damask, dem-musk, s., damast n. a., damasten; rood

damn, dem, v., (swear) vloeken; (condemn) vervloeken

damnation, dem-nee-sjun, s., verdoeming c.

damp, demp, s., vochtigheid c. a., vochtig

dance, daans, s., dans c. v., dansen

dancer, daan-s'r, s., danser c.; danseres c.

dandelion, den-di-lai-un, s., paardebloem c.

dandruff, den-druf, s., (scurf) roos c.

danger, deen-dzjur, s., gevaar n.

dangerous, deen-dzje-rus, a., gevaarlijk

dangle, deng-G'l, v., bengelen

dapper, dep-per, a., net, keurig; (sprightly)

dare, dèr, v., durven; (defy) tarten   [kwiek

daring, dèr-ing, a., vermetel, gewaagd

dark, daark, a., donker, duister; somber

darkness, daark-nis, s., duisternis c.

darling, daar-ling, s., lieveling c. a., geliefd

darn, daarn, v., stoppen. s., stop c.

darning-wool, daar-ning-woel, s., stopgaren n.

dart, daart, s., pijl c., werpspies c. v., werpen

dash, desj, s., botsing c. v., (throw) smijten; (rush) zich storten

dashing, desj-ing, a., flink, kranig

dastard, des-turd, s., lafaard c.

data, dee-ta, s.pl., gegevens n.pl.

date, deet, s., datum c.; (fruit) dadel c. v., dateren

daughter, doa-t'r, s., dochter c.

daughter-in-law, doa-t'r-in-loa, s., schoondochter c.

dauntless, doant-lis, a., onverschrokken

dawdle, doad-d'l, v., treuzelen, lummelen

dawn, doan, s., dageraad c. v., licht worden

day, dee, s., dag c.; ——break, aanbreken van de dag n.; ——light, daglicht n.

dazzle, dez-z'l, v., verblinden

deacon, die-kun, s., diaken c.

dead, ded, a., dood; ——ly, dodelijk

deaden, ded-d'n, v., verzwakken; (sound) dempen

deadlock, ded-lok, s., dode punt n., impasse c.

deaf, def, a., doof; ——en, v., verdoven

deafness, def-nis, s., doofheid c.

deal, diel, s., (business) transactie c.; (quantity) hoeveelheid c.; (wood) grenehout n. v., (trade) handelen; (treat) behandelen

dealer, die-l'r, s., handelaar c.; (cards) gever c.

dean, dien, s., deken c.

dear, dier, a., lief, dierbaar; (costly) duur. s., schat c.

dearth, deurth, s., schaarste c., gebrek n.

death, deth, s., dood c.; sterfgeval n.

debar, di-baar, v., uitsluiten; verhinderen

debase, di-bees, v., vernederen, verlagen

debate, di-beet, s., debat n. v., redetwisten

debater, di-bee-t'r, s., debater c.

debauch, di-boatsj, s., zwelgpartij c.

debauchery, di-boa-tsje-ri, s., losbandigheid c.

debenture, di-ben-tsjur, s., obligatie c.

debit, deb-bit, s., debet n. v., debiteren

debt, debt, s., schuld c.; ——or, schuldenaar c.

decadence, dek-ke-d'ns, s., verval n.

decamp, di-kemp, v., zijn biezen pakken

decant, di-kent, v., overgieten

decanter, di-ken-t'r, s., karaf c.

decapitate, di-kep-pi-teet, v., onthoofden

decay, di-kee, s., v., (decline) achteruitgang c., verval n.; (rotting) bederf n. v., vervallen; bederven

decease, di-sies, v., overlijden. s., dood c.

deceased, di-siest, a., overleden

deceit, di-siet, s., bedrog n., misleiding c.

deceitful, di-siet-foel, a., bedrieglijk

deceive, di-siev, v., bedriegen

December, di-sem-b'r, s., december c.

decency, die-sun-si, s., fatsoen n.

decennial, di-sen-jul, a., tienjarig

decent, die-sent, a., fatsoenlijk, welvoeglijk

deception, di-sep-sjun, s., bedrog n.

deceptive, di-sep-tiv, a., misleidend

decide, di-said, v., beslissen, besluiten

decided, di-sai-did, a., beslist, vastbesloten

decimal, des-si-m'l, a., tientallig. s., tiendelige
breuk c.

decipher, di-sai-f'r, v., ontcijferen, ontraadselen

decision, di-siz-zjun, s., beslissing c.

decisive, di-sai-siv, a., beslissend

deck, dek, s., dek n.; —— **out,** v., versieren

declaim, di-kleem, v., voordragen, declameren

declaration, dek-le-ree-sjun, s., verklaring c.

declare, di-klèr, v., verklaren; (customs) aangeven

declension, di-klen-sjun, s., verval n., achteruitgang c.; (gram.) verbuiging c.

decline, di-klain, s., achteruitgang c.; (prices)
prijsdaling c. v., hellen; (diminish) afnemen;
(reject) weigeren; (gram.) verbuigen

decompose, die-kum-pooz, v., ontbinden

decorate, dek-ke-reet, v., versieren; decoreren

decoration, dek-ke-ree-sjun, s., versiering c.

decorous, di-koa-rus, a., gepast, fatsoenlijk

decoy, di-koi, s., lokeend c.; (fig.) lokaas n. v.,
verlokken

decrease, di-kries, s., vermindering c. v.,
verminderen

decree, di-krie, s., bevel n. v., bevelen

decry, di-krai, v., openlijk afkeuren

dedicate, ded-di-keet, v., wijden; (devote) toewijden

deduce, di-djoes, v., afleiden

deduct, di-dakt, v., aftrekken

deduction, di-dak-sjun, s., aftrek c.; deductie c.

deed, died, s., daad c.; (document) akte c.

deem, diem, v., oordelen, achten, denken

deep, diep, a., diep; (profound) diepzinnig. **s.,**
diepte c.

deepen, die-p'n, v., verdiepen

deer, dier, s., hert n.

deface, di-fees, v., schenden, misvormen

defamation, def-fe-mee-sjun, s., laster c.

defame, di-feem, v., lasteren, smaden

default, di-foalt, s., gebrek n., verzuim n.; (business) wanbetaling c. v., in gebreke blijven; (law) niet verschijnen

defaulter, di-foal-t'r, s., wanbetaler c.

defeat, di-fiet, s., nederlaag c.; (frustration) verijdeling c. v., verslaan; verijdelen

defect, di-fekt, s., gebrek n.; ——ive, a., gebrek- [kig

defence, di-fens, s., verdediging c.

defenceless, di-fens-lis, a., weerloos

defend, di-fend, v., verdedigen, beschermen

defendant, di-fen-d'nt, s., gedaagde c.

defender, di-fen-d'r, s., verdediger c.

defensible, di-fen-si-b'l, a., verdedigbaar

defensive, di-fen-siv, a., defensief

defer, di-feur, v., uitstellen

deferential, def-fe-ren-sjul, a., eerbiedig

defiance, di-fai-'ns, s., uitdaging c.

deficiency, di-fis-sjun-si, s., gebrek n.; tekort c.

deficient, di-fis-sjunt, a., gebrekkig, ontoereikend

deficit, def-fi-sit, s., deficit n., tekort n.

defile, di-fail, s., bergpas c. v., bevuilen

define, di-fain, v., afbakenen; omschrijven

definite, def-fi-nit, a., bepaald; precies

definition, def-fi-nis-sjun, s., definitie c.

deflect, di-flekt, v., afwijken

deflection, di-fleck-sjun, s., afwijking c.

deform, di-foarm, v., misvormen, ontsieren

defraud, di-froad, v., bedriegen; beroven

defray, di-free, v., bekostigen, betalen

deft, deft, a., vlug, vaardig, handig

defunct, di-fankt, a., overleden

defy, di-fai, v., uitdagen; (resist) trotseren

degenerate, di-dzjen-ne-rit, a., ontaard. v., ontaarden

degradation, deG-Gre-dee-sjun, s., degradatie c.

degrade, di-Greed, v., degraderen; vernederen

degree, di-Grie, s., graad c.; (status) stand c.

deign, deen, v., zich verwaardigen

deject, di-djzjekt, v., ontmoedigen
dejection di-djzjek-sjun, s., neerslachtigheid c.
delay, di-lee, v., (postpone) uitstellen; (retard)
    vertragen. s., uitstel n.; vertraging c.
delectable, di-lek-te-b'l, a., verrukkelijk
delegate, del-li-Git, s., gedelegeerde c.
delete, di-liet, v., doorhalen, schrappen
deleterious, del-li-tie-ri-us, a., schadelijk
deletion, di-lie-sjun, s., doorhaling c.
deliberate, di-lib-be-rit, a., opzettelijk; (not
    hasty) bedaard. v., overwegen; (confer)
    beraadslagen
delicacy, del-li-ke-si, s., fijnheid c.; teerheid c.
delicate, del-li-kit, a., fijn; (weak) teer
delicious, di-lis-sjus, a., heerlijk
delight, di-lait, s., genot n. v., verrukken
delightful, di-lait-foel, a., verrukkelijk
delineate, di-lin-ni-eet, v., schetsen
delinquent, di-ling-kwunt, s., misdadiger c.
delirious, di-lir-ri-us, a., ijlend; to be ——, v.,
    ijlen
delirium, di-lir-ri-um, s., waanzin c., razernij c.
deliver, di-liv-v'r, v., (goods) bezorgen; (set
    free) bevrijden; (speech) houden; (letters)
    bestellen; (note) overhandigen; ——y, s.,
    (goods) bezorging c.; (letters) bestelling c.;
    (deliverance) bevrijding c.
delude, di-ljoed, v., bedriegen, misleiden
delusion, di-ljoe-zjun, s., bedrog n., misleiding c.
delve, delv, v., delven, graven
demand (di-maand, s., eis c. v., eisen, vorderen
demean (oneself), di-mien (wan-self), v., zich
    verne7deren
demeanour, di-mie-n'r, s., gedrag n., houding c.
demented, di-men-tid, a., krankzinnig
demise, di-maiz, s., overdracht c.; overlijden n.
democratic, dem-me-kret-tik, a., democratisch
demolish, di-mol-lisj, v., afbreken, slopen
demon, die-m'n, s., duivel c., boze geest c.
demonstrate, dem-m'n-street, v., bewijzen
demoralize, di-mor-re-laiz, v., demoraliseren
demur, di-meur, v., aarzelen. s., aarzeling c.

demure, di-mjoer, a., (serious) bezadigd; (prim) preuts

demurrage, di-mar-ridzj, s., overliggeld n.

den, den, s., (lair) hol n.; (cage) hok n.

denial, di-nai-ul, s., verloochening c.

denizen, den-ni-z'n, s., burger c., bewoner c.

denomination, di-nom-mi-nee-sjun, s., benoeming c.; (sect) sekte c.

denote, di-noot, v., aanduiden, aanwijzen

denounce, di-nauns, v., aanklagen

dense, dens, a., dicht; (stupid) stom

density, den-si-ti, s., dichtheid c.

dent, dent, s., deuk c. v., indeuken

dentist, den-tist, s., tandarts c.

dentistry, den-tis-try, s., tandheelkunde c.

denude, di-njoed, v., ontbloten, blootleggen

deny, di-nai, v., ontkennen; (refuse) weigeren

deodorizer, die-o-de-rai-z'r, s., ontsmettingsmiddel n.

depart, di-paart, v., vertrekken, heengaan [del n.

department, di-paart-m'nt, s., afdeling c.

departure, di-paart-sjur, s., vertrek n.; —— platform, perron van vertrek n.

depend, di-pend, v., afhangen; —— upon, zich verlaten op

dependent, di-pen-d'nt, a., afhankelijk

depict, di-pikt, v., schilderen, afbeelden

deplete, di-pliet, v., ledigen, ontlasten

depletion, di-plie-sjun, s., lediging c.

deplore, di-ploar, v., betreuren, bewenen

deport, di-poart, v., deporteren

deportment, di-poart-m'nt, s., houding c.

depose, di-pooz, v., (king) afzetten

deposit, di-poz-zit, s., (transaction) waarborgsom c.; (bank) storting c.; (sediment) bezinksel n. v., in bewaring geven; storten; bezinken

depositor, di-poz-zi-t'r, s., inlegger c.

depository, di-poz-zi-te-ri, s., bewaarplaats c.

depot, dep-po, s., depot n., opslagplaats c.

deprave, di-preev, v., (morals) bederven

deprecate, dep-pri-keet, v., ernstig afkeuren

depreciate, di-prie-sji-eet, v., (price) doen dalen

depredation, dep-pri-dee-sjun, s., plundering c.

depress, di-pres, v., neerdrukken

depression, di-pres-sjun, s., neerslachtigheid c.

deprivation, dep-pri-vee-sjun, s., beroving c.

deprive, di-praiv, v., beroven; afzetten

depth, depth, s., diepte c.

deputy, dep-joe-ti, s., afgevaardigde c.

derailment, di-reel-m'nt, s., ontsporing c.

derange, di-reendzj, v., storen, verwarren

derangement, di-reendzj-m'nt, s., storing c.

derelict, der-ri-likt, s., verlaten schip n.; (wreck) wrak n. a., verlaten; onbeheerd

deride, di-raid, v., bespotten, uitlachen

derisive, di-rai-siv, a., spottend; bespottelijk

derive, di-raiv, v., afleiden; afstammen

descend, di-send, v., neerdalen; (mountain) afdalen; (lineage) afstammen

descendant, di-send-'nt, s., afstammeling c.

descent, di-sent, s., nederdaling c.; afstamming c.

describe, dis-kraib, v., beschrijven

description, dis-krip-sjun, s., beschrijving c.

desecrate, des-si-kreet, v., ontheiligen

desert, dez-zurt, s., woestijn c. a., woest

desert, di-zeurt, v., verlaten; (mil.) deserteren; ——er, s., deserteur c.; ——ion, verlating c.; (mil.) desertie c.

deserve, di-zeurv, v., verdienen

deserving, di-zeur-ving, a., verdienstelijk

design, di-zain, v., (sketch) schetsen, ontwerpen; (intend) voorhebben. s., (purpose) plan n.; (sketch) ontwerp n.; (pattern) patroon n.; ——ing, a., listig

designate, dez-zig-neet, v., aanwijzen

designer, di-zai-n'r, s., ontwerptekenaar c.

desirable, di-zai-re-b'l, a., wenselijk

desire, di-zair, v., (wish) wensen; (covet) begeren. s., wens c.; begeerte c.

desirous, di-zai-rus, a., begerig, verlangend

desist, di-zist, v., ophouden; afzien

desk, desk, s., lessenaar c.

desolate, des-se-lit, a., verlaten; (fig.) troosteloos

despair, dis-pèr, v., wanhopen. s., wanhoop c.

despatch, dis-petsj (see dispatch)

desperate, des-pe-rit, a., (hopeless) hopeloos; (reckless) vermetel

despicable, des-pi-ke-b'l, a., verachtelijk

despise, dis-paiz, v., verachten, versmaden

despite, dis-pait, prep., ondanks, trots

despoil, dis-poil, v., plunderen; (rob) beroven

despondent, dis-pon-d'nt, a., moedeloos

despot, des-pot, s., despoot c., tiran c.

dessert, di-zeurt, s., nagerecht n., dessert n.

destination, des-ti-nee-sjun, s., bestemming c.

destine, des-tin, v., bestemmen

destiny, des-ti-ni, s., bestemming c.; noodlot n.

destitute, des-ti-tjoet, a., behoeftig

destitution, des-ti-tjoe-sjun, s., bittere armoede

destroy, dis-troi, v., vernielen, verwoesten [c.

destruction, dis-trak-sjun, s., verwoesting c.

destructive, dis-trak-tiv, a., verwoestend

desultory, des-sul-te-ri, a., onsamenhangend

detach, di-tetsj, v., losmaken

detachable, di-tetsj-ee-b'l, a., afneembaar

detail, die-teel, s., bijzonderheid c.; (trifle) kleinigheid c.

detail, di-teel, v., omstandig verhalen

detain, di-teen, v., terughouden; (prison) gevangen houden

detect, di-tekt, v., ontdekken; (see) bespeuren

detective, di-tek-tiv, s., detective c.

detention, di-ten-sjun, s., vasthouding c.

deter, di-teur, v., afschrikken, afhouden

deteriorate, di-tie-ri-e-reet, v., slechter worden

determine, di-teur-min, v., besluiten

detest, di-test, v., verafschuwen

dethrone, di-throon, v., onttronen

detonation, die-te-nee-sjun, s., ontploffing c.

detour, di-toer, s., omweg c.

detract, di-trekt, v., verminderen

detrimental, det-tri-men-t'l, a., nadelig

deuce, djoes, s., (cards) twee c.; the ———! interj., drommels!

devastate, dev-ve-steet, v., verwoesten

develop, di-vel-lup, v., ontwikkelen

development, di-vel-lup-m'nt, s., ontwikkeling c.

deviate, die-vi-eet, v., afwijken
device, di-vais, s., plan n.; (gadget) uitvinding c.
devoid, di-void, a., ontbloot, verstoken
devote, di-voot, v., toewijden, bestemmen
devour, di-vaur, v., verslinden
devout, di-vaut, a., godvruchtig, vroom
dew, djoe, s., dauw c. v., bedauwen
dexterous, deks-te-rus, a., behendig, handig
diabetes, dai-e-bie-tus, s., suikerziekte c.
diabolical, dai-e-bol-lik-'l, a., duivels
diagnose, dai-eG-nooz, v., vaststellen, constateren
diagonal, dai-eG-Ge-nul, a., overhoeks, diagonaal
diagram, dai-e-Grem, s., diagram n., figuur c.
dial, dai-ul, s., wijzerplaat c. v., (telephone) opbellen
dialect, dai-e-lekt, s., dialect n., tongval c.
dialogue, dai-e-loG, s., dialoog c., samenspraak c.
diameter, dai-em-mi-t'r, s., middellijn c.
diamond, dai-e-mund, s., diamant c.
diamonds, dai-e-munds, s.pl., (cards) ruiten c.
diarrhœa, dai-e-ri-a, s., diarree c., buikloop c.
diary, dai-e-ri, s., dagboek n.; zakagenda c.
dice, dais, s.pl., dobbelstenen c.pl.
dictate, dik-teet, v., dicteren, voorzeggen
dictionary, dik-sje-ne-ri, s., woordenboek n.
die, dai, v., sterven. s., dobbelsteen c.
diet, dai-et, s., dieet n. v., op dieet leven
differ, dif-f'r, v., (dissimilar) verschillen; (disagree) het niet eens zijn; ——ence, s., verschil n.; geschil n.; ——ent, a., verschillend
difficult, dif-fi-kult, a., moeilijk, lastig
difficulty, dif-fi-kul-ti, s., moeilijkheid c.
diffident, dif-fi-d'nt, a., schroomvallig
diffuse, dif-fjoez, v., verspreiden. a., verspreid
dig, diG, v., spitten; —— up, opgraven
digest, di-dzjest, v., verteren
digestion, dai-dzjes-tsjun, s., spijsvertering c.
dignified, diG-ni-faid, a., waardig, deftig
dignitary, diG-ni-te-ri, s., waardigheidsbekleder
dignity, diG-ni-ti, s., waardigheid c. [c.
digression, dai-Gres-sjun, s., afdwaling c.
dike, daik, s., (ditch) sloot c.; (dam) dijk c.

dilapidated, di-lep-pi-dee-tid, a., bouwvallig

dilapidation, di-lep-pi-dee-sjun, s., bouwvallig-
heid c.

dilate, di-leet, v., uitzetten, verwijden

dilatory, dil-le-tc-ri, a., talmend

dilemma, di-lem-ma, s., dilemma n.

diligence, dil-li-djuns, s., ijver c., vlijt c.

diligent, dil-li-djunt, a., ijverig, vlijtig

dilute, dai-ljoet, v., verdunnen, verslappen

dim, dim, a., (faint) dof, mat; (indistinct) schemerig, vaag. v., verduisteren; (car) dimmen

dimension, di-men-sjun, s., afmeting c., grootte

diminish, di-min-nisj, v., verminderen   [c.

dimple, dim-p'l, s., kuiltje n.

din, din, s., lawaai n., geraas n. v., verdoven

dine, dain, v., dineren, eten

dingy, din-zji, a., (dark) donker; (dirty) smerig

dining-car, dai-ning-kaar, s., restauratiewagen c.

dining-room, dai-ning-roem, s., eetzaal c.

dinner, din-n'r, s., middagmaal n., diner n.

dip, dip, s., onderdompeling c. v., indompelen;
(flag) neerlaten

diphtheria, dif-thie-ri-a, s., diphtherie c.

diplomacy, di-plo-me-si, s., diplomatie c.

dire, dair, a., verschrikkelijk, akelig

direct, di-rekt, v., (conduct) leiden; (command)
voorschrijven; (way) wijzen. a., direct; ——
ion, s., richting c.; ——ly, adv., dadelijk;
——or, s., directeur c., leider c.; ——ory,
adresboek n.

dirigible, dir-rid-zji-b'l, a., bestuurbaar

dirt, deurt, s., vuil n., slijk n.; ——y, a., vuil

disability, dis-e-bil-li-ti, s., onbekwaamheid c.

disable, dis-ee-b'l, v., ongeschikt maken

disabuse, dis-e-bjoez, v., uit de droom helpen

disadvantage, dis-ed-vaan-tidzj, s., nadeel n.

disagree, dis-e-Grie, v., het oneens zijn

disagreeable, dis-c-Grie-e-b'l, a., onaangenaam

disallow, dis-e-lau, v., weigeren, niet toestaan

disappear, dis-c-pier, v., verdwijnen

disappearance, dis-c-pier-'ns, s., verdwijning c.

disappoint, dis-e-**point,** v., teleurstellen

disappointment, dis-e-point-m'nt, s., teleur-
stelling c., tegenvaller c.

disapprove, dis-e-proev, v., afkeuren

disarm, dis-aarm, v., ontwapenen   [ning c.

disarmament, dis-aar-me-m'nt, s., ontwape-

disaster, di-zaas-t'r, s., ramp c., onheil n.

disastrous, di-zaas-trus, a., noodlottig

disburse, dis-beurs, v., betalen, uitbetalen

discard, dis-kaard, v., weggooien, afdanken

discern, di-seurn, v., onderscheiden, bespeuren

discharge, dis-tsjaardzj, v., (unload) lossen;
(gun) afschieten; (duties) vervullen; (pay)
betalen; (acquit) vrijspreken. s., lossen n.;
schot n.; vrijspraak c.; (med.) ontlasting c.

disciple, di-sai-p'l, s., leerling c., discipel c.

discipline, dis-si-plin, s., tucht c., orde c.

disclaim, dis-kleem, v., ontkennen, verwerpen

disclose, dis-klooz, v., onthullen, openbaren

disclosure, dis-klo-zjur, s., onthulling c.

discolour, dis-kal-l'r, v., verschieten, verbleken

discomfort, dis-kam-furt, s., ongemak n.

disconnect, dis-k'n-nekt, v., scheiden, uitschakelen

discontent, dis-k'n-tent, s., ontevredenheid c.

discontented, dis-k'n-ten-tid, a., ontevreden

discontinue, dis-k'n-tin-joe, v., (cease) ophouden
met; (business) opheffen; (subscription) opzeggen

discord, dis-koard, s., tweedracht c.; (sound)
wanklank c.

discount, dis-kaunt, s., korting c. v., disconteren

discourage, dis-kar-ridzj, v., ontmoedigen

discourse, dis-koars, s., voordracht c., toespraak c.

discourteous, dis-koar-ti-us, a., onhoffelijk   [c.

discover, dis-kav-v'r, v., ontdekken; ——**er, s.**,
ontdekker c.; ——**y**, ontdekking c.

discreet, dis-kriet, a., voorzichtig, tactvol

discrepancy, dis-krep-p'n-si, s., tegenstrijdigheid c.

discriminate, dis-krim-mi-neet, v., onderscheiden

discuss, dis-kas, v., bespreken

discussion, dis-**kas**-sjun, s., discussie c.

disdain, dis-**deen**, v., minachten; (scorn) ver- smaden. s., minachting c.

disdainful, dis-**deen**-foel, a., verachtelijk

disease, di-**ziez**, s., ziekte c.; —— d, a., ziek

disengaged, dis-in-**Geedzjd**, a., vrij; onbezet

disentangle, dis-in-**teng**-G'l, v., ontwarren, bevrijden

disfavour, dis-**fee**-v'r, s., ongenade c.

disfigure, dis-**fiG**-G'r, v., misvormen, verminken

disgrace, dis-**Grees**, s., ongenade c.; (shame) schande c.

disguise, dis-**Gaiz**, s., vermomming c.; (fig.) masker n. v., vermommen; (fig.) verbloemen

disgust, dis-**Gast**, s., walging c. v., doen walgen

dish, disj, s., schotel c.; (meal) gerecht n.; —— -cloth, vaatdoek c.; —— up, v., opdissen

dishearten, dis-**haar**-t'n, v., ontmoedigen

dishevelled, di-sjev-vuld, a., verward, slordig

dishonest, dis-**on**-nist, a., oneerlijk

dishonour, dis-**on**-n'r, s., oneer c. v., onteren

disillusion, dis-il-**ljoe**-zjun, v., ontgoochelen

disinclination, dis-in-kli-**nee**-sjun, s., tegenzin c.

disinfect, dis-in-**fekt**, v., ontsmetten

disinherit, dis-in-**her**-rit, v., onterven

disjointed, dis-**dzjoin**-tid, a., onsamenhangend

disk, disk, s., schijf c., discus c.

dislike, dis-**laik**, s., afkeer c. v., niet houden van

dislocate, dis-le-**keet**, v., ontwrichten

disloyal, dis-**loi**-ul, a., ontrouw, trouweloos

dismal, dis-mul, a., akelig, somber, triest

dismay, dis-**mee**, v., ontzetting c. v., doen ont-

dismiss, dis-**mis**, v., wegzenden, ontslaan [stellen

dismount, dis-**mount**, v., afstijgen

disobedient, dis-e-**bied**-j'nt, a., ongehoorzaam

disobey, dis-e-**bee**, v., niet gehoorzamen

disorder, dis-**oar**-d'r, s., wanorde c.

disown, dis-**oon**, v., niet erkennen, verloochenen

disparage, dis-**per**-ridzj, v., kleineren, afbreken

dispatch, dis-**petsj**, s., (sending) verzending c.; (message) bericht n. v., met spoed verzenden

dispel, dis-**pel**, v., verdrijven, verjagen

dispensary, dis-pen-se-ri, s., armenapotheek c.

dispensation, dis-pen-see-sjun, s., uitdeling c.; (eccl.) dispensatie c.

disperse, dis-peurs, v., verspreiden, uiteenjagen

display, dis-plee, s., vertoning c., uitstalling c.; (pomp) praal c. v., uitstallen; (exhibit) vertonen

displease, dis-pliez, v., mishagen

displeasure, dis-plez-zjur, s., misnoegen n.

disposal, dis-po-zul, s., beschikking c.

dispose (of), dis-pooz (ov), v., uit de weg ruimen

disposed, dis-poozd, a., geneigd, gestemd

disprove, dis-proev, v., weerleggen

disputable, dis-pjoe-te-b'l, a., betwistbaar

dispute, dis-pjoet, s., dispuut n. v., redetwisten

disqualify, dis-kwoa-li-fai, v., ongeschikt maken

disquiet, dis-kwai-ut, s., onrust c. v., verontrusten

disregard, dis-ri-Gaard, s., veronachtzaming c. v., veronachtzamen, negeren [c.

disrepute, dis-ri-pjoet, s., slechte naam c., oneer

disrespect, dis-ris-pekt, s., oneerbiedigheid c.

disrespectful, dis-ris-pekt-foel, a., oneerbiedig

dissatisfy, dis-set-tis-fai, v., teleurstellen

dissect, di-sekt, v., ontleden

dissent, di-sent, s., verschil van mening n.

dissimilar, di-sim-mi-l'r, a., ongelijk

dissipate, di-si-peet, v., verkwisten

dissociate, di-so-sji-eet, v., afscheiden

dissolute, dis-se-ljoet, a., losbandig

dissolve, di-zolv, v., oplossen; zich oplossen

dissuade, di-zweed, v., afraden, ontraden

distance, dis-t'ns, s., afstand c.; verte c.

distant, dis-t'nt, a., ver, verwijderd

distaste, dis-teest, s., afkeer c.; ——**ful**, a., onaangenaam; (food) onsmakelijk

distemper, dis-tem-p'r, s., hondeziekte c.

distend, dis-tend, v., opzwellen, rekken

distil, dis-til, v., sijpelen; distilleren

distinct, dis-tingkt, a., (separate) gescheiden; (clear) duidelijk; ——**ion**, s., onderscheid n.; (award) onderscheiding c.

distinguish, dis-**ting**-ɢwisj, v., onderscheiden

distort, dis-**toart,** v., verdraaien, verwringen

distract, dis-**trekt,** v., afleiden; (bewilder) verbijsteren; ——**ion,** s., afleiding c.; verwarring [c.

distrain, dis-**treen,** v., in beslag nemen [c.

distress, dis-**tres,** s., nood c. v., benauwen

distressing, dis-**tres**-sing, a., pijnlijk

distribute, dis-**trib**-joet, v., uitdelen, verdelen

district, dis-**trikt,** s., district n., streek c.

distrust, dis-**trast,** v., wantrouwen n. v., wantrouwen

disturb, dis-**teurb,** v., storen; (disquiet) verontrusten; ——**ance,** s., storing c.; (mob) beroering c.

disuse, dis-**joes,** s., onbruik n.

ditch, ditsj, s., sloot c.; (round fortress) gracht c.

ditto, dit-to, adv., dito, hetzelfde

dive, daiv, s., duik c. v., duiken

diver, dai-**v'r,** s., duiker c.

diverge, dai-**veurdzj,** v., afwijken

diverse, dai-**veurs,** a., verschillend [maak n.

diversion, dai-**veur**-sjun, s., afleiding c.; vermaak n.

divert, dai-**veurt,** v., afwenden; (amuse) vermaken

divest, di-**vest,** v., ontkleden; (deprive) beroven

divide, di-**vaid,** v., verdelen; (separate) scheiden

divine, di-**vain,** a., goddelijk. v., raden

division, di-**vi**-zjun, s., verdeling c.; (discord) verdeeldheid c.; (mil.) divisie c.

divorce, di-**voars,** s., echtscheiding c. v., scheiden

divulge, di-**valdzj,** v., bekend maken

dizzy, diz-zi, a., duizelig

do, doe, v., doen, maken

docile, do-sail, a., leerzaam; (tractable) volgzaam

dock, dok, s., dok n.; (plant) zuring c. v., dokken

dockyard, dok-jaard, s., scheepswerf c.

doctor, dok-t'r, s., (med.) dokter c.; (degree) doctor c.

doctrine, dok-trin, s., leer c.

document, dok-joe-m'nt, s., document n., akte c.

dodge, dodzj, s., kunstje n. v., ontduiken

dog, doɢ, s., hond c.; ——**ged,** a., hardnekkig

dole, dool, s., uitkering c. v., uitdelen

doleful, dool-foel, a., treurig

doll, dol, s., pop c.; ——'s house, poppenhuis n.

dome, doom, s., koepel c., gewelf n.

domestic, de-mes-tik, s., dienstbode c. a., huise-
domesticated, de-mes-ti-kee-tid, a., tam [lijk

domicile, dom-mi-sail, s., woonplaats c.

dominate, dom-mi-neet, v., overheersen

domineer, dom-mi-nier, v., de baas spelen

donation, do-nee-sjun, s., gift c.; (act) schenking

donkey, dong-ki, s., ezel c. [c.

donor, do-n'r, s., gever c., schenker c.

doom, doem, s., lot n. v., doemen

doomsday, doemz-dee, s., dag des oordeels c.

door, door, s., deur c.; (car) portier n.; ——
——-keeper, portier c.; ——-knocker, klopper
c.; ——-latch, deurklink c.; ——-mat,
deurmat c.

dormitory, doar-mi-tri, s., slaapzaal c.

dose, doos, s., dosis c. v., afpassen

dot, dot, s., punt c., stip c. v., stippelen

double, dab-b'l, a. & adv., dubbel. s., dubbele
n.; (person) dubbelganger c. v., verdubbelen

doubt, daut, s., twijfel c.; (uncertainty) onzekerheid c. v., twijfelen; ——-ful, a., twijfelachtig

douche, doesj, s., douche c.

dough, doo, s., deeg c.; (pop.) duiten c.pl.

dove, dav, s., duif c.; ——-cot, duiventil c.

dowager, dau-e-dzjur, s., douairière c.

down, daun, adv., naar beneden, neer, onder, af.
prep., langs, van . . . af. s., (feathers) dons
n.; ——-cast, a., neergeslagen; ——-fall,
val c.; (fig.) ondergang c.; ——-hill, adv.,
bergaf; ——-pour, v., stortregen c.; ——-
stairs, adv., naar beneden; beneden; ——-
wards, naar beneden

dowry, dau-ri, s., bruidsschat c.; (fig.) gave c.

doze, dooz, s., dutje n. v., dutten

dozen, daz-z'n, s., dozijn n.

drab, dreb, a., vaalbruin. s., slons c.

draft, draaft, s., (money) wissel c.; (sketch)
schets c.; (writing) ontwerp n. v., ontwerpen

drag, dreG, v., slepen.   s., sleepnet n.

dragon, dreG-G'n, s., draak c.

dragon-fly, dreG-G'n-flai, s., waterjuffer c.

dragoon, dre-Goen, s., (mil.) dragonder c.

drain, dreen, s., afvoerbuis c.; (land) afwatering c. v., afwateren; ——**age**, s., waterafvoer c.

drake, dreek, s., woerd c.

drama, dra-ma, s., drama n.

dramatic, dra-ma-tik, a., dramatisch

draper, dree-p'r, s., manufacturier c.

drastic, dres-tik, a., drastisch, radicaal

draught, draaft, s., (air) tocht c.; (drink) teug c.; (sketch) klad n.; (ship) diepgang c.; ——-**board**, dambord n.; ——**s**, pl., damspel n.

draughtsman, draafts-m'n, s., tekenaar c.

draw, droa, s., loterij c.; (game) gelijk spel n. v., (pull) trekken; (drag) slepen; (sketch) tekenen; (water) putten; (money) in ontvangst nemen; (breath) scheppen; ——**back**, s., bezwaar n.; ——**bridge**, ophaalbrug c.; ——**er**, (furniture) lade c.; (bill) trekker c.; ——**ers**, pl., (apparel) onderbroek c.; ——**ing**, trekken n.; (sketch) tekening c.; ——**ing-room**, salon c.

drawl, droal, s., geteem n. v., lijzig spreken

dread, dred, s., vrees c. v., vrezen

dreadful, dred-foel, a., vreselijk

dream, driem, s., droom c. v., dromen

dreary, drie-ri, a., somber, akelig; (place) woest

dredge, dredzj, v., dreggen. s., dreg c.

dredger, dred-zjur, s., baggermachine c.

dregs, dreGz, s., droesem c.; (fig.) uitschot n.

drench, drentsj, v., doornat maken

dress, dres, s., kleding c.; (ladies) japon c. v., aankleden; (wounds) verbinden; ——**ing**, s., (med.) verband n.; (sauce) saus c.; ——**ing-case**, toiletnécessaire c.; ——**ing-gown**, kamerjapon c.; ——**ing-room**, kleedkamer c.; ——**maker**, dameskleermaker c.

dribble, drib-b'l, v., (drop) druppelen; (saliva) kwijlen

drift, drift, s., drijfkracht c.; (snow) jachtsneeuw

c.; (sand) opeenhoping c.; (tendency) strekking c. v., drijven

drill, dril, v., (mil.) exerceren; (bore) boren. s., (mil.) drillen n.; (tool) drilboor c.

drink, dringk, v., drinken. s., drank c.

drip, drip, v., druipen. s., drup c.

dripping, drip-ping, s., (fat) braadvet n.

drive, draiv, v., drijven; (car) rijden; (urge on) voortdrijven. s., (trip) rit c.; (carriageway) oprijlaan c.; ——r, (tram) bestuurder c.; (carriage) koetsier c.

drizzle, driz-z'l, s., motregen c. v., motregenen

droll, drool, a., grappig, kluchtig. s., grapjas c.

drone, droon, s., dar c.; (fig.) luilak c. v., gonzen

droop, droep, v., laten hangen; (fig) kwijnen

drop, drop, s., druppel c. v., druppelen; (let fall) laten vallen; (fall) vallen

dropsy, drop-si, s., waterzucht c.

drought, draut, s., droogte c.; ——y, a., droog

drove, droov, s., (cattle) kudde c.

drown, draun, v., verdrinken

drowsy, drau-zi, a., slaperig, suf

drudge, dradzj, s., werkezel c. v., zwoegen

drudgery, dradzj-ri, s., gesloof n.

drug, draG, v., bedwelmen. s., bedwelmend middel n.

druggist, draG-Gist, s., drogist c.; apotheker c.

drum, dram, s., trom c. v., trommelen

drummer, dram-m'r, s., trommelslager c., tamboer c.

drunk, drangk, a., dronken; ——ard, s., dronkaard c.; ——enness, dronkenschap c.

dry, drai, a., droog. v., drogen

dryness, drai-nes, s., droogte c.

dubious, djoe-bi-us, a., twijfelachtig

duchess, dat-sjis, s., hertogin c.

duck, dak, s., eend c. v., zich bukken

due, djoe, s., (debt) schuld c.; (right) recht n. a., (owing) schuldig; (proper) behoorlijk

duel, djoe-ul, s. tweegevecht n. v., duelleren

dues, djoez, s.pl., (docks, etc.) gelden n.pl.

duet, djoe-ut, s., duet n.

duke, djoek, s., hertog c.

dull, dal, a., (stupid) dom; (boring) saai; (dim) flauw, mat; (blunt) bot; (inert) traag; (cloudy) somber

duly, djoe-li, adv., (properly) behoorlijk; (punctually) stipt

dumb, dam, a., stom; ——**found**, v., verstomd doen staan

dummy, dam-mi, s., (cards) blinde c.; (for baby) fopspeen c.; (lay-figure) ledepop c.

dump, damp, s., vuilnisbelt c. v., neergooien

dumpling, dam-pling, s., knoedel c.

dung, dang, s., mest c., drek c.

dungeon, dan-dzjun, s., kerker c.

dupe, djoep, s., slachtoffer n. v., beetnemen

duplicate, djoe-pli-kit, s., duplicaat n., afschrift n. v., verdubbelen. a., dubbel

durable, djoe-re-b'l, a., duurzaam

duration, djoe-ree-sjun, s., duur c.

during, djoe-ring, prep., gedurende, tijdens

dusk, dask, s., schemering c.; ——**y**, a., schemerig

dust, dast, s., stof n. v., afstoffen; ——**bin**, s., vuilnisbak c.; ——**er**, stofdoek c.; ——**man**, vuilnisman c.

dutiful, djoe-ti-foel, a., plichtgetrouw

duty, djoe-ti, s., plicht c.; (custom) recht n.; (officials') dienst c.

dwarf, dwoarf, s., dwerg c. v., nietig doen lijken

dwell, dwel, v., wonen; ——**upon**, uitweiden over; ——**er**, s., bewoner c.; ——**ing**, woning c.

dwindle, dwin-d'l, v., afnemen, slinken

dye, dai, v., verven. s., verf c.; ——**works**, ververij c.

dynamite, dai-ne-mait, s., dynamiet n.

dynamo, dai-ne-mo, s., dynamo c.

dysentery, dis-'n-tri, s., dysenterie c.

each, ietsj, a. & pron., elk, ieder; —— **other**, elkander

eager, ie-G'r, a., (keen) vurig; (desirous) begerig

eagerness, ie-G'r-nis, s., vuur n.; begeerte c.

eagle, ie-G'l, s., adelaar c., arend c.

ear, ier, s., oor n.; (corn) aar c.; ———**ring,** oorring c.; ———**wig,** oorworm c.

earl, eurl, s., graaf c.; ———**dom,** graafschap n.

early, eur-li, a. & adv., vroeg

earn, eurn, v., verdienen; ———**ings,** s.pl., loon n.

earnest, eur-nist, s., ernst c. a., ernstig

earth, eurth, s., aarde c.; (soil) grond c. v., (electricity) aarden; ———**enware,** s., aarde-werk n.; ———**ly,** a., aards

earthquake, eurth-kweek, s., aardbeving c.

ease, iez, s., (comfort) gemak n.; (relief) ver-lichting c.; (facility) gemakkelijkheid c. v., verlichting geven; gemakkelijker maken; **at one's** ———, op zijn gemak

easel, ie-z'l, s., schildersezel c.

easily, ie-zi-li, adv., gemakkelijk, op zijn gemak

east, iest, s., oosten n.; ———**erly,** a., oosterlijk; ———**ern,** oosters. s., oosterling c.

Easter, ies-t'r, s., Pasen c. [leunstoel c.

easy, ie-zi, a. & adv., gemakkelijk; ———**chair,** s.,

eat, iet, v., eten; (animals) vreten; (corrode) invreten; ———**able,** a., eetbaar; ———**ables,** s.pl., eetwaren c.pl.

eavesdropper, ievz-drop-p'r, s., luistervink c.

ebb, eb, s., eb c. v., ebben

ebony, eb-be-ni, s., ebbehout n.

eccentric, ek-sen-trik, a., excentriek, zonderling

echo, ek-ko, s., echo c. v., weerklinken

eclipse, i-klips, s., verduistering c. v., verduister-

economize, i-kon-ne-maiz, v., bezuinigen [en

economy, i-kon-ne-mi, s., zuinigheid c.

ecstasy, ek-ste-si, s., zielsverrukking c.

eddy, ed-di, s., (water) draaikolk c.; (wind) wervelwind c.

edge, edzj, s., (knife) snede c.; (brink) rand c. v., (sharpen) scherpen; (border) omzomen

edible, ed-di-b'l, a., eetbaar

edify, ed-di-fai, v., stichten, opbouwen

edit, ed-dit, v., perslaar maken; ———**ion,** uitgave c.; **first** ———**ion,** eerste druk c.; ———**or,** redacteur c.; ———**orial,** hoofdartikel

educate, ed-joe-keet, v., opvoeden [n.

eel, iel, s., aal c., paling c.

efface, i-fees, v., uitwissen, uitvegen

effect, i-fekt, s., uitwerking c., gevolg n. v., teweegbrengen; ——ive, a., doeltreffend; ——ual, krachtdadig

effeminate, i-fem-mi-nit, a., verwijfd

effervescent, ef-fe-ves-s'nt, a., opbruisend

efficacious, ef-fi-kee-sjus, a., krachtdadig

efficiency, i-fis-sjun-si, s., bekwaamheid c.

efficient, i-fis-sjunt, a., (person) bekwaam

effort, ef-furt, s., poging c., inspanning c.

effrontery, ef-fran-te-ri, s., onbeschaamdheid c.

effusive, ef-fjoe-siv, a., overvloedig

egg, eG, s., ei n.; ——cup, eierdopje n.

egotism, eG-Go-tizm, s., eigenliefde c.

egress, ie-Gres, s., uitgaan n.; (exit) uitgang c.

eiderdown, ai-d'r-daun, s., eiderdons n.

eight, eet, a., acht; ——een, achttien; ——eenth, achttiende; ——h, achtste; ——y, tachtig

either, ai-dh'r, a. & pron., een van beide; (each of two) elk van beide. adv., ook; —— ... or, conj., of . . . of

eject, i-dzjekt, v., uitwerpen; (expel) verdrijven

elaborate, i-leb-be-reet, v., uitwerken. a., met zorg uitgewerkt; (complicated) ingewikkeld

elapse, i-leps, v., verlopen, verstrijken

elastic, i-les-tik, a., elastiek n. a., veerkrachtig

elate, e-leet, v., opgetogen maken

elbow, el-bo, s., elleboog c. v., met de ellebogen duwen

elder, el-d'r, s., oudere c.; (tree) vlier c.

elderly, el-d'r-li, a., bejaard, oudachtig

eldest, el-dist, a., oudste. s., oudste c.

elect, i-lekt, v., verkiezen. a., uitverkoren

election, i-lek-sjun, s., verkiezing c.; (choice) keus c.

electric(al), i-lek-trik(-'l), a., electrisch

electrician, i-lek-tris-sjun, s., electricien c.

electricity, i-lek-tris-si-ti, s., electriciteit c.

electrify, i-lek-tri-fai, v., (railway) electrificeren

electroplate, i-lek-tro-pleet, v., galvanisch verzilveren. s., pleetzilver n.

elegance, el-li-G'ns, s., bevalligheid c.

elegant, el-li-G'nt, a., sierlijk, bevallig

element, el-li-m'nt, s., bestanddeel n.

elementary, el-li-m'nt-ri, a., elementair, grond...

elephant, el-li-f'nt, s., olifant c.

elevate, el-li-veet, v., opheffen; (fig.) veredelen

eleven, i-lev-v'n, a., elf; ——th, elfde

elf, elf, s., kabouter c., fee c.

elicit, i-lis-sit, v., uitlokken, ontlokken

eligible, el-lid-zji-b'l, a., verkiesbaar; wenselijk

eliminate, i-lim-mi-neet, v., verwijderen

élite, ee-liet, s., elite c., keur c.

elk, elk, s., eland c.

elm, elm, s., iep c., olm c.

elongate, ie-long-Geet, v., verlengen   [c.

elope, i-loop, v., weglopen; ——ment, s., vlucht

eloquent, el-le-kwunt, a., welsprekend

else, els, adv., anders; ——where, elders, ergens
anders

elucidate, il-joe-si-deet, v., ophelderen, verklaren

elude, il-joed, v., ontwijken, ontsnappen

elusive, il-joe-siv, a., ontwijkend, ontsnappend

emaciate, i-mee-sji-eet, v., doen vermageren

emancipate, i-men-si-peet, v., vrijmaken;
emanciperen

embalm, em-baam, v., balsemen

embankment, em-bengk-m'nt, s., dijk c., dam c.

embark, em-baark, v., inschepen; scheep gaan

embarrass, em-ber-rus, v., in moeilijkheden
brengen; (perplex) verwarren; ——ment, s.,
verlegenheid c.

embassy, em-be-si, s., ambassade c.

embellish, em-bel-lisj, v., verfraaien

embers, em-b'rz, s.pl., gloeiende as c.

embezzle, em-bez-z'l, v., verduisteren

embitter, em-bit-t'r, v., verbitteren

embody, em-bod-di, v., belichamen

embolden, em-bool-d'n, v., aanmoedigen

embrace, em-brees, v., omhelzen; (include)
insluiten

embrocation, em-bre-kee-sjun, s., smeersel n.

embroider, em-broi-d'r, v., borduren

embroidery, em-broi-de-ri, s., borduurwerk n.

embroil, em-broil, v., verwarren; (involve) verwikkelen

emerald, em-me-ruld, s., smaragd n.

emerge, i-meurdzj, v., te voorschijn komen, opkomen

emergency, i-meur-dzjun-si, s., noodtoestand c. nood c.

emetic, i-met-tik, s., braakmiddel n.

emigrant, em-mi-Grunt, s., landverhuizer c.

emigrate, em-mi-Greet, v., emigreren

eminence, em-mi-n'ns, s., hoogte c.; (title) eminentie c.

eminent, em-mi-n'nt, a., verheven, uitstekend

emissary, em-mi-se-ri, s., afgezant c.; (spy) spion c.

emit, i-mit, v., (rays) uitstralen; (eject) uitwerpen

emotion, i-mo-sjun, s., ontroering c.

emotional, i-mo-sjun-'l, a., ontroerend

emperor, em-pe-r'r, s., keizer c.

emphasis, em-fe-sis, s., nadruk c., klem c.

emphasize, em-fe-saiz, v., de nadruk leggen op

emphatic, em-fet-tik, a., nadrukkelijk

empire, em-pair, s., rijk n.; (dominion) heerschappij c.

employ, em-ploi, v., gebruiken; (engage) in dienst hebben.   s., (work) bezigheid c.; (service) dienst c.; ——**er**, wekgever c.; ——**ment**, bezigheid c., werk n.

empower, em-pau-ur, v., machtigen

empress, em-pris, s., keizerin c.

empty, em-ti, a., leeg, ledig

emulate, em-joe-leet, v., wedijveren met

emulation, em-joe-lee-sjun, s., wedijver c.; (envy) naijver c.

enable, en-ee-b'l, v., in staat stellen

enact, en-ekt, v., (decree) bepalen; (perform) opvoeren

enamel, en-em-m'l, s., email n. v., emailleren

enamoured (of), en-em-murd (ov), a., verliefd

encamp, en-kemp, v., kamperen, legeren [(op)

enchant, en-tsjaant, v., betoveren; (fig.) bekoren

enchantment, en-tsjaant-m'nt, s., betovering c.

encircle, en-seur-k'l, v., omringen, insluiten

enclose, en-klooz, v., insluiten, opsluiten

enclosure, en-klo-zjur, s., (letter) ingeslotene n.; (fence) omheining c.

encompass, en-kam-pus, v., omringen, omgeven

encore! ong-koar, interj., bis! nog eens!

encounter, en-kaun-t'r, s., ontmoeting c.; (enemy) gevecht n. v., ontmoeten, tegenko-

encourage, en-kar-ridzj, v., aanmoedigen [men

encroachment, en-krootsj-m'nt, s., inbreuk c.

encumber, en-kam-b'r, v., belemmeren, hinde-

encumbrance, en-kam-br'ns, s., hindernis c. [ren

encyclopædia, en-sai-kle-pie-di-a, s., encyclo- pedie c.

end, end, s., eind n.; (conclusion) besluit n.; (aim) doel n. v., eindigen, besluiten

endanger, en-deen-dzjur, v., in gevaar brengen

endear, en-dier, v., bemind maken

endearment, en-dier-m'nt, s., liefkozing c.

endeavour, en-dev-v'r, s., poging c. v., trachten

endive, en-div, s., andijvie c.

endless, end-lis, a., eindeloos, zonder einde

endorse, en-doars, v., endosseren

endow, en-dau, v., begiftigen, doteren   [gen n.

endurance, en- djoe-r'ns, s., uithoudingsvermo-

endure, en-djoer, v., dulden, verdragen

enema, en-ni-ma, s., klisteerspuit c.; klisteer c.

enemy, en-ni-mi, s., vijand c. a., vijandelijk

energetic, en-ne-dzjet-tik, a., energiek, krachtig

energy, en-ne-dzji, s., energie c., kracht c.

enervate, en-ne-veet, v., verzwakken

enfeeble, en-fie-b'l, v., verzwakken

enfilade, en-fi-leed, v., (mil.) enfileren

enforce, en-foars, v., afdwingen, dwingen tot

engage, en-Geedzj, v., (employ) in dienst nemen; (reserve) bespreken; (enemy) aanvallen; (bind) verbinden; (betroth) verloven

engaged, en-Geedzj-'d, a., (betrothed) verloofd; (occupied) bezig, bezet; (reserved) besproken

engagement, en-Geedzj-m'nt, s., (betrothal) ver- loving c.; (obligation) verplichting c.;

(appointment) afspraak c.; (occupation) bezigheid c.; (combat) gevecht n.

engaging, en-Gee-dzjing, a., innemend

engender, en-dzjen-d'r, v., verwekken, voortbrengen

engine, en-dzjin, s., machine c.; (rail) locomotief c.; (of car, etc.) motor c.

engineer, en-dzji-**nier,** s., ingenieur c.; (mil.) geniesoldaat c.; (ship) machinist c.

engineering, en-dzji-**nie**-ring, s., machinebouw

engrave, en-Greev, v., graveren; inprenten   [c.

engrossing, en-Gro-sing, a., boeiend

engulf, en-Galf, v., verzwelgen, verslinden

enhance, en-haans, v., verhogen, vergroten

enjoin, en-dzjoin, v., bevelen, gelasten

enjoy, en-dzjoi, v., genieten van; (rejoice in) zich verheugen in; —— **oneself,** zich amuseren

enjoyment, en-dzjoi-m'nt, s., genot n.

enlarge, en-laardzj, v., vergroten

enlargement, en-laardzj-m'nt, s., vergroting c.

enlighten, en-lai-t'n, v., inlichten, voorlichten

enlist, en-list, v., inschrijven; (army) aanwerven

enliven, en-lai-v'n, v., verlevendigen

enmity, en-mi-ti, s., vijandschap c.

ennoble, en-no-b'l, v., veredelen

enormous, i-noar-mus, a., reusachtig, enorm

enough, i-naf, a. & adv., genoeg, voldoende

enquire, in-kwair, v., (see **inquire**)

enrage, en-reedzj, v., woedend maken

enrapture, en-rept-sjur, v., in vervoering brengen

enrich, en-ritsj, v., verrijken   [gen

enrol, en-rool, v., inschrijven, registreren

ensign, en-sain, s., (flag) vlag c.; (regiment's flag) vaandel n.; (rank) onderscheidingsteken n.

enslave, en-sleev, v., tot slaaf maken

ensnare, en-snèr, v., verstrikken; (charm) lokken

ensue, en-sjoe, v., volgen, voortkomen

entail, en-teel, v., (involve) meebrengen

entangle, en-teng-G'l, v., verstrikken

enter, en-t'r, v., binnengaan; —— **upon,** aanvaarden

enterprise, en-t'r-praiz, s., onderneming c.

entertain, en-t'r-teen, v., onderhouden; (ponder) in overweging nemen; ——ment, s., onthaal
enthusiasm, en-thjoe-zi-ezm, s., geestdrift c. [n.
entice, en-tais, v., verleiden, verlokken
entire, en-tair, a., geheel, volkomen; gaaf
entitle, en-tai-t'l, v., betitelen; recht geven
entomb, en-toem, v., begraven
entrance, en-tr'ns, s., ingang c., toegang c.
entrance, en-traans, v., verrukken
entreat, en-triet, v., smeken, bidden
entrench, en-trensj, v., verschansen
entrust, en-trast, v., toevertrouwen
entry, en-tri, s., intocht c.; (way in) ingang c.
entwine, en-twain, v., ineenstrengelen
enumerate, i-njoe-me-reet, v., opsommen, optellen
envelop, en-vel-lup, v., omwikkelen, hullen
envelope, en-ve-loop, s., omslag c., enveloppe c.
envious, en-vi-us, a., jaloers, afgunstig
environs, en-vai-r'nz, s.pl., omstreken c.pl.
envoy, en-voi, s., gezant c., afgezant c.
envy, en-vi, s., nijd c. v., benijden
epicure, ep-pi-kjoer, s., epicurist c.
epidemic, ep-pi-dem-mik, s., epidemie c. a., epidemisch
episode, ep-pi-sood, s., episode c.
epistle, i-pis-s'l, s., epistel n., brief c.
epoch, ie-pok, s., tijdperk n.; tijdstip n.
equal, ie-kwul, s., gelijke c. a., gelijk. v., gelijk zijn aan; ——ity, s., gelijkheid c.; ——ize, v., gelijk maken
equator, i-kwee-t'r, s., evenaar c.
equerry, ek-kwe-ri, s., adjudant des Konings c.
equilibrium, ie-kwi-lib-bri-um, s., evenwicht n.
equip, i-kwip, v., uitrusten, toerusten
equitable, ek-kwi-te-b'l, a., billijk, onpartijdig
equity, ek-kwi-ti, s., rechtvaardigheid c.
equivalent, i-kwiv-ve-l'nt, a., gelijkwaardig
era, ie-ra, s., jaartelling c.; (epoch) tijdperk n.
eradicate, i-red-di-keet, v., uitroeien
erase, i-reez, v., uitschrappen, uitwissen
eraser, i-ree-z'r, s., radeermesje n.

erect, i-rekt, v., oprichten. a., rechtop
ermine, eur-min, s., hermelijn c.
err, cur, v., een fout begaan; (sin) zondigen
errand, er-rund, s., boodschap c.; ——-boy, loopjongen c.
erratic, er-ret-tik, a., dwalend, zwervend
erroneous, er-roon-jus, a., verkeerd, onjuist
error, er-r'r, s., vergissing c.; (fault) fout c.
eruption, i-rap-sjun, s., uitbarsting c.; (med.) uitslag c.   [c.
escape, is-keep, v., ontsnappen. s., ontsnapping
escort, is-koart, v., begeleiden. s., geleide n.
especially, is-pes-sje-li, adv., vooral
essay, es-see, s., opstel n.; (attempt) poging c. v., pogen
essential, i-sen-sjul, a, wezenlijk, werkelijk
establish, is-teb-blisj, v., oprichten; (prove) bewijzen; ——-ment, s., (institution) instelling c.
estate, is-teet, s., (land) landgoed n.; (status) rang c.; (possession) bezit n.
esteem, is-tiem, s., achting c. v., waarderen
estimate, es-ti-mit, s., (costs) begroting c.; (appraisement) schatting c. v., schatten
estrange, is-treendzj, v., vervreemden
etching, et-sjing, s., ets c.; ——-needle, etsnaald
eternal, i-teur-n'l, a., eeuwig   [c.
eternity, i-teur-ni-ti, s., eeuwigheid c.
ether, ie-th'r, s., ether c.; ——-eal, a., ijl
euphony, joe-fe-ni, s., welluidendheid c.
evacuate, i-vek-joe-eet, v., evacueren; ledigen
evade, i-veed, v., ontwijken; (pursuers) ontglippen
evaporate, i-vep-pe-reet, v., verdampen
evasive, i-vee-siv, a., ontwijkend
eve, iev, s., vooravond c.
even, ie-v'n, a., (level) effen; (regular) regelmatig; (numbers) gelijk. adv., (what is more) zelfs
evening, ie-ve-ning, s., avond c.; ——-dress, avondtoilet c. ——-prayer, avondgebed n.
evensong, ie-v'n-song, s., avonddienst c.
event, i-vent, s., gebeurtenis c.; (outcome) uit-

slag c.; ——**ful**, a., veelbewogen; ——**ually**, adv., ten slotte

ever, e-v'r, adv., (always) altijd; (at any time) ooit; ——**lasting**, a., eeuwigdurend; —— **more**, adv., steeds

every, ev-vri, a. & pron., ieder, elk; ——**body**, ——**one**, iedereen; ——**thing**, alles; —— **where**, adv., overal

evict, i-vikt, v., gerechtelijk ontzetten

evidence, ev-vi-d'ns, s., (testimony) getuigenis c.; (proof) bewijs n.; **give** ——, getuigenis afleggen

evident, ev-vi-d'nt, a., duidelijk, zichtbaar

evil, ie-vil, a., slecht. s., kwaad n.

evince, i-vins, v., bewijzen, aantonen

evoke, i-vook, v., oproepen

evolve, i-volv, v., ontvouwen, ontwikkelen

ewe, joe, s., ooi c.; ——**lamb**, ooilam n.

ewer, joe-ur, s., lampetkan c.

exact, ig-zekt, a., juist. v., eisen; ——**ing**, a., veeleisend; ——**itude**, s., nauwkeurigheid c.

exaggerate, iG-zed-zje-reet, v., overdrijven

exaggeration, iG-zed-zje-ree-sjun, s., overdrijving c.

exalt, iG-zoalt, v., verheffen, verheerlijken

examination, iG-zem-mi-nee-sjun, s., examen n.; (search) onderzoek n.; (legal) verhoor n.

examine, iG-zem-min, v., onderzoeken; ondervragen

example, iG-zaam-p'l, s., voorbeeld n.; model n.

exasperate, iG-zaas-pe-reet, v., verbitteren

excavate, eks-ke-veet, v., opgraven, uithollen

exceed, ek-sied, v., overtreffen, overschrijden

exceedingly, ek-sie-ding-li, adv., uiterst

excel, ek-sel, v., overtreffen; ——**lent**, a., uitmuntend

except, ek-sept, prep., behalve. v., uitzonderen; ——**ion**, s., uitzondering c.; **take** ——**ion** **to**, aanstoot nemen aan; ——**ional**, a. buitengewoon

excerpt, ek-seurpt, s., aanhaling c., passage c.

excess, ek-ses, s., overmaat c., overdaad c.

excessive, ek-ses-siv, a., overdadig, buitensporig
exchange, ek-tsjeendzj, s., ruil c.; (telephone) telefooncentrale c.; (rate) wisselkoers c. v., verruilen; (money) wisselen
exchequer, ek-tsjek-k'r, s., schatkist c.
excise, ek-saiz, v., uitsnijden. s., accijns c.
excitable, ek-sai-ti-b'l, a., prikkelbaar
excite, ek-sait, v., opwekken
excitement, ek-sait-m'nt, s., opwinding c.
exciting, ek-sai-ting, a., boeiend, spannend
exclaim, eks-kleem, v., uitroepen
exclamation, eks-kle-mee-sjun, s., uitroep c.
exclude, eks-kloed, v., uitsluiten
exclusive, eks-kloe-siv, a., uitsluitend
excruciating, eks-kroe-sji-ee-ting, a., zeer pijn-
exculpate, eks-kal-peet, v., vrijspreken [lijk
excursion, eks-keur-sjun, s., (trip) uitstapje n.
excuse, eks-kjoes, s., excuus n. v., verontschuldigen
execute, ek-si-kjoet, v., (perform) uitvoeren; (put to death) terechtstellen
executioner, ek-si-kjoe-sje-n'r, s., beul c.
executor, ek-si-kjoe-t'r, s., uitvoerder c.
exempt, eG-zemt, v., vrijstellen. a., vrijgesteld
exemption, eG-zem-sjun, s., vrijstelling c.
exercise, ek-se-saiz, s., oefening c.; (bodily) lichaamsbeweging c.; (school) opgave c. v., oefenen; (mil.) drillen; ——book, s., schrift n.
exert (oneself), eG-zeurt (wan-self), v., zich inspannen
exertion, eG-zeur-sjun, s., inspanning c.
exhale, eks-heel, v., uitademen; (vapour) ver-dampen
exhaust, eG-zoast, v., uitputten. s., (mech.) uit-laat c. ——ive, a., uitputtend; (thorough) grondig
exhibit, eG-zib-bit, s., bewijsstuk n.; (display) uitstalling c. v., tentoonstellen
exhibition, ek-si-bis-sjun, s., tentoonstelling c.
exhilarate, eG-zil-le-reet, v., opvrolijken
exhilarating, eG-zil-le-ree-ting, a., opvrolijkend

exhort, eG-zoart, v., aansporen; (warn) vermanen
exigency, ek-si-dzjun-si, s., nood c., behoefte c.
exile, ek-sail, s., verbanning c.; (person) ballin c. v., verbannen
exist, iG-zist, v., bestaan; ——ence, s., bestaan n.
exit, ek-sit, s., uitgang c.; (departure) heengaan n.
exodus, ek-sc-dus, s., uittocht c.
exonerate, eG-zon-ne-reet, v., verontschuldigen
exorbitant, eG-zoar-bi-t'nt, a., buitensporig
expand, ek-spend, v., uitspreiden; (develop) ontwikkelen
expansion, ek-spen-sjun, s., uitbreiding c.
expect, ek-spekt, v., verwachten; (suppose) vermoeden
expectation, ek-spek-tee-sjun, s., verwachting c.
expectorate, ek-spek-te-reet, v., opgeven
expedient, ek-spie-di-'nt, s., uitweg c. a., dienstig
expedite, ek-spi-dait, v., verhaasten
expel, ek-spel, v., verdrijven, verbannen
expend, ek-spend, v., besteden; (use up) verbruiken
expenditure, ek-spen-dit-sjur, s., uitgaven c.pl.
expense, ek-spens, s., kosten, c.pl.
expensive, ek-spen-siv, a., duur, kostbaar
experience, ek-spie-ri-'ns, s., ondervinding c. v., ondervinden, ervaren
expert, ek-speurt, s., deskundige c. a., bedreven
expire, ek-spair, v., (die) de laatste adem uitblazen; (time) verstrijken
explain, eks-pleen, v., verklaren, uitleggen
explanation, eks-ple-nee-sjun, s., verklaring c.
explicit, eks-plis-sit, a., uitdrukkelijk
explode, eks-plood, v., ontploffen
exploit, eks-ploit, v., uitbuiten. s., heldendaad c.
explore, eks-ploar, v., onderzoeken, navorsen
export, eks-poart, v., uitvoeren, exporteren
expose, eks-pooz, v., blootstellen; (photo) belichten; (unmask) ontmaskeren
exposure, eks-po-zjur, s., blootstelling c.; (photo) belichting c.
expound, eks-paund, v., verklaren, uitleggen

express, eks-pres, a., uitdrukkelijk, expres. s., exprestrein c. v., uitpersen; (utter) betuigen

expression, eks-pres-sjun, s., uitdrukking c.

expulsion, eks-pal-sjun, s., verdrijving c.

expunge, eks-pandzj, v., uitwissen

exquisite, eks-kwi-zit, a., voortreffelijk

extempore, eks-tem-pe-ri, adv., onvoorbereid

extend, eks-tend, v., zich uitstrekken; rekken

extensive, eks-ten-siv, a., uitgebreid

extenuate, eks-ten-joe-eet, v., verzachten

exterior, eks-tie-ri-ur, a., uitwendig. s., buiten-kant c.

exterminate, eks-teur-mi-neet, v., uitroeien

external, eks-teur-n'l, a., uiterlijk; uitwendig

extinct, eks-tingkt, a., geblust; (dead) uitgestor-

extinguish, eks-ting-gwisj, v., uitdoven   [ven

extort, eks-toart, v., afpersen, afdwingen

extortion, eks-toar-sjun, s., afpersing c.

extra, eks-tra, a. & adv., extra; ——ordinary, buitengewoon

extract, eks-trekt, s., extract n. v., uittrekken

extravagant, eks-trev-ve-g'nt, a., (wasteful) verkwistend; (exaggerated) overdreven

extreme, eks-triem, a., uiterst

extremely, eks-triem-li, adv., uiterst

extricate, eks-tri-keet, v., ontwarren

eye, ai, oog n.; ——ball, oogappel c.; ——brow, wenkbrauw c.; ——glass, monocle c.; ——glasses, lorgnet n.; ——lash, wimper c.; ——let, vetergaatje n.; ——lid, ooglid n.; ——sight, gezicht n.; ——witness, oog-getuige c.

fable, fee-b'l, s., fabel c.; (untruth) verzinsel n.

fabric, feb-bric, s., structuur c.; (tissue) weefsel n.

fabrication, feb-bri-kee-sjun, s., vervaardiging c.

fabulous, feb-joe-lus, a., fabelachtig

façade, fe-saad, s., voorgevel c.

face, fees, s., gezicht n.; (clock) wijzerplaat c. v., staan tegenover; (oppose) het hoofd bieden

facetious, fe-sie-sjus, a., grappig, boertig

facilitate, fe-sil-li-teet, v., vergemakkelijken

fact, fekt, s., feit n.; (deed) daad c.

factory, fek-te-ri, s., fabriek c.; factorij c.

faculty, fek-kul-ti, s., vermogen n.; (univ.) faculteit c.

fade, feed, v., (flower) verwelken; (colour) verschieten

faggot, feG-Gut, s., takkenbos c.

fail, feel, v., (disappoint) teleurstellen; (be deficient) ontbreken; (grow feeble) verzwakken; (run short) opraken; (neglect) verzuimen; (miscarry) mislukken; (exam.) niet slagen; (bankrupt) faillict gaan; **without** ——; stellig; ——**ure,** s., mislukking c.; (bankruptcy) faillict n.

faint, feent, a., zwak. s., flauwte c. v., flauw vallen

fair, fèr, s., kermis c. a., (lovely) mooi; (hair) blond; (just) billijk; (weather) helder; ——**ness,** s., billijkheid c.

fairy, fèr-ri, s., fee c.; ——**tale,** sprookje n.

faith, feeth, s., geloof n.; (confidence) vertrouwen n.; ——**ful,** a., trouw; gelovig; ——**less,** ontrouw; ongelovig

falcon, foal-k'n, s., valk c.

fall, foal, v., vallen. s., val c., vallen n.

fallacy, fel-le-si, s., bedrieglijkheid c.   [c.

false, foals, a., vals, onjuist; ——**hood,** s., leugen

falsification, foal-si-fi-kee-sjun, s., vervalsing c.

falsify, foal-si-fai, v., vervalsen

falter, foal-t'r, v., strompelen; (speech) stamelen

fame, feem, s., faam c., roem c.

famed, feemd, a., beroemd

familiar, fe-mil-jur, a., intiem; (conversant) vertrouwd

family, fem-mi-li, s., gezin n.; (relatives) familie

famine, fem-min, s., hongersnood c.   [c.

famish, fem-misj, v., uithongeren

famous, fee-mus, a., beroemd, vermaard

fan, fen, s., waaier c.; ventilator c. v., wannen

fanatic, fe-net-tik, a., dweepziek, s., dweper c.

fancy, fen-si, s., inbeelding c.; (whim) gril c.; (liking) zin c. v., zich inbeelden; houden van

fancy-ball, fen-si-boal, s., gecostumeerd bal n.

fang, feng, s., slagtand c.; (snake) gifttand c.

fantastic, fen-tes-tik, a., fantastisch

fantasy, fen-te-si, s., fantasie c.

far, faar, a. & adv., ver; —— **away,** afgelegen

farce, faars, s., klucht c., kluchtspel n.

fare, fèr, s., vracht c.; (food) kost c.

farewell, fèr-wel, s., afscheid n. interj. vaarwel!

farm, faarm, s., boerderij c. v., bebouwen

farmer, faar-m'r, s., boer c., landman c.

farrier, fer-ri-ur, s., hoefsmid c.

farther, faar-dh'r, adv., verder

fascinate, fes-si-neet, v., betoveren

fashion, fes-sjun, s., mode c.; (manner) wijze c. v., vormen; ——**able,** a., naar de mode; **in** ——, in de mode

fast, faast, a., (firm) vast; (rapid) vlug; (unfading) kleurhoudend. s., vasten c. v., vasten

fasten, fass-'n, v., vastmaken, bevestigen

fastidious, fes-tid-di-us, a., kieskeurig

fat, fet, s., vet n. a., vet, dik; ——**ten,** v., mesten

fatal, fee-t'l, a., dodelijk; noodlottig

fatality, fe-tel-li-ti, s., noodlottigheid c.

fate, feet, s., noodlot n.; (lot) lot n.; (death) dood c.; ——**d,** a., voorbestemd

father, fa-dh'r, s., vader c.; ——**-in-law,** schoonvader c.; ——**ly,** a., vaderlijk

fathom, fedh-um, s., vadem c. v., peilen

fatigue, fe-tieG, s., vermoeidheid c.; (mil.) corvee c. v., afmatten, vermoeien

fault, foalt, s., (error) fout c.; (blame) schuld c.; (defect) gebrek n.; ——**less,** a., onberispelijk

faulty, foal-ti, a., gebrekkig; verkeerd

favour, fee-v'r, s., gunst c.; (kindness) vriendelijheid c.; (preference) begunstiging c. v., begunstigen

favourable, fee-ve-re-b'l, a., gunstig

favourite, fee-ve-rit, s., gunsteling c., lieveling c. a., geliefkoosd

fawn, foan, s., jong hert n. a., geelbruin. v., vleien

fear, fier, s., vrees c. v., vrezen; ——**ful,** a.,

vreesachtig; (terrible) vreselijk; ——less, onbevreesd

feasible, fie-zi-b'l, a., doenlijk, uitvoerbaar

feast, fiest, s., feest n. v., feestvieren; smullen

feat, fiet, s., heldendaad c.; (achievement) prestatie c.

feather, fedh-ur, s., veer c.; ——ed, a., gevleugeld

feature, fiet-sjur, s., gelaatstrek c.; hoofdtrek c.

February, feb-broe-e-ri, s., februari c.

federal, fed-de-r'l, a., federaal, bonds . . .

federation, fed-de-ree-sjun, s., statenbond c.

fee, fie, s., honorarium n.; schoolgeld n. v., betalen

feeble, fie-b'l, a., zwak, krachteloos

feed, fied, v., voeden; (animals) voeren. s., voer n.

feel, fiel, v., voelen; zich voelen. s., gevoel n.

feeler, fie-l'r, s., voeler c.; (insect) voelhoorn c.

feeling, fie-ling, s., gevoel n. a., gevoelig

feign, feen, v., veinzen, huichelen

feint, feent, s., voorwendsel n.; schijnaanval c.

fell, fel, v., neervellen. s., (skin) huid c.

fellow, fel-lo, s., makker c.; (pop.) kerel c.; ——ship, kameraadschap c.; ——student, schoolmakker c.

felony, fel-le-ni, s., zware misdaad c.

felt, felt, s., vilt n.; (hat) vilten hoed c.

female, fie-meel, a., vrouwelijk. s., wijfje n.

feminine, fem-mi-nin, a., vrouwelijk; (fig.) verwijfd

fen, fen, s., ven c. & n.

fence, fens, s., omheining c.; (swordsmanship) schermkunst c. v., omheinen; (fight) scherfender, fen-d'r, s., beschutting c. [men

ferment, feur-ment, v., gisten; doen gisten. s., gist c.

fern, feurn, s., varen c.; ——y, a., vol varens

ferocious, fi-ro-sjus, a., woest, wild

ferret, fer-rit, s., fret n.; —— out, v., uitvissen

ferrule, fer-roel, s., ring c., dop c.

ferry, fer-ri, s., veer n. v., overzetten

fertile, feur-tail, a., vruchtbaar

fertilize, feur-ti-laiz, v., vruchtbaar maken

fervent, feur-v'nt, a., heet; (ardent) vurig
fester, fes-t'r, s., verzwering c. v., etteren
festival, fes-ti-v'l, s., feestdag c. a., feestelijk
festive, fes-tiv, a., feestelijk, feest . . .
festoon, fes-toen, s., slinger c., guirlande c.
fetch, fetsj, v., halen; (bring) brengen
fetter, fet-t'r, v., boeien. s., boei c., keten c.
feud, fjoed, s., vete c.; ——al, a., leenroerig [tig
fever, fie-v'r, s., koorts c.; ——ish, a., koortsach-
few, fjoe, a., weinig; a ——, enkele, enige, een
fibre, fai-b'r, s., vezel c. [paar
fickle, fik-k'l, a., wispelturig
fiction, fik-sjun, s., verzinsel n.; (book) roman c.
fictitious, fik-tis-sjus, a., verdicht; (false) onecht
fidelity, fi-del-li-ti, s., getrouwheid c., trouw c.
fidget, fid-zjit, s., onrust c. v., onrustig zijn
fidgety, fid-zji-ti, a., onrustig, gejaagd
field, field, s., veld n., akker c.; ——glass, veldkijker c.; ——marshal, veldmaarschalk c.
fiend, fiend, s., boze geest c.; ——ish, a., duivels
fierce, fiers, a., woest, wild; (cruel) wreed
fiery, fai-e-ri, a., vlammend; (ardent) vurig
fife, faif, s., fluit c., pijp c. v., pijpen
fifteen, fif-tien, a., vijftien; ——th, vijftiende
fifth, fifth, a., vijfde. (mus.) s., kwint c.
fiftieth, fif-ti-ith, a., vijftigste
fifty, fif-ti, a., vijftig
fig, fig, s., vijg c.; ——tree, vijgeboom c.
fight, fait, s., gevecht c., strijd c. v., vechten
figure, fiG-G'r, s., figuur c., gestalte c.; (image)
beeld n.; (number) cijfer n., afbeelden
figure-head, fiG-G'r-hed, s., stroman c.
filbert, fil-burt, s., hazelnoot c.
filch, filtsj, v., gappen, kapen
file, fail, s., (tool) vijl c.; (office) lias c.; (mil.)
gelid n.; (row) rij c. v., vijlen; (letters)
rangschikken
fill, fil, v., vullen; (tooth) plomberen. s., verzadi-
ging c.
filly, fil-li, s., merrieveulen n.
film, film, s., (photo) film c.; (thin layer) vlies n.
v., verfilmen; **sound** ——, s., geluidsfilm c.

filter, fil-t'r, s., filter c. v., filtreren

filth, filth, s., vuiligheid c.; ——**y,** a., vuil

fin, fin, s., (fish) vin c.; (aeroplane) kielvlak n.

final, fai-n'l, a., laatste; (decisive) beslissend

finance, fai-nens, v., financieren; ——**s,** s.pl., financiën c.pl.

financial, fai-nen-sjul, a., financieel

finch, fintsj, s., vink c.

find, faind, v., vinden; (detect) ontdekken. s., vondst c.

fine, fain, s., geldboete c. a., fijn; (beautiful) mooi. v., beboeten

finery, fai-ne-ri, s., opschik c., mooie kleren n.pl.

finger, fing-G'r, s., vinger c. v., betasten

finish, fin-nisj, v., eindigen; (complete) voltooien. s., einde n.; (completion) voltooiing c.

fir, feur, s., den c.; ——**cone,** pijnappel c.

fire, fair, v., in brand steken; (gun) schieten. s., vuur n.; (conflagration) brand c.; ——-**alarm,** brandschel c.; ——**brigade,** brandweer c.; ——**engine,** brandspuit c.; ——**escape,** brandtrap c.; ——**fly,** glimworm c.; ——**man,** brandweerman c.; (stoker) stoker c.; ——**place,** haard c.; ——**proof,** a., brandvrij; ——**works,** s.pl., vuurwerk n.

firm, feurm, s., firma c. a., vast; (steady) standvastig

first, feurst, a., eerst. adv., ten eerste, eerst

firth, feurth, s., zeearm c., brede riviermond c.

fish, fisj, s., vis c. v., vissen; ——**bone,** s., visgraat c.; ——**erman,** visser c.; ——**hook,** angel c.; ——**monger,** visverkoper c.

fishing, fisj-ing, s., vissen n.; ——**rod,** hengel c.

fissure, fis-sjur, s., kloof c., spleet c. v., splijten

fist, fist, s., vuist c. v., met de vuist slaan

fistula, fis-tjoe-la, s., fistel c.

fit, fit, s., (paroxysm) aanval c.; (caprice) bevlieging c. a., geschikt; (proper) gepast. v., (suit) passen; (adapt) geschikt maken; (erect, mount) monteren

fittings, fit-tingz, s.pl., onderdelen n.pl.

five, faiv, a., vijf

fix, fiks, v., vasthechten; (date) vaststellen. **s.,** klem c.

fixture, fiks-tsjur, s., iets spijkervast n.; (sport) datum voor de wedstrijd c.

flabby, fleb-bi, a., slap, week, zacht

flag, fleG, s., vlag c.; (flower) lis c.; (slab) plavuis c. v., bevlaggen; (languish) kwijnen; —-**ship,** s., vlaggeschip n.; —-**staff,** vlaggestok c.

flagon, fieG-G'n, s., grote fles c.

flagrant, flee-Gr'nt, a., schandelijk

flake, fleek, s., (snow) vlok c.; (rust, paint) laag c.

flaky, flee-ki, a., vlokkig, schilferachtig

flame, fleem, s., vlam c. v., ontvlammen

flank, flengk, s., zijde c., flank c. v., flankeren

flannel, flen-n'l, s., flanel n. a., flanellen

flap, flap, s., (blow) klap c.; (table) neerslaand blad n.; (hat) afhangende rand c.; (coat) pand n. v., flappen; (wings) klapwieken

flare, flèr, v., flikkeren. s., geflikker n.

flash, flesj, v., bliksemen, schitteren. s., vlam c, straal c.; —-**light,** flikkerlicht n.; (torch) zaklantaarn c.

flashy, fles-sji, a., opzichtig, fatterig

flask, flaask, s., flacon c.; veldfles c.

flat, fiet, a., vlak, plat; (market) flauw. **s.,** vlakte c.; (dwelling) etagewoning c.; (mus.) mol c.

flatten, flet-t'n, v., vlak maken; (tone) verlagen

flatter, fiet-t'r, v., vleien; —-**er,** s., vleier c.; —-**ing,** a., vleiend; —-**y,** s., vleierij c.

flavour, flee-v'r, v., kruiden. s., aroma n., geur c.

flaw, floa, s., gebrek n.; (fault) fout c.; (crack) barst c.

flax, fleks, s., vlas n.; —-**en,** a., vlaskleurig

flea, flie, s., vlo c.; —-**bite,** vlooiebeet c.

fledge, fledzj, v., veren krijgen; —-**d,** a., vlug

flee, flie, v., vluchten; (avoid) ontvluchten

fleece, flies, s., vlies n.; (sheep) vacht c.

fleet, fliet, s., vloot c. a., snel

flesh, flesj, s., vlees n.

flexible, flek-si-b'l, a., buigzaam, soepel

flicker, flik-k'r, v., flikkeren. s., geflikker n.

flight, flait, s., vlucht c.; (planes) groep c.

flimsy, flim-zi, a., (paper) dun; (weak) zwak

flinch, flintsj, v., terugdeinzen; aarzelen

fling, fling, v., gooien, smijten

flint, flint, s., keisteen c.; (lighter) vuursteentje n.

flippant, flip-p'nt, a., onbezonnen, loslippig

flirt, fleurt, s., coquette c., flirt c. v., flirten

float, floot, s., (raft) vlot n.; (angler's) dobber c. v., drijven; (ship) vlot maken

flock, flok, s., (sheep) kudde c.; (birds) zwerm c. v., samenscholen

flog, flog, v., (beat) slaan; (thrash) afranselen

flood, flad, s., vloed c.; (inundation) overstroming c. v., onder water zetten; overstromen

floor, floar, s., vloer c.; (storey) verdieping c. v., bevloeren; (strike down) neerslaan

florid, flor-rid, a., bloemrijk; (showy) opzichtig

florist, flor-rist, s., bloemist c.

floss, flos, s., floretzijde c., vlokzijde c.

flour, flaur, s., meel n., bloem c.

flourish, flar-risj, s., zwaai, c.; (writing) krul c.; (mus.) fanfare c. v., (brandish) zwaaien

flout, flaut, s., spot c. v., bespotten

flow, flo, s., vloed c.; stroom c. v., stromen

flower, flau-ur, s., bloem c. v., bloeien

fluctuate, flak-tjoe-eet, v., op en neer gaan

flue, floe, s., (pipe) afvoerbuis c.

fluency, floe-'n-si, s., vaardigheid c., vlotheid c.

fluent, floe-'nt, a., vloeiend

fluffy, flaf-fi, a., donzig, pluizig

fluid, floe-id, s., vloeistof c. a., vloeibaar

fluke, floek, s., (pop.) bof c. v., boffen

flurry, flar-ri, s., gejaagdheid c. v., zenuwachtig maken

flush, flasj, s., opwelling c.; (red face) blos c. v., (redden) doen blozen; (cleanse) uitspoelen. a., (level) effen

fluster, flas-t'r, s., verwarring c. v., verwarren

flute, floet, s., (mus.) fluit c.; ——d, a., (grooved) gegroefd

flutter, flat-t'r, v., fladderen. s., gefladder n.

fly, flai, s., vlieg c. v., vliegen; (flag) wapperen; ——**-catcher**, s., vliegenvanger c.; ——**-wheel**, vliegwiel n.

foal, fool, s., veulen n.

foam, foom, s., schuim n. v., schuimen

fob, fob, s., horlogezakje n.; **f.o.b. = free on board**, adv., vrij aan boord

focus, fo-kus, s., brandpunt n. v., stellen, richten

fodder, fod-d'r, s., voeder n. v., voeren

foe, fo, s., vijand c.

fog, foG, s., mist c.; ——**gy**, a., mistig; ——**-horn**, s., misthoorn c.

foil, foil, v., verijdelen. s., schermdegen c.

foist, foist, v., onderschuiven

fold, foold, s., (clothes) vouw c.; (sheep) kudde c. v., vouwen; (wrap round) wikkelen

foliage, fo-li-idzj, s., gebladerte n., loof n.

folk, fook, s., luitjes c.pl., mensen c.pl.

follow, fol-lo, v., volgen; (imitate) navolgen

follower, fol-lo-ur, s., volgeling c.

folly, fol-li, s., dwaasheid c., domheid c.

foment, fo-ment, v., (cherish) koesteren; (excite) aanmoedigen

fomentation, fo-men-tee-sjun, s., (med.) warme omslag c.

fond (of), fond (ov), a., verzot op, gek met

fondle, fon-d'l, v., liefkozen, strelen

font, font, s., doopvont c.; wijwaterbakje n.

food, foed, s., voedsel n.; (beasts) voer n.

fool, foel, s., dwaas c., gek c. v., bedotten; ——**-hardy**, a., roekeloos; ——**ish**, dwaas, mal

foot, foet, s., voet c.; (animal) poot c.; ——**ball**, voetbal c.; ——**board**, treeplank c.; ——**man**, lakei c.; ——**path**, voetpad n.; ——**print**, voetspoor n.; ——**step**, voetstap c.; ——**stool**, voetbankje n.

fop, fop, s., modegek c., fat c.

for, foar, conj., want. prep., voor; gedurende; om; naar; uit

forage, for-ridzj, s., voer n. v., (mil.) fourageren

forbear, foar-bèr, v. geduld hebben; (abstain

from) zich onthouden van; ——ance, s.,
geduld n.; onthouding c.; ——ing, a., verdraagzaam, toegevend

forbid, foar-bid, v., verbieden

forbidding, foar-bid-ding, a., afstotend

force, foars, s., geweld n.; (power) kracht c. v.,
(compel) dwingen; (locks, etc.) forceren

forceful, foars-foel, a., krachtig; geweldig

forceps, foar-seps, s.pl., tang c.

forcible, foar-si-b'l, a., geweldig; krachtig

ford, foard, s., doorwaadbare plaats c.; v.,
doorwaden

fore, foar, a. & adv., vooraan; to the ——, op de
voorgrond

forearm, foar-aarm, s., voorarm c.

forebode, foar-bood, v., voorspellen; vermoeden

foreboding, foar-bo-ding, s., voorgevoel n.

forecast, foar-kaast, v., voorspellen. s., weerbericht n.

forecastle, fook-sul, s., bak c., vooronder n.

foredoom, foar-doem, v., doemen

forefather, foar-fa-dh'r, s., voorvader c.

forefinger, foar-fing-G'r, s., wijsvinger c.

forego, foar-Go, v., voorafgaan

foreground, foar-Graund, s., voorgrond c.

forehead, for-rid, s., voorhoofd n.

foreign, for-rin, a., buitenlands; (strange)
vreemd

foreigner, for-ri-n'r, s., buitenlander c.

foreman, foar-m'n, s., voorman c., ploegbaas c.

foremost, foar-moost, a., voorste, eerste

forenoon, foar-noen, s., voormiddag c.

forerunner, foar-ran-n'r, s., voorloper c.

foresee, foar-sie, v., voorzien

foresight, foar-sait, s., overleg n.

forest, for-rist, s., woud n.; ——er, boswachter c.

forestall, foar-stoal, v., voorkomen

foretaste, foar-teest, s., voorsmaak c.

foretell, foar-tel, v., voorzeggen, voorspellen

forethought, foar-thoat, s., voorzorg c.

forewarn, foar-woarn, v., vooraf waarschuwen

forfeit, foar-fit, v., (life, rights) verbeuren, ver-

liezen. a., verbeurd. s., verbeurde n.; (fine)
boete c.; **play at** ——s, pand verbeuren
forge, foardzj, s., smidse c. v., smeden; (counterfeit) vervalsen; ——r, s., smeder c.; vervalser c.; ——ry, vervalsing c.
forget, f'r-Get, v., vergeten; ——ful, a., vergeetachtig; ——fulness, s., vergeetachtigheid c.; ——me-not, vergeet-mij-nietje n.
forgive, f'r-Giv, v., vergeven, kwijtschelden
forgiveness, f'r-Giv-nis, s., vergiffenis c.
forgo, foar-Go, v., zich onthouden van; opgeven
fork, foark, s., vork c.; (road) tweesprong c.
forlorn, f'r-loarn, a., verlaten; hulpeloos
form, foarm, s., (shape) vorm c.; (seat) bank c.; (class) klasse c.; (a form to fill up) formulier n. v., vormen; (mil.) formeren
formal, foar-m'l, a., formeel, vormelijk; (stiff) stijf; ——ity, s., formaliteit c.
formation, foar-mee-sjun, s., vorming c.; (planes) formatie c.
former, foar-m'r, a., vorig; ——ly, adv., vroeger
forsake, f'r-seek, v., verzaken, verlaten
forswear, foar-swèr, v., afzweren
fort, foart, s., fort n., vesting c.
forth, foarth, adv., voort; uit; buiten
forthcoming, foarth-kam-ing, a., aanstaande
forthwith, foarth-widh, adv., onmiddelijk
fortieth, foar-ti-ith, a., veertigste
fortification, foar-ti-fi-kee-sjun, s., versterking c.
fortify, foar-ti-fai, v., versterken
fortitude, foar-ti-tjoed, s., standvastigheid c.
fortnight, foart-nait, s., veertien dagen c.pl.
fortress, foar-tris, s., vesting c., sterkte c.
fortuitous, foar-tjoe-i-tus, a., toevallig
fortunate, foar-tsje-nit, a., gelukkig
fortune, foar-tsjun, s., fortuin n.; (luck) geluk c.
forty, foar-ti, a., veertig
forward, foar-wurd, adv., voorwaarts. v., (advance) bevorderen; (letter) verzenden; (re-post) doorsturen; ——ness, s., vroegtijdigheid c.; (pertness) vrijpostigheid c.
fossil, fos-sil, s., fossiel n. a., versteend

foster, fos-t'r, v., kweken; (cherish) koesteren;
——**-parents,** s.pl., pleegouders c.pl.
foul, faul, a., vuil; (air) bedorven; (play) oneerlijk
found, faund, v., stichten; (metal) gieten
foundation, faun-dee-sjun, s., grondslag c.
founder, faun-d'r, s., grondlegger c., stichter c.
foundling, faund-ling, s., vondeling c.
foundry, faun-dri, s., gieterij c.
fountain, faun-tin, s., bron c.
fountain-pen, faun-tin-pen, s., vulpen c.
four, foar, a., vier; ——**th,** vierde. s., kwart c.
fourfold, foar-foold, a., viervoudig
fourteen, foar-tien, a., veertien; ——**th,** veer-tiende
fowl, faul, s., kip c.; (poultry) gevogelte n.
fox, foks, s., vos c.; ——, v., a., sluw
foxglove, foks-glɑv, s., vingerhoedskruid n.
fraction, frek-sjun, s., breuk c.; (fragment) brok c.
fracture, frekt-sjur, s., breuk c. v., breken
fragile, fred-dzjail, a., breekbaar; (brittle) broos
fragment, freg-m'nt, s., brok c.; fragment n.
fragrance, free-gr'ns, s., geur c.
fragrant, free-gr'nt, a., geurig, welriekend
frail, freel, a., teer; (weak) zwak
frame, freem, s., bouw c.; geraamte n. v., bouwen
framework, freem-weurk, s., raam n.; geraamte
franchise, frent-sjaiz, s., stemrecht n. [n.
frank, frengk, a., oprecht, openhartig
frantic, fren-tik, a., razend, dol
fraternal, fre-teur-n'l, a., broederlijk
fraud, froad, s., bedrog n.; (person) bedrieger c.
fraudulent, froa-djoe-l'nt, a., bedrieglijk
fray, free, v., verslijten. s., strijd c., twist c.
freak, friek, s., gril c.; (monster) gedrocht n.
freckle, frek-k'l, s., sproet c.
freckled, frek-k'ld, a., bespikkeld
free, frie, a., vrij. v., bevrijden; ——**dom,** s., vrijheid c.; ——**mason,** vrijmetselaar c.; ——**thinker,** vrijdenker c.; —— **trade,** vrijhandel c.
freeze, friez, v., vriezen; bevriezen

freight, freer, s., (load) lading c.; (cost) vracht c. v., laden; bevrachten

frenzy, fren-zi, s., waanzin c., razernij c.

frequency, frie-kw'n-si, s., gedurige herhaling c.

frequent, frie-kw'nt, a., herhaald. v., omgaan met

fresh, fresj, a., vers, fris; ——**ness**, s., versheid c.

fret, fret, v., (eat away) wegvreten; (irritate) prikkelen; ——**ful**, a., kribbig; ——**saw**, s., figuurzaag c.; ——**work**, snijwerk n.

friar, frai-ur, s., monnik c.; ——**y**, klooster n.

friction, frik-sjun, s., wrijving c.

Friday, frai-di, s., vrijdag c.

friend, frend, s., vriend c.; (girl) vriendin c.; ——**liness**, vriendelijkheid c.; ——**ly**, a., vriendelijk; vriendschappelijk; ——**ship**, s., vriendschap c.

fright, frait, s., schrik c., vrees c.

frighten, frait-'n, v., doen schrikken

frightful, frait-foel, a., verschrikkelijk

frigid, frid-dzjid, a., koud, kil, ijzig

frill, fril, s., plooikraag c. v., plooien

fringe, frindzj, s., franje c.; (border) rand c.

frisky, fris-ki, a., dartel, vrolijk

fritter, frit-t'r, s., poffertje n.; —— **away**, v., verbeuzelen; (money) verkwisten

frivolous, friv-ve-lus, a., beuzelachtig

frizzle, friz-z'l, v., krullen; (fry) braden

fro, fro, adv., to and ——, heen en weer

frock, frok, s., (woman's) jurk c.; (monk's) pij c.

frog, frog, s., kikker c., kikvors c.

frolic, frol-lik, s., pretje n., grap c.

from, from, prep., van; uit; van . . . af; door

front, front, s., voorste gedeelte n.; (war) front n. v., staan tegenover. a., voorste; (first) eerste

frontier, fron-tjur, s., grens c.

frost, frost, s., vorst c.; (hoar-frost) rijp c. v., bevriezen; ——**bitten**, a., bevroren

frosty, fros-ti, a., vriezend

froth, froth, s., schuim n. v., doen schuimen

frown, fraun, s., frons c. v., het voorhoofd fronsen

frugal, froe-G'l, a., matig, zuinig, sober

fruit, froet, s., vrucht c.; fruit n.

fruiterer, froe-te-r'r, s., fruithandelaar c.

fruitful, froet-foel, a., vruchtbaar

fruition, froe-is-sjun, s., genot n.; (fulfilment) vervulling c.

fruitless, froet-lis, a., vruchteloos

frustrate, fras-treet, v., verijdelen; hinderen

fry, frai, v., (fish, potatoes) bakken; (egg, meat) braden

fuchsia, fjoe-sje, s., foksia c.

fuel, fjoe-'l, s., brandstof c.; (fig.) voedsel n.

fugitive, fjoe-dzji-tiv, s., vluchteling c.

fugue, fjoeG, s., fuga c.

fulcrum, fal-krum, s., steunpunt n.

fulfil, foel-fil, v., vervullen; volbrengen

fulfilment, foel-fil-m'nt, s., vervulling c.

full, foel, a., vol; (satiated) verzadigd

fullness, foel-nis, s., volheid c.; volledigheid c.

fully, foel-li, adv., geheel, volledig

fulsome, foel-sum, a., walglijk

fume, fjoem, s., damp c.; (smoke) rook c. v., roken

fun, fan, s., grap c.; (jollity) pret c.

function, fangk-sjun, s., ambt n.; (ceremony) plechtigheid c. v., functionneren

functionary, fangk-sje-ne-ri, s., ambtenaar c.

fund, fand, s., fonds n. v., funderen

fundamental, fan-de-men-t'l, a., fundamenteel. s., grondbeginsel n., basis c.

funeral, fjoe-ne-r'l, s., begrafenis c.; lijkstoet c.

funnel, fan-n'l, s., (to convey liquids) trechter c.; (steamship) pijp c.; (air) luchtkoker c.

funny, fan-ni, a., grappig; (queer) raar

fur, feur, s., bont n., pels c.; (coat) bontjas c.

furbish, feur-bisj, v., polijsten; poetsen

furious, fjoe-ri-us, a., woedend, razend

furlough, feur-lo, s., verlof n.

furnace, feur-nis, s., smeltoven c., oven c.

furnish, feur-nisj, v., verschaffen; (equip) uitrus-

furniture, feur-nit-sjur, s., meubelen n.pl.   [ten

furrier, far-ri-ur, s., bontwerker c.

furrow, far-ro, s., voor c.; (wrinkle) rimpel c.

further, feur-dh'r, a. & adv., verder. **v.,** bevorderen

furtherance, feur-dhe-r'ns, s., bevordering c.

furtive, feur-tiv, a., heimelijk

fury, fjoe-ri, s., woede c.; (frenzy) razernij c.

fuse, fjoez, s., lont c.; (electric) zekering c. **v.** smelten; samensmelten

fusee, fjoe-zie, s., windlucifer c.

fuss, fas, s., drukte c., ophef c. **v.,** druk doen

fustian, fas-ti-'n, s., fustein n.; (fig.) bombast c.

fustiness, fas-ti-nis, s., mufheid, c., dufheid c.

fusty, fas-ti, a., muf, duf

futile, fjoe-tail, a., nutteloos; (worthless) waardeloos

future, fjoet-sjur, a., toekomstig. **s.,** toekomst c.

gable, Gee-b'l, s., gevelspits c.

gadfly, Ged-flai, s., horzel c., brems c.

gaff, Gef, s., visspeer c.; (ship) gaffel c.

gag, GaG, s., knevel c.; (stage) improvisatie c. **v.,** knevelen; (stage) woorden inlassen

gaiety, Gee-i-ti, s., vrolijkheid c., pret c.

gain, Geen, v., (win) winnen; (obtain) verkrijgen; (clock) voorlopen; (attain) bereiken. **s.,** winst c.; (profit) voordeel c.

gait, Geet, s., gang c., pas c.

gaiter, Gee-t'r, s., slobkous c.

galaxy, Gel-luk-si, s., melkweg c.

gale, Geel, s., storm c.

gall, Goal, s., gal c.; (nut) galnoot c. **v.,** verbitteren

gallant, Gel-l'nt, a., dapper; (courtly) hoffelijk

gallantry, Gel-l'n-tri, s., (courage) dapperheid c.; (courtliness) hoffelijkheid c.

gallery, Gel-le-ri, s., galerij c.

galling, Goal-ling, a., kwetsend, ergerlijk

galloon, Ge-loen, s., galon n., boordlint n.

gallop, Gel-lup, s., galop c. **v.,** galopperen

gallows, Gel-looz, s., galg c.

galore, Ge-loar, adv., in overvloed

galosh, Ge-losj, s., overschoen c.

galvanism, Gel-ve-nizm, s., galvanisme n.

gamble, Gem-b'l, v., gokken. **s.,** gokkerij c.

gambler, Gem-bl'r, s., speler c., gokker c.

gambol, Gem-bul, s., sprong c. v., huppelen c.

game, geem, s., spel n.; (animals) wild n. a., moedig, flink; ——keeper, s., jachtopziener c.

gaming-house, Gee-ming-haus, s., speelhuis n.

gammon, Gem-mun, s., gerookte ham c.; (deception) bedriegerij c.; (humbug) onzin c.

gamut, Gem-mut, s., toonladder c.

gander, Gen-d'r, s., gent c., mannetjesgans c.

gang, Geng, s., (workmen) ploeg c.; (robbers) bende c.

gangway, Geng-wee, s., (passage) doorgang c.; (ship) loopplank c.

gaol, dzjeel (see jail)

gap, Gep, s., gat n., opening c.; (mountains) kloof c.

gape, Geep, v., gapen, geeuwen; —— at, aangapen

garage, Ger-raazj, s., garage c.

garb, Gaarb, s., gewaad n., dracht c. v., kleden

garbage, Gaar-bidzj, s., afval c.; (fig.) vuil n.

garden, Gaar-d'n, s., tuin c. v., tuinieren; —— er, s., tuinman c.; ——-party, tuinfeest n.

gargle, Gaar-G'l, v., gorgelen c., gorgeldrank c.

garish, Gèr-isj, a., (gaudy) opzichtig; (dazzling) flikkerend

garland, Gaar-lund, s., krans c. v., bekransen [hel

garlic, Gaar-lik, s., knoflook n.

garment, Gaar-m'nt, s., kledingstuk n.

garnish, Gaar-nisj, s., versiering c. v., versieren

garret, Ger-rit, s., zolderkamertje n.; vliering c.

garrison, Ger-ri-s'n, s., garnizoen n.

garrulity, Ge-roe-li-ti, s., praatachtigheid c.

garrulous, Ger-roe-lus, a., praatziek

garter, Gaar-t'r, s., kouseband c.

gas, Ges, s., gas n. v., vergassen; —— attack, s., gasaanval c.; ——-cooker, gasfornuis n.

gaseous, Ges-si-us, a., gasachtig, gas . . .

gash, Gesj, s., gapende wonde c. v., opensnijden

gasp, Gaasp, s., hijgen n. v., naar adem snakken

gastric, Ges-trik, a., gastrisch, maag . . .

gasworks, Ges-weurks, s.pl., gasfabriek c.

gate, Geet, s., poort c., hek n., ingang c.

gather, Gedh-ur, v., bijeenbrengen; (pluck)

plukken; (infer) afleiden; ——ing, s., bijeenkomst c.

gaudy, Goa-di, a., (colours) bont; (showy) opzichtig

gauge, Geedzj, s., (size) standaardmaat c.; (tool)
peilstok c.; (rails) spoorwijdte c. v., meten,
peilen; (estimate) schatten

gaunt, Goant, a., (lean) mager; (grim) grimmig

gauntlet, Goant-lit, s., schermhandschoen c.

gauze, Goaz, s., gaas n.; (haze) waas n.

gawky, Goa-ki, a., onhandig, lomp. s., lummel c.

gay, Gee, a., vrolijk, opgewekt; (colours) kleurig

gaze, Geez, v., staren. s., starende blik c.

gazelle, Ge-zel, s., gazelle c.

gazette, Ge-zet, s., Staatscourant c.

gear, Gier, s., (tools) gereedschappen c.pl.; (car)
versnelling c.; (harness) tuig n.; ——box,
versnellingsbak c.

gelatin(e), dzjel-le-tin, s., gelatine c.

gelding, Gel-ding, s., ruin c.

gem, dzjem, s., juweel n., edelsteen c.

gender, dzjen-d'r, s., geslacht n.

general, dzjen-ne-r'l, a., algemeen. s., generaal c.

generalize, dzjen-ne-re-laiz, v., generaliseren

generally, dzjen-ne-re-li, adv., gewoonlijk

generate, dzjen-ne-reet, v., voortbrengen, verwekken

generation, dzjen-ne-ree-sjun, s., geslacht n.;
(propagation) voortplanting c.

generosity, dzjen-ne-ros-si-ti, s., (liberality)
mildheid c.; (magnanimity) edelmoedigheid c.

generous, dzjen-ne-rus, a., edelmoedig; mild

genial, dzjie-ni-ul, a., hartelijk; (climate) zacht

genius, dzjie-ni-us, s., genie n.; (spirit) geest c.

genteel, dzjen-tiel, a., deftig; (refined) beschaafd

gentile, dzjen-tail, s., niet-Jood c., heiden c.

gentility, dzjen-til-li-ti, s., deftigheid c.

gentle, dzjen-t'l, a., zacht; (kindly) vriendelijk;
——man, s., heer c.; ——ness, zachtheid c.

gently, dzjent-li, a., zachtjes; vriendelijk

genuine, dzjen-joe-in, a., echt, onvervalst

genuineness, dzjen-joe-in-nis, s., echtheid c.

geography, dzji-oG-Gre-fi, s., aardrijkskunde c.
geology, dzji-ol-le-dzji, s., geologie c.
geometry, dzji-om-mi-tri, s., meetkunde c.
geranium, dzji-reen-jum, s., geranium, c.
germ, dzjeurm, s., kiem c. v., ontkiemen
germinate, dzjeur-mi-neet, v., ontkiemen
gesticulate, dzjes-tik-joe-leet, v., gesticuleren
gesture, dzjest-sjur, s., gebaar n.
get, Get, v., (obtain) krijgen; (earn) verdienen; (fetch) halen; (induce) overhalen; (reach) aankomen; (become) worden; —— **back**, (receive back) terugkrijgen; —— **down**, (alight) afstappen; (descend) naar beneden gaan; —— **in**, binnenkomen; (step in) instappen; —— **off**, (alight) afstappen; (escape) er afkomen; —— **on**, (progress) opschieten; —— **out**, eruit komen; eruit halen; —— **up**, opstaan
geyser, Gie-z'r, s., geiser c.
ghastly, Gaast-li, a., akelig; (pale) doodsbleek
gherkin, Geur-kin, s., augurkje n.
ghost, Goost, s., geest c.; ——**ly**, a., spookachtig
giant, dzjai-'nt, s., reus c.; ——**ess**, reuzin c.
gibberish, dzjib-be-risj, s., brabbeltaal c.
gibbet, dzjib-bit, s., galg c. v., ophangen
gibe, dzjaib, s., spotternij c. v., spotten
giddiness, Gid-di-nis, s., duizeligheid c.
giddy, Gid-di, a., duizelig; (fickle) onbezonnen
gift, Gift, s., (talent) gave c.; (present) geschenk n.
gifted, Gif-tid, a., begaafd; begiftigd
gigantic, dzhai-Gen-tik, a., reusachtig
giggle, GiG-G'l, v., gichelen. s., gegichel n.
gild, Gild, v., vergulden; ——**ing**, s., verguldsel n.
gill, Gil, s., (fish) kieuw c.; (fowl) lel c.
gilt, Gilt, a., verguld. s., verguldsel n.
gimlet, Gim-lit, s., spitsboor c. v., boren [c.
gin, dzjin, s., jenever c.; (snare) strik c.; (trap) val
ginger, dzjin-dzjur, s., gember c.; ——**bread**, peperkoek c.
gipsy, dzjip-si, s., Zigeuner c., Zigeunerin c.
giraffe, dzji-raaf, s., giraffe c.
gird, Geurd, v., omgorden; ——**at**, spotten met

girder, Geur-d'r, s., dwarsbalk c.
girdle, Geur-d'l, s., gordel c., band c.
girl, Geurl, s., meisje n.; ——**hood,** meisjesjaren n.pl.
girth, Geurth, s., (strap) buikriem c.; (circumference) omvang c. v., (horse) singelen
gist, dzjist, s., hoofdpunt n., kern c.
give, Giv, v., geven; (hand) aangeven; (present) schenken; —— **in,** toegeven; —— **up,** opgeven
giver, Giv-v'r, s., gever c.
gizzard, Giz-zurd, s., spiermaag c.; (fig.) strot c.
glacier, Glee-sjur, s., gletsjer c.
glad, Gled, a., blij, verheugd
gladden, Gled-d'n, v., verblijden, verheugen
glade, Gleed, s., open ruimte in een bos c.
glance, Glaans, s., blik c. v., kijken
gland, Glend, s., klier c.
glare, Glèr, s., verblindende glans c.; (fierce stare) woeste blik c. v., hel schijnen; woest kijken
glaring, Glèr-ing, a., schel, oogverblindend; (eyes) vlammend; (injustice) schreeuwend; (error) grof
glass, Glaas, s., glas n.; (mirror) spiegel c.; ——**es,** bril c.; ——**paper,** schuurpapier n.; ——**ware,** glaswerk n.; ——**works,** glasfabriek c.; ——**y,** a., glazig; (smooth) spiegelglad
glaze, Gleez, v., van glas voorzien. s., glazuur n.
glazier, Glee-zi-ur, s., glazenmaker c.
gleam, Gliem, s., glans c.; (ray) straal c. v., blinken, glanzen; ——**y,** a., blinkend
glean, Glien, v., aren lezen; ——**er,** s., arenlezer c.
glee, Glie, s., vrolijkheid c.
glen, Glen, s., bergdal n.
glib, Glib, a., vlot, rad van tong
glide, Glaid, v., glijden. s., glijden
glider, Glai-d'r, s., (aircraft) zweefvliegtuig n.
glimmer, Glim-m'r, v., flikkeren. s., schijnsel n.
glimpse, Glimps, s., vluchtige blik c.
glint, Glint, v., glinsteren. s., glinstering c.
glisten, Glis-s'n, v., schitteren, fonkelen
glitter, Glit-t'r, v., schitteren. s., schittering c.

gloat (on), Gloob (on), v., met wrede wellust beschouwen

globe, Gloob, s., (ball) bol c.; (earth) aardbol c.

globular, Glob-joe-l'r, a., bolvormig

gloom, Gloem, s., duisternis c.; (melancholy) droefgeestigheid c.; ——y, a., donker, duister; droefgeestig

glorify, Gloa-ri-fai, v., verheerlijken

glorious, Gloa-ri-us, a., (illustrious) roemrijk; (magnificent) heerlijk, prachtig

glory, Gloa-ri, s., roem c.; (splendour) pracht c.; —— in, v., zich beroemen op

gloss, Glos, s., (lustre) glans c. v., doen schitteren; —— over, vergoelijken; ——y, a., glanzend

glove, Glʌv, s., handschoen c.

glover, Glʌv-v'r, s., handschoenmaker c.

glow, Glo, s., gloed c. v., gloeien

glue, Gloe, s., lijm c. v., lijmen, plakken

glum, Glʌm, a., nors, somber, triest

glut, Glʌt, v., overladen. s., oververzadiging c.

glutton, Glʌt-t'n, s., gulzigaard c.

gluttonous, Glʌt-t'n-us, a., gulzig

gnarl, naarl, s., knoest c.; ——ed, a., knoestig

gnash, nesj, v., knarsen; —— one's teeth, knarsetanden

gnat, net, s., mug c.

gnaw, noa, v., knabbelen, afknagen

go, Go, v., gaan; —— away, weggaan; —— back, teruggaan; —— down, naar beneden gaan; (sink) ondergaan; —— for, halen; (attack) te lijf gaan; —— off, weggaan; (gun) afgaan; (decline) achteruitgaan; —— out, uitgaan; —— up, opstijgen; —— without, het stellen zonder

goad, Good, s., prikkel c. v., aanzetten

goal, Gool, s., (aim) doel n.; (football) goal c.

gobble, Gob-b'l, v., (turkey) klokken; (guzzle) schrokken; —— r, s., kalkoen c.; schrokker c.

goblet, Gob-blit, s., bokaal c.

goblin, Gob-blin, s., kabouter c., boze geest c.

God, God, s., God c.; (idol) afgod c.; ——child, petekind n.; ——dess, godin c.; ——father, peetoom c.; ———-fearing, a., godvrezend; ———less, goddeloos; ———liness, s., godsvrucht c.; ———ly, a., godvruchtig; ———mother, s., meter c.; ———send, buitenkansje [n.

goggle-eyed, GOG-Glaid, a., puiloogig

goggles, GOG-Gulz, s.pl., stofbril c.

goitre, GOI-t'r, s., kropgezwel n.

gold, Goold, s., goud n.; ———en, a., gouden; ———finch, s., putter c.; ———fish, goudvis c.; ———leaf, bladgoud n.; ———smith, goudsmid c.

golf, Golf, s., golfspel n.; ———er, golfspeler c.

golf-links, Golf-lingks, s.pl., golfbaan c.

gong, Gong, s., gong c.; (bell) bel c.

good, Goed, a., goed. s., goed n.; (profit) voordeel n.; ———bye, interj., adieu!; ———morning, goedenmorgen; ———day, goedendag; ———night, welterusten

Good Friday, Goed frai-di, s., Goede Vrijdag c.

good-natured, Goed-neet-sjurd, a., goedaardig

goodness, Goed-nis, s., goedheid c.; (virtue) deugd c.

goods, Goedz, s.pl., goederen n.pl.

goods-train, Goedz-treen, s., goederentrein c.

good-will, Goed-will, s., welwillendheid c.; (business) klandizie c., relaties c.pl.

goose, Goes, s., gans c.; (fig.) uilskuiken n.

gooseberry, Goes-be-ri, s., kruisbes c.

gore, Goar, s., geronnen bloed n.; (of a garment) geer c. v.; (pierce) doorboren; geren

gorge, Goardzj, s., keel c.; (ravine) bergengte c. v., opslokken; zich volproppen

gorgeous, Goar-dzjus, a., prachtig, schitterend

gorilla, Ge-ril-la, s., gorilla c.

gorse, Goars, s., steekbrem c.

gosling, Goz-ling, s., gansje n.

gospel, Gos-p'l, s., evangelie n.

gossamer, Gos-se-m'r, s., herfstdraden c.pl.

gossip, Gos-sip, v., kletsen. s., gebabbel n.; (person) kletskous c.

gouge, Gaudzj, v., gutsen; uitsteken

gout, Gaut, s., jicht c.; ———y, a., jichtig

govern, Gᴀv-vurn, v., besturen; ——**ess,** s., gouvernante c.; ——**ment,** regering c.; ——**or,** bestuurder c.; (colony) gouverneur c.; (mech.) regulateur c.

gown, Gaun, s., japon c.; (official) toga c.

grab, Greb, v., grijpen. s., (mech.) vanghaak c.

grace, Grees, s., genade c.; (charm) bevalligheid c.; ——**ful,** a., bevallig; ——**less,** (manner-less) onbeschaamd; (depraved) verdorven

gracious, Gree-sjus, a., genadig

gradation, Gre-dee-sjun, s., schakering c.

grade, Greed, s., graad c.; kwaliteit c.

gradient, Gree-di-'nt, s., (slope) helling c.

gradual, Gred-joe-ul, a., geleidelijk

graduate, Gred-joe-eet, v., in graden verdelen; (university) promoveren; s., gegradueerde c.

graft, Graaft, s., ent c. v., enten

grain, Green, s. graankorrel c.; (corn) koren n.; (particle) greintje n.; (wood) draad c.

grammar, Grem-m'r, s., spraakkunst c.

granary, Gren-ne-ri, s., korenschuur c.

grand, Grend, a., (great) groot; (important) voornaam; ——**child,** s., kleinkind n.; ——**daughter,** kleindochter c.; ——**father,** grootvader c.; ——**mother,** grootmoeder c.; ——**son,** kleinzoon c.

grange, Greendzj, s., herenboerderij c.

grant, Graant, v., (allow) toestaan; (confer on) verlenen. s., (gift) schenking c.

grape, Greep, s., druif c.; ——**fruit,** pompel-moes c.; ——**shot,** schroot n.; ——**stone,** druivepit c.

grapple, Grep-p'l, s., (hook) enterhaak c. v., vastklemmen; ——**with,** worstelen met

grasp, Graasp, v., grijpen; (mentally) begrijpen. s., greep c.; ——**ing,** a., inhalig

grass, Graas, s., gras n.; (lawn) grasveld n.; ——**hopper,** sprinkhaan c.; ——**y,** a., grasrijk

grate, Greet, v., raspen; (brakes, wheels) knarsen. s., rooster c.; (grating) traliewerk n.

grateful, Greet-foel, a., dankbaar, erkentelijk

gratefulness, Greet-foel-nis, s., dankbaarheid c.
gratification, Gret-ti-fi-kee-sjun, s., bevrediging
gratify, Gret-ti-fai, v., bevredigen, voldoen [c.
gratifying, Gret-ti-fai-ing, a., aangenaam
grating, Gree-ting, s., traliewerk n. a., knarsend
gratis, Gree-tis, adv., gratis, kosteloos
gratitude, Gret-ti-tjoed, s., dankbaarheid c.
gratuitous, Gre-tjoe-i-tus, a., gratis, kosteloos;
   (without motive) ongemotiveerd
gratuity, Gre-tjoe-i-ti, s., gift c.; (tip) fooi c.
grave, Greev, s., graf n. a., (serious) ernstig;
   (solemn) plechtig; ——**digger,** s., doodgraver c.; ——**stone,** grafsteen c.; ——**yard,**
   kerkhof n.
gravel, Grev-v'l, s., grint n., kiezelzand n.
gravitate, Grev-vi-teet, v., neigen, overhellen
gravity, Grev-vi-ti, s., (weight) gewicht n.;
   (seriousness) ernst c.; (physics) zwaarte-
   kracht c.
gravy, Gree-vi, s., vleesnat n.; (sauce) jus c.
graze, Greez, v., weiden; (touch slightly) even
   aanraken
grease, Gries, s., vet n., smeer c. v., smeren
greasy, Grie-zi, a., smerig; (oily) vettig; (roads)
   glibberig
great, Greet, a., groot; (important) belangrijk
greatness, Greet-nis, s., grootheid c.
greed, Gried, s., (avarice) hebzucht c.; (gluttony)
   gulzigheid c.; ——**y,** a., hebzuchtig; gulzig
green, Grien, s., groen n.; (plot of grass) grasveld
   n. a., groen. v., groen maken; ——**grocer,**
   s., groenteboer c.; ——**house,** brocikas c.;
   ——**ish,** a., groenachtig; ——**s,** s.pl., groente
greet, Griet, v., groeten; ——**ing,** s., groet c. [c.
grenade, Gri-need, s., handgranaat c.
grey, Gree, a., grijs; (ashy) grauw
greyhound, Gree-haund, s., hazewind c.
grief, Grief, s., smart c., droefheid c.
grievance, Grie-v'ns, s., grief c.
grieve, Griev, v., treuren; (distress) bedroeven
grievous, Grie-vus, a., pijnlijk; (grave) zwaar
grill, Gril, s., rooster c. v., roosteren, braden

grim, Grim, a., streng; (cruel) wreed

grimace, Gri-**mees**, s., grijns c. v., grijnzen

grime, Graim, s., (dirt) vuil n.; (soot) roet n.

grin, Grin, s., grijnslach c. v., grinniken

grind, Graind, v., malen; (sharpen) slijpen

grinder, Grain-d'r, s., slijper c.

grip, Grip, s., greep c. v., vasthouden

gripe, Graip, s., vat c., greep c.; ———s, koliek c.

grisly, Griz-li, a., griezelig, akelig

grist, Grist, s., maalkoren n.

grit, Grit, s., (gravel) steengruis n.

gritty, Grit-ti, a., zanderig

groan, Groon, v., kreunen, zuchten. s., gekreun n.

groats, Groots, s.pl., grutten c.pl.

grocer, Gro-s'r, s., kruidenier c.

grocery, Gro-se-ri, s., kruidenierswinkel c.

grog, GroG, s., grog c.; ———gy, a., onvast op de benen

groin, Groin, s., lies c.; (arch) graatrib c.

groom, Groem, s., stalknecht c., kamerheer c.

groove, Groev, s., groef c., gleuf c. v., groeven

grope, Groop, v., tastend zoeken, rondtasten

gross, Groos, a., (thick) dik; (coarse) ruw; (vulgar) plat. s., (12 dozen) gros n.; ——— weight, bruto gewicht n.

ground, Graund, v., baseren; (naut.) stranden. s., grond c.; ———floor, benedenverdieping c.; ———less, a., ongegrond; ———s, s.pl., (park) aanleg c.; ———work, grondslag c.

group, Groep, s., groep c. v., groeperen

grouse, Graus, s., korhoen n. v., (pop.) kankeren

grovel, Grov-v'l, v., kruipen

grow, Gro, v., groeien; (cultivate) kweken; ———er, s., kweker c.; ———n up, a., volwassen; ———th, s., groei c.; (increase) toeneming c.; (product) product n.

growl, Graul, s., gebrom n. v., brommen

grub, Grab, s., larve c., made c.

grudge, Gradzj, s., wrok c. v., misgunnen

gruel, Groe-ul, s., dunne pap c.

gruesome, Groe-sum, a., ijselijk, griezelijk

gruff, Graf, a., nors, bars; (hoarse) schor

grumble, Grăm-b'l, v., morren

grumbler, Grăm-bl'r, s., brompot c.

grunt, Grănt, v., knorren. s., geknor n.

guarantee, Ger-r'n-tie, s., waarborg c.; garantie c.; (bail) borg c. v., waarborgen

guard, Gaard, s., wacht c.; (railway) conducteur c.; (prison) bewaker c. v., bewaken; beschermen; ——ed, a., voorzichtig; (circumspect) omzichtig; ——ian, s., bewaker c.; (trustee) voogd c.

guess, Ges, v., raden. s., gissing c.

guess-work, Ges-weurk, s., gissing c., gegis n.

guest, Gest, s., gast c.; genodigde c.

guidance, Gai-d'ns, s., leiding c.; geleide n.

guide, Gaid, v., leiden. s., gids c.; (book) reisgids

guild, Gild, s., vereniging c.; (trade) gilde n. [c.

guile, Gail, s., (deceit) bedrog n.; (cunning) list c.

guilt, Gilt, s., schuld c.; ——y, a., schuldig

guinea, Gin-ni, s., guinje c.; ——fowl, parelhoen n.; ——pig, Guinees biggetje n.

guise, Gaiz, s., gedaante c.; (semblance) schijn c.

guitar, Gi-taar, s., gitaar c.

gulf, Gălf, s., golf c.; (abyss) afgrond c.

gull, Găl, s., zeemeeuw c. v., beetnemen

gullet, Găl-lit, s., slokdarm c., keel c.

gulp, Gălp, v., slokken. s., slok c.

gum, Găm, s., gom c. v., gommen

gums, Găms, s.pl., tandvlees, n.

gun, Găn, s., geweer n.; (cannon) kanon n.; ——ner, artillerist c.; ——powder, buskruit n.

gunsmith, Găn-smith, s., geweermaker c.

gurgle, Geur-g'l, v., klokken, klateren

gush, Găsj, s., uitstorting c. v., gutsen

gust, Găst, s., windvlaag c.; (passion) vlaag c.

gut, Găt, s., darm c.; (strait) zeeëngte c.

gutter, Găt-t'r, s., goot c.

guy, Gai, s., (effigy) vogelverschrikker c.

gymnasium, dzim-nee-zjum, s., gymnastiek-zaal c.

gymnastics, dzim-nes-tiks, s.pl., gymnastiek c.

N.B.—De letter H wordt altijd duidelijk uitgesproken, behalve in de enkele woorden die
met een § aangegeven worden.

haberdasher, heb-be-des-sjur, s., winkelier in
ellewaren, garen, band, kant, etc. c.
habit, heb-bit, s., gewoonte c.; (dress) kleed n.
habitable, heb-bi-te-b'l, a., bewoonbaar
habitual, he-bit-joe-ul, a., gewoon
hack, hek, v., hakken. s., (cut) snede c.; (horse)
hackneyed, hek-nied, a., afgezaagd   [knol c.
haddock, hed-duk, s., schelvis c.
hag, heg, s., heks c.; ——**gard,** a., wild; afgetobd
haggle, heG-G'l, v., pingelen, afdingen
hail, heel, s., hagel c.; (call) roep c. v., hagelen;
(salute) begroeten; (taxi) aanroepen. interj.,
heil!
hair, hèr, s., haar n., haren n.pl.; ——**brush,**
haarborstel c.; ——**dresser,** kapper c.;
——**pin,** haarspeld c.; ——**y,** a., harig
hake, heek, s., stokvis c.
hale, heel, a., gezond; (robust) flink, kloek
half, haaf, s., helft c.   a. & adv., half
halfpenny, hee-pe-ni, s., halve stuiver c.
halibut, hel-li-bƏt, s., heilbot c.
hall, hoal, s., zaal c.; (entry) vestibule c.;
——**mark,** stempel c.; ——**porter,** portier c.
hallow, hel-lo, v., heiligen, wijden   [n.
hallucination, hel-joe-si-nee-sjun, s., zinsbedrog
halo, hee-lo, s., heiligenkrans c.; stralenkrans c.
halt, hoalt, s., stilstand c.; (a stop) halte c. v.,
halt laten houden; halt houden
halter, hoal-t'r, s., halster c.; (rope) strop c.
halve, haav, v., halveren, in tweeën delen
ham, hem, s., ham c.; (thigh) dij c.
hamlet, hem-lit, s., gehucht n.
hammer, hem-m'r, s., hamer c. v., hameren
hammock, hem-muk, s., hangmat c.
hamper, hem-p'r, s., sluitmand c. v., belemmeren
hand, hend, s., hand c.; (clock) wijzer c. v.,
overhandigen; ——**bag,** s., handtasje n.;
——**bill,** strooibiljet n.; ——**cuff,** handboei

c.; ——ful, handvol c.; ——kerchief, zakdoek c.; ——le, handvat c.; (knob) deurknop
c. v., betasten; (manipulate) behandelen;
——made, a., met de hand gemaakt; ——
rail, leuning c.

handsome, hend-sum, a., mooi, knap; royaal

handy, hen-di, a., handig; (near) bij de hand

hang, heng, v., hangen; —— up, ophangen

hangar, heng-Gaar, s., hangar c., loods c.

hangman, heng-m'n, s., beul c.

hanker, heng-k'r, v., hunkeren, haken

happen, hep-p'n, v., gebeuren, plaats hebben

happily, hep-pi-li, adv., gelukkig

happiness, hep-pi-nis, s., geluk n.; (bliss) gelukzaligheid c.

happy, hep-pi, a., gelukkig; (joyful) blij

harangue, he-reng, s., heftige rede c. v., toe-
spreken, een redevoering houden

harass, her-rus, v., kwellen; (exhaust) afmatten

harbinger, haar-bin-dzjur, s., voorloper c.

harbour, haar-b'r, s., haven c. v., herbergen

hard, haard, a., hard; (difficult) moeilijk; (severe)
streng; (cruel) wreed

harden, haar-d'n, v., verharden; zich verharden

hardihood, haar-di-hoed, s., onversaagdheid c.

hardly, haard-li, adv., nauwelijks, bijna niet

hardness, haard-nis, s., hardheid c.

hardship, haard-sjip, s., (privation) ontbering
c.; (discomfort) ongemak n.; (injury) onrecht

hardware, haard-wèr, s., ijzerwaren c.pl. [n.

hardy, haar-di, a., gehard; (bold) stoutmoedig

hare, hèr, s., haas c.; ——lip, hazelip c.

harlequin, haar-li-kwin, s., harlekijn c.

harlot, haar-lut, s., hoer c.

harm, haarm, s.; (injury) letsel n.; (damage)
schade c. v., schaden; kwaad doen; ——ful,
a., schadelijk; ——less, onschadelijk; (un-
harmed) onbeschadigd [mend

harmonious, haar-moon-jus, a., overeenstem-

harmonize, haar-me-naiz, v., overeenstemmen

harness, haar-nis, s., paardetuig n. v., inspannen; (forces) aanwenden

harp, haarp, s., harp c. v., op de harp spelen

harpoon, haar-poen, s., harpoen c. v., harpoeneren

harrow, her-ro, s., eg c. v., eggen; (torment) kwellen

harsh, haarsj, a., (severe) streng; (colour, sound) scherp; (rough) ruw; (unfeeling) hardvochtig

hart, haart, s., hert n.

harvest, haar-vist, s., oogst c. v., oogsten

hash, hesj, s., hachee c.; (mess) knoeiboel c.

hassock, hes-suk, s., knielkussen n.; bosje gras n.

haste, heest, s., haast c.; (rashness) overijling c.

hasten, hees-t'n, v., zich haasten; (speed up) verhaasten

hastily, hees-ti-li, adv., haastig; overijld

hat, het, s., hoed c.; ——box, hoededoos c.; ——brush, hoedeborstel c.; ——rack, kapstok c.; ——ter, hoedenverkoper c.; (maker) hoedenmaker c.

hatch, hetsj, v., broeden. s., (naut.) luik n.

hatchet, het-sjit, s., bijl c., bijltje n.

hate, heet, v., haten; het land hebben aan

hateful, heet-foel, a., hatelijk; gehaat

hatred, hee-trid, s., haat c., vijandschap c.

haughtiness, hoa-ti-ness, s., hoogmoed c., trots c.

haughty, hoa-ti, a., hoogmoedig, trots

haul, hoal, v., (pull) trekken; (drag along) slepen. s., trek c.; (catch) vangst c.

haunch, hoantsj, s., heup c.; (meat) bout c.

haunt, hoant, v., spoken; (frequent) veelvuldig bezoeken. s., verblijfplaats c.; (animals') hol n.

have, hev, v., hebben; houden; (cause) laten

haven, hee-v'n, s., haven c.; (refuge) toevluchtshaversack, hoa-ve-sek, s., broodzak c. [oord n.

havoc, hev-vuk, s., verwoesting c.

hawk, hoak, s., havik c. v., venten

hawker, hoa-k'r, s., venter c., leurder c.

hawthorn, hoa-thoarn, s., hagedoorn c.

hay, hee, s., hooi n.; ——fever, hooikoorts c.; ——loft, hooizolder c.; ——making, hooien n.; ——rick, hooiberg c.

hazard, hez-zurd, s., (chance) kans c.; (risk) risico n.; (game) hazardspel n. v., wagen

hazardous, hez-zurd-us, a., gewaagd

haze, heez, s., waas n.; (vapour) damp c.

hazel, hee-z'l, s., hazelaar c. a., lichtbruin

hazel-nut, hee-z'l-nɑt, s., hazelnoot c.

hazy, hee-zi, a., wazig, vaag; (mental) beneveld

he, hie, pron., hij

head, hed, s., hoofd n.; (animal) kop c.; (top) top c.; (chief) chef c.; (source) oorsprong c.; ——**ache,** hoofdpijn c.; ——**ing,** opschrift n.; ——**land,** voorgebergte n.; ——**light,** koplicht n.; ——**long,** a., hals over kop; ——**master,** s., directeur c.; ——**quarters,** pl., (mil.) hoofdkwartier n.; (central office) hoofdkantoor n.; ——**strong,** a., koppig; ——**waiter,** s., oberkellner c.; ——**way,** vooruitgang c.

heady, hed-di, a., onstuimig; (wine) koppig

heal, hiel, v., genezen; ——**ing,** a., heilzaam

health, helth, s., gezondheid c.; ——**y,** a., gezond

heap, hiep, s., hoop c. v., ophopen

hear, hier, v., horen; ——**er,** s., toehoorder c.; ——**ing,** gehoor n.; (court) behandeling c.; ——**say,** horen zeggen n.

hearse, heurs, s., lijkwagen c.

heart, haart, s., hart n.; (core) kern c.; (courage) moed c.; ——**broken,** a., gebroken door smart; ——**burn,** s., zuur in de maag n.; ——**ily,** adv., hartelijk; ——**less,** a., harteloos; ——**s,** s.pl., (cards) harten c.

hearth, haarth, s., haard c.

heat, hiet, s., hitte c. v., verhitten; ——**er,** s., verwarmingstoestel n.; ——**ing,** verwarming [c.

heath, hieth, s., heide c.

heathen, hie-dh'n, s., heiden c. a., heidens

heather, hedh-ur, s., heidekruid n.

heave, hiev, v., opheffen; (anchor) lichten; (sigh) slaken

heaven, hev-v'n, s., hemel c.; ——**ly,** a., hemels

heaviness, hev-vi-nis, s., zwaarte c.; loomheid c.

heavy, hev-vi, a., zwaar; (weather) drukkend

hedge, hedzj, s., heg c.; ——**hog**, egel c.
heed, hied, v., letten op. s., aandacht c.; ——**ful**, a., behoedzaam; ——**less**, zorgeloos
heel, hiel, s., hiel c.; (shoe) hak c.
hefty, hef-ti, a., sterk, gespierd
heifer, hef-f'r, s., vaars c.
height, hait, s., hoogte c.; (summit) hoogtepunt n.
heighten, hai-t'n, v., verhogen
heinous, hee-nus, a., afschuwelijk
§heir, èr, s., erfgenaam c.; ——**ess**, erfgename c.
§heirloom, èr-loem, s., erfstuk n.
hell, hel, s., hel c.; ——**ish**, a., hels
helm, helm, s., roer n.; ——**sman**, roerganger c.
helmet, hel-mit, s., helm c.
help, help, s., hulp c. v., helpen; (assist) bijstaan; ——**er**, s., helper c.; ——**ful**, a., behulpzaam
helpless, help-lis, a., hulpeloos
hem, hem, s., zoom c. v., zomen; ——**in**, omringen
hemisphere, hem-mis-fier, s., halfrond n.
hemlock, hem-lok, s., dollekervel c.
hemorrhage, hem-me-ridzj, s., bloeding c.
hemp, hemp, s., hennep c.
hen, hen, s., kip c., hen c.; (female bird) pop c.; ——**house**, kippenhok n.; ——**roost**, hoenderrek n.
hence, hens, adv., van hier; (thus) vandaar
henceforth, hens-foarth, adv., voortaan
her, heur, pron., haar
heraldry, her-rul-dri, s., wapenkunde c.
herb, heurb, s., kruid n.
herbalist, heurb-be-list, s., kruidkenner c.
herd, heurd, s., kudde c. v., bijeendrijven [c.
herdsman, heurdz-m'n, s., herder c., veehoeder
here, hier, adv., hier; ——**about**, hier in de buurt; ——**after**, hierna. s., hiernamaals n.; ——by, adv., hierbij; ——**in**, hierin; ——**of**, hiervan; ——**on**, hierop; ——**to**, hierbij; ——**tofore**, eertijds; ——**upon**, hierop; ——**with**, hiermede
hereditary, hi-red-di-te-ri, a., erfelijk
heresy, her-ri-si, s., ketterij c.

heretic, her-ri-tik, s., ketter c.
hermetical, heur-met-tik-'l, a., luchtdicht
hermit, heur-mit, s., kluizenaar c.
hermitage, heur-mit-eedzj, s., kluis c.
hernia, heur-ni-a, s., breuk c.
hero, hie-ro, s., held c.; ——ic, a., heldhaftig
heroine, her-ro-in, s., heldin c.
heroism, her-ro-izm, s., heldenmoed c.
herring, her-ring, s., haring c.
hers, heurz, pron., van haar, de hare, het hare
herself, heur-self, pron., zijzelf, haarzelf, zich
hesitate, hez-zi-teit, v., aarzelen
hesitation, hez-zi-**tee**-sjun, s., aarzeling c.
hew, hjoe, v., (hack) hakken; (cut down) vellen
hiccough, hiccup, hik-kap, v., hikken; s., hik c.
hide, haid, s., huid c., vel n. v., verbergen
hideous, hid-di-us, a., afschuwelijk
hiding, hai-ding, s., verbergen n.; (beating) pak
    slaag n.; ——**place,** schuilplaats c.
high, hai, a., hoog; (meat) sterk; ——**er,** a.,
    hoger; ——**est,** hoogst; ——**lander,** s.,
    Hooglander c.; ——**ness,** hoogte c.; (title)
    hoogheid c.; ——**way,** straatweg c.
hilarity, hi-**ler**-ri-ti, s., vrolijkheid c.
hill, hil, s., heuvel c.; ——**y,** a., heuvelachtig
hilt, hilt, s., (sword) gevest n.; (dagger) heft n.
him, him, pron., hem; ——**self,** hijzelf, zichzelf
hind, haind, s., hinde c. a., achterste, achter . . .
hinder, hin-d'r, v., verhinderen; hinderen
hindermost, hain-d'r-moost, a., achterste
hindrance, hin-dr'ns, s., hinderpaal c.
hinge, hindzj, s., hengsel n., scharnier c.
hint, hint, s., wenk c. v., laten doorschemeren
hip, hip, s., heup c.
hire, hair, v., huren. s., huur c.; (payment) loon n.
his, hiz, pron., zijn, van hem, de zijne, het zijne
hiss, his, v., sissen; (persons) fluiten
historian, his-**tor**-ri'n, s., geschiedschrijver c.
historic(al), his-**tor**-rik(-'l), a., historisch
history, his-te-ri, s., geschiedenis c.
hit, hit, s., slag c. v., slaan; (target, etc.) treffen
hitch, hitsj, s., ruk c.; (obstacle) storing c.; (naut.)

knoop c. v., (pull up) optrekken; (hook on) vasthaken; (make fast) vasthechten

hither, hidh-ur, adv., hierheen; ——to, tot nu [toe

hive, haiv, s., bijenkorf c.

hoar, hoar, a., wit, grijs; ——frost, s., rijp c.; ——y, a., grijs; (fig.) eerbiedwaardig

hoard, hoard, v., hamsteren. s., voorraad c.

hoarding, hoar-ding, s., (fence) schutting c.

hoarse, hoars, a., hees, schor

hoax, hooks, s., (popperij c. v., foppen [ren

hobble, hob-b'l, v., strompelen; (horse) kluiste-

hobby, hob-bi, s., stokpaardje n.

hock, hok, s., rijnwijn c.; (hough) hakpees c.

hoe, ho, s., schoffel c. v., schoffelen

hog, hoG, s., varken c.; (fig.) zwijn n.

hogshead, hoGz-hed, s., okshoofd n.

hoist, hoist, v., oplichten; (flag) hijsen. s., hijstoestel n.

hold, hoold, s., greep c.; (power) macht c.; (ship) scheepsruim n. v., houden; (contain) bevatten; (possess) in zijn bezit hebben; —— **back,** achterhouden; ——er, s., (owner) bezitter c.; (receptacle) reservoir n.; (tenant) pachter c.; —— **good,** v., gelden; ——ing, s., pachthoeve c.; (property) bezit n.; —— **on,** v., volharden; —— **over,** uitstellen

hole, hool, s., gat n.; (den) hol n.

holiday, hol-li-di, s., feestdag c.

holidays, hol-li-deez, s.pl., vakantie c.

holiness, ho-li-nis, s., heiligheid c.

hollow, hol-lo, s., holte c. a., hol; (insincere) onoprecht. v., uithollen

holly, hol-li, s., hulst c.

holy, ho-li, a., heilig; —— **water,** s., wijwater n.; —— **week,** Goede Week c.

homage, hom-midzj, s., hulde c. v., huldigen

home, hoom, s., thuis n.; (homeland) geboorteland n. adv., naar huis; at ——, thuis; ——less, a., dakloos; ——ly, huiselijk; **to be ——sick,** heimwee hebben; ——ward, adv., huiswaarts; ——ward bound, a., op de thuisreis

homœopathic, ho-mi-e-peth-ik, a., homeopa-
thisch

hone, hoon, s., wetsteen c. v., wetten   [c.

honest, on-nist, a., eerlijk; ——y, s., eerlijkheid

honey, han-ni, s., honing c.; ——moon, huwelijksreis c.; ——suckle, kamperfoelie c.

honorary, on-ne-re-ri, a., honorair, ere . . .

honour, on-n'r, s., eer c. v., eren; ——able, a.,
eervol; (upright) rechtschapen

hood, hoed, s., kaper c.; (motor) kap c.

hoodwink, hoed-wingk, v., misleiden

hoof, hoef, s., hoef c.; ——ed, a., gehoefd

hook, hoek, s., haak c. v., vasthaken; (catch) aan
de haak slaan; ——s and eyes, haken en
ogen pl.

hoop, hoep, s., hoepel c.; hoepelrok c.

hoot, hoet, s., (horn) getoeter n.; (owl) geschreeuw
n. v., toeteren; schreeuwen; ——at, uitjou-
wen

hop, hop, s., sprongetje n.; (plant) hop c. v.,
hinken; (frisk) huppelen; hop plukken

hope, hoop, s., hoop c. v., hopen; ——ful, a.,
hoopvol; ——less, hopeloos

horizon, he-rai-z'n, s., gezichtskring c.

horizontal, hor-ri-zon-t'l, a., horizontaal

horn, hoarn, s., hoorn c. a., hoornen

hornet, hoar-nit, s., horzel c.

horrible, hor-ri-b'l, a., afschuwelijk

horrid, hor-rid, a., afgrijselijk, gruwelijk

horrify, hor-ri-fai, v., met afschuw vervullen

horror, hor-r'r, s., (shudder) huivering c.;
(dread) afschrik c.

horse, hoars, s., paard n.; (clothes) droogrek n.;
——on——back, adv., te paard; ——hair, s.,
paardehaar n.; ——man, ruiter c.; ——-
-power, paardekracht c. (abbrev. P.K.);
——race, wedren c.; ——shoe, hoefijzer
n.; ——whip, rijzweep c.

hose, hooz, s., (rubber tube) slang c.

hosier, ho-zjur, s., handelaar in wollen goed c.

hosiery, ho-zje-ri, s., (stockings) kousen c.pl.

hospitable, hos-pi-te-b'l, a., gastvrij

hospital, hos-pi-t'l, s., ziekenhuis n.

host, hoost, s., gastheer c.; (innkeeper) waard c.;
(multitude) menigte c.; (eccl.) hostie c.;
——**ess,** gastvrouw c.; (innkeeper) waardin c.

hostage, hos-tidzj, s., gijzelaar c.

hostel, hos-t'l, s., (students) kosthuis n.

hostile, hos-tail, a., vijandelijk

hot, hot, a., heet; (ardent) vurig; (fierce) heftig

hotel, ho-tel, s., hotel n.

hothouse, hot-haus, s., broeikas c.

hound, haund, s., jachthond c. v., achtervolgen

§hour, aur, s., uur n.; ——**ly,** a., ieder uur, per uur

house, haus, s., huis n.; ——**agent,** huizenmake-
laar c.; ——**hold,** huisgezin n.; ——**keeper,**
huishoudster c.; ——**maid,** werkmeid c.;
——**of Commons,** Lagerhuis n.

hovel, hov-v'l, s., hut c., krot n.

hover, hov-v'r, v., fladderen, zweven

how, hau, adv., hoe; ——**ever,** conj., echter.
adv., hoe . . . ook; ——**far?** hoe ver?
much? ——**many?** hoeveel?

howl, haul, s., gehuil n. v., huilen, janken

hub, hab, s., naaf c.; (fig.) middelpunt n.

huddle, had-d'l, v., dooreengooien. s., warboel c.

hue, hjoe, s., tint c.; (shade) kleurschakering c.;
to raise a —— and cry, houdt de dief
roepen

hug, hag, v., knuffelen; (cherish) koesteren

huge, hjoedzj, a., kolossaal, reusachtig

hulk, halk, s., oud onttakeld schip n.

hull, hal, s., (pod) schil c., dop c.; (ship) romp c.

hum, ham, v., (bee) zoemen; (engine) snorren;
(man) neuriën. s., gezoem n.; gesnor n.;
geneurie n.

human, hjoe-m'n, a., menselijk

humane, hjoe-meen, a., menslievend

humanity, hjoe-men-ni-ti, s., mensheid c.;
(kindness) menslievendheid c.

humble, ham-b'l, a., nederig; (modest) bescheiden

humidity, hjoe-mid-di-ti, s., vochtigheid c.

humiliate, hjoe-mil-li-eet, v. vernederen

humiliation, hjoe-mi-li-ee-sjun, s., vernedering

humorous, hjoe-me-rus, a., grappig, luimig [c.

humour, hjoe-m'r, s., (mood) stemming c.;
(temper) luim c.; (wit) humor c. v., toegeven
aan

hunch, hantsj, s., (hump) bult c.; (lump) homp c.

hunchback, hantsj-bek, s., gebochelde c.

hundred, han-drud, a., honderd. s., honderdtal
n.; ——**th,** a., honderdste; ——**weight,** s.,
centenaar c.

hunger, hang-G'r, s., honger c. v., hongeren

hungry, hang-Gri, a., hongerig; be ——, honger
hebben

hunt, hant, v., jagen. s., jacht c.; ——**er,** jager c.

hurdle, heur-d'l, s., horde c.; (racing) hek n.

hurl, heurl, v., slingeren, werpen

hurricane, har-ri-k'n, s., orkaan c.

hurry, har-ri, s., haast c. v., haasten; zich haasten

hurt, heurt, v., (wound) wonde c.; (injury) letsel
n.; (damage) nadeel n. v., wonden; benadelen; (cause pain) pijn doen; (feelings) krenken; ——**ful,** a., nadelig

husband, haz-b'nd, s., echtgenoot c., man c.

hush, hasj, interj., st! stil!; ——**up,** v., stilhouden

husk, hask, s., schil c., dop c. v., doppen

husky, has-ki, a., (voice) schor, hees

hustle, has-s'l, v., verdringen; (jostle) duwen

hut, hat, s., hut c.; (mil.) barak c.

hutch, hatsj, s., (rabbits) konijnenhok n.

hyacinth, hai-e-sinth, s., hyacint c.

hydrant, hai-drunt, s., standpijp c.

hydraulic, hai-drol-lik, a., hydraulisch

hydro, hai-dro, ——**gen,** s., waterstof c.;
——**gen bomb,** waterstofbom c.; ——**pathic,**
waterkuurinrichting c.; ——**phobia,** watervrees c.; ——**plane,** watervliegtuig n.

hygienic, hai-dzjie-nik, a., hygiënisch

hymn, him, s., gezang n., hymne c.

hyphen, hai-f'n, s., koppelteken n.

hypocrisy, hi-**pok**-kre-si, s., huichelarij c.

hypocrite, hip-pe-krit, s., huichelaar c.

hysterical, his-ter-ri-k'l, a., hysterisch

I, ai, pron., ik

ice, ais, s., ijs n.; ——**berg**, ijsberg c.; ——**bound**, a., ingevroren; ——**cream**, s., ijsco

icicle, ai-si-k'l, s., ijskegel c.   [c.

icy, ai-si, a., ijsachtig; (very cold) ijskoud

idea, ai-die-e, s., denkbeeld n.; (notion) begrip n.

ideal, ai-diel, s., ideaal n.   a., denkbeeldig; (perfect) ideaal; ——**ize**, v., idealiseren

identical, ai-den-tik-'l, a., gelijk, identiek

identify, ai-den-ti-fai, v., identificeren

identity, ai-den-ti-ti, s., identiteit c.

idiom, id-di-um, s., taaleigen n.; dialect n.

idiot, id-di-ut, s., idioot c.; ——**ic**, a., idioot

idle, ai-d'l, a., (unemployed) nietsdoend; (lazy) lui; (vain) ijdel, v., leeglopen; ——**ness**, s., ledigheid c.; ——**r**, leegloper c.

idol, ai-d'l, s., afgod c.; ——**ize**, v., verafgoden

idyll, ai-dil, s., idylle c.; ——**ic**, a., idyllisch

if, if, conj., indien, als; (whether) of; **even** ——,

ignite, ig-nait, v., in brand steken   [zelfs al

ignition, ig-nis-sjun, s., (motor) ontsteking c.

ignoble, ig-no-b'l, a., onedel; (base) gemeen

ignominious, ig-ne-min-ni-us, a., schandelijk

ignominy, ig-ne-mi-ni, s., oneer c., schande c.

ignorance, ig-ne-r'ns, s., onwetendheid c.

ignore, ig-noar, v., negeren; voorbijzien

ill, il, a., ziek; (nausea) misselijk.   adv., slecht, kwalijk; ——**ness**, s., ziekte c.

illegal, il-lie-g'l, a., onwettig

illegible, il-led-zji-b'l, a., onleesbaar

illegitimate, il-li-dzjit-ti-mit, a., onwettig

illiterate, il-lit-te-rit, a., ongeletterd

illogical, il-lod-zji-k'l, a., onlogisch

illuminate, il-loe-mi-neet, v., verlichten

illumination, il-loe-mi-nee-sjun, s., verlichting

illusion, il-loe-zjun, s., zinsbegoocheling c.   [c.

illusory, il-loe-se-ri, a., bedrieglijk; denkbeeldig

illustrate, il-le-street, v., toelichten

illustration, il-le-stree-sjun, s., illustratie c.

illustrious, il-las-tri-us, a., beroemd, vermaard

image, i-midzj, s., beeld n.; (likeness) evenbeeld n.

imagination, i-med-zji-nee-sjun, s., verbeelding c.; (power) verbeeldingskracht c.

imagine, i-med-zjin, v., zich voorstellen

imbecile, im-bi-siel, s., idioot c.

imbibe, im-baib, v., drinken; (absorb) opzuigen

imbue, im-bjoe, v., drenken; (fig.) vervullen

imitate, im-mi-teet, v., nabootsen, namaken

immaculate, im-mek-joe-lit, a., onbevlekt

immaterial, im-me-tie-ri-'l, a., onstoffelijk

immature, im-me-tjoer, a., onrijp, onvolkomen

immeasurable, im-mez-zje-re-b'l, a., onmeetbaar; (enormous) onmetelijk

immediate, im-mie-djeet, a., onmiddelijk; (very near) naast; ——ly, adv., onmiddelijk

immense, im-mens, a., onmetelijk, oneindig

immensity, im-men-si-ti, s., onmetelijkheid c.

immerse, im-meurs, v., onderdompelen

immigrant, im-mi-Gr'nt, s., immigrant c.

immigrate, im-i-Greet, v., immigreren

imminent, im-mi-n'nt, a., dreigend; ophanden

immoderate, im-mod-de-rit, a., onmatig

immodest, im-mod-dist, a., (lacking modesty) onbescheiden; (improper) onbetamelijk

immoral, im-mor-r'l, a., onzedelijk

immortal, im-moar-t'l, a., onsterfelijk

immortalize, im-moar-te-laiz, v., vereeuwigen

immovable, im-moe-ve-b'l, a., onbeweeglijk

immune, im-mjoen, a., immuun, onvatbaar

immunity, im-mjoe-ni-ti, s., immuniteit c.

immure, im-mjoer, v., insluiten, opsluiten

imp, imp, s., duivelskind n.; (little rascal) rakker c.

impact, im-pekt, s., stoot c.; (collision) botsing c.

impair, im-pèr, v., (damage) benadelen; (weaken) verzwakken

impale, im-peel, v., spietsen

impart, im-paart, v., mededelen; (bestow) ver-

impartial, im-paar-sjul, a., onpartijdig [lenen

impassable, im-pa-se-b'l, a., onbegaanbaar

impassive, im-pes-siv, a., ongevoelig

impatience, im-pee-sjuns, s., ongeduld n.

impatient, im-pee-sjunt, a., ongeduldig

impeach, im-pietsj, v., beschuldigen

impeachment, im-**pietsj**-m'nt, s., beschuldiging c.

impecunious, im-pi-**kjoe**-ni-us, a., zonder geld

impede, im-**pied**, v., belemmeren, bemoeilijken

impediment, im-**ped**-di-m'nt, s., belemmering c.; (in speech), spraakgebrek n.

impel, im-**pel**, v., aandrijven, aanzetten

impending, im-**pen**-ding, a., ophanden zijnd; (threatening) dreigend

imperative, im-**per**-ri-tiv, s., (gram.) gebiedende wijs c. a., gebiedend; (urgent) dringend

imperfect, im-**peur**-fikt, s., onvoltooid verleden tijd c. a., onvolmaakt; (incomplete) onvolkomen; ——**ion,** s., onvolmaaktheid c.; onvolkomenheid c.

imperial, im-**pie**-ri-'l, a., keizerlijk; rijks . . .

imperil, im-**per**-ril, v., in gevaar brengen

imperishable, im-**per**-ri-sje-b'l, a., onvergankelijk

impersonate, im-**peur**-se-neet, v., verpersoonlijken

impertinence, im-**peur**-ti-n'ns, s., onbeschaamdheid c.

impertinent, im-**peur**-ti-n'nt, a., onbeschaamd

impervious, im-**peur**-vi-us, a., ondoordringbaar

impetuous, im-**pet**-joe-us, a., onstuimig, heftig

impetus, im-pi-tus, s., stuwkracht c.; aandrift c.

impiety, im-**pai**-e-ti, s., goddeloosheid c.

impious, im-pi-us, a., goddeloos, profaan

implant, im-**plaant**, v., (fig.) inprenten

implement, im-**ple**-m'nt, s., gereedschap n.

implicate, im-**pli**-keet, v., insluiten

implicit, im-**plis**-sit, a., onvoorwaardelijk

implore, im-**ploar**, v., smeken; afsmeken

imply, im-**plai**, v., insluiten; (hint) laten doorschemeren

impolite, im-pe-**lait**, a., onbeleefd

import, im-**poart**, v., invoeren. s., invoer c. ——**duties,** pl., invoerrechten n. pl.; ——**er,** importeur c.

importance, im-**poar**-t'ns, s., belang n. [teur c.

important, im-**poar**-t'nt, a., belangrijk

importune, im-**poar**-tjoen, v., lastig vallen

impose, im-pooz, v., opleggen; —— **upon**, bedriegen

imposing, im-po-zing, a., indrukwekkend

imposition, im-pe-zis-sjun, s., oplegging c.; (tax) belasting c.; (school) strafwerk n.

impossibility, im-pos-si-bi-li-ti, s., onmogelijkheid c.

impossible, im-pos-si-b'l, a., onmogelijk

impostor, im-pos-t'r, s., bedrieger c.

impotent, im-pe-t'nt, a., machteloos; impotent

impound, im-paund, v., opsluiten; (legal) beslag leggen op

impoverish, im-pov-ve-risj, v., verarmen

impracticable, im-prek-ti-ke-b'l, a., ondoenlijk

imprecation, im-pri-kee-sjun, s., verwensing c.

impregnable, im-preg-ne-b'l, a., onneembaar

impress, im-pres, s., (mark) stempel c.; (imprint) afdruk c. v., stempelen; afdrukken; (mind) indruk maken; —— **ion**, s., (mind) indruk c.; —— **ive**, a., indrukwekkend

imprint, im-print, s., afdruk c.; (mark) stempel c. v., drukken; (mind) inprenten

imprison, im-priz-z'n, v., gevangen zetten

imprisonment, im-priz-z'n-m'nt, s., gevangenschap c.

improbable, im-prob-be-b'l, a., onwaarschijnlijk

improper, im-prop-p'r, a., ongeschikt; ongepast

impropriety, im-pre-prai-e-ti, s., ongeschiktheid c.; (indecency) ongepastheid c.

improve, im-proev, v., verbeteren; —— **ment**, s., verbetering c.; (progress) vooruitgang c.

improvident, im-prov-vi-d'nt, a., zorgeloos

imprudent, im-proe-d'nt, a., onvoorzichtig

impudence, im-pjoe-d'ns, s., schaamteloosheid c.

impudent, im-pjoe-d'nt, a., schaamteloos

impulse, im-pals, s., stoot c.; opwelling c.

impure, im-pjoer, a., onzuiver; (morally) onkuis

impurity, im-pjoe-ri-ti, s., onzuiverheid c.

impute, im-pjoet, v., wijten, toeschrijven

in, in, prep., in; naar; bij; aan; op; over; met

inability, in-e-bil-li-ti, s., onbekwaamheid c.

inaccessible, in-ek-ses-si-b'l, a., ongenaakbaar
inaccuracy, in-ek-joe-re-si, s., onnauwkeurigheid c.
inaccurate, in-ek-joe-rit, a., onnauwkeurig
inadequate, in-ed-di-kwit, a., ontoereikend
inadvertent, in-ud-veur-t'nt, a., onoplettend
inane, in-een, a., (vacant) leeg; (silly) zinloos
inanimate, in-en-ni-mit, a., levenloos
inapt, in-ept, a., ongeschikt; ongepast
inasmuch as, in-ez-m**a**tsj-ez, conj., aangezien
inaudible, in-oa-di-b'l, a., onhoorbaar
inaugurate, in-oaG-joe-reet, v., (official) installeren; (commence) openen
inborn, inbred, in-boarn, **in-**bred, a., aangeboren
incalculable, in-kel-kjoe-le-b'l, a., onberekenbaar
incapable, in-kee-pe-b'l, a., onbekwaam
incapacitate, in-ke-pes-si-teet, v., ongeschikt maken
incapacity, in-ke-pes-si-ti, s., onbekwaamheid c.
incarnation, in-kaar-nee-sjun, s., verpersoonlijking c.; (eccl.) menswording c.
incautious, in-koa-sjus, a., onvoorzichtig
incense, in-sens, v., vertoornen; ——d, a., woedend
incense, in-sens, s., wierook c. v., bewieroken
incentive, in-sen-tiv, s., aansporing c.
incessant, in-ses-s'nt, a., onophoudelijk
inch, intsj, s., Engelse duim c.
incident, in-si-d'nt, s., voorval n.
incidental, in-si-dent-'l, a., toevallig
incision, in-siz-zjun, s., insnijding c.
incite, in-sait, v., aansporen, ophitsen
incivility, in-si-vil-li-ti, s., onbeleefdheid c.
inclination, in-kli-nee-sjun, s., neiging c.
incline, in-klain, v., (tilt) hellen; (bow) buigen; (be prone) geneigd zijn. s., helling c.
include, in-kloed, v., insluiten
inclusive, in-kloe-siv, a., inclusief
incoherent, in-ko-hie-r'nt, a., onsamenhangend
income, in-k'm, s., inkomen n.; ——-tax, inkomstenbelasting c.

incoming, in-ka_m_-ming, a., binnenkomend; (succeeding) nieuw; (tide) opkomend

incommode, in-ke-mood, v., lastig vallen

incommodious, in-ke-mo-di-us, a., lastig

incomparable, in-kom-pe-re-b'l, a., weergaloos

incompatible, in-k'm-pet-ti-b'l, a., onverenigbaar

incompetent, in-kom-pi-t'nt, a., onbevoegd

incomplete, in-k'm-pliet, a., onvolledig

incomprehensible, in-kom-pri-hen-si-b'l, a., onbegrijpelijk; (boundless) onbegrensd

inconceivable, in-k'n-sie-ve-b'l, a., onbegrijpelijk; (unimaginable) ondenkbaar

inconclusive, in-k'n-kloe-siv, a., niet afdoend

incongruous, in-kong-Groe-us, a., ongepast

inconsiderable, in-k'n-sid-de-re-b'l, a., onbeduidend

inconsiderate, in-k'n-sid-de-rit, a., onbezonnen

inconsistent, in-k'n-sis-t'nt, a., tegenstrijdig

inconsolable, in-k'n-so-le-b'l, a., ontroostbaar

inconstant, in-kon-st'nt, a., wispelturig

inconvenience, in-k'n-vien-juns, v., last aandoen. s., ongemak n., ongerief n.

inconvenient, in-k'n-vien-junt, a., lastig

incorporate, in-koar-pe-reet, v., verenigen

incorrect, in-ke-rekt, a., onnauwkeurig; fout

incorrigible, in-kor-rid-zji-b'l, a., onverbeterlijk

increase, in-kries, v., (augment) vermeerderen; (wages) verhogen; (size) toenemen. s., (growth) groei c.; (augmentation) vermeerdering c.

incredible, in-kred-di-b'l, a., ongelofelijk

incredulous, in-kred-joe-lus, a., ongelovig

incriminate, in-krim-mi-neet, v., beschuldigen

inculcate, in-ka_l_-keet, v., inprenten

incumbent (on), in-ka_m_-b'nt (on), a., rustend op

incur, in-keur, v., oplopen

incurable, in-kjoe-re-b'l, a., ongeneeslijk

indebted, in-det-tid, a., met schulden beladen; (obliged) verplicht

indecent, in-die-s'nt, a., onfatsoenlijk

indecision, in-di-siz-zjun, s., besluiteloosheid c.

indecisive, in-di-**sai**-siv, a., onbeslist

indecorous, in-**dek**-ke-rus, a., onwelvoeglijk

indeed, in-**died**, adv., inderdaad, waarlijk

indefatigable, in-di-**fet**-ti-Ge-b'l, a., onvermoeibaar

indefensible, in-di-**fen**-si-b'l, a., onverdedigbaar

indefinite, in-**def**-fi-nit, a., onbepaald

indelible, in-**del**-li-b'l, a., onuitwisbaar

indelicate, in-**del**-li-kit, a., onkies, grof

indemnify, in-**dem**-ni-fai, v., schadeloos stellen;
—— **against**, vrijwaren voor

indemnity, in-**dem**-ni-ti, s., vergoeding c. [heid c.

independence, in-di-**pen**-d'ns, s., onafhankelijk-

independent, in-di-**pen**-d'nt, a., onafhankelijk

indescribable, in-dis-**krai**-be-b'l, a., onbeschrijfelijk

indestructible, in-dis-**trak**-ti-b'l, a., onverwoestbaar

index, in-deks, s., index c.; (finger) wijsvinger c.

india-rubber, in-dje-**rab**-b'r, s., gummi n. & c.

indicate, in-di-keet, v., aanduiden, aanwijzen

indication, in-di-**kee**-sjun, s., aanwijzing c.

indicator, in-di-kee-t'r, s., (mech.) wijzer c.

indict, in-dait, v., aanklagen

indifference, in-**dif**-fr'ns, s., onverschilligheid c.

indifferent, in-**dif**-fr'nt, a., onverschillig

indigestible, in-di-**djes**-ti-b'l, a., onverteerbaar

indigestion, in-di-**djest**-sjun, s., indigestie c.

indignant, in-**diG**-n'nt, a., verontwaardigd

indignity, in-**diG**-ni-ti, s., belediging c.

indigo, in-di-Go, s., indigo n. & c.

indirect, in-di-**rekt**, a., niet rechtstreeks

indiscreet, in-dis-**kriet**, a., onbezonnen; indiscreet

indiscriminate, in-dis-**krim**-mi-nit, a., geen onderscheid makend; ——**ly**, adv., zonder onderscheid

indispensable, in-dis-**pen**-se-b'l, a., onmisbaar

indisposed, in-dis-**poozd**, a., ongenegen; ongesteld

indisposition, in-dis-pe-**zis**-sjun, s., ongesteldheid c.; (aversion) afkeer c.

indisputable, in-dis-pjoe-te-b'l, a., onbetwistbaar

indistinct, in-dis-tingkt, a., onduidelijk

indistinguishable, in-dis-ting-Gwi-sje-b'l, a., niet te onderscheiden

indite, in-dait, v., opstellen; (write) schrijven

individual, in-di-vid-joe-ul, a., individueel. s., enkeling c.; individu n.

indolent, in-de-l'nt, a., traag, vadsig

indoors, in-doarz, adv., binnen, binnenshuis

induce, in-djoes, v., bewegen; teweegbrengen

inducement, in-djoes-m'nt, s., beweegreden c.

indulge, in-daldzj, v., toegeven aan

indulgent, in-dal-dzj'nt, a., toegeeflijk

industrial, in-das-tri-ul, a., industrieel

industrious, in-das-tri-us, a., ijverig, vlijtig

industry, in-dus-tri, s., ijver c.; industrie c.

inebriate, in-ie-bri-it, a., dronken

ineffective, in-if-fek-tiv, a., vruchteloos

inefficient, in-if-fis-sjunt, a., ongeschikt

inept, in-ept, a., onbekwaam; (stupid) dwaas

inequality, in-i-kwol-li-ti, s., ongelijkheid c.

inert, in-eurt, a., log, loom; (sluggish) traag

inestimable, in-es-ti-me-b'l, a., onschatbaar

inevitable, in-ev-vi-te-b'l, a., onvermijdelijk

inexact, in-iG-zekt, a., onnauwkeurig, onjuist

inexcusable, in-iks-kjoe-ze-b'l, a., onvergeeflijk

inexhaustible, in-iG-zoas-ti-b'l, a., onuitputtelijk

inexpedient, in-iks-pie-di-'nt, a., ondienstig

inexpensive, in-iks-pen-siv, a., goedkoop

inexperience, in-iks-pie-ri-'ns, s., onervarenheid c.; ———d, a., onervaren

inexplicable, in-eks-pli-ke-b'l, a., onverklaarbaar

inexpressible, in-iks-pres-si-b'l, a., onuitspre-[kelijk

infallible, in-fel-li-b'l, a., onfeilbaar

infamous, in-fe-mus, a., berucht; schandelijk

infamy, in-fe-mi, s., eerloosheid c.; schande c.

infancy, in-f'n-si, s., kindsheid c.

infant, in-f'nt, s., kindje n.; (law) minderjarige c.

infantry, in-f'n-tri, s., infanterie c. [c.

infatuation, in-fet-joe-ee-sjun, s., verdwaasdheid

infect, in-fekt, v., besmetten; ——ious, a., besmettelijk

infer, in-feur, v., afleiden; (imply) insluiten

inference, in-fe-r'ns, s., gevolgtrekking c.

inferior, in-fie-ri-ur, a., minder; minderwaardig

infernal, in-feur-n'l, a., hels, duivels

infest, in-fest, v., onveilig maken; (harass) teisteren

infidel, in-fi-d'l, a., ongelovig. s., ongelovige c.

infinite, in-fi-nit, a., oneindig

infirm, in-feurm, a., zwak; (irresolute) weifelend; ——ary, s., ziekenzaal c.; ziekenhuis n.

inflame, in-fleem, v., doen ontvlammen; (med.) ontsteken

inflammable, in-flem-me-b'l, a., brandbaar

inflammation, in-fle-mee-sjun, s., ontsteking c.

inflate, in-fleet, v., opblazen; (tyres) oppompen; (prices) opdrijven

inflexible, in-flek-si-b'l, a., onbuigbaar; (unyielding) onverzettelijk

inflict, in-flikt, v., (blow) toebrengen; (punishment) opleggen

inflow, in-flo, s., instroming c., toevloed c.

influence, in-floe-'ns, s., invloed c. v., invloed hebben op, beïnvloeden

influential, in-floe-en-sjul, a., invloedrijk

influenza, in-floe-en-za, s., griep c.

influx, in-flaks, s., instroming c., toevloed c.

inform, in-foarm, v., mededelen; ——al, a., niet officieel; ——ation, s., mededeling c.; (news) bericht n.

infrequent, in-frie-kw'nt, a., zeldzaam

infringe, in-frindzj, v., schenden; (law) overtreden; ——ment, s., schending c.; overtreding c.

infuriate, in-fjoe-ri-eet, v., woedend maken

infuse, in-fjoez, v., ingieten; (tea) laten trekken

ingenious, in-dzjie-jus, a., vindingrijk

ingenuity, in-dzji-njoe-i-ti, s., vernuft n.

ingenuous, in-dzjen-joe-us, a., ongekunsteld

ingot, ing-Gut, s., baar c., staaf c.

ingrained, in-Greend, a., ingeworteld

ingratiate (oneself), in-Gree-sji-eet (**wɒn-self**)
v., trachten in de gunst te komen [c.
ingratitude, in-Gret-ti-tjoed, s., ondankbaarheid
ingredient, in-Grie-di-'nt, s., bestanddeel n.
ingrowing, in-Gro-ing, a., ingroeiend
inhabit, in-heb-bit, v., bewonen; **able**, a.,
bewoonbaar; **ant**, s., inwoner c.
inhale, in-heel, v., inademen; (smoke) inhaleren
inherent, in-hie-r'nt, a., onafscheidelijk verbonden
inherit, in-her-rit, v., erven
inheritance, in-her-rit-'ns, s., erfenis c.
inhospitable, in-hos-pi-te-b'l, a., ongastvrij
inhuman, in-hjoe-m'n, a., onmenselijk
iniquitous, i-nik-kwi-tus, a., onrechtvaardig
initial, i-nis-sjul, s., eerste letter c. a., voorste
initiate, i-nis-sji-eet, v., inwijden
inject, in-dzjekt, v., inspuiten
injection, in-dzek-sjun, s., inspuiting c.
injudicious, in-dzjoe-dis-sjus, a., onverstandig
injunction, in-dzjɒngk-sjun, s., bevel n.
injure, in-dzjur, v., benadelen; kwetsen
injurious, in-dzjoe-ri-us, a., nadelig; krenkend
injury, in-dzje-ri, s., onrecht n.; letsel n.
injustice, in-dzjɒs-tis, s., onrechtvaardigheid c.
ink, ingk, s., inkt c.; **stand**, inktkoker c.
inlaid, in-leed, a., ingelegd
inland, in-lend, a., binnenlands. s., binnenland n.
inlet, in-let, s., ingang c.; (creek) kreek c.
inmate, in-meet, s., medebewoner c.
inmost, in-moost, a., binnenste; (most secret)
geheimste
inn, in, s., herberg c.; **keeper**, herbergier c.
inner, in-n'r, a., inwendig, innerlijk
innocent, in-ne-s'nt, a., onschuldig
innocuous, i-nok-joe-us, a., onschadelijk
innovation, i-ne-vee-sjun, s., nieuwigheid c.
innumerable, i-njoe-me-re-b'l, a., ontelbaar
inoculate, i-nok-joe-leet, v., inenten; (tree) enten
inoffensive, in-e-fen-siv, a., onschadelijk
inopportune, i-nop-pe-tjoen, a., ongelegen
inquest, in-kwest, s., (coroner's) lijkschouwing c.

inquire, in-kwair, v., informeren [n.

inquiry, in-kwai-ri, s., vraag c.; (law) onderzoek

inquisition, in-kwi-zis-sjun, s., onderzoek n.

inquisitive, in-kwiz-zi-tiv, a., nieuwsgierig

inroad, in-rood, s., vijandelijke aanval c.

insane, in-seen, a., krankzinnig

insanity, in-sen-ni-ti, s., krankzinnigheid c.

insatiable, in-see-sji-e-b'l, a., onverzadelijk

inscribe, in-skraib, v., inschrijven; opschrijven

inscription, in-skrip-sjun, s., opschrift n.

insect, in-sekt, s., insect c.

insecure, in-si-kjoer, a., onveilig

insensible, in-sen-si-b'l, a., ongevoelig; (unconscious) bewusteloos

inseparable, in-sep-pe-re-b'l, a., onscheidbaar

insert, in-seurt, v., invoegen; (advertisement)
plaatsen; ——**ion,** s., invoeging c.; plaatsing c.

inside, in-said, s., binnenkant c. adv., naar binnen

insidious, in-sid-di-us, a., verraderlijk

insight, in-sait, s., inzicht n.

insignificant, in-siG-ni-fi-k'nt, a., onbeduidend

insincere, in-sin-sier, a., onoprecht

insinuate, in-sin-joe-eet, v., insinueren

insipid, in-sip-pid, a., smakeloos, flauw

insist (on), in-sist (on), v., aandringen (op)

insolence, in-se-l'ns, s., onbeschaamdheid c.

insolent, in-se-l'nt, a., onbeschaamd

insolvent, in-sol-v'nt, a., insolvent

inspect, in-spekt, v., onderzoeken; ——**ion,** s.,
onderzoek n.; ——**or,** inspecteur c.

inspiration, in-spi-ree-sjun, s., ingeving c.

inspire, in-spair, v., inademen; ingeven

install, in-stoal, v., installeren; (apparatus) plaatsen; ——**ation,** s., installatie c.; plaatsing c.

instalment, in-stoal-m'nt, s., termijn c.; (part)
gedeelte; **by** ——**s,** op afbetaling

instance, in-st'ns, s., voorbeeld n.; geval n.

instant, in-st'nt, s., ogenblik n. a., (urgent)
dringend; ——**aneous,** ogenblikkelijk; ——
ly, adv., onmiddellijk

instead of, in-sted ov, adv., in plaats van

instep, in-step, s., wreef c.

instigate, in-sti-Geet, v., ophitsen; aansporen
instil, in-stil, v., indruppelen; inprenten
instinct, in-stingkt, s., instinct n.
institute, in-sti-tjoet, v., stichten. s., instelling c.
instruct, in-strakt, v., (teach) onderrichten; (command) gelasten; ——ion, s., onderwijs n.; (command) opdracht c.
instrument, in-stroe-m'nt, s., instrument n. [nig
insubordinate, in-sub-oar-di-nit, a., weerspan-
insufferable, in-saf-fe-re-b'l, a., onverdraaglijk
insufficient, in-se-fisj-unt, a., onvoldoende
insulation, in-sjoe-lee-sjun, s., isolatie c.
insult, in-salt, v., beledigen. s., beleding c.
insurance, in-sjoe-r'ns, s., verzekering c.
insure, in-sjoer, v., verzekeren
insurrection, in-se-rek-sjun, s., opstand c.
intellect, in-ti-lekt, s., verstand n.
intelligence, in-tel-li-dzj'ns, s., verstand n.
intelligent, in-tel-li-dzj'nt, a., verstandig
intemperate, in-tem-pe-rit, a., onmatig
intend, in-tend, v., van plan zijn, bedoelen
intense, in-tens, a., krachtig, hevig
intent, in-tent, s., bedoeling c. a., ingespannen; ——ion, s., voornemen n.; ——ional, a., opzettelijk
inter, in-teur, v., begraven; ——ment, s., be-grafenis c.
inter, in-t'r, prep., onder; ——cept, v., onder-scheppen; ——change, ruilen; ——course, s., omgang c.; ——dict, v., verbieden; ——est, s., belang n.; (money) rente c. v., interesseren; ——esting, a., interessant; ——fere, v., tussen beide komen; ——fere with, (hinder) belemmeren; ——ference, s., inmenging c.; (radio) storing c.; ——lace, v., ineenstrengelen; ——loper, s., onder-kruiper c.; ——lude, tussenspel n.; ——mediate, a., tussenliggend; ——mingle, v., vermengen; ——mission, s., onderbreking c.; ——mittent, a., afwisselend; ——mix, v., vermengen; ——national, a., interna-tionaal; ——rupt, v., onderbreken; ——val,

s., tussentijd c.; (theatre) pauze c.; ——vene,
v., tussenbeide komen; (space, time) liggen
tussen; ——vention, s., tussenkomst c.;
——view, onderhoud n.; (for news) interview n. v., interviewen

interior, in-tie-ri-ur, a., inwendig. s., binnenste
intern, in-teurn, v., interneren [n.
internal, in-teur-n'l, a., innerlijk; binnenlands
interpret, in-teur-prit, v., uitleggen; (translate)
vertolken; ——er, s., tolk c.
interrogate, in-ter-re-Geet, v., ondervragen
intestate, in-tes-tit, a., zonder testament
intestine, in-tes-tin, s., darm c.
intimacy, in-ti-me-si, s., vertrouwelijkheid c.
intimate, in-ti-mit, a., vertrouwelijk, intiem
intimate, in-ti-meet, v., te kennen geven
intimation, in-ti-mee-sjun, s., kennisgeving c.
intimidate, in-tim-mi-deet, v., vrees aanjagen
into, in-toe, prep., in; tot
intolerable, in-tol-le-re-b'l, a., ondraaglijk
intoxicate, in-tok-si-keet, v., dronken maken
intrepid, in-trep-pid, a., onverschrokken
intricate, in-tri-kit, a., ingewikkeld
intrigue, in-trieG, s., gekonkel n. v., intrigeren
intriguer, in-trie-G'r, s. intrigant c.
intrinsic, in-trin-sik, a., innerlijk, wezenlijk
introduce, in-tre-djoes, v., inleiden; (people)
voorstellen
introductory, in-tre-dak-te-ri, a., inleidend
intrude, in-troed, v., indringen; storen
intruder, in-troe-d'r, s., indringer c.
intuition, in-tjoe-is-sjun, s., intuïtie c.
inundation, in-an-dee-sjun, s., overstroming c.
inure, i-njoer, v., harden; (accustom) gewennen
invade, in-veed, v., binnenvallen; ——r, s.,
vijandelijke indringer c.
invalid, in-ve-lied, s., zieke c.; (mil.) invalide c.;
——chair, rolstoel c.
invalid, in-vel-lid, a., ongeldig
invaluable, in-vel-joe-e-b'l, a., onschatbaar
invariable, in-vèr-ri-e-b'l, a., onveranderlijk
invasion, in-vee-zjun, s., inval c., invasie c.

inveigle, in-vieɢ-ɢ'l, v., verlokken, verleiden
invent, in-vent, v., uitvinden; ——ion, s., uit-
    vinding c.; (lie) verzinsel n.; ——or, uit-
    vinder c.
inventory, in-vun-tri, s., inventaris c.
invert, in-veurt, v., omkeren, omzetten
invest, in-vest, v., bekleden; (money) beleggen
investigate, in-ves-ti-ɢeet, v., onderzoeken
investment, in-vest-m'nt, s., geldbelegging c.
investor, in-ves-t'r, s., geldbelegger c.
inveterate, in-vet-te-rit, a., ingeworteld
invigorate, in-viɢ-ɢe-reet, v., versterken
invincible, in-vin-si-b'l, a., onoverwinnelijk
invisible, in-viz-zi-b'l, a., onzichtbaar
invitation, in-vi-tee-sjun, s., uitnodiging c.
invite, in-vait, v., uitnodigen; uitlokken
invoice, in-vois, s., factuur c. v., factureren
invoke, in-vook, v., inroepen, aanroepen
involuntary, in-vol-l'n-te-ri, a., onwillekeurig
involve, in-volv, v., wikkelen; verwikkelen
inward, in-wurd, a., inwendig. adv., naar binnen
iodine, ai-e-dien, s., jodium n.
I.O.U., ai o joe, s., schuldbekentenis c.
iris, ai-ris, s., iris c.
irksome, eurk-sum, a., vervelend, ergelijk
iron, ai-urn, s., ijzer n.; (flat) strijkijzer n. v.,
    strijken; ——monger, s., handelaar in ijzer-
    waren c.; ——works, pl., ijzerfabriek c.
ironical, ai-ron-ni-k'l, a., ironisch
irony, ai-re-ni, s., ironie c.   [zoenlijk
irreconcilable, i-rek-k'n-sai-le-b'l, a., onver-
irregular, i-reɢ-joe-l'r, a., onregelmatig
irrelevant, i-rel-li-v'nt, a., niet toepasselijk
irreproachable, i-ri-proot-sje-b'l, a., onberis-
    pelijk
irresistible, i-ri-zis-ti-b'l, a., onweerstaanbaar
irrespective, i-ris-pek-tiv, a., ongeacht
irresponsible, i-ris-pon-si-b'l, a., onverantwoor-
    delijk
irretrievable, i-ri-trie-ve-b'l, a., onherstelbaar
irreverent, i-rev-ve-r'nt, a., oneerbiedig
irrigate, ir-ri-ɢeet, v., besproeien

irritable, ir-ri-te-b'l, a., prikkelbaar
irritate, ir-ri-teet, v., irriteren, prikkelen
irruption, i-rap-sjun, s., inval c.
isinglass, ai-zing-Glaas, s., vislijm c.
island, ai-l'nd, s., eiland n.; ——er, eilandbe- woner c.
isle, ail, s., eiland n.; ——t, eilandje n.
isolate, ai-se-leet, v., afzonderen, isoleren
isolation, ai-se-lee-sjun, s., afzondering c.
issue, is-joe, v., (publish) uitgeven; (flow out) uitstromen; (end) eindigen. s., (flow) uit- stroming c.; (offspring) nakomelingen c.pl.; (outcome) uitslag c.; (publication) uitgave c.
isthmus, is-mus, s., landengte c.
it, it, pron., het
italic, i-tel-lik, a., cursief; in ——s, cursief
itch, itsj, s.; v., jeuk c. v., jeuken
item, ai-tem, s., (programme) nummer n.; (agenda) punt n.; (news) bericht n.; (bill)
itinerant, i-tin-ne-r'nt, a., rondreizend [post c.
its, its, pron., zijn; haar
itself, it-self, pron., zich, zich zelf
ivory, ai-ve-ri, s., ivoor n. a., ivoren
ivy, ai-vi, s., klimop c.

jabber, dzjeb-b'r, v., brabbelen, kakelen [kracht c.
jack, dzjek, s., (cards) boer c.; (mech.) domme-
jackal, dzjek-oal, s., jakhals c.; (fig.) handlanger c.
jackdaw, dzjek-doa, s., kerkkauw c.
jacket, dzjek-kit, s., jas c., jasje n.
jade, dzjeed, s., (horse) oude knol c. v., afjakkeren
jag, dzeG, s., uitsteeksel n. tand c. v., tanden
jail, dzjeel, s., gevangenis c.; ——er, cipier c.
jam, dzjem, s., jam c.; (traffic) opstopping c.; (radio) storing c. v., drukken, klemmen; storen
jangle, dzjeng-G'l, s., wanklank c. v., rammelen
January, dzjen-joe-e-ri, s., januari c.
jar, dzjaar, s., pot c., fles c.; (sound) wanklank c. v., knarsen; (shake) doen trillen
jaundice, dzjoan-dis, s., geelzucht c.
jaw, dzjoa, s., kaak c. v., (pop.) zwammen

jay, dzjee, s., Vlaamse gaai c.
jealous, dzjel-lus, a., jaloers; ——**y,** s., afgunst c.
jeer, dzjier, v., schimpen; (mock) bespotten
jelly, dzjel-li, s., gelei c.; ——**-fish,** kwal c.
jeopardize, dzjep-pe-daiz, v., in gevaar brengen
jeopardy, dzjep-pe-di, s., gevaar n.
jerk, dzjeurk, s., stoot c.; (tug) ruk c. v., rukken
jersey, dzjeur-zi, s., sporttrui c., trui c.
jest, dzjest, v., schertsen. s., scherts c.
jester, dzjes-t'r, s., grappenmaker c.; nar c.
jet, dzjet, s., git n.; (spirt) straal c. v., spuiten;
    ——**-fighter,** s., straaljager c.; ——**-plane,**
    straalvliegtuig n.
jettison, dzjet-ti-s'n, v., overboord werpen
jetty, dzjet-ti, s., pier c. a., gitzwart, gitachtig
Jew, dzjoe, s., Jood c.; ——**ess,** Jodin c.
jewel, dzjoe-il, s., juweel n., edelsteen c.; ——**ler,**
    juwelier c.; ——**lery,** juwelen n.pl.
jig, dzjig, s., horlepijp c. v., dansen; hossen
jilt, dzjilt, v., de bons geven, laten zitten
jingle, dzjing-G'l, v., rinkelen. s., gerinkel n.
job, dzjob, s., karwei c.; (post) baantje n.
jobber, dzjob-b'r, s., (stocks) effectenhandelaar c.
jockey, dzjok-ki, s., jockey c. v., bedriegen
jocular, dzjok-joe-l'r, a., grappig, schertsend
join, dzjoin, v., samenvoegen; (unite) verenigen;
    (army) dienst nemen in; (club) lid worden
    van; ——**in,** meedoen
joiner, dzjoi-n'r, s., schrijnwerker c.
joint, dzjoint, s., verbinding c.; (body) gewricht
    n.; (carpentry) voeg c.; (meat) stuk vlees n.
    a., verbonden; gemeenschappelijk
jointly, dzjoint-li, adv., gezamelijk   [maken
joke, dzjook, s., grap c., scherts c. v., grappen
joker, dzjo-k'r, s., grappenmaker c.
jolly, dzjol-li, a., vrolijk, lollig
jolt, dzjolt, v., horten, stoten. s., schok c.
jostle, dzjos-s'l, v., stoten, dringen
journal, dzjeur-n'l, s., dagboek n.; (paper) dag-
    blad n.; ——**ism,** journalistiek c.; ——**ist,**
    journalist c.
journey, dzjeur-ni, s., reis c. v., reizen

jovial, dzjo-vjul, a., vrolijk, opgewekt

joy, dzjoi, s., vreugde c.; ——**ful**, a., blij

jubilant, dzjoe-bi-l'nt, a., juichend, jubelend

jubilee, dzjoe-bi-lie, s., jubileum n.

judge, dzjadzj, s., rechter c.; (critic) kenner c. v., rechtspreken; ——**ment**, s., oordeel n.

judicial, dzjoe-dis-sjul, a., gerechtelijk

judicious, dzjoe-dis-sjus, a., verstandig

jug, dzjaG, s., kruik c., kan c.

juggle, dzjaG-G'l, v., goochelen

juggler, dzjaG-l'r, s., goochelaar c.

juice, dzjoes, s., sap n.

juicy, dzjoe-si, a., sappig

july, dzjoe-lai, s., juli c. [boel c.

jumble, dzjam-b'l, v., dooreengooien. s., warjump, dzjamp, s., sprong c. v., springen; (omit) overslaan; ——**er**, s., springer c.; (blouse) jumper c.; (sailors) matrozenkiel c.

junction, dzjangk-sjun, s., verbinding c.; (railway) knooppunt n.

juncture, dzjangk-sjur, s., verbindingspunt n.

june, dzjoen, s., juni c.

jungle, dzjang-G'l, s., rimboe c.

junior, dzjoen-j'r, a., jonger. s., jongere c.

juniper, dzjoe-ni-p'r, s., jeneverbes c.

jurisdiction, dzjoe-ris-dik-sjun, s., rechtsbevoegdheid c.; jurisdictie c.

juror, dzjoe-r'r, s., gezworene c., jurylid n.

jury, dzjoe-ri, s., jury c., gezworenen c.pl.

just, dzjast, a., rechtvaardig. adv., juist; (a moment ago) net; (barely) enkel maar; ——**ice**, s., rechtvaardigheid c.; (judge) rechter c.; ——**ification**, rechtvaardiging c.; ——**ify**, v., rechtvaardigen; ——**ly**, adv., met recht

jut, dzjat, v., uitsteken. s., uitsteeksel n.

jute, dzjoet, s., jute c.

juvenile, dzjoe-vi-nail, a., jeugdig, jong

kangaroo, keng-Ge-roe, s., kangoeroe c.

keel, kiel, s., kiel c.; (coal-barge) kolenschuit c.

keen, kien, a., (sharp) scherp; (acute) hevig; (piercing) doordringend; (eager) vurig

keep, kiep, s., kost c. v., (retain) houden; (preserve) bewaren; (protect) beschermen; ——**back,** achterhouden; ——**er,** s., bewaker c.; ——**off,** v., afweren; ——**sake,** s., aandenken n.; ——**to,** v., zich houden aan

keg, keG, s., vaatje n.

kennel, ken-n'l, s., hondehok n.; hok n.

kerbstone, keurb-stoon, s., trottoirband c.

kernel, keur-n'l, s., kern c.

kettle, ket-t'l, s., ketel c.; ——**drum,** pauk c.

key, kie, s., sleutel c.; ——**board,** klavier n.; ——**hole,** sleutelgat n.; ——**note,** grondtoon c.

kick, kik, s., trap c., schop c. v., trappen

kid, kid, s., jonge geit c.; ——**glove,** glacé handschoen c.

kidnap, kid-nep, v., ontvoeren; (child) stelen

kidney, kid-ni, s., nier c.

kill, kil, v., doden; (slaughter) slachten

kiln, kiln, s., kalkoven c.

kin, kin, s., bloedverwantschap c.; ——**dred,** a., verwant; ——**sfolk,** s., familie c.; ——**sman,** bloedverwant c.; ——**swoman,** bloedverwante c.

kind, kaind, s., soort c., aard c. a., vriendelijk, goed; ——**ness,** s., vriendelijkheid c.; (favour) dienst c.

kindle, kin-d'l, v., ontsteken; ontvlammen

king, king, s., koning c.; ——**dom,** koninkrijk n.

kipper, kip-p'r, s., gerookte haring c.

kiss, kis, s., kus c., zoen c. v., kussen, zoenen

kit, kit, s., uitrusting c.; (tub) vaatje n.

kitchen, kit-sjin, s., keuken c.

kite, kait, s., (bird) wouw c.; (toy) vlieger c.

kitten, kit-t'n, s., katje n. v., jongen

knack, nek, s., slag c., handigheid c.

knapsack, nep-**sek,** s., knapzak c., ransel c.

knave, neev, s., schurk c.; (cards) boer c.

knead, nied, v., kneden; (fig.) vormen

knee, nie, s., knie c.; ——**breeches,** pl., kniebroek c.; ——**cap,** knieschijf c.; (cover) kniebeschermer c.

kneel, niel, v., knielen

knell, nel, s., doodsklok c.

knickers, nik-k'rz, s.pl., (ladies, boys) broek c.

knife, naif, s., mes n. v., doorsteken   [c.

knight, nait, s., ridder c.; ——**hood,** ridderschap

knit, nit, v., breien; ——**ting,** s., breiwerk n.

knob, nob, s., knobbel c.; (door) deurknop c.

knock, nok, v., kloppen; (beat) slaan; —— **against,** stoten tegen; ——**down,** neer-slaan; (car) aanrijden; ——**er,** s., klopper c.

knoll, nol, s., heuveltje n.

knot, not, s., knoop c.; (tie) strik c. v., knopen

knotty, not-ti, a., (wood) knoestig; netelig

know, no, v., weten; (be acquainted with) kennen

knowledge, nol-lidzj, s., kennis c.

knuckle, nak-k'l, s., knokkel c.; (joint) schenkel c.

label, lee-b'l, s., etiket n.; (luggage) label c.

laboratory, leb-be-re-te-ri, s., laboratorium n.

laborious, le-boar-ri-us, a., werkzaam; moei-zaam

labour, lee-b'r, s., arbeid c.; (workers) arbeiders c.pl. v., arbeiden; ——**er,** s., arbeider c.

laburnum, le-beur-num, s., goudenregen c.

lace, lees, s., kant c.; (galloon) lint n.; (shoe) veter c. v., vastrijgen

lacerate, les-se-reet, v., verscheuren

lack, lek, s., (shortage) gebrek n.; (need) behoefte

lackey, lek-ki, s., lakei c.   [c.

lacquer, lek-k'r, s., lak n. v., lakken

lad, led, s., jongen c., knaap c.

ladder, led-d'r, s., ladder c.

lading, lee-ding, s., lading c.; **bill of ——,** connossement n.

ladle, lee-d'l, s., potlepel c. v., opscheppen

lady, lee-di, s., dame c.; ——**bird,** lievenheers-beestje n.

lag, leG, v., dralen; —— **behind,** achterblijven

lagoon, le-Goen, s., lagune c.

lair, lèr, s., leger n.; (den) hol n.

lake, leek, s., meer n.

lamb, lem, s., lam n. v., lammeren

lame, leem, a., kreupel. v., kreupel maken

lament, le-ment, v., weeklagen. s., weeklacht c.

lamp, lemp, s., lamp c.; (street) lantaarn c.

lance, laans, s., lans c. v., doorsteken

land, lend, s., land n.; (estate) landerijen c.pl. v., landen; ——ing, s., landing c.; (stairs) trapportaal n.; ——ing-place, landings-plaats c.; ——lady, (lodgings) hospita c.; (inn) waardin c.; ——lord, (land-owner) landheer c.; (inn) waard c.; (house-owner) huisbaas c.; ——mark, grenspaal c.; (naut.) landteken n.; ——scape, landschap n.; ——slide, aardverschuiving c.

lane, leen, s., landweg c.; (alley) steeg c.

language, leng-Gwidzj, s., taal c.

languid, leng-Gwid, a., lusteloos, loom

languish, leng-Gwisj, v., wegkwijnen; smachten

lank, lengk, a., schraal; ——y, lang en mager

lantern, len-t'rn, s., lantaarn c.

lap, lep, s., schoot c.; (sports) ronde c. v.,

lapel, le-pel, s., lapel c.   [oplikken

lapse, leps, v., vervallen. s., (time) verloop n.

larceny, laar-se-ni, s., diefstal c.

lard, laard, s., varkensreuzel c.

larder, laar-d'r, s., provisiekamer c.

large, laardzj, a., groot; (ample) ruim, breed

lark, laark, s., leeuwerik c.; (fun) pret c.

lash, lesj, s., (whip) zweepkoord n.; (stroke) slag c.; (eye) wimper c. v., zwepen; (tie) vastsjorren

lassitude, les-si-tjoed, s., moeheid c.

last, laast, v., duren. s., leest c. a., laatst; (most recent) vorig; ——ing, duurzaam, bestendig

latch, letsj, s., klink c. v., op de klink doen

latchkey, letsj-kie, s., huissleutel c.

late, leet, a., laat; (belated) te laat; (former) vorig; (deceased) wijlen

lately, leet-li, adv., onlangs, kort geleden

latent, lee-t'nt, a., verborgen, slapend

lathe, leedh, s., draaibank c.

lather, ledh-ur, s., zeepsop n. v., inzepen

latitude, let-ti-tjoed, s., breedte c.; (extent) omvang c.

latter, let-t'r, a., laatste, laatstgenoemde

lattice, let-tis, s., traliewerk n.

laudable, loa-de-b'l, a., prijzenswaardig

laugh, laaf, s., lach c. v., lachen; ——**able,** a., belachelijk; ——**ing-stock,** s., voorwerp van bespotting n.; ——**ter,** gelach n.

launch, loansj, s., tewaterlating c.; (boat) barkas c. v., te water laten; (hurl) slingeren

laundress, loan-dris, s., wasvrouw c.

laundry, loan-dri, s., wasserij c.; (clothes) was c.

laureate, loa-ri-it, s., (poet) hofdichter c.

laurel, loa-r'l, s., laurier c.; lauwerkrans c.

lavatory, lev-ve-te-ri, s., wasplaats c.; (W.C.) toilet n., W.C. c.

lavender, lev-vin-d'r, s., lavendel c.

lavish, lev-visj, a., kwistig. v., kwistig uitdelen

law, loa, s., wet c.; ——**ful,** a., rechtmatig; ——**less,** wetteloos; (person) losbandig; ——**suit,** s., proces n.; ——**yer,** advocaat c.; rechtsgeleerde c.

lawn, loan, s., grasperk n.; —— **tennis,** tennis n.

lax, leks, a., (loose) los; (not strict) laks

laxative, lek-se-tiv, s., laxeermiddel n.

lay, lee, v., leggen; (set) zetten; (table) dekken

layer, lee-ur, s., (stratum) laag c.; (hen) leghen c.

layman, lee-m'n, s., leek c.

laziness, lee-zi-nis, s., luiheid c.

lazy, lee-zi, a., lui; (slothful) vadsig

lead, led, s., lood n.; (plummet) dieplood n. a., loden. v., met lood bedekken

lead, lied, v., leiden; (command) aanvoeren; (induce) er toe brengen; (cards) uitkomen; (to be first) bovenaan staan; ——**er,** s., leider c.; ——**ership,** leiding c.; ——**ing,** a., eerste; (principal) voornaamste; ——**ing article,** s., hoofdartikel n.

leaf, lief, s., blad n.; ——**let,** blaadje n.

leafy, lie-fi, a., bladerrijk

league, lieG, s., bond c.; (naut.) zeemijl c.

leak, liek, s., lek n. v., lek zijn, lekken

lean, lien, a., mager. v., leunen; (incline) over-hellen; —— **on,** steunen op

leap, liep, v., springen. s., sprong c.; ——**frog**, haasje-over n.; ——**year**, schrikkeljaar n.

learn, leurn, v., leren; (hear) vernemen; ——**ed**, a., geleerd; ——**er**, s., leerling c.; ——**ing**, geleerdheid c.

lease, lies, s., (letting) verhuring c.; (contract) huurcontract n. v., huren; (land) pachten

leash, liesj, s., koppel c. v., koppelen

least, liest, a., minste; **at** ——, ten minste

leather, ledh-ur, s., leer n. a., leren

leave, liev, s., verlof n. v., (depart) weggaan; (desert) verlaten; (bequeath) nalaten; —— **behind**, achterlaten; —— **off**, ophouden met; (clothes) uitlaten; —— **out**, weglaten; —— **to**, (hand over) overlaten

lecture, lek-tsjur, s., lezing c.; (university) college n.; (reprimand) berisping c. v., een lezing houden; ——**r**, s., lector c.

ledge, ledzj, s., richel c.; (rock) bergrand c.

ledger, led-zjur, s., grootboek n.

leech, lietsj, s., bloedzuiger c.

leek, liek, s., prei c., look n.

leer, lier, v., gluren, lonken

left, left, a. & adv., links; ——**handed**, a., links

leg, leG, s., been n.; (trousers) pijp c.; (meat) bout

legacy, leG-Ge-si, s., erfenis c. [c.

legal, lie-G'l, a., wettelijk; ——**ize**, v., wettigen

legation, li-Gee-sjun, s., gezantschap n.

legend, lie-dzjunt, s., legende c.; opschrift n.

legging, leG-Ging, s., beenkap c.

legible, led-zji-b'l, a., leesbaar

legion, lie-dzjun, s., legioen n.

legislate, led-zjis-leet, v., wetten maken

legislation, led-zjis-lee-sjun, s., wetgeving c.

legitimacy, li-dzjit-ti-me-si, s., rechtmatigheid c.; (parentage) wettigheid c.

legitimate, li-dzjit-ti-mit, a., rechtmatig; (just) gerechtvaardigd; (parentage) wettig

leisure, lez-zjur, s., vrije tijd c.

leisurely, lez-zjur-li, adv., op zijn gemak

lemon, lem-m'n, s., citroen c.

lemonade, lem-m'n-eed, s., limonade c.

lend, lend, v., lenen

length, length, s., lengte c.; (duration) duur c.; (size) grootte c.; ———**en,** v., verlengen; ———**ways,** adv., in de lengte; ———**y,** a., lang; (prolix) langdradig

leniency, lie-ni-un-si, s., toegevendheid c.

lenient, lie-ni-unt, a., toegevend, zacht

lens, lenz, s., lens c.

Lent, lent, s., vasten c., vastentijd c.

lentil, len-til, s., linze c.

leopard, lep-purd, s., luipaard c.

leper, lep-p'r, s., melaatse c.

leprosy, lep-pre-si, s., melaatsheid c.

leprous, lep-prus, a., melaats

less, les, a. & adv., minder. prep., (deducting) min

lessee, les-sie, s., huurder c.; (land) pachter c.

lessen, les-s'n, v., verminderen; afnemen

lesson, les-s'n, s., les c.; ———**book,** leerboek n.

let, let, v., laten; (allow) toestaan; (house) verhuren; to ———, te huur; ——— **down,** teleurstellen

letter, let-t'r, s., brief c.; (alphabet) letter c.; ———**box,** brievenbus c.; ——— **of credit,** credietbrief c.

lettuce, let-tis, s., sla c., salade c.

level, lev-v'l, a., horizontaal; (even) gelijk; (flat) vlak. v., gelijk maken; (raze) slechten. s., hoogte c.; (of the sea) zeespiegel c.; (level country) vlakte c.; ———**crossing,** overweg c.

lever, lie-v'r, s., hefboom c.

levity, lev-vi-ti, s., lichtzinnigheid c.

levy, lev-vi, s., (tax) heffing c.; (troops) lichting c. v., heffen; lichten

lewd, ljoed, a., ontuchtig; ———**ness,** s., ontucht c.

liability, lai-e-bi-li-ti, s., aansprakelijkheid c.

liable, lai-e-b'l, a., (responsible) verantwoordelijk; (subject) blootgesteld; ——— **to,** geneigd

liar, lai-ur, s., leugenaar c. [tot

libel, lai-b'l, s., schotschrift n. v., belasteren

libellous, lai-be-lus, a., lasterlijk

liberal, lib-be-r'l, a., royaal; (ample) ruim

liberate, lib-be-reet, v., bevrijden

liberty, lib-be-ti, s., vrijheid c.

librarian, lai-**brèr**-i-un, s., bibliothecaris c.

library, lai-bre-ri, s., bibliotheek c.

licence, lai-s'ns, s., (leave) verlof n.; (drinks) vergunning c.; (car) rijbewijs n.; (irregular behaviour) losbandigheid c.

license, lai-s'ns, v., vergunning geven

licentious, lai-sen-sjus, a., losbandig

lick, lik, v., likken; —— **up,** oplikken

lid, lid, s., deksel n.; **eye** ——, ooglid n.

lie, lai, s., (untruth) leugen c. v., liegen

lie, lai, s., ligging c. v., liggen; —— **about,** rondslingeren; —— **down,** gaan liggen

lieutenant, lef-ten-n'nt, s., luitenant c.

life, laif, s., leven n.; ——**belt,** reddingsgordel c.; ——**boat,** reddingsboot c.; ——**insur-ance,** levensverzekering c.; ——**less,** a., levenloos; (dead) dood; ——**like,** levensge-trouw; ——**long,** levenslang; ——**size,** levensgroot; ——**time,** s., levensduur c.; **in my** ——**time,** bij mijn leven

lift, lift, v., (raise) opheffen; (eyes) opslaan; (hand) opsteken. s., lift c.; (rise in status) promotie c.

light, lait, s., licht n. a., licht. v., (kindle) aansteken; (illuminate) verlichten; (brighten) schitteren; ——**en,** verlichten; ——**er,** s., (flint) aansteker c.; (boat) lichter c.; ——**house,** vuurtoren c.; ——**ing,** verlichting c.; ——**ness,** gemakkelijkheid c.

lightning, lait-ning, s., bliksem c.; ——**-con-ductor,** bliksemafleider c.

like, laik, v., houden van, graag hebben. a., gelijk; (resembling) gelijkend; ——**lihood,** s., waarschijnlijkheid c.; ——**ly,** adv., waar-schijnlijk; ——**ness,** s., gelijkenis c.; portret n.; ——**wise,** adv., eveneens

liking, lai-king, s., zin c., voorliefde c.

lilac, lai-luk, s., sering c. a., (colour) lila

lily, lil-li, s., lelie c.; —— **of the valley,** lelietje van dalen n.

limb, lim, s., (anatomy) lid n.

lime, laim, s., **kalk** c.; (bird-lime) vogellijm c.;

(fruit) limoen c.; (tree) linde c.; ——juice, limoensap n.; ——light, kalklicht n.; **be in the** ——light, de algemene aandacht trekken

limit, lim-mit, s., grens c. v., begrenzen; (restrict) beperken; ——ed, a., beperkt; Ltd. Co., s., naamloze vennootschap c.

limp, limp, v., hinken. a., (soft) slap

limpet, lim-pit, s., napslak c.

line, lain, s., lijn c.; (rail) spoorlijn c.; (business) branche c.; (fishing) snoer n.; (rope) touw n.; (print) regel c.; (row) rij c. v., (garment) [voeren

lineage, lin-ni-idzj, s., geslacht n.

linen, lin-nin, s., linnen n. a., linnen

liner, lai-n'r, s., lijnboot c.

linger, ling-G'r, v., talmen

lingering, ling-G'r-ring, a., langdurig

linguist, ling-Gwist, s., taalkundige c.

lining, lai-ning, s., (of clothes) voering c.

link, lingk, v., verbinden. s., schakel c.

links, lingks, s.pl., (cuff) manchetknopen c.pl.

linnet, lin-nit, s., vlasvink c., kneu c.

linoleum, li-nool-jum, s., linoleum n.

linseed, lin-sied, s., lijnzaad n.

lint, lint, s., pluksel n., pluis c.

lion, lai-un, s., leeuw c.; ——ess, leeuwin c.

lip, lip, s., lip c.; ——stick, lippenstift c.

liquefy, lik-kwi-fai, v., vloeibaar maken

liqueur, li-keur, s., likeur c.

liquid, lik-kwid, s., vloeistof c. a., vloeibaar

liquidate, lik-kwi-deet, v., liquideren; (debts) vereffenen

liquidation, li-kwi-dee-sjun, s., vereffening c.

liquor, lik-k'r, s., (fluid) vocht n.; (alcoholic drink) sterke drank c.; (cookery) aftreksel n.

liquorice, lik-ke-ris, s., zoethout n.

lisp, lisp, v., lispelen. s., gelispel n.

list, list, s., lijst c.; (naut.) slagzijde c. v., (naut.) slagzijde hebben

listen, lis-s'n, v., luisteren; ——er, s., luisteraar c.; —— in, v., (radio) luisteren

literal(ly), lit-te-r'l(-li), a. & adv., letterlijk

literary, lit-te-re-ri, a., letterkundig

literature, lit-te-re-tsjur, s., letterkunde c.

lithograph, lith-e-Graaf, s., steendruk c.

litigate, lit-ti-Geet, v., procederen

litigation, li-ti-Gee-sjun, s., proces n., geding n.

litter, lit-t'r, s., (stretcher) draagstoel c.; (rubbish) rommel c.; (untidiness) warboel c.; (straw) strooisel n.; (animals) worp c. v., van stro voorzien

little, lit-t'l, a., (size) klein; (quantity) **weinig**; (time) kort. adv., weinig

live, liv, v., leven; (reside) wonen

live, laiv, (see **alive**)

lively, laiv-li, a., levendig; (gay) vrolijk

liver, liv-v'r, s., lever c.   [houderij c.

livery, liv-ve-ri, s., livrei c.; ——**stable,** stal-

livid, liv-vid, a., loodkleurig; (very pale) doodsbleek

living, liv-ving, s., leven n.; (livelihood) kostwinning c. a., levend

lizard, liz-zurd, s., hagedis c.

load, lood, v., laden. s., lading c.; (burden) **last** c.

loaf, loof, v., (about) leeglopen, rondslenteren. s., (bread) brood n.; ——**sugar,** broodsuiker c.

loafer, lo-f'r, s., leegloper c.

loam, loom, s., leem n.; ——**y,** a., leemachtig

loan, loon, v., lenen. s., lening c.; (thing lent) geleende n.; **on** ——, to leen

loathe, loodh, v., verafschuwen, walgen van

loathing, lo-dhing, s., walg c., weerzin c.

loathsome, lodh-sum, a., walglijk, afschuwelijk

lobby, lob-bi, s., (hall) voorzaal c.; (theatre) foyer c.

lobe, loob, s., (ear) lel c.; (leaf) lob c.

lobster, lob-st'r, s., zeekreeft c.

local, lo-k'l, a., plaatselijk; ——**ity,** s., **plaats** c.

locate, lo-keet, v., plaatsen, vestigen

lock, lok, s., slot n.; (canal, etc.) sluis c.; (hair) lok c. v., op slot doen; ——**et,** s., medaillon n.; —— **in,** v., opsluiten; ——**up,** v., opsluiten; ——**jaw,** s., mondklem c.; —— **out,** v., buitensluiten; ——**smith,** s., slotenmaker c.

locomotive, lo-ke-mo-tiv, s., locomotief c.

locum tenens, lo-kum tie-nenz, s., plaatsvervanger c.

locust, lo-kust, s., sprinkhaan c.

lodge, lodzj, s., portierswoning c.; (masonic) loge c. v., (accommodate) herbergen; (reside) wonen; ——r, s., inwonende c.

lodging, lod-zjing, s., huisvesting c.

loft, loft, s., zolder c.; ——y, a., hoog, verheven

log, loG, s., (wood) blok n.; ——book, logboek n.

logic, lod-zjik, s., logica c.; ——al, a., logisch

loin, loin, s., lende c.; (meat) lendestuk n.

loiter, loi-t'r, v., treuzelen; ——er, s., treuzelaar

loll, lol, v., lummelen; (tongue) uitsteken   [c.

loneliness, loon-li-nis, s., eenzaamheid c.

lone(ly), loon(-li), a., eenzaam

long, long, a., lang; —— for, v., verlangen naar; ——ing, s., verlangen n.; (yearning) hunkering c.

longitude, lon-dzi-tjoed, s., lengte c.; (degree of ——), lengtegraad c.

look, loek, s., blik c. v., kijken; (appear) er uitzien; —— after, (take care of) zorgen voor; —— at, kijken naar; ——er-on, s., toeschouwer c.; —— for, v., zoeken; (expect) verwachten; ——ing-glass, s., spiegel c.; —— out, v., uitkijken; ——round, omkijken

loom, loem, s., weefgetouw n. v., opdoemen

loop, loep, s., (noose) lus c.; ——hole, kijkgat n.; (fort) schietgat n.; (fig.) achterdeurtje n.; ——ing the loop, duikeling c.

loose, loes, a., los; (morals) los; ——n, v., losmaken

loot, loet, v., plunderen. s., buit c.

lop, lop, v., (prune) snoeien; ——off, wegkappen

loquacious, le-kwees-sjus, a., babbelziek

Lord (the), loard, (God) de Heer

Lord's Prayer, loardz prè-ur, s., Onze Vader n.

lord, loard, s., heer c., meester c.; (peer) lord c.

lorry, lor-ri, s., (motor) vrachtauto c.

lose, loez, v., verliezen; (play away) verspelen; (train) missen; ——r, s., verliezer c.

Lost Property Office, lost prop-pe-ti of-fis, s., bureau van gevonden voorwerpen n.

lot, lot, s., lot n.; (portion) portie c.; —— **of,** heel

lotion, lo-sjun, s., wasmiddel n. [wat

lottery, lot-te-ri, s., loterij c.

loud, laud, a., luid; (colours) opzichtig; —— **-speaker,** s., (radio) luidspreker c.

lounge, laundzj, s., (couch) ligstoel c. v., slenteren

louse, laus, s., luis c.

lout, laut, s., pummel c., lummel c.

love, lav, v., beminnen; (like) houden van. s., liefde c.; —— **liness,** beminnelijkheid c.; —— **ly,** a., lief, beminnelijk; —— **r,** s., minnaar c.; (of books, etc.) liefhebber c.

low, lo, a., laag; (voice) zacht; (pulse) zwak; (bow) diep; (vulgar) plat. v., (cattle) loeien

lower, lo-ur, v., (prices) verlagen; (flag) strijken

lowland, lo-lend, s., laagland n.

loyal, loi-ul, a., trouw; —— **ty,** s., getrouwheid c.

lozenge, loz-zindzj, s., tabletje n.

lubricate, loe-bri-keet, v., smeren, oliën

lucid, loe-sid, a., schitterend; (clear) helder

luck, lak, s., (chance) toeval n.; (good fortune) geluk n.

lucky, lak-ki, a., gelukkig

ludicrous, loe-di-krus, a., belachelijk

luggage, lag-Gidzj, s., bagage c.; —— **-ticket,** bagagereçu n.; —— **-van,** bagagewagen c.

lukewarm, loek-woarm, a., lauw

lull, lal, v., (child) in slaap wiegen; (soothe) sussen; (wind) luwen. s., (calm) stilte c.

lullaby, lal-le-bai, s., wiegelied n.

lumbago, lam-bee-Go, s., lendepijn c., spit n.

lumber, lam-b'r, s., rommel c.; (wood) timmerhout n.

luminous, loe-mi-nus, a., lichtgevend, stralend

lump, lamp, s., klomp c.; —— **y,** a., kloddereig

lunacy, loe-ne-si, s., krankzinnigheid c.

lunar, loe-n'r, a., van de maan, maan . . .

lunatic, loe-ne-tik, s., krankzinnige c.; —— **asylum,** gekkenhuis n.

lunch(eon), lansj(-un), s., lunch c. v., lunchen

lung, lᴀng, s., long c.
lurch, leurtsj, v., slingeren. s., plotselinge slinger
c.; to leave in the ——, in de steek laten
lure, ljoer, v., verlokken. s., lokaas n.
lurid, ljoe-rid, a., akelig; (colour) vaalbleek
lurk, leurk, v., loeren
luscious, lᴀs-sjus, a., lekker; (fulsome) walglijk
lust, lᴀst, s., zinnelijke lust c.; (desire) begeerte c.
v., begeren; ——ful, a., wellustig
lustre, lᴀs-t'r, s., glans c.; (pendant) luchter c.
lute, loet, s., luit c.
luxurious, lᴀɢ-zoe-ri-us, a., weelderig
luxury, lᴀk-sje-ri, s., weelde c., luxe c.
lying-in, lai-ing-in, s., bevalling c.
lymph, limf, s., lymphe c.
lynch, lintsj, v., lynchen

macaroni, mek-ke-ro-ni, s., macaroni c.
macaroon, mek-ke-roen, s., bitterkoekje n.
mace, mees, s., (staff) staf c.; (spice) foelie c.
machine, me-sjien, s., machine c.; ——ry,
machinerieën c.pl.; ——gun, mitrailleur c.
machinist, me-sjie-nist, s., machineconstructeur
mackerel, mek-krul, s., makreel c. [c.
mackintosh, mek-kin-tosj, s., regenjas c.
mad, med, a., gek; (frantic) dol; ——man, s.,
gek c.; ——ness, krankzinnigheid c.; dolheid
madam, med-dum, s., mevrouw c. [c.
magazine, meɢ-ɢe-zien, s., magazijn n.;
(periodical) tijdschrift n.
maggot, meɢ-ɢut, s., made c.
magic, med-zjik, s., toverkunst c. a., toverachtig
magistrate, med-zjis-trit, s., politierechter c.
magnanimity, meɢ-ne-ni-mi-ti, s., grootmoe-
digheid c.
magnanimous, meɢ-nen-ni-mus, a., grootmoedig
magnesia, meɢ-nie-sje, s., magnesia c.
magnet, meɢ-nit, s., magneet c.; ——ic, a.,
magnetisch; ——ism, s., magnetisme n.;
——ize, v., magnetiseren
magneto, meɢ-nie-to s., magneet c.
magnificent, meɢ-nif-fi-s'nt a., prachtig

magnify, meG-ni-fai, v., vergroten; ——**ing glass,** s., vergrootglas n.

magnitude, meG-ni-tjoed, s., (size) grootte c.

magpie, meG-pai, s., ekster c.

mahogany, mc-hoG-Ge-ni, s., mahoniehout n.

Mahometan, me-hom-mi-t'n, (see **Mohamme-dan**)

maid, meed, s., (girl) meisje n.; (virgin) maagd c.; (servant) meid c.; **old** ——, oude vrijster c.

maiden, mee-d'n, s., meisje n.; maagd c.

mail, meel, s., post c.; (armour) maliënkolder c. v., posten; ——**bag,** s., postzak c.; ——**plane,** postvliegtuig n.

maim, meem, v., verminken

main, meen, a., voornaamste. s., (water, gas) hoofdleiding c.; ——**land,** vasteland n.

maintain, meen-teen, v., (uphold) handhaven; (defend) verdedigen; (assert) beweren

maintenance, meen-ti-n'ns, s., onderhoud n.

maize, meez, s., maïs c., Turkse tarwe c.

majestic, me-dzjes-tik, a., majestueus

majesty, med-zjes-ti, s., majesteit c.

major, mee-dzjur, s., majoor c.; (of age) meer-derjarige c. a., groter; (age) meerderjarig; ——**ity,s.,meerderheid** c.; meerderjarigheid c.

make, meek, s., fabrikaat n. v., maken; (manu-facture) vervaardigen; ——**believe,** s., aanstellerij c.; ——**r,** fabrikant c.; ——**shift,** hulpmiddel n.; ——**up,** (face) grime c.

making, mee-king, s., vervaardiging c.

malady, mel-le-di, s., ziekte c.

malaria, me-lèr-i-a, s., malaria c.

male, meel, a., mannelijk. s., mannetje n.

malediction, mel-li-dik-sjun, s., vervloeking c.

malevolent, me-lev-ve-l'nt, a., kwaadwillig

malice, mel-lis, s., boosaardigheid c.

malicious, me-lis-sjus, a., boosaardig

malign, me-lain, v., belasteren. a., verderfelijk

malignant, me-liG-n'nt, a., kwaadwillig

maligner, me-lai-n'r, s., lasteraar c.

malinger, me-ling-G'r, v., zich ziek houden

mallet, mel-lit, s., houten hamer c.

malt, moalt, s., mout n. v., mouten
maltreat, mel-**triet**, v., mishandelen
mammal, mem-m'l, s., zoogdier n.
man, men, s., mens c.; man c. v., bemannen;
  -**hood,** s., mannelijkheid c.; (age) mannelijke
  leeftijd c.; ——**kind,** menshed c.; ——**ly,** a.,
  mannelijk; ——**servant,** s., bediende c.;
  ——**slaughter,** manslag c.
manacle, men-ne-k'l, s., handboei c.
manage, men-nidzj, v., (conduct) leiden;
  (handle) hanteren; (control) beheren; (accomplish) het klaarspelen; ——**ment,** s.,
  leiding c.; (board) bestuur n.; ——**r,** bestuurder c., directeur c.
mandate, men-deet, s., bevel n., bevelschrift n.
mandoline, men-de-lien, s., mandoline c.
mane, meen, s., manen c.pl.
manger, men-dzjur, s., voerbak c., krib c.
mangle, meng-G'l, s., mangel c. v., mangelen
mania, mee-ni-a, s., manie c.; ——**c,** maniak c.
manicure, men-ni-kjoer, s., manicure c.
manifest, men-ni-fest, a., klaarblijkelijk. s.,
  scheepsmanifest n. v., openbaren
manifold, men-ni-foold, a., veelvuldig
manipulate, me-nip-joe-leet, v., hanteren [c.
manner, men-n'r, s., manier c.; (habit) gewoonte
manners, men-n'rz, s.pl., goede manieren c.pl.
manœuvre, me-noe-v'r, s., manœuvre c. v.,
  manœuvreren
manor, mee-n'r, s., riddergoed n.; landgoed n.
mansion, men-sjun, s., herenhuis n. [tel c.
mantelpiece, men-t'l-pies, s., schoorsteenman-
mantle, men-t'l, s., mantel c.; (gas) gloeikousje
  n.; (fig.) dekmantel c. v., bedekken
manual, men-joe-ul, s., handboek n.; ——
  labour, handenarbeid c.
manufactory, men-joe-fek-te-ri, s., fabriek c.
manufacture, men-joe-fekt-sjur, s., fabrikaat n.
  v., vervaardigen; ——**r,** s., fabrikant c.
manure, me-njoer, s., mest n. v., mesten
manuscript, men-joe-skript, s., manuscript n.
many, men-ni, a.pl., veel, vele; —— a, menig

MAP 483 MAS

map, mep, s., landkaart c. v., in kaart brengen

maple, mee-p'l, s., ahorn c., esdoorn c.

mar, maar, v., bederven; (disfigure) ontsieren

marble, maar-b'l, s., marmer n.; (toy) knikker c.

March, maartsj, s., maart c.

march, maartsj, v., marcheren. s., mars c.

marchioness, maar-tsje-nis, s., markiezin c. [c.

mare, mèr, s., merrie c.; **night**——, nachtmerrie

margarine, maar-dzje-rien, s., margarine c.

margin, maar-dzjin, s., rand c.; ——al, a., rand . . .; ——al notes, s.pl., kanttekeningen

marigold, mer-ri-Goold, s., goudsbloem c. [c.pl.

marine, me-rien, s., marinier c. a., zee . . .

mariner, mer-ri-n'r, s., matroos c., zeeman c.

maritime, mer-ri-taim, a., kust . . ., zee . . .

mark, maark, s., (sign) teken n.; (impression) merkteken n.; (at school) punt n. v., tekenen; (distinguish) onderscheiden; ——ing-ink, s., merkinkt c.

market, maar-kit, s., markt c. v., markten

marmalade, maar-me-leed, s., marmelade c.

marmot, maar-m't, s., marmot c.

maroon, me-roen, a., kastanjebruin

marquee, maar-kie, s., grote tent c.

marquess, maar-kwis, s., markies c.

marriage, mer-ridzj, s., huwelijk n.

marrow, mer-ro, s., merg n.; (fig.) pit c.

marry, mer-ri, v., trouwen

marsh, maarsj, s., moeras c.

marshal, maar-sjul, s., maarschalk c.

marten, maar-tin, s., marter c.

martial, maar-sjul, a., krijgshaftig; **court**——, s., krijgsraad c.; —— **law**, staat van beleg c.

martyr, maar-t'r, s., martelaar c. v., martelen

martyrdom, maar-t'r-dum, s., martelaarschap n.

marvel, maar-v'l, v., zich verwonderen. s., wonder n.

marvellous, maar-v'l-lus, a., wonderbaar

masculine, mes-kjoe-lin, a., mannelijk

mash, mèsj, v., fijnstampen

mask, maask, v., vermommem. s., masker n.

mason, mee-s'n, s., steenhouwer c.; (freemason) vrijmetselaar c.; ——ic, a., vrijmetselaars ...; ——ry, s., (stone) metselwerk n.

masquerade, mes-ke-reed, v., zich vermommen. s., maskerade c.

mass, mes, s., massa c.; (eccl.) Mis c.

massacre, mes-se-k'r, s., bloedbad n., moord c.

massage, mes-saazj, s., massage c. v., masseren

massive, mes-siv, a., massief, zwaar

mast, maast, s., mast c.

master, maas-t'r, v., zich meester maken van. s., meester c.; heer c.; (college) hoofd n.; ——ful, a., bazig; ——ly, meesterlijk; ——piece, s., meesterstuk n.

masticate, mes-ti-keet, v., kauwen

mastiff, maas-tif, s., bulhond c.

mat, met, s., mat c. a., (colour) mat, dof

match, metsj, s., lucifer c.; (contest) wedstrijd c.; (marriage) huwelijk n.; (equal) gelijke c. v., (colours) bij elkaar passen; (equal) evenaren; (oppose) tegenover elkaar stellen

matchless, metsj-lis, a., weergaloos

mate, meet, s., maat c., makker c.; (work) gezel c.; (naut.) stuurman c. v., paren

material, me-tie-ri-ul, s., materiaal n.; (cloth) stof c.

materialize, me-tie-ri-e-laiz, v., verstoffelijken

maternal, me-teur-n'l, a., moederlijk, moeder...

mathematics, meth-i-met-tiks, s.pl., wiskunde c.

matrimony, met-tri-me-ni, s., huwelijk n.

matrix, mee-triks, s., baarmoeder c.

matron, mee-tr'n, s., (hospital) directrice c.

matter, met-t'r, s., stof c.; (substance) materie c.; (affair) zaak c.; (pus) etter c. v., van belang zijn; (discharge pus) etteren

matting, met-ting, s., matwerk n.

mattress, met-tris, s., matras c. [rijpen

mature, me-tjoer, a., rijp; (bills) vervallen. v.,

maturity, me-tjoe-ri-ti, s., rijpheid c.; vervaltijd

maul, moal, s., slegel c. v., toetakelen [c.

mauve, moov, a., mauve, licht paars

maxim, mek-sim, s., leerspreuk c.

maximum, mek-si-mum, s., maximum n.

May, mee, s., mei c.

may, mee, v., (permission, wish) mogen; (possibility) kunnen; ——be, adv., misschien

mayor, mèr, s., burgemeester c.

maze, meez, s., doolhof c.; (bewilderment) verbijstering c.

me, mie, pron., mij

meadow, med-do, s., weide c., weiland n.

meagre, mie-g'r, a., (scanty) schraal

meal, miel, s., maaltijd c.; (flour) meel n.

mean, mien, v., (intend) bedoelen; (signify) betekenen. a., gering; (low) laag; (stingy) krenterig

meaning, mie-ning, s., bedoeling c.; (sense) betekenis c.; ——less, a., zonder zin, zinledig

means, mienz, s.pl., middel n.; (income) inkomsten c.pl.

meanwhile, mien-wail, adv., ondertussen

measles, mie-z'lz, s.pl., mazelen c.pl.

measure, mez-zjur, v., meten; (survey) opmeten; (clothes) de maat nemen. s., maat c.; (rod) maatstaf c.; ——ment, afmeting c.

meat, miet, s., vlees n.

mechanic, mi-ken-nik, s., werktuigkundige c.; ——al, a., machinaal; ——s, s.pl., werktuigkunde c.

mechanism, mek-ke-nizm, s., mechanisme n.

medal, med-d'l, s., medaille c.

meddle, med-d'l, v., zich bemoeien

mediæval, med-di-ie-v'l, a., middeleeuws

mediate, mie-di-eet, v., bemiddelen

medical, med-di-k'l, a., medisch, geneeskundig

medicine, med-di-sin, s., medicijn c.; geneeskunde c.

mediocre, mie-di-o-k'r, a., middelmatig

meditate, med-di-teet, v., overdenken

medium, mie-di-um, s., midden n.; (means) middel n.; (person) tussenpersoon c. a., middelmatig

meek, miek, a., zachtmoedig; (submissive) gedwee

meerschaum, mier-sjum, s., meerschuim n.
meet, miet, v., ontmoeten; (obligations) voldoen aan; (expenses) bestrijden; ——**ing,** s., ontmoeting c.; (gathering) vergadering c.
melancholy, mel-l'n-ke-li, s., zwaarmoedigheid c. a., zwaarmoedig, droefgeestig
mellow, mel-lo, a., sappig, rijp
melodious, mi-**lood**-jus, a., welluidend
melody, mel-le-di, s., melodie c.
melon, mel-l'n, s., meloen c.
melt, melt, v., smelten; (fig.) vertederen
member, mem-b'r, s., lid n.; (parliament) afgevaardigde c.; ——**ship,** lidmaatschap n.
memento, me-**men**-to, s., aandenken n.
memoirs, mem-waarz, s.pl., memoires c.pl.
memorandum, mem-me-**ren**-dum, s., aantekening c.; ——**book,** notitieboekje n.
memorial, mi-**moa**-ri-ul, s., gedenkteken n.
memory, mem-me-ri, s., geheugen n.; herinnering c.
menace, men-nis, v., dreigen. s., dreiging c.
menagerie, mi-**ned**-zje-ri, s., beestenspel n.
mend, mend, v., herstellen; (socks) stoppen
mendacious, men-**dee**-sjus, a., leugenachtig
menial, mie-ni-ul, s., knecht c. a., dienstbaar
mental, men-t'l, a., geestelijk, verstandelijk
mention, men-sjun, v., vermelden, noemen
menu, men-joe, s., menu n., spijskaart c.
mercantile, meur-k'n-tail, a., handels ...
merchandise, meur-tsj'n-daiz, s., koopwaar c.
merchant, meur-tsj'nt, s., koopman c.; ——**fleet,** koopvaardijvloot c.
merciful, meur-si-foel, a., barmhartig
mercury, meur-kjoe-ri, s., kwikzilver n.
mercy, meur-si, s., barmhartigheid c., genade c.
mere, mier, a., louter, zuiver, niets anders dan
merge, meurdzj, v., doen opgaan; opgaan
meridian, me-**rid**-di-un, s., meridiaan c.
merit, mer-rit, v., verdienen. s., verdienste c.; ——**orious,** a., verdienstelijk; ——**s,** s.pl., essentiële n.
mermaid, meur-meed, s., meermin c.

merriment, mer-ri-m'nt, s., vrolijkheid c.

merry, mer-ri, a., vrolijk, lustig

mesh, mesj, s., maas c.; ——es, pl., netwerk n.

mesmerize, mez-me-raiz, v., hypnotiseren

mess, mes, v., bevuilen. s., (muddle) warboel c.; (dirt) vuiligheid c.; (mil.) menage c.; (naut.) bak c.

message, mes-sidzj, s., boodschap c.

messenger, mes-sin-dzjur, s., boodschapper c.

metal, met-t'l, s., metaal n.

metallic, met-tel-lik, a., metaalachtig

meteor, miet-jur, s., meteoor c.

meter, mie-t'r, s., gasmeter c.

method, meth-ud, s., methode c.

methylated (spirit), meth-i-lee-tid (spir-rit), s., brandspiritus c.

metropolis, mi-trop-pe-lis, s., hoofdstad c.

mica, mai-ke, s., mica n., glimmer n.

Michaelmas, mik-k'l-mus, s., St. Michiel c.

microscope, mai-krus-koop, s., microscoop c.

middle, mid-d'l, s., midden n. a., middelste; ——aged, van middelbare leeftijd; ——-class, s., burgerklasse c.; ——man, tussen-

midge, midzj, s., mug c.; (fig.) dwerg c. [persoon c.

midget, mid-zjit, s., dwergje n.

midnight, mid-nait, s., middernacht c.

midshipman, mid-sjip-m'n, s., adelborst c.

midst, midst, in the —— of, prep., te midden van

midwife, mid-waif, s., vroedvrouw c.

mien, mien, s., voorkomen n., uiterlijk n.

might, mait, s., macht c., kracht c.

mighty, mait-i, a., machtig

mignonette, min-je-net, s., reseda c.

migrate, mai-Greet, v., verhuizen, trekken

mild, maild, a., zacht; (jokes) flauw

mildew, mil-djoe, s., schimmel c.

mile, mail, s., Engelse mijl c.; ——stone, mijlpaal c.

military, mil-li-te-ri, a., militair, krijgs . .

milk, milk, s., melk c. v., melken

milky, mil-ki, a., melkachtig; ——way s., Melkweg c.

mill, mil, v., malen.   s., molen c.; (factory)
miller, mil-l'r, s., molenaar c.   [fabriek c.
milliner, mil-li-n'r, s., modiste c.
millinery, mil-li-ne-ri, s., modeartikelen n.pl.
million, mil-jun, s., miljoen n.; ———aire,
     miljonair c.
mimic, mim-mik, v., nadoen.   s., nabootser c.
mind, maind, s., (intellect) verstand n.; (memory)
     herinnering c.; (thoughts) gedachten c.pl.
     v., (heed) letten op; ———ful, a., indachtig
mine, main, pron., van mij, de mijne, het mijne
mine, main, s., mijn c.
miner, mai-n'r, s., mijnwerker c.
mineral, min-ne-r'l, s., delfstof c.
mingle, ming-G'l, v., mengen; zich mengen
miniature, min-je-tsjur, s., miniatuur c.
minimize, min-ni-maiz, v., verkleinen
minister, min-nis-t'r, s., (cabinet) minister c.;
     (of religion) predikant c.
ministry, min-nis-tri, s., ministerie n.
mink, mink, s., nerts c.; (fur) nertsbont n.
minor, mai-n'r, s., minderjarige c.   a., (less)
     minder; (slight) gering; (junior) jonger   [c.
minority, mai-nor-ri-ti, s., (number) minderheid
minstrel, min-str'l, s., minstreel c.
mint, mint, s., munt c.   v., munten
minuet, min-joe-et, s., menuet n.
minus, mai-nus, prep., min.   s., minteken n.
minute, min-nit, s., minuut c.
minute, mai-njoet, a., gering; (precise) haarfijn
miracle, mir-re-k'l, s., wonder n., mirakel n.
miraculous, mi-rek-joe-lus, a., wonderdadig
mirage, mi-raazj, s., luchtspiegeling c.
mire, mair, s., modder c.   v., bemodderen
mirror, mir-r'r, s., spiegel c.   v., weerkaatsen
mirth, meurth, s., vrolijkheid c.; ———ful, a.,
     vrolijk
misadventure, mis-ed-vent-sjur, s., ongeluk n.
misapprehension, mis-ep-pri-hen-sjun, s., mis-
     verstand n.
misappropriate, mis-e-pro-pri-eet, v., zich
     wederrechtelijk toeëigenen

misbehave, mis-bi-heev, v., zich misdragen
miscarriage, mis-ker-ridzj, s., mislukking c.;
(birth) miskraam c.; (justice) rechterlijke
dwaling c.
miscarry, mis-ker-ri, v., mislukken, niet slagen
miscellaneous, mi-si-leen-jus, a., gemengd
mischief, mis-tsjif, s., kattekwaad n.; (harm)
kwaad n.
mischievous, mis-tsji-vus, a., ondeugend
misconduct, mis-kon-dukt, s., wangedrag n.;
(law) overspel n.; (mismanagement) wanbe-
heer n.
misconstruction, mis-k'n-strak-sjun, s., verkeerde opvatting c.; verkeerde uitlegging c.
miscount, mis-kaunt, v., zich vertellen
miscreant, mis-kri-'nt, s., misbaksel n.
misdeed, mis-died, s., misdaad c.
misdemeanour, mis-di-mie-n'r, s., misdrijf n.
misdirect, mis-di-rekt, v., verkeerd wijzen;
(letter) verkeerd adresseren
miser, mai-z'r, s., vrek c.; ——ly, a., gierig
miserable, miz-ze-re-b'l, a., ellendig
misery, miz-ze-ri, s., ellende c.
misfit, mis-fit, s., niet passend kledingstuk n.
misfortune, mis-foar-tsjun, s., ongeluk n.
misgiving, mis-giv-ving, s., angstig voorgevoel n.
misgovern, mis-gav-vurn, v., slecht besturen
misguide, mis-gaid, v., misleiden
mishap, mis-hep, s., ongeval n., ongeluk n.
misinform, mis-in-foarm, v., verkeerd inlichten
misjudge, mis-dzjadzj, v., verkeerd oordelen
mislay, mis-lee, v., zoek maken [bedriegen
mislead, mis-lied, v., misleiden; (deceive)
mismanage, mis-men-nidzj, v., slecht besturen
misplace, mis-plees, v., misplaatsen
misprint, mis-print, s., drukfout c. [spreken
mispronounce, mis-pre-nauns, v., verkeerd uit-
misrepresent, mis-rep-pri-zent, v., een verkeerde voorstelling geven van
miss, mis, v., (train) missen; (school) verzuimen;
(fail to hit) misslaan; (omit) overslaan;
——ing, a., vermist

Miss, mis, s., mejuffrouw c.

missile, mis-sail, s., werptuig n.; projectiel n.

mission, mis-sjun, s., missie c.; (embassy) gezantschap n.; ——ary, missionaris c.

misstatement, mis-steet-m'nt, s., onjuiste opgave c.

mist, mist, s., nevel c.; ——y, a., nevelig

mistake, mis-teek, s., vergissing c. v., zich vergissen; ——n, a., verkeerd; (misdirected)

Mister, (Mr.) mis-t'r, s., mijnheer c. [verdoold

mistletoe, misl-to, s., maretak c.

mistress, mis-tris, s., (Mrs.) mevrouw c.; (of the house) vrouw des huizes c.; (school) onderwijzeres c.

mistrust, mis-trast, v., wantrouwen. s., wantrouwen n.

misunderstand, mis-an-d'r-stend, v., misverstaan; ——ing, s., misverstand n.

misuse, mis-joez, v., misbruiken; mishandelen

mitigate, mit-ti-Geet, v., verzachten, verlichten

mitre, mai-t'r, s., mijter c.

mix, miks, v., mengen; ——ed, a., gemengd; ——ture, s., mengsel n.; —— with, v., omgaan met

moan, moon, v., kreunen. s., gekreun n.

moat, moot, s., gracht c.

mob, mob, s., gepeupel n.; (crowd) menigte c.

mobile, mo-bail, a., beweeglijk

mobilize, mo-bi-laiz, v., mobiliseren

mock, mok, v., bespotten; —— at, spotten met; ——ery, s., bespotting c.; ——ingly, adv., spottend

mode, mood, s., (way) wijze c.; (fashion) mode c.

model, mod-d'l, s., model n. v., modeleren

moderate, mod-de-reet, v., matigen. a., matig

moderation, mod-de-ree-sjun, s., matigheid c.

modern, mod-durn, a., modern, hedendaags

modest, mod-dist, a., bescheiden; (coy) zedig

modify, mod-di-fai, v., (alter) wijzigen

Mohammedan, mo-hem-mi-d'n, s., Mohammedaan c.

moist, moist, a., vochtig; ——en, v., bevochtigen

moisture, mois-tsjur, s., vochtigheid c.
mole, mool, s., mol c.; (mark) moedervlek c.; (jetty) havendam c.; ——**hill,** molshoop c.
molest, me-lest, v., lastig vallen
molten, mool-t'n, a., gesmolten [belang n.
moment, mo-m'nt, s., ogenblik n.; (importance)
momentous, mo-men-tus, a., gewichtig
momentum, mo-men-tum, s., stuwkracht c.
monarch, mon-nurk, s., vorst c.
monarchy, mon-ne-ki, s., monarchie c.
monastery, mon-ne-stri, s., klooster n.
Monday, man-di, s., maandag c.
monetary, man-ni-te-ri, a., geldelijk
money, man-ni, s., geld n.; ——**box,** spaarpot c.; ——**changer,** wisselaar c.; ——**lender,** geldschieter c.; ——**order,** postwissel c.
mongrel, mang-Gr'l, s., bastaard c.
monk, mangk, s., monnik c.
monkey, mang-ki, s., aap c.; ——**nut,** apenootje n.
monocle, mon-nok-k'l, s., monocle c.
monogram, mon-ne-Grem, s., monogram n.
monoplane, mon-ne-pleen, s., eendekker c.
monopolize, me-nop-pe-laiz, v., monopoliseren
monopoly, me-nop-pe-li, s., monopolie c.
monotonous, me-not-te-nus, a., eentonig
monster, mon-st'r, s., monster n., gedrocht n.
monstrous, mon-strus, a., monsterachtig
month, manth, s., maand c.; ——**ly,** a., maandelijks
monument, mon-joe-m'nt, s., gedenkteken n.
mood, moed, s., stemming c.; (temper) luim c.; (gram.) wijs c.; ——**y,** a., humeurig
moon, moen, s., maan c.; ——**light,** maanlicht n.; ——**shine,** maneschijn c.
Moor, moer, s., Moor c.; ——**ish,** a., Moors
moor, moer, s., heide c. v., (boat) vastleggen
mop, mop, s., zwabber c. v., zwabberen
mope, moop, v., kniezen. ; s., kniesoor c. [c.pl.
moral, mor-r'l, a., zedelijk; ——**s,** s.pl., zeden
morass, me-res, s., moeras n.
moratorium, mor-re-to-ri-um, s., moratorium n.

morbid, moar-bid, a., ziekelijk, ziekte . . .

more, moar, a. & adv., meer; once ——, nog eens

moreover, moa-ro-v'r, adv., bovendien

morning, moar-ning, s., morgen c.; voormiddag

morocco, me-rok-ko, s., marokijnleer n.   [c.

morose, me-roos, a., knorrig, gemelijk

morphia, moar-fi-e, s., morfine c.

morsel, moar-s'l, s., hapje n., stukje n.

mortal, moar-t'l, s., sterveling c. a., sterfelijk;
(deadly) dodelijk; ——**ity,** s., sterfelijkheid c.

mortar, moar-t'r, s., metselkalk c.; (gun) mortier c.

mortgage, moar-Gidzj, s., hypotheek c.

mortgagee, moar-Ge-dzji, s., hypotheekhouder c.

mortification, moar-ti-fi-kee-sjun, s., verster-
ving c.; (humiliation) vernedering c.; (med.)
koudvuur n.

mortuary, moar-tjoe-e-ri, s., lijkenhuisje n.

mosaic, me-zee-ik, s., mozaïek n.

mosque, mosk, s., moskee c.

mosquito, mos-kie-to, s., muskiet c.

moss, mos, s., mos n.

most, moost, a. & adv., meest

mostly, moost-li, adv., meestal

moth, moth, s., nachtvlinder c.; (clothes—moth)
mot c.

mother, madh-ur, s., moeder c.; ——hood,
moederschap n.; ——**in-law,** schoonmoeder
c.; —— **of pearl,** paarlemoer n.; ——**ly,** a.,
moederlijk

motion, mo-sjun, s., beweging c.; (proposal)
voorstel n.; ——**less,** a., bewegingloos

motive, mo-tiv, s., beweegreden c. a., bewegend

motor, mo-t'r, s., motor c.; (car) auto c.;
——**bus,** autobus c.; ——**cycle,** motorfiets c.;
——**ing,** autorijden n.; ——**ist,** automobilist

mottled, mot-t'ld, a., gevlekt, gespikkeld   [c.

motto, mot-to, s., motto n., zinspreuk c.

mould, moold, s., (matrix) gietvorm c.; (mildew)
schimmel c.; (earth) teelaarde c. v., vormen;
——**er,** s., vormer c.; ——**y,** a., beschimmeld

moult, moolt, v., (birds) ruien; (animals) verharen

mound, maund, s., heuveltje n., wal c.

mount, maunt, s., berg u.; (horse) rijdier n.; (frame) montuur c. v., (climb) klimmen; (ascend) stijgen; ——ed, a., (on horseback) bereden

mountain, main-tin, s., berg c.; ——eer, bergbewoner c.; ——ous, a., bergachtig; —— range, s., bergketen c.

mourn, moarn, v., treuren; ——er, s., rouwdrager c.; ——ful, a., treurig; ——ing, s., rouw c.; (apparel) rouwkleding c.

mouse, maus, s., muis c.; ——trap, muizenval c.

moustache, me-staasj, s., snor c., knevel c.

mouth, mauth, s., mond c.; (animal) muil c.; (river) monding c.; ——ful, mondvol c.

mouth-piece, mauth-pies, s., mondstuk n.

movable, moe-ve-b'l, a., beweeglijk, beweegbaar

move, moev, v., bewegen; (shift) verplaatsen; (rouse) opwekken. s., (games) zet c.; (removal) verhuizing c.; ——ment, beweging c.; (mus.) tempo n.

mow, mo, v., maaien; ——er, s., maaier c.

much, matsj, a., veel. adv., zeer, erg, veel

mud, mad, s., modder c.; ——dy, a., modderig

muddle, mad-d'l, s., warboel c.

mudguard, mad-gaard, s., spatbord n.

muffle, maf-f'l, v., inbakeren; (sound) dempen

muffler, maf-fl'r, s., das c.

mug, mag, s., kroes c.

mulatto, mjoe-let-to, s., mulat c.

mulberry, mal-be-ri, s., moerbezie c.

mule, mjoel, s., muildier n.; (fig.) stijfkop c.

multifarious, mal-ti-fèr-i-us, a., velerlei

multiplication, mal-ti-pli-kee-sjun, s., vermenigvuldiging c.

multiply, mal-ti-plai, v., zich vermenigvuldigen; (arithmetic) vermenigvuldigen

multitude, mal-ti-tjoed, s., menigte c. [n.

mumble, mam-b'l, v., mompelen. s., gemompel

mummery, mam-me-ri, s., maskerade c.

mummy, mam-mi, s., mummie c.

mumps, mamps, s.pl., bof c.

munch, mansj, v., hoorbaar kauwen
municipal, mjoe-nis-si-p'l, a., gemeentelijk, stads . . .
munificent, mjoe-nif-fi-s'nt, a., vrijgevig
munitions, mjoe-nis-sj'nz, s.pl., krijgsvoorraad c.
murder, meur-d'r, s., moord c. v., vermoorden;
——**er,** s., moordenaar c.; ——**ess,** moordenares c.; ——**ous,** a., moorddadig
murky, meur-ki, a., donker; (dismal) somber
murmur, meur-m'r, v., mompelen. s., gemompel n.
muscle, mas-s'l, s., spier c.; (strength) spierkracht c.
muse, mjoez, v., mijmeren. s., (goddess) muze c.
museum, mjoe-zi-um, s., museum n.
mushroom, masj-roem, s., eetbare paddestoel c.
music, mjoe-zik, s., muziek c.
musical, mjoe-zik-'l, a.; muzikaal
musician, mjoe-zis-sjun, s., musicus c.   [c.
musk, mask, s., muskus c.; ——**rat,** muskusrat
musket, mas-kit, s., geweer n., musket n.
muslin, maz-lin, s., neteldoek n., mousseline n.
mussel, mas-s'l, s., mossel c.
must, mast, v., moeten. s., (wine) most c.
mustard, mas-turd, s., mosterd c.
muster, mas-t'r, v., monsteren. s., monstering c.
musty, mas-ti, a., schimmelig
mute, mjoet, a., stom. s., stomme c.
mutilate, mjoe-ti-leet, v., verminken
mutineer, mjoe-ti-nier, s., muiter c.
mutinous, mjoe-ti-nus, a., oproerig   [rij c.
mutiny, mjoe-ti-ni, s., opstand c.; (ship) muite-
mutter, mat-t'r, v., mopperen. s., gemopper n.
mutton, mat-t'n, s., schapenvlees n.
mutual, mjoe-tjoe-ul, a., wederkerig, wederzijds
muzzle, maz-z'l, s., (snout) snuit c.; (for dogs) muilband c.; (gun) tromp c.
my, mai, pron., mijn
myrrh, meur, s., mirre c.
myrtle, meur-t'l, s., mirt c.
myself, mai-self, pron., ikzelf, mijzelf, zelf
mysterious, mis-tie-ri-us, a., geheimzinnig

mystery, mis-te-ri, s., geheim n.; raadsel n.
mystify, mis-ti-fai, v., foppen, bedotten
myth, mith, s., mythe c.; (fiction) verzinsel n.
mythology, mi-thol-le-dzji, s., mythologie c.

nag, neG, s., hit c. v., vitten; (scold) bekijven
nail, neel, s., nagel c. v., vastspijkeren; ——
——brush, s., nagelborstel c.; ——file, nagel-
vijltje n.
naive, na-iev, a., naïef, ongekunsteld
naked, nee-kid, a., naakt, bloot; (bare) kaal
name, neem, s., naam c.; Christian ——, voornaam c.; sur ——, achternaam c. v., noemen;
——less, a., onbekend
namely, neem-li, adv., namelijk
namesake, neem-seek, s., naamgenoot c.
nap, nep, s., dutje n.; take a ——, v., een dutje
nape, neep, —— of the neck, nek c. [doen
naphtha, nef-tha, s., nafta c.
napkin, nep-kin, s., servet n.; (baby's) luier c.
narcissus, naar-sis-sus, s., narcis c.
narcotic, naar-kot-tik, s., verdovingsmiddel n.
narrate, ner-reet, v., vertellen, verhalen
narrative, ner-re-tiv, s., verhaal n.
narrow, ner-ro, a., eng, nauw; ——minded,
bekrompen; ——ness, s., nauwheid c.
nasal, nee-z'l, a., van de neus, neus . . .
nasturtium, ne-steur-sjum, s., waterkers c.
nasty, naas-ti, a., (dirty) vies; (obscene) gemeen
nation, nee-sjun, s., natie c.; volk n.
national, nes-sje-n'l, a., nationaal
nationality, nes-sje-nel-li-ti, s., nationaliteit c.
native, nee-tiv, s., inboorling c., inlander c.
natural, net-sje-r'l, a., natuurlijk. s., idioot c.
naturalization, net-sjre-lai-zee-sjun, s., natura-
lisatie c.
nature, neet-sjur, s., natuur c.; (character)
karakter n.
naught, noat, s., niets n., nul c.
naughty, noa-ti, a., stout, ondeugend
nauseous, noa-sji-us, a., walglijk
nautical, noa-ti-k'l, a., zee . . ., scheepvaart . .

naval, nee-v'l, —— officer, s., zeeofficier c.; —— **victory,** overwinning op zee c.

navel, nee-v'l, s., navel c.; (centre) middelpunt n.

navigate, nev-vi-Geet, v., varen; bevaren

navigation, nev-vi-Gee-sjun, s., scheepvaart c.

navigator, nev-vi-Gee-t'r, s., zeevaarder c.

navvy, nev-vi, s., grondwerker c.

navy, nee-vi, s., marine c., zeemacht c.

nay, nee, adv., ja zelfs

near, nier, adv. & prep., nabij, dichtbij. **a.,** dichtbij zijnd. **v.,** naderen; ——**ly,** adv., bijna; ——**ness,** s., nabijheid c.; —— **sighted, a.,** bijziend

neat, niet, a., (spruce) keurig; (smart) knap; (undiluted) onvermengd; ——**ness,** s., netheid c.

necessarily, nes-si-sèr-ri-li, adv., noodzakelijk

necessary, nes-si-se-ri, a., noodzakelijk, nodig

necessitate, ni-ses-si-teet, v., noodzaken

necessity, ni-ses-si-ti, s., noodzaak c.; (want) behoefte c.

neck, nek, s., hals c.; ——**lace,** halssnoer n.; ——**tie,** das c.

need, nied, v., nodig hebben. s., nood c.; behoefte c.

needful, nied-fool, a., nodig. s., nodige n. [c.

needle, nie-d'l, s., naald c.; ——**woman,** naaister c.

needless, nied-lis, a., onnodig, nodeloos

needy, nie-di, a., behoeftig; (poor) armoedig

negation, ni-Gee-sjun, s., ontkenning c.

negative, neG-Ge-tiv, a., ontkennend. s., ontkenning c.

neglect, ni-Glekt, v., verzuimen. s., verzuim n.

negligence, neG-Gli-dzjuns, s., nalatigheid c.

negotiate, ni-Go-sji-eet, v., onderhandelen; (bills) verhandelen; (loan) sluiten

negotiation, ni-Go-sji-ee-sjun, s., onderhandeling c.; (bills) verhandeling c.

negress, nie-Gris, s., negerin c.

negro, nie-gro, s., neger c. a., neger . . .

neigh, nee, v., hinniken. s., gehinnik n.

neighbour, nee-b'r, s., buurman c.; ——**hood,**

buurt c.; ——ing, a., naburig; ——ly, als
goede buren

neither, nai-dh'r, pron., geen van beide. **conj.**
& adv., ook . . . niet

nephew, nev-joe, s., neef c.

nerve, neurv, s., zenuw c.; (courage) moed c.

nervous, neur-vus, a., zenuwachtig; (timid) bang

nest, nest, s., nest n. v., zich nestelen

nestle, nes-s'l, v., lekker gaan liggen

net, net, s., net n. v., in een net vangen. a., netto;
nett weight, s., netto gewicht n.

nettle, net-t'l, s., brandnetel c.

neuralgia, njoe-rel-dzje, s., zenuwpijn c.

neuritis, njoe-rai-tis, s., zenuwontsteking c.

neuter, njoe-t'r, a., onzijdig

neutral, njoe-tr'l, a., neutraal. s., neutrale c.

never, nev-v'r, adv., nooit; ——more, nooit
meer; ——theless, niettemin

new, njoe, a., nieuw

news, njoez, s., nieuws n.; (radio) nieuwsberichten
n.pl.; ——agent, krantenverkoper c.; ——
paper, krant c.

next, nekst, a., naast. adv., daarna

nib, nib, s., (pen) punt c.

nibble, nib-b'l, v., knabbelen; (fish) bijten

nice, nais, a., (dainty) kieskeurig; (fine) lekker

nick, nik, s., kerf c., keep c.

nickel, nik-k'l, s., nikkel n. a., nikkelen

nickname, nik-neem, s., bijnaam c.

nicotine, nik-ke-tien, s., nicotine c.

niece, nies, s., nicht c., nichtje n.

niggard, niG-Gurd, s., vrek c.; ——ly, a., vrekkig

night, nait, s., nacht c.; ——dress, nachtjapon c.;
——fall, het vallen van de avond n.; ——
ingale, nachtegaal c.; ——ly, a., nachtelijk;
——mare, s., nachtmerrie c.

nimble, nim-b'l, a., vlug, kwiek, rap

nine, nain, a., negen; ——teen, negentien; ——
teenth, negentiende; ——tieth, negentigste;
——ty, negentig

ninth, nainth, a., negende

nip, nip, v., knijpen; (cold) bijten. s., kneep c.

nipple, nip-p'l, s., speen c.; tepel c.
nitrate, nai-trit, s., salpeterzuurzout n.
nitrogen, nai-tre-dzjun, s., stikstof c.
no, no, a., geen. adv., neen. s., neen c.
nobility, no-bil-li-ti, s., adel c.; adelstand c.
noble, no-b'l, a., adelijk; (character) edel
nobleman, no-b'l-m'n, s., edelman c.
nobody, no-be-di, pron., niemand. s., nul c.
nod, nod, v., knikken. s., knik c.; knikje n.
noise, noiz, s., geluid n.; (din) lawaai n.
noiseless, noiz-les, a., geluidloos
noisy, noi-zi, a., luidruchtig, druk
nominal, nom-mi-n'l, a., nominaal; in naam
nominate, nom-mi-neet, v., benoemen
nominee, nom-mi-nie, s., benoemde c.
non-commissioned officer, non-ke-mi-sjund of-fi-s'r, s., onderofficier c.
none, nan, pron. & a., geen
nonplussed, non-plast, a., perplex
nonsense, non-s'ns, s., onzin c.
non-skid, non-skid, a., niet slippend
non-stop, non-stop, a., (train) doorgaand; (show) doorlopend; (plane) zonder tussenlanding
nook, noek, s., hoek c.; (cosy place) gezellig plekje
noon, noen, s., middag c. [n.
noose, noes, s., lus c., strik c. v., verstrikken
nor, noar, conj., noch, en ook niet
normal, noar-m'l, a., normaal, gewoon
north, noarth, s., noorden n.; ——**erly,** a., noorderlijk
nose, nooz, s., neus c. v., ruiken, snuffelen
nostril, nos-tril, s., neusgat n.
not, not, adv., niet
notable, no-te-b'l, a., merkwaardig
notary, no-te-ri, s., notaris c.
notch, notsj, v., inkepen. s., inkeping c.
note, noot, s., noot c.; (letter) briefje n.; ——**-book,** aantekenboekje n.; ——**-paper,** postpapier n.
noted, no-tid, a., vermaard, beroemd
noteworthy, noot-weur-dhi, a., opmerkenswaardig

nothing, n*a***th-ing,** pron., niets. adv., volstrekt niet

notice, no-tis, v., opmerken. s., aandacht c.; (announcement) aankondiging c.

noticeable, no-ti-se-b'l, a., merkbaar

notify, no-ti-fai, v., bekend maken

notion, no-sjun, s., begrip n.; (idea) denkbeeld n.

notoriety, no-te-rai-e-ti, s., beruchtheid c.

notorious, no-toa-ri-us, a., berucht; (well-known) bekend

notwithstanding, not-with-**sten**-ding, prep., ondanks, niettegenstaande. adv., niettemin

nought, no*a***t,** s., niets n., nul c.

noun, naun, s., (gram.) zelfstandig naamwoord n.

nourish, nar-risj, v., voeden; (cherish) koesteren; ——**ing,** a., voedzaam; ——**ment,** s., voedsel

novel, nov-v'l, s., roman c. a., nieuw [n.

novelist, nov-ve-list, s., romanschrijver c.

novelty, nov-v'l-ti, s., nieuwigheid c.

November, no-vem-b'r, s., november c.

novice, nov-vis, s., nieuweling c.; (eccl.) novice c.

now, nau, adv., nu, nou; —— **and then,** nu en

nowadays, nau-e-deez, adv., tegenwoordig [dan

nowhere, no-wèr, adv., nergens

noxious, nok-sjus, a., schadelijk, verderfelijk

nozzle, noz-z'l, s., (spout) tuit c.; (snout) snuit c.

nucleus, njoe-kli-us, s., kern c.

nude, njoed, a., naakt, bloot

nudge, n*a***dzj,** v., zachtjes aanstoten. s., duwtje n.

nugget, n*a***G-Git,** s., goudklomp c., klomp c.

nuisance, njoe-s'ns, s., last c., lastpost c.

null, n*a***l,** a., nietig; ——**ify,** v., nietig verklaren

numb, n*a***m,** a., verkleumd; (sensation) gevoelloos

number, n*a***m-b'r,** v., nummeren; (count) tellen. s., (many) aantal n.; (figure) getal n.; (No.) nummer n.; ——**less,** a., talloos

numbness, n*a***m-nis,** s., verstijving c.

numerous, njoe-me-rus, a., talrijk

nun, n*a***n,** s., non c.; ——**nery,** nonnenklooster n.

nuptial, n*a***p-sjul,** a., huwelijks . . .; bruilofts . . .

nuptials, n*a***p-sjulz,** s.pl., bruiloft c.

nurse, neurs, s., verpleegster c.; (male) verpleger

c.; (maid) kindermeisje n.   v., verplegen;
(suckle) zogen; (foster) koesteren
nursery, neur-se-ri, s., kinderbewaarplaats c.;
(plants) kwekerij c.; ———rhyme, baker-
rijmpje n.

nut, nat, s., noot c.; (of screw) moer c.
nutcrackers, nat-krek-k'rz, s.pl., notenkraker c.
nutmeg, nat-meG, s., notemuskaat c.
nutriment, njoe-tri-m'nt, s., voedsel n.
nutritious, njoe-tris-sjus, a., voedzaam
nutshell, nat-sjel, s., notedop c.; in a ———, in
een paar woorden

oak, ook, s., eik c.   a., eikehouten
oakum, o-kum, s., werk n.
oar, oar, s., roeiriem c.; ———sman, roeier c.
oasis, o-ee-siz, s., oase c.
oath, ooth, s., eed c.; (curse) vloek c.   [n.
oats, oots, s.pl., haver c.; rolled ———, havermout
obdurate, ob-djoe-rit, a., verstokt, verhard
obedience, o-bie-djuns, s., gehoorzaamheid c.
obedient, o-bie-djunt, a., gehoorzaam
obese, o-bies, a., zwaarlijvig, corpulent
obesity, o-bie-si-ti, s., zwaarlijvigheid c.
obey, o-bee, v., gehoorzamen   [n.
obituary, o-bit-joe-e-ri, s., (notice) doodsbericht
object, ub-dzjekt, v., (oppose) zich verzetten
tegen; (raise objections) tegenwerpingen
maken
object, ob-dzjikt, s., voorwerp n.; (aim) doel n.;
(gram.) voorwerp n.; ———ion, tegenwerping
c.; ———ionable, a., verwerpelijk; ———ive, s.,
objectief n.
obligation, ob-bli-Gee-sjun, s., verplichting c.
obligatory, o-bliG-Ge-te-ri, a., verplicht
oblige, e-blaidzj, v., verplichten; (compel) dwin-
obliging, e-blaid-zjing, a., vriendelijk   [gen
obliterate, e-blit-te-reet, v., uitwissen
oblivion, e-bliv-vi-un, s., vergetelheid c.
oblivious, e-bliv-vi-us, a., vergeetachtig
oblong, ob-long, a., langwerpig. s., rechthoek c.
obnoxious, ub-nok-sjus, a., aanstotelijk

obscene, ub-sien, a., onzedelijk, gemeen

obscure, ub-skjoer, a., donker. v., verdonkeren

observance, ub-zeur-v'ns, s., inachtneming c.

observant, ub-zeur-v'nt, a., (alert) oplettend

observation, ob-z'r-vee-sjun, s., waarneming c.

observatory, ub-zeur-ve-tri, s., sterrenwacht c.

observe, ub-zeurv, v., waarnemen; (rules) nako-

obsolete, ob-se-liet, a., verouderd   [men

obstacle, ob-ste-k'l, s., hindernis c.

obstinacy, ob-sti-ne-si, s., hardnekkigheid c.

obstinate, ob-sti-nit, a., hardnekkig, koppig

obstreperous, ub-strep-pe-rus, a., luidruchtig

obstruct, ub-**strakt,** v., verstoppen; (bar) versperren; **——ion,** s., verstopping c.; ver-
sperring c.

obtain, ub-teen, v., verkrijgen

obtrude, ub-troed, v., opdringen; zich opdringen

obtrusive, ub-troe-siv, a., opdringend

obtuse, ub-tjoes, a., bot; (stupid) stompzinnig

obviate, ob-vi-eet, v., uit de weg ruimen

obvious, ob-vi-us, a., klaarblijkelijk, duidelijk

occasion, e-kee-zjun, s., gelegenheid c.; (cause)
aanleiding c.   v., veroorzaken; **——al,** a.,
toevallig; **——ally,** adv., nu en dan

occult, e-**kalt,** a., verborgen; (secret) geheim

occupation, ok-kjoe-pee-sjun, s., bezigheid c.;
(mil.) bezetting c.

occupier, ok-kjoe-pai-ur, s., bezitter c.; (tenant)
bewoner c.

occupy, ok-kjoe-pai, v., (possess) bezitten;
(space) beslaan; (mil.) bezetten; (a post)
bekleden; (house) bewonen; **—— oneself in,**
zich bezig houden met

occur, e-keur, v., gebeuren; (be met with) zich
voordoen; **—— to one,** bij iemand opkomen

occurrence, e-kar-r'ns, s., voorval n.

ocean, o-sjun, s., oceaan c.

ochre, o-k'r, s., oker c.

o'clock, e-klok, adv., . . . uur

octagonal, ok-teG-Ge-n'l, a., achthoekig

octave, ok-teev, s., octaaf n.; octaafdag c.

October, ok-to-b'r, s., oktober c.

oculist, ok-joe-list, s., oogarts c.
odd, od, a., (number) oneven; (strange) raar
oddly, od-li, adv., vreemd
odds, odz, s.pl., (inequality) ongelijkheid c.; (advantage) voordeel n.; —— **and ends**, stukken en brokken
odious, ood-jus, a., afschuwelijk, hatelijk
odium, o-di-um, s., haat c., afschuw c.
odour, o-d'r, s., reuk c.; (fragrance) geur c.
of, ov, prep., van; **all** —— **us**, wij allen
off, of, adv., eraf, weg. prep., van. a., verder
offal, of-f'l, s., afval n.; (carrion) kreng n.
offence, e-fens, s., belediging c.; (law) vergrijp n.
offend, e-fend, v., beledigen; (to sin) misdoen
offensive, e-fen-siv, a., beledigend. s., (mil.) offensief n.
offer, of-f'r, v., aanbieden. s., aanbod n.; (bid) bod n.; ——**ing**, offerande c.; (sacrifice) offer n.
office, of-fis, s., (function) ambt n.; (place) kantoor n.
officer, of-fi-s'r, s., ambtenaar c.; (mil.) officier c.
official, e-fis-sjul, a., ambtelijk. s., ambtenaar c.
officious, e-fis-sjus, a., bemoeiziek
offspring, of-spring, s., nakomelingen c.pl.
often, of-f'n, adv., dikwijls, vaak
ogle, o-G'l, v., lonken. s., lonk c.
oil, oil, s., olie c. v., oliën, smeren
oil-cloth, oil-kloth, s., wasdoek n.
ointment, oint-m'nt, s., zalf c.
old, oold, a., oud; ——**fashioned**, ouderwets
olive, ol-liv, s., olijf c. a., olijfkleurig
omelet, om-lit, s., omelet c.; eierstruif c.
omen, o-m'n, s., voorteken n. v., voorspellen
ominous, om-mi-nus, a., onheilspellend
omission, o-mis-sjun, s., (leave out) weglating c.; (neglect) verzuim n.
omit, o-mit, v., weglaten; (neglect) verzuimen
omnibus, om-ni-bus, s., omnibus c.
omnipotent, om-nip-pe-t'nt, a., almachtig
on, on, prep., (upon) op; (date) op; (foot, horse) te. adv., (onward) voort, verder

once, wʌns, adv., eenmaal, eens; **all at ——,** plotseling; **at ——,** dadelijk; (simultaneously) tegelijk; **—— more,** nog eens

one, wʌn, a., een. pron., men; **any ——,** iemand; **no ——,** niemand; **some ——,** iemand

onerous, on-ne-rus, a., lastig, bezwaarlijk

oneself, wʌn-self, pron., zich, zichzelf, zelf

onion, ʌn-jun, s., ui c.

only, oon-li, adv., alleen, slechts; pas. a., enig

onslaught, on-sloat, s., aanval c.

onward, on-wurd, adv., vooruit

onyx, on-niks, s., onyx n. & c.

ooze, oez, v., sijpelen. s., modder c.

opal, o-p'l, s., opaal c.

opaque, o-peek, a., ondoorschijnend

open, o-p'n, v., openen; zich openen. a., open; (frank) openhartig; (liable) blootgesteld

opening, o-p'ning, s., opening c.

opera, op-pe-ra, s., opera c.; **——glass,** toneelkijker c.; **——hat,** klakhoed c.; **——house,** operate, op-pe-reet, v., opereren [opera c.

operation, op-pe-ree-sjun, s., operatie c.

operator, op-pe-ree-t'r, s., operateur c.; (telephone) telefonist c.

ophthalmia, of-thel-mi-a, s., oogontsteking c.

opiate, o-pi-it, s., slaapmiddel n.

opinion, o-pin-jun, s., mening c., oordeel n.

opium, oop-jum, s., opium n. & c.

opossum, e-pos-sum, s., buidelrat c.

opponent, e-po-n'nt, s., tegenstander c.

opportune, op-p'r-tjoen, a., gelegen, geschikt

opportunity, op-p'r-tjoe-ni-ti, s., gelegenheid c.

oppose, e-pooz, v., stellen tegenover; weerstaan

opposite, op-pe-zit, s., tegendeel n. adv., tegenover

opposition, op-pe-zis-sjun, s., oppositie c.

oppress, e-pres, v., onderdrukken; **——ion,** s., onderdrukking c.; **——ive,** a., drukkend

optician, op-tis-sjun, s., opticien c.

option, op-sjun, s., keus c.; **——al,** a., naar keuze

opulence, op-joe-l'ns, s., rijkdom c.

opulent, op-joe-l'nt, a., rijk; overvloedig

or, oar, conj., of; **either ... or,** of ... of
oral, oa-r'l, a., mondeling
orange, or-rindzj, s., sinaasappel c. a., oranje
orator, or-re-t'r, s., redenaar c.
oratory, or-re-te-ri, s., kapel c., huiskapel c.
orb, oarb, s., (globe) bol c.; (ring) kring c.
orchard, oar-tsjurd, s., boomgaard c.
orchestra, oar-kis-tra, s., orkest n.
orchid, oar-kid, s., orchidee c.
ordain, oar-deen, v., verordenen; (eccl.) wijden
ordeal, oar-diel, s., vuurproef c.
order, oar-d'r, s., orde c.; (goods) bestelling c.;
    (command) bevel n.; (sequence) volgorde c.;
    (rank) stand c. v., ordenen; (goods) bestellen;
    (command) bevelen
orderly, oar-d'r-li, a., orderlijk. s., ordonnans c.
ordinary, oar-di-ne-ri, a., gewoon, alledaags
ordnance, oard-n'ns, s., geschut n.
ore, oar, s., erts n.
organ, oar-G'n, s., orgaan n.; (mus.) orgel n.
organic, oar-Gen-nik, a., organisch
organization, oar-Ge-nai-zee-sjun, s., organisatie
organize, oar-Ge-naiz, v., organiseren   [c.
orgy, oar-dzji, s., braspartij c., orgie c.
orient, oa-ri-'nt, s., oosten n.
oriental, oa-ri-en-t'l, a., oosters. s., oosterling c.
origin, or-ri-dzjin, s., oorsprong c.; (birth)
    afkomst c.; ——al, a., oorspronkelijk
originate, e-rid-zji-neet, v., voortbrengen; ontstaan
ornament, oar-ne-m'nt, s., sieraad n. v., tooien
ornamental, oar-ne-men-t'l, a., versierend
orphan, oar-f'n, s., wees c.; ——age, weeshuis n.
orthodox, oar-the-doks, a., orthodox
orthography, oar-thoG-Gre-fi, s., juiste spelling c.
oscillate, os-si-leet, v., schommelen
ostentatious, os-ten-tee-sjus, a., opzichtig
ostler, os-l'r, s., stalknecht c.
ostrich, os-tritsj, s., struisvogel c.
other, adh-ur, a., ander; **the —— day,** adv.,
    onlangs; **the —— one,** de andere c.; ——
    wise, adv., anders

otter, ot-t'r, s., otter c.

ought, oat, v., moeten, behoren

ounce, auns, s., ons n. (28.35 gr.) [onze

our, aur, pron., ons; ——s, van ons, de onze, het

ourselves, aur-selvz, pron., wijzelf, onszelf, zelf

out, aut, adv., uit, eruit; (away) weg; (outside) buiten; ——**bid,** v., meer bieden dan; ——**break,** s., uitbarsting c.; ——**burst,** uitbarsting c.; ——**cast,** verstoteling c.; ——**cry,** geschreeuw n.; protest n.; ——**do,** v., overtreffen; ——**fit,** s., uitrusting c.; ——**fitter,** leverancier van uitrustingen c.; ——**goings,** pl., uitgaven c.pl.; ——**grow,** v., ontgroeien; ——**last,** langer duren dan; ——**law,** s., vogelvrij verklaarde c. v., vogelvrij verklaren; ——**lay,** s., uitgave c.; ——**let,** uitweg c.; ——**line,** schets c.; ——**live,** v., overleven; ——**look,** s., uitkijk c.; (fig.) kijk c.; ——**lying,** a., afgelegen; ——**number,** v., in aantal overtreffen; ——**post,** s., voorpost c.; ——**put,** productie c.; ——**rage,** gewelddaad c.; ——**rageous,** a., gewelddadig; ——**right,** adv., ronduit; ——**run,** v., voorbijlopen; ——**side,** c., buitenkant c. adv. & prep., buiten; ——**size,** a., abnormaal groot; ——**skirts,** s.pl., (town) buitenwijken c.pl.; ——**standing,** a., markant; (debts) uitstaand; ——**ward,** uitwendig. adv., naar buiten; ——**ward bound,** (shipping) op de uitreis; ——**wit,** v., te slim af zijn

oval, o-v'l, a., ovaal, eirond. s., ovaal n.

oven, ɑv-v'n, s., oven c.

over, o-v'r, prep., over; boven; over . . . heen; bij. adv., over; (past) voorbij; ——**alls,** s.pl., werkbroek c.; ——**bearing,** a., aanmatigend; ——**board,** adv., overboord; ——**cast,** a., betrokken; ——**charge,** v., te veel rekenen; ——**coat,** s., overjas c.; ——**come,** v., overwinnen; ——**do,** overdrijven; ——**dose,** s., al te grote dosis c.; ——**due,** a., (late) te laat; (debt) achterstallig; ——**flow,** v., overstro-

men; ——grow, groeien over; ——hang,
hangen over; ——haul, grondig nazien;
——hear, toevallig horen; ——land, a. &
adv., over land; ——lap, v., gedeeltelijk
bedekken; ——load, overladen; ——look,
overzien; (disregard) over 't hoofd zien;
——power, overweldigen; ——rate, overschatten; ——rule, (set aside) verwerpen;
——run, overschrijden; ——sea, a., overzees; ——seer, s., opzichter c.; ——sight,
toezicht n.; (error) vergissing c.; ——sleep,
v., zich verslapen; ——step, overschrijden;
——take, inhalen; ——throw, omverwerpen;
——time, s., overuren n.pl.; ——ture,
(mus.) ouverture c.; ——turn, v., omwerpen;
(fall) omslaan; ——weight, s., overgewicht
n.; ——whelm, (v., overstelpen; (crush)
verpletteren; ——work, te hard laten werken;
zich overwerken. s., overmatig werk n.
owe, o, v., schuldig zijn; te danken hebben
owing, o-ing, a., schuldig; —— to, prep., ten
gevolge van
owl, aul, s., uil c.; ——ish, a., uilachtig
own, oon, a., eigen. v., bezitten; (admit) toegeven
owner, o-n'r, s., eigenaar c.
ox, oks, s., os c.
oxygen, ok-si-dzjun, s., zuurstof c. [kerij c.
oyster, ois-t'r, s., oester c.; ——bed, oesterkwe-
ozone, o-zoon, s., ozon n.

pace, pees, v., stappen. s., stap c., pas c.
pacific, pe-sif-fik, a., vredelievend
pacify, pes-si-fai, v., bedaren, stillen
pack, pek, v., inpakken; pakken s., pak n.; (load)
last c.; (cards) spel n.; (gang) bende c.;
(hounds) troep c.; ——age, verpakking
c.; ——et, pakje n.
pact, pekt, s., verdrag n., verbond n.
pad, ped, v., opvullen. s., (stuffing) opvulsel n.;
(for writing) onderlegger c.; (animal's foot)
poot c.; ——ding, (fill up) bladvulling c.
paddle, ped-d'l, v., pagaaien; (feet, hands)

voorliefde hebbend voor; ——ity, s., par-
tijdigheid c.

participate, paar-tis-si-peet, v., deelnemen

participle, paar-ti-si-p'l, s., deelwoord n.

particle, paar-ti-k'l, s., deeltje n.; greintje n.

particular, p'r-tik-joe-l'r, a., bijzonder; (personal) persoonlijk; (exact) nauwkeurig; (fastidious) kieskeurig. s., bijzonderheid c.

parting, paar-ting, s., afscheid n.; (hair) scheiding c.

partition, paar-tis-sjun, s., scheidsmuur c.

partly, paart-li, adv., gedeeltelijk, deels

partner, paart-n'r, s., maat c.; (business) vennoot c.; ——ship, bennootschap c.

partridge, paar-tridzj, s., patrijs c.

party, paar-ti, s., partij c.; (social) gezelschap n.

pass, paas, v., voorbijgaan; (at cards) passen; (examination) slagen voor; (a bill) aannemen. s., pas c.

passage, pes-sidzj, s., doorgang c.; (voyage) overtocht c.; (of a book) passage c.

passbook, paas-boek, s., kassiersboekje n.

passenger, pes-sin-dzjur, s., passagier c.

passer-by, paas-s'r-bai, s., voorbijganger c.

passion, pes-sjun, s., hartstocht c.; (anger) woede c.; ——ate, a., hartstochtelijk

passover, paas-o-v'r, s., Joods Paasfeest n.

passport, paas-poart, s., paspoort n.

past, paast, prep., voorbij; over. a., verleden. s., verleden n.

paste, peest, s., (dough) deeg c.; (adhesive) stijfsel n.; (gem) valse diamant c. v., plakken

pastime, paas-taim, s., tijdverdrijf c.

pastor, paas-t'r, s., zielenherder c.

pastry, pees-tri, s., gebak n.; ——cook, banketbakker c.

pasture, paas-tsjur, s., (ground) weiland n.; (grass) gras n.

pat, pet, v., tikken. s., tikje n.; (butter) stukje n.

patch, petsj, s., lap c. v., oplappen

patent, pee-t'nt, s., patent n. v., patenteren; —— leather, s., lakleer n.

paternal, pe-teur-n'l, a., vaderlijk

path, paath, s., pad n., weg c.

pathetic, pe-thet-tik, a., aandoenlijk, gevoelvol

patience, pee-sj'ns, s., geduld n.

patient, pee-sj'nt, a., geduldig. s., patiënt c.

patriot, pet-tri-ut, s., patriot c., vaderlander c.

patriotic, pet-tri-ot-tik, a., vaderlandslievend

patrol, pe-trool, s., patrouille c. v., patrouilleren

patronize, pet-tre-naiz, v., begunstigen

pattern, pet-turn, s., model n.; (sample of cloth) staal n.

patty, pet-ti, s., pasteitje n.

paunch, poantsj, s., buik c.

pauper, poa-p'r, s., arme c.

pause, poaz, s., onderbreking c. v., pauseren

pave, peev, v., bestraten; ——ment, s., trottoir n.

pavilion, pe-vil-jun, s., paviljoen n., tent c.

paw, poa, s., poot c.; klauw c. v., krabben

pawn, poan, s., pand n.; (chess) pion c. v., verpanden; ——broker, s., lommerdhouder c.

pay, pee, s., betaling c.; (wages) loon n. v., betalen; ——able, a., betaalbaar; ——er, s., betaler c.; ——ment, betaling c.

pea, pie, s., erwt c.

peace, pies, s., vrede c.; (rest) rust c.

peaceful, pies-foel, a., vredig

peach, pietsj, s., perzik c.; ——tree, perzikboom c.

peacock, pie-kok, s., pauw c. [c.

peak, piek, s., spits c., top c.; (cap) klep c.

peal, piel, s., (bells) gelui n.; (thunder) donderslag c. v., schallen; doen schallen

peanut, pie-nat, s., apenootje n.; ——butter, pindakaas c.

pear, pèr, s., peer c.; ——tree, pereboom c.

pearl, peurl, s., parel c.; ——y, a., parelachtig

peasant, pez-z'nt, s., boer c.; ——ry, boerenstand c.

peat, piet, s., turf c.

pebble, peb-b'l, s., kiezelsteen c.

peck, pek, v., pikken; ——at, pikken in

peculiar, pi-kjoe-li-ur, a., bijzonder; (queer) zonderling; ——ity, s., eigenaardigheid c.

pecuniary, pi-kjoe-ni-e-ri, a., geldelijk

pedal, ped-d'l, s., pedaal n. v., trappen

pedantic, pi-den-tik, a., schoolmeesterachtig

pedestal, ped-dis-t'l, s., voetstuk n.

pedestrian, pi-des-tri-un, s., voetganger c.

pedigree, ped-di-Grie, s., stamboom c.

pedlar, ped-l'r, s., marskramer c.

peel, piel, s., schil c. v., schillen

peep, piep, v., gluren; (squeak) piepen. s., blik c.

peer, pier, v., turen, kijken. s., edelman c.;
———**age,** adelstand c.; ———**less,** a., weergaloos

peevish, pie-visj, a., korzelig, knorrig

peg, peG, s., pin c.; (violin) schroef c.; (washing) klemhoutje n.; (hats, etc.) kapstok c.

pellet, pel-lit, s., balletje n.

pelt, pelt, v., gooien. s., huid c.; (fur) vacht c.

pen, pen, s., pen c.; (sheep) schaapskooi c.;
———**holder,** pennehouder c.; ———**knife,** zakmesje n.

penal, pie-n'l, a., strafbaar; ——— **servitude,** s., dwangarbeid c.

penalty, pen-n'l-ti, s., straf c.; (fine) boete c.

penance, pen-n'ns, s., boete c.; biecht c.

pencil, pen-sil, s., potlood n.

pendant, pen-d'nt, s., hanger c.; luchter c.

pending, pen-ding, a., hangende. prep., gedu-

pendulum, pen-djoe-lum, s., slinger c. [rende

penetrate, pen-ni-treet, v., doordringen

penguin, peng-Gwin, s., pinguin c.; vetgans c.

peninsula, pe-nin-sjoe-la, s., schiereiland n.

penitent, pen-ni-t'nt, s., biechteling c. a., boetvaardig

penniless, pen-ni-lis, a., arm, zonder geld

pension, pen-sjun, s., pensioen n.; jaargeld n.

pensioner, pen-sje-n'r, s., gepensionneerde c.

pensive, pen-siv, a., peinzend

penurious, pi-njoe-ri-us, a., karig; (stingy) gierig

people, pie-p'l, s., mensen c.pl.; (nation) volk n. v., bevolken

pepper, pep-p'r, s., peper c.; ———**mint,** pepermunt c.

per, peur, prep., per; ——— **cent,** adv., percent

perambulator, pe-rem-bjoe-lee-t'r, s., **kinder-**
wagen c.
perceive, p'r-siev, v., merken, waarnemen
perception, p'r-sep-sjun, s., waarneming c.
perch, peurtsj, s., (roost) roest c.; (fish) **baars c.**
perchance, p'r-tsjaans, adv., misschien
perdition, p'r-dis-sjun, s., ondergang c.
peremptory, per-r'm-te-ri, a., beslissend
perfect, peur-fikt, a., volmaakt. v., volmaken;
perfectionneren; ——ion, s., volmaaktheid c.
perfidious, p'r-fid-di-us, a., trouweloos
perfidy, peur-fi-di, s., trouweloosheid c.
perforate, peur-fe-reet, v., doorboren
perform, p'r-foarm, v., (accomplish) volbrengen; (fulfil) vervullen; (function) verrichten;
(a play) opvoeren; ——ance, s., (stage)
uitvoering c.
perfume, peur-fjoem, s., parfum n.; (scent)
perfume, p'r-fjoem, v., parfumeren [geur c.
perhaps, p'r-heps, adv., misschien
peril, per-ril, s., gevaar n.; ——ous, a., gevaarlijk
period, pie-ri-ud, s., periode c.; ——ical, tijdschrift n. a., periodiek
periscope, per-ris-koop, s., periscoop c.
perish, per-risj, v., omkomen; (decay) vergaan;
(die) sterven; ——able, a., vergankelijk
perjury, peur-dzje-ri, s., meineed c.
permanent, peur-me-n'nt, a., blijvend, bestendig
permeate, peur-mi-eet, v., doordringen
permission, p'r-mis-sjun, s., verlof n.
permit, p'r-mit, v., toestaan, veroorloven
permit, peur-mit, s., vergunning c.
pernicious, peur-nis-sjus, a., verderfelijk
perpendicular, peur-pen-dik-kjoe-l'r, a., loodrecht
perpetrate, peur-pi-treet, v., bedrijven
perpetual, peur-pet-joe-ul, a., eeuwigdurend
perplex, p'r-pleks, v., verwarren, onthutsen
perquisite, peur-kwi-zit, s., fooi c.
persecute, peur-si-kjoet, v., vervolgen
persecution, peur-si-kjoe-sjun, s., vervolging c.
perseverance, peur-si-vie-r'ns, s., volharding c.

persevere, peur-si-vier, v., volharden

persist, p'r-sist, v., hardnekkig volhouden

person, peur-s'n, s., persoon c.; ——**al**, a., persoonlijk; ——**ality**, s., persoonlijkheid c.; ——**ate**, v., de rol spelen van; ——**ify**, verpersoonlijken

perspective, p'r-spek-tiv, s., perspectief n.

perspicacity, peur-spi-kes-si-ti, s., schranderheid c.

perspiration, peur-spi-ree-sjun, s., transpiratie

perspire, p'r-spair, v., transpireren [c.

persuade, p'r-sweed, v., overreden

persuasion, p'r-swee-zjun, s., overreding c.

pert, peurt, a., brutaal; (brisk) levendig

pertain (to), peur-teen (toe), v., behoren tot;

pertinent, peur-ti-n'nt, a., toepasselijk [aangaan

perturb, p'r-teurb, v., storen, verwarren

perverse, p'r-veurs, a., slecht; onhandelbaar

pervert, p'r-veurt, v., verdraaien; (corrupt) bederven

pest, pest, s., lastpost c.; ——**er**, v., lastig vallen

pet, pet, v., vertroetelen. s., lievelingsdier n.

petal, pet-t'l, s., bloemblad n.

petition, pi-tis-sjun, s., verzoek n.

petitioner, pi-tis-sjun-'r, s., verzoeker c.

petrify, pet-tri-fai, v., doen verstenen; verstenen

petrol, pet-trul, s., benzine c.

petroleum, pi-trool-jum, s., petroleum c.

petticoat, pet-ti-koot, s., onderrok c.

petty, pet-ti, a., gering, onbeduidend

pew, pjoe, s., kerkbank c.

pewter, pjoe-t'r, s., (tankard) tinnen kan c.

phantom, fen-tum, s., spook n.; (vision) droom-

phase, feez, s., fase c. [beeld n.

pheasant, fez-z'nt, s., fazant c.

phenomenon, fi-nom-mi-n'n, s., verschijnsel n.

phial, fai-ul, s., flesje n.

philosopher, fi-los-se-f'r, s., wijsgeer c.

phlegm, flem, s., slijm n.; (coolness) koelheid c.

phonograph, fo-ne-Graaf, s., fonograaf c.

phosphate, fos-feet, s., fosfaat c.

phosphorus, fos-fe-rus, s., fosfor c.

photograph, fo-te-Graaf, s., foto c. v., fotograferen

photographer, fo-toG-Gre-f'r, s., fotograaf c.

phrase, freez, s., uitdrukking c.

physic, fiz-zik, s., geneeskunde c.; ——al, a., natuurkundig; ——ian, s., dokter c. [c.

piano, pjen-no, s., piano c.; **grand——,** vleugel

pick, pik, v., hakken; (pluck) plukken; (teeth) peuteren in; (choose) uitkiezen. s., houweel n.; ——pocket, zakkenroller c.; —— up, v., oppikken

pickle, pik-k'l, v., pekelen; ——s, s.pl., ingemaakt zuur n.

picnic, pik-nik, s., picknick c. v., picknicken [n.

picture, pik-tsjur, s., schilderij c.; (image) beeld

pie, pai, s., pastei c.

piece, pies, s., stuk n.; ——meal, adv., bij stukken en brokken; ——work, s., stukpied, paid, a., bont, gevlekt [werk n.

pier, pier, s., (jetty) havenhoofd n.

pierce, piers, v., doordringen, doorsteken

piercing, pier-sing, a., doordringend

piety, pai-e-ti, s., vroomheid c.

pig, piG, s., varken n.; ——sty, varkenshok n.

pigeon, pid-zjun, s., duif c.; ——hole, vakje n.

pig-iron, piG-ai-urn, s., ruw ijzer n.

pike, paik, s., (fish) snoek c.; (weapon) piek c.

pilchard, pil-tsjurd, s., pelser c.

pile, pail, s., (heap) stapel c. v., ophopen; (load) laden; ——s, s.pl., aambeien c.pl.

pilfer, pil-f'r, v., gappen, kapen

pilgrim, pil-Grim, s., pelgrim c.

pilgrimage, pil-Grim-eedzj, s., bedevaart c.

pill, pil, s., pil c.; (fig.) bittere pil c.

pillage, pil-lidzj, s., plundering c.

pillar, pil-l'r, s., pilaar c.; (column) zuil c.

pillory, pil-le-ri, s., schandpaal c.

pillow, pil-lo, s., hoofdkussen n.

pilot, pai-lut, s., (ship) loods c.; (plane) piloot c.

pimple, pim-p'l, s., puist c., puistje n.

pin, pin, s., speld c.; (peg) pin c. v., vastspelden

pinafore, pin-ne-foar, s., boezelaar c.

pincers, pin-s'rz, s.pl., nijptang c.

pinch, pintsj, v., knijpen. s., kneep c.

pine, pain, s., pijnboom c.; —— **for,** v., smachten naar; —— **away,** wegkwijnen; ——**apple,** s., ananas c.

pinion, pin-jun, v., kortwieken. s., (mech.) rondsel n.

pink, pingk, s., anjelier c. a., rose

pinnacle, pin-ne-k'l, s., spits torentje n.

pint, paint, s., pint c. (0.57 liter)

pioneer, pai-e-nier, s., pionier c., baanbreker c.

pious, pai-us, a., vroom, godsvruchtig

pip, pip, s., (fruit) pit c.; (disease) pip c.

pipe, paip, s., pijp c.; (tube) buis c.

pirate, pai-rit, s., zeerover c.; roofschip n.

pistol, pis-t'l, s., pistool n.

piston, pis-t'n, s., zuiger c.; (mus.) klep c.

pit, pit, s., kuil c.; (theatre) parterre n.

pitch, pitsj, s., pek n.; (height) hoogte c.; (mus.) toonhoogte c. v., (tent) opslaan; (fix) bevestigen; (throw) werpen; (ship) stampen

pitcher, pit-sj'r, s., (tool) pik c.; (jug) kruik c.

pitchfork, pitsj-foark, s., hooivork c.

piteous, pit-ti-us, a., beklagenswaardig

pitfall, pit-foal, s., valkuil c.

pith, pith, s., merg n.; (vigour) kracht c.

pitiable, pit-ti-e-b'l, a., jammerlijk

pitiful, pit-ti-foel, a., medelijdend

pitiless, pit-ti-lis, a., meedogenloos

pity, pit-ti, s., medelijden n.; **what a ——l** hoe jammer!

pivot, piv-v't, s., spil c.; —— **upon,** v., draaien

placard, plek-kaard, s., aanplakbiljet n. [om

placate, plee-keet, v., gunstig stemmen

place, plees, s., plaats c.; (spot) plek c.; (house) huis n. v., plaatsen

placid, ples-sid, a., rustig, kalm

plagiarism, pleed-zji-e-rism, s., plagiaat n.

plague, pleeG, s., pest c.; (fig.) plaag c.

plaice, plees, s., schol c.

plain, pleen, s., vlakte c. a., (evident) duidelijk; (simple) eenvoudig; (looks) lelijk

plaint, pleent, s., (legal) aanklacht c.; ——iff, eiser c., aanklager c.; ——ive, a., klagend

plait, plet, s., vlecht c.; (fold) vouw c. v., vlechten

plan, plen, s., plan n.; (scheme) ontwerp n. v., schetsen; (contrive) beramen

plane, pleen, v., schaven. s., schaaf c.; (tree)

planet, plen-nit, s., planeet c. [plataan c.

plank, plengk, s., dikke plank c.

plant, plent, v., planten. s., plant c.; (factory) bedrijfsmaterieel n.; ——ation, plantage c.

plaster, plaas-t'r, v., pleisteren. s., pleister n.; —— of Paris, gips c.

plate, pleet, v., (silver) verzilveren; (gild) ver-gulden. s., bord n.; (metal) plaat c.; (silver-ware) tafelzilver n.; ——glass, spiegelglas n.

platform, plet-foarm, s., podium n.; (station) perron n.

platinum, plet-ti-num, s., platina n.

play, plee, v., spelen. s., spel n.; (theatre) toneel-stuk n.; ——er, speler c.; (stage) toneel-speler c.; ——ful, a., speels; ——ground, s., speelplaats c.; ——ing-cards, pl., speel-kaarten c.pl.

plea, plie, s., (excuse) verontschuldiging c.; (legal) pleit n.

plead, plied, v., pleiten; (plead guilty) bekennen

pleasant, plez-z'nt, a., aangenaam

please, pliez, v., bevallen. interj., als 't u belieft

pleased, pliezd, a., blij; (gratified) tevreden

pleasing, plie-zing, a., aangenaam

pleasure, plez-zjur, s., genoegen n., plezier n.

pledge, pledzj, s., onderpand n.; (promise) belofte c. v., verpanden; (promise) beloven

plenipotentiary, plen-ni-pe-ten-sje-ri, a., gevol-machtigd. s., gevolmachtigde c.

plenty, plen-ti, s., overvloed c. adv., overvloedig

pleurisy, ploe-ri-si, s., pleuris c.

pliable, plai-e-b'l, a., buigzaam; (fig.) plooibaar

pliers, plai-urz, s.pl., buigtang c., vouwtang c.

plight, plait, s., toestand c., staat c.

plod, plod, v., (work) ploeteren; —— along voortsukkelen; ——der, s., ploeteraar c.

plot, plot, s., (conspiracy) samenzwering c.; (ground) stuk grond n.; (story) intrige c. v., samenspannen

plotter, plot-t'r, s., samenzweerder c.

plough, plau, v., ploegen. s., ploeg c.

ploughman, plau-m'n, s., boer c.

plover, pluv-v'r, s., pluvier c.

pluck, pluk, v., rukken; plukken. s., (fig.) moed c.

plug, plaɢ, v., dichtstoppen. s., prop c.; (electric) stekker c.; **sparking ——**, bougie c.

plum, plam, s., pruim c.; **——tree**, pruime- [boom c.

plumage, ploe-midzj, s., gevederte n.

plumb, plam, s., schietlood n. v., peilen

plumber, plam-m'r, s., loodgieter c.

plump, plamp, a., mollig; (fleshy) vlezig

plunder, plan-d'r, v., plunderen. s., buit c.

plunderer, plan-de-r'r, s., plunderaar c.

plunge, plandzj, v., dompelen, storten

plural, ploe-r'l, s., meervoud n. a., meervoudig

plus, plas, adv., plus. s., plusteken n.

plush, plasj, s., pluche c.

ply, plai, s., (fold) vouw c.; (layer) laag c. v., (a trade) uitoefenen; (go to and fro) heen en weer gaan

pneumatic, njoe-met-tik, a., pneumatisch

pneumonia, njoe-moon-ja, s., longontsteking c.

poach, pootsj, v., stropen; **——er**, s., stroper c.

pocket, pok-kit, s., zak c.

pod, pod, s., dop c., peul c. v., doppen

poem, po-im, s., gedicht n.

poet, po-it, s., dichter c.; **——ess**, dichteres c.

poetry, po-i-tri, s., dichtkunst c., poëzie c.

point, point, v., (finger) wijzen met; (sharpen) aanpunten; **—— out**, aanwijzen. s., (tip) punt c.; (position, item) punt n.; **——er**, wijzer c.; (hint) aanwijzing c.

poise, poiz, v., balanceren. s., evenwicht n.

poison, poi-z'n, s., vergift n. v., vergiftigen

poisonous, poi-z'n-as, a., vergiftig

poke, pook, v., stoten; (fire) oppoken. s., stoot c., duw c.; **——r**, pook c.; (cards) pokerspel n.

pole, pool, s., paal c.; (arctic) pool c.

police, pe-lies, s., politie c.; ——**man**, politieagent c.; —— **station,** politiebureau n.

policy, pol-li-si, s., staatsbeleid n.; (insurance)
polis c.

polish, pol-lisj, s., (gloss) glans c.; (substance)
politoer n.; (shoes) schoenpoets c. v., poetsen

polite, pe-lait, a., beleefd; ——**ness,** s., beleefdheid c.

political, pe-lit-ti-k'l, a., staatkundig, politiek

politician, pol-li-tis-sjun, s., staatsman c.

politics, pol-li-tiks, s.pl., politiek c.

poll, pool ,s., (election) stemming c.; —— **for,**
v., stemmen op

pollute, pe-ljoet, v., bevuilen

pomade, pe-maad, s., pommade c.

pomegranate, pom-Gren-nit, s., granaatappel c.

pomp, pomp, s., praal c.; ——**ous,** a., deftig

pond, pond, s., vijver c., plas c.

ponder, pon-d'r, v., peinzen; ——**ous,** a., zwaar

pontiff, pon-tif, s., Paus c.; opperpriester c.

pony, po-ni, s., pony c.

poodle, poe-d'l, s., poedel c.

pool, poel, s., poel c.; (puddle) plas c.; (cards) pot
c. v., verenigen, bij elkaar leggen

poop, poep, s., achterdek n.

poor, poer, a., arm, armoedig

poorness, poer-nes, s., armoede c.

pop, pop, v., poffen, knallen. s., knal c., klap c.

Pope, poop, s., Paus c.

poplar, pop-pl'r, s., populier c.

poplin, pop-plin, s., popeline c.

poppy, pop-pi, s., klaproos c., papaver c.

populace, pop-pjoe-lis, s., volk n.

popular, pop-pjoe-l'r, a., populair, volks . . .

populate, pop-pjoe-leet, v., bevolken

population, pop-pjoe-lee-sjun, s., bevolking c.

populous, pop-pjoe-lus, a., dicht bevolkt

porcelain, poars-lin, s., porselein n.

porch, poartsj, s., voorportaal n.

porcupine, poar-kjoe-pain, s., stekelvarken n.

pore, poar, s., porie c.; —— **over,** v., vlijtig

pork, poark, s., varkensvlees n.   [bestuderen

porous, poa-rus, a., poreus

porpoise, poar-pus, s., bruinvis c.

porridge, por-ridzj, s., meelpap c.

port, poart, s., (wine) portwijn c.; (harbour) haven c.; (naut.) bakboord n.; ——**hole,** patrijspoort c.

portable, poar-te-b'l, a., draagbaar

portend, poar-tend, v., voorspellen

porter, poar-t'r, s., (door) portier c.; (luggage) kruier c.; ——**age,** draagloon n.

portfolio, poart-fo-li-o, s., portefeuille c.

portion, poar-sjun, s., deel m. v., verdelen

portly, poart-li, a., deftig; (stout) gezet

portmanteau, poart-men-to, s., valies n.

portrait, poar-trit, s., portret n.; schildering c.

portray, poar-tree, v., afschilderen

pose, pooz, s., houding c.; (affected) aanstellerij c. v., poseren; zich aanstellen

position, pe-zis-sjun, s., positie c.; (rank) stand c.

positive, poz-zi-tiv, a., positief; (definite) stellig

possess, pe-zes, v., bezitten, hebben

possession, pe-zes-sjun, s., bezit n.; bezitting c.

possessor, pe-zes-s'r, s., bezitter c., eigenaar c.

possibility, pos-si-bil-li-ti, s., mogelijkheid c.

possible, pos-si-b'l, a., mogelijk

possibly, pos-si-bli, adv., mogelijk, misschien

post, poost, v., (letter) posten. s., post c.; (pole) paal c.; (position) betrekking c.; ——**age,** port n.; ——**card,** briefkaart c.; ——**date,** v., later dateren; ——**free,** a., franco; ——**man,** postbode c.; ——**master,** post-directeur c.; ——**mortem,** lijkschouwing c.; ——**office,** postkantoor n.; ——**pone,** v., uitstellen; ——**script,** s., naschrift n.

poster, poos-t'r, s., aanplakbiljet n.

posterior, pos-tie-ri-ur, a., volgend, later

posterity, pos-ter-ri-ti, s., nageslacht n.

posture, pos-tsjur, s., houding c.; (state) staat c.

pot, pot, s., pot c. v., (plants) potten

potash, pot-tesj, s., potas n.

potato, pe-tee-to, s., aardappel c.

potent, po-t'nt, a., machtig, sterk

potion, po-sjun, s., drank c., drankje n.

pottery, pot-te-ri, s., aardewerk n.; pottenbak-
kerij c.

pouch, pautsj, s., zak c., tas c.

poulterer, pool-te-r'r, s., poelier c.

poultice, pool-tis, s., pap c. v., pappen

poultry, pool-tri, s., pluimvee n.

pounce, pauns, s., klauw c.; —— **upon,** v., neerschieten op

pound, paund, s., pond n. v., fijn stampen.

pour, poar, v., gieten; —— **out,** (serve) inschen-

pout, paut, v., pruilen. s., gepruil n. [ken

poverty, pov-ve-ti, s., armoede c.

powder, pau-d'r, v., poederen. s., poeder n.

powder-puff, pau-d'r-paf, s., poederkwast c.

power, pau-ur, s., (bodily) kracht c.; (mental)
macht c.; ——**ful,** a., machtig; ——**less,**
machteloos

practicable, prek-ti-ke-b'l, a., uitvoerbaar

practical, prek-ti-k'l, a., praktisch; feitelijk

practice, prek-tis, s., praktijk c.; (custom) gewoonte c.; (exercise) oefening c.

practise, prek-tis, v., zich oefenen; oefenen

practitioner, prek-tis-sje-n'r, s., (med.) prakti-
zerend geneesheer c.

praise, preez, v., prijzen, loven. s., lof c. [dig

praiseworthy, preez-weur-dhi, a., prijzenswaar-

prance, praans, v., (horse) steigeren; (man) trots
stappen

prank, prengk, s., dolle streek c. v., uitdossen

prattle, pret-t'l, v., babbelen. s., gebabbel n.

prawn, proan, s., steurgarnaal c.

pray, pree, v., bidden, smeken; (beg) verzoeken

prayer, prè-ur, s., gebed n.; ——**book,** gebedenboek n.; the **Lord's Prayer,** het Onze
Vader

preach, prietsj, v., preken; ——**er,** s., predikant c.

precarious, pri-kèr-i-us, a., onzeker, wankel

precaution, pri-koa-sjun, s., voorzorg c.

precede, pri-sied, v., voorafgaan

precedence, pri-sie-d'ns, s., voorrang c.

precedent, pri-sie-d'nt, a., voorafgaand

precept, prie-sept, s., lering c.; stelregel c.; (law) mandaat n.; —or, leermeester c.
precincts, prie-singktz, s.pl., omgeving c.
precious, pres-sjus, a., kostbaar; (metal) **edel**
precipice, pres-si-pis, s., steile rots c.
precipitate, pri-sip-pi-teet, a., haastig. v., storten
precise, pri-sais, a., nauwkeurig, juist
precision, pri-siz-zjun, s., nauwkeurigheid c.
preclude, pri-kloed, v., uitsluiten; (prevent) voorkomen
precocious, pri-ko-sjus, a., vroegrijp
predatory, pred-de-te-ri, a., roofzuchtig; roof...
predecessor, prie-dis-ses-s'r, s., voorganger c.
predicament, pri-dik-ke-m'nt, s., hachelijke positie c.
predicate, pred-di-kit, s., (gram.) gezegde n.
predict, pri-dikt, v., voorspellen, voorzeggen
prediction, pri-dik-sjun, s., voorspelling c.
predominant, pri-dom-mi-n'nt, a., overheersend
pre-eminent, prie-em-mi-n'nt, a., uitmuntend
preface, pref-fis, s., voorwoord n.; prefatie c.
prefect, prie-fekt, s., prefect c.; (school) monitor
prefer, pri-feur, v., verkiezen, liever hebben [c.
preferable (to), pref-fe-re-b'l (toe), a., verkieslijk
preference, pref-fe-r'ns, s., voorkeur c.
prefix, prie-fiks, s., voorvoegsel n.
pregnancy, preG-n'n-si, s., zwangerschap c.
pregnant, preG-n'nt, a., zwanger; (animals) drachtig; (significant) betekenisvol
prejudice, pred-zjoe-dis, s., vooroordeel n.; (harm) nadeel n.; v., benadelen; **without —,** onder voorbehoud
prejudiced, pred-zjoe-dist, a., bevooroordeeld
prejudicial, pred-zjoe-dis-sjul, a., nadelig
prelate, prel-lit, s., prelaat c., kerkvoogd c.
preliminary, pri-lim-mi-ne-ri, a., inleidend. s., inleiding c., voorbereiding c.
prelude, prel-joed, s., voorspel n.
premature, prem-me-tjoer, a., te vroeg, ontijdig
premeditate, pri-med-di-teet, v., vooraf beramen

premier, prem-mjer, a., eerste. s., eerste minister c.

premises, prem-mi-siz, s.pl., pand n., huis n.

premium, priem-jum, s., premie c.; (prize) prijs c.   [c.

preparation, prep-pe-**ree**-sjun, s., voorbereiding

prepare, pri-pèr, v., voorbereiden; (food) bereiden

prepay, pri-pee, v., vooruitbetalen; (postage) frankeren

prepossessing, prie-pe-**zes**-sing, a., innemend

preposterous, pri-pos-te-rus, a., onzinnig

prerogative, pri-roG-Ge-tiv, s., voorrecht n.   [n.

presage, pres-sidzj, s., voorteken n.; voorgevoel

prescribe, pris-kraib, v., voorschrijven

prescription, pris-krip-sjun, s., (med.) voorschrift n.

presence, prez-z'ns, s., tegenwoordigheid c.; —— **of mind**, tegenwoordigheid van geest c.

present, pri-zent, v., presenteren; (offer) aanbieden

present, prez-z'nt, s., geschenk n. a., tegenwoordig; ——**ation**, s., voorstelling c.; (gift) aanbieding c.; ——**ly**, adv., dadelijk

presentiment, pri-zen-ti-m'nt, s., voorgevoel n.

preservation, prez-z'r-**vee**-sjun, s., instandhouding c.

preserve, pri-zeurv, v., in stand houden; (defend) beschermen; (fruit, etc.) inmaken. s., ingemaakte vruchten c.pl.; (game) wildpark n.

preside, pri-zaid, v., voorzitten

president, prez-zi-d'nt, s., president c.; (chairman) voorzitter c.

press, pres, s., pers c.   v., drukken; (squeeze) uitknijpen; (urge) aandrijven; ——**ing**, a., dringend; ——**man**, s., journalist c.

pressure, pres-sjur, s., druk c.; (fig.) pressie c.

presume, pri-zjoem, v., vermoeden, veronderstellen

presumption, pri-zam-sjun, s., aanmatiging c.

pretence, pri-tens, s., voorwendsel n.

pretend, pri-tend, v., voorwenden, doen alsof
pretentious, pri-ten-sjus, a., aanmatigend
pretext, prie-tekst, s., voorwendsel n.
pretty, prit-ti, a., mooi, aardig, lief
prevail, pri-veel, v., heersen; (be current) over-heersend zijn; —— **over**, de overhand hebben op
prevalent, prev-ve-l'nt, a., heersend
prevaricate, pri-ver-ri-keet, v., uitvluchten zoeken
prevent, pri-vent, v., verhinderen; ——**ion**, s., verhindering c.; ——**ive** a., verhinderend
previous, priev-jus, a., voorafgaand, vorig
prevision, pri-viz-zjun, s., vooruitzien n.
prey, pree, s., prooi c., buit c. v., plunderen
price, prais, s., prijs c.; ——**less**, a., onschatbaar
prick, prik, s., prik c. v., prikken; ——**ly**, a., stekelig
prickle, prik-k'l, s., prikkel c., stekel c.
pride, praid, s., trots c.
priest, priest, s., priester c.
prig, priG, s., verwaande kwibus c.
prim, prim, a., vormelijk, preuts, stijf [ste
primary, prai-me-ri, a., eerst; (main) voornaam-
primate, prai-mit, s., (eccl.) primaat c.
prime, praim, s., (of life) bloei c.; (of period) bloeitijd c. a., (first) eerste; (quality) prima. v., (coach) africhten; —— **minister**, s., eerste minister c.; ——**r**, boek voor beginners
primitive, prim-mi-tiv, a., primitief [n.
primrose, prim-rooz, s., sleutelbloem c.
prince, prins, s., prins c.; (ruler) vorst c.; ——**ly**, a., vorstelijk; ——**ss**, s., prinses c.
principal, prin-si-p'l, s., hoofd n.; (chief) chef c.; (school) rector c. a., voornaamste
principle, prin-si-p'l, s., oorsprong c.; grond-beginsel n.; **on** ——, uit principe
print, print, s., druk c.; (photo) afdruk c. v., drukken; ——**er**, s., drukker c.; ——**ing**, drukkunst c.; ——**ing-works**, drukkerij c.
prior, prai-ur, s., prior c. a., vroeger; (first) eerste

priority, prai-**or**-ri-ti, s., voorrang c.

priory, **prai**-e-ri, s., priorij c.

prism, prizm, s., prisma n.; ——**atic**, a., prismatisch

prison, **priz**-z'n, s., gevangenis c.; ——**er**, gevangene c.

privacy, **prai**-ve-si, s., afzondering c.

private, **prai**-vit, s., gewoon soldaat c. a., (personal) persoonlijk; (secret) geheim; (confidential) vertrouwelijk; (one's own) eigen

privation, prai-**vee**-sjun, s., ontbering c.

privilege, **priv**-vi-lidzj, s., voorrecht n. v., bevoorrechten

privy, **priv**-vi, a., geheim. s., privaat n.

prize, praiz, s., prijs c. v., op prijs stellen

pro, pro, prep., vóór; —— **and con**, vóór en tegen

probable, **prob**-be-b'l, a., waarschijnlijk

probation, pre-**bee**-sjun, s., proeftijd c.; (trial) beproeving c.; ——**er**, (nurse) leerling-verpleegster c.; (eccl.) novice c.

probe, proob, v., nauwkeurig onderzoeken

probity, **prob**-bi-ti, s., eerlijkheid c.

problem, **prob**-blim, s., probleem n., vraagstuk n.

procedure, pre-**sied**-jur, s., werkwijze c.

proceed, pre-**sied**, v., voortgaan; ——**s**, s.pl., opbrengst c.; ——**ings**, pl., werkzaamheden c.pl.; (legal) gerechtelijke stappen c.pl.

process, **pro**-ses, s., proces n.; (course) verloop n.

procession, pre-**ses**-sjun, s., stoet c.; (eccl.) processie c.

proclaim, pre-**kleem**, v., afkondigen, verkondigen

proclamation, prok-kle-**mee**-sjun, s., afkondiging c.

proclivity, pre-**kliv**-vi-ti, s., neiging c.

procrastination, pro-kres-ti-**nee**-sjun, s., uitstel n.

procurable, pre-**kjoe**-re-b'l, a., verkrijgbaar [n.

procure, pre-**kjoer**, v., verschaffen, verkrijgen

prod, prod, s., por c. v., porren, prikken

prodigal, **prod**-di-G'l, a., verkwistend. s., verkwister c.

prodigious, pre-**did**-zjus, a., wonderbaar

prodigy, prod-di-dzji, s., wonder n.

produce, pre-djoes, v., voortbrengen

produce, prod-joes, s., voortbrengsel n.

producer, pre-djoe-s'r, s., producent c.; (film) regisseur c.

product, prod-dukt, s., produkt n.; resultaat n.

production, pre-dak-sjun, s., produktie c.

profane, pre-feen, a., profaan. v., profaneren

profess, pre-fes, v., belijden; (teach) doceren; ——ion, s., beroep n.; (eccl.) professie c.; ——ional, (sports) beroepsspeler c.; ——or, professor c.

proficiency, pre-fis-sjun-si, s., bekwaamheid c.

proficient, pre-fis-sjunt, a., bekwaam, vaardig

profile, pro-fail, s., profiel n.

profit, prof-fit, s., voordeel n. v., van nut zijn; ——able, a., voordelig; ——eer, s., afzetter c., woekerwinstmaker c.

profligate, prof-fli-Git, a., losbandig. s., losbol c.

profound, pre-faund, a., grondig; (deep) diep

profuse, pre-fjoes, a., kwistig; (copious) rijk

prognosticate, proG-nos-ti-keet, v., voorspellen

programme, pro-Grem, s., programma n.

progress, pro-Gres, s., voortgang c.

progress, pre-Gres, v., vooruitgaan

prohibit, pre-hib-bit, v., verbieden

prohibition, pro-i-bis-sjun, s., verbod n.

project, prod-zjekt, s., plan n., ontwerp n.

project, pre-dzjekt, v., werpen; (plan) beramen; (jut out) uitsteken; ——ile, s., projectiel n.; ——ion, uitstek n.

proletarian, pro-li-tèr-i-un, s., proletariër c.

prologue, pro-loG, s., proloog c.

prolong, pre-long, v., verlengen, rekken

promenade, prom-mi-naad, s., wandeling c.; (place) promenade c. v., wandelen

prominent, prom-mi-n'nt, a., uitstekend

promiscuous, pre-mis-kjoe-us, a., gemengd

promise, prom-mis, v., beloven. s., belofte c.

promissory note, prom-mi-se-ri noot, s., promesse c.

promote, pre-moot, v., bevorderen; (foster)

aankweken; ——r, s., bevorderaar c.;
company ——, oprichter c.

promotion, pre-mo-sjun, s., bevordering c.

prompt, prompt, a., vaardig; (not late) stipt. v.,
(stage) souffleren; (urge) aanzetten

prompter, prompt-'r, s., souffleur c.

prone, proon, a., vooroverliggend; —— to,
geneigd tot

prong, prong, s., hooivork c., gaffel c.

pronoun, pro-noun, s., voornaamwoord n.

pronounce, pre-nauns, v., uitspreken [c.

pronunciation, pre-nan-si-ee-sjun, s., uitspraak

proof, proef, s., bewijs n.; proef c.; (printer's)
drukproef c. a., bestand

prop, prop, s., steun c., stut c. v., steunen

propagate, prop-pe-Geet, v., voortplanten

propel, pre-pel, v., voortdrijven

propeller, pre-pel-l'r, s., schroef c.

proper, prop-p'r, a., (one's own) eigen; (fit)
geschikt; (decent) fatsoenlijk; ——ty, s.
eigendom n.; (landed) landgoed n.

prophecy, prof-fi-si, s., voorspelling c.

prophesy, prof-fi-sai, v., voorspellen [c.

prophet, prof-fit, s., profeet c.; ——ess, profetes

propitious, pre-pis-sjus, a., gunstig

proportion, pre-poar-sjun, s., verhouding c.;
(portion) deel n.

proposal, pre-po-z'l, s., voorstel n.; (marriage)
huwelijksaanzoek n.

propose, pre-pooz, v., voorstellen; aanbieden

proprietor, pre-prai-e-t'r, s., eigenaar c.

proprietress, pre-prai-e-tris, s., eigenares c.

propriety, pre-prai-e-ti, s., gepastheid c.

proscribe, pre-skraib, v., verbannen

prose, prooz, s., proza n.

prosecute, pros-si-kjoet, v., (law) vervolgen

prosecution, pros-si-kjoe-sjun, s., vervolging c.

prosecutor, pros-si-kjoe-t'r, s., aanklager c.

prospect, pros-pekt, s., uitzicht n.

prospective, pre-spek-tiv, a., toekomstig

prospectus, pre-spek-tus, s., prospectus n.

prosper, pros-p'r, v., gedijen, bloeien

prosperity, pros-per-ri-ti, s., voorspoed c.
prosperous, pros-pe-rus, a., voorspoedig
prostitute, pros-ti-tjoet, s., prostituée c.
prostrate, pros-trit, a., vooroverliggend; **(grief)** gebroken; (humbly) ootmoedig
prostrate, pros-treet, v., neerwerpen; (oneself) een knieval doen
prostration, pros-tree-sjun, s., voetval c.; (med.) uitputting c.
protect, pre-tekt, v., beschermen
protection, pre-tek-sjun, s., bescherming c.
protest, pro-test, s., protest n.
protest, pre-test, v., protesteren; betuigen
protract, pre-trekt, v., rekken, verlengen
protrude, pre-troed, v., uitsteken
proud, praud, a., fier; (haughty) hovaardig
provable, proe-ve-b'l, a., bewijsbaar
prove, proev, v., bewijzen; op de proef stellen
proverb, prov-veurb, s., spreekwoord n.
provide, pre-vaid, v., verschaffen
provided (that), pre-vai-did (dhet), conj., mits
providence, prov-vi-d'ns, s., vooruitziendheid c.
provident, prov-vi-d'nt, a., vooruitziend; zuinig
provider, pre-vai-d'r, s., leverancier c.
province, prov-vins, s., provincie c.; (sphere) sfeer c.
provision, pre-viz-zjun, s., voorziening c.
provisional, pre-viz-zje-n'l, a., voorlopig
provisions, pre-viz-zjuns, s.pl., proviand c.
provocation, prov-ve-kee-sjun, s., tarting c.
provoke, pre-vook, v., opwekken; (defy) tarten
prow, prau, s., voorsteven c.
prowess, prau-is, s., dapperheid c., moed c.
prowl, praul, v., rondsluipen
proximity, prok-sim-mi-ti, s., nabijheid c.
proxy, prok-si, s., volmacht c.; (person) gevol-machtigde c.; by ——, bij volmacht
prude, proed, s., preutse vrouw c.; ——nce, voorzichtigheid c.; ——nt, a., voorzichtig; verstandig; ——ry, s., preutsheid c.
prudish, proe-disj, a., preuts
prune, proen, s., pruimedant c. v., snoeien

prussic acid, pras-sik es-sid, s., blauwzuur n.

pry, prai, v., (peer) gluren; (spy) snuffelen

psalm, saam, s., psalm c.

pseudonym, sjoe-de-nim, s., pseudoniem n.

psychology, sai-kol-le-dzji, s., psychologie c.

public, pab-blik, s., publiek n.   a., publiek; ——**an,** s., tollenaar c.; (inn) herbergier c.; ——**-house,** herberg c.

publication, pab-bli-kee-sjun, s., bekendmaking c.; (books, papers, etc.) uitgave c.

publish, pab-blisj, v., bekend maken; (banns) afkondigen; (books) uitgeven; ——**er,** s., uitgever c.

pucker, pak-k'r, v., rimpelen. s., rimpel c.

pudding, poe-ding, s., beuling c.; **black** ——, bloedworst c.

puddle, pad-d'l, s., poel c., plas c. v., knoeien

puerile, pjoe-e-rail, a., kinderachtig

puff, paf, s., (breath) zuchtje n.; (wind) windstoot c. v., snuiven; (pant) hijgen; (pipe) paffen; (inflate) opblazen; ——**y,** a., opgeblazen

pug, pag, s., (dog) mopshond c.; ——**nacious,** a., strijdlustig; ——**-nose,** s., mopneus c.

pugilist, pjoe-dzji-list, s., bokser c.

pull, poel, s., trekken n.; (tug) ruk c.; (handle) handvat n. v., trekken; (tug) rukken; (trigger) aftrekken; —— **down,** neerhalen; (demolish) afbreken; —— **out,** uittrekken; —— **up,** optrekken

pullet, poe-lit, s., jonge kip c.

pulley, poe-li, s., katrol c.; (belt) riemschijf c.

pulp, palp, v., tot moes maken. s., (of fruit) vlees n.; (soft mass) weke massa c.; **wood——,** houtpap c.

pulpit, poel-pit, s., preekstoel c.

pulse, pals, s., pols c. v., kloppen

pulverize, pal-ve-raiz, v., fijnstampen

pumice-stone, pam-mis-stoon, s., puimsteen c.

pump, pamp, s., pomp c. v., pompen

pun, pan, s., woordspeling c. v., woordspelingen maken

punch, pantsj, v., (strike) stompen; (tickets)

knippen. s., (drink) punch c.; (tool) drevel c.; (Punch and Judy show) poppenkast c.

punctilious, pangk-til-li-us, a., overdreven nauwgezet

punctual, pangk-tjoe-ul, a., stipt, punctueel

punctuate, pangk-tjoe-eet, v., interpungeren

punctuation, pangk-tjoe-ee-sjun, s., punctuatie

puncture, pangk-tsjur, s., prik c.; (tyre) lek n. [c.

pungency, pan-dzjun-si, s., scherpheid c.

pungent, pan-dzjunt, a., scherp, bijtend

punish, pan-nisj, v., straffen; (chastise) kastijden; ——able, s., strafbaar; ——ment, s., straf c.

punitive, pjoe-ni-tiv, a., straffend; straf . . .

punt, pant, s., vlet c. v., voortbomen

puny, pjoe-ni, a., klein, nietig, zwak

pupil, pjoe-pil, s., leerling c.; (eye) oogappel c.

puppet, pap-pit, s., marionet c.; (fig.) speelpop c.

puppy, pap-pi, s., jonge hond c.; (fig.) kwibus c.

purchase, peur-tsj's, v., kopen. s., koop c., inkoop c.; ——r, koper c., afnemer c.

pure, pjoer, a., zuiver; (chaste) kuis, rein

purgative, peur-Ge-tiv, s., purgeermiddel n.

purgatory, peur-Ge-te-ri, s., vagevuur n.

purge, peurdzj, v., zuiveren; (med.) purgeren

purify, pjoe-ri-fai, v., reinigen, zuiveren

purity, pjoe-ri-ti, s., zuiverheid c.

purlieus, peur-ljoez, s.pl., buurt c.

purloin, peur-loin, v., stelen, gappen

purple, peur-p'l, s., purper n. a., purperkleurig

purport, peur-purt, s., (intention) bedoeling c.; (meaning) betekenis c. v., voorgeven

purpose, peur-pus, s., (aim) doel n.; (intention) bedoeling c. v., zich voornemen

purposely, peur-pus-li, adv., expres

purr, peur, v., spinnen

purse, peurs, s., beurs c., portemonnaie c.

purser, peur-s'r, s., (naut.) administrateur c.

pursuant (to), p'r-sjoe-'nt (toe), a., overeenkomstig

pursue, p'r-sjoe, v., achtervolgen; (aim) nastreven

pursuit, p'r-sjoet, s., achtervolging c.   [ven

purveyor, peur-vee-ur, s., leverancier c.

pus, *pas*, s., etter c.
push, poesj, v., duwen; (jostle) dringen; (impel) voortdrijven. s., duw c.; (pressure) druk c.
pushing, poesj-ing, a., ondernemend
puss, poes, s., poes c.
put, poet, v., (lay) leggen; (place) plaatsen; (set) zetten; (question) stellen; —— **across**, overzetten; —— **aside**, op zij zetten; —— **off**, (delay) uitstellen; —— **on**, (clothes) aantrekken; —— **out**, (lamp) uitdoen
putrefy, pjoe-tri-fai, v., verrotten, bederven
putrid, pjoe-trid, a., verrot, bedorven
putty, *pat*-ti, s., stopverf c.
puzzle, *paz*-z'l, v., verbijsteren. s., raadsel n.; (perplexity) verlegenheid c.; **crossword** ——, kruiswoordraadsel n.
pyjamas, pe-dzja-muz, s.pl., pyjama c.
pylon, pai-l'n, s., poort c.; (aerodrome) mast c.
pyramid, pir-re-mid, s., pyramide c.
python, paith-un, s., python c.

quack, kwek, v., kwaken. s., gekwaak n.; (doctor) kwakzalver c.; ——**ery**, kwakzalverij c.
quadrille, kwe-*dril*, s., quadrille c.
quadruped, kwod-droe-ped, s., viervoeter c.
quadruple, kwod-droe-p'l, a., viervoudig
quagmire, kweG-mair, s., moeras n., poel c.
quail, kweel, s., kwartel c. v., de moed verliezen
quaint, kweent, a., zonderling, eigenaardig
quake, kweek, v., beven; **earth**——, s., aardbeving c.
Quaker, kwee-k'r, s., Kwaker c.
qualification, kwol-li-fi-kee-sjun, s., geschiktheid c.
qualify, kwol-li-fai, v., bevoegd maken; beperken
quality, kwol-li-ti, s., kwaliteit c.; (characteristic) eigenschap c.
quandary, kwon-de-ri, s., dilemma n.
quantity, kwon-ti-ti, s., hoeveelheid c.; aantal n.
quarantine, kwor-r'n-tien, s., quarantaine c.
quarrel, kwor-r'l, s., ruzie c. v., twisten
quarrelsome, kwor-r'l-sum, a., twistziek

quarry, kwor-ri, s., steengroeve c.; (prey) wild n.
quarter, kwoar-t'r, s., kwart n.; (moon, hour) kwartier n.; (of a town) wijk c.; (of a year) kwartaal n.; ——ly, a. & adv., driemaandelijks
quarter-master, kwoar-t'r-maas-t'r, s., kwartiermeester c.
quartet, kwoar-tet, s., kwartet n.
quartz, kwoarts, s., kwarts n.
quash, kwosj, v., onderdrukken; (a verdict) vernietigen
quaver, kwee-v'r, v., trillen. s., (mus.) achtste [noot c.
quay, kie, s., kaai c., kade c.
queen, kwien, s., koningin c.; (cards) vrouw c.
queer, kwier, a., vreemd, raar; (ill) onwel
quell, kwel, v., onderdrukken; (allay) stillen
quench, kwentsj, v., blussen; (thirst) lessen
querulous, kwer-roe-lus, a., klagend, knorrig
query, kwie-ri (see **question**)
quest, kwest, v., zoeken. s., onderzoek n.
question, kwest-sjun, s., vraag c.; (doubt) twijfel c. v., vragen; (interrogate) ondervragen; (doubt) betwijfelen; ——able, a., twijfelachtig; —— mark, s., vraagteken n.
queue, kjoe, s., rij c. v., in de rij staan
quibble, kwib-b'l, s., (evasion) uitvlucht c. v., uitvluchten zoeken
quick, kwik, a., (swift) vlug, snel; (lively) levendig; —— en, v., (animate) bezielen; (hasten) verhaasten; ——lime, s., ongebluste kalk c.; ——ness, vlugheid c.; levendigheid c.; ——sands, drijfzand n.; ——silver, kwikzilver n.
quiet, kwai-ut, a., rustig, stil. s., rust c., stilte c.
quill, kwil, s., schacht c.; (pen) veren pen c.
quilt, kwilt, s., gewatteerde deken c.
quince, kwins, s., kweepeer c., kwee c.
quinine, kwi-nien, s., kinine c.
quire, kwair, s., (paper) boek n.
quit, kwit, a., vrij. v., verlaten; ——s, adv., quitte
quite, kwait, adv., helemaal, heel, zeer
quiver, kwiv-v'r, s., pijlkoker c.; (tremble) trilling c. v., trillen, beven [n.
quoit, koit, s., werpring c.; ——s, pl., ringwerpen

quota, kwo-ta, s., evenredig deel n.

quotation, kwo-tee-sjun, s., (citation) aanhaling c.; (price) prijsnotering c.

quote, kwoot, v., aanhalen; (prices) noteren

rabbi, reb-bai, s., rabbijn c., rabbi c.

rabbit, reb-bit, s., konijn n.

rabble, reb-b'l, s., gepeupel n., grauw n.

rabid, reb-bid, a., razend, woest; (dog) dol

rabies, ree-biez, s., hondsdolheid c.

race, rees, v., rennen, snellen. s., (breed) ras n.; (contest) wedloop c.; ——course, renbaan c.; ——horse, renpaard n.; ——r, (man) hardloper c.; (car) renwagen

rack, rek, s., rek n.; (luggage) bagagenet n.; (torture) pijnbank c. v., folteren

racket, rek-kit, s., raket n.

radiant, ree-di-'nt, a., stralend

radiate, ree-di-eet, v., uitstralen

radiator, ree-di-ee-t'r, s., radiator c.

radio, ree-di-o, s., radio c.

radish, red-disj, s., radijs c.

radium, ree-di-um, s., radium n.

radius, ree-di-us, s., straal c.

raffle, ref-f'l, s., loterij c. v., verloten

raft, raaft, s., vlot n. v., vlotten

rafter, raaf-t'r, s., dakspar c. [ruw

rag, reG, s., vod c.; ——ged, a., haveloos; (rough)

rage, reedzj, s., woede c. v., woeden, razen

raid, reed, s., inval c.; air——, luchtaanval c.; police——, politie-inval c. v., een inval doen

rail, reel, s., (bar) staaf c.; (stairs) leuning c.; (ship) reling c. v., schelden, schimpen; ——ing, s., geschimp n.; ——lery, scherts c.

railway, reel-wee, s., spoorweg c.

rain, reen, v., regenen. s., regen c.; ——bow, regenboog c.; ——coat, regenjas c.; ——fall, regenval c.; ——y, a., regenachtig

raise, reez, v., doen rijzen; (lift) optillen; (set upright) overeind zetten; (voice) verheffen; (eyes) opslaan; (monument) oprichten; (cattle) fokken; (family) grootbrengen;

(increase) verhogen; (doubt) **opperen;** (question) opwerpen

raisin, ree-z'n, s., rozijn c.   [harken

rake, reek, s., hark c.; (person) losbol c. v.,

rally, rel-li, v., (collect) verzamelen. s., verzameling c.

ram, rem, s., ram c.; (battering) stormram c.; (naut.) ramschip n. v., heien

ramble, rem-b'l, v., rondzwerven; (mind) ijlen. s., zwerftocht c.

rampant, rem-p'nt, a., (fig.) uitgelaten; (rife) heersend

rampart, rem-purt, s., wal c.; (defence) bolwerk n.

rancid, ren-sid, a., (bacon) ranzig; (butter) sterk

rancour, reng-k'r, s., wrok c.; **bear** ——, wrok koesteren

random, ren-dum, at ——, adv., op goed geluk af

range, reendzj, v., rangschikken. s., (fire-arms) draagwijdte c.; (voice) omvang c.; (kitchen) fornuis n.; **rifle** ——, schietbaan c.; **mountain** ——, bergketen c.

ranger, reen-dzjur, s., zwerver c.

rank, rengk, v., opstellen. a., (rancid) ranzig; (strong smelling) sterk riekend. s., rij c.; (mil.) gelid n.; (degree) graad c.; (social) stand c.; —— **and file,** de minderen c.pl.

rankle, reng-k'l, v., etteren; (fig.) knagen

ransack, ren-sek, v., doorzoeken; (plunder) plunderen

ransom, ren-sum, s., losgeld n. v., vrijkopen

rap, rep, v., (hit) slaan; (knock) kloppen. s., (tap) tik c.; (knock) geklop n.

rapacious, re-pee-sjus, a., roofzuchtig; gierig

rape, reep, v., verkrachten. s., verkrachting c.

rapid, rep-pid, a., snel, vlug; ——**ity,** s., snelheid c.; ——**s,** pl., stroomversnelling c.

rapier, ree-pi-ur, s., rapier n.

rapture, rept-sjur, s., verrukking c.

rare, rèr, a., zeldzaam; (air) ijl

rarity, rèr-i-ti, s., zeldzaamheid c.; dunheid c.

rascal, raas-k'l, s., schurk c.; schelm c.

rash, resj, s., (skin) huiduitslag c. a., (hasty) overijld; (reckless) onbezonnen

rasher, res-sjur, s., schijfje n.

rasp, raasp, v., raspen. s., rasp c.; (sound) gekras

raspberry, raaz-be-ri, s., framboos c.   [n.

rat, ret, s., rat c.; ————**trap,** ratteval c.

rate, reet, s., (proportion) verhouding c.; (exchange) koers c.; (price) prijs c.; (speed) snelheid c.; (tax) gemeentebelasting c. v., (value) taxeren; **at any** ————, adv., in ieder geval

rather, ra-dh'r, adv., liever; (sooner) eerder

ratify, ret-ti-fai, v., bekrachtigen

ratio, ree-sji-o, s., verhouding c.

ration, res-sjun, s., rantsoen n.; portie c.

rational, res-sje-n'l, a., redelijk; (wise) verstandig

rattle, ret-t'l, v., ratelen, rammelen. s., ratel c.; (toy) rammelaar c.; (noise) geratel n.; (death) gereutel n.

rattlesnake, ret-t'l-sneek, s., ratelslang c.   [c.

ravage, rev-vidzj, v., verwoesten. s., verwoesting

rave, reev, v., ijlen, razen; ———— **about,** dwepen met

raven, ree-v'n, s., raaf c.

ravenous, ree-ve-nus, a., vraatzuchtig; (famished) uitgehongerd

ravine, re-vien, s., ravijn n.

raving, ree-ving, a., razend; ———— **mad,** stapelgek

ravish, rev-visj, v., verkrachten; (delight) verrukken; ————**ing,** a., verrukkelijk

raw, roa, a., rauw; (cotton) ruw; (leather) ongelooid; (weather) guur; (inexperienced) onervaren; ———— **materials,** s.pl., grondstoffen c.pl.

ray, ree, s., straal c.; ———— **of light,** lichtstraal c.

raze, reez, v., uitwissen; (demolish) slechten

razor, ree-z'r, s., scheermes n.; ————**-blade,** scheermesje n.; ————**-strop,** scheerriem c.; **safety** ————, scheerapparaat n.

reach, rietsj, v., bereiken. s., bereik n.

react, ri-ekt, v., reageren; —— **against,** zich verzetten tegen; ——**ion,** s., reactie c.

read, ried, v., lezen; ——**er,** s., lezer c.; (book) leesboek n.; ——**ing,** lezen n.; (matter) lectuur c.

readily, red-di-li, adv., gaarne; (easily) gemakkelijk

ready, red-di, a., klaar; (willing) bereid; (quick) vlug; (able) vaardig; ——**made clothes,** s.pl., confectie c.

real, riel, a., werkelijk; (genuine) echt; —— **estate,** s., onroerende goederen n.pl.; ——**ly,** adv., werkelijk

realize, ri-e-laiz, v., beseffen; (sell) te gelde **realm,** relm, s., koninkrijk n., rijk n. [maken

ream, riem, s., riem c.

reap, riep, v., (cut) maaien; (gather) oogsten; ——**er,** s., maaier c.; ——**ing-machine,** maaimachine c.

rear, rier, v., (children) grootbrengen; (cattle) fokken; (plants) kweken; (prance) steigeren. s., achterkant c.; (mil.) achterhoede c. [c.

rear-admiral, rier-ed-mi-r'l, s., schout-bij-nacht

reason, rie-z'n, v., redeneren. s., (intellect) verstand n.; (motive) reden c.; (cause) oorzaak c.; ——**able,** a., redelijk; (price) billijk

reassure, ri-es-sjoer, v., geruststellen

rebate, ri-beet, s., korting c., aftrek c.

rebel, reb-b'l, s., oproerling c. a., oproerig

rebel, ri-bel, v., oproer maken; ——**lion,** s.,

rebound, ri-baund, v., terugspringen [oproer n.

rebuff, ri-baf, v., afwijzen. s., afwijzing c.

rebuke, ri-bjoek, v., berispen. s., berisping c.

recall, ri-koal, v., terugroepen; (mind) herinneren

recapitulate, ric-ke-pit-joe-leet, v., samenvatten

recede, ri-sied, v., terugwijken, teruggaan

receipt, ri-siet, s., ontvangst c.; kwitantie c.

receive, ri-siev, v., ontvangen; (accept) aannemen; ——**r,** s., ontvanger c.; (stolen goods) heler c.

recent, rie-s'nt, a., van de laatste tijd; (new) nieuw; ——**ly,** adv., onlangs; in de laatste tijd

receptacle, ri-sep-te-k'l, s., vergaarbak c.

reception, ri-sep-sjun, s., ontvangst c.; (guests) receptie c.

recess, ri-ses, s., opschorting c.; (creek) inham c.

recipe, res-si-pi, s., recept n.

reciprocate, ri-sip-pre-keet, v., beantwoorden

recital, ri-sai-t'l, s., opsomming c.; (tale) verhaal

recite, ri-sait, v., opsommen; voordragen   [n.

reckless, rek-lis, a., roekeloos; woest

reckon, rek-k'n, v., rekenen; (regard) beschouwen

reclaim, ri-kleem, v., terugeisen; (land) droog-leggen

recline, ri-klain, v., liggen; achterover leunen

recluse, ri-kloes, s., kluizenaar c.

recognition, rek-ke-Gnis-sjun, s., herkenning c.; (appreciation) waardering c.

recognize, rek-ke-Gnaiz, v., herkennen; waar-deren

recoil, ri-koil, v., terugspringen. s., (gun) terug-stoot c.

recollect, rek-ke-lekt, v., zich herinneren

recollection, rek-ke-lek-sjun, s., herinnering c.

recommence, rie-ke-mens, v., weer beginnen

recommend, rek-ke-mend, v., aanbevelen; ——ation, s., aanbeveling c.

recompense, rek-k'm-pens, v., belonen; vergel-den. s., vergelding c.

reconcile, rek-k'n-sail, v., verzoenen

reconnoitre, rek-ke-noi-t'r, v., verkennen

reconsider, rie-k'n-sid-d'r, v., weder overwegen

record, ri-koard, v., aantekenen; registreren

record, rek-koard, s., aantekening c.; document n.; (gramophone) grammofoonplaat c.; (sport) record n.; (law) verleden n.

recoup, ri-koep, v., schadeloos stellen

recourse, ri-koars, s., toevlucht c.

recover, ri-kʌv-v'r, v., (regain) terugkrijgen; (health) herstellen; ——y, s., herstel n.

re-cover, ri-kʌv-v'r, v., opnieuw bedekken

recreation, rek-kri-ee-sjun, s., ontspanning c.; (diversion) vermaak n.; —— ground, speel-plaats c.

recruit, ri-**kroet**, s., rekruut c. v., rekruteren
rectangular, rek-**teng**-Gjoe-l'r, a., rechthoekig
rectify, **rek**-ti-fai, v., herstellen, verbeteren
rector, **rek**-t'r, s., pastoor c.; dominee c.
recumbent, ri-**kam**-b'nt, a., liggend, leunend
recuperate, ri-**kjoe**-pe-reet, v., herstellen
recur, ri-**keur**, v., terugkeren; zich herhalen
red, red, a., rood; ――**breast**, s., roodborstje n.;
――**den**, v., rood maken; (blush) blozen;
――**dish**, a., roodachtig; ――**hot**, gloeiend
heet; ――**ness**, s., roodheid c.
redeem, ri-**diem**, v., (to buy back) terugkopen;
(mortgage) aflossen; (promise) vervullen;
(soul) verlossen
redemption, ri-**demp**-sjun, s., (debt) aflossing c.
redouble, ri-**dab**-b'l, v., verdubbelen
redress, ri-**dres**, v., herstellen. s., herstel c.
reduce, ri-**djoes**, v., terugbrengen; (lessen) verminderen; (weaken) verzwakken; (prices)
verlagen
reduction, ri-**dak**-sjun, s., vermindering c.;
[(prices) reductie c.
reed, ried, s., riet n.
reef, rief, s., rif n.; (sail) reef c. v., reven
reek, riek, s., (smoke) rook c.; (vapour) damp c.;
(stench) stank c., v., roken; dampen; stinken
reel, riel, s., haspel c.; (spool) klos c. v., wankelen
refer (to), ri-**feur** (toe), v., verwijzen naar;
(apply) zich beroepen op; (consult books)
raadplegen
referee, ref-fe-**rie**, s., scheidsrechter c.
reference, **ref**-fe-r'ns, s., verwijzing c.; (mention)
vermelding c.; (person) getuige c.; (testimonial) getuigschrift n.; **with ―― to**, met
betrekking tot
refine, ri-**fain**, v., zuiveren; (fig.) beschaven;
――**d**, a., gezuiverd; beschaafd; ――**ment**,
s., beschaafdheid c.; (elegance) verfijning c.
re-fit, rie-**fit**, v., opnieuw uitrusten
reflect, ri-**flekt**, v., (mirror) weerkaatsen; (ponder) nadenken; ――**ion**, s., weerschijn c.;
(thought) bespiegeling c.; (reproach) verwijt
n.; ――**or**, reflector c.

reform, ri-foarm, v., hervormen; (moral) bekeren. s., verbetering c.; ——**ation,** (eccl.) hervorming c.

refrain, ri-freen, v., zich bedwingen. s., refrein n.

refresh, ri-fresj, v., verfrissen; (memory) opfrissen

refreshment, ri-fresj-m'nt, s., verkwikking c.

refrigerator, ri-frid-zje-ree-t'r, s., ijskast c.

refuge, ref-fjoedzj, s., (place) toevluchtsoord n.

refugee, ref-fjoe-dzjie, s., vluchteling c.

refund, ri-fand, v., terugbetalen

refusal, ri-fjoe-z'l, s., weigering c.

refuse, ri-fjoez, v., weigeren

refuse, ref-fjoes, s., uitschot n., afval c.

regain, ri-Geen, v., herkrijgen, herwinnen

regal, rie-G'l, a., koninklijk, vorstelijk

regale, ri-Geel, v., onthalen

regard, ri-Gaard, v., beschouwen; (esteem) achten; (concern) betreffen. s., blik c.; (esteem) achting c.; (heed) aandacht c.; **with** —— **to,** met betrekking tot; **kind** ——**s,** pl., beste groeten; ——**less,** a., achteloos

regatta, ri-Get-te, s., roeiwedstrijd c.

regenerate, ri-dzjen-ne-reet, v., doen herleven

regent, rie-dzj'nt, s., regent c.; regentes c.

regiment, red-zji-m'nt, s., regiment n.

region, rie-dzjun, s., streek c.; (sphere) sfeer c.

register, red-zjis-t'r, s., register n.; (list) lijst c. v., inschrijven; (letter) aantekenen

registrar, red-zjis-traar, s., ambtenaar van de burgerlijke stand c.

registration, red-zjis-tree-sjun, s., registratie c.; (letter) aantekening c.

registry, red-zjis-tri, s., registratiekantoor n.; **servants'** ——, verhuurkantoor n.

regret, ri-Gret, v., betreuren. s., spijt c.

regrettable, ri-Gret-te-b'l, a., betreurenswaardig

regular, reG-joe-l'r, a., regelmatig; geregeld

regulate, reG-joe-leet, v., regelen, ordenen [n.

regulation, reG-joe-lee-sjun, s., (rule) voorschrift

rehearsal, ri-heur-s'l, s., (stage) repetitie c.
rehearse, ri-heurs, v., (stage) repeteren
reign, reen, v., regeren. s., regering c.
reimburse, rie-im-beurs, v., terugbetalen
rein, reen, s., teugel c. v., beteugelen
reindeer, reen-dier, s., rendier n.
reinforce, rie-in-foars, v., versterken
reinstate, rie-in-steet, v., in ere herstellen
reinsure, rie-in-sjoer, v., herverzekeren
reject, ri-dzjekt, v., verwerpen; (refuse) afwijzen
rejoice, ri-dzjois, v., verheugen; zich verheugen
rejoicing, ri-dzjoi-sing, s., vreugde c.
rejuvenate, ri-dzjoe-vi-neet, v., verjongen
relapse, ri-leps, v., terugvallen. s., terugval c.
relate, ri-leet, v., verhalen; ——d, a., verwant
relation, ri-lee-sjun, s., (reference) betrekking c.; (kinship) bloedverwant c.; ——ship, verwantschap c.
relax, ri-leks, v., verslappen; (abate) afnemen
relaxation, ri-lek-see-sjun, s., ontspanning c.
relay, ri-lee, v., (radio) relayeren
release, ri-lies, v., vrijlaten. s., bevrijding c.
relent, ri-lent, v., zich laten vermurwen
relentless, ri-lent-lis, a., meedogenloos
relevant, rel-li-v'nt, a., toepasselijk
reliable, ri-lai-e-b'l, a., betrouwbaar
reliance, ri-lai-'ns, s., vertrouwen n.
relic, rel-lik, s., overblijfsel n.; (eccl.) relikwie c.
relief, ri-lief, s., verlichting c.; (pain) leniging c.; (mil.) aflossing c.; (siege) ontzet n.
relieve, ri-liev, v., verlichten; steunen; aflossen
religion, ri-lid-zjun, s., godsdienst c.
religious, ri-lid-zjus, a., godsdienstig; vroom
relinquish, ri-ling-kwisj, v., opgeven, afstaan
relish, rel-lisj, s., smaak c. v., smaak vinden in
reluctance, ri-lak-t'ns, s., tegenzin c.
reluctant, ri-lak-t'nt, a., onwillig, afkerig [op
rely (on), ri-lai (on), v., vertrouwen op, steunen
remain, ri-meen, v., blijven; ——der, s., rest c.
remand, ri-maand, v., terugzenden in voorarrest
remark, ri-maark, v., opmerken. s., opmerking c.
remarkable, ri-maar-ke-b'l, a., merkwaardig [c.

remedy, rem-mi-di, s., geneesmiddel n.   v., verhelpen; (cure) genezen

remember, ri-mem-b'r, v., zich herinneren

remembrance, ri-mem-br'ns, s., herinnering c.

remind (of), ri-maind (ov), v., herinneren aan

remit, ri-mit, v., (money) overmaken; (fine) kwijtschelden

remittance, ri-mit-t'ns, s., overmaking c.

remnant, rem-n'nt, s., overblijfsel n.

remonstrate, ri-mon-street, v., protesteren

remorse, ri-moars, s., wroeging c.

remote, ri-moot, a., afgelegen; afgezonderd

removal, ri-moe-v'l, s., (furniture) verhuizing c.

remove, ri-moev, v., (furniture) verhuizen; (take away) verwijderen; (dismiss) ontslaan

remunerate, ri-mjoe-ne-reet, v., belonen

remunerative, ri-mjoe-ne-re-tiv, a., lonend

rend, rend, v., verscheuren; (split) splijten

render, ren-d'r, v., (return) teruggeven; (service) bewijzen; (aid) verlenen; ——ing, s., (version) vertaling c.

renegade, ren-ni-Geed, s., afvallige c.

renew, ri-njoe, v., vernieuwen

renewal, ri-njoe-'l, s., vernieuwing c.

renounce, ri-nauns, v., afstand doen van

renovate, ren-ne-veet, v., vernieuwen

renown, ri-naun, s., roem c.; ——ed, a., beroemd

rent, rent, v., huren. s., huur c.; (tear) scheur c.

renunciation, ri-nan-si-ee-sjun, s., verzaking c.

reorganize, rie-oar-Ge-naiz, v., reorganiseren

repair, ri-pèr, v., herstellen. s., reparatie c.

reparation, rep-pe-ree-sjun, s., schadeloosstelling c.

repartee, re-paar-tie, s., gevat antwoord n.

repeal, ri-piel, v., intrekken. s., intrekking c.

repeat, ri-piet, v., herhalen. s., herhaling c.

repel, ri-pel, v., terugdrijven; (be repulsive) afstoten

repellent, ri-pel-l'nt, a., weerzinwekkend

repent, ri-pent, v., berouw hebben

repetition, rep-pe-tis-sjun, s., herhaling c.

replace, ri-plees, v., (substitute) vervangen

replenish, ri-plen-nisj, v., aanvullen

reply, ri-plai, v., antwoorden. s., antwoord n.

report, ri-poart, s., rapport n.; (rumour) gerucht n.; (bang) knal c. v., melden, berichten

reporter, rep-pri-zent, 'r, s., verslaggever c.

repose, ri-pooz, v., uitrusten. s., rust c.

repository, ri-poz-zi-te-ri, s., bewaarplaats c.

represent, rep-pri-zent, v., voorstellen; (agent) vertegenwoordigen; ——ation, s., voorstelling c.; (agency) vertegenwoordiging c.; ——ative, vertegenwoordiger c.

reprieve, ri-priev, v., uitstel verlenen

reprimand, rep-pri-maand, v., berispen. s., berisping c.

reprint, rie-print, s., herdruk c. v., herdrukken

reprisal, ri-prai-z'l, s., vergelding c.

reproach, ri-prootsj, v., verwijten. s., verwijt n.

reprobate, rep-pre-bit, s., verworpeling c.

reproduce, rie-pre-djoes, v., zich voortplanten

reproduction, rie-pre-dak-sjun, s., reproduktie c.

reproof, ri-proef, s., berisping c., verwijt n.

reprove, ri-proev, v., berispen, terechtwijzen

reptile, rep-tail, s., reptiel n. a., kruipend

republic, ri-pab-blik, s., republiek c.

repudiate, ri-pjoe-di-eet, v., verwerpen; verstoten

repugnant, ri-pag-n'nt, a., weerzinwekkend

repulse, ri-pals, v., (enemy) afslaan

repulsive, ri-pal-siv, a., afstotend; waglijk

reputation, rep-joe-tee-sjun, s., goede naam c.

repute, ri-pjoet, s., vermaardheid c.

request, ri-kwest, s., verzoek n. v., verzoeken

require, ri-kwair, v., (need) nodig hebben; (claim) vorderen; ——ment, s., behoefte c.

requisite, rek-kwi-zit, a., vereist. s., vereiste c.

rescue, res-kjoe, v., redden. s., redding c.

research, ri-seurtsj, s., onderzoeking c.

resemble, ri-zem-b'l, v., gelijken op

resent, ri-zent, v, kwalijk nemen; ——ful, a., lichtgeraakt; haatdragend; ——ment, s., wrok c.

reserve, ri-zeurv, s., (restraint) gereserveerdheid

c. v., bewaren; (seats) bespreken; (rights) voorbehouden

reservoir, rez-z'r-vwaar, s., reservoir n.

reside, ri-zaid, v., wonen, resideren

residence, rez-zi-d'ns, s., woonplaats c. [tig

resident, rez-zi-d'nt, s., inwoner c. a., woonach-

resign, ri-zain, v., ontslag nemen; (a right) opgeven; —— **oneself,** berusten

resin, rez-zin, s., hars n.; —— **ous,** a., harsachtig

resist, ri-zist, v., weerstaan; —— **ance,** s., verzet

resolute, rez-ze-ljoet, a., vastberaden [n.

resolution, rez-ze-ljoe-sjun, s., besluit n.

resolve, ri-zolv, v., besluiten; (solve) oplossen

resort, ri-zoart, s., (expedient) hulpmiddel n.; **holiday**——, vacantieoord n.; —— **to,** v., zijn toevlucht nemen tot

resound, ri-zound, v., weerklinken, weergalmen

resource, ri-soars, s., hulpbron c.

resources, ri-soar-sus, s.pl., middelen n.pl.

respect, ri-pekt, v., eerbiedigen; (esteem) achten. s., eerbied c.; (esteem) achting c.; —— **ability,** achtenswaardigheid c.; —— **able,** a., achtenswaardig; ——**ful,** eerbiedig; ——**ing,** prep., betreffende

respite, res-pit, s., uitstel n.; (rest) rust c.

respond, ris-pond, v., (reply) antwoorden

respondent, ris-pon-d'nt, s., (law) gedaagde c.

response, ris-pons, s., antwoord n.

responsibility, ris-pon-si-bil-li-ti, s., verant-woordelijkheid c.; aansprakelijkheid c.

responsible, ris-pon-si-b'l, a., verantwoordelijk

rest, rest, s., (remainder) rest c.; (repose) rust c.; (pause) pauze c. v., rusten; ——**ful,** a., rus-tig; ——**ive,** koppig; ——**less,** onrustig

restaurant, res-to-rant, s., restaurant n.; ——-**car,** restauratiewagen c.

restore, ris-toar, v., (give back) teruggeven; (heal) genezen; (repair) herstellen

restrain, ris-treen, v., (check) beteugelen

restraint, ris-treent, s., (check) beteugeling c.; (constraint) dwang c.

restrict, ris-trikt, v., beperken

restriction, ris-trikt-sjun, s., beperking c.

result, ri-zalt, v., voortkomen. s., (consequence) gevolg n.; (issue) afloop c.; (outcome) resul-

resume, ri-zjoem, v., weer beginnen   [taat n.

resumption, ri-zamp-sjun, s., hervatting c.

resurrection, rez-ze-rek-sjun, s., verrijzenis c.

retail, ri-teel, v., in 't klein verkopen. s., klein-handel c. ——er, kleinhandelaar c.

retain, ri-teen, v., (keep) houden; (remember) onthouden

retaliate, ri-tel-li-eet, v., wraak nemen

retard, ri-taard, v., vertragen; (delay) uitstellen

reticent, ret-ti-s'nt, a., terughoudend

retinue, ret-tin-joe, s., gevolg n., stoet c.

retire, ri-tair, v., zich terugtrekken; (from office) zijn ontslag nemen

retirement, ri-tair-m'nt, s., ontslagneming c.

retort, ri-toart, v., vinnig antwoorden

retract, ri-trekt, v., terugtrekken   [c.

retreat, ri-triet, v., zich terugtrekken. s., aftocht

retrench, ri-trensj, v., (mil.) verschansen

retrieve, ri-triev, v., terugvinden; (loss) weer goedmaken; (by dog) apporteren

return, ri-teurn, v., (come back) terrugkomen; (go back) teruggaan; (give back) teruggeven. s., terugkeer c.; —— **ticket,** retourkaartje n.

returns, ri-teurnz, s.pl., (commercial) omzet c.

reveal, ri-viel, v., onthullen; openbaren

revel, rev-v'l, v., zwelgen. s., braspartij c.

revenge, ri-vendzj, v., wreken. s., wraak c.

revenue, rev-vin-joe, s., inkomsten c.pl.

reverse, ri-veurs, v., omkeren; (engine) om-zetten. s., tegendeel n.; (misfortune) tegen-spoed c.; (mil.) nederlaag c. a., omgekeerd; (contrary) tegengesteld

revert, ri-veurt, v., terugkeren, terugkomen

review, ri-vjoe, v., (revise) herzien; (look back on) terugzien op; (troops) inspecteren; (a book) bespreken. s., herziening c.; terugblik c.; inspectie c.; boekbespreking c.

revile, ri-vail, v., schimpen, smaden

revise, ri-vaiz, v., herzien; (correct) nazien

revision, ri-**viz**-zjun, s., herziening c.

revive, ri-**vaiv**, v., doen herleven; herleven

revoke, ri-**vook**, v., herroepen; (cards) niet
bekennen   [c.

revolt, ri-**voolt**, v., in opstand komen. s., opstand

revolution, rev-ve-**ljoe**-sjun, s., revolutie c.;
(rotation) omwenteling c.

revolve, ri-**volv**, v., omwentelen

revolver, ri-**volv**-'r, s., revolver c.

reward, ri-**woard**, v., belonen. s., beloning c.

rheumatism, **roe**-me-tizm, s., reumatiek c.

rhinoceros, rai-**nos**-se-rus, s., neushoorn c.

rhubarb, **roe**-baarb, s., rabarber c.

rhyme, raim, s., rijm n. v., rijmen

rib, rib, s., rib c.; (of umbrella) balein c.

ribbon, **rib**-b'n, s., lint n.; (strip) strook c.

rice, rais, s., rijst c.

rich, ritsj, a., rijk; (food) machtig

riches, **ritsj**-iz, s.pl., rijkdom c.

rickets, **rik**-kits, s., Engelse ziekte c.

rickety, **rik**-ki-ti, a., wankel; (weak) zwak

rid, rid, v., bevrijden; **to get —— of**, afkomen van

riddle, **rid**-d'l, s., raadsel n. v., zeven; (perforate)
doorzeven

ride, raid, v., rijden

rider, **rai**-d'r, s., berijder c.; (horse) ruiter c.

ridge, ridzj, s., bergrug c.; (of a roof) nok c.

ridicule, **rid**-di-kjoel, v., belachelijk maken

ridiculous, ri-**dik**-joe-lus, a., belachelijk

rifle, **rai**-f'l, s., geweer n. v., (rob) beroven

rift, rift, s., (crack) spleet c.; (cleft) scheur c.

rig, riG, s., (ship) tuig n. v., kleden

right, rait, s., recht n. v., (set upright) overeind
zetten; (correct) verbeteren. a., recht; (correct) juist; (not left) rechts; (just) billijk;
(lawful) rechtmatig; (true) waar. adv., recht;
all ——, in orde!; on your ——, aan uw
rechterhand

rigid, **rid**-zjid, a., stijf, strak; (stern) streng

rigorous, **riG**-Ge-rus, a., streng; (harsh) hard

rigour, **riG**-G'r, s., strengheid c.; hardheid c.

rim, rim, s., rand c.; (wheel) velg c. v., omranden

rind, raind, s., (peel) schil c.; (bacon) zwoerd n.
ring, ring, s., ring c. v., bellen; luiden
ringleader, ring-lie-d'r, s., belhamel c.
rinse, rins, v., omspoelen; s., spoeling c.
riot, rai-ut, s., relletje n.; (revel) braspartij c.
rip, rip, v., (tear) openscheuren; (split) splijten
ripe, raip, a., rijp; ——n, v., rijp worden
ripple, rip-p'l, v., rimpelen; (brook) kabbelen
rise, raiz, v., opstaan; (stand up) gaan staan;
    (revolt) in opstand komen. s., rijzing, c.;
    (sun) opgang c.; (salary) verhoging c.
risk, risk, s., gevaar n., risico n. v., riskeren
rite, rait, s., ritus c.
rival, rai-v'l, s., mededinger c.
river, riv-v'r, s., rivier c., stroom c.
rivet, riv-vit, s., klinknagel c. v., vastklinken
road, rood, s., weg c.
roam, room, v., ronddolen, rondzwerven
roar, roar, v., (lion) brullen; (wind) huilen
roast, roost, v., roosteren; (coffee) branden
rob, rob, v., beroven; ——ber, s., rover c.
robbery, rob-be-ri, s., diefstal c., roof c.
robe, roob, s., staatsiemantel c., toga c.
robin, rob-bin, s., roodborstje n.
robust, ro-bast, a., krachtig, sterk, fors
rock, rok, s., rots c.; (cliff) klif n. v., schommelen;
    (cradle) wiegen; ——y, a., rotsachtig
rocket, rok-kit, s., raket c., vuurpijl c.
rod, rod, s., stok c., staf c.; (birch) roede c.
roe, ro, s., (deer) ree c.; (fish) viskuit c.
rogue, rooG, s., schurk c.; (wag) guit c.; ——ry,
    schurkenstreken c.pl.; guitigheid c.
roll, rool, s., rol c.; (bread) broodje n.; (list) lijst
    c. v., rollen; (drum) roffelen; ——call, s.,
    appèl n.; ——er, wals c.; ——er-skate,
    rolschaats c.
romance, re-mens, s., romantisch verhaal n.
romp, romp, v., stoeien
roof, roef, s., dak n.; (vehicle) kap c.
rook, roek, s., roek c.; (chess) kasteel n.
room, roem, s., kamer c.; (space) ruimte c.
roomy, roe-mi, a., ruim; (spacious) wijd

roost, roest, s., roest n.   v., op stok gaan
root, roet, s., wortel c.   v., omwroeten
rope, roop, s., touw n., koord n.
rosary, ro-ze-ri, s., rozenkrans c.
rose, rooz, s., roos c.; (nozzle) sproeier c.
rosemary, rooz-me-ri, s., rosmarijn c.
rosy, ro-zi, a., rooskleurig; (flushing) blozend
rot, rot, s., verrotting c.   v., verrotten
rotate, ro-teet, v., draaien; doen draaien
rotten, rot-t'n, a., verrot, bedorven
rouge, roezj, s., rode verf c.
rough, raf, a., (not smooth) ruw; (rugged) ruig;
    (harsh) streng; (road) oneffen; (sea) woest;
    —— **copy,** s., klad n.
round, raund, a., rond.   v., afronden. s., (circle)
    kring c.; (sphere) bol c.; (slice) snee c.; ——
    about, adv., rondom.   s., draaimolen c.;
    —— **ness,** rondheid c.
rouse, rauz, v., wakker maken; (stir up) aanporren
rout, raut, v., (mil.) op de vlucht drijven.   s.,
route, roet, s., weg c., route c.   [vlucht c.
routine, roe-tien, s., sleur c., routine c.
rove, roov, v., zwerven; ——**r,** s., zwerver c.
row, ro, v., roeien. s., rij c.; (series) reeks c.
row, rau, s., (noise) herrie c.; (quarrel) ruzie c.
royal, roi-ul, a., koninklijk; ——**ist,** s., konings-
    gezinde c.; ——**ty,** koningschap n.
rub, rab, v., wrijven; —— **down,** —— **off,**
    afschuren; ——**ber,** s., rubber c.; **india-**
    rubber, gummi c.
rubbish, rab-bisj, s., puin n.; (trash) bocht n.
ruby, roe-bi, s., robijn c.
rudder, rad-d'r, s., roer n., roerblad n.
ruddy, rad-di, a., rossig; (complexion) blozend
rude, roed, a., (rough) ruw, grof; (boorish) lomp
rudiment, roe-di-m'nt, s., grondbeginsel n.
rue, roe, v., betreuren; ——**ful,** a., treurig
ruffian, raf-jun, s., schurk c., woesteling c.
ruffle, raf-f'l, v., verwarren. s., plooi c.
rug, raG, s., reisdeken c.; (hearth) haarkleedje n.
rugged, raG-Gid, a., ruig, ruw; (bumpy) hobbelig
ruin, roe-in, v., verwoesten. s., ondergang c.

rule, roel, v., liniëren; (govern) regeren. s., regel c.; (government) bestuur n.
ruler, roel-'r, s., liniaal c.; bestuurder c.
rum, ram, s., rum c.
rumble, ram-b'l, v., rommelen, dreunen
rummage, ram-midzj, v., doorsnuffelen
rumour, roe-m'r, s., gerucht n., praatje n.
run, ran, v., lopen; (rush) rennen; (flee) weglopen; (flow) vloeien. s., loop c.; ———away, (horse) op hol geslagen paard n.
rupture, rapt-sjur, s., breuk c.
rural, roe-r'l, a., landelijk; plattelands . . .
rush, rasj, s., (run) geren n.; (onslaught) bestorming c.; (water) geruis n. v., (hurry) voortsnellen; (run) rennen; (flow rapidly) stromen; ——— at, losstormen op
Russian leather, ras-sj'n ledh-ur, s., juchtleer n.
rust, rast, s., roest n. v., verroesten; ———y, a., roestig
rustic, ras-tik, a., landelijk. s., boer c.
rustle, ras-s'l, s., geruis n. v., ruisen
rut, rat, s., wagenspoor n.; (groove) groef c.
rye, rai ,s., rogge c.

sable, see-b'l, s., (fur) sabelbont n. a., zwart
sabre, see-b'r, s., sabel c. v., neersabelen
sack, sek, s., zak c.; (mil.) plundering c. v., plunderen
sacrament, sek-kre-m'nt, s., sacrament n.
sacred, see-krid, a., heilig; (consecrated) gewijd
sacrifice, sek-kri-fais, s., offer n. v., offeren
sad, sed, a., treurig; ———ness, s., droefheid c.
saddle, sed-d'l, v., zadelen. s., zadel n.
saddler, sed-dl'r, s., zadelmaker c.
safe, seef, a., veilig; (reliable) betrouwbaar. s., brandkast c.; (strong room) kluis, c.; ———guard, v., beveiligen. s., beveiliging c.; ———ty, veiligheid c.; ———ty-razor, veiligheidsscheermes n.
sag, seG, v., doorzakken
sagacious, se-Gee-sjus, a., scherpzinnig
sage, seedzj, s., wijze c.; (herb) salie c.

sail, seel, s., zeil n. v., zeilen; (leave) afvaren

sailing, seel-ing, s., zeilen n.; (departure) afvaart c.

sailor, seel-'r, s., matroos c.

saint, seent, a., heilig. s., heilige c.

sake, seek, s., for the —— of, ter wille van

salad, sel-l'd, s., sla c.; ——-dressing, salade-saus c.

salary, sel-le-ri, s., salaris n.

sale, seel, s., verkoop c.; (clearance) uitverkoop c.; ——able, a., verkoopbaar; ——sman, s., verkoper c.

salient, see-li-'nt, a., (jutting) uitstekend

saliva, se-lai-ve, s., speeksel n.

sallow, sel-lo, a., ziekelijk bleek, vuilgeel

salmon, sem-mun, s., zalm c. a., zalmkleurig

saloon, se-loen, s., zaal c.; (ship) grote kajuit c.

salt, soalt, s., zout n. a., zout; ——cellar, s., zoutvaatje n.

salute, se-ljoet, v., groeten. s., (mil.) saluut c.

salvage, sel-vidzj, v., bergen. s., berging c.

salvation, sel-vee-sjun, s., redding c.; (souls) verlossing c.; —— Army, Leger des Heils n.

salver, sel-v'r, s., presenteerblad n.

same, seem, a., zelfde; (identical) gelijk

sample, saam-p'l, s., monster n. v., keuren, proeven

sanctify, sengk-ti-fai, v., heilig maken

sanction, sengk-sjun, v., bekrachtigen. s., bekrachtiging c.

sanctity, sengk-ti-ti, s., heiligheid c.   [asyl n.

sanctuary, sengk-tjoe-e-ri, s., heiligdom n.;

sand, send, s., zand n.; ——y, a., zandig; (hair) rossig

sandal, sen-d'l, s., sandaal c.

sandpaper, send-pee-p'r, s., schuurpapier n.

sandwich, send-witsj, s., belegde boterham c.

sane, seen, a., gezond van geest; (sensible) verstandig

sanguine, seng-Gwin, a., bloedrood; (fig.) hoopvol

sanitary, sen-ni-te-ri, a., gezondheids . . .; —— towel, s., banddoek c.

sanity, sen-ni-ti, s., gezond verstand n.
sap, sep, s., plantensap n. v., (health) ondermijnen
sapper, sep-p'r, s., sappeur c.
sapphire, sef-fair, s., saffier c. a., saffieren
sarcasm, saar-kezm, s., sarcasme n.
sarcastic, saar-kes-tik, a., sarcastisch
sardine, saar-dien, s., sardientje n., sardine c.
sash, sesj, s., (band) sjerp c.; ——-**window,**
schuifraam n.
satchel, set-sjul, s., (school) boekentas c.
satiate, see-sji-eet, v., verzadigen
satin, set-tin, s., satijn n. a., satijnen
satire, set-tair, s., satire c., hekeldicht n.
satisfaction, set-tis-fek-sjun, s., voldoening c.;
(reparation) genoegdoening c.; (contentment)
tevredenheid c.
satisfactory, set-tis-fek-te-ri, a., bevredigend
satisfy, set-tis-fai, v., voldoen aan
saturate, set-sje-reet, v., verzadigen, drenken
Saturday, set-t'r-di, s., zaterdag c.
satyr, set-t'r, s., satyr c., sater c.
sauce, soas, s., saus c.; ——-**pan,** stoofpan c.
saucer, soa-s'r, s., schoteltje n., bordje n.
saunter, soan-t'r, v., slenteren
sausage, soa-sidzj, s., worstje n.
savage, sev-vidzj, s., wilde c. a., wild; (cruel)
wreed
save, seev, v., (rescue) redden; (redeem) verlossen;
(preserve) bewaren; (lay aside) sparen
saving, see-ving, a., spaarzaam, zuinig. s., redding
c.; besparing c.; ——-s, pl., spaarcenten c.pl.
Saviour, seev-jur, s., Heiland c. Verlosser c.
savoury, see-ve-ri, a., smakelijk. s., tussenge-
saw, soa, s., zaag c. v., zagen [recht n.
say, see, v., zeggen; ——-ing, s., gezegde n.
scabbard, skeb-burd, s., schede c.
scaffold, skef-fuld, s., (building) steiger c.;
(execution) schavot n.; ——-ing, steigerwerk
scald, skoald, s., brandwonde c. v., branden [n.
scale, skeel, s., (fish) schub c.; (measure) maatstaf
c.; (mus.) toonladder c. v., (fish) schrappen;
(climb) beklimmen

scales, skeelz, s.pl., weegschaal c.
scallop, skol-lup, s., schulp c. v., uitschulpen
scalp, skelp, s., scalp c. v., scalperen
scamp, skemp, s., deugniet c. v., afroffelen
scamper, skem-p'r, v., hollen. s., gehol n.
scan, sken, v., onderzoeken; (verse) scanderen
scandal, sken-d'l, s., (offence) ergernis c.; (disgrace) schande c.; (malicious gossip) laster c.;
——ous, a., schandelijk; lasterlijk
scanty, sken-ti, a., schaars, krap, gering
scapegoat, skeep-Goot, s., zondenbok c.
scar, skaar, s., litteken n. v., met een litteken bedekken
scarce, skèrs, a., schaars; ——ly, adv., nauwelijks
scarcity, skèr-si-ti, s., schaarste c., gebrek n.
scare, skèr, v., verschrikken; —— away, wegjagen; ——crow, s., vogelverschrikker c.
scarf, skaarf, s., das c.; sjerp c.
scarlet, skaar-lit, s., scharlaken n.; (colour) scharlakenrood n.; ——fever, roodvonk n.
scathing, skee-dhing, a., vernietigend
scatter, sket-t'r, v., rondstrooien; uiteenjagen
scavenger, skev-ven-dzur, s., straatveger c.
scene, sien, s., toneel n.
scenery, sien-ri, s., decor n.; (landscape) landschap n.
scent, sent, s., (smell) geur c.; (perfume) parfum n.; (trail) spoor n. v., ruiken; parfumeren
sceptical, skep-ti-k'l, a., twijfelzuchtig
sceptre, sep-t'r, s., schepter c., staf c.
schedule, sjed-djoel, s., lijst c., tabel c.
scheme, skiem, s., plan n. v., beramen
schism, sizm, s., scheuring c., schisma n. [c.
scholar, skol-l'r, s., geleerde c.; (pupil) leerling
scholarship, skol-l'r-sjip, s., geleerdheid c.; (allowance) studiebeurs c.
school, skoel, s., school c.; ——master, schoolmeester c.; ——mistress, onderwijzeres c.
schooner, skoe-n'r, s., schoener c.
sciatica, sai-et-ti-ka, s., ischias c., heupjicht c.
science, sai-'ns, s., wetenschap c.
scientific, sai-'n-tif-fik, a., wetenschappelijk

scissors, siz-z'rz, s.pl., schaar c.   [met
scoff, skof, s., bespotting c.; —— **at,** v., spotten
scold, skoold, v., bekijven. s., feeks c.
scoop, skoep, s., schep c., schop c. v., scheppen
scope, skoop, s., gezichtskring c.; (aim) doel n.
scorch, skoartsj, v., schroeien, verzengen
score, skoar, s., (bill) rekening c.; (number)
    twintigtal n.; (games) stand c. v., (cut) ker-
    ven; (register) aantekenen
scorn, skoarn, v., verachten. s., verachting c.
scornful, skoarn-foel, a., minachtend
scoundrel, skaun-dr'l, s., schurk c.
scour, skaur, v., schuren; (clean) reinigen
scourge, skeurdzj, s., gesel c. v., geselen [der c.
scout, skaut, s., verkenner c.; **boy**——, padvin-
scowl, skaul, v., het voorhoofd fronsen
scraggy, skreG-Gi, a., mager, spichtig, schriel
scramble, skrem-b'l, s., (struggle) worsteling c.
    v., (climb) klauteren; —— **for,** vechten om
scrap, skrep, s., (bit) stukje n.; (cutting) uitknip-
    sel n.; (refuse) afval c. v., afdanken
scrape, skreep, v., schrapen. s., gekras n.
scratch, skretsj, v., krabben; (cancel) schrappen.
    s., schram c.; —— **out,** v., uitkrabben;
    (word) doorhalen
scream, skriem, v., gillen; (with laughter) gieren.
    s., gil c.
screen, skrien, s., scherm n.; (motor-car) voor-
    ruit c.; (cinema) witte doek n. v., (protect)
    beschutten; (hide) verbergen
screw, skroe, s., schroef c. v., vastschroeven;
    ——**driver,** s., schroevedraaier c.
scribble, skrib-b'l, v., krabbelen. s., gekrabbel n.
Scripture, skript-sjur, s., heilige Schrift c.
scroll, skrool, s., rol c.; (ornament) krul c.
scrub, skrab, v., schrobben. s., (underwood)
    struikgewas n.
scruple, skroe-p'l, s., gewetensbezwaar n.
scrupulous, skroep-joe-lus, a., angstvallig
scrutinize, skroe-ti-naiz, v., nauwkeurig onder-
    zoeken
scuffle, skaf-f'l, v., plukharen. s., vechtpartij c.

scull, ska**l,** s., (oar) riem c. v., roeien

scullery, ska**l-le-ri,** s., bijkouken c.

sculptor, ska**lp-t'r,** s., beeldhouwer c.

sculpture, ska**lpt-sjur,** s., beeldhouwkunst c.

scum, ska**m,** s., schuim n.; (refuse) uitschot n.

scurf, skeurf, s., (on scalp) roos c.

scurfy, skeur-fi, a., vol roos

scurvy, skeur-vi, a., scheurbuik c. a., gemeen

scuttle, ska**t-t'l,** s., kolenbak c.; (hatch) luik n.

scythe, saidh, s., zeis c. v., maaien

sea, sie, s., zee c.; ——gull, zeemeeuw c.; ——man, zeeman c.; ——sick, a., zeeziek; ——side, s., zeekant c.; ——weed, zeewier n.; ——worthy, a., zeewaardig

seal, siel, s., zegel n.; (animal) zeehond c. v., verzegelen; ——ing-wax, s., zegellak n.

sealskin, siel-skin, s., robbevel n.

seam, siem, s., naad c.; (scar) litteken n. v., aaneennaaien; ——stress, s., naaister c.

sear, sier, v., (wither) verdorren; (scorch) schroeien

search, seurtsj, v., (examine) doorzoeken; (garments) fouilleren. s., doorzoeking c.; onderzoek n.; ——light, zoeklicht n.

season, sie-z'n, s., jaargetijde n.; (period of activities) seizoen n. v., (spice) kruiden; (timber) laten drogen; ——able, a., gelegen; ——ing, s., kruiderij c.; ——ticket, abonnementskaart c.

seat, siet, s., zitplaats c.; (bottom of chair) zitting c.; (chair) stoel c.; (bench) bank c.

secluded, si-kloe-did, a., afgezonderd

seclusion, si-kloe-zjun, s., afzondering c.

second, sek-k'nd, s., seconde c. a., (numeral) tweede. v., (support) steunen; ——ary, a., ondergeschikt; ——hand, tweedehands; ——ly, adv., ten tweede

secrecy, sie-kri-si, s., geheimhouding c.

secret, sie-krit, s., geheim n. a., geheim

secretary, sek-kri-te-ri, s., secretaris c.

secrete, si-kriet, v., verbergen; (glands) afscheiden; **secretion,** si-krie-sjun, s., afscheiding c. [den

sect, sekt, s., sekte c.
section, sek-sjun, s., snijding c.; (part) deel n.
sector, sek-t'r, s., sector c.
secular, sek-joe-l'r, a., wereldlijk; eeuwenoud
secure, si-kjoer, a., veilig. v., beveiligen
security, si-kjoe-ri-ti, s., veiligheid c.
sedate, si-deet, a., rustig, bezadigd
sedative, sed-di-tiv, s., pijnstillend middel n.
sedentary, sed-d'n-te-ri, a., zittend
sediment, sed-di-m'nt, s., bezinksel n.
sedition, si-dis-sjun, s., opruiing c.; oproer n.
seditious, si-dis-sjus, a., opruiend; oproerig
seduce, si-djoes, v., verleiden
seducer, si-djoes-'r, s., verleider c.
see, sie, v., zien; (understand) inzien; (call on)
opzoeken; (interview) spreken; (receive) ontvangen; —— **through,** doorzien
seed, sied, s., zaad n.
seek, siek, v., zoeken; (strive) streven naar
seem, siem, v., schijnen; ——**ly,** a., betamelijk
seethe, siedh, v., koken, zieden
seize, siez, v., vatten, grijpen [c.
seizure, sie-zjur, s., beslaglegging c.; (fit) aanval
seldom, sel-d'm, adv., zelden
select, si-lekt, v., uitkiezen. a., uitgelezen
selection, si-lekt-sjun, s., (choice) keus c.;
(number of things) selectie c.
self, self, s., persoon c.; one——, pron., zich;
——**conscious,** a., zelfbewust; (shy) verlegen; ——**ish,** zelfzuchtig; ——**ishness,** s.,
zelfzucht c.; ——**starter,** (motor) auto-
matische starter c.
sell, sel, v., verkopen; ——**er,** s., verkoper c.
semblance, sem-bl'ns, s., schijn c., gelijkenis c.
semi, sem-mi, half . .; ——**circle,** s., halve
cirkel c.; ——**colon,** puntkomma c.
seminary, sem-mi-ne-ri, s., seminarie n.
semolina, sem-me-lie-na, s., griesmeel n.
senate, sen-nit, s., senaat c.
send, send, v., zenden, sturen; —— **away,**
wegzenden; —— **back,** terugzenden; ——**er,**
s., afzender c.; —— **for,** v., laten halen;

—— **off,** afzenden; —— **on,** doorzenden;
—— **up,** naar boven sturen; (prices) opdrijven

senile, sie-nail, a., seniel, van de oude dag
senior, sien-jur, s., oudere c. a., ouder; (in rank) oudste; —— **clerk,** s., eerste bediende c.
sensation, sen-see-sjun, s., gewaarwording c.; (feeling) gevoel n.; (stir) sensatie c.
sense, sens, s., zin c.; (reason) verstand n.
senseless, sens-les, a., bewusteloos; (foolish) dwaas, onzinnig
sensible, sen-si-b'l, a., verstandig; merkbaar
sensitive, sen-si-tiv, a., fijngevoelig
sensual, sen-sjoe-ul, a., zinnelijk
sentence, sen-t'ns, s., zin c.; (law) vonnis n.
sentiment, sen-ti-m'nt, s., gevoel n.; (sentimentality) sentimentaliteit c.
sentimental, sen-ti-m'nt-t'l, a., sentimenteel
sentinel, sen-ti-n'l, s., schildwacht c.
sentry, sen-tri, s., schildwacht c.; ——**-box,** schilderhuisje n.
separate, sep-pe-reet, v., scheiden; a., afzonder-
separation, sep-pe-ree-sjun, s., scheiding c. [lijk
September, sep-tem-b'r, s., september c.
septic, sep-tik, a., septisch, bederf veroorzakend
sequel, sie-kwul, s., vervolg n.; (result) gevolg n.
sequence, sie-kw'ns, s., volgorde c.; (series) reeks c.
serenade, ser-ri-need, s., serenade c.
serene, si-rien, a., (calm) kalm; (clear) helder
serge, seurdzj, s., serge c.
sergeant, saar-dzjunt, s., sergeant c.; wachtmeester c.
serial, sie-ri-ul, a., volg . . .; s., (story) feuilleton
series, sie-riez, s., reeks c., serie c. [n.
serious, sie-ri-us, a., ernstig; belangrijk
sermon, seur-m'n, s., preek c.
serpent, seur-p'nt, s., slang c.
servant, seur-v'nt, s., knecht c.; (maid) meid c.; **civil** ——, ambtenaar c.
serve, seurv, v., dienen; (at table) opdienen; (be useful) dienstig zijn; (tennis) serveren

service, seur-vis, s., dienst c.; (attendance) bediening c.; (Divine) kerkdienst c.; ——**able,** a., dienstig; (useful) nuttig

servile, seur-vail, a., (cringing) slaafs

servitude, seur-vi-tjoed, s., slavernij c.; (penal) dwangarbeid c.

session, ses-sjun, s., zitting c.

set, set, v., zetten; (place) plaatsen; (plant) planten; (arrange) schikken; (clock) gelijkzetten; (watch, net) uitzetten; (table) dekken; (razor) aanzetten; (task) opgeven; (example) geven; (tune, pace) aangeven; (jewels) vatten; (sun) ondergaan. s., stel n.; (series) serie c.; (group) troep c. **tea**——, **dinner**——, servies n.; **wireless**——, radiotoestel n.; —— **(dog) at,** (de hond) aanhitsen tegen; —— **on fire,** in brand steken

settee, set-tie, s., sofa c., canapé c.

settle, set-t'l, v., (establish) vestigen; (decide) beslissen; (affairs) regelen; (accounts) vereffenen; (a dispute) bijleggen; (become stable) tot rust komen

settlement, set-t'l-m'nt, s., vestiging c.; regeling c.; vereffening c.; (colony) kolonie c.

settler, set-l'r, s., kolonist c.

seven, sev-v'n, a., zeven; ——**teen,** zeventien; ——**th,** zevende; ——**ty,** zeventig

sever, sev-v'r, v., scheiden; (cut off) afsnijden

several, sev-vr'l, a., verscheiden

severe, si-vier, a., (stern) streng; (pain) hevig

severity, si-ver-ri-ti, s., strengheid c.; hevigheid c.

sew, so, v., naaien; ——**ing,** s., naaien n.; (needlework) naaiwerk n.; ——**ing-cotton,** naaigaren n.; ——**ing-machine,** naaimachine c.

sewage, sjoe-idzj, s., rioolwater n.

sewer, sjoe-ur, s., riool n.

sex, seks, s., geslacht n.; ——**ual,** a., geslachtelijk

sexton, seks-tun, s., koster c.; (digger) doodgraver c.

shabby, sjeb-bi, a., haveloos; (action) gemeen

shackle, sjek-k'l, s., boei c. v., boeien

shade, sjeed, s., schaduw c.; (colour) schakering

c.; (lamp) kap c.; (fire) scherm. v., beschaduwen

shadow, sjed-do, s., schaduw c.   v., als een schaduw volgen

shady, sjee-di, a., schaduwrijk; (fig.) verdacht

shaft, sjaaft, s., (stem) schacht c.; (mine) mijnschacht c.; (ray, beam) straal c.; (handle) steel c.

shaggy, sjeG-Gi, a., ruig, ruigharig

shake, sjeek, v., schudden; (tremble) beven; (fig.) schokken

shaky, sjee-ki, a., wankel; (uncertain) onzeker

shallow, sjel-lo, a., ondiep. s., ondiepte c.

sham, sjem, s., schijn c.   a., onecht. v., veinzen

shame, sjeem, s., schaamte c.; (disgrace) schande c.   v., beschamen; ——ful, a, schandelijk; ——less, schaamteloos

shampoo, sjem-poe, s., hoofdwassing c.; hoofdwasmiddel n.

shamrock, sjem-rok, s., klaverblad c.

shape, sjeep, s., vorm c.   v., vormen, maken

share, sjèr, v., delen. s., aandeel n.; (plough) ploegschaar c.; ——holder, aandeelhouder c.

shark, sjaark, s., haai c.   v., bedriegen

sharp, sjaarp, a., scherp; (pointed) spits; (acute) hevig; (steep) steil; (shrill) schel; ——en, v., scherpen; (pencil) aanpunten; ——ness, s., scherpte c.

sharper, sjaar-p'r, s., bedrieger, c., afzetter c.

shatter, sjet-t'r, v., verbrijzelen; (nerves) schokken

shave, sjeev, v., scheren; zich scheren   [ken

shaving, sjee-ving, s., scheren n.; ——brush, scheerkwast c.

shavings, sjee-vingz, s.pl., krullen c.pl.

shawl, sjoal, s., sjaal c., omslagdoek c.

she, sjie, pron., zij, ze. s., (female) wijfje n.

sheaf, sjief, s., (corn) schoof c.; (papers) bundel c.

shear, sjier, v., scheren; ——s, s.pl., grote schaar c.

sheath, sjieth, s., (scabbard) schede c.   [c.

shed, sjed, s., loods c., keet c.   v., (blood) vergieten; (tears) storten; (horns, skin) afwerpen; (hair) verliezen

sheen, sjien, s., glans c., schittering c.

sheer, sjier, a., zuiver, puur; (steep) steil

sheet, sjiet, s., (bed) beddelaken n.; (paper) blad n.; (metal) plaat c.; ——**lightning**, weerlicht n.

shelf, sjelf, s., plank c.

shell, sjel, s., (hard) schaal c., schelp c.; (soft) bolster c.; (mil.) granaat c. v., schillen; (mil.) beschieten; ——**fish**, s., schaaldier n.

shelter, sjel-t'r, s., beschutting c. v., beschutten; (give lodging) onderdak geven

shepherd, sjep-p'rd, s., herder c.

shepherdess, sjep-p'rd-es, s., herderin c.

sheriff, sjer-rif, s., sheriff c.

sherry, sjer-ri, s., sherrywijn c.

shield, sjield, s., schild n. v., beschermen

shift, sjift, v., (remove) verplaatsen; (change) veranderen. s., verplaatsing c.; verandering c.; (workmen) ploeg c.

shilling, sjil-ling, s., shilling c.

shin, sjin, s., scheen c.

shine, sjain, s., glans c. v., schijnen; (be bright) schitteren; (be eminent) uitschitteren

shingle, sjing-G'l, s., kiezelsteen c.; (roof) dakspaan c. v., (hair) kort knippen

ship, sjip, s., schip n. v., inschepen; verschepen ——**broker**, s., scheepsmakelaar c.; ——**ment**, verscheping c.; ——**owner**, reder c.; ——**ping**, (traffic) scheepvaart c.; ——**wreck**, schipbreuk c.

shire, sjair, s., graafschap n.

shirk, sjeurk, v., lijntrekken. s., lijntrekker c.

shirt, sjeurt, s., overhemd n.; (women) blouse c.

shiver, sjiv-v'r, v., rillen. s., rilling c.

shoal, sjool, s., (crowd) menigte c.; (fish) **school** c.; (shallow) ondiepte c., zandbank c.

shock, sjok, s., schok c.; (hair) ruige haarbos c. v., schokken; (give offence) aanstoot geven; ——**absorber**, s., schokbreker c.; ——**ing**, a., ergerlijk

shoddy, sjod-di, s., kunstwol c. a., prullig

shoe, sjoe, s., schoen c.; (horse) hoefijzer n. **v.,**

(horse) beslaan; ——**black**, s., schoenpoetser c.; ——**horn**, schoenlepel c.; ——**maker**, schoenmaker c.; ——**polish**, schoenpoets c.

shoot, sjoet, v., schieten; (kill) doodschieten; (bud) uitschieten. s., (hunt) jachtpartij c.; (sprout) scheut c.; ——**ing**, s., schieten n.; ——**ing-star**, vallende ster c.

shop, sjop, s., winkel c.; (workshop) werkplaats c. v., winkelen; ——**keeper**, s., winkelier c.; ——**ping**, winkelen n.; ——**walker**, winkelchef c.

shore, sjoar, s., kust c., oever c. v., stutten

short, sjoart, a., kort; (small) klein; (curt) kortaf; ——**age**, s., tekort n.; ——**en**, v., verkorten; ——**hand**, s., stenografie c.; ——**ly**, adv. (soon) spoedig; (curtly) kortaf; ——**ness**, s., kortheid c.; ——**sighted**, a., bijziend; (fig.) kortzichtig

shot, sjot, s., schot n.; (pellet) hagel c.; (billiards) stoot c.; (football) schop c.; (marksman) scherpschutter c.

shoulder, sjool-d'r, s., schouder c. v., (push) met de schouder duwen; ——**strap**, s., schouderband c.

shout, sjaut, s., schreeuw c. v., schreeuwen

shove, sjav, s., stoot c., duw c. v., stoten

shovel, sjav-v'l, s., schop c. v., scheppen

show, sjo, s., (spectacle) vertoning c.; (exhibition) tentoonstelling c. v., laten zien; —— **in**, binnen laten; ——**room**, s., toonzaal c.; ——**y**, a., opzichtig

shower, sjau-ur, s., bui c.; ——**bath**, stortbad n., douche c.; ——**y**, a., buiig, regenachtig

shred, sjred, s., stukje n. v., versnipperen

shrew, sjroe, s., feeks c.

shrewd, sjroed, a., schrander

shriek, sjriek, s., gil c. v., gillen

shrill, sjril, a., schel. v., schel klinken

shrimp, sjrimp, s., garnaal c.; (fig.) peuter c.

shrine, sjrain, s., relikwieënkastje n.; heiligdom n.

shrink, sjringk, v., krimpen; —— **at**, huiveren voor; —— **back**, terugdeinzen

shrivel, sjriv-v'l, ——— up, v., verschrompelen
shroud, sjraud, s., doodkleed n. v., omhullen [c.
Shrove Tuesday, sjroov-tjoez-di, s., vastenavond
shrub, sjrab, s., struik c.; ——— bery, bosje n.
shrug, sjraG, v., (shoulders) de schouders ophalen
shudder, sjad-d'r, s., huivering c. v., huiveren
shuffle, sjaf-f'l, v., (gait) sloffen; (cards) schudden
shun, sjan, v., vermijden, schuwen
shunt, sjant, v., (train) rangeren
shut, sjat, v., sluiten, dichtdoen; ——ter, s., blind n.; (photo) sluiter c.
shuttle, sjat-t'l, s., (sewing) schuitje n.
shy, sjai, a., schuw; (horse) schichtig. v., schichtig worden; ——ness, s., schuwheid c.
sick, sik, a., ziek; misselijk; beu; ——en, v., ziek worden; misselijk worden; ——ly, a., ziekelijk; ——ness, s., ziekte c.
sickle, sik-k'l, s., sikkel c.
side, said, s., zijde c., kant c. v., partij kiezen;
——board, s., buffet n.; ——car, zijspan n.; ——slip, slippen n. v., slippen; ——ways, adv., zijwaarts; on the one ———, enerzijds; on the other ———, anderzijds
siding, sai-ding, s., zijspoor n., wisselspoor n.
siege, siedzj, s., beleg n., belegering c.
sieve, siv, s., zeef c. v., zeven, ziften
sift, sift, v., ziften; (scrutinize) onderzoeken
sigh, sai, s., zucht c. v., zuchten
sight, sait, v., te zien krijgen; (aim) mikken. s., gezicht n.; (spectacle) schouwspel n.; (gun) vizier n.; at first ———, op het eerste gezicht; by ———, van aanzien; ——s, s.pl., bezienswaardigheden c.pl.
sign, sain, s., teken n.; (board) uithangbord n. v., ondertekenen; ——post, s., handwijzer c.
signal, siG-n'l, s., sein n.; signaal n. v., seinen
signature, siG-ne-tsjur, s., handtekening c.
significant, siG-nif-fi-k'nt, a., betekenisvol
signification, siG-ni-fi-kee-sjun, s., betekenis c.
signify, siG-ni-fai, v., aanduiden; (mean) betekenen

silence, sai-l'ns, s., stilte c. **v.,** tot zwijgen brengen

silent, sai-l'nt, a., stil, zwijgend

silk, silk, s., zijde c.; ——**en, a.,** zijden; (like silk) zacht als zij; ——**worm, s.,** zijderups c.

sill, sil, s., (door) drempel c.; (window) vensterbank c.

silly, sil-li, a., onnozel, dwaas, dom

silver, sil-v'r, s., zilver n. **a.,** zilveren. **v.,** verzilveren

similar, sim-mi-l'r, a., gelijk; —— **to,** gelijkend op

similarity, si-mi-ler-ri-ti, s., gelijkheid c.

simile, sim-mi-li, s., vergelijking c.

simmer, sim-m'r, v., zachtjes koken

simple, sim-p'l, a., gewoon; ——**minded,** eenvoudig

simplicity, sim-plis-si-ti, s., eenvoud c. [voudig

simplify, sim-pli-fai, v., vereenvoudigen

simultaneous, si-mul-teen-jus, a., gelijktijdig

sin, sin, s., zonde c. **v.,** zondigen; ——**ful, a.,** zondig; ——**less,** zondeloos; ——**ner, s.,** zondaar c.

since, sins, adv. & prep., sedert. **conj.,** aangezien

sincere, sin-sier, a., oprecht; (genuine) echt

sinew, sin-joe, s., pees c.; ——**s, pl.,** spierkracht c.

sing, sing, v., zingen; ——**er, s.,** zanger c.

singe, sindzj, v., schroeien

single, sing-G'l, a., enkel; (unmarried) ongetrouwd. **s.,** (ticket) enkele reis c.; ——**-handed, a.,** alleen, zonder hulp; —— **out, v.,** uitkiezen

singly, sing-Gli, adv., afzonderlijk; alleen

singular, sing-Gjoe-l'r, a., enkelvoudig. **s.,** enkelvoud n.

sinister, sin-nis-t'r, a., onheilspellend

sink, singk, v., zinken; (cause to sink) tot zinken brengen; (a well) boren. **s.,** gootsteen c.

sip, sip, s., teugje n. **v.,** met kleine teugjes drinken

siphon, sai-f'n, s., hevel c. **v.,** hevelen

sir, seur, s., mijnheer c.; (title) Sir c.

siren, sai-r'n, s., sirene c.

sirloin, seur-loin, s., lendestuk n.

sister, sis-t'r, s., zuster c.

sister-in-law, sis-t'r-in-loa, s., schoonzuster c.

sit, sit, v., zitten; (hatch) broeden; —— **down,** gaan zitten; ——**ting,** s., (session) zitting c.; (eggs for hatching) broedeieren n.pl.; ——**ting-room,** huiskamer c.

site, sait, s., (building) bouwterrein n.

situated, sit-joe-ee-tid, a., gelegen

situation, sit-joe-ee-sjun, s., situatie c.; (location) plaats c., ligging c.

six, siks, a., zes; ——**teen,** zestien; ——**teenth,** zestiende; ——**th,** zesde; ——**tieth,** zestigste; ——**ty,** zestig

size, saiz, s., grootte c.; (measure) maat c.; (dimensions) afmetingen c.pl.; (glue) lijmwater n. v., sorteren; (glue) lijmen

skate, skeet, v., schaatsenrijden. s., schaats c.; (fish) vleet c.

skater, skee-t'r, s., schaatsenrijder c.

skein, skeen, s., (thread, yarn) streng c.

skeleton, skel-li-t'n, s., geraamte n.

sketch, sketsj, s., schets c. v., schetsen

skewer, skjoe-ur, s., vleespen c. v., vaststeken

skid, skid, v., (car) slippen. s., slippen n.

skiff, skif, s., skiff n.

skilful, skil-foel, a., handig, bekwaam

skill, skil, s., handigheid c., bekwaamheid c.

skim, skim, v., afschuimen; (cream) afromen

skin, skin, s., huid c., vel n.; (peel) schil c. v., (flay) villen; (peel) schillen

skip, skip, v., huppelen; (omit) overslaan

skipper, skip-p'r, s., schipper c.

skirmish, skeur-misj, s., schermutseling c.

skirt, skeurt, s., rok c.; (edge) rand c.

skittle, skit-t'l, s., kegel c.; ——s, pl., kegelspel n.

skull, skol, s., schedel c.

skunk, skangk, s., stinkdier n.; (fig.) smeerlap c.

sky, skai, s., lucht c.; (firmament) hemel c.; ——**light,** dakraam n.; ——**scraper,** wolkenkrabber c.

slab, sleb, s., (marble) plaat c.; (stone) platte steen c.

slack, slek, s., (trade) slapte c. a., slap; (tardy) traag

slacken, slek-'n, v., verslappen; (pace) vertragen

slam, slem, v., hard dichtslaan. s., harde slag c.

slander, slen-d'r, s., laster c. v., lasteren

slanderer, slen-d'r-'r, s., lasteraar c.

slang, sleng, s., gemeenzame taal c.

slant, slaant, s., helling c. v., hellen; (cause to slant) doen hellen; ——ing, a., schuin

slap, slep, v., een klap geven. s., klap c.

slash, slesj, s., houw c., snee c.; (slit) split n. v., houwen; (lash) slaan

slate, sleet, s., lei c. a., leien; (colour) leikleurig. v., met leien dekken; ——pencil, s., griffel c.

slaughter, sloa-t'r, s., slachten n. v., slachten; (massacre) vermoorden; ——er, s., slachter c.; ——house, slachthuis n.

slave, sleev, s., slaaf c.; (female) slavin c. v., slaven, zwoegen; ——ry, s., slavernij c.

slay, slee, v., doden, doodslaan, slachten

sledge, sledzj, s., slede c. v., sleeën; (convey) per slede vervoeren; ——hammer, s., voorhamer c.

sleek, sliek, a., glad, zacht; (oily) zalvend

sleep, sliep, v., slapen. s., slaap c.; ——ing-car, slaapwagen c.; ——less, a., slapeloos; ——lessness, s., slapeloosheid c.; ——y, a., slaperig

sleet, sliet, s., natte sneeuw c., natte hagel c.

sleeve, sliev, s., mouw c.; (mech.) mof c.

sleigh, slee, s., arreslede c. v., arren

sleight, slait, s., —— of hand, goochelarij c.

slender, slen-d'r, a., slank; (scanty) schraal

slice, slais, s., (bread) sneetje n.; (ham, etc.) schijfje n.; (share) part n. v., in sneetjes snijden

slide, slaid, s., (ice) glijbaan c.; (microscope) glaasje n. v., glijden; (slip) uitglijden

slight, slait, s., geringschatting c. a., (slender) tenger; (insignificant) onbeduidend. v., geringschatten [doen

slim, slim, a., slank. v., een vermageringskuur

slime, slaim, s., (mud) slib c.; (snails) slijm n.

slimy, slai-mi, a., glibberig; (filthy) vuil

sling, sling, s., slinger c. v., slingeren

slink (away), slingk (e-wee), v., wegsluipen

slip, slip, v., uitglijden; ——pery, a., glad

slipper, slip-p'r, s., pantoffel c., slof c.

slit, slit, s., spleet c. v., splijten

sloe, slo, s., sleepruim c.

slop, slop, v., morsen; ——s, s.pl., waswater n.

slope, sloop, s., helling c. v., glooien

slot, slot, s., gleuf c.; (track) spoor n.

sloth, slooth, s., luiheid c.; (animal) luiaard c.

slouch, slautsj, v., slungelen. s., slungelige gang c.

slough, slau, s., poel c., moeras n.

slovenly, slav-v'n-li, a., slonzig, slordig

slow, slo, a., langzaam; **to be** ——, v., (watch) achter zijn; ——**train,** s., boemeltrein c.

slug, slaG, s., naakte slak c.; ——**gard,** luilak c.

sluggish, slaG-Gisj, a., lui, traag

sluice, sloes, s., sluis c.; (water) sluiswater n.

sluice-gate, sloes-Geet, s., sluisdeur c.

slum, slam, s., achterbuurt c., slop n. [c.

slumber, slam-b'r, v., sluimeren. s., sluimering

slump, slamp, s., plotselinge sterke daling c.

slur, sleur, v., onduidelijk uitspreken. s., vlek c.

slush, slasj, s., modderige sneeuw c.

slut, slat, s., slons c., sloerie c.

sly, slai, a., sluw; (roguish) schalks

smack, smek, s., (slap) **klap** c.; (boat) smak c. v., (slap) slaan; (lips) smakken met

small, smoal, a., klein; (petty) gering

smallpox, smoal-poks, s., pokken c.pl.

smart, smaart, a., (keen) scherp; (clever) gevat; (spruce) net gekleed. v., pijn doen

smash, smesj, s., (collision) botsing c.; (commercial) bankroet n. v., verbrijzelen; ruïneren

smattering, smet-te-ring, s., oppervlakkige kennis c.

smear, smier, s., vlek c. v., insmeren; (soil) besmeuren

smell, smel, s., reuk c. v., ruiken; stinken; ——**ing-salts,** s.pl., reukzout n.

smelt, smelt, v., smelten. s., (fish) spiering c.
smile, smail, s., glimlach c. v., glimlachen
smite, smait, v., slaan; (afflict) kwellen
smoke, smook, s., rook c. v., roken; ——less, a., rookloos; ——r, s., roker c.
smoky, smo-ki, a., rokerig, walmend [strijken
smooth, smoedh, a., glad; (soft) zacht. v., glad-
smother, smadh-ur, v., verstikken. s., walm c.
smoulder, smool-d'r, v., smeulen. s., smeulen n
smudge, smadzj, s., vlek c.; smet c. v., bevlekken
smug, smaG, a., zelfvoldaan
smuggle, smaG-G'l, v., smokkelen
smuggler, smaG-Gl'r, s., smokkelaar c.
smut, smat, s., roetvlek c.; ——ty, a., vuil
snack, snek, s., lichte maaltijd c.
snail, sneel, s., huisjesslak c.
snake, sneek, s., slang c.
snap, snep, v., (break) afknappen; (crack) knap-pen; (bite) happen; (snarl) snauwen. s., knak c.; hap c.; snauw c.
snapshot, snep-sjot, s., kiek c.
snare, snèr, s., strik c. v., verstrikken
snarl, snaarl, v., snauwen; (growl) grommen
snatch, snetsj, s., greep c.; (short spell) ogenblikje n. v., grijpen; ——at, grijpen naar
sneak, sniek, s., gluiperd c. v., gluipen; (creep) kruipen; ——away, wegsluipen; ——y, a., gluiperig
sneer, snier, v., grijnslachen. s., grijns c.
sneeze, sniez, v., niezen. s., niezen n.
sniff, snif, v., snuffelen, opsnuiven
snip, snip, v., afsnijden, afknippen
snipe, snaip, s., snip c.; ——r, sluipschutter c.
snob, snob, s., poen c.; —**bish,** a., poenig
snore, snoar, v., snurken. s., gesnurk n.
snort, snoart, v., snuiven. s., gesnuif n.
snout, snaut, s., snuit c., snoet c.
snow, sno, s., sneeuw c. v., sneeuwen; —**drop,** s., sneeuwklokje n.; —**flake,** sneeuwvlok c.
snub, snab, v., afsnauwen. s., snauw c. a., stomp
snub-nose, snab-nooz, s., stompneus c.
snuff, snaf, s., snuifje n. v., snuiven

snug, snᴀɢ, a., gezellig, knus, behaaglijk
so, so, adv., zo, aldus, zodanig. conj., dus, derhalve
soak, sook, v., weken; (drench) doornat maken
soap, soop, s., zeep c. v., inzepen
soar, soar, v., omhoog vliegen, zich verheffen
sob, sob, v., snikken. s., snik c.
sober, so-b'r, a., sober; (sane) verstandig
sociable, so-sje-b'l, a., gezellig [n.
social, so-sjul, a., sociaal; ——**ism,** s., socialisme
society, se-sai-e-ti, s., maatschappij c.; genootschap n.
sock, sok, s., sok c.; (sole) losse binnenzool c.
socket, sok-kit, s., (mech.) sok c., mof c.; (eye)
kas c.
sod, sod, s., zode c.
soda, so-da, s., soda c.; ——**water,** spuitwater n.
soft, soft, a., zacht; ——**en,** v., zacht maken;
zacht worden; ——**ness,** s., zachtheid c.
soil, soil, s., grond c., land n.; (stain) smet c.
v., besmetten; bevuilen
sojourn, sod-zjeurn, s., tijdelijke verblijfplaats c.
v., tijdelijk verblijven
solace, sol-lis, s., troost c. v., troosten
solder, sol-d'r, v., solderen. s., soldeersel n.
soldier, sool-dzjur, s., soldaat c.
sole, sool, s., zool c.; (fish) tong c. v., zolen. a.,
enig, enkel
solemn, sol-lum, a., plechtig; (serious) ernstig
solicit, se-lis-sit, v., vragen; lastig vallen
solicitor, se-lis-si-t'r, s., rechtskundig adviseur c.
solicitude, se-lis-si-tjoed, s., bezorgdheid c.
solid, sol-lid, a., (firm) stevig; (sound) degelijk
solidify, se-lid-di-fai, v., vast maken; vast worden
solitary, sol-li-te-ri, a., eenzaam; (single) enkel
solitude, sol-li-tjoed, s., eenzaamheid c.
soluble, sol-joe-b'l, a., oplosbaar
solution, se-ljoe-sjun, s., oplossing c.
solve, solv, v., oplossen
solvency, sol-v'n-si, s., solvabiliteit c.
solvent, sol-v'nt, a., solvent; oplossend
sombre, som-b'r, a., somber, donker
some, sᴀm, pron., iets, wat; enige, sommige.

a., de een of ander; een zekere; (a little) een beetje. adv., (about) ongeveer; ——body, s., iemand; ——how, adv., op de een of andere wijze; ——thing, s., iets; ——times, adv., soms; ——what, enigszins; ——where, ergens

somersault, sam-m'r-soalt, s., salto mortale c.

somnambulist, som-nem-bjoe-list, s., slaap-wandelaar c.

son, san, s., zoon c.; ——in-law, schoonzoon c.

sonata, se-na-ta, s., sonate c.

song, song, s., lied n.; (bird) gezang n.

soon, soen, adv., spoedig; as —— as, zodra

soot, soet, s., roet n. v., met roet bedekken

soothe, soedh, v., kalmeren, verzachten

sorcerer, soar-se-r'r, s., tovenaar c.

sorcery, soar-se-ri, s., toverij c., hekserij c.

sordid, soar-did, a., smerig; (mean) gemeen

sore, soar, s., pijnlijke plek c. a., pijnlijk

sorrel, sor-r'l, s., zuring c. a., rossig

sorrow, sor-ro, s., smart c. v., treuren

sorrowful, sor-ro-foel, a., treurig, droevig

sorry, sor-ri, a., bedroefd; (paltry) armzalig; I am ——, 't spijt me

sort, soart, s., soort c. v., sorteren

soul, sool, s., ziel c.

sound, saund, s., geluid n., klank c. v., klinken, weerklinken. a., (healthy) gezond; (thorough) grondig. adv., (asleep) vast; ——film, s., geluidsfilm c.

soundings, saun-dingz, s.pl., (naut.) diepten c.pl.

soup, soep, s., soep c.

sour, saur, a., zuur; (peevish) nors

source, soars, s., bron c.; (origin) oorsprong c.

south, sauth, s., zuiden n. a. & adv., zuidelijk

southerly, sadh-ur-li, a., & adv., zuidelijk

souvenir, soe-ve-nier, s., souvenir n.

sovereign, sov-vrin, s., heerser c., opperheer c. a., oppermachtig; (supreme) hoogst; (effective) probaat

sow, so, v., zaaien; ——er, s., zaaier c.

sow, sau, s., zeug c.

space, spees, s., ruimte c.; (time) tijdruimte c.

spacious, spee-sjus, a., wijd, ruim

spade, speed, s., spade c., schop c.; (cards) schoppen c.

span, spen, s., span c.; (plane) vleugelbreedte c.; (bridge) spanwijdte c. v., overspannen

spangle, speng-G'l, s., lovertje n.

spaniel, spen-jul, s., spaniel c., patrijshond c.

spanner, spen-n'r, s., schroefsleutel c.

spar, spaar, v., boksen. s., (naut.) rondhout n.

spare, spèr, v., sparen; (dispense with) 't stellen zonder. a., (meagre) schraal; (left over) overtollig; —— **part,** s., reservedeel n.; —— **room,** logeerkamer c.; —— **time,** vrije tijd c.

sparing, spèr-ing, a., (frugal) zuinig

spark, spaark, s., vonk c. v., vonken

sparking-plug, spaar-king-plaG, s., bougie c.

sparkle, spaar-k'l, v., fonkelen; (wine) parelen. s., gefonkel n.; (glitter) glans c.

sparrow, sper-ro, s., mus c.; ——**hawk,** sperspasm, spezm, s., kramp c.; (fig.) vlaag c. [wer c.

spasmodic, spez-mod-dik, a., krampachtig

spats, spets, s.pl., slobkousen c. pl.

spatter, spet-t'r, v., bespatten

spawn, spoan, s., kuit c. v., kuit schieten

speak, spiek, v., spreken; ——**er,** s., spreker c.

spear, spier, s., speer c., lans c. v., spietsen

special, spes-sjul, a., bijzonder; extra; ——**ity,** s., specialiteit c.; —— **train,** extra trein c.

specie, spie-sjie, s., baar goud n.; ——**s,** soort c.

specification, spes-si-fi-kee-sjun, s., nauwkeurige opgave c.

specify, spes-si-fai, v., specificeren [n.

specimen, spes-si-min, s., voorbeeld n., staaltje

specious, spie-sjus, a., schoonschijnend

speck, spek, s., vlekje n., spikkel c. v., vlekken

spectacle, spek-te-k'l, s., schouwspel n.

spectacles, spek-te-k'ls, s.pl., bril c.

spectator, spek-tee-t'r, s., toeschouwer c.

spectre, spek-t'r, s., spook n.

speculate, spek-joe-leet, v., peinzen; (bank) speculeren

speech, spietsj, s., spraak c.; (address) toespraak c.; ——less, a., sprakeloos; (dumb) stom
speed, spied, s., spoed c., snelheid c. v., snellen
speedy, spie-di, a., snel; (quick) spoedig
spell, spel, v., spellen. s., betovering c.
spend, spend, v., (money) uitgeven; (time) doorbrengen; (squander) verkwisten; ——thrift, s., verkwister c.
sphere, sfier, s., bol c.; (globe) globe c.; (extent) omvang c.; (area) gebied n.
spice, spais, s., specerij c. v., kruiden
spicy, spai-si, a., gekruid; (fig.) pittig
spider, spai-d'r, s., spin c.
spike, spaik, s., ijzeren punt c. v., vastspijkeren
spill, spil, v., (milk) morsen; (blood) vergieten
spin, spin, v., spinnen; ——ning-wheel, s., spinnewiel n.
spinach, spin-nitsj, s., spinazie c.
spinal, spai-n'l, a., ruggegraats . . .
spindle, spin-d'l, s., spoel c.; (shaft) spil c.
spine, spain, s., ruggegraat c.
spinster, spin-st'r, s., oude vrijster c.
spiral, spai-r'l, a., spiraalvormig. s., spiraal c.
spire, spair, s., (church) torenspits c.
spirit, spir-rit, s., geest c.; (vitality) levenslust c.; (courage) moed c.; (alcohol) sterke drank c.; ——ed, a., levendig; (courageous) moedig; ——ual, geestelijk; ——ualist, s., spiritist c.
spit, spit, v., spuwen. s., braadspit n.
spite, spait, s., wrok c. v., ergeren; ——ful, a., kwaadaardig; **in** —— **of,** conj., ondanks, trots
spittle, spit-t'l, s., speeksel n., spuug n.
spittoon, spit-toen, s., kwispedoor n. & c.
splash, splesj, v., bespatten. s., geplas n.
splendid, splen-did, a., schitterend, prachtig
splendour, splen-d'r, s., pracht c., praal c.
splint, splint, s., (med.) spalk c. v., spalken
splinter, splin-t'r, s., splinter c. v., versplinteren
split, split, v., splijten. s., spleet c.
spoil, spoil, v., bederven; (plunder) roven
spoils, spoilz, s.pl., buit c.
spoke, spook, s., spaak c.

spokesman, spooks-m'n, s., woordvoerder c.
sponge, spa**ndzj,** s., spons c. v., afsponsen
sponsor, spon-s'r, s., borg c.; (baptism) peter c.
spontaneous, spon-teen-jus, a., spontaan
spool, spoel, s., spoel c.; klos c.
spoon, spoen, s., lepel c.; **——ful,** lepelvol c.
sport, spoart, s., sport c.; (fun) pret c.; **——ive,**
a., vrolijk, speels; **——sman,** s., sportlief-
hebber c.
spot, spot, s., (stain) vlek c.; (place) plekje n.
v., bevlekken; (detect) ontdekken
spotless, spot-les, a., smetteloos
spout, spaut, s., (gutter) goot c.; (vessel) tui c.;
(jet) straal c. v., spuiten, gutsen
sprain, spreen, v., verstuiken; s., verstuiking c.
sprat, spret, s., sprot c.
sprawl, sproal, v., nonchalant liggen
spray, spree, s., (branch) takje n.; (water) stuif-
water n. v., besproeien; **——er,** s., sproeier c.
spread, spred, v., spreiden; (be extended) zich
uitstrekken; (news) verspreiden; (on bread)
smeren [n.
sprig, sprig, s., (twig) twijgje n.; (nail) spijkertje
sprightly, sprait-li, a., levendig, opgewekt
spring, spring, s., (season) lente c.; (leap) sprong
c.; (water) bron c.; (metal) veer c. v.,
springy, spring-i, a., veerkrachtig [springen
sprinkle, spring-k'l, v., besprenkelen
sprout, spraut, s., spruitje n. v., uitspruiten
spur, speur, s., spoor c. v., aansporen
spurious, spjoe-ri-us, a., vals, onecht
spurn, speurn, v., wegtrappen. s., verachting c.
spy, spai, s., spion c. v., spionneren
squabble, skwob-b'l, v., kibbelen. s., gekibbel n.
squad, skwod, s., groep c.; **——ron,** (mil.) eska-
dron n.; (naval) eskader n.; (air) escadrille c.
squalid, skwol-lid, a., smerig; (base) gemeen
squall, skwoal, s., windvlaag c. v., gillen
squalor, skwol-l'r, s., vuil n., vuilheid c.
squander, skwon-d'r, v., verkwisten
square, skwèr, a., vierkant. s., vierkant n.; (in
town) plein n.

squash, skwosj, v., verpletteren. s., gedrang n.

squat, skwot, v., hurken. a., (dumpy) gedrongen

squeak, skwiek, v., piepen. s., gepiep n.

squeeze, skwiez, v., uitknijpen; (extort) afpersen

squint, skwint, v., scheel zien. a., scheel

squirrel, skwir-r'l, s., eekhoorn c.

squirt, skweurt, v., spuiten. s., spuit c.

stab, steb, v., doorsteken. s., steek c.

stability, ste-bil-li-ti, s., stabiliteit c.

stable, stee-b'l, s., stal c. a., stabiel, vast

stack, stek, s., (heap) hoop c.; (hay) mijt c.; (chimney) schoorsteen c. v., opstapelen

staff, staaf, s., staf c.; (pole) stok c.

stag, steG, s., mannetjeshert n.

stage, steedzj, s., (theatre) toneel n.; (period) fase c.

stagger, steG-G'r, v., wankelen; versteld doen

stagnate, steG-neet, v., stilstaan [staan

staid, steed, a., ernstig, bezadigd

stain, steen, s., (blot) vlek c.; (character) schande c. v., bevlekken; beitsen; ——less, a., smetteloos; (steel) roestvrij

stair, stèr, s., trede c.; ——s, pl., trap c.

stake, steek, s., paal c.; (punishment) brandstapel c.; (wager) inzet c. v., afbakenen; (wager) verwedden

stale, steel, a., (bread) oudbakken; (liquor) verschaald

stalk, stoak, s., stengel c. v., statig stappen

stall, stoal, s., (booth) kraam c.; (theatre) box c.

stalwart, stoal-wurt, a., flink, fors

stamina, stem-mi-na, s., uithoudingsvermogen

stammer, stem-m'r, v., stotteren [n.

stammerer, stem-m'r-'r, s., stotteraar c.

stamp, stemp, s., stempel c.; (postage) postzegel c. v., stempelen; (letter) frankeren; (foot) stampen

stampede, stem-pied, s., wilde vlucht c.

stand, stend, s., stand c.; (stop) halte c.; (resistance) weerstand c. v., staan; (endure) verdragen; ——ing, s., stand c., rang c. a. blijvend; ——ing-room, s., staanplaats c.

standard, sten-durd, s., (flag) vaandel n.; (criterion) maatstaf c.; (school) klasse c. a., standaard . . .

standstill, stend-stil, s., stilstand c.

staple, stee-p'l, a., voornaamste. s., kram c.

star, staar, s., ster c.

starry, staar-ri, a., met sterren bezaaid

starboard, staar-board, s., stuurboord n.

starch, staartsj, s., stijfsel n. v., stijven

stare, stèr, v., staren. s., starende blik c.

starling, staar-ling, s., spreeuw c.

start, staart, s., begin n.; (shock) schok c. v., beginnen; (alarm) ontstellen; (set out) vertrekken; (motor) aanzetten

startle, staar-t'l, v., doen schrikken

starvation, staar-vee-sjun, s., verhongering c.

starve, staarv, v., honger lijden

state, steet, v., opgeven, mededelen. s., staat c.; (condition) toestand c.; (pomp) staatsie c.; ——ly, a., statig; ——ment, s., verklaring c.; (account) uiteenzetting c.; ——sman, staatsman c.

station, stee-sjun, s., (railway) station n.; (position) rang c.; (place) plaats c. v., plaatsen

stationary, stee-sje-ne-ri, a., stationnair, vast

stationer, stee-sje-n'r, s., handelaar in schrijfbehoeften c.; ——y, schrijfbehoeften c.pl.

statistics, ste-tis-tiks, s.pl., statistiek c.

statue, stet-joe, s., standbeeld n.

statute, stet-joet, s., verordening c.; (law) wet c.

staunch, stoansj, a., sterk, hecht; (loyal) trouw

stave, steev, s., duig c.; —— in, v., indrukken

stay, stee, s., verblijf n. v., (remain) blijven

stead, sted, s., plaats c.; **in** —— **of,** in plaats van

steadfast, sted-faast, a., standvastig, trouw

steady, sted-di, a., (firm) vast; (constant) standvastig; (weather) bestendig. interj., kalmpjes!

steak, steek, s., runderlapje n.

steal, stiel, v., stelen

stealth, stelth, s., heimelijkheid c.; **by** ——, heimelijk

steam, stiem, s., stoom c.; ——**er, stoomboot** c.

steel, stiel, s., staal n. a., stalen, van staal

steep, stiep, a., steil. v., (soak) indopen

steeple, stie-p'l, s., spitse toren c.

steer, stier, v., sturen. s., stierkalf n., var c.

steerage, stie-ridzj, s., tussendek n.

stem, stem, s., stengel c.; (ship) boeg c. v., stuiten

stench, stensj, s., stank c.

step, step, v., stappen. s., stap c.; (stair) trede c.; ——**father,** stiefvader c.; ——**mother,** stiefmoeder c.

sterile, ster-rail, a., onvruchtbaar

sterilize, ster-ri-laiz, v., onvruchtbaar maken

sterling, steur-ling, a., echt, onvervalst

stern, steurn, a., streng, hard. s., achtersteven c.

stevedore, stie-vi-doar, s., stuwadoor c.

stew, stjoe, v., stoven. s., gestoofd vlees n.

steward, stjoe-wurd, s., (estate) rentmeester c.; (ship) hofmeester c.; (plane) steward c.

stick, stik, s., stok c. v., (pierce) doorsteken; (fasten) vastmaken; (adhere) kleven

sticky, stik-ki, a., kleverig

stiff, stif, a., stijf; stroef; ——**en,** v., stijf maken

stifle, stai-f'l, v., stikken; doen stikken

stigmatize, stiG-me-taiz, v., brandmerken

stile, stail, s., (step) overstap c.; (door) stijl c.

still, stil, v., stillen, kalmeren. a., stil. adv., nog, nog altijd; (yet) toch. s., distilleerketel c.

stimulate, stim-mjoe-leet, v., aansporen, aanzetten

sting, sting, v., steken; (nettle) branden. s., steek c.; stekel c.

stingy, stin-dzji, a., vrekkig, gierig

stink, stingk, v., stinken. s., stank c.

stint, stint, v., karig zijn met [n.

stipend, stai-p'nd, s., bezoldiging c., stipendium

stipulate, stip-joe-leet, v., bedingen, bepalen

stipulation, stip-joe-lee-sjun, s., bediging c.

stir, steur, v., roeren; (rouse) opwekken

stirrup, stir-r'p, s., stijgbeugel c.

stitch, stitsj, v., stikken; (sew) naaien. s., steek c.

stock, stok, s., (tree) stam c.; (gun) lade c.; (family) geslacht n.; (fund) fonds n.; (flower) violier c.; (store) voorraad c. v., (store) inslaan; (supply) voorzien; —— **book**, s., magazijnboek n.; ——**broker**, effectenmakelaar c.; ——**exchange**, effectenbeurs c.; ——**s**, pl., effecten n.pl.

stocking, stok-king, s., kous c.

stoke, stook, v., stoken; ——**r**, s., stoker c.

stolid, stol-lid, a., flegmatisch; (slow) traag

stomach, stǎm-muk, s., maag c.; ——**ache**, maagpijn c.

stone, stoon, s., steen c.; (fruit) pit c. v., stenigen; (fruit) van pitten ontdoen

stool, stool, s., kruk c.; (feet) voetenbankje n.

stoop, stoep, v., zich bukken; (fig.) zich verlagen

stop, stop, v., stoppen; (tooth) plomberen; (obstruct) versperren; (salary) inhouden; (work) staken; (halt) blijven staan; (cease) ophouden; (remain) blijven. s., pauze c.; (obstruction) belemmering c.; (punctuation) leesteken n.; —— **up**, v., verstoppen; ——**per**, s., stop c.

storage, stoa-ridzj, s., opberging c.

store, stoar, s., voorraad c.; (shop) magazijn n. v., inslaan

stork, stoark, s., ooievaar c.

storm, stoarm, s., storm c. v., stormen

stormy, stoarm-mi, a., stormachtig

story, stoa-ri, s., (floor) verdieping c.; (narrative) verhaal n.; (untruth) leugentje n.

story-book, stoa-ri-boek, s., vertelselboek n.

stout, staut, a., (strong) stevig; (corpulent) dik

stove, stoov, s., kachel c.; (range) fornuis n.

stow, stov, v., leggen, bergen

stowaway, sto-e-wee, s., verstekeling c.

straggle, streG-G'l, v., (wander away) afdwalen

straight, street, a., recht; (honest) eerlijk. adv., rechtuit; (directly) rechtstreeks; ——**en**, v., recht maken; ——**forward**, a., oprecht

strain, streen, v., spannen; (distort) verdraaien; (muscle) verrekken; (filter) filtreren. s., spanning c.; verdraaiing c.; verrekking c.; (tune) melodie c.

strainer, stree-n'r, s., vergiet n.

strait, street, a., nauw; ——s, s.pl., zeestraat c.

strand, strend, s., strand n.; (hair) haarlok c.; (rope) streng c. v., laten stranden

strange, streendzj, a., vreemd; (odd) zonderling

stranger, streen-dzjur, s., vreemdeling c.

strangle, **streng**-G'l, v., worgen

strap, strep, s., riem c. v., vastmaken

straw, stroa, s., stro n.; ——berry, aardbei c.

stray, stree, v., afdwalen. s., verdwaald dier n.

streak, striek, s., streep c.; ——y, a., gestreept

stream, striem, s., stroom c. v., stromen

street, striet, s., straat c.

strength, strength, s., kracht c., macht c.

strengthen, streng-th'n, v., versterken

strenuous, stren-joe-us, a., krachtig, energiek

stress, stres, s., (pressure) druk c.; (tension) spanning c.; (emphasis) nadruk c. v., de nadruk leggen op

stretch, stretsj, v., uitstrekken; (be extended) zich uitstrekken. s., uitgestrektheid c.; (effort) inspanning c.

stretcher, stretsj-'r, s., draagbaar c.

strew, stroe, v., strooien, uitstrooien

strict, strikt, a., strikt, stipt; (severe) streng

stride, straid, v., schrijden. s., schrede c.

strife, straif, s., twist c., strijd c.

strike, straik, v., (hit) slaan; (match) aansteken; (lightning) inslaan; (cease work) staken. s., staking c.; —— out, v., (delete) doorhalen

striker, **straik**-'r, s., (of work) staker c.

string, string, s., touwtje n.; (violin) snaar c.

stringency, strin-dzj'n-si, s., strengheid c.

strip, strip, s., strook c. v., (undress) uitkleden

stripe, straip, s., streep c. v., strepen

strive, straiv, v., streven; (fight) strijden

stroke, strook, s., (blow) slag c.; (pen) haal c.; (paralysis) verlamming c. v., strelen

stroll, strool, s., wandeling c. v., kuieren

strong, strong, a., sterk; (cigar) zwaar; (butter) ranzig

strop, strop, s., scheerriem c. v., aanzetten

structure, **strakt**-sjur, s., bouw c.

struggle, straG-G'l, v., zwoegen; (contend) worstelen. s., zwoegen n.; worsteling c.

strut, strat, v., trots stappen. s., trotse gang c.

stubborn, stab-burn, a., hardnekkig, halsstarrig

stud, stad, s., (knob) knop c.; (collar) boordeknoopje n.; (breeding) stoeterij c. v., beslaan

student, stjoe-d'nt, s., student c.

studio, stjoe-di-o, s., atelier n.; (radio) studio c.

studious, stjoe-di-us, a., leergierig, vlijtig

study, stad-di, v., studeren. s., studie c.

stuff, staf, v., volstoppen; (birds) opzetten; (cooking) farceren. s., stof c.; ——ing, vulsel n.; ——y, a., bedompt

stumble, stam-b'l, v., struikelen

stump, stamp, s., (tree) stronk c.; (butt) eindje n.

stun, stan, v., bedwelmen; (amaze) verbazen

stunt, stant, a., in de groei belemmeren

stupefy, stjoe-pi-fai, v., bedwelmen; (amaze) verbluffen

stupendous, stjoe-pen-dus, a., verbazingwekkend

stupid, stjoe-pid, a., dom; ——ity, s., domheid c.

stupor, stjoe-p'r, s., bedwelming c., verdoving c.

sturdy, steur-di, a., stoer, fors, sterk

sturgeon, steur-dzjun, s., steur c.

stutter, stat-t'r, v., stotteren. s., gestotter n.

sty, stai, s., varkenshok n.; (eye) strontje n.

style, stail, s., stijl c.

stylish, stai-lisj, a., elegant, deftig

subdue, sub-djoe, v., onderwerpen; (soften) temperen; ——d, a., (tone) gedempt; (colour) zacht

subject, sab-dzjikt, v., onderwerpen. s., onderwerp n.; (national) onderdaan c.; ——ion, onderwerping c.; —— to, afhankelijk van; (liable) blootgesteld aan

subjunctive, sub-dzjangk-tiv, s., aanvoegende

sublime, se-blaim, a., verheven, subliem [wijs c.

submarine, sab-me-rien, s., onderzeeër c.

submerge, sub-meurdzj, v., onderdompelen

submission, sub-mis-sjun, s., onderwerping c.

submit, sub-mit, v., onderwerpen; (offer) voorleggen

subordinate, sub-oar-di-nit, a., ondergeschikt

subpœna, sub-pie-na, s., dagvaarding c.

subscribe, sub-skraib, v., ondertekenen; (contribute) bijdragen; (papers) zich abonneren

subscriber, sub-skraib-'r, s., ondertekenaar c.; abonnee c.

subscription, sub-skrip-sjun, s., ondertekening c.; bijdrage c.; abonnement n.

subsequent, sab-si-kw'nt, a., volgend, later

subservient, sub-seur-vi-'nt, a., dienstig

subside, sub-said, v., zinken; (abate) bedaren

subsidiary, sub-sid-je-ri, a., hulp . . .; bijkomstig

subsidy, sab-si-di, s., bijdrage c., subsidie c.

subsist, sub-sist, v., bestaan; —— on, leven van

substance, sab-st'ns, s., zelfstandigheid c.; (essence) wezen n.; (wealth) vermogen n.

substantial, sub-sten-sjul, a., wezenlijk; (solid) degelijk; (meal) stevig; (important) belangrijk

substantiate, sub-sten-sji-eet, v., (prove) bewijzen

substantive, sab-st'n-tiv, s., zelfstandig naamwoord n.

substitute, sab-sti-tjoet, s., (person) plaatsvervanger c.; (thing) surrogaat n.

subterranean, sab-te-ree-ni-'un, a., onderaards

subtle, sat-t'l, a., fijn, subtiel; (crafty) sluw

subtract, sub-trekt, v., aftrekken

suburb, sab-beurb, s., voorstad c., buitenwijk c.

subway, sab-wee, s., perrontunnel c.

succeed, suk-sied, v., (follow) komen na; (be heir to) opvolgen; (achieve) slagen

success, suk-ses, s., succes n.; —— ful, a., voorspoedig; —— ion, s., opvolging c.; —— or, opvolger c.

succour, sak-k'r, s., hulp c. v., helpen

succumb, se-kam, v., bezwijken

such, satsj, pron., degene. a., zulk, zo'n

suck, sak, v., zuigen; —— le, zogen

suction, sak-sjun, s., zuiging c.

sudden, sad-d'n, a., plotseling, onverhoeds

sue, sjoe, v., gerechtelijk vervolgen

suet, sjoe-it, s., niervet n.

suffer, saf-f'r, v., lijden; (endure) ondergaan; —— **-er** s., lijder c.; —— **-ing**, lijden n. a., lijdend

suffice, se-fais, v., voldoende zijn

sufficient, se-fis-sjunt, a., voldoende, genoeg

suffocate, saf-fe-keet, v., smoren, verstikken

suffrage, saf-fridzj, s., kiesrecht n.; (vote) stem c.

sugar, sjoe-G'r, s., suiker c.; —— **-basin**, suikerpot c.; —— **-cane**, suikerriet n.

suggest, se-dzjest, v., suggereren; (propose) voorstellen; —— **-ion**, s., suggestie c.; voorstel n.; —— **-ive**, a., suggestief

suicide, soe-i-said, s., zelfmoord c.

suit, sjoet, v., passen. s., (clothes) pak n.; (law) proces n.; —— **-able**, a., gepast; —— **-or**, s., vrijer c.

suite, swiet, s., (retinue) gevolg n.; (set) reeks c.; (furniture) ameublement n.

sulk, salk, v., pruilen; —— **-y**, a., pruilerig

sullen, sal-l'n, a., nors, knorrig

sulphur, sal-f'r, s., zwavel c.

sultry, sal-tri, a., zwoel, drukkend

sum, sam, s., som c.; —— **up**, v., optellen

summary, sam-me-ri, s., samenvatting c. a., beknopt

summer, sam-m'r, s., zomer c.

summit, sam-mit, s., top c., kruin c.   [vaarden

summon, sam-m'n, v., ontbieden; (law) dag-

summons, sam-m'ns, s., dagvaarding c.

sumptuous, samp-tjoe-us, a., kostbaar, prachtig

sun, san, s., zon c.; —— **-beam**, zonnestraal c.; —— **-dial**, zonnewijzer c.; —— **-ny**, a., zonnig; —— **-rise**, s., zonsopgang c.; —— **-set**, zonsondergang c.; —— **-shine**, zonneschijn c.; —— **-stroke**, zonnesteek c.

Sunday, san-di, s., zondag c.

sundries, san-driz, s.pl., diversen c.pl.

sundry, san-dri, a., diverse, allerlei

sunken, sang-k'n, a., (cheeks) ingevallen; (eyes) diepliggend

super, sjoe-p'r, s., (theatre) figurant c.; —— **-abundant**, a., overloedig; —— **-annuation**.

s., pensioen n.; ——cillious, a., hooghartig; ——ficial, oppervlakkig; ——fine, extrafijn; ——intend, v., toezicht houden; ——intendent, s., opzichter c.; ——natural, a., bovennatuurlijk; ——sede, v., vervangen; ——vise, het toezicht hebben over; ——vision, s., toezicht n.

superb, sjoe-peurb, a., groots, prachtig

superfluous, sjoe-peur-floe-us, a., overtollig

superior, sjoe-pie-ri-ur, s., superieur c. a., (higher) hoger; (better) beter; (upper) boven

superlative, sjoe-peur-le-tiv, s., overtreffende trap c.

superstition, sjoe-p'r-stis-sjun, s., bijgeloof n.

superstitious, sjoe-p'r-stis-sjus, a., bijgelovig

supper, sap-p'r, s., avondeten c.

supplant, se-plaant, v., verdringen

supple, sap-p'l, a., soepel; (docile) gedwee

supplement, sap-pli-m'nt, s., bijvoegsel n.

supplier, se-plai-ur, s., leverancier c.

supply, se-plai, s., levering c.; (stock) voorraad c. v., leveren; ——with, voorzien van

support, se-poart, s., (prop) stut c.; (aid) steun c. v., (sustain) ondersteunen; (endure) verduren

suppose, se-pooz, v., veronderstellen   [c.

supposition, sap-pe-zis-sjun, s., veronderstelling

suppress, se-pres, v., onderdrukken

supremacy, sjoe-prem-me-si, s., oppergezag n.

supreme, sjoe-priem, a., hoogst, opperst

surcharge, seur-tsjaardzj, v., extra laten betalen; (overload) overladen. s., (postage) opdruk c.

sure, sjoer, a., zeker; ——ty, s., (bail) borg c.

surf, seurf, s., branding c.

surface, seur-fis, s., oppervlakte c.

surge, seurdzj, v., golven. s., grote golf c.

surgeon, seur-dzjun, s., chirurg c.

surgery, seur-dzje-ri, s., heelkunde c.

surgical, seur-dzji-k'l, a., heelkundig

surly, seur-li, a., knorrig, nors

surmise, seur-maiz, v., vermoeden. s., gissing c.

surmount, seur-maunt, v., te boven komen

surname, seur-neem, s., achternaam c.

surpass, seur-**paas**, v., overtreffen

surplus, seur-plus, s., overschot n.

surprise, s'r-**praiz**, v., verrassen. s., verrassing c.

surrender, se-ren-d'r, s., (mil.) overgave c. v., zich overgeven; (cede) afstaan

surround, se-**raund**, v., omringen; (mil.) omsingelen

surroundings, se-**raund**-ings, s.pl., omgeving c.

survey, seur-**vee**, v., overzien; (land) opmeten. s., overzicht n.; opmeting c.; **——or**, landmeter c.; (inspector) opzichter c.

survival, seur-vai-v'l, s., overleving c.

survive, seur-vaiv, v., overleven

survivor, seur-vai-v'r, s., overlevende c.

susceptible, se-sep-ti-b'l, a., ontvankelijk; (sensitive) gevoelig

suspect, se-**spekt**, v., verdenken; (distrust) wantrouwen. s., verdachte c.

suspend, se-**spend**, v., ophangen; (defer) uitstellen

suspender, se-spend-'r, s., sokophouder c.

suspense, se-**spens**, s., onzekerheid c.

suspension, se-spen-sjun, s., ophanging c.; schorsing c.; uitstel n.; **——bridge**, hangbrug c.

suspicion, se-spis-sjun, s., verdenking c.

suspicious, se-spis-sjus, a., wantrouwig; verdacht

sustain, se-steen, v., (hold up) ophouden; (support) ondersteunen; (suffer) verdragen; (uphold) hooghouden

sustenance, sas-ti-n'ns, s., levensonderhoud n.

swagger, sweG-G'r, v., opscheppen. s., opschepperij c.

swallow, swol-lo, v., slikken. s., (gullet) slokdarm c.; (bird) zwaluw c.

swamp, swomp, s., moeras n. v., vol water laten lopen

swan, swon, s., zwaan c.

swarm, swoarm, s., zwarm c. v., (bees) zwermen; (throng) krioelen

sway, swee, v., (swing) zwaaien; (waver) schommelen; (influence) beïnvloeden. s., zwaai c.; schommeling c.; invloed c.

swear, swèr, v., zweren; (curse) vloeken

sweat, swet, s., zweet n. v., zweten

sweep, swiep, v., vegen. s., schoorsteenveger c.

sweeper, swie-p'r, s., veger c.

sweet, swiet, s., bonbon c., snoepje n. a., zoet; ——**bread,** s., zwezerik, c.; ——**en,** v., zoet maken; ——**heart,** s., lieveling c.; ——**meats,** pl., suikergoed n.; ——**smelling,** a., geurig

swell, swel, s., (sea) deining c. v., zwellen; ——**ing,** a., zwellend. s., (tumour) gezwel n.

swerve, sweurv, v., afwijken, afdwalen

swift, swift, a., vlug, snel

swim, swim, v., zwemmen

swindle, swin-d'l, v., zwendelen. s., zwendel c., oplichterij c.; ——**r,** oplichter c.

swine, swain, s., varken n., zwijn n.

swing, swing, s., zwaai c.; (child's) schommel c. v., zwaaien; schommelen

switch, switsj, s., (twig) takje n.; (electrical) schakelaar c. v., (train) rangeren; ——**off,** (light) uitdraaien; ——**on,** (light) aandraaien

swivel, swiv-v'l, s., wartel c.

swoon, swoen, v., bezwijmen. s., bezwijming c.

swoop (down), swoep (daun), v., neerschieten

sword, soard, s., zwaard n.

sworn, swoarn, a., beëdigd; (enemies) gezworen

syllable, sil-le-b'l, s., lettergreep c.

syllabus, sil-le-bus, s., program n., leerplan n.

symbol, sim-bul, s., symbool n., zinnebeeld n.

symmetry, sim-me-tri, s., symmetrie c.

sympathetic, sim-pe-thet-tik, a., medegevoelend

sympathize, sim-pe-thaiz, v., medegevoelen

sympathy, sim-pe-thi, s., medegevoel n.

symptom, simp-tum, s., verschijnsel n., teken n.

synchronize, sing-kre-naiz, v., (clocks) gelijkzetten

syndicate, sin-di-kit, s., syndicaat n.

synonymous, si-non-ni-mus, a., synoniem

syphilis, sif-fi-lis, s., syphilis c.
syphon, sai-f'n, s., hevel c.
syringe, sir-rindzj, s., spuit c. v., spuiten
syrup, sir-rup, s., stroop c., siroop c.
system, sis-tim, s., systeem n.; (body) gestel n.

tabernacle, teb-be-nek-k'l, s., tabernakel n.
table, tee-b'l, s., tafel c.; (list) tabel c.; ———
-cloth, tafellaken n.; ———cover, tafelkleed
n.; ———land, tafelland n.; ———spoon,
eetlepel c.
tablet, teb-blit, s., tablet n.; (memorial) gedenk-
plaat c.
tack, tek, s., (nail) spijkertje n. v., vastspijkeren;
(stitch) rijgen; (sailing) laveren
tackle, tek-k'l, s., takel c.; gerei n. v., (set to
work) aanpakken
tact, tekt, s., tact c.; ———ful, a., tactvol; ———ics,
s.pl., tactiek c.; ———less, a., tactloos
tadpole, ted-pool, s., kikkervisje n.
tag, teG, s., aanhangsel n. v., aanhechten
tail, teel, s., staart c.; (coat) slip c.
tailor, tee-l'r, s., kleermaker c.
taint, teent, s., smet c., vlek c. v., besmetten
take, teek, v., nemen; (medicine, fortress) innemen; (accept) aannemen; ——— after, aarden
naar; ——— away, wegnemen; ——— off,
afnemen
takings, tee-kingz, s.pl., ontvangsten c.pl.
tale, teel, s., verhaal n.; (fictitious) vertelsel n.
talent, tel-l'nt, s., talent n., begaafdheid c.
talk, toak, s., gesprek n. v., praten, spreken
talkative, toa-ke-tiv, a., praatziek
tall, toal, a., (tree) hoog; (man) groot
tallow, tel-lo, s., talk c., kaarsvet n.
tally, tel-li, s., kerfstok c. v., (agree) kloppen
talon, tel-l'n, s., klauw c.
tame, teem, a., tam; (docile) gedwee; (dull) saai.
v., temmen; ———ness, s., tamheid c.; ———r,
temmer c.
tamper (with), tem-p'r (widh), v., knoeien met
tan, ten, s., taankleur c. v., looien; (sunburn)

bruinen; ——ner, s., looier c.; ——nery, looierij c.

tangerine, ten-dzje-rien, s., mandarijntje n.
tangible, ten-dzji-b'l, a., voelbaar, tastbaar
tangle, teng-G'l, s., verwarring c. v., verwarren
tank, tengk, s., reservoir n.; (mil.) tank c.
tankard, teng-kurd, s., drinkkan c.
tantalize, ten-te-laiz, v., tantaliseren
tantamount, ten-te-maunt, a., gelijkwaardig
tap, tep, s., (cock) kraan c.; (rap) tikje n. v., (strike lightly) tikken; (barrel) tappen
tape, teep, s., band c.; (telegraph) strook papier c.; ——worm, lintworm c.; red——, bureaucratie c.
taper, tee-p'r, s., waspit c. v., spits toelopen
tapestry, tep-pis-tri, s., wandtapijt n.
tar, taar, s., teer n. v., teren
tardiness, taar-di-nis, s., traagheid c.
tardy, taar-di, a., (slow) traag; (late) laat
tare, tèr, s., tarra c.; (weed) voederwikke c.
target, taar-Git, s., mikpunt n.
tariff, ter-rif, s., tarief n.
tarnish, taar-nisj, v., dof worden. s., dofheid c.
tarpaulin, taar-poa-lin, s., geteerd zeildoek n.
tart, taart, s., vruchtentaart c. a., zuur, wrang
task, taask, s., taak c., karwei n.
tassel, tes-s'l, s., kwastje n.; (in book) lint n.
taste, teest, s., smaak c. v., smaken; (try) proeven; ——ful, a., smakelijk; ——less, smakeloos
tasty, tees-ti, a., lekker, smakelijk
tatter, tet-t'r, s., lomp c., vod c.
tattered, tet-t'rd, a., haveloos
tattle, tet-t'l, v., babbelen. s., gebabbel n.
tattoo, te-toe, v., tatoueren. s., tatouering c.; (mil.) taptoe c.
taunt, toant, s., hoon c., smaad c. v., honen
tavern, tev-vurn, s., herberg c.
tawdry, toa-dri, a., smakeloos, opzichtig
tax, teks, s., belasting c. v., belasten
taxi, tek-si, s., taxi c. v., (plane) taxiën
tea, tie, s., thee c.; ——pot, theepot c.
teach, tietsj, v., onderwijzen; ——er, s., onder-

wijzer c.; (woman) onderwijzeres c.; ——ing, onderwijs n.

team, tiem, s., (horses) span n.; (group) ploeg c.
tear, tèr, s., scheur c. v., scheuren
tear, tier, s., traan c.; ——ful, a., schreiend
tease, tiez, v., plagen. s., plaaggeest c.
teat, tiet, s., tepel c.; (dummy) speen c.
technical, tek-ni-k'l, a., technisch
tedious, tie-di-us, a., vervelend; (dull) saai
tedium, tie-di-um, s., verveling c.; saaiheid c.
teem, tiem, v., wemelen, krioelen
teethe, tiedh, v., tanden krijgen
teetotaller, tie-toot-l'r, s., geheelonthouder c.
telegram, tel-li-Grem, s., telegram n.
telegraph, tel-li-Graaf, v., telegraferen
telephone, tel-li-foon, s., telefoon c. v., telefoneren
telescope, tel-lis-koop, s., verrekijker c.
television, tel-li-vi-zjun, s., televisie c.
tell, tel, v., vertellen; (order) bevelen
temper, tem-p'r, s., temperament n. v., temperen
temperance, tem-pe-r'ns, s., matigheid c.
temperate, tem-pe-rit, a., matig, gematigd
temperature, tem-prit-sjur, s., temperatuur c.
tempest, tem-pist, s., hevige storm c.
temple, tem-p'l, s., tempel c.; (head) slaap c.
temporary, tem-pe-re-ri, a., tijdelijk
tempt, temt, v., verleiden
temptation, temt-tee-sjun, s., verleiding c.
ten, ten, a., tien
tenable, ten-ne-b'l, a., houdbaar
tenacious, ti-nee-sjus, a., vasthoudend; (tough) taai
tenacity, ti-nes-si-ti, s., vasthoudendheid c.
tenancy, ten-n'n-si, s., huur c.; (land) pacht c.
tenant, ten-n'nt, s., huurder c.; (land) pachter c.
tend, tend, v., (patient) oppassen; —— to, een neiging hebben tot
tendency, tend-'n-si, s., neiging c.
tender, ten-d'r, s., tender c.; (offer) aanbod n. a., teer; (meat) mals; (sensitive) teergevoelig; (loving) liefhebbend. v., aanbieden

tenement, ten-ni-m'nt, s., woning c.

tennis, ten-nis, s., tennis n.

tenor, ten-n'r, s., tenor c.; (purport) inhoud c.

tense, tens, s., (gram.) tijd c. a., strak

tension, ten-sjun, s., spanning c.

tent, tent, s., tent c.

tentative, ten-te-tiv, a., bij wijze van proef

tenth, tenth, a., tiende

tenure, ten-joer, s., eigendomsrecht n., bezit n.

tepid, tep-pid, a., lauw; ——**ity,** s., lauwheid c.

term, teurm, s., (word) term c.; (time) termijn c.;
  (quarter) trimester n.; ——**s,** pl., voorwaarden

terminate, teur-mi-neet, v., beëindigen [c.pl.

terminus, teur-mi-nus, s., eindstation n.

terrace, ter-ris, s., terras n.

terrible, ter-ri-b'l, a., verschrikkelijk

terrific, te-rif-fik, a., schrikwekkend

terrify, ter-ri-fai, v., schrik aanjagen

territory, ter-ri-te-ri, s., gebied n. [ren

terror, ter-r'r, s., angst c.; ——**ize,** v., terrorise-

terse, teurs, a., pittig; (concise) beknopt

test, test, s., toetssteen c.; proef c.; (examination)
  proefwerk n.   v., (try) toetsen; ——**ify,**
  getuigenis afleggen; ——**imonial,** s., getuigschrift n.; (gift) huldeblijk n.; ——**imony,**
  bewijs n.

Testament, tes-te-m'nt, s., Testament n.

testicle, tes-ti-k'l, s., testikel c.

tether, tedh-ur, s., tuier c.   v., tuieren

text, tekst, s., tekst c.; ——**book,** leerboek n.

textile, teks-tail, a., textiel; (woven) gewoven

texture, tekst-sjur, s., weefsel n.; structuur c.

than, dhen, conj., dan

thank, thengk, v., danken; —— **you,** dank u;
  (after offer) alstublieft; ——**ful,** a., dankbaar;
  ——**less,** ondankbaar; ——**s,** s.pl., dank c.;
  ——**s to,** prep., dank zij; ——**sgiving,** s.,
  dankzegging c.

that, dhet, conj., dat.   pron., (common gender)
  die; (neuter) dat

thatch, thetsj, s., rieten dak n.   v., met riet dekken

thaw, thoa, s., dooi c.   v., dooien

the, dhe, art., de; (neuter singular) het; the . . .
the . . ., hoe . . . hoe . . ., example: the later
the better, hoe later hoe beter

theatre, thi-e-t'r, s., schouwburg c.

thee, dhie, pron., jou, je; to ——, aan jou

theft, theft, s., diefstal c.

their, dhèr, pron., hun; (feminine) haar; ——s,
de hunne, de hare; (neuter) het hunne, het
hare

them, dhem, pron., hen; (feminine) ze; to ——,
hun; haar

theme, thiem, s., thema n., onderwerp n.

themselves, dhem-selvz, pron., zelf, zichzelf

then, dhen, adv., toen; (next) dan, daarop

thence, dhens, adv., vandaar, daaruit

thenceforth, dhens-foarth, adv., van die tijd af

theology, thi-ol-le-dzji, s., godgeleerdheid c.

theoretical, thi-e-ret-ti-k'l, a., theoretisch

theory, thi-e-ri, s., theorie c.

there, dhèr, adv., daar; ——after, daarna; ——
by, daardoor; ——fore, daarom; ——upon,
daarop

thermal, theur-m'l, a., warmte . . .; (springs) heet

thermometer, theur-mom-mi-t'r, s., thermometer c.

these, dhiez, pron., deze

thesis, thie-sis, s., thesis c.

they, dhee, pron., zij, ze

thick, thik, a., dik; ——en, v., dik maken

thicket, thik-k't, s., kreupelbosje n.

thickness, thik-nis, s., dikte c.

thief, thief, s., dief c.

thieve, thiev, v., stelen

thigh, thai, s., dij c.

thimble, thim-b'l, s., vingerhoed c.

thin, thin, a., dun; (lean) mager; (sparse) schaars.
v., verdunnen; ——ness, s., dunheid c.

thine, dhain, pron., jouw; de jouwe; het jouwe

thing, thing, s., ding n.; (matter) zaak c.

think, thingk, v., denken; (believe) geloven; ——
of, denken van; (remember) denken aan;
—— over, nadenken over

third, theurd, a., derde; ——ly, adv., ten derde

thirst, theurst, s., dorst c.; ——y, a., dorstig

thirteen, theur-tien, a., dertien

thirteenth, theur-tienth, a., dertiende

thirtieth, theur-ti-ith, a., dertigste

thirty, theur-ti, a., dertig

this, dhis, pron., deze; (neuter) dit

thistle, this-s'l, s., distel c.

thong, thong, s., riem c.

thorn, thoarn, s., doorn c.; ——y, a., doornachtig

thorough, thar-re, a., volledig; (perfect) volmaakt; ——bred, volbloed; ——fare, s., doorgang c.; (road) weg c.; no ——fare, afgesloten rijweg

those, dhooz, pron., die

thou, dhau, pron., jij, gij

though, dho, conj., hoewel, ofschoon

thought, thoat, s., gedachte c.; ——ful, a., nadenkend; (pensive) peinzend; (kind) attent; ——less, gedachteloos; (inconsiderate) onbezonnen

thousand, thau-z'nd, a., duizend

thousandth, thau-z'ndth, a., duizendste

thrash, thresj, v., afranselen

thrashing, thresj-ing, s., pak ransel n.

thread, thred, s., draad c. v., (string up) aanrijgen; ——bare, a., kaal, versleten

threat, thret, s., dreiging c.; ——en, v., dreigen

threatening, thret-te-ning, a., dreigend

three, thrie, a., drie; ——fold, a., drievoudig

thresh, thresj, v., dorsen; ——er, s., dorsmachine

threshold, thres-sjoold, s., drempel c.   [c.

thrice, thrais, a., driemaal

thrift, thrift, s., zuinigheid c.; ——less, a., verkwistend; ——y, zuinig; (thriving) voorspoedig

thrill, thril, v., ontroeren; (vibrate) doortrillen. s., ontroering c.; trilling c.; ——ing, a., spannend

thrive, thraiv, v., gedijen; (success) voorspoed hebben

throat, throot, s., hals c.; (gullet) keel c.

throb, throb, v., bonzen; (heart) kloppen

throes, throoz, s.pl., barensweeën n.pl.

throne, throon, s., troon c.   v., op de troon plaatsen

throng, throng, s., gedrang n. v., zich verdringen

throttle, throt-t'l, v., worgen. s., strot c., keel c.; (valve) smoorklep c.

through, throe, prep., door; ——**out,** adv., helemaal; (everywhere) overal; ——**-train,** s., directe trein c.

throw, thro, s., worp c. v., werpen; (cast down) neerwerpen; (cast off) afwerpen

thrush, thrasj, s., lijster c.

thrust, thrast, v., stoten, steken. s., steek c.

thud, thad, s., bons c., plof c. v., bonzen

thumb, tham, s., duim c.

thump, thamp, v., (to strike) stompen; slaan. **s.,** stomp c.; slag c.; (sound) bons c.

thunder, than-d'r, v., donderen. s., donder c.; ——**bolt,** bliksemstraal c.; ——**storm,** onweer n.

Thursday, theurz-di, s., donderdag c.

thus, dhas, adv., dus, zo

thwart, thwoart, v., dwarsbomen; (frustrate) verijdelen

thy, dhai, pron., jouw

thyme, taim, s., tijm c.

tick, tik, v., tikken. s., tik c.; (cover) beddetijk c.

ticket, tik-kit, s., (train, bus) kaartje n.; (of admission) toegangskaartje n.; (label) prijsetiket n.; season——, abonnementskaart c.

tickle, tik-k'l, v., kietelen. s., gekietel n.

ticklish, tik-klisj, a., netelig, teer

tidal, tai-d'l, a., getij . . .; —— **wave, s.,** vloedgolf c.

tide, taid, s., getij n.; (flood) vloed c.

tidings, tai-dingz, s.pl., tijding c., bericht n.

tidy, tai-di, a., netjes, zindelijk. v., opknappen

tie, tai, s., das c.; (bond) band c. v., (fasten) vastbinden; (knot) knopen; (bind) binden

tier, tier, s., rij c.; (theatre) rang c.

tiff, tif, s., kleine ruzie c.

tiger, tai-G'r, s., tijger c.

tight, tait, a., (close) dicht; (garments) strak, nauw; **air——,** luchtdicht; **——en,** v., spannen; (a screw) aandraaien; **water——,** a., waterdicht; **——s,** s.pl., spanbroek c.

tile, tail, s., (roof) dakpan c. (floor) tegel c.

till, til, s., geldlade c. v., bebouwen. conj., totdat. prep., tot, tot aan; **——now,** adv., tot nu toe

tiller, til-l'r, s., landbouwer c.; (naut.) roerpen c.

tilt, tilt, v., (tip) kantelen. s., schuine stand c.

timber, tim-b'r, s., timmerhout n.

time, taim, v., regelen. s., tijd c.; keer c. (three times, drie keer, etc.); (mus.) maat c.; **——-keeper,** chronometer c.; (sport) tijjdopnemer c.; **——ly,** a. & adv., tijdig; **——-table,** s., dienstregeling c.

timid, tim-mid, a., verlegen, bedeesd

tin, tin, s., tin n.; (can) busje n. v., vertinnen; (can) inmaken. a., tinnen; **——foil,** s., bladtin n.; **——plate,** blik n. [c.

tincture, tingkt-sjur, s., tinctuur c.; (tinge) kleur

tinge, tindzj, s., kleur c.; (fig.) tikje n. v., tinten

tingle, ting-G'l, v., tintelen; (ears) tuiten

tinkle, ting-k'l, v., tingelen. s., getingel n.

tinsel, tin-s'l, s., klatergoud n. a., opzichtig

tint, tint, s., tint c. v., tinten

tiny, tai-ni, a., heel klein, nietig

tip, tip, s., puntje n.; (gentle hit) tikje n.; (hint) wenk c.; (gratuity) fooi c. v., (tilt) kantelen; (reward) een fooi geven; **on ——toe,** adv., op de tenen

tire, tair, s., (band) band c. v., vermoeien; (bore) vervelen; **——d,** a., vermoeid; **——of,** v., 't beu worden; **——some,** a., vermoeiend; (boring) vervelend

tissue, tis-sjoe, s., weefsel n.; **——-paper,** zijde-papier n.

tithe, taidh, s., tiend n.

title, tai-t'l, s., titel c.; (right) recht n.; **——-deed,** eigendomsbewijs n.; **——-page,** titelblad n.

titter, tit-t'r, v., gichelen. s., gegichel n.

to, toe, prep., aan; (direction) naar; (comparison) [bij

toad, tood, s., pad c.

toast, toost, s., geroosterd brood n.; (drinking) heildronk c. v., roosteren; —— **to**, drinken op

tobacco, to-bek-ko, s., tabak c.; ——**nist**, tabaksverkoper c.; ——**pouch**, tabakszak c.

to-day, te-dee, adv., vandaag, heden

toe, to, s., teen c.; (boot, shoe) neus c.

toffee, tof-fi, s., toffee c.

together, te-Gedh-ur, adv., samen, tegelijk

toil, toil, v., zwoegen. s., gezwoeg n.

toiler, toi-l'r, s., zwoeger c.

toilet, toi-lit, s., toilet n.

token, to-k'n, s., teken n.; (mark) kenteken n.

tolerable, tol-le-re-b'l, a., draaglijk

tolerance, tol-le-r'ns, s., verdraagzaamheid c.

tolerant, tol-le-r'nt, a., verdraagzaam

tolerate, tol-le-reet, v., verdragen, dulden

toll, tool, s., (tax) tol c.; (bell) gelui n. v., luiden

tomato, te-ma-to, s., tomaat c.

tomb, toem, s., graf n.; ——**stone**, grafsteen c.

tomboy, tom-boi, s., robbedoes c., wildzang c.

tomcat, tom-ket, s., kater c.

tomfoolery, tom-foe-le-ri, s., gekheid c.

to-morrow, te-mor-ro, adv., morgen

tomtit, tom-tit, s., pimpelmees c.

ton, ton, s., ton c.; ——**nage**, scheepsruimte c.

tone, toon, s., toon c.; (tinge) tint c.

tongs, tongz, s., tang c.

tongue, tang, s., tong c.; (speech) spraak c.; (language) taal c.; ——**tied**, a., sprakeloos,

tonic, ton-nik, s., versterkend middel n. [stom

to-night, te-nait, adv., vanavond; vannacht

tonsil, ton-sil, s., amandel c.

tonsilitis, ton-si-lai-tis, s., amandelontsteking c.

too, toe, adv., te; (also) ook; —— **much**, te veel

tool, toel, s., werktuig n., gereedschap n.

tooth, toeth, s., tand c.; ——**ache**, tandpijn c.; ——**brush**, tandenborstel c.; ——**paste**, tandpasta c.; ——**pick**, tandenstoker c.

top, top, s., top c.; (mountain, head) kruin c.; (table) hoofd n.; (highest position) hoogste plaats c.; (apex) toppunt n.; (toy) tol c. a., (principal) voornaamste; (first) eerste; **on** ——, bovenaan; ——**-boots**, s.pl., kaplaarzen c.pl.; ——**-hat**, hoge hoed c.

topic, top-pik, s., onderwerp n., thema n.

topple, top-p'l, v., tuimelen, omvallen

topsy-turvy, top-si-teur-vi, adv., op zijn kop

torch, toartsj, s., toorts c.; (electric) zaklantaarn c.

torment, toar-m'nt, s., marteling c., foltering c.

torment, toar-ment, v., martelen, folteren

tornado, toar-nee-do, s., wervelstorm c.

torpedo, toar-pie-do, v., torpederen. s., torpedo c.; ——**-boat**, torpedojager c.

torpid, toar-pid, a., verdoofd; (sluggish) traag

torpor, toar-p'r, s., verdoving c.; traagheid c.

torrent, tor-r'nt, s., stortvloed c.

torrid, tor-rid, a., verzengd, brandend

tortoise, toar-tus, s., schildpad c.

torture, toart-sjur, s., foltering c. v., folteren

toss, tos, s., gooi c., worp c. v., gooien; (coin) opgooien; (hay) keren; —— **about**, heen en weer slingeren

total, to-t'l, s., totaal n. a., totaal, geheel. v. optellen

totter, tot-t'r, v., wankelen, waggelen

tottery, tot-te-ri, a., wankel, waggelend

touch, tøtsj, s., (contact) aanraking c.; (sense) gevoel n. v., aanraken; voelen; ——**ing**, a., roerend; ——**y**, lichtgeraakt

tough, tøf, a., taai; (firm) stevig

tour, toer, s., rondreis c.; (ramble) uitstapje n. v., een rondreis maken; (a country) afreizen; ——**ist**, s., toerist c.; ——**nament**, concours n.

tout, taut, s., klantenlokker c. v., klanten lokken [n.

tow, to, v., (haul) slepen. s., (flax) werk n.; ——**age**, slepen n.; ——**rope**, sleeptouw n.

towards, te-woardz, prep, in de richting van; (in relation to) jegens; (with respect to) met het oog op

towel, tau-ul, s., handdoek c. v., zich afdrogen

tower, tau-ur, s., toren c. v., zich hoog verheffen

town, taun, s., stad c.; ——**hall**, stadhuis n.

toy, toi, s., speelgoed n. v., (trifle) beuzelen
trace, trees, s., (harness) streng c.; (track) spoor
n. v., nasporen; (draw) ontwerpen
tracing, tree-sing, s., schets c., tekening c.
tracing-paper, tree-sing-pee-p'r, s., calqueerpapier n.
track, trek, s., (trace) spoor n.; (race) baan c.;
(railway) spoorbaan c. v., nasporen
tract, trekt, s., uitgestrektheid c.; ——ion, trekken n.; ——or, tractor c.
trade, treed, s., handel c.; (craft) ambacht n. v.,
handel drijven; ——mark, s., handelsmerk
n.; ——sman, winkelier c.; ——union,
vakvereniging c.
tradition, tre-dis-sjun, s., overlevering c.
traditional, tre-dis-sje-n'l, a., traditioneel
traduce, tre-djoes, v., belasteren
traffic, tref-fik, s., verkeer n. v., handelen
tragedian, tre-dzjie-di-un, s., treurspeldichter c.
tragedy, tred-zji-di, s., treurspel n., tragedie c.
tragic, tred-zjik, a., tragisch, treurspel . . .
trail, treel, s., sleep c.; (track) spoor n. v., slepen;
(follow track) nasporen; ——er, s., (vehicle)
aanhangwagen c.
train, treen, v., grootbrengen; (animals) dresseren;
(sport) trainen; (mil.) drillen; (practise) zich
oefenen. s., (railway) trein c.; (dress) sleep
c.; ——ing, opleiding c.; (sport) training c.
traitor, tree-t'r, s., verrader c.
tram, trem, s., tram c.
tramp, tremp, s., vagebond c.; (walk) voetreis c.
trample, trem-p'l, v., vertrappen, trappen
trance, traans, s., schijndood c.; (rapture) verrukking c.
tranquil, treng-kwil, a., kalm, rustig
transact, tren-zekt, v., verrichten; (do business)
zaken doen; ——ion, s., verrichting c.; zaak c.
transcribe, tren-skraib, v., (copy) overschrijven
transfer, trens-feur, v., (property) overmaken;
(convey) overbrengen; (person) verplaatsen.
s., overmaking c.; overbrenging c.; verplaatsing c.; ——paper, overdrukpapier n.

transform, trens-foarm, v., omvormen
transgress, trens-Gres, v., overtreden
tranship, tren-sjip, v., overladen, overschepen
transit, **tren**-sit, s., doorgang c.; doorvoer c.
translate, trens-leet, v., vertalen
translation, trens-lee-sjun, s., vertaling c.
translator, trens-lee-t'r, s., vertaler c.
transmit, trens-mit, v., overzenden; overleveren
transparent, trens-pèr-'nt, a., doorzichtig
transpire, trens-pair, v., uitwasemen
transport, trens-poart, v., vervoeren; verrukken
transport, **trens**-poart, s., vervoer n.; verrukking
transpose, trens-pooz, v., verplaatsen   [c.
transverse, trens-veurs, a., dwars
trap, trep, s., val c.   v., vangen
trap-door, trep-doar, s., luik n.
trappings, trep-pingz, s.pl., opschik c., praal c.
trash, tresj, s., afval c.; (nonsense) onzin c.
trashy, tres-sji, a., prullig, waardeloos
travel, trev-v'l, v., reizen; —ler, s., reiziger c.
traverse, trev-v'rs, v., doorkruisen. a., dwars
trawler, troa-l'r, s., treiler c.
tray, tree, s., presenteerblad n.
treacherous, tret-sje-rus, a., verraderlijk
treachery, tret-sje-ri, s., trouweloosheid c.
treacle, trie-k'l, s., stroop c.
tread, tred, v., treden. s., tred c., stap c.
treason, trie-s'n, s., verraad n.
treasure, trez-zjur, s., schat c. v., waarderen
treasurer, trez-zje-r'r, s., schatbewaarder c.
treasury, trez-zje-ri, s., schatkist c.
treat, triet, v., behandelen; (entertain) trakteren;
   (negotiate) onderhandelen. s., onthaal n.
treatise, triet-iez, s., verhandeling c.
treatment, triet-m'nt, s., behandeling c.
treaty, trie-ti, s., verdrag n.; contract n.
treble, treb-b'l, a., drievoudig. v., verdrievoudi-
   gen. s., (mus.) sopraan c.
tree, trie, s., boom c.; family ——, stamboom c.
trellis, trel-lis, s., latwerk n., traliewerk n.
tremble, trem-b'l, v., beven, rillen. s., rilling c.
tremendous, tri-men-dus, a., verschrikkelijk

tremulous, trem-joe-lus, a., bevend, rillend
trench, trensj, s., greppel c.; (mil.) loopgraaf c.
trend, trend, s., neiging c. v., neigen
trespass, tres-pus, v., op verboden terrein komen.
   s., overtreding c.; ——**er,** overtreder c.
trestle, tres-s'l, s., schraag c., bok c.
trial, trai-ul, s., proef c.; (law) verhoor n.
triangle, trai-eng-G'l, s., driehoek c.
triangular, trai-eng-Gjoe-l'r, a., driehoekig
tribe, traib, s., stam c., geslacht n.
tribunal, tri-bjoe-n'l, s., rechtbank c.
tribune, tri-bjoen, s., spreekgestoelte n.
tributary, trib-bjoe-te-ri, s., (river) zijrivier c.
tribute, trib-bjoet, s., schatting c.; (gift) huldeblijk n.
trick, trik, s., kunstgreep c.; (prank) poets c.;
   (stratagem) list c.; (habit) aanwensel n.;
   (cards score) slag c. v., bedriegen; ——**ery,**
   s., bedotterij c.; ——**ster,** bedrieger c.
trickle, trik-k'l, v., druppelen; **s.,** straaltje n.
trifle, trai-f'l, s., kleinigheid c. v., beuzelen
trifling, trai-fling, a., onbeduidend
trigger, triG-G'r, s., trekker c.
trill, tril, s., trilling c. v., trillend zingen
trim, trim, v., (hair) bijknippen; (dress) afzetten.
   a., keurig, netjes; ——**ming, s.,** garneersel n.
Trinity, trin-ni-ti, s., Drieëenheid c.
trinket, tring-kit, s., kleinood n.
trio, trie-o, s., trio n.
trip, trip, v., trippelen; (stumble) struikelen;
   (err) een fout maken. **s.,** (journey) uitstapje n.
tripe, traip, s., pens c.; (fig.) snert c.
triple, trip-p'l, a., drievoudig, driedelig
triplets, trip-plits, s.pl., drieling c.
tripod, trai-pod, s., drievoet c.
tripper, trip-p'r, s., plezierreiziger c.
triumph, trai-umf, s., triomf c., zegepraal c.
trivial, triv-vi-ul, a., onbeduidend
trolley, trol-li, s., lorrie c.; (electric) contactrol c.
trombone, trom-boon, s., schuiftrompet c.
troop, troep, v., zich verzamelen. **s.,** troep c.
trooper, troe-p'r, s., (mil.) cavalerist c.

troopship, troep-sjip, s., transportschip n.

trophy, tro-fi, s., zegeteken n.; tropee c.

tropical, trop-pi-k'l, a., tropisch

tropics, trop-piks, s.pl., tropen c.pl.

trot, trot, s., draf c. v., draven; ——**ter,** s., (horse) harddraver c.; (pig) varkensspoot c.

trouble, trab-b'l, s., (affliction) verdriet n.; (worry) zorg c.; (disturbance) verwarring c.; (ailment) kwaal c.; (inconvenience) ongemak n. v., (disturb) in beroering brengen; (molest) lastig vallen; (afflict) kwellen; (bother) zich bekommeren

troublesome, trab-b'l-sam, a., lastig, moeilijk

trough, trof, s., trog c., drinkbak c.

trounce, trauns, v., afrossen, afstraffen

trousers, trau-z'rz, s.pl., broek c.

trout, traut, s., forel c.

trowel, trau-ul, s., troffel c.; (garden) schopje n.

truant, troe-unt, s., spijbelaar c.; play ——, v., spijbelen

truce, troes, s., wapenstilstand c.

truck, trak, s., handkar c.; (train) open wagen c.

truckle, trak-k'l, v., zich slaafs onderwerpen

truculent, trak-joc-l'nt, a., woest, wreed, wild

trudge, tradzj, v., zich voortslepen

true, troe, a., waar; (faithful) trouw

truffle, traf-f'l, s., truffel c.

truism, troe-izm, s., gemeenplaats c.

trump, tramp, s., troef c. v., troeven

trumpery, tram-pe-ri, a., waardeloos, prullig

trumpet, tram-pit, s., trompet c.

truncheon, tran-zjun, s., gummistok c.

trunk, trangk, s., (tree) stam c.; (body) romp c.; (travelling) koffer c.; (elephant) slurf c.; —— **call,** interlocaal gesprek n.

truss, tras, s., bundel c.; (surgical) breukband c. v., opbinden

trust, trast, s., vertrouwen n.; (combine) trust c. v., vertrouwen; (entrust) toevertrouwen

trustee, tras-tie, s., beheerder c.

trustworthy, trast-weur-dhi, a., betrouwbaar

truth, troeth, s., waarheid c.

try, trai, v., proberen; (overtax) veel vergen van;
(law) berechten; ——ing, a., lastig, moeilijk
tub, tab, s., tobbe c.; (bath) badkuip c.
tube, tjoeb, s., buis c., pijp c.; (paint, etc.) tube c.
tuck, tak, s., plooi c.; (trousers) omslag c. v.,
plooien; (sleeves) opstropen; —— in, instop-
pen
Tuesday, tjoez-di, s., dinsdag c.
tuft, taft, s., bosje n.
tug, taG, s., ruk c. v., trekken; rukken aan;
——boat, s., sleepboot c.; —— of war,
trouwtrekken n.
tuition, tjoe-is-sjun, s., onderricht n.
tulip, tjoe-lip, s., tulp c.
tumble, tam-b'l, v., tuimelen; (rumple) verfrommelen
tumbler, tam-bl'r, s., (glass) bekerglas n.
tumour, tjoe-m'r, s., gezwel n. [n.
tumult, tjoe-malt, s., tumult n.; (uproar) oproer
tune, tjoen, s., wijsje n., deuntje n. v., stemmen
tuneful, tjoen-foel, a., welluidend
tunic, tjoe-nik, s., (mil.) uniformjas c.
tuning-fork, tjoe-ning-foark, s., stemvork c.
tunnel, tan-n'l, s., tunnel c. v., een tunnel maken
tunny, tan-ni, s., tonijn c.
turbine, teur-bain, s., turbine c.
turbot, teur-but, s., tarbot c.
turbulent, teur-bjoe-l'nt, a., onstuimig, **woelig**
tureen, tjoe-rien, s., soepterrine c.
turf, teurf, s., zode c.; (peat) turf c.
turkey, teur-ki, s., kalkoen c.
Turkish, teur-kisj, a., Turks
turmoil, teur-moil, s., verwarring c., beroering c.
turn, teurn, v., draaien, wenden. s., draai c.;
(change) ommekeer c.; (bend) bocht c.;
(order of sequence) beurt c.; —— about, v.,
zich omkeren; —— aside, afwenden;
——back, terugkeren; ——coat, s., overloper c.;
——er, draaier c.; ——ing, zijstraat c.;
(bend) bocht c.; ——ing-point, keerpunt
n.; —— into, v., veranderen in; —— off,
(gas, etc.) afdraaien; (wireless) afzetten;

—— **on**, (gas, etc.) opendraaien; (wireless) aanzetten; —— **out**, (gas, etc.) uitdraaien; (expel) wegsturen; —— **over**, zich omkeren; (pages) omslaan. s., (trade) omzet c.; —— **to**, v., zich wenden tot

turnip, teur-nip, s., raap c., knol c.

turnstile, teurn-stail, s., tourniquet c.

turpentine, teur-p'n-tain, s., terpentijn c.   [c.

turret, tar-rit, s., torentje n.; (gun) geschutstoren

turtle, teur-t'l, s., zeeschildpad c.; ——**dove**, tortelduif c.; **turn** ——, v., omslaan

tusk, task, s., slagtand c. v., doorboren

tussle, tas-s'l, s., vechtpartij c. v., vechten

tutor, tjoe-t'r, s., huisonderwijzer c. v., onderwijzen

twang, tweng, s., getingel n.; (nasal sound) neusklank c. v., tingelen; door de neus spreken

tweezers, twie-z'rz, s.pl., haartangetje n.

twelfth, twelfth, a., twaalfde

twelve, twelv, a., twaalf

twentieth, twen-ti-ith, a., twintigste

twenty, twen-ti, a., twintig

twice, twais, adv., tweemaal, twee keer

twig, twiG, s., takje n., twijgje n.

twilight, twai-lait, s., schemering c.

twill, twil, s., keper c. v., keperen

twin, twin, a., tweeling . . .; ——**s,** s.pl., tweeling c.

twine, twain, s., bindgaren n. v., zich kronkelen

twinge, twindzj, s., steek c.; (remorse) wroeging c. v., steken; (conscience) knagen

twinkle, twing-k'l, v., flikkeren; (eyes) knippen met

twirl, tweurl, v., ronddraaien. s., draaiing c.

twist, twist, v., vlechten; (distort) verdraaien

twit, twit, v., berispen. s., berisping c.

twitch, twitsj, s., zenuwtrekking c. v., trekken

twitter, twit-t'r, v., tjilpen. s., getjilp n.

two, toe, a., twee; ——**fold,** tweevoudig

type, taip, s., (model) voorbeeld n.; (printing) letter c. v., typen

typewriter, taip-rai-t'r, s., schrijfmachine c.

typhoid, tai-foid, s., typhus c.

typical, tip-pi-k'l, a., typisch, zinnebeeldig

typist, tai-pist, s., typist c.; (lady) typiste c.

typography, tai-poG-Gre-fi, s., drukkunst c.

tyrannical, ti-**ren**-ni-k'l, a., tiranniek

tyrannize, tir-re-naiz, v., tiranniseren

tyrant, tai-r'nt, s., tiran c., dwingeland c.

tyre, tair, s., band c.

ubiquitous, joe-**bik**-kwe-tus, a., alomtegenwoor-
udder, ad-d'r, s., uier c.   [dig

ugliness, aG-li-nis, s., lelijkheid c.

ugly, aG-li, a., lelijk; (menacing) dreigend

ulcer, al-s'r, s., ettergezwel n.; (fig.) kanker c.

ulcerate, al-se-reet, v., zweren, etteren

ulterior, al-tie-ri-ur, a., verderop gelegen

ultimate, al-ti-mit, a., laatste, uiterste

ultimatum, al-ti-**mee**-tum, s., ultimatum n.

ultimo, al-ti-mo, adv., van de vorige maand

ultra, al-tra, a., uiterst, ultra

umbrella, am-**brel**-la, s., paraplu c.

umbrella-stand, am-**brel**-la-stend, s., paraplu-
stander c.

umpire, am-pair, s., scheidsrechter c.

unabashed, an-e-besjt, a., niet verlegen

unabated, an-e-bee-tid, a., onverminderd

unable, an-ee-b'l, a., niet in staat, onbekwaam;
  to be ——, v., niet kunnen

unacceptable, an-ek-sep-te-b'l, a., onaannemelijk

unaccountable, an-e-koun-te-b'l, a., onverklaarbaar

unacquainted, an-e-kween-tid, a., onbekend

unaffected, an-e-fek-tid, a., ongekunsteld

unaided, an-ee-did, a., zonder hulp

unalterable, an-oal-te-re-b'l, a., onveranderlijk

unaltered, an-oal-t'rd, a., onveranderd   [c.

unanimity, joe-ne-**nim**-mi-ti, s., eenstemmigheid

unanimous, joe-nen-ni-mus, a., eenstemmig

unanswerable, an-aan-se-re-b'l, a., onweerlegbaar

unapproachable, an-e-proot-sje-b'l, a., ongenaakbaar

unarmed, *an*-aarmd, a., ongewapend
unassailable, *an*-e-see-le-b'l, a., onaantastbaar
unattainable, *an*-e-tee-ne-b'l, a., onbereikbaar
unattended, *an*-e-ten-did, a., zonder gevolg
unavoidable, *an*-e-voi-de-b'l, a., onvermijdelijk
unaware, *an*-e-wèr, a., zich niet bewust
unawares, *an*-e-wèrz, adv., onverwachts
unbearable, *an*-bèr-e-b'l, a., ondraaglijk
unbecoming, *an*-bi-**kam**-ing, a., ongepast;
    (dress) niet goed staand
unbeliever, *an*-bi-lie-v'r, s., ongelovige c.
unbend, *an*-bend, v., ontspannen; zich ontspan-
    nen
unbending, *an*-ben-ding, a., onbuigzaam, stijf
unbiassed, *an*-bai-ust, a., onbevooroordeeld
unbleached, *an*-blietsjt, a., ongebleekt
unblemished, *an*-blem-misjt, a., onbevlekt
unbounded, *an*-baun-did, a., onbegrensd
unbreakable, *an*-bree-ke-b'l, a., onbreekbaar
unburden, *an*-beur-d'n, v., ontlasten
unbutton, *an*-bat-t'n, v., losknopen
uncalled for, *an*-koald foar, a., onnodig
uncanny, *an*-ken-ni, a., griezelig, angstwekkend
uncared for, *an*-kèrd-foar, a., verwaarloosd
unceasing, *an*-sie-sing, a., onophoudelijk
uncertain, *an*-seur-tin, a., onzeker
unchangeable, *an*-tsjeen-dzje-b'l, a., onveran-
    derlijk
uncivil, *an*-siv-vil, a., onbeleefd, lomp
unclaimed, *an*-kleemd, a., niet opgeëist
uncle, *ang*-k'l, s., oom c.
unclean, *an*-klien, a., vuil
uncomfortable, *an*-kam-f'r-te-b'l, a., ongemak-
    kelijk
uncommon, *an*-kam-m'n, a., ongewoon
unconcern, *an*-k'n-seurn, s., onverschilligheid c.
unconditional, *an*-k'n-dis-sje-n'l, a. onvoor-
    waardelijk
uncongenial, *an*-k'n-dzjie-ni-ul, a., onsym-
    pathiek
unconscionable, *an*-kon-sje-ne-b'l, a., geweten-
    loos; (excessive) overdreven

unconscious, *a*n-kon-sjus, a., bewusteloos; (unaware) onbewust

uncontrollable, *a*n-k'n-tro-le-b'l, a., niet te controleren; (unmanageable) onhandelbaar

unconventional, *a*n-k'n-ven-sje-n'l, a., ongedwongen, vrij

uncork, *a*n-koark, v., ontkurken

uncouth, *a*n-koeth, a., lomp, onhandig   [van

uncover, *a*n-kav-v'r, v., de bedekking wegnemen

uncultivated, *a*n-k*a*l-ti-vee-tid, a., onbebouwd

undated, *a*n-dee-tid, a., niet gedateerd

undaunted, *a*n-doan-tid, a., onverschrokken

undeceive, *a*n-di-siev, v., uit de droom helpen

undecided, *a*n-di-sai-did, a., onbeslist

undefiled, *a*n-di-faild, a., onbesmet

undelivered, *a*n-di-liv-v'rd, a., niet afgeleverd

undeniable, *a*n-di-nai-e-b'l, a., onloochenbaar

under, *a*n-d'r, adv. & prep., onder, beneden; —— **age**, a., minderjarig; ——**clothing**, s., ondergoed n.; ——**done**, a., niet gaar; ——**estimate**, v., onderschatten; ——**fed**, a., ondervoed; ——**go**, v., ondergaan; (suffer) lijden; ——**graduate**, s., student c.; ——**ground**, a., ondergronds. s., (railway) ondergrondse spoorweg c.; ——**hand**, a., onderhands; ——**line**, v., onderstrepen; ——**mine**, v., ondermijnen; ——**neath**, prep., onder. adv., hieronder; ——**paid**, a., slecht betaald; ——**rate**, v., onderschatten; ——**sell**, onder de waarde verkopen; ——**sign**, ondertekenen; ——**sized**, a., onder de gemiddelde grootte; ——**stand**, v., verstaan; ——**standing**, s., verstand n.; (agreement) afspraak c.; ——**state**, v., beneden de waarheid blijven; ——**study**, s., doublure c.; ——**take**, v., ondernemen; ——**taker**, s., (funeral) begrafenisondernemer c.; ——**taking**, onderneming c.; ——**tone**, gedempte toon c.; ——**wear**, ondergoed n.; ——**world**, onderwereld c.; ——**writer**, assuradeur c.

undeserved, *a*n-di-zeurvd, a., onverdiend

undesirable *a*n-di-zai-re-b'l, a., ongewenst

undignified, *an*-diG-ni-faid, a., zonder waardigheid

undiminished, *an*-di-min-nisjt, a., onverminderd

undismayed, *an*-dis-meed, a., onverschrokken

undisturbed, *an*-dis-teurbd, a., ongestoord

undo, *an*-doe, v., ongedaan maken; (untie) losmaken

undoing, *an*-doe-ing, s., (ruin) ondergang c.

undoubted, *an*-dau-tid, a., ongetwijfeld

undress, *an*-dres, v., uitkleden; zich uitkleden

undue, *an*-djoe, a., (improper) onbehoorlijk

undulating, *an*-djoe-lee-ting, a., golvend

unduly, *an*-djoe-li, adv., onbehoorlijk

unearned, *an*-eurnd, a., onverdiend

unearth, *an*-eurth, v., opgraven; (fig.) opsnorren

unearthly, *an*-eurth-li, a., (weird) spookachtig

uneasy, *an*-ie-zi, a., onbehaaglijk; (worried) ongerust

uneducated, *an*-ed-joe-kee-tid, a., onopgevoed

unemployed, *an*-em-ploid, a., werkloos

unemployment, *an*-em-ploi-m'nt, s., werkloosheid c.

unequal, *an*-ie-kwul, a., ongelijk

unequalled, *an*-ie-kwuld, a., ongeëvenaard

unerring, *an*-eu-ring, a., onfeilbaar

uneven, *an*-ie-v'n, a., ongelijk; (road) oneffen

unexpected, *an*-ek-spek-tid, a., onverwacht

unfailing, *an*-fee-ling, a., niet falend, zeker

unfair, *an*-fèr, a., onbillijk, oneerlijk

unfaithful, *an*-feeth-foel, a., ontrouw

unfaltering, *an*-foal-te-ring, a., onwankelbaar

unfasten, *an*-fa-s'n, v., losmaken, openmaken

unfathomable, *an*-fedh-e-mc-b'l, a., onpeilbaar

unfavourable, *an*-fee-ve-re-b'l, a., ongunstig

unfeeling, *an*-fie-ling, a., ongevoelig, wreed

unfit, *an*-fit, a., ongeschikt; (improper) ongepast

unflagging, *an*-fleG-Ging, a., onverflauwd

unflinching, *an*-flin-sjing, a., onwrikbaar

unfold, *an*-foold, v., ontvouwen; (fig.) openbaren

unforeseen, *an*-foar-sien, a., onvoorzien

unfortunate, *an*-foar-tsje-nit, a., ongelukkig

unfortunately, *a*n-foar-tsje-nit-li, adv., on-
gelukkigerwijze
unfounded, *a*n-faun-did, a., ongegrond
unfriendly, *a*n-frend-li, a., onvriendelijk
unfulfilled, *a*n-foel-fild, a., onvervuld
unfurl, *a*n-feurl, v., (flag) ontplooien
unfurnished, *a*n-feur-nisjt, a., ongemeubileerd
ungainly, *a*n-Geen-li, a., onbevallig, lelijk
ungrateful, *a*n-Greet-ful, a., ondankbaar
unguarded, *a*n-Gaar-did, a., onbewaakt
unhappy, *a*n-hep-pi, a., ongelukkig
unharness, *a*n-haar-nis, v., uitspannen
unhealthy, *a*n-hel-thi, a., ongezond
unheard, *a*n-heurd, a., niet gehoord; —— of,
ongehoord
unheeded, *a*n-hie-did, a., veronachtzaamd
unhinge, *a*n-hindzj, v., uit de hengsels lichten;
(fig.) van streek brengen
unhurt, *a*n-heurt, a., ongedeerd
uniform, joe-ni-foarm, s., uniform n. a., gelijkvormig; (equal) gelijk
uniformity, joe-ni-foarm-i-ti, s., gelijkheid c.
unimaginable, *a*n-i-med-zji-ne-b'l, a., ondenkbaar
unimpaired, *a*n-im-pèrd, a., ongeschonden
unimpeachable, *a*n-im-piet-sje-b'l, a., onberispelijk
unimportant, *a*n-im-poar-t'nt, a., onbelangrijk
uninhabitable, *a*n-in-heb-bi-te-b'l, a., onbewoonbaar
unintelligible, *a*n-in-tel-li-dzji-b'l, a., onbegrijpelijk
unintentional, *a*n-in-ten-sje-n'l, a., onopzettelijk
uninviting, *a*n-in-vai-ting, a., niet aanlokkelijk
union, joen-jun, s., vereniging c.; (league) unie c.
unique, joe-niek, a., enig, uniek
unit, joe-nit, s., eenheid c.
unite, joe-nait, v., verenigen; zich verenigen
unity, joe-ni-ti, s., eenheid c., eendracht c.
universal, joe-ni-veur-s'l, a., algemeen
universe, joe-ni-veurs, s., heelal n.
university, joe-ni-veur-si-ti, s., universiteit c.

unjust, *an*-dzj*a*st, a., onrechtvaardig

unkind, *an*-kaind, a., onvriendelijk

unknown, *an*-noon, a., onbekend

unlawful, *an*-loa-foel, a., onwettig

unless, *an*-les, conj., tenzij, indien . . . niet

unlike, *an*-laik, a., ongelijk, anders dan

unlikely, *an*-laik-li, adv., onwaarschijnlijk

unlimited, *an*-lim-mi-tid, a., onbeperkt

unload, *an*-lood, v., ontladen, lossen

unlock, *an*-lok, v., ontsluiten

unlooked for, *an*-loekt foar, a., onverwacht

unlucky, *an*-lak-ki, a., ongelukkig

unmannerly, *an*-men-n'r-li, a., ongemanierd

unmarried, *an*-mer-rid, a., ongehuwd

unmerciful, *an*-meur-si-foel, a., onbarmhartig

unmistakable, *an*-mis-tee-ke-b'l, a., onmisken-

unmoved, *an*-moevd, a., onbewogen   [baar

unnatural, *an*-net-sje-r'l, a., onnatuurlijk

unnecessary, *an*-nes-si-se-ri, a., nodeloos

unnerve, *an*-neurv, v., ontzenuwen, verlammen

unnoticed, *an*-no-tist, a., onopgemerkt   [baar

unobtainable, *an*-ub-tee-ne-b'l, a., onverkrijg-

unoccupied, *an*-ok-joe-paid, a., (person) niet

    bezig; (house) onbewoond; (place) onbezet

unopposed, *an*-op-poozd, a., ongehinderd

unpack, *an*-pek, v., uitpakken

unpardonable, *an*-paar-de-ne-b'l, a., onvergeef-

    lijk

unpleasant, *an*-plez-z'nt, a., onaangenaam

unpopular, *an*-pop-joe-l'r, a., impopulair

unprecedented, *an*-pres-si-den-tid, a., weerga-

unprepared, *an*-pri-pèrd, a., onvoorbereid [loos

unproductive, *an*-pre-d*a*k-tiv, a., improductief

unprofitable, *an*-prof-fi-te-b'l, a., onvoordelig

unpromising, *an*-prom-mi-sing, a., weinig

    belovend

unpropitious, *an*-pre-pis-sjus, a., ongunstig

unprotected, *an*-pre-tek-tid, a., onbeschermd

unprovided, *an*-pre-vai-did, a., niet voorzien

unpunctual, *an*-p*a*ngk-tjoe-ul, a., niet stipt

unquestionable, *an*-kwest-sje-ne-b'l, a., ont-

    twijfelbaar

unravel, *a*n-rev-v'l, v., uitrafelen; (fig.) ontknopen

unread, *a*n-red, a., ongelezen; (person) onbelezen

unreadable, *a*n-rie-de-b'l, a., onleesbaar

unreasonable, *a*n-rie-ze-ne-b'l, a., onredelijk

unrelated, *a*n-ri-lee-tid, a., niet verwant

unrelenting, *a*n-ri-len-ting, a., onverbiddelijk

unreliable, *a*n-ri-lai-e-b'l, a., onbetrouwbaar

unremitting, *a*n-ri-mit-ting, a., aanhoudend

unreserved, *a*n-ri-zeurvd, a., (frank) vrijmoedig

unrest, *a*n-rest, s., onrust c.

unrestrained, *a*n-ri-streend, a., onbeteugeld

unrestricted, *a*n-ri-strik-tid, a., onbeperkt

unripe, *a*n-raip, a., onrijp

unroll, *a*n-rool, v., afrollen, ontrollen

unruly, *a*n-roe-li, a., onhandelbaar

unsafe, *a*n-seef, a., onveilig

unsaleable, *a*n-see-le-b'l, a., onverkoopbaar

unsatisfactory, *a*n-set-tis-fek-te-ri, a., onbevredigend

unscrew, *a*n-skroe, v., losschroeven

unscrupulous, *a*n-skroe-pjoe-lus, a., gewetenloos

unseasonable, *a*n-sie-ze-ne-b'l, a., ontijdig [loos

unseemly, *a*n-siem-li, a., onbetamelijk

unseen, *a*n-sien, a., ongezien

unselfish, *a*n-sel-fisj, a., onbaatzuchtig

unsettled, *a*n-set-t'ld, a., (weather) onbestendig; (account) onbetaald; (disturbed) verward

unshaken, *a*n-sjee-k'n, a., onwrikbaar

unshrinkable, *a*n-sjring-ke-b'l, a., krimpvrij

unshrinking, *a*n-sjring-king, a., onversaagd

unsightly, *a*n-sait-li, a., onooglijk, lelijk

unskilful, *a*n-skil-foel, a., onbekwaam

unskilled, *a*n-skild, a., ongeschoold

unsociable, *a*n-so-sje-b'l, a., ongezellig

unsold, *a*n-soold, a., onverkocht

unsolicited, *a*n-se-lis-si-tid, a., ongevraagd

unsolved, *a*n-solvd, a., onopgelost

unstinted, *a*n-stin-tid, a., onbeperkt

unsuccessful, *a*n-s'k-ses-foel, a., zonder succes

unsuitable, *a*n-sjoe-te-b'l, a., ongepast

unsuited, *a*n-sjoe-tid, a., ongeschikt

unsurpassed, *an*-s'r-paast, a., onovertroffen
untack, *an*-tek, v., losmaken, losrijgen
untamed, *an*-teemd, a., ongetemd, wild
untarnished, *an*-taar-nisjt, a., vlekkeloos
untenable, *an*-ten-ne-b'l, a., onhoudbaar
untenanted, *an*-ten-n'n-tid, a., onverhuurd
unthankful, *an*-thengk-foel, a., ondankbaar
unthinking, *an*-thing-king, a., onnadenkend
untidy, *an*-tai-di, a., slordig, onordelijk
untie, *an*-tai, v., losknopen, losmaken
until, *an*-til, prep., tot, tot aan. conj., totdat
untimely, *an*-taim-li, a., ongelegen
untiring, *an*-tai-ring, a., onvermoeid
untold, *an*-toold, a., onverteld; ongeteld
untouched, *an*-tatsjt, a., ongeroerd
untranslatable, *an*-trens-lee-te-b'l, a., onvertaal-
untried, *an*-traid, a., onbeproefd   [baar
untrodden, *an*-trod-d'n, a., onbetreden
untrue, *an*-troe, a., onwaar; (disloyal) ontrouw
untrustworthy, *an*-trast-weur-dhi, a., onbe-
            trouwbaar
untruth, *an*-troeth, s., onwaarheid c.
untwist, *an*-twist, v., losdraaien, ontwinden
unusual, *an*-joe-zjoe-ul, a., ongewoon
unvaried, *an*-vèr-id, a., onveranderd
unveil, *an*-veel, v., onthullen
unwarranted, *an*-wor-r'n-tid, a., ongewettigd;
            (not justified) onverantwoord
unwavering, *an*-wee-ve-ring, a., standvastig
unwelcome, *an*-wel-kum, a., onwelkom
unwell, *an*-wel, a., ongesteld, onwel
unwholesome, *an*-hool-sum, a., ongezond
unwieldy, *an*-wiel-di, a., log, lomp, zwaar
unwilling, *an*-wil-ling, a., onwillig
unwind, *an*-waind, v., afwinden, loswinden
unwise, *an*-waiz, a., onverstandig, onwijs
unwittingly, *an*-wit-ting-li, adv., onbewust
unworthy, *an*-weur-dhi, a., onwaardig
unwrap, *an*-rep, v., losmaken, loswikkelen
unwritten, *an*-rit-t'n, a., ongeschreven
unyielding, *an*-jiel-ding, a., onverzettelijk
up, *ap*, prep., op. adv., op, omhoog, boven; ——

and down, op en neer; —— here, hierboven; —— there, daarboven; —— to, tot aan, tot op

upbraid, *a*p-breed, v., verwijten

upheaval, *a*p-hie-v'l, s., omwenteling c.

uphill, *a*p-hil, a., bergop; (troublesome) moeilijk

uphold, *a*p-hoold, v., (support) steunen; (maintain) handhaven

upholster, *a*p-hool-st'r, v., stofferen

upholsterer, *a*p-hool-st'r-'r, s., stoffeerder c.

upkeep, *a*p-kiep, s., (maintenance) onderhoud n.; (costs) kosten c.pl.

upland, *a*p-lend, s., hoogland n.

uplift, *a*p-lift, v., optillen, opheffen

upon, e-pon, prep., op. adv., erop

upper, *a*p-p'r, a., hoger, opper; ——hand, s., overhand c.; ——most, a., hoogst, bovenst; —— part, s., bovengedeelte n.

upright, *a*p-rait, a., rechtopstaand; (honest) oprecht. s., stijl c.; (piano) pianino c.

uprising, *a*p-rai-zing, s., opstand c.

uproar, *a*p-roar, s., herrie c, lawaai n.

uproot, *a*p-roet, v., ontwortelen; (fig.) uitroeien

upset, *a*p-set, v., omgooien; (disturb) in de war brengen

upside, *a*p-said, —— down, onderste boven; (in disorder) in de war

upstairs, *a*p-stêrz, adv., boven; to go ——, v., naar boven gaan

upstart, *a*p-staart, s., parvenu c.

upwards, *a*p-wurdz, adv., opwaarts, naar boven

urban, *a*r-b'n, a., stedelijk, stads . . .

urchin, eur-tsjin, s., rakker c, kwajongen c.

urge, eurdzj, v., voortdrijven; (exhort) aansporen; (insist on) aandringen op. s., aandrang c.

urgency, eur-dzjun-si, s., dringende noodzakelijkheid c.

urgent, eur-dzjunt, a., dringend, urgent

urine, joe-rin, s., urine c.

urn, eurn, s., urn c., vaas c.

us, *a*s, pron., ons

use, joez, v., gebruiken; (apply) aanwenden; —— up, verbruiken

use, joes, s., gebruik n.; (utility) nut n.; (custom) gewoonte c.; ——ful, a., nuttig; ——less, nutteloos; ——d to, (accustomed) gewoon aan

usher, *as*-sj'r, s., portier c.; —— in, v., binnenleiden

usual, joe-zjoe-ul, a., gewoon, gebruikelijk

usurp, joe-zeurp, v., zich wederrechtelijk toeëigenen

usurper, joe-zeurp-'r, s., overweldiger c.

usury, joe-zje-ri, s., woeker c.

utensil, joe-ten-sil, s., gereedschap n.

utility, joe-til-li-ti, s., nut n., nuttigheid c.

utilize, joe-ti-laiz, v., benutten, nuttig besteden

utmost, *at*-moost, a., uiterste, hoogste

utter, *at*-t'r, v., uiten. a., totaal, volslagen

utterance, *at*-t'r-'ns, s., uiting c.

uttermost, *at*-t'r-moost, a., uiterste, hoogste

vacancy, vee-k'n-si, s., (emptiness) leegte c.; (gap) leemte c.; (vacant post) vacature c.

vacant, vee-k'nt, a., vacant; (house) leegstaand

vacate, ve-keet, v., (post) neerleggen; (house) ontruimen

vacation, ve-kee-sjun, s., (holiday) vakantie c.

vaccinate, vek-si-neet, v., inenten

vacillate, ves-sil-leet, v., wankelen; (hesitate) weifelen

vacuum, vek-joe-um, s., ledige ruimte c.; —— cleaner, stofzuiger c.

vagabond, veG-Ge-b'nd, s., vagebond c.

vagary, ve-Gèr-i, s., nuk c., gril c.

vague, veeG, a., vaag, onbepaald

vain, veen, a., ijdel; in ——, tevergeefs

vainglory, veen-Glor-ri, s., ijdelheid c.

vale, veel, s., dal n., vallei c.

valet, vel-lit, s., bediende c.

valiant, veel-junt, a., moedig, dapper

valid, vel-lid, a., geldig; (sound) deugdelijk

valley, vel-li, s., dal n., vallei c.

valorous, vel-le-rus, a., moedig, dapper

valuable, vel-joe-e-b'l, a., waardevol

valuation, vel-joe-ee-sjun, s., **schatting** c.

value, vel-joe, s., waarde c. v., schatten

valuer, vel-joe-ur, s., schatter c., taxateur c.

valve, velv, s., klep c.; (radio) lamp c.; (tube) ventiel n.

vamp, vemp, s., bovenleer n.; (patch) lap c. v., (patch) oplappen; (mus.) improviseren

vampire, vem-pair, s., vampier c.

van, ven, s., bestelwagen c.; (mil.) voorhoede c.

vane, veen, s., weerhaan c.; (windmill) wiek c.

vanilla, ve-nil-le, s., vanille c.

vanish, ven-nisj, v., verdwijnen

vanity, ven-ni-ti, s., ijdelheid c.

vanquish, veng-kwisj, v., overwinnen

vapour, vee-p'r, s., damp c., wasem c.

variable, vèr-i-e-b'l, a., veranderlijk

variance, vèr-i-'ns, s., onenigheid c.

variation, vèr-i-ee-sjun, s., afwijking c.

varicose vein, ver-ri-koos veen, s., spatader c.

varied, vèr-id, a., gevarieerd

variegated, vèr-i-Gee-tid, a., veelkleurig

variety, ve-rai-i-ti, s., verscheidenheid c.; (theatre) variété c.

various, vèr-i-us, a., verscheiden, verschillend

varnish, vaar-nisj, s., vernis n., lak n.; (fig.) vernisje n., v., vernissen, lakken

vary, vèr-i, v., (change) veranderen; (diversify) variëren; (differ) verschillen

vase, vaaz, s., vaas c.

vaseline, vez-zi-lien, s., vaseline c.

vast, vaast, a., reusachtig, onmetelijk

vat, vet, s., vat n. v., vaten

vault, voalt, s., gewelf n.; (cellar) kelder c.; (burial) grafkelder c. v., (jump) springen

veal, viel, s., kalfsvlees n.

veer, vier, v., vieren; (wind) omlopen

vegetables, ved-zji-te-b'lz, s.pl., groenten c.pl.

vegetarian, ved-zji-tèr-i-un, s., vegetariër c.

vegetation, ved-zji-tee-sjun, s., plantengroei c.

vehement, vie-i-m'nt, a., hevig, heftig, vurig

vehicle, vie-i-k'l, s., voertuig n.

veil, veel, s., sluier c. v., met een sluier bedekken; (cloak) bemantelen

vein, veen, s., ader c.; (mood) stemming c.

vellum, vel-lum, s., kalfsperkament n.

velocity, vi-los-si-ti, s., snelheid c.

velvet, vel-vit, s., fluweel n. a., fluwelen

velveteen, vel-vi-tien, s., katoenfluweel n.

vendor, ven-d'r, s., verkoper c.

veneer, vi-nier, v., fineren. s., fineer n.; (fig.) vernisje n.

venerable, ven-ne-re-b'l, a., eerbiedwaardig

veneration, ven-ne-ree-sjun, s., verering c.

venereal, vin-nie-ri-ul, a., venerisch

vengeance, ven-dzjuns, s., wraak c.; with a ——, duchtig

venial, vie-ni-ul, a., vergeeflijk

venison, ven-ni-z'n, s., wildbraad n.

venom, ven-n'm, s., venijn n.

venomous, ven-n'm-us, a., venijnig

vent, vent, s., luchtgat n.; (outlet) uitweg c.; give —— to, v., lucht geven aan

ventilate, ven-ti-leet, v., ventileren

ventilator, ven-ti-lee-t'r, s., ventilator c.

ventriloquist, ven-tril-le-kwist, s., buikspreker c.

venture, vent-sjur, s., waagstuk n. v., wagen

venturesome, vent-sjur-s'm, a., (risky) gewaagd; (bold) stout

veracity, vi-res-si-ti, s., waarheidsliefde c.

veranda, ve-ren-da, s., veranda c.

verb, veurb, s., werkwoord n.

verbal, veur-b'l, a., letterlijk; (oral) mondeling

verbatim, veur-bee-tim, adv., woord voor woord

verbose, veur-boos, a., breedsprakig

verdant, veur-d'nt, a., groen

verdict, veur-dikt, s., (of jury) uitspraak c.

verdigris, veur-di-Gris, s., kopergroen n.

verge, veurdzj, s., (brink) rand c.; (rod) roede c.

verger, veur-dzjur, s., stafdrager c.

verify, ver-ri-fai, v., staven, bevestigen

vermilion, v'r-mil-jun, s., vermiljoen n.

vermin, veur-min, s., ongedierte n.; (fig.) tuig n.

vernacular, v'r-nek-joe-l'r, s., landstaal c.

versatile, veur-se-tail, a., (talent) veelzijdig

verse, veurs, s., vers n.; (poetry) poëzie c.

versed, veurst, a., bedreven, ervaren
version, veur-sjun, s., (translation) vertaling c.; (account) lezing c.
versus, veur-sus, prep., tegen, tegenover
vertical, veur-ti-k'l, a., verticaal, loodrecht
vertigo, veur-ti-GO, s., duizeling c.
very, ver-ri, adv., heel, zeer; precies (the very same, precies hetzelfde)
vessel, ves-s'l, s., vat n.; (ship) vaartuig n.   [tigen
vest, vest, s., hemd n. v., bekleden; (endow) begif-
vestige, ves-tidzj, s., spoor n., overblijfsel n.
vestments, vest-m'nts, s.pl., misgewaden n.pl.
vestry, ves-tri, s., sacristie c.
veteran, vet-te-r'n, s., oudgediende c.
veterinary, vet-tc-ri-ne-ri, a., veeartsenijkundig;
  ——**-surgeon,** s., veearts c.
veto, vie-to, s., veto n. v., verbieden
vex, veks, v., plagen; ——**ation,** s., plagerij c.; ——**atious,** a., hinderlijk
via, vai-e, prep., via, over
viaduct, vai-e-dakt, s., viaduct n.
viaticum, vai-et-ti-kum, s., (eccl.) Teerspijze c.
vibrate, vai-breet, v., vibreren; slingeren
vibration, vai-bree-sjun, s., vibreren n.; slinge-ring c.
vicar, vik-k'r, s., dominee c.; plaatsvervanger c.
vicarage, vik-ke-ridzj, s., pastorie c.
vice, vais, s., ondeugd c.; (defect) gebrek n.; (mech.) bankschroef c.; ——**-admiral,** vice-admiraal c.; ——**-president,** vice-president c.; ——**-roy,** onderkoning c.
vicinity, vi-sin-ni-ti, s., buurt c., nabijheid c.
vicious, vis-sjus, a., slecht; (defective) gebrekkig; (dog, etc.) vals; ——**ness,** s., slechtheid c.
victim, vik-tim, s., slachtoffer n.; ——**ize,** v., tot slachtoffer maken; (dupe) bedriegen
victor, vik-t'r, s., overwinnaar c.; ——**ious,** a., zegevierend; ——**y,** s., overwinning c.
victual, vit-t'l, v., proviandeeren
victuals, vit-t'lz, s.pl., levensmiddelen n.pl.
vie, vai, v., wedijveren, mededingen
view, vjoe, s., gezicht n.; (prospect) uitzicht n.;

(opinion) **opvatting** c.; (intention) **bedoeling** c. v., bezien; (regard) **beschouwen**

vigil, vid-zjil, s., vigilie c.; ——ance, waakzaamheid c.; ——ant, a., waakzaam

vigorous, vig-Ge-rus, a., sterk, krachtig

vile, vail, a., laag, verachtelijk

vilify, vil-li-fai, v., zwart maken, belasteren

village, vil-lidzj, s., dorp n.

villager, vil-li-djur, s., dorpsbewoner c.

villain, vil-lin, s., schurk c.; ——ous, a., schurkachtig; ——y, s., schurkenstreek c.

vindicate, vin-di-keet, v.; (maintain) handhaven; (justify) rechtvaardigen; (prove) bewijzen

vindication, vin-di-kee-sjun, s., handhaving c.; rechtvaardiging c.; bewijs n.

vindictive, vin-dik-tiv, a., wraakgierig

vindictiveness, vin-dik-tiv-nes, s., wraakzucht c.

vine, vain, s., wijnstok c.

vinegar, vin-ni-G'r, s., azijn c.

vineyard, vin-jurd, s., wijngaard c.

vintage, vin-tidzj, s., wijnoogst c.   [ontwijden

violate, vai-e-leet, v.; (law) overtreden; (profane)

violence, vai-e-l'ns, s., geweld n., gewelddaad c.

violet, vai-e-lit, a., paars. s., viooltje n.

violin, vai-e-lin, s., viool c.; ——ist, violist c.

viper, vai-p'r, s., adder c.; (fig.) serpent n.

virgin, vur-dzjin, s., maagd c. a., maagdelijk

virile, vir-rail, a., mannelijk; (strong) krachtig

virtual, veur-tjoe-ul, a., feitelijk

virtually, veur-tjoe-ul-li, adv., practisch

virtue, veur-tjoe, s., deugd c.; (chastity) kuisheid c.

virtuous, veur-tjoe-us, a., deugdzaam; kuis c.

virulent, vir-joe-l'nt, a., vergiftig, venijnig

visa, vie-za, s., visum n.

viscount, vai-kaunt, s., burggraaf c.

visibility, vi-zi-bil-li-ti, s., zicht n.

visible, viz-zi-b'l, a., zichtbaar   [n.

vision, viz-zjun, s., gezicht n.; (apparition) visioen

visit, viz-zit, s., bezoek n. v., bezoeken; ——ing-card, s., visitekaartje n.; ——or, bezoeker c.

vital, vai-t'l, a., (essential) essentieel; ——ity, s., levenskracht c.; ——s, s.pl., edele delen n.pl.

vitiate, vis-sji-eet, v., bederven; vervalsen

vitriol, vit-tri-ul, s., vitriool n. & c.

vivacious, vi-vee-sjus, a., levendig, opgewekt

vivacity, vi-ves-si-ti, s., levendigheid c.

vivid, viv-vid, a., levendig; (bright) helder

vivify, viv-vi-fai, v., verlevendigen

vixen, vik-s'n, s., wijfjesvos c.; (fig.) feeks c.

viz. = namely, neem-li, adv., namelijk

vocabulary, ve-keb-joe-le-ri, s., woordenlijst c.; (command of words) woordenschat c.

vocal, vo-k'l, a., stem . . .; —— chords, s.pl., stembanden c.pl.

vocation, vo-kee-sjun, s., beroep n.; (call) roeping c.

vociferous, vo-sif-fe-rus, a., luidruchtig

vogue, voog, s., mode c.; in ——, in zwang

voice, vois, s., stem c.

void, void, a., leeg; (null) nietig. s., leemte c.

volatile, vol-le-tail, a., vervliegend

volcano, vol-kee-no, s., vulkaan c.

volley, vol-li, s., (mil.) salvo n.; (fig.) stroom c.

volt, voolt, s., (electricity) volt c.

voluble, vol-joe-b'l, a., woordenrijk

volume, vol-joem, s., deel n.; (bulk) volume n.

voluminous, ve-ljoe-mi-nus, a., omvangrijk

voluntary, vol-l'n-te-ri, a., vrijwillig

volunteer, vol-l'n-tier, s., vrijwilliger c.

voluptuous, ve-lap-tjoe-us, a., wellustig

vomit, vom-mit, v., braken. s., braaksel n.

voracious, va-ree-sjus, a., vraatzuchtig

vortex, voar-teks, s., draaikolk c.

vote, voot, s., stem c. v., stemmen

voter, vo-t'r, s., kiezer c.

vouch, vautsj, v., getuigen; —— for, instaan voor

voucher, vaut-sjur, s., (document) bewijsstuk n.

vow, vau, s., gelofte c. v., plechtig beloven

vowel, vau-ul, s., klinker c.

voyage, voi-idzj, s., zeereis c. v., reizen

vulcanite, val-ke-nait, s., eboniet n.

vulgar, val-G'r, a., plat, ordinair, laag

vulnerable, val-ne-re-b'l, a., kwetsbaar

vulture, valt-sjur, s., gier c.

wabble, wob-b'l, v., waggelen; (waver) weifelen

wad, wod, s., prop c. v., opvullen

wadding, wod-ding, s., opvulsel n.; (cottonwool) watten c.pl.

waddle, wod-d'l, v., waggelen

wade, weed, v., waden; —— **through,** doorwaden

wafer, wee-f'r, s., wafel c.; (eccl.) hostie c.

wag, weG, s., grappenmaker c. v., (head) schudden met; (tail) kwispelen met   [n.

wage, weedzj, v., (war) voeren; ——s, s.pl., loon

wager, wee-dzjur, s., weddingschap c. v., wedden

waggle, weG-G'l, v., heen en weer schudden

waggon, weG-G'n, s., wagen c.; (railway) wagon c.

waif, weef, s., (child) verwaarloosd kind n.

wail, weel, s., weeklacht c. v., weeklagen

waist, weest, s., middel n.; ——**coat,** vest c.

wait, weet, v., wachten; (at table) bedienen; ——**er,** s., kellner c.; —— **for,** v., wachten op; ——**ing,** s., wachten n.; (service) bediening c.; ——**ing-room,** wachtkamer c.; ——**ress,** kellnerin c.; —— **upon,** v., bedienen

waive, weev, v., afzien van, laten varen   [nen

wake, week, v., ontwaken; (rouse) wakker maken, wekken. s., (ship's) zog n., kielwater n.

walk, woak, v., lopen; (stroll) wandelen. s., wandeling c.; ——**er,** wandelaar c.; ——**ing-tour,** wandeltocht c.

wall, woal, s., muur c. v., ommuren; ——**flower,** s., muurbloem c.; ——**paper,** behangselpapier n.

wallet, wol-lit, s., portefeuille c.

wallow, wol-lo, v., zich wentelen

walnut, woal-nat, s., walnoot c.; (tree) noteboom c.

walrus, woal-ras, s., walrus c.

waltz, woals, s., wals c. v., walsen

wander, won-d'r, v., zwerven; (rave) ijlen

wane, ween, v., verminderen; (moon) afnemen

want, wont, s., (lack) gebrek n.; (need) behoefte c.; (poverty) armoede c. v., (lack) gebrek hebben aan; (need) nodig hebben; (desire) verlangen

wanton, won-t'n, a., (sportive) speels; (unre-strained) uitgelaten; (lustful) wulps. s., licht-ekooi c.

war, woar, s., oorlog c. v., oorlog voeren; ——like, a., oorlogzuchtig; ——loan, s., oorlogs-lening c.; ——office, Ministerie van Oorlog n.; ——ship, oorlogsschip n.

warble, woar-b'l, v., kwelen; ——r, s., zanger c.

ward, woard, s., (minor) pupil c.; (hospital) zaal c.; ——en, (guardian) opziener c.; (college) hoofd n.; ——er, cipier c.; —— off, v., afweren; ——ress, s., gevangenbewaarster c.; ——robe, kleerkast c.; (clothes) garderobe c.; ——room, officierskajuit c.

ware, wèr, s., waar c.; ——house, pakhuis n.

warily, wèr-i-li, adv., voorzichtig, behoedzaam

warm, woarm, a., warm. v., warm maken; warm worden

warmth, woarmth, s., warmte c.

warn, woarn, v., waarschuwen; ——ing, s., waarschuwing c.

warp, woarp, v., kromtrekken; (fig.) verdraaien

warrant, wor-r'nt, s., (guarantee) waarborg c.; (authorization) machtiging c.; (writ of arrest) bevel tot inhechtenisneming n.; (voucher) bewijsstuk n. v., waarborgen; machtigen; (justify) wettigen; ——y, s., garantie c.

warrior, wor-ri-ur, s., krijgsman c., krijger c.

wart, woart, s., wrat c.

wary, wèr-i, a., voorzichtig, behoedzaam

wash, wosj, v., wassen; zich wassen. s., was c.; ——basin, waskom c.; ——erwoman, wasvrouw c.; ——ing, (laundry) wasgoed n.; ——stand, wastafel c.

washer, wos-sj'r, s., (mech.) sluitring c.

wasp, wosp, s., wesp c.

waste, weest, s., (squandering) verspilling c.; (refuse) afval c.; (desert) woestijn c. v., ver-spillen; (devastate) verwoesten; —— away, wegkwijnen; ——ful, a., verkwistend c.; ——paper basket, s., prullenmand c.

watch, wotsj, s., horloge n.; (guard) wacht c.;

(vigilance) waakzaamheid c. v., waken; (keep guard) de wacht houden; (observe) gadeslaan; ——**ful**, a., waakzaam; ——**maker**, s., horlogemaker c.; ——**man**, waker c.; ——**over**, v., waken over; ——**word**, s., wachtwoord n.

water, woa-t'r, v., (cattle) drenken; (flowers) begieten; (land) besproeien. s., water n.; hot——**bottle**, warme kruik c.; ——**closet**, W.C. c.; ——**colour**, waterverf c.; (painting) aquarel c.; ——**cress**, waterkers c.; ——**fall**, waterval c.; ——**jug**, waterkruik c.; ——**level**, waterstand c.; (instrument) waterpas n.; ——**lily**, waterlelie c.; ——-**line**, waterlijn c.; ——**logged**, a., vol water; ——**mark**, s., (paper) watermerk n.; ——**proof**, a., waterdicht; ——-**tank**, s., water-reservoir n.; ——**tight**, a., waterdicht; ——**y**, waterig

watering, woa-te-ring, s., begieten n.; ——**can**, gieter c.; ——-**place**, wed n.; -(town) badplaats c.

wave, weev, s., golf c. v., golven; (flag) wapperen; (handkerchief) wuiven met; (hair) onduleren

waver, wee-v'r, v., waggelen; (hesitate) weifelen

wavy, wee-vi, a., golvend, gegolfd

wax, weks, s., was n. v., met was bestrijken; (polish) boenen; (become) worden; ——-**candle**, s., waskaars c.; ——**works**, pl., wassenbeelden n.pl.

way, wee, s., weg c.; (direction) richting c.; (manner) manier c.; —— **in**, ingang c.; ——**lay**, v., belagen; —— **out**, s., uitgang c.; —— **through**, doorgang c.

wayward, wee-wurd, a., weerspannig, eigenzinnig

we, wie, pron., wij, we

weak, wiek, a., zwak; ——**en**, v., verzwakken; ——**ening**, s., verzwakking c.; ——**ling**, zwakkeling c.; ——**ness**, zwakheid c.

weal, wiel, s., welzijn n.; (wale) striem c.

wealth, welth, s., rijkdom c.; ——**y**, a., rijk [van

wean, wien, v., spenen; —— **from**, vervreemden

weapon, wep-p'n, s., wapen n.

wear, wèr, s., (wear and tear) slijtage c.; (clothes) kleding c. v., dragen; slijten; —— out, (clothes) afdragen; (exhaust) uitputten

weariness, wie-ri-nis, s., vermoeidheid c.; (boredom) verveling c.

weary, wie-ri, a., vermoeid; (boring) vervelend. v., vermoeien; vervelen

weasel, wie-z'l, s., wezel c.

weather, wedh-ur, s., weer n.; ——beaten, a., verweerd; ——bound, door het weer opgehouden; ——forecast, s., weervoorspelling c.; ——report, weerbericht n.

weave, wievv, v., weven; ——r, s., wever c.

web, web, s., (fabric) weefsel n.; (cobweb) web n.; ——footed, a., met zwempoten

wed, wed, v., huwen; ——ding, s., bruiloft c.; ——ding-cake, bruiloftstaart c.; ——ding-ring, trouwring c.

wedge, wedzj, s., wig c. v., een wig slaan in; —— in, indrijven

wedlock, wed-lok, s., huwelijk n.

Wednesday, wenz-di, s., woensdag c.

weed, wied, s., onkruid n. v., wieden

week, wiek, s., week c.; ——day, werkdag c.; ——end, weekeinde n.; ——ly, a. & adv., wekelijks

weep, wiep, v., schreien; ——ing willow, s. treurwilg c.

weevil, wie-vil, s., korenworm c.

weigh, wee, v., wegen; (ponder) overwegen; ——t, s., gewicht n.; (burden) last c.; ——ty, a., zwaar; (important) gewichtig

weir, wier, s., stuwdam c.

weird, wierd, a., griezelig; (queer) vreemd

welcome, wel-kum, s., welkom n. a., welkom. v., verwelkomen

weld, weld, v., lassen, aaneensmeden

welfare, wel-fèr, s., welvaart c.

well, wel, s., put c. a. & adv., wel, goed. interj., well goed!; ——being, s., welzijn n.; ——bred, a., beschaafd; —— done, goed gaar; ——wisher, s., vriend c.

welt, welt, s., striem c.

wend, wend, —— **one's way**, v., voortschrijden

west, west, s., westen n.; —— **erly**, a., westelijk

wet, wet, s., nat n.   a., nat   v., nat maken

wet-nurse, wet-neurs, s., min c.

whack, wek, v., afranselen. s., mep c.

whale, weel, s., walvis c.; —— **bone**, balein c.

whaler, wee-l'r, s., walvisvaarder c.

wharf, woarf, s., aanlegplaats c., kaai c.

what, wot, pron., wat, wat voor, welk; —— **ever**, wat ook, al wat; —— **kind of**, wat voor, wat voor een

wheat, wiet, s., tarwe c., weit c.

wheedle, wie-d'l, v., vleien, flikflooien

wheel, wiel, s., wiel n., rad n.   v., (convey) per as vervoeren; (revolve) wentelen; —— **-barrow**, (s), kruiwagen c.; —— **-wright**, wagenmaker c.

wheezy, wie-zi, a., aamborstig, hijgend

whelk, welk, s., wulk c.

when, wen, adv. & pron., wanneer; —— **ce**, adv., vanwaar; —— **ever**, telkens wanneer, wanneer ook

where, wèr, adv. & pron., waar; —— **about(s)**, adv., waar ergens. s., verblijfplaats c.; —— **as**, conj., terwijl daarentegen; —— **at**, adv., waarop; —— **by**, waardoor; —— **fore**, waarom; —— **in**, waarin; —— **on**, waarop; —— **to**, waartoe

wherever, wèr-ev-v'r, adv., waar ook

whet, wet, v., wetten; (appetite) opwekken

whether, wedh-ur, conj., of

which, witsj, pron., welk; —— **ever**, welk ook

while, wail, conj., terwijl. s., tijdje n.

whim, wim, s., gril c.; —— **sical**, a., grillig

whimper, wim-p'r, v., grienen

whine, wain, v., temen. s., geteem n.

whip, wip, s., zweep c.   v., wippen; (eggs) kloppen

whirl, weurl, v., ronddraaien. s., dwarreling c.; —— **pool**, draaikolk c.; —— **wind**, wervelwind c.

whisk, wisk, v., (sweep) vegen; (eggs) kloppen.

s., (brush) borstel c.; (egg beater) eierklopper
c.; —— away, v., wegijlen

whiskers, wis-k'rz, s.pl., bakkebaard c.; (cat) snor

whisky, wis-ki, s., whisky c.　　　　　　　　[c.

whisper, wis-p'r, v., fluisteren. s., gefluister n.

whist, wist, s., whist n.

whistle, wis-s'l, v., fluiten. s., (sound) gefluit n.;
(instrument) fluitje n.

whit, wit, s., zier c., jota c.

white, wait, a., wit. s., witte kleur c.; ——**wash,**
witkalk c. v., witten

whither, widh-ur, adv., waarheen

whiting, wai-ting, s., wijting c.

Whitsuntide, wit-s'n-taid, s., Pinksteren c.

whiz, wiz, v., sissen, snorren. s., gesis n.

who, hoe, pron., wie; die; ——**ever,** wie ook, al
wie; ——m, wie; die; ——se, wiens; (plural)
wier; ——**soever,** al wie, wie ook

whole, hool, s., geheel n. a., heel; ——**sale,** s.,
groothandel c.; ——**some,** a., gezond

wholly, ho-li, adv., geheel, totaal

whoop, hoep, v., schreeuwen. s., geschreeuw n.

whooping-cough, hoe-ping-kof, s., kinkhoest c.

whore, hoar, s., hoer c. v., hoereren

why, wai, adv., waarom. interj., wel!

wick, wik, s., pit c.

wicked, wik-kid. a., slecht, zondig

wickedness, wik-kid-nis, s., slechtheid c.

wicker, wik-k'r, s., rijs n., wilgetakje n.

wide, waid, a., wijd; (spacious) ruim; ——
-**awake, klaar wakker;** ——**ly,** adv., wijd;
ruim; ——**n,** v., verwijden; wijder worden;
——-**spread,** a., wijd verspreid

widow, wid-do, s., weduwe c.

widower, wid-do-'r, s., weduwnaar c.

width, width, s., breedte c., wijdte c.

wield, wield, v., hanteren; (power) uitoefenen

wife, waif, s., vrouw c., echtgenote c.

wig, wig, s., pruik c.

wild, waild, a., wild, woest; (furious) woedend;
(frantic) dol

wilderness, wil-d'r-nis, s., wildernis c.

wile, wail, s., list c.　v., verlokken　　[zinnig
wilful, wil-foel, a., moedwillig; (stubborn) eigen-
will, wil, s., wil c.; (legal) testament n.　v., willen;
　(future) zullen; (bequeath) vermaken
willing, wil-ling, a., gewillig, bereid
willingness, wil-ling-nis, s., bereidwilligheid c.
will-o'-the-wisp, wil-le-dhe-**wisp**, s., dwaallicht-
　je n.
willow, wil-lo, s., wilg c.　　　　[kwaadschiks
willy nilly, wil-li nil-li, adv., goedschiks of
wily, wai-li, a., slim, sluw
win, win, v., winnen; ——**ner**, s., winnaar c.;
　——**ning**, a., (manners) innemend; ——
　ning-post, s., eindpaal c.; ——**nings**, pl.,
　winst c.
wince, wins, v., huiveren. s., huivering c.
winch, wintsj, s., windas n.; (crank) kruk c.
wind, waind, v., winden; (twist) draaien; ——**ing**,
　a., kronkelend; ——**up**, v., (clock) opwinden;
　(business) liquideren
wind, wind, s., wind c.; ——**fall**, (fig.) meeval-
　lertje n.; ——**mill**, windmolen c.; ——**pipe**,
　luchtpijp c.; ——**ward**, adv., windwaarts;
　——**y**, a., winderig
windlass, wind-les, s., windas n.
window, win-do, s., venster n., raam n.
wine, wain, s., wijn c.; ——**bottle**, wijnfles c.
wing, wing, s., vleugel c.; (vane) molenwiek c.
wink, wingk, v., knipogen; (flicker) flikkeren
winter, win-t'r, s., winter c.　v., overwinteren
wipe, waip, v., afvegen; afdrogen
wire, wair, s., draad c.　v., met draad vastmaken
wireless, wair-lis, a., draadloos. s., radio c.; (tele-
　graphy) draadloze telegrafie c.　v., draadloos
wisdom, wis-dum, s., wijsheid c.　　[telegraferen
wise, waiz, a., wijs
wish, wisj, s., wens c.　v., wensen, verlangen
wishful, wisj-foel, a., wensend, verlangend
wisp, wisp, s., bundeltje n.; (hair) piek c.
wistaria, wis-tèr-i-a, s., blauweregen c.
wistful, wist-foel, a., weemoedig, droefgeestig
wit, wit, s., geestigheid c.; (intelligence) verstand

n.; (person) geestig man; ——ticism, geestigheid c.; ——ty, a., geestig

witch, witsj, s., heks c.; ——craft, hekserij c.

with, widh, prep., met; ——draw, v., terugtrekken; zich terugtrekken; ——hold, terughouden; (keep from) onthouden; ——in, prep. & adv., binnen; ——out, prep., zonder. adv., buiten; ——stand, v., weerstaan

wither, widh-ur, v., verwelken; doen verwelken

withering, widh-e-ring, a., (look) vernietigend

witness, wit-nis, s., (evidence) getuigenis c.; (person) getuige c. v., getuigen

wizard, wiz-z'rd, s., tovenaar c.

wobble, wob-b'l, see **wabble**

woe, wo, s., wee c.; ——ful, a., treurig

wolf, woelf, s., wolf c.; she——, wolvin c.

woman, woe-m'n, s., vrouw c.; ——hood, vrouwelijke staat c.; ——ly, a., vrouwelijk

womb, woem, s., baarmoeder c.

wonder, won-d'r, s., wonder n.; (astonishment) verwondering c. v., zich verwonderen; (feel curiosity) benieuwd zijn

wonderful, wʌn-d'r-foel, a., wonderlijk

woo, woe, v., vrijen met; ——er, s., vrijer c.

wood, woed, s., hout n.; (forest) bos n.; ——bine, wilde kamperfoelie c.; ——cock, houtsnip c.; ——en, a., houten; ——pecker, s., specht c.; ——y, a., bosrijk

wool, woel, s., wol c.; ——len, a., wollen

woolly, woe-li, a., wollig, wolachtig

word, weurd, v., onder woorden brengen. s., woord n.; (news) bericht n.; ——ing, bewoordingen c.pl.; — of honour, erewoord n.

work, weurk, v., werken. s., werk n.; arbeid c.; (occupation) bezigheid c.

worker, weur-k'r, s., werkman c.

workhouse, weurk-haus, s., armenhuis n.

working, weur-king, s., werking c.; (mine, quarry) exploitatie c. a., werkend; ——expenses, s.pl., bedrijfskosten c.pl.

workman, weurk-m'n, s., arbeider c.; ——ship, bekwaamheid c.; (finish) afwerking c.

works, weurkz, s.pl., fabriek c.; (mech.) werk n.

workshop, weurk-sjop, s., werkplaats c.

world, weurld, s., wereld c.; ——ly, a., werelds

worm, weurm, s., worm c.; (screw) schroefdraad

worm-eaten, weurm-ie-t'n, a., wormstekig [c.

worry, war-ri, v., kwellen; (be anxious) zich bezorgd maken. s., kwelling c.; (care) zorg c.; (solicitude) bezorgdheid c.

worse, weurs, a. & adv., erger, slechter

worship, weur-sjip, s., aanbidding c.; (divine service) godsdienstoefening c. v., aanbidden

worst, weurst, a., slechtst, ergst. adv., het slechtst, het ergst

worsted, woes-tid, s., (yarn) kamgaren n.

worth, weurth, a., waard. s., waarde c.; ——ily, adv., waardig; ——less, a., waardeloos; (person) verachtelijk; —— while, adv., de moeite waard

worthy, weur-thi, a., achtenswaardig

would-be, woed-bie, a., zogenaamd

wound, woend, s., wonde c., v., verwonden

wrangle, reng-G'l, v., krakelen. s., gekrakeel n.

wrap, rep, v., wikkelen; (fig.) hullen. s., omhulsel n.; ——ped, a., (absorbed) verzonken; ——per, s., (book) kaft c.; (postal) kruisband c.

wrath, roath, s., toorn c.; ——ful, a., toornig

wreath, rieth, s., krans c.

wreathe, riedh, v., omkransen; vlechten

wreck, rek, s., schipbreuk c.; (destroyed vessel) wrak n. v., schipbreuk doen lijden; (destroy) verwoesten; ——age, s., (debris) wrakhout n.; **be** ——ed, v., schipbreuk lijden

wren, ren, s., winterkoninkje n.

wrench, rensj, s., ruk c.; (tool) schroefsleutel c.; (sprain) verstuiking c.; (fig.) pijnlijke scheiding c. v., rukken; verstuiken; (distort)

wrestle, res-s'l, v., worstelen [verdraaien

wrestler, res-s'lr, s., worstelaar c.

wretch, retsj, s., (unhappy person) stakker c.; (mean person) ellendeling c.; ——ed, a., ellendig; ——edness, s., ellende c.

wriggle, riG-G'l, v., wriemelen, wriggelen

wring, ring, v., (hands) wringen; (clothes) uitwringen; (neck) omdraaien; (pervert) verdraaien

wrinkle, ring-k'l, s., rimpel c., plooi c. v., rim

wrist, rist, s., pols c., polsgewricht n. [pelen

writ, rit, s., bevelschrift n.

write, rait, v., schrijven; ——**r,** s., schrijver c.

writhe, raidh, v., zich kronkelen

writing, rai-ting, s., geschrift n.; **hand**——, handschrift n.; **in** ——, adv., schriftelijk; ——**-case,** s., schrijfmap c.; ——**-pad,** sousmain c.; ——**-paper,** schrijfpapier n.; ——**-table,** schrijftafel c.

written, rit-t'n, a. & p.p., geschreven

wrong, rong, a., verkeerd; (wicked) slecht. s., (evil) kwaad n.; (injustice) onrecht n. v., onrecht aandoen; **be** ——, ongelijk hebben

wroth, roath, a., woedend, vertoornd

wry, rai, a., scheef, verdraaid; —— **face,** s., zuur gezicht n.; ——**neck,** scheve hals c.; (bird) draaihals c.

Xmas (=**Christmas**), **kris-mus,** s., Kerstmis c.

X-ray, eks-ree, s., röntgenstraal c.; (photo) röntgenfoto c. v., doorlichten

xylophone, zai-le-foon, s., xylophoon c.

yacht, jot, s., jacht n.; ——**ing,** zeilsport c.

yard, jaard, s., plaats c.; (measure) Engelse el c.; **ship**——, scheepstimmerwerf c.; **timber**——, houtloods c.

yarn, jaarn, s., garen n.; (tale) verhaal n.

yawn, joan, v., geeuwen. s., geeuw c.

year, jier, s., jaar n.; ——**ling,** éénjarig dier n. a., éénjarig; ——**ly,** a. & adv., jaarlijks

yearn, jeurn, v., smachten, vurig verlangen; ——**ing,** s., smachtend verlangen n.

yeast, jiest, s., gist c.

yell, jel, v., gillen, schreeuwen. s., gil c.

yellow, jel-lo, a., geel. s., geel n.

yelp, jelp, v., keffen. s., gekef n.

yes, jes, adv., ja
yesterday, jes-t'r-di, adv., gisteren
yet, jet, adv., nog, tot nog toe; (nevertheless) toch.
conj., maar, doch; **not** ——, nog niet
yew, joe, s., taxis c.; (wood) taxishout n.
yield, jield, s., opbrengst c. v., (produce) voortbrengen; (surrender) overgeven; (give way) wijken
yoke, jook, s., juk n. v., het juk aandoen
yokel, jo-k'l, s., boerenkinkel c., pummel c.
yolk, jook, s., dooier c.
yonder, jon-d'r, a., ginds. adv., daarginds
you, joe, pron., u; (fam.) jij, je; (fam. plural) jullie
young, jang, a., jong; **the** ——, s., jeugd c.;
(animals) jongen c.pl.; ——**er,** a., jonger; (of two) jongste
youngster, jang-st'r, s., knaap c., jochie n.
your, joer, pron., uw; (fam.) je, jouw; ——**s,** de
uwe; (neuter) het uwe; (fam.) de jouwe, het jouwe; ——**self,** u, zelf, uzelf; (fam.) jij, zelf, jijzelf; ——**selves,** u, zelf, uzelf; (fam.) jullie, zelf, jullie zelf
youth, joeth, s., jeugd c.; (young man) jongeling
c.; ——**ful,** a., jeugdig; —— **hostel,** s., jeugdherberg c.
Yule-tide, joel-taid, s., Kersttijd c.

zeal, ziel, s., vurige ijver c.
zealous, zel-lus, a., ijverig; (ardent) vurig
zebra, zie-bra, s., zebra c.
zenith, zen-nith, s., zenit n.; (fig.) toppunt n.
zero, zie-ro, s., nul c.; (thermometer) nulpunt n.
zest, zest, s., animo c.; (enjoyment) genot n.
zinc, zingk, s., zink n. v., met zink bekleden
zip-fastener, zip-faas-n'r, s., ritssluiting c.
zone, zoon, s., zone c., luchtstreek c.
zoology, zo-ol-le-dzi, s., dierkunde c.

hugo

Pocket Dictionaries

French–English/English–French
German–English/English–German
Spanish–English/English–Spanish
Italian–English/English–Italian
Dutch–English/English–Dutch
Russian–English/English–Russian
Turkish–English/English–Turkish

English Pocket Dictionary

Tourist Phrasebooks

French, German, Spanish, Italian,
Greek, Portuguese, Yugoslav,
Turkish, Arabic, Japanese, Thai,
Chinese, Russian, Swedish, Danish
and Dutch.

*Essential words and phrases for most
holiday travel situations.*